W9-CKS-776

Collective Behavior

Erich Goode

Collective Behavior

State University of New York, Stony Brook

Erich Goode

Saunders College Publishing

A Harcourt Brace Jovanovich College Publisher

Fort Worth Philadelphia San Diego New York Orlando Austin San Antonio
Toronto Montreal London Sydney Tokyo

For Barbara

Acquisitions Editor: Rick Roehrich
Manuscript Editor: Zanae Rodrigo
Designer: Marjorie Taylor
Art Editor: Cindy Robinson
Production Manager: Mandy Van Dusen

Copyright © 1992 by Harcourt Brace Jovanovich, Inc.

All rights reserved. No part of this publication may be reproduced or transmitted in any form or by any means, electronic or mechanical, including photocopy, recording or any information storage and retrieval system, without permission in writing from the publisher.

Requests for permission to make copies of any part of the work should be mailed to: Permissions Department, Harcourt Brace Jovanovich, Inc., 8th Floor, Orlando, Florida 32887.

ISBN: 0-15-500033-0

Library of Congress Catalog Card Number: 91-77957

Printed in the United States of America

Photo Credits:

Page 23: Reuters/Bettman Newsphotos; 35: c 1990 Kevin Vessel/All Rights Reserved; 59: AP/Wide World Photos; 77: c 1989 Peter Turnley/Black Star; 125: AP/Wide World Photos; 211: Keith Meyers/The New York Times; 235: c V. Ivleva/Magnum Dist.; 238: AP/Wide World Photos; 309: c Sergio Dorantes/The New York Times; 315: AP/Wide World Photos; 359: c Mike Geissinger/The New York Times; 374: NY Times/Don Hogan Charles; 425: c BartonSilverman/The New York Times; 451: Copyright by Les Stone/SYGMA; 475: AP/Wide World Photos.

PREFACE

In Salt Lake City, three teenagers are trampled to death by a crowd attending a heavy metal rock concert. In Haiti, a rumor, later discovered to be false, circulates that certain individuals were agents of the despised Duvalier dictatorship; four of the accused are lynched by an angry mob, and the police kill six protestors. In Los Angeles, two planes collide and, in one, 17 passengers are trampled to death in a frenzied rush to escape from the smoke-filled aircraft. In Rio de Janeiro, 70,000 people fill a stadium and scream, sing, and sway to a throbbing samba beat and a swirl of dancing, costumed marchers. In upstate New York, stories circulate about a satanic cult whose members supposedly engage in animal sacrifice.

These events are examples of collective behavior. But they represent some of its more sensationalistic, headline-grabbing instances. In the past, collective behavior has been thought to be frenzied and destructive. We now know that it is just as likely to be exemplified by far less destructive, more controlled behavior: the rebuilding of a community after an earthquake, the everyday gossip that dominates the stories friends tell one another, the clothing styles we adopt, the gimmicky toys we purchase and give to our children—or keep for ourselves, the founding of a new social movement, or the perception that a miracle has taken place.

The field of collective behavior has been controversial since its inception. This book is unlikely to resolve the controversy. Of late, practitioners of bordering fields have attempted to carve collective behavior up like a Thanksgiving turkey and carry off the pieces, until nothing remains but a denuded carcass. In my view, they are "throwing out the baby with the bathwater." I have attempted to reclaim some of the meat of those carried-off portions, to reclaim the full scope of the field for serious and exciting sociological investigation.

The disaster specialists are busy studying the predictable, structural features of organizations that arise before, during, and after disasters. They and others seem to deny that "unscheduled events" disrupt community life in disasters. They wish to *tame* disasters, to strip them of their terror and devastation.

The social movement specialists are emphatic in arguing that social movement activity is rational, predictable from prior institutional involvements and commitments, and, above all, a structural and organizational phenomenon. Suddenly, as if by fiat, Nazis, Ku Klux Klanners, pre-Revolutionary Bolsheviks, and members of the Nation of Islam become brothers and sisters under the skin with the Democratic National Committee and Young Republicans. The fervor, passion, anguish, and fury that boils up in many social movement activists is ignored, swept under the rug, explained away.

Specialists in crowds and social gatherings are busy counting, tabulating, and calculating only that which can be seen and measured, and seem to have forgotten that social behavior is predicated on the seemingly unfathomable bedrock of human meaning.

In this book, I attempt to dig for some of collective behavior's classic roots, but, at the same time avoid some of its myths and misconceptions. If I am asked what approach I adopt in this book, my response would have to be: Its approach is eclectic. But insofar as some recent practitioners have moved away from some of the field's classic concerns with spontaneity and extrainstitutionality and—yes—emotionality, I have to admit to having become disenchanted with these developments. If I am asked with which sociologists this book's approach in most congenial, which ones have had the most influence on its content, my response would have to be John Lofland and Gary Marx. I owe a debt of gratitude to them for their work and their insights.

More specifically, I would like to thank almost uncountable friends and colleagues who assisted me in one way or another with the preparation of this book. Among them I must include: Nachman Ben-Yehuda, Jeffrey Victor, David Bouchier, Aldon Morris, Robert Bartholomew, Fred Davis, James Stewart, James Jasper, Jonathan Cohen, Gene Lebovics, Fred Weinstein, Mayer Zald, William Thompson, Robert McAulay, George Kirkpatrick, Gary Alan Fine, Lewis Killian, Robert Bass, Stacey Leuci, and Barbara Weinstein. Two figures deserve special mention; their comments were surely "above and beyond the call of duty" demanded by mere colleagueship: Mike Schwartz and Marcello Truzzi. I feel guilty that my demand for their time deflected their attention away from their own work, but I am glad that they bestowed it upon me and on this book. I feel doubly guilty that the chapter on paranormal beliefs that Marcello read and commented on in such loving detail could not appear in this book. But that simply exemplifies one of life's spontaneous, unscheduled events, and as such, must be counted an instance of collective behavior.

Erich Goode

CONTENTS

PART ONE

INTRODUCTION TO COLLECTIVE BEHAVIOR

Stalin loved applause, and it was bestowed on him lavishly. In the *Gulag*, [Alexander] Solzhenitsyn describes a district party conference at which everyone rose to applaud the great leader. The applause continued for ten minutes and still no one could risk being the first one to stop applauding. Finally, the director of a paper factory sat down, permitting all others to follow suit. That night the director was arrested. He was reminded in the process never to be the first to stop applauding. In written transcripts of such occasions the phrase "stormy applause" provides no precise data about duration, other than the occasional use of "prolonged." However, the individuals responsible for the set of records containing Stalin's speeches evidently dared not abbreviate the applause, which covers an entire side of one record. . . .

Stormy applause bestowed on others upset Stalin. . . . [Anna] Akhmatova [one of 20th century Russia's most esteemed and beloved poets] had been put in jeopardy by an incident that occurred in May 1944 when she was returning to Leningrad from her wartime refuge in Tashkent. She stopped briefly in Moscow to recite her poetry to a large audience at the Polytechnic Museum. The audience evidently rose to its feet when she came out on stage. According to Nadezhda Mandelstam [writer and wife of poet Ossip Mandelstam], Andrei Zhdanov [Stalin's deputy of culture] reported this to Stalin, who supposedly asked, "Who organized this standing ovation?" (Sheldon, 1990, pp. xi, xvi)

As the actors [in the play, *Waiting for Lefty*] began to speak [Clifford] Odets' stingingly authentic dialogue . . . audience members found themselves swept up in a drama they seemed to know intimately, from deep inside themselves, even though they'd never heard a word of it before. They gasped. . . . They cheered. . . . They murmured sadly. . . . They jeered. . . . They laughed sympathetically. . . . Swept up by the passion they had aroused, the actors were no longer acting. "They were being carried along as if by an exultantcy of communication such as I have never witnessed in the theater before," wrote [Harold] Clurman [the director of the play]. The playwright was awed by the emotional conflagration he'd ignited. . . . "Suddenly . . . the audience and the actors were at one with each other." As the play mounted to its climax, the intensity of feelings on- and offstage became almost unbearable. . . . [When a character asked the question] "Well, what's the answer?", [as planned, three members of the audience, including the playwright] began shouting "Strike!" "LOUDER!" [the actor yelled] "and, one by one, from all over the auditorium, individual voices called out, "Strike!" Suddenly, the entire audience, some 1,400 people rose and and roared, "Strike! Strike!" The actors froze, stunned by the spontaneous demonstration. The militant cries gave way to cheers and applause so thunderous the cast was kept on stage for forty-five minutes to receive the crowd's inflamed tribute. "When they couldn't applaud any more, they stomped their feet," said Ruth Nelson [one of the actresses in the play]. "All I could think was 'My God, they're going to bring the balcony down!' It was terrible, it was so beautiful." The actors were all weeping. . . . "The audience wouldn't leave," said Cheryl Crawford [the play's casting director]. "I was afraid they were going to tear the seats out and throw them on the stage." When the astounded stage manager finally rang down the curtain, they remained out front, talking and arguing about the events in a play that seemed as real to them as their own lives. Actors and playwright were overwhelmed and a little frightened by the near-religious communion they had just shared. . . . [The actors and the playwright] emerged onto [the street] to find clusters of people still gathered outside, laughing, crying, hugging each other, clapping their hands. "There was almost a sense of pure madness about it," Morris Carnovsky [an actor] felt. (Smith, 1990, pp. 197–199)

Spontaneous applause and laughter, riots, miracles, joyous, ecstatic crowds, disasters, rumors, gossip, belief in fantastic happenings, fads, fashion, crazes, some demonstrations, some strikes, and some aspects of social movements—these are the stuff of collective behavior. The field studies some extraordinary—and some quite ordinary—phenomena. Collective behavior is an integral part of the lives of all of us. Television news and the print media are filled with accounts of episodes of collective behavior; we all experience many types and examples of it at some time in our lives. Moreover, most of us regard collective behavior events as worthy of our attention; we usually pay close attention when some form of it is discussed. And yet, in spite of its importance, collective behavior has not been studied as intensively as it should have been; it occupies an almost marginal place in sociology, social psychology, anthropology, political science, and the other social sciences.

The systematic study of collective behavior as a distinct phenomenon is little more than a century old, and the now-dominant views of it have existed for barely a generation. Theories that were taken for granted in the past are discredited today. The *earliest* view of collective behavior (Mackay, 1932; LeBon, 1982; Park, 1972; Blumer, 1939), universally regarded as obsolete, held that it was distinctly different from ordinary, everyday, conventional behavior—more irrational, more emotional (even frenzied), completely spontaneous, disorganized, disruptive, and totally without rules or boundaries. This view stated that, at times, for no rational reason, large numbers of people became obsessed about something that was previously alien to them; they suddenly cast off society's norms and excitedly engaged in unusual, reckless, delusional behavior. Collective behavior represented the operation of "mob psychology," the product of the "madness of crowds." Why did they do it? After all, there was little to recommend the behavior aside from the fact that others were doing it and, when the mania passed, most of those who engaged in it wondered what the fuss had been all about. This older school tended to explain collective behavior by invoking causes that sounded negative, pathological, and very much like a sickness—a process analogous to a "contagion"; to social or individual strain; to primitive, animalistic, or "herd" instincts; to alienation; or to ignorance, stupidity, and the like.

This view of collective behavior is now universally regarded as obsolete— the "myth of the madding crowd" (McPhail, 1991). The newer and clearly more valid view of collective behavior is that the distinction between it and ordinary, everyday, conventional behavior is not so sharp or clear-cut as was previously believed. There is a fuzziness or a blurring of the demarcation between the two. Collective behavior is not necessarily a pathological phenomenon, not necessarily irrational or highly emotional, rarely frenzied, not completely spontaneous, and by no means normless. In fact, there are strong parallels between collective and conventional behavior; the two cannot be placed in totally distinct realms. People are bound by rules in both contexts; they are influenced by what others do and believe to be right when engaging in collective behavior—just as they do when engaging in conventional behavior. Collective behavior is not a realm apart or distinct from what we do in the more routine aspects of our lives. At the same time, many observers feel (Lofland, 1985; Marx, 1980; Marx and Wood, 1975; Bainbridge, 1989) that the field of collective behavior *does* exist, that relatively spontaneous, relatively noninstitutional behavior *is* a phenomenon worthy of sociological study.

It has become fashionable of late to insist that collective behavior does not exist, that "two coherent realms"—that is, collective and institutional behavior—cannot be distinguished, that no "inner logic permeates" the various behaviors that fall under the collective behavior umbrella (Morris and Herring, 1987, pp. 146, 147), that there is "no real difference" between collective behavior and ordinary, everyday behavior (Couch, 1968; Miller, 1985, pp. 10–11). There are several assumptions built into this claim. First, that all legitimate sociological phenomena are permeated with an "inner logic" and coherence, that any category of behavior that does not meet this criterion is not a legitimate sociological phenomenon. Second, that collective behavior is not permeated with this "inner logic," or is significantly less so than categories of behavior that should be regarded as legitimate sociological phenomena. Third, that a single, coherent explanation can account for all legitimate sociological phenomena. And fourth, that all behavior is enacted by individuals who are involved in conventional sociological institutions and organizations—family, education, religion, work, and so on—and therefore, no one launches into behavior (even that incorrectly designated as collective behavior) without having that fact influence every detail of their actions.

These assumptions range from irrelevant to completely false. It is possible that *no* sociological phenomenon exists that is "permeated" with an "inner logic" such that a single explanation can account for all its varieties. *All* types of behavior designated with a specific name display variety: politics, murder, marriage, urbanization, social movements, deviance, crime, rape, economic activity, religious observance. Not one possesses a coherence such that a single explanation can account for its infinite variety. Insisting that collective behavior must hew to a criterion not met by any other sociological phenomenon in existence is unrealistic. The field of collective behavior is simply a broad umbrella that allows us to study a range of fascinating phenomena. While no coherent theory can explain all varieties and cases of collective behavior, all phenomena designated by the term do share at least two fundamental characteristics in common: They all are relatively spontaneous and relatively noninstitutionalized.

It cannot be stressed too strongly that "spontaneous" does not mean uncaused, incomprehensible, totally impulsive, or appearing out of nowhere for no reason whatsoever (Miller, 1985, pp. 30–31). Rosenthal and Schwartz (1989, p. 54), in discussing the emergence of social movements, draw an analogy with the "spontaneous" combustion of oily rags; in the latter case, the appearance of a seemingly uncaused conflagration is due to certain specifiable prior conditions. "Similarly, on occasion, groups of people will engage in actions that are largely unpremeditated, but nevertheless *mediated by identifiable forces and preexisting structures*" (p. 54; my emphasis). Even collective behavior—less organizationally and institutionally bound than social movement activity—emerges out of, and is mediated by, "identifiable forces and preexisting structures." No behavior mysteriously bursts out of nowhere, totally uncaused or lacking in links to existing social structures.

At the same time, most explanations of the causes of collective behavior (and to a lesser extent, social movement activity) are done *post hoc*—that is, after the fact, not before. While the "spontaneous" combustion of oily rags could have been predicted in advance (as can much conventional behavior), the same is *not* true of most forms of collective behavior. Can anyone seriously argue that "streaking"—regardless of how elegantly it may have been accounted for after the fact (Evans and Miller, 1975; Anderson, 1977; Aguirre, Quarantelli, and Mendoza, 1988)—could have been predicted in advance? Clearly not, for no one was able to make such a prediction at the time. No doubt, streakers *were* influenced by their institutional involvements—the fact that they were relatively young, tended to be college students, were more likely to be male than female, were influenced by what the members of their friendship network were doing, and so on. And yet, who can say that streaking was precisely or even fundamentally similar to genuine conventional, institutional behavior, such as attending class, stopping at a red light, or making a purchase at a store? Such a claim would be invalid. Can anyone seriously argue that the two examples of spontaneous audience reaction cited at the beginning of this section are *in no discernible fashion* distinctly different from ordinary, everyday behavior—tying one's shoes, purchasing groceries, mailing a letter? Like Stalin, some sociologists cannot imagine any behavior being genuinely spontaneous, cannot distinguish between the applause coercively granted to him and that spontaneously and voluntarily granted to the beloved poet Akhmatova.

Rosenthal and Schwartz (1989, pp. 40–41, 54) refer to spontaneous ("seeming extraorganizational") behavior as *impromptu* and *unpremeditated,* and insist that such behavior typically has institutional roots. This point is well-taken, but it ignores the fact that much behavior is *not* impromptu, *is* premeditated, is *highly* predictable, and has *deeper* and *stronger* institutional roots than that behavior widely referred to as collective behavior. In other words, while "spontaneous" is not a precise antonym for "organized" or "institutionally rooted," *spontaneity is a matter of degree.* Collective behavior and some social movement activity are higher on both the spontaneity and the extra-institutionality dimensions than behaviors that are generally referred to as "conventional," "institutional," and "organizational." To the extent that behavior is lacking in spontaneity and extra-institutionality, it is *not* a form of collective behavior; to the extent that a given instance of social movement activity is lacking in these qualities, likewise, it is *not* an example of collective behavior.

It must be strongly emphasized that collective behavior *is* different from ordinary, everyday behavior; the two cannot be equated, as some have done (McPhail, 1978; Couch, 1968, 1970). If they were identical, there would be no such field as collective behavior; the study of what is called collective behavior would be swallowed up by the study of social or institutional behavior in general, as McPhail (1991, pp. 158ff) wishes to do. To quote Marx and Wood, "The excesses of those who saw collective behavior as totally unlike conventional behavior . . . should not now be counterbalanced by seeing it as exactly the same" (1975, p. 368). To those who argue that there are "no differences" between collective and ordinary behavior, the question automatically arises: Why use the term "collective" behavior at all? Why not say that all behavior is "social" behavior, and leave it at that? The answer is obvious: There *is* something different about collective behavior—and this will be the subject matter of this book. To say that collective behavior is not as different as was previously believed cannot be equated with saying that the two are identical; to argue that collective behavior is not totally spontaneous is not the same thing as arguing that it is just as organized and planned out as any other type of behavior; to agree that collective behavior is bound by rules is not to go on to make the more extavagant claim that these rules are exactly the same as those that operate in everyday life. Marx (1980, pp. 259–261) refers to the denial of difference between collective and conventional behavior as an example of "Type I Errors"; in the view of much of the field, it is a basic fallacy.

Participants in all forms of collective behavior are entangled in conventional structures, institutions, and organizations although, obviously, to varying degrees, depending on the activity in question. However, prior entanglements neither *predict* nor *prevent* their enactment of certain forms of collective behavior. The critics of the reality of collective behavior make the mistake of assuming an automatic extrapolation from involvement with conventional structures to behavior generally called collective, and assume that such involvement negates the reality of the latter or generates behavior of a certain sort in a mechanical fashion. Simply because people are involved with conventional structures does not mean that whatever they do in every area of life cannot therefore be regarded as collective behavior, that is, relatively spontaneous and relatively noninstitutionalized. To show that collective behavior generally has institutional roots is not enough; to make this case, it is necessary to show that these roots are *just as strong* for behavior that is generally referred to as collective behavior as for behavior regarded as conventional and institutional. No critic of the field has been able to make this comparison. And, as the chapters of this book will show, this is most decidedly not the case.

Our lives are governed by norms, by rules and regulations as to what we should and should not do. For most of us, these norms become incorporated into our sense of right and wrong. But at times, for many of us, these traditional norms no longer seem appropriate or relevant in certain contexts, and a new definition of an appropriate line of action emerges to guide our behavior. Some of us launch off in this new, somewhat different direction; we end up doing things that we didn't do just a few days before, indeed, things that we ourselves might very well have regarded as silly, wrong, excessive, inappropriate, or unusual. And yet, while we were doing them, all of us agreed that it was the right thing to do; at the time, no one regarded himself or herself as a deviant or a criminal. We know, when we gossip about someone, that our communication is a bit different from what we say under most ordinary circumstances. We know that certain rules of appropriate behavior during an extreme emergency are not the same as those in everyday life. We know when people are transported with ecstasy while listening to their favorite rock star, seeing a hero in action, or witnessing a religious vision, that their demeanor is different from the way it is when they open a can of tuna fish or read a physics textbook. When an angry crowd storms the presidential palace in a far away land and executes the dictator, everyone agrees that this is not "business as usual." Behavior of this sort is *not* a result of social "disorganization," a "breakdown" of society or a sector of it, or anomie. Instead, it shows that cultures are incapable of dictating behavior that is appropriate for any and all circumstances, that humans are creative in their interpretation of what behavior is appropriate in a given context, and that what is regarded as the appropriate behavior in certain contexts changes over time, often radically.

The field of collective behavior studies actions that are relatively spontaneous and noninstitutionalized. "Spontaneous" refers to their unpremeditated, unplanned, unpredictable quality; "noninstitutionalized" refers to the fact that, in comparison with most forms of behavior, they tend to be less tied down by traditional norms and rules. In the midst of a collective behavior event, we can't quite be sure what's going to happen next. In contrast, when we see people making a purchase in a store, working at their desks or at a machine, attending class, or checking a book out of the library, we have a fairly good idea (within limits, of course) as to what's going to happen from one moment to the next—and so do the participants. On the other hand, with the behavior we describe in this book, this is far less likely to be the case. Such behavior is far more volatile, fleeting, unpredictable; participants are significantly less likely to follow traditional norms.

But remember: No behavior is completely spontaneous. No actors are completely free of normative constraint; in fact, a major assumption that guides our view of collective behavior is that, in engaging in it, participants continue to be influenced by norms, although they are nontraditional and emergent in character. And no collective behavior participants are free from institutional entanglements. Even if behavior in a noninstitutional setting is not tied down by traditional, conventional norms, all participants eventually return to a world in which traditional, conventional norms are influential, and this acts back on future collective behavior in important ways. Simply because, in a given context, two people gossip and create a certain nonnormative interpretation about the events they are discussing, in the long run, they are not completely free to believe and act on that novel, spontaneously arrived-at interpretation. The fact is, they must confront other people and real-world events *with* that novel interpretation, which may be found wanting and may have to be revised. If we believe that we have seen a miraculous vision, again, that belief will be acted back upon by the reactions of the social world in which we live—our friends, acquaintances, relatives, colleagues, and the power hierarchy of the religion with which we are affiliated. In this sense, *all* collective behavior can be said to have one foot in the conventional world. *At the same time*, this "institutional acting-back" on collective behavior is a matter of degree, and varies from one type to another, as we'll see throughout this book. The traditional, institutionalized world is less likely to act back on certain individuals who have engaged in certain types of collective behavior than is true of others.

Much of the most innovative recent research in the field has moved away from its classic root emphasis on spontaneity and extrainstitutionality. To be more precise, aspects of several subjects classically investigated by the field of collective behavior have been shown to be less spontaneous, more institutionalized and normatively bound, more predictable and tightly organized than has been previously thought. This is especially the case in at least three major areas of collective behavior: crowd behavior, behavior in disasters, and social movements. This means that these three areas only partly overlap with—and, at best, have one foot *in* and one foot *out of*—the field of collective behavior.

Crowd behavior (or, in McPhail's terminology, 1991, pp. 152–154, 162–163, the behavior of "gatherings"), as we'll see in Part II, is far from ruleless and normless. How crowds are formed, break apart, and what they do and don't do, are all governed by *assembling processes* or mechanisms (McPhail, 1991; p. 152ff, 1992). Some observers feel this makes it necessary to look at collective behavior in a very different fashion (Miller, 1985, pp. 42ff). I do not share this view. Indeed, *to the extent that* the behavior of some crowds is predictable, normative, and lacking in spontaneity, it cannot be referred to as collective behavior at all. As McPhail himself, says, conveying a somewhat different meaning, not all crowds are examples of collective behavior. Crowds are not in and of themselves collective behavior; they may be the site for or the locus of collective behavior—or they may not. Crowds provide the *raw material* out of which some forms of collective behavior spring, but *most* crowds never engage in collective behavior, as it is defined here. The study of crowd behavior does not force us to reconceptualize collective behavior so much as it forces us to rethink the relationship between crowds and gatherings on the one hand and collective behavior on the other.

McPhail (1991, 1992) even goes so far as to argue that the term *collective behavior* should be equated with *social behavior generally*, that is, "two or more persons, engaged in one or more behaviors . . . ., judged common or concerted, on one or more dimensions" (p. 159)—what Howard S. Becker refers to as "doing things together" (1986). Lofland, 1981, refers to what McPhail calls collective behavior as "merely the study of human coordination," 1985, p. 40. Examples would include a boxing match, a couple making love, the weekly purchase of one's groceries, a lecture in a sociology course, a parade, and the building of a bridge. While such activities are indeed worthy of study, it is not clear that we add anything by calling them "collective" behavior rather than *social* behavior. In my estimation, regardless of what the field is called, there remains an intriguing area worthy of study—relatively spontaneous, relatively noninstitutional behavior. Attempting to define this field of study out of existence does not gainsay the fact that a fascinating realm of social behavior out there in the real world exists that cries out for attention.

Sociologists who focus more or less exclusively on external behavior are troubled by the fact that it is difficult to determine precisely the existence of certain subjectively based concepts in the material world. Hence, they retreat to a more or less mechanistic and measureable set of concepts. For instance, McPhail (1991, pp. 156, 158, 159, 187, and 149–186, *passim*) finds it impossible to accept the reality of the traditional view of collective behavior as spontaneous in part because its reality cannot be determined with any degree of precision. For McPhail, the actor's subjective experience is "impenetrable" (p. 159). To my mind, and to most observers in the field, what this demonstrates is not so much a problem with the concepts of spontaneity and extrainstitutionality as a disagreement between strict behaviorists and sociologists who feel that the subjectivistic dimension, although more difficult to study than overt actions—and only overt actions—is worthy of study, that a sociology stripped of it is no sociology at all.

In a parallel fashion, recent disaster research has emphasized the organized responses that communities, bureaucracies, and government agencies mount to meet the challenge of disasters (Dynes, DeMarchi, and Pelanda, 1987; Kreps, 1989). Again, *to the extent that* such organizational responses are predictable, planned, normatively bound, and lacking in spontaneity, *they do not qualify* as instances of collective behavior. Of course, *no* disaster is completely predictable; there will *always* be an element of surprise in any disaster. Still, when disaster organizations rehearse their responses to a number of natural and humanly created disaster contingencies to the point where everything goes as planned, it is difficult to refer to what happened as an example of collective behavior. The more chaos a disaster creates, the more ambiguous the situations in which disaster victims and relief workers find themselves, the more inventive and spontaneous human behavior has to be to meet the challenges a disaster poses and the more that we have collective behavior on our hands. Again, as with crowds, disasters are not *themselves* forms of collective behavior, nor are responses to disasters necessarily or by definition examples of collective behavior. It is when disasters create circumstances that force us to be creative together that collective behavior makes its appearance.

As we'll see in Part V, social movements, too, have been looked at in recent years in a very different light from the classic view. Here, however, there is an difference: While much of the field has sought to retain the study of crowds and disasters in their entirety, to a great extent, social movements and collective behavior have been severed from one another. Most of the "young Turks" in the study of social movements (Zald and McCarthy, 1987; McAdam, 1982; McAdam, McCarthy, and Zald, 1988; Jenkins, 1986; Morris, 1984; Morris and Herring, 1987; Morris and Mueller, 1991) approach the phenomenon by focusing on goals, tactics, organization, resources, and outcomes—a very different approach from that adopted by the field's classic writers. It could very well be that social movements are most fruitfully approached with the aid of these variables and concepts, but to the extent that this is true, they are *not* forms of collective behavior. The more organized social movements are, the more predictable the behavior of their members, and the more cooperation that exists between social movements and mainstream institutions, the less that they can be referred to as collective behavior. Most of the practitioners who work with this newer approach recognize this fact, and regard social movements and collective behavior as two separate fields.

It seems to me that recent researchers in these three areas—the study of "assembling processes," the study of disasters, and the study of social movements—have thrown the baby out with the bathwater. That is, practitioners of each field have carved out a sector that once was an integral part of the field of collective behavior, and now assume that nothing of the original field remains. While they are correct in their view that what they study is not, strictly speaking, what was once defined as collective behavior, an area does remain, is substantial, and is worthy of study. It is possible that these carving-up and throwing-out processes were prompted by the universally accepted view that the LeBon-Park-Blumer view of the crowd specifically and collective behavior generally are invalid (McPhail, 1991, p. 152). But agreeing that *one view* of collective behavior is invalid does not mean that the field does not exist—or that the element of spontaneity must be extracted or ignored, and that collective behavior be equated with social behavior generally.

Collective behavior is both apart from and yet integral to ordinary, every-day, conventional behavior. It is different enough to warrant a distinct field of study; at the same time, it is also general enough to be integral to the lives of all of us. We all engage in it, we all are subject to it, and knowing about it reveals secrets that govern social life in general.

What is collective behavior? What are its basic characteristics? How does it get started? What social conditions encourage it? Who engages in it—and who doesn't? What do specific types or forms of collective behavior look like? Is it possible to explain collective behavior as a general phenomenon, or does each type require a separate explanation? Can we predict the out-break of collective behavior in advance? What kind of an impact does it have on its participants and on society generally? Do different types of collective behavior have different kinds of impact? Do some leave a legacy, while oth-ers disappear without a trace? This book will explore and attempt to answer questions such as these. It will be an introduction to one of the most inter-esting of all imaginable areas of human life. Such an exploration cannot fail to fascinate; I hope that, in addition, it will also inform and enlighten.

References

Aguirre, B. E., Enrico L. Quarantelli, and Jorge L. Mendoza. 1988. "The Collective Behavior of Fads: The Characteristics, Effects, and Career of Streaking." *American Sociological Review*, 53 (August): 569–584.

Anderson, William A. 1977. "The Social Organization and Social Control of a Fad." *Urban Life*, 6 (July): 221–240.

Bainbridge, William Sims. 1989. In Rodney Stark, *Sociology* (3rd ed.). Belmont, Calif.: Wadsworth, pp. 608–640.

Becker, Howard S. 1986. *Doing Things Together: Selected Papers.* Evanston, Ill.: Northwestern University Press.

Blumer, Herbert. 1939. "Collective Behavior." In Robert E. Park (ed.), *Outline of the Principles of Sociology* (1st ed.). New York: Barnes & Noble, pp. 221–279.

Couch, Carl J. 1968. "Collective Behavior: An Examination of Some Stereotypes." *Social Problems*, 15 (Winter): 310–322.

Couch, Carl J. 1970. "Dimensions of Association in Collective Behavior Episodes." *Sociometry*, 33 (4): 457–471.

Dynes, Russell R., Bruna DeMarchi, and Carlo Pelanda (eds.). 1987.

Sociology of Disasters: Contribution of Sociology to Disaster Research. Milan, Italy: Franco Angeli.

Evans, Robert R., and Jerry L. L. Miller. 1975. "Barely an End in Sight." In Robert R. Evans (ed.), *Readings in Collective Behavior* (2nd ed.). Chicago: Rand McNally, pp. 401–417.

Jenkins, J. Craig. 1986. "Stirring the Masses: Indigenous Roots of the Civil Rights Movement." *Contemporary Sociology*, 15 (May): 354–357.

Kreps, Gary A. (ed.). 1989. *Social Structure and Disaster.* Newark, Del.: University of Delaware Press.

LeBon, Gustave. 1982 (originally published in 1895). *The Crowd: A Study of the Popular Mind.* Marietta, Georgia: Larlin.

Lofland, John. 1981. "Collective Behavior: The Elementary Forms." In Morris Rosenberg and Ralph H. Turner (eds.), *Social Psychology: Sociological Perspectives.* New York: Basic Books, pp. 411–446.

Lofland, John. 1985. *Protest: Studies of Collective Behavior and Social Movements.* New Brunswick, N.J.: Transaction Books.

Mackay, Charles. 1932 (originally published in 1841, 1st ed., and 1852, 2nd ed.). *Extraordinary Popular Delusions and the Madness of Crowds.* New York: L. C. Page.

Marx, Gary T. 1980. "Conceptual Problems in the Field of Collective Behavior." In Hubert M. Blalock, Jr., *Sociological Theory and Research: A Critical Appraisal.* New York: Free Press, pp. 258–274.

Marx, Gary T., and James L. Wood. 1975. "Strands of Theory and Research in Collective Behavior." *Annual Review of Sociology*, 1: 363–428.

McAdam, Doug. 1982. *Political Process and the Development of Black Insurgency*, 1930–1970. Chicago: University of Chicago Press.

McAdam, Doug, John D. McCarthy, and Mayer D. Zald. 1988. "Social Movements." In Neil J. Smelser (ed.). *Handbook of Sociology.* Newbury Park, Calif.: Sage, pp. 695–737.

McPhail, Clark. 1978. "Toward a Theory of Collective Behavior." Unpublished paper presented at the Symposium on Symbolic Interaction, University of South Carolina, Columbia, March 17.

McPhail, Clark. 1991. *The Myth of the Madding Crowd.* New York: Aldine de Gruyter.

McPhail, Clark. 1992. *Acting Together: The Organization of Crowds.* New York: Aldine de Gruyter.

Miller, David L. 1985. *Introduction to Collective Behavior.* Belmont, Calif.: Wadsworth.

Morris, Aldon D. 1984. *The Origins of the Civil Rights Movement: Black Communities Organizing for Change.* New York: Free Press.

Morris, Aldon D., and Cedric Herring. 1987. "Theory and Research in Social Movements: A Critical Review." In Samuel Long (ed.), *Political Behavior Annual.* Norwood, N.J.: Ablex, pp. 137–198.

Morris, Aldon D., and Carol Mueller (eds.). 1991. *Frontiers of Social Movement Theory.* New Haven, Conn.: Yale University Press.

Park, Robert E. 1972 (principal essay originally published in 1904). *The Crowd and the Public and Other Essays.* Chicago: University of Chicago Press.

Rosenthal, Naomi, and Michael Schwartz. 1989. "Spontaneity and Democracy in Social Movements." *International Movement Research,* 2: 33–59.

Sheldon, Richard. 1990. "Introduction to Enlarged and Updated Edition." In Vera Dunham, *In Stalin's Time: Middleclass Values in Soviet Fiction* (enlarged and updated ed.). Durham, N.C.: Duke University Press, pp. xi–xxiv.

Smith, Wendy. 1990. *Real Life Drama: The Group Theater in America.* New York: Alfred Knopf.

Zald, Mayer N., and John D. McCarthy (eds.). 1987. *Social Movements in Organizational Society: Collected Essays.* New Brunswick, N.J.: Transaction Books.

CHAPTER

1

WHAT IS COLLECTIVE BEHAVIOR?

L ate in 1988, a letter warning of a new form of LSD distribution began to turn up in northern New Jersey. It was said to have been written by a member of the Union City police department. Soon after, at the invitation of the supposed author of the letter, it was reprinted and distributed by school, health, and law enforcement officials in a number of districts and jurisdictions throughout the northeastern United States. The letter read, in part:

> A form of tattoo called "BLUE STAR" is being sold to school children. It is a small sheet of paper containing blue stars the size of a pencil eraser. Each star is soaked with LSD. Each star can be removed and placed in the mouth. THE LSD CAN ALSO BE ABSORBED THROUGH THE SKIN SIMPLY BY HANDLING THE PAPER. [In addition, there are also] brightly colored paper tabs resembling postage stamps [that] have pictures of Superman, butterflies, clowns, Mickey Mouse and other Disney characters on them. . . . This is a new way of selling ACID by appealing to young children. A young child could happen upon these and have a fatal "trip." . . . A red stamp called "RED PYRAMID" is also being distributed along with "MICRO DOT" in various colors [as is] another kind called "WINDOW PANE" which has a grid that can be cut out. THESE ARE ALL LACED WITH DRUGS. . . . If you or your children see any of the above

> DO NOT HANDLE!!! THESE DRUGS ARE KNOWN TO REACT [sic] VERY QUICKLY and SOME ARE LACED WITH STRYCH-NINE. Symptoms are: hallucinations, severe vomiting, uncontrolled laughter, mood change, and change in body temperature. GET TO THE HOSPITAL AS SOON AS POSSIBLE AND CALL POLICE.

Within five weeks, the story of the LSD-impregnated stickers was declared to be a hoax; "there are no stickers," said a spokesperson for the federal Drug Enforcement Administration. "It's a very poor practical joke," he added. It is unlikely that enough of the drug could be put on the tattoos for it to have a hallucinogenic effect if absorbed through the skin, the official declared. Exactly how the rumor got started isn't clear; "the trail of the LSD tattoos fades into vapor as it is followed. No one can point to the source of the letter nor the time it started. Despite the persistent rumors that someone knows someone who saw the stickers or who had a child who was affected by a sticker, no witness has ever surfaced." When one school official called the police department from which the letter supposedly emanated, "they said it [the LSD in tattoos] was real. They said that this is out there," the official stated. She could not recall with whom she spoke, however. Another school official said that the stickers are "apparently present and available" locally. When asked how he knew this, he said that two students in his district "were apprehended. They had these stickers and they got them at a rock concert." Several concerned parents said that the reason why they reacted so strongly and quickly to the LSD letter was that: "Drugs are everywhere today. . . . You just can't assume that your child is safe" (Kolata, 1988, pp. B1, B5). However, to this day, concrete evidence of the LSD-impregnated tattoos has never been located.

In June, 1983, an unusual, peculiar-looking doll was introduced on the American children's toy market: the Cabbage Patch doll. It proved to be an immediate success; during its first full year of commercial availability, sales of the dolls totaled over $500 million, and the following year's sales grossed some $600 million. Demand for the dolls could scarcely be satisfied. When a new shipment arrived at a local store parents crowded, pushed, and shoved to get their hands on one; near-riots broke out in dozens of stores nationwide. Stores generally sold out of them within minutes. But by 1986, sales of the dolls were less than half—$250 million—what they had been in their peak year, and in 1987, sales fell again by half to a weak $125 million. Between 1985 and 1986, the company's net income plummeted from a net profit of $65 million to $110 million in the loss column; in 1987, the company once again lost over $100 million. In 1988, the manufacturer of the Cabbage Patch dolls, Coleco Industries, unable to cope with the abruptness of the "boom and bust" cycle of its doll sales, and severely hurt by the slump in its revenues, filed for bankruptcy (Crudele, 1986; Feder, 1988). In 1990, Coleco sold its rights to the Cabbage Patch doll to Hasbro, another toy manufacturer, which hoped to profit from its long-term and more modest institutionalized, as opposed to its past intense and more faddish, sales.

On June 10, a few hours after the ruling party had certified Roh Tae Woo as its presidential candidate, hundreds of thousands of protesters took to the streets in cities all over South Korea demanding direct elections. The government assumed that the rallies and demonstrations, as in the past, would be largely confined to radicals and students, and would be "easily contained." However, this time, "things were different. It was not just that the rally was bigger than previous ones. For the first time, there were also undeniable signs of solid middle class support. . . . People of all ages and backgrounds were obviously dissatisfied with the slow pace of political development." Their demonstrations continued daily for over a week, reaching "a fever pitch" on the night of the 18th. "Downtown Seoul looked like a war zone as tens of thousands of demonstrators took control of the streets, overpowering entire units of riot policemen who had run out of tear gas." In a city a few miles south of Seoul, a protester commandeered a bus and plowed it into a line of officers, killing one. At that point, the mood of the police turned ugly; several units demanded military assistance, and in some quarters, martial law was expected momentarily. On June 19th, the President, Chun Doo Hwan, issued a decree ordering troops to take positions outside the capital (Haberman, 1987, p. 6).

A few hours before troops were scheduled to move into Seoul, President Chun pulled them back. Through his figurehead Prime Minister, a "stern warning" was issued on national television; if the riots did not stop, it was stated, "extraordinary measures" would be taken. The statement was interpreted by most observers to mean that the ruling party would consider serious compromises that had been rejected previously. Within two weeks, opposition demands for direct presidential elections, the release of political prisoners, and the granting of civil liberties to political dissidents, were approved. Suddenly, Mr. Roh, the ruling party's candidate, found that he had to mount a campaign for the presidency instead of having it handed to him. Likewise, the opposition found that it, too, had to launch a presidential campaign and contemplate organizing for the possibility of taking office. While the eventual election of Mr. Roh by a plurality—two feuding left-wing candidates split the bulk of the remaining votes, ensuring that neither would win—touched off more protests for a brief period, the intensity of the violence of June was not repeated. Almost miraculously, as a result of a series of protests and demonstrations, South Korea stepped into a period of democratic elections (Haberman, 1987, p. 6).

_____ DEFINING COLLECTIVE BEHAVIOR _____

Rumors and legends, fads, and collective protest—these and other social phenomena make up the subject matter of the field of collective behavior. *Collective behavior* is the relatively spontaneous, unstructured, extrainstitutional behavior of a fairly large number of individuals. *Extrainstitutional* means that behavior of this type deviates from the established, normative, institutionalized patterns of everyday life. It also tends to have one foot planted outside society's mainstream structures and institutions, such as the educational system, traditional religious bodies, politics and government, and the mass media. Collective behavior operates in situations in which there are no, or few, adequate, clear-cut definitions as to what to do from mainstream culture or where those definitions fail to determine participants' behavior. The examples detailed above all operate outside the stable, patterned structures of society. They reflect, like all collective behavior, the "maverick" side of human life. Compared with conventional, everyday life, collective behavior is less inhibited and more spontaneous, more changeable and less structured, shorter-lived and less stable. Of course, like most distinctions, the one between collective behavior and conventional, everyday behavior is a matter of degree, one of shades of gray, not a black-or-white affair. The two blend into one another, filling out a spectrum from completely structured at one end to almost completely unstructured at the other—with most behavior falling somewhere between the two. Collective behavior is relatively unstructured, but it is not wholly so. In short, collective behavior is somewhat different from, *but not wholly discontinuous with*, conventional, institutional behavior.

Rather than thinking of collective behavior as a clear-cut, readily identifiable and definable phenomenon, it is perhaps more fruitful to identify a number of dimensions that distinguish collective behavior from conventional, everyday behavior. There are no hard and fast rules explicitly spelling out what it is; different experts define it somewhat differently. At the same time, that does not mean that there are no differences between the two. While there are some observers who hold the position that collective behavior is no different from more conventional, institutionalized behavior (Miller, 1985, pp. 10–11; Couch, 1968; McPhail, 1978, 1991, 1992), it is clear that their conception of collective behavior is far broader than the mainstream of the field. Go over the examples discussed above: Are these ordinary, everyday events? Are the rules for what one is supposed to do as clear-cut and as explicit during riots and demonstrations, spreading rumors, adopting fads, and relating myths and legends as they are for going to class, making a purchase in a store, voting in an election, and telling someone about something when all the facts are available? It is easy to see that collective behavior is at least somewhat different from what we regard as ordinary, conventional behavior.

I have been contrasting collective behavior with *conventional* behavior. This implies that collective behavior is relatively unconventional, that it violates the norms of mainstream culture. This is true, of course, but its relationship with conventional values, beliefs, and practices is extremely complex. Collective behavior may be urged by newly developed norms that arose because traditional practices simply don't seem to work any longer in the eyes of some members of the society. In the past generation, there has been a certain religious and spiritual longing that remains unfulfilled among some of society's younger members, and unconventional or "new" religions have stepped in to fill that void (Appel, 1983; Bromley and Shupe, 1981). Collective behavior may arise because traditional norms are in conflict with certain desired values in a specific situation. We learn that "thou shalt not steal," but when one sees others looting during a blackout, and no one is getting caught, it is difficult to avoid temptation, and one may very well join in with others who are looting (Curvin and Porter, 1979). Often, collective behavior takes place when mainstream norms do not indicate a particular course of action in a certain situation; in order to act, one must innovate.

For example, in many disasters, within broad limits, it is not clear just what one must do to survive. Often, one's course of action could not have been predicted from society's conventional norms. "Improvising is the key activity in disaster response." Activities that are later thought of as nonnormative "are better understood as behavior organized under adverse and deteriorating" conditions (Miller, 1985, pp. 171, 175). In short, there is a "complex character" in the relationship between established norms and collective behavior, rather than a "total discontinuity" (Turner, 1964, p. 383).

It should be emphasized that, while collective behavior typically stands outside institutionalized patterns of behavior, participants in collective behavior are not necessarily isolated from the conventional members of the society or from the society's mainstream culture. In fact, typically, collective behavior participants *are* the conventional members of the society; they are integrated into the conventional society in ways that criminals and deviants, for the most part, are not. Most participants in collective behavior see what they are doing as acceptable and conventional; most have not totally rejected society's norms or beliefs—they have simply redefined them, put their special spin on them. For example, a participant in a fad tends not to see himself or herself outside society's mainstream and, except for that one characteristic, is usually quite conventional. While most collective behavior participants recognize that some members of mainstream society will define them as "kooks," they see what they do as completely normal and in no way threatening of the social order.

In sum, *conventional, everyday behavior tends to be relatively* organized, structured, planned, predictable, enduring, stable, institutionalized, normative, and familiar. In contrast, *collective behavior tends to be relatively* unorganized, unstructured, spontaneous, unpredictable, short-lived, "extra-institutional," nonnormative, unconventional, and unfamiliar.

Collective behavior has a second quality in addition to its spontaneity and relatively unstructured character. This is implied in the word *collective.* Collective behavior is not the behavior of isolated individuals acting on their own; it is the behavior of individuals acting *with* and *in relation to* one another. When someone does something fairly unique on his or her own, without being directly influenced by others to do it, and does not talk about it with others, this can be referred to as *individual* behavior; when the same thing is done by a number of other individuals, again, without direct influence from others, sociologists call it *parallel* behavior. In parallel behavior, each person "is doing the same thing for the same reason, but each is doing it alone" (Bainbridge, 1989, p. 613). But when that behavior is engaged in in the concrete presence of others, or is directly influenced by others, and becomes the basis for a group bond (and, of course, it is spontaneous and unstructured), sociologists refer to it as *collective* behavior. As with the difference between conventional and collective behavior, the line between individual and parallel behavior, and that between parallel and collective behavior, are not sharp or clear-cut; again, these are matters of degree, spectrums rather than either-or, black-or-white affairs. In collective behavior, people communicate with one another "and influence each other's actions so that they end up doing somewhat similar things in a somewhat unified way" (Bainbridge, 1989, p. 613).

It must be stressed that its group character does *not* distinguish collective behavior from conventional behavior; like all social behavior, collective behavior is "doing things together" (Becker, 1986; McPhail, 1991, 1992). Though collective behavior is a group-influenced product, most conventional behavior, too, is a group product. The idea that an "intensification of group control over the individual" when collective behavior takes place "may be an illusion" (Turner, 1964, p. 382). In the respect that collective behavior is a group product, it is no different from ordinary, everyday behavior.

Still, some forms of behavior *are* less influenced by the group than others. When an individual throws a brick through the window of a building, that is individual behavior; when a thousand people all over the country, uninfluenced by one another's behavior, individually and on their own, throw bricks through windows, that is parallel behavior. But if a crowd gathers outside a government building and demands reforms, begins milling about and shouting, becomes enraged that officials do not address their demands, grabs bricks and throws them through windows, storms the building and kidnaps several officials inside—that is collective behavior. In the first two cases, we have individuals acting on their own; in the third, we have a genuine *group* of individuals acting together, in concert. Even in crowds, people may engage in behavior *in common* without necessarily engaging in behavior *in concert* (McPhail, 1991, pp. 49–51).

If one person wears purple clothes, that is individual behavior; if a number of individuals in different places do the same thing, again, each uninfluenced by the others, that is parallel behavior. If wearing purple clothes becomes the basis of a new fashion, which is adopted by a substantial number of individuals, and that fashion to some extent becomes the basis for how people relate to one another, that is collective behavior. If one person sees something in the night sky he or she believes is a flying saucer, that is individual behavior; if a number of isolated people have the same experience, but are not aware of the experiences of others, that is parallel behavior. However, if the people who have had this experience talk to others about it, try to get them to believe in its validity, meet others who share the experience in common, affirm their belief as a result of this interaction, form clubs on the basis of the experience and the belief, argue with skeptics about the validity of what they saw, get together and demand that the government do something about the problem of flying saucers—this is a form of collective behavior. While there may be many cases that are difficult to categorize, there also are many cases that clearly belong in one category or another—individual, parallel, or collective behavior.

_____ SETTINGS OF COLLECTIVE BEHAVIOR _____

In 1901, a French sociologist named Gabriel Tarde published a book titled _L'Opinion et la foule_, which means, in English, _The Public and the Crowd_ (Tarde, 1969). In this book, Tarde distinguished between two quite different social collectivities—one, the public, which is scattered and diffuse and connected only by a common interest in a specific issue, and the other, the crowd, which is compact and whose members are physically together in the same place at the same time. The public, Tarde wrote, is a modern creation and exists only by virtue of the mass media; the crowd has existed wherever and whenever humans have congregated in substantial numbers. And, while a given individual can—and always does—belong to several publics simultaneously, one can belong to only one crowd at a time. These characteristics impart a special quality to publics and crowds that make them distinctly different social phenomena. Although Tarde misunderstood exactly how publics and crowds differed (he believed the public to be skeptical and rational, and crowds, fanatical and irrational), he did put his finger on a crucial and fundamental distinction for the field of collective behavior, one that can be ignored only at the observer's intellectual peril. Moreover, he disagreed with his contemporary, Gustave LeBon, who claimed that the modern age is the age of crowds; in contrast, Tarde argued, insightfully and, in my estimation, accurately, that the 20th century is the age not of crowds but of publics (1969, p. 281). In any case, this distinction between publics and crowds will guide the observations of much of this book.

Today, the field of collective behavior distinguishes between collective behavior that takes place in compact, spatially proximate, more or less face-to-face settings or _crowds_ (or temporary gatherings), and diffuse, spacially dispersed social settings, which are called _masses_ and _publics_. In crowds, people are in the same place at the same time; in masses and publics, people are geographically scattered. (One book-length and supposedly general discussion of collective behavior, Perry and Pugh, 1978, does not deal with diffuse collectivities at all.) This distinction is important because many crucial processes that take place in crowds do not take place in masses and publics, and vice versa; moreover, different types of collective behavior take place in each of these settings. Of course, like practically everything else in social life, the line between a crowd and a mass or a public is not always clear-cut. Sometimes a crowd is so large, scattered, and diffuse that it is made up of clusters of smaller crowds, each reacting in the same way to an event or a stimulus. Still, the physical proximity of the members of a crowd is what makes it a unique setting in which collective behavior can take place. Likewise, the geographical dispersal of publics and masses creates a unique setting in which certain kinds of collective behavior are likely to emerge.

CROWDS

When we use the term "crowd," we do *not* imply an endorsement of any of the myths and misconceptions commonly held about it—that they act in a uniform fashion, in one way only, that they continue to act a certain way, that they are frequently conflictual and violent, and so on (McPhail, 1991, pp. 162–163). There is no need to scrap the term "crowd" and come up with a new one—one expert suggests "gathering" or "temporary gathering" (McPhail, 1991, pp. 152–154). To us, the "crowd" and the "gathering" are synonymous. According to a classic typology, there are four basic types of crowds (Blumer, 1969, pp. 78–85): *casual, conventional, expressive,* and *acting* crowds. As with all social phenomena, these types blend into one another; most crowds contain something of a "mix" of types. Above all, in classifying a crowd, we must not fall into the fallacy of "the illusion of unanimity" (Turner and Killian, 1972, p. 22; 1987, p. 26; McPhail, 1991, pp. 71, 162). At the same time, most crowds *can* be classified according to the behavior or orientation of the majority of their members. The people streaming into and out of Times Square minute by minute is different from an audience at a classical music concert, whose members, in turn, do not act precisely like the audience at a "heavy metal" concert, who, likewise, behave differently from a lynching mob. While the four basic crowd types do not characterize all gatherings, they do characterize a great many.

Casual Crowds. These are loosely structured, made up of people who just happen to be in the same place at the same time. They are united solely by physical proximity and not (or not necessarily) by common interests or goals. As previously noted, an example is the crowd that gathers daily in and around Times Square in New York. Its members come and go, some "hang out" and look around for a time, but still, even though they are physically present in a certain spot at a certain time, they have no common bond and no common identity. The members of such a crowd can enter and leave it at any time. Occasionally, a precipitating event—such as an arrest, a fight, or an accident—can generate a common focus of attention and thus give its members some sense of common identity. Still, the members of casual crowds have little else in common except their physical location. Under most circumstances, casual crowds are not acting out a form of collective behavior. There are normative, institutionalized rules for behavior in casual and conventional crowds, and most people follow them.

Conventional Crowds. These come together for a common, specific purpose—such as to attend a lecture, hear a concert, or watch a movie or a play. Conventional crowds tend to be normatively governed; their members observe the rules that decree what is, and what is not, appropriate in such settings. Generally, a movie audience does not throw rocks at the screen, and students attending a lecture do not try to beat up the professor. Of course, under certain conditions, a conventional crowd could become very unconventional; the movie the crowd has paid to see never appears on the screen,

There are many remarkable and revealing features of political riots and demonstrations. One is that they show that regimes that appear to be deeply entrenched and fully institutionalized are often extremely vulnerable, unstable, and rest on little more than the shaky loyalty of government troops. Some regimes, in fact, are little more than a "house of cards" that tumble in the face of widespread, popular, collective protest. Here, Rumanian demonstrators help bring down the Ceaucescu regime.

or the professor the students have come to hear arbitrarily decides to fail everyone in the class (see the boxed insert on page 105, "From Conventional to Expressive to Acting Crowd"). Still, to the extent that crowds are conventional, they are not enacting collective behavior.

Expressive Crowds. These may have gathered for a specific purpose, but they differ from conventional crowds in that their main purpose is belonging to the crowd itself. Crowd activity for its members is an end in itself, not just a means. In conventional crowds, the audience wants to watch the movie or hear the lecture; being part of the audience is secondary or irrelevant. In expressive crowds, the audience also wants to be a member of the crowd, and participate in crowd behavior—to scream, shout, cheer, clap, and stomp their feet. People do not, for example, attend a political rally chiefly to be enlightened by the speaker; they assemble for the purpose of expressing an emotion, a belief, a sentiment through the crowd and its behavior. Fans do not go to a rock concert for the sole purpose of listening to the music; just as important is participating in crowd spectacle and all it entails. Naturally, the line between a conventional and an expressive crowd is fuzzy. Under certain conditions, a conventional crowd can become an expressive crowd. An especially bitter loss by the home team or a bad call by a referee or an umpire can turn ordinarily law-abiding fans into an angry, screaming assembly. Most sporting events and rock concerts have both conventional and expressive elements, which means that their members form a transitional or in-between type of crowd.

Acting Crowds.   These engage in overt behavior, aside from simply milling around. Revolutions, lynchings, violent demonstrations, and mass lootings provide examples of acting crowds. Acting crowds are often referred to by observers who mistrust them as "mobs." An acting crowd, as its name implies, *does* something. The act the crowd engages in may have been planned in advance, or emerged in the crowd setting or the milling process itself. Most likely, it is a little of both, or one or the other, depending on the crowd in question or the specific members of the crowd we are referring to. Crowds do not act with a single mind; we should never forget that they are made up of a large number of distinct and different individuals. In most acting crowds, some people act and some do not. However, people acting together can—and actually do—do things that the same number of people acting alone could never do. Crowds are more than the sum of their parts, and it would be proper to say, for example, that "a crowd" stormed the embassy, assassinated the dictator, looted the store, or attacked the police.

As we saw in the introduction to this part of the book, *not all crowd behavior is collective behavior.* Simply because a substantial number of people gather in the same place at the same time does *not* mean that they necessarily engage in spontaneous, extrainstitutional behavior. Many crowds provide the *settings* for collective behavior (though most do not) just as publics or diffuse collectivities may (or may not) constitute a locus of collective behavior. Convergent or assembling behavior is eminently worthy of study in its own right, but crowds cannot be *equated with* collective behavior, or even one *type* of collective behavior.

PUBLICS

Spatially dispersed collectivities are often referred to as *masses* and *publics.* Masses and publics are generally defined as *a large and heterogeneous number of people who are geographically scattered and whose attention is focused on a particular stimulus, issue, or phenomenon.* Exactly how much they interact with one another is a matter of degree and depends on the issue or phenomenon in question; the members of some masses and publics are more loosely interconnected than others. Still, for all masses and publics there is *some* degree of interconnectedness.

The Mass.   Until recently, the concepts of "mass" and "public" were distinguished. A *mass* was defined as a number of anonymous, isolated, heterogeneous individuals who have little contact with one another, and who react to a given stimulus in a parallel, not a collective fashion. A *public* was seen as scattered individuals who are also focused on a given stimulus, but who have some contact with one another (Blumer, 1969, pp. 85–91ff; Miller, 1985, p. 21). During the generation just before and just after the Second World

War, there was concern that the United States had become a "mass society," a nation of dispersed and essentially anonymous, disconnected individuals, subject to the same problems and participating in the same behavior, but socially isolated from one another. The concept that many people have of how the "mass media" operate follows this line of thinking; millions of individuals supposedly watch television or read a newspaper story in isolation, without influencing one another.

However, later generations of sociologists realized that collective behavior does not work in this fashion; as it was originally conceived (Blumer, 1939, 1969, pp. 85–89), mass behavior scarcely exists at all. When geographically dispersed people are exposed to a common stimulus or phenomenon, such as a TV show, they typically watch it with others, discuss it, and engage in social interaction about it. Hardly anyone lives in the kind of isolated, atomistic social world defined by the original formulation of the term "mass"; the members of practically no mass (or public) are lacking in interaction and social contact with others. Behavior that is spatially dispersed generally takes place in *clusters* of groups and collectivities. From now on, I will use the two terms "mass" and "public" as synonyms to refer to essentially the same phenomenon. Masses and publics are *diffuse collectivities.*

Publics vs Crowds. Clearly, masses and publics are different from crowds. While in a crowd setting, a given individual may have direct face-to-face interaction with dozens, perhaps hundreds of people, and indirect, second- or third-hand interaction with many more thousands. Apart from the crowd—in a mass or a public setting—instant access to other people is limited to a much smaller number. Going about one's daily rounds, one may talk to a friend on the phone, meet several acquaintances for coffee, interact with colleagues at work, talk to fellow students before and after class, watch and discuss television news with roommates, and so on. Each setting affords an opportunity for certain types of collective behavior to take place. But, again, each setting is very different from a crowd; each entails a fairly small number of individuals. Yet for each, the people who sustain the collective behavior tend to be large in number and stand outside the group of which one is a part. For instance, one may have read a rumor about a celebrity in a gossip column, or seen the 6 o'clock news on television.

The mass and the public can be thought of as a kind of *immense potential audience* that stands ready to react to messages, events, or stimuli. While, for most stimuli, it is nearly always much larger than the typical crowd, it is also very scattered and physically disconnected. The interest its members have in certain issues is what binds it together into a collectivity, however geographically separated they may be. In short, the mass or the public is a kind of "spiritual collectivity, a dispersal of individuals who are physically separated and whose cohesion is entirely mental" (Tarde, 1969, p. 277).

The Mass Media. Masses and publics cannot flourish without certain "technological requisites" (Clark, 1969, p. 53). Exclusive face-to-face interaction with individuals who are interested in and focused on a particular issue is a slow and cumbersome way of spreading a message. Imagine you acquired evidence proving that a well-known politician routinely takes bribes to ignore the illegal dumping of toxic waste in local waters. How could you communicate this to others on a strictly face-to-face basis without using any technological inventions? The fact is, you couldn't get the message to very many people; in addition, it would take a long time even for a few hundred people to find out about it. On the other hand, think of how you could spread the message if you had modern technology at your disposal. Of course, you'd use the telephone, and chances are, you'd also get in your car and travel to other locations to tell others about it. But the single invention that could spread the news of your discovery faster than any other is the *mass media,* or *mass communications.* You could tell a newspaper reporter about it and get the story into tomorrow's edition; you could tell a TV reporter about it and get it on the six o'clock news. In this way, thousands, perhaps millions, of people could learn about your discovery.

Thus, the mass media *generate* masses and publics, that is, create large audiences who simultaneously receive the same messages, some of whom will react in similar ways. Not all the news is equally important to every member of a newspaper readership or a television audience; some of us will ignore a particular story and find another fascinating, while others will react in the opposite fashion. Moreover, some of the audience will react in one way, will approve of what someone said, while other segments of the audience will react quite differently, disapprovingly. Still, by sending out the same message to millions of individuals, a mass or a public may be created or reinforced in relation to a certain issue, problem, question, or phenomenon.

While crowds possess *immediacy,* masses and publics have *range;* while crowds have *density* and *compactness,* masses and publics are *scattered* and *diffuse.* While what happens in a crowd is *instantly* communicated to its members, what happens in masses and publics—without the aid of mass communications—is communicated only in a slower, more indirect fashion, as in the case of gossip and rumor, weeks later; in the case of fad and fashion, weeks or months afterward, and so on. To put things another way, the communication process *within the immediate context of the crowd* is rapid, but that same mode of communication—basic, face-to-face interaction—if applied to publics, is extremely slow and inefficient. On the other hand, given the scattered nature of the collectivity, only technologically facilitated mass communication in publics is as rapid. Again, certain kinds of collective behavior are possible only in a crowd, and other types only take place in masses and publics.

Publics as Sites for Collective Behavior.   Masses and publics are only sites or *locations* for collective behavior, just as crowds are; they are not, *in and of themselves,* collective behavior. In fact, a great deal of conventional behavior takes place in masses and publics. When elections are held every two or four years, that is conventional behavior; there are rules and laws and norms governing proper procedure with respect to elections and, in many countries of the world, they are followed. When customers go to the supermarket day after day, week after week, and purchase groceries, that is conventional behavior. When worshippers attend traditional religious services and observe according to their respective faiths, that is conventional behavior. But we have cases of collective behavior on our hands when a mass movement overthrows the electoral process and sweeps a dictator into office; when a product catches on like wildfire, sells millions of units one year and, a year later, becomes so unpopular that it is taken off the market; and when, practically overnight, a new religion seizes millions of fervent believers to follow its message. Again, masses and publics are only the *sites* or *locations* of some forms of collective behavior, they are not collective behavior by themselves. Masses and publics enact conventional *as well as* collective behavior, although, here, it is specifically the collective behavior that they enact with which we are interested.

Overlapping Publics.   It must be emphasized that, unlike the crowd, a specific individual may be a member of *a number of different and overlapping publics* simultaneously. If you pay attention to a presidential campaign, you are part of a *political* public; if you buy clothes and are concerned with changes in styles, you are part of the *fashion* public; if you are concerned about the lives of celebrities, you are part of a certain *gossip* public; if you follow the latest trends in "crystal power," psychic healing, or astrology, you are a member of what might be called the *paranormal* public. Someone else—for instance, your roommate—may be part of some of these publics, but not others. He or she may care intensely about politics and follow it closely, wear the same clothes day after day or year after year and be unaware of fashion trends, be totally unconcerned about the doings of famous people, and practice all manner of paranormal beliefs. In the case of your roommate, he or she would be a member of some publics, but not others.

Publics and Social Networks.   Much collective behavior takes place in masses and publics, that is, among geographically scattered individuals. For example, fads and fashion are "mass" behavior. Though a fad may take place nationwide, or even worldwide, and the stimulus for a given individual to participate may have originated from an impersonal source—such as television—fads are almost always sustained through informal, interpersonal group interaction. Most fad adherents know others who follow a fad, tend to have closer and more frequent social contact with other fad adherents, and often use the fad as a basis or a criterion for a social relationship. Rumor and gossip, likewise, may have originated from the mass media, but they are always sustained interpersonally among clusters of intimates or acquaintances. Unusual, novel, and short-lived beliefs tend to arise in and are maintained by social networks. Even the collective actions originally discussed as forms of atomistic "mass" behavior—reactions to a murder trial, mass migrations, the mass media, a gold rush, land booms (Blumer, 1969, p. 88)—were in fact generated and sustained in groups. In all masses and publics, mutual influence can be seen; individuals in clusters or groups influence one another. They talk about a given phenomenon, exchange information, feelings, and beliefs, and this talk influences their behavior. Of course, the dynamics of behavior that takes place in a scattered, more loosely connected collectivity—some of whose members are densely and intensely connected socially—and a crowd are quite different, which is why they have to be examined separately.

COLLECTIVE BEHAVIOR
AND SOCIAL MOVEMENTS

Social movements have often been investigated side-by-side with collective behavior. In fact, in the past, the study of social movements has often been regarded as a subfield of collective behavior; most collective behavior textbooks contain at least one chapter on social movements (for instance, Lang and Lang, 1961; Turner and Killian, 1987; Perry and Pugh, 1978; Miller, 1985). Social movements may be thought of as *organized efforts by a substantial number of people to change, or to resist change, in some major aspect or aspects of society.* The civil rights movement is an example of a social movement. It is the organized effort on the part of Blacks, and some whites, to improve the social and economic position of African-Americans. The pro-democracy student movement in China is an example of a social movement. Its goals include the establishment of direct elections for political representatives, more say by the mass of the people in the political process, freedom of speech and the press, and the exercise of certain civil rights and liberties. There is a vigorous animal rights movement in the United States, with several million supporters, who regard animals as an oppressed category of beings. Activists demand more humane treatment of animals by humans, and they insist on an end to medical experiments on animals, indecent treatment of farm animals, hunting animals for sport, and killing them for their hides and skins. Women's liberation is another example of a social movement. Its goal is to improve the social and economic condition of women in the United States and around the world.

The *traditional* view, also called the *classical* or *collective behavior* approach (Blumer, 1939, 1969, pp. 99–120; Lang and Lang, 1961, Chapters 16, 17; Turner and Killian, 1957, 1972, 1987, Part 4; Smelser, 1962, Chapters IX, X), sees social movements as a form of collective behavior; it sees no fundamental differences between them, especially when they are in the initial stages of formation. Some of the same explanations that can account for the rise and fall of the hula hoop, a popular product fad in the 1950s, can also explain revolutions, the emergence of the civil rights movement, and why the Nazis arose in Germany in the 1920s and took power in the 1930s. Thus, social movements, like collective behavior, are spontaneous, dynamic, fluid, and emergent phenomena; social movements, like collective behavior, are nonnormative and extrainstitutional, and, like collective behavior, are relatively unstructured and unorganized.

The more recent conflict-oriented, *politico-rational*, or "superrational" (for this term, see Killian, 1980, pp. 278ff; I have combined Killian's "politico-rationalistic" and his "superrationalistic" perspectives) approach to the study of social movements sees things almost exactly the other way around: It *deemphasizes* the similarities between collective behavior and social movements and *emphasizes* the similarities between social movement participation and mainstream, institutional, political, and, especially organizational behavior (McCarthy and Zald, 1973; Zald and McCarthy, 1987; Oberschall, 1973; Jenkins, 1986; Morris and Herring, 1987). In this view, there is more similarity between participation in the civil rights movement and the behavior of representatives of the Republican party, for example, than there is between the former and fashion in clothing or participation in certain fads, such as streaking and break-dancing. The politico-rational approach to the study of social movements sees social movement participation as ruled mainly by rational, purposive, goal-oriented motives, as is true of mainstream organizational behavior; it emphasizes the question of the outcome of specific movement strategies, especially the attainment of movement goals; and it sees resources, power, social organization, and leadership as a crucial set of dimensions that determine the attainment of movement goals. These are all questions that the classical collective behavior approach to the study of social movements usually ignored.

SIMILARITIES

Regardless of which of these approaches we adopt or how these two areas are studied, social movements and collective behavior possess both similarities and differences. Three characteristics they have in common are of central importance. First of all, both are *dynamic*: They reflect or help to generate social change. A highly stable, strongly traditional society tends to have very little collective behavior and few social movements. Highly fluid, changing societies have both. In short, both represent something of a break with the past and the present, although in different ways. Second, both have an *extrainstitutional* element—that is, both violate mainstream society's established norms, institutions, and traditional values. Both, in some way or another, affront the notion of what "ought to be" that is held by the respectable, traditional, conventional, conforming members of the society. Both reflect the "maverick" side of social life. And third, both collective behavior and social movements are *collective* phenomena—they are engaged in by interactions with others. They are group creations. Collective behavior and social movements are always the product of actions, reactions, and interactions with and in the midst of other people.

DIFFERENCES

Just as collective behavior and social movements share some characteristics in common, they also possess qualities that are different as well. The differences include their *duration* or *time span, degree of organization, degree of spontaneity versus planning, relationship to the social order*, and *intentionality of participants.*

Duration or Time Span.   Collective behavior tends to be relatively transitory and short-lived, whereas social movements are usually more enduring. Riots last for an hour, a day or two, occasionally longer; the life span of a rumor may be a few weeks or a few months, rarely longer; a fad may last a few weeks, a few months, occasionally a few years, and very rarely a decade. (Some forms of collective behavior may come and go in cycles, however.) In contrast, many social movements stay around for decades, and some may survive for centuries. The civil rights movement emerged in the 1950s and 1960s (though its roots go back much further); women's liberation came about in the 1960s (though, again, various feminist organizations went back half a century or more before that). Karl Marx (1818–1883) and Friedrich Engels (1820–1895), wrote their influential book, *The Communist Manifesto,* in 1848, and thus the communist and socialist movements, and the labor movement, have been with us for at least a century and a half. By their very nature, collective behavior is comparatively short-lived; social movements tend to be more enduring.

Degree of Organization.   Collective behavior is relatively unorganized and unstructured, whereas social movements are relatively structured and organized. A corollary of this difference is that collective behavior is typically leaderless; there is little or no formal differentiation into leaders and followers. On the other hand, social movements tend to have leaders and active participants. To put things a bit differently: *To the extent that* unconventional, dynamic, social behavior is organized and is divided into leaders and followers, it is likely to be part of a social movement; *to the extent that* it is relatively unorganized and leaderless, it is more likely to be a form of collective behavior. There was or is no "organization" of break-dancers, graffiti artists, or purchasers of slap bracelets. To the extent that there are leaders of these fads, they are informal and not formal leaders. In contrast, a social movement tends to be represented by social movement *organizations*, and these organizations are usually differentiated into leaders, participants, and supporters.

Degree of Spontaneity Vs. Planning.   While both collective behavior and social movements are dynamic phenomena, the nature of their dynamism is somewhat different. Collective behavior is more spontaneous, while the dynamism of social movements tends to be planned. No one can predict what fad will be adopted next year. (Though manufacturers do try to put certain products on the market, and convince customers to buy them; they usually fail to know in advance how well they will sell.) No one could have predicted the huge success of video games in the 1970s to early 1980s, their precipitous decline in the middle 1980s, and their comeback in the late 1980s. While *some* aspects of collective behavior can be predicted (for instance, that rumor is more likely to be about important people and phenonema than unimportant ones), most cannot. Since social movements are more organized, they tend to be more planned, and hence, more aspects of them can be predicted. For example, rallies and demonstrations sponsored by social movement organizations are usually planned out in advance, and much, although not all, of what happens during them is also planned. Of course, the success of a social movement cannot be predicted or planned in advance—as is true of many phenomena or products generated by a conventional organization.

Relationship to the Social Order. Both collective behavior and social movements are somewhat unconventional. The difference is that, whereas collective behavior stands a bit outside the social order, but rarely challenges it directly, social movements tend to directly challenge the social order. Collective behavior is usually irrelevant to politics and ideology (although, occasionally—as in riots, for instance—they do challenge the existing order). Gossip and rumor may support or question the authority structure, but most likely it skirts or ignores it; most gossip and rumor is about friends or celebrities, and it rarely threatens the status quo in any substantial way. In contrast, although social movements are politically all over the map, they exist because their members believe that something is wrong with the way things are. (Or they believe that, if they don't act, something will *become* seriously wrong.) Their leadership and members say to established authority, you aren't doing your job very well; *here's* what ought to be done. Although social movements are rarely revolutionary, in the sense that they aim to overthrow the existing power structure from top to bottom, and some are conservative or even reactionary with respect to the existing regime, they all offer at least an implicit criticism of the status quo.

Intentionality of Participants. For the most part, participants in collective behavior are relatively nonpurposive and expressive; they are more concerned with the expression of emotion or with enacting certain behavior than with the attainment of a specific, concrete goal. In contrast, participants in social movements tend to be intentional, instrumental, and purposeful in seeking to attain specific goals. They may go about it in an ineffective way—that is, the goals they seek may be unattainable through the means they employ or they may be unattainable, period; still, they do set out to achieve those goals in a more or less intentional fashion. To put things another way, concrete goals loom larger in social movement participation than they do in collective behavior; in the latter, the attainment of specific goals is secondary, rather than primary. When a fan screams in ecstasy at a football rally or a rock concert, no specific goal or aim is sought; emotional release is an end in itself. In contrast, when the members of a given organization march and shout at a political demonstration, they generally have something in mind that they want to achieve by their participation.

The relationship of social movements to collective behavior is so important that the last part of this book is devoted to the subject. The approach adopted here is different from, and breaks with, both the older, classical, or "collective behavior" approach and the newer "politico-rational" approach. I do not believe all or even most social movement participation can be characterized by the same explanations that account for participation in most forms of collective behavior. In that respect, I believe the "collective behavior" approach is faulty. On the other hand, in contrast with the "politico-rational" approach, I do not believe social movement participation *can be assumed to be* more similar to mainstream political and organizational processes than to most forms of collective behavior. This depends on the social movement in question and, for that matter, the individual participant's participation as well. While social movements can be studied *as* purposive, goal-oriented organizations, this does not mean that, *in all cases*, this is the most productive way of studying them.

THE QUESTION OF RATIONALITY

Collective behavior phenomena are often thought of as "irrational." When people refer to gossip and rumor, it is nearly always in a pejorative, critical way; the very terms imply triviality and falseness. Fad (especially) and fashion (to some extent), too, are often referred to in a negative way, as if participating in them is, by their very nature, silly, useless, and illogical. Most commentary on riots emphasizes the rioters' irrational behavior; their supposed empty and counterproductive destructiveness is usually focused on, rather than the purposes that participants may have had in mind when they took part in the rioting. Most people either implicitly or explicitly criticize participation in collective behavior as irrational when they discuss it. In so doing, one dismisses and stigmatizes both the behavior and its participants.

In fact, participation in collective behavior is no more irrational than is participation in conventional, conforming behavior. The terms "rational" and "irrational" tend to be used in a fairly loose way by most people; they have a variety of meanings to many of us. Before applying rationality to collective behavior, it is necessary to introduce three relevant concepts: first, the notion of *means-ends rationality*, second, the distinction between *irrationality* and *nonrationality*, and third, the distinction between *individual* and *collective rationality*.

MEANS-ENDS RATIONALITY

Means-ends rationality refers to the fact that the selection of a specific means to attain a specific goal or end is rational *to the extent that* it may reasonably be expected to achieve that end, given what we know about the relationship between cause and effect. If I seek to achieve wealth (a specific end or goal) by chanting a magical incantation (the means I have chosen to attain that end), I am very *unlikely* to be successful, given what we know about how wealth is usually attained. Under most circumstances, chanting alone will not result in great wealth. Thus, it can be said that this behavior is irrational from the point of view of means-ends rationality. Notice that such behavior (chanting) is not irrational in general—only in relation to the attainment of this specific goal. It may lead to other goals, such as relaxation. Notice also that we cannot say that the person who pursues wealth through chanting is irrational, since we do not know anything about the many other things that this person does or believes. Every one of us engages in a mixture of rational and irrational behavior, although with most of us, it may be more one than the other. In addition, it is just possible that chanting, *in combination with more instrumental actions,* may have some personal impact on the chanter's actions, and hence, on his or her likelihood of achieving great wealth. Thus, an action that appears on the surface to be quite irrational may actually prove to be far less so when examined closely.

It is important to point out that we all have a variety of goals in mind, and not just one. Often, the way we seek to attain one will contradict the attainment of another. Let's say that I have as one of my goals living to the age of 100. Let's say further that I am a heavy smoker. It might seem that my goal is contradicted by my behavior, since smokers typically live shorter, unhealthier lives than nonsmokers, and smoking is causally related to ill health and premature death. We might conclude that my behavior is irrational from the point of view of the relationship between means and ends. This would be true if a long life were the *only* goal I sought. But let's also say that I enjoy smoking very much; it is pleasureable to me, and pleasure is one of my goals. In this case, the different goals I seek will contradict one another; the attainment of one threatens or cancels out the attainment of another. Here, the rationality of my smoking behavior is difficult, if not impossible, to calculate since, in making such a calculation, it is necessary to take into account the attainment of more than one goal.

If a New Guinea tribesman decides not to use a steel ax (in spite of the fact that it chops trees down faster and with less effort) but continues to use a stone ax because that is what his ancestors used, his behavior is irrational *only* if that single goal is considered. (And only within the context of Western empirical rationality.) The tribesman may correctly feel that his fellow tribesmen will disapprove of his using the steel ax; since their approval is important to him, he refuses to do so. When the total complex of all the goals and values the tribesman holds are considered, refusing to use the steel ax may actually be quite rational. It is only as measured by the the value of chopping efficiency—a Western notion not necessarily shared elsewhere—that such behavior can be deemed irrational. According to other, non-Western values, it may be quite rational. Someone who professes to value freedom but, when outside prison walls, continuously engages in a life of crime and, as a consequence, is arrested and spends more time behind bars than free, may not, strictly speaking, be "irrational" in his actions, since there may be enormous gratifications in engaging in crime that provide a powerful motivation to that individual's behavior (Katz, 1988).

"IRRATIONALITY" VS. NONRATIONALITY

Means-ends rationality says nothing about the rationality *of ends them-selves*. Ends or goals are neither rational nor irrational. No matter how irra-tional a goal might seem to you, there is simply no way of judging ends in themselves as irrational. Let's say my goal is to get high, or intoxicated. That goal is, in itself, neither rational nor irrational. (Of course, if it is a means to a different goal, it could be rational *or* irrational, depending on the goal we're talking about.) But we can refer to *means to attain that goal* as rational or irrational. If I try to get high by drinking a glass of ordinary tap water, that would be quite irrational because drinking water cannot get me high. On the other hand, taking LSD to get high would be quite *rational*, because all evi-dence points to the fact that this is a very *effective* means to attain the partic-ular end I have in mind. But the end of getting high, in and of itself, is nei-ther rational nor irrational—unless we specify *further* ends which getting high may be a means of attaining. If we are selecting a means for the pur-pose of attaining academic success, let's say, getting high would undoubted-ly be an irrational means, because evidence suggests that it will not help us attain that particular goal.

This discussion indicates that much collective behavior that is dubbed "irrational" is really *nonrational*, that is, *it does not enter into the means-ends scheme at all*, and thus, cannot be declared to be irrational. For instance, fads such as stuffing a number of people into a telephone booth, streaking, flag-pole sitting, buying hula hoops, going on "panty raids," buying Cabbage Patch dolls, playing video games, or cutting up and then swallowing pieces of an entire Volkswagen micro-bus, are, in and of themselves, neither rational nor irrational. If one's goal is simply engaging in the activities themselves, then there is no way of evaluating their rationality or irrationality. If one's goal is having fun, attracting attention, being sociable and engaging in an activity with others whose company one enjoys, or getting into *The Guinness Book of World Records*, then such activities may be quite rational, because engaging in them may very well be an effective means of attaining one of those ends. On the other hand, if curing cancer is one's goal, it is probably irrational to hold a crystal in one's hand for that purpose, since evidence suggests that that partic-ular means cannot achieve this specific goal. However, many fads are simply ends in themselves and are no more rational than earning a great deal of mon-ey, seeking fame, love, or respect from others, or wanting to have children.

THE POSSESSION OF RELEVANT INFORMATION

The means-ends rationality scheme assumes that the actor has full, rele-vant knowledge of the situation in which he or she acts, and full knowledge of the consequences of his or her actions. This may not be the case. It is common knowledge that, by itself, one cannot become wealthy by chanting, get high as a consequence of drinking a glass of water, excel academically by taking LSD, or cure illness by fondling a crystal. But many outcomes are not

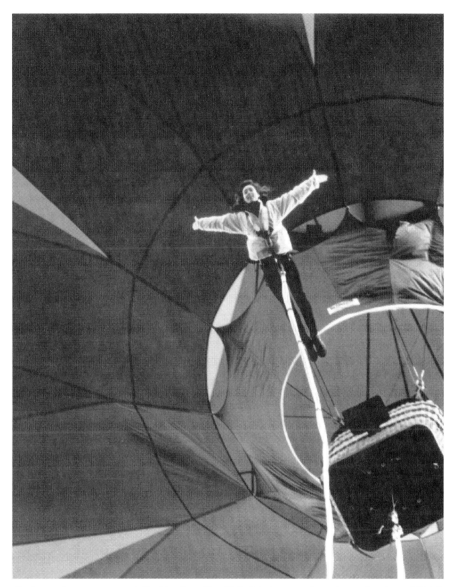

Perhaps the most recent "institutionalized" fad is bungee jumping—leaping off high places with a rubber cord attached to one's legs or midsection. Is this activity "irrational," as most people believe, or nonrational, as the field of collective behavior argues?

so obvious. The individual making a decision may not know all the relevant facts; they may not even be available. Knowledge of the cause-and-effect connections in a given situation may be attained only after all the facts are revealed.

For instance, was it irrational to flee the area around the Three Mile Island nuclear plant after an accident occurred there in 1979, as has been suggested

(Slovic, Fischoff, and Lichtenstein, 1980, p. 48)? Some 200,000 local residents fled to another area to avoid being contaminated, but evidence now suggests that contamination of the area was minimal, and that no one outside the plant was injured by the accident (Diamond, 1989). Was it irrational *not* to flee the area of the Chernobyl nuclear plant in the Soviet Union, after an accident there in 1986? Most local residents stayed put, but we now know that contamination was extensive, and the number of premature deaths over a lifetime, downwind from the plant as a result of that contamination, may eventually number in the tens, possibly in the hundreds, of thousands. Our consideration of the rationality of either action is based on what we know now, *after* the fact of each accident, when the facts are more certain than they were at the time. But when each accident occurred, few knew what the facts were—that Three Mile Island would be less serious than local residents suspected, or that Chernobyl would be more serious. (The picture is further complicated by the fact that local behavior in the case of Chernobyl was strongly influenced by what the authorities did—and didn't—do.)

Again, in the heat of action, in the absence of verifiable information, engaging in a particular action to achieve a given goal (in this case, physical survival) may not be in the least bit irrational. After all, what if Three Mile Island *had* turned out to be as serious as Chernobyl, or Chernobyl as unserious as Three Mile Island? No one can know these things in advance, without the evidence that is usually lacking at the time. Hence, taking, or refusing to take, a certain action to avoid disaster may seem perfectly rational at the time; only in hindsight are we able to say that a given action was rational or irrational. After-the-fact hindsight is referred to as "Monday morning quarterbacking"; it is a basic fallacy.

Of course, it is also true that certain outcomes are highly unlikely, even in advance of complete knowledge. Again, drinking water to get high and holding crystals to achieve health provide examples. But what if the likelihood of an outcome resulting from a given action is not zero, or nearly so, but one in two? One in 10? One in 100—or one in a million? Is it irrational to purchase a lottery ticket when the chance of winning a jackpot is as remote as it is in large state lotteries? Clearly, it is irrational to *expect* to win, but if, with full awareness of the odds, one purchases a ticket and *hopes* to win? Hardly anyone would call that action irrational, and yet, the relationship between the means (buying a ticket) and the end (winning a jackpot) is exceedingly tenuous. After all, many of us reason, *someone* must win—why not me?—and moreover, the cost is quite low. So why is it irrational? Is joining a small social movement that has practically no hope of achieving its stated goals irrational? History is replete with cases of successful small social movements. (Even though failure is much more common.) Someone who doesn't like taking chances may regard such behavior as irrational, but such a view would be extremely limited. The point is, designating actions as rational or irrational isn't such an easy job as first appears.

Some observers (Killian, 1980, p. 281) argue that it is a fallacy to claim that we can identify any "objective" reality, and presumably, by extension, we cannot determine whether any ends can be achieved by any means the actor chooses. But in fact, we all operate *as if* an objective reality existed, and some of our expectations are far more likely to be verified than others. While our knowledge about the world is never complete, always to some degree tentative, and based on degrees of certainty rather than absolute certainty, given the nature of the available evidence, certain views of how the world works are highly likely to be wrong. It is entirely reasonable to call such views irrational, again, from the point of view of Western empirical science, that is, from the point of view of what we know given the information at our disposal.

At the same time, the term "irrational" should not be applied indiscriminately to the phenomena we are looking at. Often what one person thinks is irrational will seem perfectly rational to another. Applying objective criteria to determine what's rational and irrational is rarely an easy task. When we look at examples of collective behavior, we should not assume that they are irrational just because they are different from ordinary, everyday behavior. As measured by such criteria, given what we know, collective behavior is probably no more irrational than conventional behavior. Most behavior and most beliefs are neither rational nor irrational; for most of the phenomena we look at, the question of rationality is quite irrelevant.

INDIVIDUAL VS. COLLECTIVE RATIONALITY

All researchers of collective behavior and, especially, social movements, make a distinction between *individual* and *collective* rationality. What I've been discussing so far is rationality exclusively from the point of view of one individual's choices among a variety of means to attain a specific, concrete end. However, there is a second kind of rationality to be considered: collective rationality. Most contemporary research, especially that on social movements, collective protests, riots, and the like, focus on the latter, not the former. The distinction becomes relevant as a result of the following theoretical problem, the "free rider" problem (Olson, 1965). When a collective effort achieves a specific goal, everyone in a given category may benefit, *regardless of whether or not they made an effort to attain it.*

Let's say that you recognize that a cleaner environment will make life better for everyone, including yourself. Further, let's say, a social movement exists to clean up the environment. And finally, let's say you are considering joining that movement to help in this campaign. Is your participation in this social movement rational? The answer is, from the point of view of individual rationality, no, it is *not* rational. Why not? The fact is, in all likelihood, your participation will not make any difference at all; if the movement is successful in cleaning up the environment, you can simply benefit from everyone else's efforts. By not lifting a finger to help, the air and water are cleaner, and you didn't have to expend any time, effort, or energy, to make it that way—others did it for you. Thus, *their* behavior is irrational and *yours* is rational. You have gotten a "free ride." This "free rider" problem raises an important question: If most people act on the basis of rationality, then why should anyone bother to participate in any social movement to make this a better world in which to live? In fact, from the point of view of individual rationality, it is distinctly *irrational* (Olson, 1965).

There are two answers to the "free rider" problem. First, in any collective effort, there must be more inducements ("spin-offs" or *selective incentives*) than simply the attainment of its goals; they are rewards that are available *only if* one participates (Oliver, 1980). People must be motivated to participate by a "hidden agenda," for instance, sociability, camaraderie, the respect of one's peers, the avoidance of punishment by one's peers for not joining the struggle, the intrinsic excitement of the collective activity itself. For instance, the labor movement may achieve higher wages for all workers—including "free riders"—but there may be incentives available *only* to dues-paying members, such as pension plans, health benefits, grievance procedures (Macy, 1990, p. 810). In addition, there may be *negative* inducements, that is, one may be punished for *not* participating—being ridiculed by one's peers, for instance.

Second, no collective action can get off the ground and have any impact unless there is a "critical mass" of participants (Oliver, Marwell, and Teixeira, 1985); that is, a sufficiently large body of activists dedicated to achieving a given collective goal that makes the enterprise viable. There is an awareness by individuals who are most committed to a given goal that, unless they take steps to achieve it, the goal cannot be achieved. This is the view, "If you don't do it, nobody else will" (Oliver, 1984). Such an appeal often has a great deal of impact on individuals who wish to see a given goal attained. In fact, some people may even feel that if many others are working to attain a given goal, there's no point in participating themselves, but if none or few are doing so, that's the time to roll up their sleeves and *do* something. Moveover, the attainment of certain goals may only require a small band of dedicated activists; in many cases, the fact that most people who profit from their efforts are doing nothing to help the cause may be irrelevant. As long as there are enough individuals operating on the basis of collective rationality, the individual rationality of the "free riders" will not hamper their efforts. Such collective actions make it possible for certain collective goals to be sought and attained. (For a detailed discussion of the question of rationality in a form of behavior that overlaps with collective behavior, see Rule, 1989.)

TEN STEREOTYPES ABOUT COLLECTIVE BEHAVIOR

More than a generation ago, sociologist Carl Couch (1968) discussed ten stereotypes that were once widely held about crowds—suggestibility, destructiveness, irrationality, emotionality, mental disturbance, lower-class participation, spontaneity, creativity, lack of self-control, and antisocial behavior. These stereotypes derived in part from the earliest theorists in the field, Gustave LeBon in particular, but they were also simply part of the gen-

eral intellectual baggage that observers carried around with them a generation or more ago. Couch's comments still apply to a large extent, but they
require some qualification. Applied to collective behavior, they imply that
collective behavior is "no different" from ordinary, routine, institutional
behavior. If that were true, there would be nothing distinctive about collective behavior, it would not exist as a separate field, and there would be no
point in studying it. Let's look at Couch's stereotypes and see if his criticisms
of them still apply. (While he focuses almost entirely on the crowd, we'll be
looking at collective behavior generally.) When we examine each stereotype,
we should be asking ourselves two questions. The first is: Is this a necessary,
universal, or *defining* characteristic of collective behavior? And the second: Is
collective behavior *more likely* to possess this characteristic than normative or
institutional behavior?

Suggestibility. Individuals acting in normative, institutionalized settings
routinely take the suggestions of others. When interacting with others, we
nearly always take them into account. Such behavior is *social* behavior; in
that sense, behavior is always collective. In the vast majority of all settings,
we are influenced, either directly or indirectly, by what others do and say. In
this respect, engaging in collective behavior is no different from engaging in
conventional behavior. Some measure of "suggestibility" is an inherent characteristic of *all* social life, and that includes both collective and more fully
institutionalized behavior. In all likelihood, people are no more suggestible
in a crowd than when enacting conventional, institutional behavior, and they
are more suggestible when enacting collective behavior than when enacting
conventional, institutional behavior as well.

Destructiveness. Very few crowds are destructive. In fact, even in cases
where they are, such as riots, the legal and conventional actions of the
authorities result in more destructiveness and a greater loss of human life
than the behavior that generated the actions of the authorities in the first
place (Couch, 1968, pp. 313–315). A great many forms of behavior that are
traditional and conventional are destructive, such as warfare, oppression and
exploitation, and racism and sexism. Taken on an act-by-act basis, crowd
behavior is probably no more destructive than is conventional behavior.
Although it is part and parcel of the stereotype of crowd behavior, destructiveness should be cast aside as one of its distinguishing characteristics. The
same applies to collective behavior generally: It is no more destructive than
conventional behavior; in fact, it is highly likely that the latter has produced
a far greater magnitude of human destructiveness than the former.

Irrationality. As measured by the means-ends rationality scheme, both
crowd behavior and collective behavior are probably no more "irrational"
than institutional behavior, as we just saw. With each realm, there are
instances and types that are quite rational, and others that are quite irrational.
For instance, as we'll see, research shows that in disasters, most people's
behavior is "rational," that is, they usually engage in behavior that increases

their chances of survival and the survival of others. They very rarely act in such a way as to increase the danger or damage that a catastrophe presents or causes. In cases of mass looting, many participants manage to obtain what they want—the goods they steal, for example. Still, rationality should not be part of our *definition* of collective—*or* institutional—behavior; collective and institutional behavior may be either rational *or* "irrational." Most people use the term "rationality" and "irrationality" in a very loose fashion, to refer to anything that strikes them as bizarre or unacceptable. As Couch says (p. 315), many so-called irrational acts or beliefs form the basis of tomorrow's social institutions.

Emotionality.   While much crowd (and collective) behavior is emotionally charged, so is a great deal of normative behavior—for instance, the love that husband and wife, or two lovers, feel for one another. Riots, protests, victory celebrations, religious ecstasy, disasters, gossip and rumor, telling and believing certain legends and myths, holding unusual and nonnormative beliefs, fads and crazes, social movements—all of these collective behavior phenomena are characteristically locuses of intense emotion. Thus, while collective behavior generally can be characterized by emotionality in a typical case, and, in all likelihood, it is more so than the typical instance of normative, institutional behavior, this is *not* a characteristic that marks the two forms of behavior off from one another in any *absolute* sense. If we were to examine a wide range of forms of collective behavior—fad and fashion, demonstrations, riots, and other collective violence, gossip and rumor, religious ecstasy and other ecstatic crowds, legends and paranormal beliefs, behavior during disasters—participants would be *more likely* to exhibit a high level of emotionality than is true of *most* institutionalized behavior. Thus, the difference is comparative, not absolute; relative rather than definitional. However, Couch's point is well taken: Crowd behavior cannot be *characterized* by emotionality.

Mental Disturbance.   Participants in crowd *and* collective behavior are no more "mentally disturbed" than are individuals who participate in conventional, institutional behavior. While LeBon's late-19th century characterization of the crowd (discussed in Chapter 2) made it seem, collectively, very much like a person who has gone insane, it is clear that the earliest observers of crowd phenomena seriously misunderstood its nature and dynamics. It is unlikely that most seriously ill people could even engage in most forms of crowd or collective behavior. Mental disturbance is a totally inappropriate characteristic to attach to the phenomena we'll be looking at.

Lower-class Participation.   As we'll see in detail at various points in this book, participants in most forms of crowd and collective behavior are *not* usually drawn from the lowest socioeconomic segments of society. Racial disturbances, for example, usually attract a wide cross-section of the minority community, and rioters tend to be a bit better educated than their peers who do not riot. Disasters tend to strike whole communities, not just the poor; fads and fashion and gossip and rumor have participants up and down the social class and educational ladder. An over-representation of lower-class participants in collective behavior is a myth; anyone holding it should discard it immediately.

Spontaneity. While Couch is correct in pointing out that much crowd behavior is planned in advance (p. 319), not all crowd behavior is collective behavior, as we've seen in this chapter. Collective behavior is, by its very nature and by definition, relatively spontaneous. To the extent that it is organized and planned out, it is not collective behavior. Of course, all the planning in the world can't generate a riot without a substantial number of dedicated rioters; most riots have at least a measure of spontaneity. Collective behavior has an emergent quality to it that is lacking in most (although certainly not all) institutional behavior. While spontaneity is part of the stereotype of collective behavior, it is, in fact, an accurate assessment. At the same time, Couch is correct in his critique as it applies specifically to crowd behavior: *Crowd* behavior (as distinguished from *collective* behavior) is no more spontaneous than behavior that does not take place in crowds.

Creativity. Although Couch (pp. 319–320) emphasizes that innovation is probably no more characteristic of collective behavior phenomena than of everyday, institutional behavior, again, he focuses entirely on crowds. *From the point of view of mainstream norms and values*, it must be said that collective behavior *is* more creative and innovative than traditional, institutional behavior. This does not mean that, in some abstract sense, collective behavior participants are more open-minded or creative than those who engage in conventional behavior. In fact, many forms of collective behavior, such as holding paranormal beliefs, are to some degree *insulated from* innovation and creativity in that they are relatively immune to new information. Belief in miracles has not changed much in content or form in the two or three millenia it has been widely held. In many ways, gossip and rumor affirm traditional beliefs and preserve the status quo more than they challenge them. But collective behavior is *itself* a form of innovation, and in this sense, it *is* more creative than institutional behavior. Collective behavior "fills in the gaps" that exist because conventional, institutional patterns do not answer questions that many people want answered. While collective behavior is to some degree a *manifestation* of social change, for the most part, most forms of collective behavior represent only extremely tiny steps to change society— often, small-scale social change that results in more large-scale stability. Thus, as applied to collective behavior generally, while Couch is correct if creativity is regarded in the abstract, he is wrong if creativity is defined strictly *in relation to* mainstream norms, beliefs, and values—and here, collective behavior *is* more creative than mainstream culture. On the other hand, Couch's point applies specifically to crowds and here, I would agree: Crowd behavior is no more "creative" than social behavior generally.

Lack of Self-Control. As Couch points out (p. 320), much crowd (and collective) behavior is less a manifestation of a lack of self-control than it is an

TABLE 1-1   TEN STEREOTYPES OF COLLECTIVE BEHAVIOR: ARE THEY RIGHT?

	Defining Characteristics	Relative Characteristics
Suggestibility	No	No
Destructiveness	No	No
Irrationality	No	No
Emotionality	No	Yes
Mental Disturbance	No	No
Lower-Class Participation	No	No
Spontaneity	Yes	Yes
Creativity	No	Yes
Lack of Self-Control	No	No
Antisocial	No	No

inability of authorities to control the behavior of participants. Control has simply shifted to a different social location, it has not disappeared. In fact, much crowd (and, again, collective) behavior demonstrates a great deal of group control. Collective behavior exists *because* the individual is sensitive to group pressures and directives, not in spite of it. This element of the stereotype is completely inaccurate, and Couch's criticism is valid.

Antisocial Behavior. Claiming that crowd and collective behavior are antisocial assumes that participants are insensitive to the norms and beliefs of the group. In reality, while some may engage in behavior that is contrary to what tradition or the authorities want them to do, they are always influenced by the members of a particular collective. Moreover, some forms of collective behavior do as much, perhaps in a more indirect fashion, to support tradition and the authorities as does institutional behavior. Anti-social behavior is an element of the prevailing stereotype of collective behavior that must be cast aside and quickly forgotten.

In sum, although Couch is entirely correct with respect to the inaccuracy and inappropriateness of all elements of the *crowd* behavior stereotype, if we were to extend his argument to collective behavior *generally*, we find that only seven of his objections (suggestibility, destructiveness, irrationality, mental disturbance, lower-class participation, lack of self-control and antisocial behavior), hold up entirely, one of his objections is off the mark in the sense that the stereotype is actually largely correct—with respect to spontaneity—and two (emotionality and creativity) are partly correct (Table 1-1). Collective behavior is a bit different from ordinary, routine, conventional behavior; that is why we study it and find it interesting. It is *by definition* more spontaneous, *often* (although not always) more creative, and it is *usually* (although, again, not necessarily) more emotional. Thus, some elements of the stereotype are correct, although most are false. In correcting the stereotype, it is important, as we saw earlier, not to "throw the baby out with the bathwater."

SUMMARY

Collective behavior tends to be relatively unorganized, unstructured, spontaneous, unpredictable, short-lived, extrainstitutional, nonnormative, and unconventional behavior. It is behavior that is enacted when tradition no longer seems relevant or binding, when actors find the old norms incapable of satisfying what they want. Collective behavior takes over in situations in which there are no, or few, adequate or clear-cut definitions as to what to do from mainstream culture. At the same time, collective behavior is not totally normless or wild, impulsive behavior. It is not a product of social disorganization or anomie. Collective behavior is, above all, a product of group norms, except that the group and the norms that influence our behavior are a bit different from the conventional, mainstream groups and norms that usually do so. Most enactors of collective behavior are fairly conventional in most areas of life other than their collective behavior. Riots, demonstrations, ecstatic crowds and miracles, behavior in disasters, gossip and rumor, the emergence of legends, fad, fashion, and crazes provide instances of collective behavior.

Collective behavior takes place in at least two settings—*crowds* or *compact* collectivities, and *publics* or *diffuse* collectivities. Crowds are made up of a fairly substantial number of people in the same place at the same time. Casual and conventional crowds rarely generate collective behavior; expressive and acting crowds often do. By themselves, crowds cannot be regarded as coterminous with collective behavior, although they do display fascinating dynamics that must be studied. Publics have their attention focused on a given stimulus and are scattered all over a vast geographical area, although they generally cluster into small gatherings of intimates. More than any other single factor, the mass media have vastly expanded the size of publics and speeded up the communication processes that take place within them.

Social movements are organized efforts by a substantial number of people to change or resist change in a major aspect of society. In the past, collective behavior and social movements were studied as aspects of the same phenomenon; in fact, social movements were seen as a *type* of collective behavior. Today, most scholars see at least as many differences as similarities between them. Both tend to be dynamic, institutional, and collective. On the other hand, in contrast to social movements, collective behavior tends to be relatively short-lived, unorganized, spontaneous, and its actors tend to be less intentional and goal-oriented.

A number of stereotypes, some held by past scholars, have supposedly characterized crowd behavior and, by extension, collective behavior as well—suggestibility, destructiveness, irrationality, emotionality, mental disturbance, lower-class participation, spontaneity, creativeness, lack of self-control, and antisocial behavior. As applied to collective behavior, all of these stereotypes are false except three—emotionality, spontaneity, and creativeness. Collective behavior is, *by definition*, more spontaneous than everyday, conventional, institutional behavior, and is *more likely to be* more emotional and creative.

The study of collective behavior is fascinating and rewarding. It is one of the most dynamic and exciting areas of social life. An examination of collective behavior reveals important and enlightening social processes. It is an aspect of the lives of all of us, and knowing how it is generated tells us a great deal about how society works. We cannot help but be enlightened by its study.

References

Appel, Willa. 1983. *Cults in America: Programmed for Paradise.* New York: Holt, Rinehart & Winston.

Bainbridge, William Sims. 1989. "Collective Behavior and Social Movements." In Rodney Stark, *Sociology* (3rd ed.). Belmont, Calif.: Wadsworth, pp. 608–640.

Becker, Howard S. 1986. *Doing Things Together: Selected Papers.* Evanston, Ill.: Northwestern University Press.

Blumer, Herbert. 1939. "Collective Behavior." In Robert E. Park (ed.), *Outline of the Principles of Sociology* (1st ed.). New York: Barnes & Noble, pp. 221–279.

Blumer, Herbert. 1969. "Collective Behavior." In Alfred McClung Lee (ed.), *Principles of Sociology* (3rd ed.). New York: Barnes & Noble, pp. 67–120.

Bromley, David G., and Anson D. Shupe, Jr. 1981. *Strange Gods: The Great American Cult Scare.* Boston: Beacon Press.

Clark, Terry N. (ed.). 1969. "Introduction" to *Gabriel Tarde on Communication and Social Influence.* Chicago: University of Chicago Press, pp. 1–69.

Couch, Carl J. 1968. "Collective Behavior: An Examination of Some Stereotypes." *Social Problems,* 15 (Winter): 310–322.

Crudele, John. 1986. "After the Cabbage Patch Kids." *The New York Times,* August 23, pp. 29, 41.

Curvin, Robert, and Bruce Porter. 1979. *Blackout Looting!* New York: Gardner Press.

Diamond, Stuart. 1989. "TMI: 10 Years Later: How a Nuclear Accident Changed a Town and an Industry." *Newsday*, March 26, pp. 5, 20, 22.

Feder, Barnaby J. 1988. "Coleco Fails to Fend Off Chapter 11." *The New York Times*, July 13, pp. D1, D4.

Haberman, Clyde. 1987. "Fury and Turmoil: Days That Shook Korea." *The New York Times*, July 6, pp. 1, 6.

Jenkins, J. Craig. 1986. "Stirring the Masses: Indigenous Roots of the Civil Rights Movement." Review of Aldon Morris, *The Origins of the Civil Rights Movement: Black Communities Organizing for Change*. New York: Free Press, 1984, in *Contemporary Sociology*, 15 (May): 354–357.

Katz, Jack. 1988. *Seductions of Crime: Moral and Sensual Attractions in Doing Evil*. New York: Free Press.

Killian, Lewis M. 1980. "Theory of Collective Behavior: The Mainstream Revisited." In Hubert M. Blalock, Jr. (ed.), *Sociological Theory and Research: A Critical Appraisal*. New York: Free Press, pp. 275–289.

Kolata, Gina. 1988. "Rumor of LSD-Tainted Tattoos Called Hoax." *The New York Times*, December 9, pp. B1, B5.

Lang, Kurt, and Gladys Engel Lang. 1961. *Collective Dynamics*. New York: Thomas Y. Crowell.

Macy, Michael W. 1990. "Learning Theory and the Logic of Critical Mass." *American Sociological Review*, 55 (December): 809–826.

Marx, Gary T. 1980. "Conceptual Problems in the Field of Collective Behavior." In Hubert M. Blalock, Jr. (ed.), *Sociological Theory and Research: A Critical Appraisal*. New York: Free Press, pp. 258–274.

Marx, Gary T., and James L. Wood. 1975. "Strands of Theory and Research in Collective Behavior." *Annual Review of Sociology*, 1: 363–428.

McCarthy, John D., and Mayer N. Zald. 1973. *The Trends of Social Movements in America: Professionalization and Resource Mobilization*. Morristown, N.J.: General Learning Press.

McPhail, Clark. 1978. "Toward a Theory of Collective Behavior." Unpublished paper presented at the Symposium on Symbolic Interaction, University of South Carolina, Columbia, March 17.

McPhail, Clark. 1991. *The Myth of the Madding Crowd*. New York: Aldine de Gruyter.

McPhail, Clark. 1992. *Acting Together: The Organization of Crowds.* New York: Aldine de Gruyter.

Miller, David L. 1985. *Introduction to Collective Behavior.* Belmont, Calif.: Wadsworth.

Morris, Aldon, and Cedric Herring. 1987. "Theory and Research in Social Movements: A Critical Review." In Samuel Long (ed.), *Political Behavior Annual.* Norwood, N.J.: Ablex, pp. 137–198.

Oberschall, Anthony. 1973. Social Conflict and Social Movements. Englewood Cliffs, N.J.: Prentice-Hall.

Oliver, Pamela. 1980. "Rewards and Punishments for Selective Inducements for Collective Actions: Theoretical Investigations." *American Journal of Sociology,* 85 (May): 1356–1375.

Oliver, Pamela. 1984. "'If You Don't Do It, Nobody Else Will': Active and Token Contributors to Local Collective Action." *American Sociological Review,* 49 (October): 601–610.

Oliver, Pamela, Gerald Marwell, and Ruy Teixeira. 1985. "A Theory of the Critical Mass. I. Interdependence, Group Heterogeneity, and the Production of Collective Action." *American Journal of Sociology,* 91 (November): 522–556.

Olson, Mancur. 1965. *The Logic of Collective Action.* Cambridge, Mass.: Harvard University Press.

Perry, Joseph B., Jr., and Meredith D. Pugh. 1978. *Collective Behavior: Response to Stress.* St. Paul: West.

Rule, James B. 1989. "Rationality and Non-Rationality on Militant Collective Action." *Sociological Theory,* 7 (Fall): 145–160.

Slovic, Paul, Baruch Fischoff, and Sarah Lichtenstein. 1980. "Risky Assumptions." *Psychology Today,* 14 (June): 44–48.

Smelser, Neil J. 1962. *Theory of Collective Behavior.* New York: Free Press.

Tarde, Gabriel. 1969. "The Public and the Crowd" (originally published in 1901). In Terry N. Clark (ed.), *Gabriel Tarde on Communication and Social Influence.* Chicago: University of Chicago Press, pp.277–294.

Turner, Ralph H. 1964. "Collective Behavior." In Robert E. L. Faris (ed.), *Handbook of Modern Sociology.* Chicago: Rand McNally, pp. 382–425.

Turner, Ralph H., and Lewis M. Killian. 1957. *Collective Behavior.* Englewood Cliffs, N.J.: Prentice-Hall.

Turner, Ralph H., and Lewis M. Killian. 1972. *Collective Behavior* (2nd ed.). Englewood Cliffs, N.J.: Prentice-Hall.

Turner, Ralph H., and Lewis M. Killian. 1987. *Collective Behavior* (3rd ed.). Englewood Cliffs, N.J.: Prentice-Hall.

Zald, Mayer N., and John D. McCarthy. 1987. *Social Movements in Organizational Society: Collected Essays.* New Brunswick, N.J.: Transaction Books.

CHAPTER
2

THEORIES OF COLLECTIVE BEHAVIOR

WHAT IS A THEORY?

The dictionary defines a theory as *an explanation for a general class of phenomena.* In the social sciences, the term theory is used in two different ways: first, in the dictionary's sense of a general explanation, and second, in the much broader sense of an *approach* or *perspective.* In contrast to a genuine theory, an approach or perspective rarely spells out in detail just how the phenomena it looks at are caused or can be explained. An approach or a perspective is simply a *way of looking* at a given phenomenon. It says, "Here are some things to focus on when we look at this phenomenon; they will reveal a great deal about it." For example—as we saw—the classical or traditional approach to the relationship between collective behavior and social movements said that social movements are more similar to collective behavior than they are different; the "politico-rational" approach says that the differences between the two phenomena are stronger than the similarities. Neither says anything about *how* or *why* these phenomena arise and, hence, cannot be called theories in the strict or dictionary sense of the word. In the field of collective behavior, perspectives sometimes are loosely called theories, and sometimes what is called a theory really *is*—following the dictionary's definition—a true explanation.

To the popular mind, the term *theory* has a pejorative connotation; it is often equated with wild speculation, that is, guesswork without any factual basis. To a scientist, in contrast, a theory is not wild speculation at all, but an attempt to account for facts that are observed. "Theories are structures of ideas that explain and interpret facts" (Gould, 1984, p. 254). In other words, theory and fact do *not* stand at the opposite end of a spectrum. Instead, theories may be general explanations *in addition to* being factually supported. A good example of this is the theory of evolution; it is an explanation for the origin of species, and, *in addition*, nearly every biologist and geologist in the world accepts it as factually verified. Evolution thus is *both* a theory *and* a fact. On the other hand, *some* theories or general explanations have received little or *no* factual support. Here, we would have to include the "lunar cycle" theory—that the phases of the moon cause people to commit crimes and to go crazy (Lieber, 1978)—which has no factual support at all and has, in fact, been completely discredited (Hines, 1988, pp. 156–158). In short, "theory" and "fact" are not opposites; they are two independent but partly overlapping concepts.

In the field of collective behavior, we have a number of perspectives or theories that address or attempt to account for the phenomena we're looking at. Four of them—contagion theory, convergence theory, the emergent norm theory, and value-added theory—are fairly general, and include pretty much all collective behavior phenomena in their scope (although most focus far more on crowd behavior than the behavior of masses and publics). And four of them—rational calculus or game theory, the threshold model, the SBI or social behavioral/interactionist theory, and resource mobilization—are more specialized, and explain a more limited range of collective behavior phenomena, or explain only a particular aspect of collective behavior. Some of these are more approaches and perspectives than theories, while others are genuine theories. For that reason, I'll refer to them as both theories *and* perspectives or approaches. Still, we should keep in mind the fact that they all contain at least one or more theories in the scientific sense.

The study of collective behavior emerged in the 19th century in Europe. The first book describing collective behavior phenomena in any detail was written by Charles Mackay (1814–1889), a Scottish poet, journalist, and songwriter. First published in 1841, it was titled *Memoirs of Extraordinary Popular Delusions.* (In later editions and printings, its title changed.) In it, Mackay described such phenomena as the Crusades; prophecies; astrology; fortune telling; the "witch mania" of Renaissance Europe; belief in haunted houses; popular admiration for thieves and bandits; political and religious control of hair and beard styles; and "tulipomania," or the economic craze that gripped the Netherlands in the 1600s, which entailed the buying and selling of tulip bulbs at incredibly high and, supposedly, wildly inflated prices. Mackay's argument was that nations, "like individuals, have their whims and their peculiarities, their seasons of excitement and recklessness, when they care not what they do." Whole communities, he asserted, "suddenly fix their minds upon one object, and go mad in its pursuit; millions of people become simultaneously impressed with one delusion, and run after it, until their attention is caught by some new folly more captivating than the first" (1932, p. xix). Mackay's approach was entirely atheoretical and unsystematic; he had no general explanation for the behavior he described. Other than making the claim that people "think in herds," "go mad in herds," and "only recover their senses slowly, and one by one" (1932, pp. xx), Mackay had little to say about *how* or *why* the behavior he described arose, was sustained, or died out. Moreover, he focused entirely on "irrational" behavior; he did not understand that much behavior that he would have considered rational followed similar lines, that is, was influenced by "herd" or collective sentiments. In addition, some of the irrational behavior he described had traditional, institutional origins and did not suddenly burst forth and then quickly die out as he claimed. Although he examined a number of phenomena still fascinating to contemporary researchers of collective behavior, Mackay has had virtually no impact on contemporary thinking in the field.

GUSTAVE LEBON:
A MAJOR PRECURSOR OF THE FIELD

The first author who, it is felt by many, put forth an analysis of phenomena now examined by the field of collective behavior was Gustave LeBon (1841–1931). It is difficult today to imagine LeBon's impact when he was alive. LeBon was extremely prolific, publishing a large number of works on extremely diverse subjects, from equitation to the education of children, but it was his book *The Crowd* that remains LeBon's most popular work. First published in 1895 and translated into English in 1897, this book remains in print today. LeBon's views on the crowd—in fact, his views on most subjects—were profoundly conservative, even reactionary. He mistrusted the crowd; for LeBon, that included not only revolutionary crowds, but such democratic institutions as juries, "electoral crowds," and parliamentary assemblies as well.

LeBon believed that an "organized" or "psychological" crowd was subject to *the law of mental unity* (1982, p. 2). Members of such a crowd lose their individuality and become transformed into a homogeneous entity; they are subject to the contagion of the other members of the crowd (p. 10). Individually, they may be cultivated, educated, and intelligent; as the members of a crowd, however, they can be characterized by stupidity (p. 9), suggestibility (p. 10), impulsivity and "irresistible impetuosity" (p. 11), barbarism (p. 12), "irritability, incapacity to reason, the absence of judgment and of the critical spirit, the exaggeration of the sentiment" (p. 16), credulity (pp. 20f), and intolerance (p. 37). Members of the crowd are like a hypnotized individual in the hands of a hypnotist. "The conscious personality has entirely vanished; will and discernment are lost" (p. 11). In a crowd, every member is like "an automaton who has ceased to be guided by his will" (p. 12). The individual in a crowd has become someone who "descends several rungs in the ladder of civilisation," a "creature acting by instinct" (p. 12). LeBon also believed that the "special characteristics of crowds" are to be found in "inferior forms of evolution—in women, savages, and children" (p. 16).

It must be said that LeBon also believed the crowd to be capable of heroic and "very lofty acts of devotion, sacrifice, and disinterestedness, of acts much loftier indeed than those of which the isolated individual is capable" (p. 42). In a crowd, the feelings of impulsivity, suggestibility, and invulnerability give members the courage to act, regardless of the nature of that act. Because of the crowd, Christians marched on the Crusades and French soldiers defended native soil against the encroachment of foreigners (both of which LeBon approved of). Thus, while crowds occasionally engage in noble acts, these are impulsive, unthinking, unreflective acts, without any real intellectual, moral, and spiritual foundation; they have been stimulated by strong leaders and mob contagion, not the merits of the case in question. Although he mentioned both good and bad actions of crowds, overwhelmingly, LeBon emphasized the savage and destructive rather than the noble and productive side of crowds; "crowds," he said, "are only powerful for destruction" (p. xviii). He believed in "the mental inferiority of all collectivities, whatever their composition" (p. 191). "The work of a crowd is always inferior," he says, "to that of an isolated individual" (p. 210). As a consequence, LeBon leaves us with the negative side of crowds, "the purely destructive nature of their power" (p. xviii), rather than the more balanced view we might have received had he been less ideologically biased.

LeBon was a member of a circle of largely aristocratic, right-wing, antidemocratic thinkers who lived in France during the years following the Paris Commune of 1871, which Karl Marx called "the first modern revolution." Their hostility to crowds stemmed from their view that both crowds and democracy are evil because they both put brute, unreasoning power in the hands of the masses. The Comte de Gobineau, a theorist of racial superiority, believed that Paris still housed "a profoundly perverted population, multitudinous and seething with rage." The Comtesse de Segur claimed that there were tens of thousands of radicals scattered around Paris "ready again to massacre and pillage." Leconte de Lisle urged: "Deport this Parisian rabble—men, women, and children!" (Lebovics, 1988, pp. 33, 34). However, these antidemocratic writers believed that, in spite of any measures the government might take against the masses, their elitist culture was doomed; it was, unavoidably, as LeBon pointed out, "the era of crowds" (LeBon, 1982, pp. xiii–xxii). Clearly, LeBon simply articulated the views of a substantial and influential segment of French society who held elitist, reactionary, even racist views, and who profoundly mistrusted the actions of the crowd, the mob, the great masses of the people. Their feeling was that it should be the elite, not the masses, who wield power; when the masses seize power, civilization as they knew it would be destroyed. LeBon ends his book on the crowd with this gloomy generalization: "To pass in pursuit of an ideal from the barbarous to the civilized state, and then, when this ideal has lost its virtue, to decline and die, such is the cycle of the life of a people" (1982, p. 219).

LeBon's views are not taken seriously today. One reason is that his contempt for democratic innovations is shared by practically no one nowadays. His elitist views, so contemptuous of the mass of the people in any society, sound archaic, a relic of a bygone age. "Civilisations," he said, "have only been created and directed by a small intellectual aristocracy, never by crowds" (p. xviii). He expressed a number of ideas that the contemporary reader would regard as racist. For instance, he claimed that Latin (by that he meant French, Italian, Portuguese, and Spanish) crowds are far more emotional and irrational than Anglo-Saxon crowds, and react far more violently to small things (p. 20). He also claimed that it didn't much matter what form of government a nation had; each would come to its own decisions, because politics are "the expression of the unconscious aspirations of the race"; "institutions and government play but a small part in the life of a people" because they "are guided in the main by . . . their race, that is, by [an] inherited residue of qualities" (p. 192). His evaluation of women as inferior to, and more emotional than, men—crowds, he said, "are everywhere distinguished by feminine characteristics" (p. 20)—marks his ideas as profoundly sexist and obsolete.

Moreover, LeBon has no real explanation of crowd behavior; his claim to offering a theory of the crowd is weak. Early in his book, he makes a distinction between a simple "gathering of individuals" who lack a common sentiment or focus and the mental unity he regarded as so important, and what he called the "organized" or the "psychological" crowd, which possesses these very characteristics. Since it is not the mere fact of a large number of people in the same place at the same time that creates the "psychological" crowd, exactly what is it? "To acquire the special characteristics of such a crowd, the influence is necessary of certain predisposing causes of which we shall have to determine the nature" (p. 2). However, LeBon is extremely sketchy about what these conditions are. For all his tough-sounding, cynical language, he failed to provide an adequate job of explanation. LeBon mentioned three factors that facilitate true crowds: (1) the emergence of capitalism, the destruction of feudalism, and the "entry of the popular classes into political life" (p. xv and *passim*); (2) the persuasion of crowd leaders (pp. 112–140); and (3) occasions that draw large numbers of people together (pp. 1, 2, and *passim*). However, except for his discussion on leaders, what he had to say on the generation of "psychological" crowds was unfocused, sketchy, and inadequate.

Even if he had managed more adequately to analyze the conditions that transform a large, heterogeneous gathering of people into an "organized" and "psychological" crowd characterized by "mental unity," it is clear that his theory is little more than a "single-factor explanation" of history (Miller, 1985, p. 20). He ignores all other factors (except what he refers to as race)—form of government, organizational factors, economic conditions, natural resources, ideology, urbanness, religion, and personal variables and individual variation—in short, any other dimensions except insofar as they might bring people together. It is the crowd that is the explanatory variable, and *only* the crowd; and yet, as we have seen, LeBon had no idea what generates a real crowd.

Today, LeBon's theory seems simple, crude, and empirically wrong; in fact, by the 1930s, his writings had "fallen into theoretical disrepute" (Zygmunt, 1986, p. 26). And yet, as Robert Merton (1960) has said, LeBon put his finger on some important intellectual problems, although he was incapable of solving them. He identified the fact that not all behavior follows institutional rules. Although he wrote at a time long before the field of collective behavior had been identified, he recognized the fact that the same generalizations that apply to routine, conventional behavior may not be capable of dealing with more spontaneous, less organized, less normatively controlled behavior. While his ideas are not taken seriously by anyone working in it today, LeBon is recognized as a forerunner of, or a *precursor* to, the field of collective behavior.

CONTAGION OR TRANSFORMATION THEORY

In addition to being the most important precursor of the field of collective behavior, LeBon may also be regarded as the "father" of contagion theory. *Contagion theory*, referred to by some as the *transformation hypothesis* (McPhail, 1991, pp. 13ff), seeks to explain how people in collectivities come to behave *uniformly, intensely,* and *at variance with their usual patterns* (Turner, 1964, p. 384). The explanation that all contagion theorists use is that, in a collectivity, mechanisms such as imitation, suggestion, and emotional contagion operate, in addition to "anonymity and restricted attention, which neutralize ordinary behavior anchorages" (Turner, 1964, p. 384). In a crowd, people are *transformed* from the way they are in their ordinary, everyday lives, much like the good Dr. Jekyl was transformed into the evil Mr. Hyde. Contagion theory clearly borrows its imagery from the field of medicine; one person or a group of persons "infect" others with their intense mood and emotional behavior in much the same way a disease is transmitted. The result is an "epidemic" of collective excitement. Collective excitement, like diseases, is said to be "contagious." In the early years of writings on collective behavior—and LeBon's work provides a clear-cut example—it was thought of as an almost exclusively undesirable, pathological phenomenon, with undesirable causes and consequences. This view is not intrinsic to the notion of crowd influence—after all, we can imagine any manner of positive *and* negative sentiments, leading to both positive and negative behavior, communicated in a group setting. Still, the roots of the contagion perspective lie in the disease analogy.

Gustave LeBon can be regarded as a "crude" or primitive contagion theorist for, as we saw, he did not elucidate the precise mechanism by which collectivities of people acquire the crowd characteristics he elaborated, and he worked with a unicausal theory of the impact of crowds. Robert Park (1864–1944) imported LeBon's views on the crowd to the United States. (Park received his Ph.D. from the University of Heidelberg in Germany.) Following Gabriel Tarde (1843–1904), Park made the crucial distinction—which is also maintained in this book—between the crowd and the public. Unfortunately and fatally for his views on collective behavior, Park (like Tarde) held that the public, being made up of diverse, heterogeneous and overlapping views, groups, and categories, tends to generate rational, prudent discussion of issues, while the crowd, which is homogeneous and cohesive, is uncritical and impulsive. Views among crowd members tend to be reinforced and amplified in a "circular form of interaction." In a crowd, individuals act "impersonally"; they do not feel responsible for their actions. The crowd does not discuss, says Park, "and hence it does not reflect. It simply 'mills.' Out of this milling process a collective impulse is formed which dominates all members of the crowd" (Park and Burgess, 1921, p. 385).

A more contemporary and detailed version of contagion theory was put forth by Park's student Herbert Blumer (1900–1987). Blumer (1939, 1969) attempts to locate the mechanism of social contagion—just how a mood of collective excitement is spread—in a form of social interaction he calls a *circular reaction*. (Incidentally, Blumer never used the phrase, "contagion theory.") It is generated in the following fashion. All people have certain "impulses, desires, or dispositions." At times, these aspirations cannot be fulfilled. Consequently, such people experience "discomfort, frustration, insecurity, and usually . . . alienation or loneliness. This inner tension, in the absence of regulated means for its release, will express itself usually through random and uncoordinated activity." Such a psychic state of restlessness by itself does not generate collective behavior, though it may cause individual or parallel behavior. It is only when that state of individual restlessness becomes communicated with others that it "becomes contagious" and generates a state of general "social unrest." In contrast with the state of individual restlessness that meets no sympathetic audience, "social unrest has a reciprocal character," that is, "its display awakens a similar condition of restlessness on the part of others, and there occurs mutual reinforcement of this state as the individuals interact with each other" (1969, p. 72).

Social unrest is marked by three basic characteristics. The first is that people gripped by it have an "urge to act," but they are unsure of what it is they seek; consequently, they "move about in an erratic and aimless way." The second characteristic of social unrest is that people experience "an excited feeling, usually in the form of vague apprehensions, alarm, fears, insecurity, eagerness, or aroused pugnacity." Such excited feelings are "conducive to rumors and to exaggerated views and perceptions." The third characteristic of social unrest is "the irritability and increased suggestibility of people." Such an emotional state leads to greater instability, a shorter attention span, and greater malleability and receptivity to new stimuli and ideas (1969, p. 73).

During periods of unrest, three basic types of social interaction develop. They are, in Blumer's words, "the elementary mechanisms of collective behavior," that is, "they appear spontaneously and naturally, they are the simplest and earliest ways in which people interact in order to act together, and they usually lead to more advanced and more complicated forms" (1969, pp. 74, 75). These social interactions are *milling, collective excitement*, and *social contagion.*

Milling.   In milling, "individuals move around amongst one another in aimless and random fashion, such as in the interweaving of cattle or sheep who are in a state of excitement." Milling makes the individuals in such interaction "more sensitive and responsive to one another," and "decreasingly responsive" to other "objects and events which would ordinarily concern them. . . . People in this state are much more disposed to act together, under the influence of a common impulse or mood, than they are to act separately" (p. 75).

Collective Excitement.   The second type of mechanism of collective behavior is collective excitement, which Blumer referred to as "a more intense form of milling," "a speeding up of the milling process." Here, the excited behavior of some members of the collectivity cannot be ignored by others. It compels attention and makes for a "loss of normal control." Under the influence of collective excitement, "people become more emotionally aroused and more likely to be carried away by impulses and feelings. . . . In collective excitement, individuals may embark on lines of conduct which previously they would not likely have thought of, much less dared to undertake" (pp. 75, 76).

Social Contagion.   "Where collective excitement is intense and widespread, there is every likelihood for some kind of social contagion to take place. Social contagion refers to the relatively rapid, unwitting, and nonrational dissemination of a mood, impulse, or form of conduct." This state generates such forms of collective behavior as crazes, fads, and manias. "In its extreme forms, it has the character of a social epidemic" (1969, p. 76), such as the tulip mania, discussed by Mackay, patriotic war hysteria, and speculative financial panics. Social contagion "attracts and infects individuals, many of whom originally are merely detached and indifferent spectators and bystanders." As such onlookers—the "merely curious" or the "mildly interested"—"catch the spirit of excitement and become more attentive to the behavior, they become more inclined to engage in it." Under such conditions, the behavior in question will "spread like wildfire" (p. 77).

Blumer's contagion theory may be compared and contrasted with LeBon's on at least five major points. Blumer's approach shares two weaknesses with LeBon's, as well as one strength, and makes two advances beyond LeBon's perspective. First and second, the weaknesses. Like LeBon, Blumer saw collective behavior as a largely *pathological* and *irrational* phenomenon; it is generated under conditions of individual frustration and social disorganization and unrest, it is irrational and highly emotionally charged behavior. Blumer offers no positive or constructive examples. And second, Blumer saw unity in the crowd where, in actual fact, crowds and other collectivities tend to be diverse, far from unified. Third, as to the strength: Like LeBon, Blumer recognized the fact that collective behavior (as it turns out, like social behavior in general—which neither would have admitted) has an "emergent" or "generative" quality (Zygmunt, 1986, p. 27); it is behavior that is *qualitatively different* from that which isolated individuals would have engaged in, removed from contact with other members of a collectivity. Fourth and fifth, as to Blumer's contributions. Unlike LeBon, Blumer identified some of the social *mechanisms* by which crowd mood intensifies, one being social interaction with like-minded individuals. And, also unlike LeBon, Blumer expanded the notion of collectives that can have an influence over the individual to include not only crowds, but *publics* and *masses* as well, that is, individuals who are tied together by means of the mass media. Thus, while Blumer's version of contagion theory represents a couple of steps beyond LeBon's, it also shares at least one of its flaws—its focus on negative or pathological examples, causes, and consequences.

Today, contagion theory—whether Blumer's or LeBon's version—is not looked upon with much favor in the field of collective behavior. There are six problems with it. First, contagion theory tended to focus on unusual and extreme cases that most observers would regard as destructive and irrational—riots, for instance, or frenzied rallies attending the speeches of demagogic politicians. Clearly, there are other forms of collective behavior, as we'll see in the later chapters of this book. Contagion theory contains a smuggled-in bias about the nature of collective behavior phenomena that is not borne out in real life. Contagion is a *process*; it refers to the communication of a certain mood in a collectve setting. Why should that mood always be of a violent, destructive nature? (Even LeBon's few supposedly positive examples referred to violent events, such as religious and patriotic wars.) Why can't an ecstatic or a nonviolent mood be communicated to the members of a crowd or a public? The fact is, it can, and contagion theorists failed to realize this.

Second, since contagion theory never bothered to look at what the members of crowds were actually doing, it made an unwarranted assumption about crowd *unity* or *uniformity*. Once you were a member of a frenzied crowd, how could you fail to get caught up in the frenzy? In fact, in most crowds, even those that are described as frenzied, people are not uniformly emotional, nor do their members act in anything like a uniform fashion. There are, of course exceptions, but, for the most part, a close look even at acting crowds shows much variation in what its members are doing, including a great deal of nonparticipation (Miller, 1985, p. 46).

Third and fourth: Contagion theory made the unwarranted assumption that people in crowds are more suggestible in large part because they are more *anonymous*. The member of a crowd is a tiny particle in a vast, powerful mass, unknown and unrecognizable by the other members; they can do anything they want because, being anonymous, they are *unaccountable*. While such a formulation may appeal to common sense, it is completely false, as it turns out. Crowd members, like publics, tend to be in gatherings with others whom they know and whose opinions they value. They are far from anonymous or unaccountable for their actions (Aveni, 1977; McPhail, 1991, p. 14).

Fifth, contagion theory assumes that there is an iron-clad rule that, once like-minded individuals gather and begin to get whipped up into an intense emotional state, this mood will inevitably *escalate* and translate into some kind of behavioral outlet, such as a riot. But, as we'll see, not only is the *deescalation* of crowd or public excitement and behavior likely, it happens far more often than does its opposite.

Moreover, and this is contagion theory's sixth problem, it gives no indication of just what crowds, publics, or masses are likely to do in a given situation. Under what circumstances does crowd excitement translate into crowd behavior? Into crowd inaction? Under what circumstances do the members of a given public, aroused over a given issue, act on it? Under what circumstances does a potentially explosive issue simply fizzle out? Or get redefined and change direction? Contagion theory does not explain when and how contagion is activated. Properly speaking, contagion theory isn't a real theory at all; what it does is supply a mechanism that operates under a very limited set of circumstances, but it doesn't spell out what those circumstances are. It may be true that the mood of a large number of members of a crowd or a public is *sometimes* or *often* communicated to individuals in that crowd or public who did not originally feel it. However, it is quite another to argue that this process *always* occurs. As matters stand, contagion is a tautology, an example of circular reasoning: If crowds get whipped up into an emotional frenzy and are stirred to act, they are seized by contagion; if they do not do so, they are not so seized. To know *how*, *when*, and *under what circumstances* this process occurs, it is necessary to move beyond contagion theory.

CONVERGENCE OR PREDISPOSITION THEORY

Contagion theory makes the assumption that all like-minded individuals in a given collective situation will be swept up by the fervor of others. *Convergence theory*, which is also called the *predisposition hypothesis* (McPhail, 1991, pp. 43ff), offers a contrasting approach. Convergence theory is a "kinds of people" theory of collective behavior. It says that the way people act in crowds or publics is an expression or outgrowth of *who they are ordinarily.* It argues that like-minded people come together in, or *converge* on, a certain location where collective behavior can and will take place, where individuals can act out tendencies or traits that they had in the first place (Allport, 1924, p. 292; Dollard et al., 1939). Being in a crowd simply gives its members an excuse to reveal their "true selves" (Turner, 1964, p. 387). In short, to the convergence theorist, collective behavior is "the simultaneous release of already existing predispositions" (Turner and Killian, 1987, p. 19).

The earliest and crudest version of convergence theory is that *all* people have at least the potential for engaging in collective behavior, such as rioting, because in doing so they are expressing the savage, brutal, primitive instincts that all of us share. The only difference among us is our ability to cover up or inhibit those savage impulses. *All* humans are basically animals in disguise, and our savagery will express itself at the appropriate time and place. Cultivation and education may repress these impulses, but under the right cir-

What happens when a quarter of a million bikers descend on a small town in South Dakota? Chances are the townspeople—and the bikers—are in for a few surprises. It is unlikely that their norms and values will fully prepare them for the unexpected encounters they are likely to have.

cumstances, they will burst forth. If an opportunity arises, our destructive instincts will overwhelm us and force us to engage in brutal, destructive, irrational, and highly emotional behavior. Here, the "convergence" of people into a collective behavior situation is the coming together of *any and all people*, regardless of their characteristics. We *all* have a propensity for engaging in destructive mob behavior, although some of us choose not to place ourselves in situations that would permit this to happen. Clearly, Sigmund Freud's theory of psychoanalysis holds to a position very much like this position.

A somewhat more sophisticated version of convergence theory would argue that *certain kinds of people* have the propensity to engage in *certain kinds of behavior*. Thus, following convergence theory, the crowds of screaming, seething teenage fans at rock concerts are acting out behavior that expresses their everyday selves, be it because intense emotionalism and a tendency toward violence is a general adolescent trait, or because the specific adolescents who attend rock concerts tend to be more emotional and violent than those who don't. Individuals who lynched Blacks in the South in the 1920s and 1930s were poor whites with low incomes, little education, and criminal records; the reasons they instigated or joined the lynchings had to do with *who they were* (Cantril, 1941, pp. 78ff), not because they got together, got whipped up into an emotional frenzy, and acted in a violent, racist fashion. The people who rioted and looted during civil disturbances of the 1960s were lower-class Black males gripped by feelings of uncertainty, insecurity, purposelessness, and frustration engaged in "rampages of destructiveness and lawlessness" (Bolce, 1982, pp. 139, 140). Convergence theory argues that a *certain kind of individual* is drawn to *a certain kind of gathering* and engages in *a certain kind of behavior*—collective behavior.

Today, it is impossible to agree with LeBon, who argued that *any* member of a mob, regardless of his or her background, will act in the same violent, irrational fashion. Clearly, the characteristics of the participants have *something* to do with whether or not they engage in collective behavior. Among the Islamic fundamentalists mourning the death of the Ayatolla Khomeini, described in Chapter 4, a nonbeliever was extremely unlikely to have felt or displayed the emotion that gripped the vast majority of the crowd; clearly, religious belief had something to do with feeling and acting that way. The English toughs, skinheads, and hooligans who go to soccer games and engage in violent behavior are, overwhelmingly, young working-class or unemployed males who also engage in violent behavior in their everyday lives; soccer games happen to be a *locus* of their behavior, not a cause of it (Hazleton, 1989a, 1989b). An extremely conservative business executive is very unlikely to get caught up in fads such as skateboarding, video games, and break-dancing; even if he or she had the time, a brain surgeon is unlikely to sit on a flagpole for 400 days nonstop simply because a lot of people have begun doing it. No one would argue that personal characteristics or predispositions have *nothing* to do with engaging in certain forms of collective behavior. People find certain activities appealing *in part* because of preexisting tendencies that they have.

One major—indeed, fatal—flaw in the convergence or predisposition explanation of collective behavior is that, like contagion theory, it focuses exclusively on destructive and irrational examples. Convergence theorists have not bothered to examine the *full range* of crowd or collective behavior and hence, never bothered to find out that *most* instances of what they are talking about *contradict* their views. In point of fact, crowd violence is quite rare relative to the immense number of temporary gatherings that assemble, but it is practically the *only* type of crowd this school examines. In addition, and also in common with contagion theorists, convergence theory assumes crowd unanimity, now known to be false. The assumption that all people in a given gathering have come because they have a predisposition to act violently, and that all so assembled do so, is empirically false. We now know that crowds are extremely heterogeneous, both in background and in behavior.

Moreover, preexisting tendencies, even where they are related to some forms of behavior, do *not* explain collective behavior—they only give us one very small and simple piece of a very large and complex puzzle. As we'll see later on in the book, participation in many forms of collective behavior *cannot* be predicted from the characteristics of individuals. For example, participants in the 1977 New York City blackout looting, taken as a whole, represented a cross-section of the minority community; an adequate explanation for why it took place is dependent on which *stage* of the looting we are talking about (Curvin and Porter, 1979). Engaging in the urban civil disorders of the 1960s was related to only a very few individual attributes, and the connection with most of those that common sense would tell us were related were in fact not empirically verified (McPhail, 1971). And the simple fact is, even when people with certain "preexisting tendencies" do get together in crowds, violence is still extremely rare. Consider, for example, the fact that sporting events are attended heavily by young, working-class men, a high proportion of whom have been violent under certain circumstances; out of thousands of such events that take place daily worldwide, only a tiny fraction ever break out into overt violence. Clearly, then, something other than "preexisting tendencies" is responsible for the few events where such violence does erupt.

The image that once dominated thinking about revolutions and other political insurrections was that the poorest, most disadvantaged, most criminally inclined, and most unstable members of a society are the ones who are most active in overthrowing the government. Indeed, such a theory appeals to common sense, and would certainly be endorsed by the convergence theorist. In a study of the French Revolution, however, Rudé (1959) found that the revolutionary crowds were made up, for the most part, not of the poorest segment of society, but of shopkeepers, craftsmen, wage earners—individuals who would be classified as working and lower-middle class. These were people with jobs, a salary, a fixed address, and no criminal record. Moreover, most of the leaders of the French Revolution were professionals, successful and affluent owners of businesses, and even landowners. Clearly, the usual preexisting characteristics to explain engaging in political revolt had little or nothing to do with participating in the French Revolution.

Even if collective behavior is in part an expression of preexisting latent tendencies, *if these tendencies cannot find an appropriate set of circumstances to be expressed*, they cannot translate into action. The individual does not create a crowd, a mass, or a public in the first place; although such gatherings may crop up from time to time, they are never tailor-made for a specific individual's characteristics. Behavior in any situation is never determined solely or even mainly by prior individual characteristics or tendencies. Hardly anyone launches a series of actions regardless of the situations in which they are located or the reactions of others. Clearly, for instance, someone's likelihood of engaging in collective behavior in a crowd setting is strongly influenced by factors such as the size of the crowd and what it is doing in the first place (Sullivan, 1977; Granovetter, 1978). It is fallacious to impute causality to individual characteristics without reference to social context.

In short, although we cannot ignore individual characteristics in playing a role in influencing participation in collective behavior phenomena, they do not tell the whole story. Indeed, they may not even tell a major part of the story. Individuals do not create the social conditions within which they operate; often, it is social conditions to which they respond, and not their individual characteristics that are telling them what to do. The same individual, facing two different sets of conditions, will act one way in one and an entirely different way in the other. To understand why collective behavior arises, is sustained, and dies out, we must move beyond the individual.

EMERGENT NORM THEORY

The *emergent norm* perspective (Turner and Killian, 1957, 1972, 1987; Turner, 1964; Killian, 1980) offers a critique of most of the major assumptions of both contagion and convergence theories. Although there are differences between contagion and convergence theory, both perspectives: (1) see collective behavior as irrational, destructive, and highly emotional; (2) they see the behavior of individual participants, and their emotional states, as fairly uniform and unanimous; and (3) they generally see collective behavior as the violation of conventional norms.

Emergent norm theory sees each of these assumptions as false. It argues three principal points: (1) collective behavior is no more irrational, destructive, or emotional than conventional behavior; (2) crowds are far more heterogeneous and diverse than casual, unthinking observers believe; and (3) participation in collective behavior does not violate mainstream norms as much as revise them in the light of a novel, unique situation for which conventional norms are not provided or relevant (the new norms "emerging" in the new context).

Emergent norm theorists start with the issue of "how meaning is constructed" (Turner and Killian, 1987, p. 27); that is, how people come to see beliefs as true, values as relevant, norms as binding, and behavior as acceptable. They argue that meaning does not arise from the individual as a result of independent cognition, or solely from the material world, but as a consequence of interaction with others. Instead, most of our beliefs about what's good and true are learned as a result of human contact. We see things the way we do in large part because of the groups in which we are involved and the relations we have with others. This does not mean that we are exact carbon copies of others who share our group memberships. Every one of us retains our own special individuality and uniqueness, but we are all powerfully influenced by the general society in which we grew up, the categories to which we belong, and the social circles in which we move.

A set of classic experiments verifies this view (Sherif, 1936; Sherif and Harvey, 1952). Subjects were placed in dark rooms, able to see only a tiny pinpoint of light. Though the light did not move, it appeared to, because observers had no "anchorages" in the background. (This is called the "autokinetic" phenomenon or effect.) Alone, each subject estimated the distance and direction that the light supposedly moved; each subject had his or her own standard individual estimate. Then, individuals were put into the dark rooms in groups, and, together, they discussed the movement of the light. In this situation, *group* norms evolved—somewhat different for each group—with respect to where and how far the light moved. These were widely divergent from each subject's original individual estimates. In a group setting, after discussing the light with others, individuals said to themselves, "Before, I thought I saw the light move from left to right about two feet, but since the others see it moving from right to left about a foot, I guess that's what I see now." In other words, *a different or revised interpretation of what was happening emerged out of group interaction.*

Then, the researchers introduced a wrinkle in the experiment. Subjects were placed in two different kinds of rooms. One was small and the subjects had a chance to look around the room before it became dark, that is, to orient themselves to the anchorages in the room. Another was large and subjects were led into it in blindfolds so that they had no idea of the size of the room or what was in it. The first set of conditions was regarded as a *less uncertain* condition, and the second, a *more uncertain* condition. In the *more* uncertain condition, subjects were more subject to group estimates: In comparison with the less uncertain condition, their group estimates converged more, and their original individual judgments of the direction and distance of the light were more likely to be set aside. In short, the more uncertain the condition, the more *susceptible* individuals are to the suggestions of others, and the more *influence* the group has.

The same process takes place in collective behavior, emergent norm theorists argue. Collective behavior is not so much a result of *freedom from* the contraints of convention as it is *the emergence of a new norm in normatively ambiguous situations.* Conventional norms do not spell out in detail everything that one should and shouldn't do in every situation that arises in one's life. Individuals often find themselves in situations in which the old norms don't seem to fit or work very well. Conventional norms seem ambiguous, irrelevant, or contradictory. It's not that normative controls in general cease to exist; it's that new norms arise when old ones don't work.

In a collective behavior situation, people get together in a more or less novel situation or gathering. The situation is normatively ambiguous; it isn't clear what the right thing to do is. They act and interact with one another and communicate with one another about the circumstances they face. Out of this interaction, definitions of right and wrong, what to do and what not to do, begin to emerge—definitions that are a bit different from the definitions they may have learned since childhood. They revise their definition of the situation based on their judgment and the judgments of others. And they engage in behavior *based* on that revised definition. Most people who participate in collective behavior don't think, "I'm violating the norms I grew up with." They are more likely to say, "If anyone else were in this same situation, they'd do pretty much the same thing we're doing." Individuals in a given collectivity supply or seek *justifications* for their course of action; communication in a group setting entails a search to apply a particular norm to a situation in which the individual finds himself or herself.

Let's take an obvious example. Imagine that a disaster, such as a tornado, has struck a community. Groups of relief workers are going through the community to help the victims. One group comes to a house where they look inside and see a woman lying unconscious on the floor and a small baby by her side, crying. The door is locked and they cannot get in without doing some damage to it. They quickly talk the matter over and agree the owners wouldn't mind if they broke down the door. Routine norms say, don't trespass, don't destroy property. But here, we have something of a novel situation, a situation in which traditional, conventional norms no longer apply. These individuals come together and agree that a different course of action is called for; they arrive at a norm that says break the door down! Human life is a lot more important than property! In less obvious situations, the same process occurs when disaster workers must technically steal property, such as a truck, in order to facilitate helping others. Again, the old norms don't work very well in a new situation; new norms are called for, norms that are not so much a *violation* of conventional morality as a collective *redefinition* of it. Interestingly, as we'll see in a few chapters, research shows that, in most disasters, very few people panic or engage in unlawful behavior such as looting. The prediction of contagion theorists would be that most people would panic in a disaster, the panic of each person feeding off the panic of others. But this is clearly *not* what happens; in fact, most people are fairly rational and cooperative in disasters, something that emergent norm theory would have predicted.

Looting in civil disturbances provides another good illustration of emergent norm theory. It should be said that there is no single type of looter, and no single explanation can account for the looting of all who do it. (See the boxed insert in this chapter on the 1977 New York City blackout looting to understand how different theories of collective behavior explain the actions of different looters.) Still, one major process that takes place during looting is *the emergence of new norms in an unusual situation where the old ones don't work*. Looting is rarely simply opportunistic behavior, that is, people stealing to take advantage of the fact that they are unlikely to be caught. In fact, there are many situations in which apprehension is unlikely and looting is very rare—in disasters, for instance. At the same time, it is extremely widespread during civil disturbances, such as riots and other uprisings against exploitation and oppression that take place in minority communities. Moreover, the looting that does take place during disasters is the work of solitary, isolated *individuals*, not groups, and tends to be perpetrated by *outsiders*, rarely residents of the community in which the disaster takes place. The looting that takes place during civil disorder tends to be the work of *groups* or *collectivities*, most of whom live in the community that is experiencing the disturbance (Quarantelli and Dynes, 1970).

The question is why? Why is looting widespread during civil disturbances and very rare in natural disasters? The fact is, in a disaster, norms are strongly opposed to taking advantage of the misfortune of others; it is not possible for norms supporting such an action to emerge out of a disaster situation.

Individuals who do it are regarded as deviants and are condemned by the overwhelming majority of the community, and other communities as well. In contrast, in civil disturbances, community norms support looting from stores. Looting at such a time and in such a situation is regarded by many as expropriating goods in retaliation for the exploitation of which minority residents feel they have been victims. Looting is redefined as "taking what's rightfully mine." Property norms become redefined; liquor, clothing, electronic equipment belong to the stores' owners only because they have ripped off the community. Now it's time to turn around and exact some justice! Looting is felt to be an uprising against oppressive conditions, a symbolic blow against white exploitation. As such, it has widespread community support (Quarantelli and Dynes, 1970; Turner and Killian, 1987, pp. 93–94).

Another crucial point that emergent norm theory makes is that crowds and other collectivities are less unanimous than both contagion and convergence theories would predict. Not only would contagion theory predict that people would panic during disasters, it also predicts that people would react pretty much the same way in a disaster. Again, crowd unity is a feature of contagion theory. In fact, in disasters, there is a wide *range* of actions and reactions, depending on how each individual links up with the disaster; each set of participants plays a different role in the disaster—victims, returnees, helpers, the curious, and so on (Turner and Killian, 1987, pp. 30–31). We cannot predict how people will react unless we know in what specific way they are part of the overall picture.

The same logic applies to crowds generally. Contagion theory perpetrates "the illusion of unanimity"; emergent norm theory emphasizes the *diversity* of crowds, that crowds are, for the most part, a motley crew, a mixed assemblage. Some members of a crowd are active participants; others are onlookers, bystanders, and passersby; still others come to cheer on the participants; and others come to jeer rather than cheer. In May 1970, students held a demonstration at Kent State University to protest the American government's invasion of Cambodia. The governor of Ohio called in the National Guard to maintain order. At one point, the guardsmen, mostly young and inexperienced, feared physical danger to themselves. Panicking, they began to fire indiscriminately into the crowd. But the crowd, as emergent norm would have predicted, was not a homogeneous assemblage; it was a mixed group of individuals, made up of an "active core," who shouted insults and threw dirt and rocks at the guardsmen; "cheerleaders," who egged the participants on; and "spectators," who simply watched what was going on. The guardsmen, like most people who look at crowds, imagined that they were face-to-face with a large, homogeneous, ugly crowd. In fact, the area the guardsmen fired upon was made up mostly of spectators. As a result of their inability to understand the situation, and their belief in "the illusion of unanimity," four students lay dead that day on the Kent State University campus (Lewis, 1972).

And lastly, emergent norm theory argues that a collective setting does not necessarily generate ever-increasing hysteria and stimulation; a deescalation of crowd excitement is, in fact, more likely than its escalation. The emergent norms that arise in a particular collective setting may very well call for certain *limits* on the behavior of its members. The image that convergence and, especially, contagion theory hold is that, in a collective setting, individuals become increasingly frenzied and out of control. But emergent collective norms may *demand* certain kinds of control in a given setting.

A good example of this principle took place in the pro-democracy uprising in Tiananmen Square in Beijing in the Spring of 1989. At its peak, roughly a million protesters thronged the square, carried signs and chanted slogans and, even, for a time, prevented soldiers from entering. And yet, throughout the demonstration, a certain sense of decorum was maintained. (It must be said that, when the protest was crushed by the government, some participants did attack and even kill soliders who were seen attacking or killing demonstrators.) On May 24th, the huge portrait of Mao Zedong that hangs above the gate to the Forbidden City was spattered with paint. Since Mao is in many ways a symbol of the conservative old Communist China the students and workers were protesting against, it might have been reasonable to assume that this portrait would have become a target of their wrath. Exactly the reverse was true. Mao is such a revered figure in China that attacking the portrait was seen as a desecration, even by the protesters. When the portrait was defaced, the protesters disclaimed responsibility for the act and in fact identified and turned the culprits who did it over to the police. As we now know, however, such restraint did not help the demonstrators much when government tanks rolled in ten days later, crushed the rebellion, and killed hundreds, perhaps thousands, who were in the square.

One of the largest anti-Vietnam demonstrations was held in October 1967 in Washington; nearly a quarter of a million people showed up for it. A group of protesters was camped out in the backyard of a residence in Georgetown. A young man approached the group and said that he had a supply of cherry bombs that he would give to the protesters "if they would throw them at police and soldiers during Saturday's rally at the Lincoln Memorial." One protester "pointed out how stupidly dangerous it would be to discharge fireworks around nervous and trigger-happy soliders." A young woman in the group "offered a rather vulgar plan for disposing" of the explosives; at that point, the young man left. The next evening, at a rally on the steps of the Pentagon, there was "shouting, shoving, kicking, and the use of night sticks and gun butts as troops moved into the crowd sitting before them." Each time the television floodlights came on, the clamor ceased. At one point, protesters at the rear of the crowd began to throw fruit and soda cans and other trash at the soldiers. Protesters seated nearest the soldiers "shouted for the barrage to cease." Finally one protester with a loud voice shouted, "If you want action, come up here and sit in the first row. Otherwise knock it off!" The protesters cheered and then chanted, "Peace now!" After that, nothing more was thrown at the soldiers (Miller, 1985, pp. 23–24).

As these two examples illustrate, collective behavior is not a frenzied, out-of-control, ever-escalating violation of conventional norms. Crowd behavior does not necessarily or inevitably move in an increasingly violent or irrational direction. Newly emerging norms in a given situation may control or restrain the crowd of the collective. The convergence and contagion perspectives assume that crowds are made up of individuals who egg one another on in the direction of increasingly violent, irrational, and destructive acts. In contrast, the emergent norm perspectives shows that the process is not necessarily unidirectional. A certain level of violence, or certain specific violent acts, may very well contradict the crowd's sense of proper behavior. Simply being in a crowd does not give everyone license to go on a rampage. All crowds are marked by some restraint, although that takes place within the normative limits of each specific crowd. Of course, *some* crowds *do* commit extremely violent and destructive acts, but, again, specifically those that are within *their* normative limitations.

Even though it is universally recognized to represent a theoretical advance over the contagion and convergence perspectives, emergent norm theory has not met with universal acceptance. Perhaps the most forceful criticism that has been lodged against this approach is that it is an example of a tautology, or circular reasoning. It *defines* collective behavior in precisely the same way it *explains* it. What is collective behavior? It is behavior "in which usual conventions cease to guide social action and people collectively transcend, bypass, or subvert established patterns and structures" (Turner and Killian, 1987, p. 3). In other words, what it *is* and *how it is caused* are exactly the same thing. Collective behavior *is* behavior that takes place under the governance of emergent norms, and collective behavior *is caused by* the governance of emergent norms. Clearly, this is an example of circular reasoning, which means that it is not a true explanation or scientific theory (McPhail, 1991, p. 98). Moreover, Turner and Killian's assumption that people enact collective behavior as a consequence of revised norms may not even be true. It is not clear that people who engage in collective behavior in general hold norms that are significantly different from those who do so. It is likely that emergent norm theory is overly ambitious; it probably works better for some types of collective behavior than others. As a result, it should be regarded as a partial, rather than a general, theory.

VALUE-ADDED THEORY

One of the most ambitious theories of collective behavior was put forth in the early 1960s by sociologist Neil Smelser. It is called the *value-added theory* (1962). This approach isolates six determining factors, or conditions, that make for collective behavior: structural conduciveness, structural strain, generalized beliefs, precipitating factors, mobilization for action, and operation of social control. If these conditions are missing, collective behavior will not occur; if they are present, it is almost sure to do so. Each individual condition increases the likelihood that collective behavior will take place; the absence of any condition sharply decreases that likelihood. These factors form a sequence; each step generates the conditions that make the next step possible.

Structural Conduciveness. The major aspects of a social structure must promote or allow collective behavior; if these aspects are missing, it cannot take place. For instance, mass looting can take place only in a materialistic society, in which people value the possession of goods. Likewise, there must be retail stores that stock goods that can be stolen by looters. In a small hunting and gathering society, which has neither stores nor much in the way of material possessions, looting is impossible. The Wall Street stock market crash of 1929, largely a product of several collective behavior processes, was possible only in a society in which stocks and bonds are traded on the market and form a basis for financial speculation.

Structural Strain. Smelser argues that collective behavior is problem-solving behavior. Faced with what he calls structural strain—stress, deprivation, threats, or uncertainty of some sort—people respond in ways that attempt to alleviate the problem. Prison inmates who experience intolerable conditions and feel that nothing is being done to improve them may erupt in a riot; inmates in prisons with more intolerable conditions are more likely to riot than inmates living in prisons with more favorable living conditions. Rival gangs of Black and white teenage boys may engage in gang warfare in neighborhoods where racial tension is high; in neighborhoods with a lower level of racial tension, gang warfare is far less likely. In Argentina in 1989, with rampant inflation pushing food prices up by the hour and families unable to put food on the table, crowds looted supermarkets and grocery stores all over the country (Gorman, 1989). Collective behavior attempts to relieve tensions felt by individuals living in a situation of structural strain.

Generalized Beliefs. By itself, strain is not enough to generate collective behavior. Smelser argues that strain must be accompanied by a belief that points to the specific *problem* and to a particular *solution*. Both may, of course, be mythical; beliefs need not be valid for people to act on them, as long as they are widely held. For instance, in the 1920s and 1930s, hundreds, perhaps thousands, of Blacks were lynched by angry white mobs in the South (and some in the North as well). These actions were fueled by racist beliefs about the inferiority of Blacks, their "proper place" in a white-dominated society, and what to do with them if they stepped out of line. Mass looting in poor neighborhoods is often based on the (usually correct) belief that stores located in them charge higher prices than stores in more affluent areas, and on the looters' belief that they have not received their fair share of the nation's material wealth. In several Soviet republics, such as Latvia, Lithuania, Estonia, Uzbekistan, Armenia, and Georgia, demonstrations and rioting broke out in the late 1980s and early 1990s because many of their residents held (and still hold) the generalized belief that they should be independent nations with a more independent political relationship with Moscow.

Precipitating Factors. In most cases, collective behavior is set off by triggering events or precipitating factors. A 1983 riot at the Ossining Correctional Facility ("Sing Sing"), a maximum security state prison, was touched off by a guard who showed up an hour late to let inmates out of their cells for a recreational period (Mack, 1983). In 1988 and 1989, in Tibet, once an independent country but, since 1959, a largely unwilling province of China, a series of demonstrations broke out which eventually led to the imposition of martial law by Beijing. The demonstrations were generated by a specific event. On December 10th, International Human Rights Day, a monk began to parade through the streets of Lhasa carrying the Tibetan flag, an illegal act. When the police tried to wrench the flag from his hands, he resisted; shots were fired, and the monk was killed. From then until March, when martial law was imposed, demonstrations appeared regularly. After that, Tibetians had to carry permits to go everywhere, including shopping and going to work; people were warned that anyone who assembled would be shot (Crossette, 1989).

In 1980, in Miami, four white police officers were acquitted in the fatal beating of a Black man in their custody; news of this decision sparked a riot in the Black community of Liberty City in which 14 died, 200 were injured, and arson and looting persisted for days afterwards. Often, the precipitating event seems major in hindsight, such as the killing in Tibet, but, just as often, it seems out of proportion to the reaction, such as a scuffle with the police and an arrest following a traffic ticket, which is what generated the civil disorders in the Watts community of Los Angeles in 1965. The situation prior to the event may resemble a "powder keg" ready to explode, and so the precipitating event is a pretext for action, rather than a cause.

Mobilization for Action.   Collective behavior is usually inspired by leaders who take initiative, or the mass media, which can spread news of events, pass on rumors, or inspire beliefs and attitudes throughout a community. The 1977 blackout looting began on a widespread basis only after a small number of street hustlers mobilized passersby to follow their example. (See the boxed insert in this chapter on the looting.) The protest in Tiananmen Square in Beijing in 1989 began with a core of roughly 10,000 students, who set an example for others; at its peak, roughly a million protesters filled the square. In the 1980 Liberty City riot, rumors and news stories about the police officers' aquittal mobilized the Black community's hostile feelings toward their economic and political plight.

Operation of Social Control.   Typically, if controls or restraints discouraging collective behavior are absent, it is free to take place. In the case of the 1977 blackout looting, during much of the time formal social control was almost entirely absent. For the first three hours of the blackout, the police did not have enough officers on the street to deal effectively with the looters. Said one precinct captain, "By the time we got enough men to do anything that night, it was already too late" (Curvin and Porter, 1979, p. 58). A rumor that the police were not arresting anyone spread through the streets. By the time the police began arresting looters in large numbers, the professional criminals had already made off with the most valuable merchandise. Most of the people arrested were teenagers out for a good time and working-class people scrambling for whatever happened to be lying around. Those who

FIGURE 2-1   VALUE-ADDED THEORY

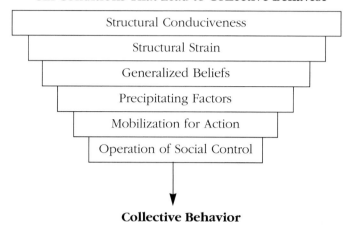

Six Conditions That Lead to Collective Behavior

- Structural Conduciveness
- Structural Strain
- Generalized Beliefs
- Precipitating Factors
- Mobilization for Action
- Operation of Social Control

↓

Collective Behavior

profited most from the looting stood the lowest chance of being arrested, while those who profited least were the most likely to be caught (Curvin and Porter, 1979, p. 58). On the other hand, the protest in Tibet against Chinese rule in 1989 began because formal social control was too *severe*, not too lax. Police action resulted in the death of a monk, which generated sporadic demonstrations for three months until the Chinese imposed martial law.

If Smelser's value-added model could be depicted in a diagram, it would look very much like a giant funnel, with structural conduciveness at one end and collective behavior at the other as the end product of these six conditions (Figure 2-1).

COLLECTIVE BEHAVIOR

While Smelser's model seems to make a great deal of sense at first glance, some reflection raises questions about its value and validity. Some elements of the model are so broad as to be commonsensical and obvious, while other elements seem necessary for some types of collective behavior, but not others.

Of course there must be "structural conduciveness" for collective behavior, otherwise it will not occur: No material goods, no looting; no financial speculation, no stock market crash; no clothing, no fashion in clothing; no flagpoles, no fad of flagpole sitting; little or no social change, social differentiation, or contact with other societies, no social movements. It would be hard to argue with these generalizations; still, they are so obvious as to be trite. At the same time, some structural factors may not be quite as obviously necessary as the existence of a market economy or a stock market, and their influence on certain forms of collective behavior, likewise, may not be obvious. In such cases, Smelser's emphasis on structural factors would represent a contribution to the field.

Of course there must be "generalized beliefs" to support participation in certain collective behavior: People do not act mindlessly, and their behavior is usually generated on the premise that action has something to do with belief. Some examples of such beliefs: Blacks are oppressed, whites are the oppressors; whites are kind, patient, and good, Blacks are ungrateful, pushy, and bad; "they" have too much, "we" deserve more; the Virgin Mary appears in a vision to those who are virtuous; humans do not have the right to torture animals or kill them for sport; abortion is murder; science can't explain everything; anything is possible. These and countless other beliefs support certain types of collective behavior phenomena. As Smelser says, as with every one of his conditions or elements, these beliefs are necessary for collective behavior, but they do not guarantee its occurrence. Beliefs have circulated for generations about the existence of extraterrestrial creatures on or flying around earth, but only if the other conditions fall into place is such a belief a catalyst for collective behavior (1962, p. 16). Still, again, the assumption that certain beliefs are necessary for certain actions seems intuitively obvious. However, once again, searching out the connections between generalized beliefs and their influence on collective behavior may be a tricky and complex matter. In such cases, Smelser's focus on this factor represents a major contribution to the field. Moreover, with many forms of collective behavior, differences in belief do *not* distinguish collective behavior participants from nonparticipants.

While "structural conduciveness" and "generalized beliefs" do seem genuinely—although obviously—necessary for at least some forms of collective behavior, the other four conditions do not.

Why must "structural strain" be a necessary precondition for the appearance of or participation in collective behavior? Here, we can look at structural strain both on the individual and on the societal level. On the individual level, were the parents who purchased Cabbage Patch dolls suffering from some form of strain? The only strain they felt was contemplating the possibility of not being able to purchase something their children wanted very much. Do people who pass on gossip and rumor do so because they experience strain? They value information about things that are important to them, and often, that information is difficult to obtain. Still, do they suffer *strain?* Well, not necessarily. Do those who gossip and pass on rumor do so *because* they suffer from strain—more so than individuals who don't gossip or pass on rumors? This is very unlikely; at the very least, evidence on the relationship between strain and participation in a wide range of collective behavior phenomena would have to be presented to make this case plausible.

It is mainly on the societal level that Smelser examines strain: Are *societies* that are marked by a great deal of structural strain—"ambiguities, deprivations, conflicts, and discrepancies" (p. 16)—ones in which collective behavior is widespread? If you define structural strain broadly enough, it exists in all societies; however, in some, it is deeper and more intense than it is in others. Participation in some activities is clearly generated in part by strain; riots, demonstrations, protests, and social movement participation take place because some people are unhappy about the way things are and want to make them better. At the same time, are social movement activists and participants more likely to recognize this strain any more than individuals who are inactive? As we'll see in Part 5, recent research on social movements questions this age-old assumption. Moreover, it is difficult to see structural strain underlying many fads and much fashion (aside from the division of society into "in" and "out" crowds), much rumor and gossip (aside from the lack of availability of the information being sought or passed on), some ecstatic crowds, belief in some paranormal phenomena, and most processes of public opinion. Structural strain is one of those classic assumptions shoring up how most people think about participation in collective behavior that just doesn't seem to hold up under close scrutiny.

Are "precipitating factors" necessary for collective behavior to take place? As we saw, it is for some. The three-month long series of sporadic demonstrations in Tibet between December 1988 and March 1989 was touched off by the police killing a monk who was carrying a Tibetan flag; they ended only with the imposition of martial law. Moreover, rumor or a news story of certain events can generate certain kinds of collective behavior, such as a riot, exemplified by the riots in 1980 by residents of Liberty City, Florida, after hearing the news of the acquittal of white police officers who killed a Black man in their custody. Some forms of collective behavior get started as a result of certain events, that is, the collective behavior phenomenon is *about* the event in the first place. A good example of this is gossip. Gossip began circulating about Senator Kennedy's auto accident on Chappaquiddick Island because of the accident itself. Clearly, this is tautological, that is, true by definition, and cannot be regarded as an explanation of anything.

But what was the "precipitating factor" in the Cabbage Patch doll fad? The commercial availability of the doll itself? *News* of its availability? News of its *scarcity?* Where is the precipitating factor in most fashion? The announcement of the style in question? Manufacturers like to generate "events" when they introduce fashion and product fads to make them seem more desirable to the public, but that does not explain why some are popular and others are not. What is the "precipitating factor" in the thousands of contemporary legends about events that, in all likelihood, never happened, but which are told as true? (We'll explore contemporary legends in Chapter 8.) For most of them, there isn't any such specific factor. Again, this precondition is necessary for some collective behavior phenomena but not others.

The same holds for "mobilization for action." Again, some activities do require, and are characterized by, such mobilization—a call to action, an announcement at a meeting, the example of leaders. But how is gossip and rumor "mobilized"? Well, someone tells another person something that he or she hasn't heard about and considers interesting; when this happens a lot, it's called gossip or rumor. How are fashion and product fads "mobilized"? Well, they are developed by a manufacturer; introduced onto the market; and announced and advertised so that media hype is generated about them—and some catch on, while some don't. Is the "mobilization" for fads and fashions that become successful any different from those that don't? Probably not. Does "mobilization" explain anything here? Again, probably not.

For some forms of collective behavior, the "operation of social control" is clearly relevant—the blackout looting that took place in New York City in 1977; the demonstrations in Tibet in 1988 and 1989; the student and worker unprisings in China that took place in the Spring of 1989; the demonstrations that took place in Seoul, South Korea in 1987; the massive and widespread demonstrations that occurred in Eastern Europe in 1989; many, probably most, prison riots. But is it *too much* or *too little* social control that is causal in collective behavior? What the authorities do may stimulate or inhibit participation in collective behavior—but exactly how isn't clear from the theory. Moreover, the authorities are *uninterested* in many forms of collective behavior—again, fads, fashion, gossip, most rumor, most urban legends, most paranormal phenomena, some miracles and other ecstatic forms of collective behavior. It is difficult to see the relevance of the role of formal social control in many collective behavior phenomena.

In sum, Smelser's theory of collective behavior is partly true, but obvious, and partly invalid, because it is clearly overextended. It is very likely that the theory works a great deal better for crowd phenomena, which Smelser focuses on, than for the behavior of masses and publics, and that parts of it work better for behavior that is relevant to social movements than for some of the less purposive, less organized forms of collective behavior that we'll be looking at in this book. In fact, Smelser's theory has made several important contributions to contemporary thinking on social movements. At the same time, the value-added approach was intended to be a theory of collective behavior *in general*, and so, for that reason, must be regarded as not completely successful.

SPECIALIZED THEORIES OF COLLECTIVE BEHAVIOR

There are four major theories of collective behavior that apply to some collective behavior phenomena or its aspects but not others. These are the rational calculus or game theory, the threshold model, the social behavioral/interactionist (SBI) theory, and the resource mobilization perspective. None offers the grand, general sweep that the four classic theories just discussed do, and yet, most of them are more likely to be factually verified *within their own limited scope* than the older theories are.

THE RATIONAL CALCULUS OR GAME THEORY

Rational calculus or game theory theorizes about collective actions, especially those that are political, that attempt to attain a specific goal. It emphasizes crowd behavior, but assumes that it is relevant for more diffuse collective actions as well. In addition, it seems most focused on social movement activity. Still, some of the actions analyzed by game theory do fit our delineation of collective behavior, such as looting and rioting. This theory, model, or perspective argues that people weigh the costs and benefits of their behavior in a careful, rational, calculating fashion; they arrive at a course of action that maximizes their reward and minimizes their costs (Berk, 1974a, pp. 67–75, 1974b), a practice known as the *minimax strategy* (1974b, p.364). It is the contention of gaming theorists that crowd behavior is no different from behavior in other contexts; both are equally rational or dominated by minimax strategies.

In this model or theory, people are seen as rational actors. In the end, they decide to do that which yields the desired end with the least risk. Even such actions as looting and rioting usually result in important payoffs, such as the goods that are stolen or political goals that may be achieved. Moreover, people tend to avoid incurring a great deal of cost—not monetary cost alone, but all the other things that people find undesirable as well, such as getting injured, arrested, or socially ostracized. If a riot breaks out, for example, a potential participant immediately begins thinking about what he or she would receive by joining in, and what the risks are. If this weighing process results in an assessment that produces more potential benefits than potential costs, the individual will take part in the riot; if the individual comes up with more costs than benefits, he or she does not take part. Game theory sees collective action as a means by which individuals or groups attain desired goals. Of course, these goals may be individually held, as in looting a store to steal merchandise, or held by an entire collective, such as the members of a movement or a group when they overthrow a government.

Before we look at the validity of game theory, several qualifications are in order. First, there is a great deal of variation in what people see as desirable ends or goals. One person's goal may seem silly and irrational to another. As we saw in the first chapter, we cannot call someone's goal irrational simply because *we* do not see it as desirable. To a hunter, the goals of the animal rights movement, which aims to end or reduce the willful suffering and killing of animals, make no sense at all. To someone who supports a given administration or regime, a demonstration protesting it seems counterproductive. Still, we cannot apply the rationality scheme to people's goals, ends, or values. Collective action is seen by this approach as a means *to attain specific goals;* it is *not* a scheme to analyze the rationality *of the goals themselves.* We take the goals as a given, and determine whether people's actions are a rational means of attaining them. The rationality or irrationality of certain goals is outside the scope of the theory.

Second, people may be factually *mistaken* in their calculation of the likelihood of attaining a given goal, or the likelihood of incurring a given cost, as a result of their action. Game theory does not assert that everyone who acts has all the facts relevant to the situation at his or her disposal; all it says is that people weigh pluses and minuses according to what they know, or think they know. I may decide to take part in a riot on Pennsylvania Avenue in front of the White House because I've heard that the president will be there and will be influenced by our message. But it's possible I'm wrong; the president could be out of town, or he may be completely unsympathetic to my movement's cause, or he may even decide *against* our cause as a result of our riot. All of these things are possible. Still, game theory does not say that all actors are completely correct about the consequences of their actions, only that they take cost, benefit, and risk into account.

What are we to make of the rational calculus theory? After all the necessary qualifications have been registered, it seems extremely unlikely that all or even most people weigh cost and benefit in the way that game theory suggests (Perry and Pugh, 1978, p. 37). Unless we were to define *everything* people do as the quest for ends they hold dear, which would make our theory true by definition, a tautology, it is clear that *much* of what we do is *not* ruled by a rational calculus. Some of what we do, in fact, may *undermine* our goals, especially our collective goals. Much of what we do is what we "have to do" on principle; we do it *knowing* that we will fail, or that it makes our attainment of a goal we seek difficult or impossible. The young men and women who threw rocks at Russian tanks in Hungary in 1956, and in Czechoslovakia in 1968, knew that their action entailed a huge risk to life and limb, and would not achieve their desired end—the pull-out of Soviet troops from their countries. It was a spontaneous action, one that seems almost innocent of rational calculation; in fact, it seems quite irrational from the perspective of game theory. But it was something they had to do to express their feelings.

In June, 1989, the Chinese government decided to crush the student-led pro-democracy demonstrations that were being held in Tiananmen Square in Beijing. The army was sent in, and between 500 and 1,000 protesters were killed. At one point, as a column of tanks rolled through the square, a single man walked to the lead tank and stood there, blocking its path. "There he stood, implausibly resolute in his white shirt, an unknown Chinese man facing down a lumbering column of tanks." The lead tank tried to turn, first to the right, then to the left, to avoid running over the man, but each time he stepped into its path; then it stopped, unsure of what to do next. "Why are you here?" the man shouted to the soliders inside. "You have done nothing but create misery. My city is in chaos because of you" (Talbott, 1989, p. 10). Finally, some other protesters grabbed and spirited him off, and the tanks continued rumbling through the square.

Here again it is difficult to reconcile what this man did with the tenets of rationality theory. Was what he did an attempt to achieve a specific, concrete goal? Did he imagine the soldiers in the tank would get out, step down, shake his hand, and stop their repression of the rebellion? What was it, exactly, this man was trying to achieve? Was he simply trying to express himself, overcome by the anguish and rage he felt at the destruction of the movement he supported? If his action was rational, what about the demonstrators who took him away? Were they doing something different simply because they had more realistic information about the consequences of his action? Again, it is stretching the concept of rationality beyond all limits to assume that this man's action fits the assumptions of game theory. Of course, as game theorists themselves point out, self-expression may be an end in itself (Berk, 1974a, p. 74) and may stand aside from or even contradict *other* goals, such as the preservation of one's life or overthrowing an oppressive regime. But such qualifications are often tacked on *after the fact.* Figuring out which goal a given action rationally pursues or expresses is often a tricky business and is usually impossible to predict in advance. In McPhail's words, "the minimax principle is but one set of instructions people . . . give themselves in some situations. But it is a very limited set of instructions, insufficient for virtually all the complex individual and social behaviors in which human beings engage" (1991, p. 125).

Another problem the rational calculus model runs into is the *risky shift* phenomenon. Years ago it was discovered that when a decision is reached after group deliberation, such a decision tends be riskier than if a decision is made individually. The reason is that a group decision diffuses responsibility for an undesirable outcome, whereas, if the individual alone makes the choice, he or she is solely responsible for its outcome (Kogon and Wallach, 1967). For instance, in five-card draw poker any player knows that drawing one card to an inside straight is a sucker's bet; the risk of losing is far greater than the likelihood of winning in that situation. And yet, when seven players discuss a hand together, they are more likely to make the sucker's bet and draw to an inside straight than is the single player making the decision alone. While later research has produced mixed results and suggested more complex conclusions (Billig et al., 1988, p. 13), it is clear that a strictly rational calculation does not characterize group decisions as to whether or not to take part in collective behavior. The members of a crowd do not necessarily act to minimize risk and maximize rewards. In fact, much crowd behavior, and much collective behavior, seems to work almost precisely in the opposite direction of that predicted by the rational calculus position; that is, in many cases, the crowd may be *less* rational than the individual.

It is true that some collective actions are rational—assuming that we can all agree as to just what this means. It is true that some actors engaging in collective behavior do weigh the cost, benefit, and risk of their actions carefully. But in truth, this process is an empirical question; as to whether people do it in real life is something that must be investigated in each concrete case. To hold it as an assumption is unrealistic. Many actions do not fit this assumption. No matter how we define rationality, if our formulation is not a tautology, true by definition, many collective actions will be found to stray far beyond the bounds of strict rationality. People have many motives for doing things, and the rational attainment of specific goals is only one of them. At best, game theory must be regarded as a narrow, partial, and specialized explanation, valid for certain types or aspects of collective behavior and not others. It is difficult to take it seriously as a general explanation. Still, it is possible that the rational calculus approach is more valuable in studying social movements than in helping us understand most of the collective behavior we'll be looking at in this book. However, it must be emphasized that the

Crowd size is a major factor in the threshold theory of collective behavior. At the height of the pro-democracy demonstrations that took place in 1989, more than a million protesters crowded into Tienanmen Square.

view of collective behavior as generally rational offers a powerful corrective to the even more mistaken view that it is always or typically irrational. In fact, one observer holds that for at least one form of action that overlaps heavily with collective behavior, collective militant action, the shift that took place some 25 years ago from seeing it as irrational to seeing it as rational represented "an authentic theoretical revolution" (Rule, 1989, p. 145).

THE THRESHOLD MODEL

The threshold model (Sullivan, 1977; Granovetter, 1978) argues that collective behavior is *not* a simple outcome of the norms, motives, and preferences of individual actors; we can know everything there is to know about all of the individuals who are poised to engage in collective behavior without being able to predict successfully whether a given episode of it will actually take place. Even with the complete knowledge of individuals, there is "still a great deal to be done"; the outcome of a given situation "cannot be determined by any simple counting of preferences" (Granovetter, 1978, p. 1421). The threshold model is strongly influenced by and overlaps with, but is not identical to, the rational calculus or gaming approach (Berk, 1974a, pp. 71–73).

The threshold model applies to behavior that has the following qualities.

First, there must be some sort of flow of communication or information from one person to another. *Second*, the behavior must be binary, that is, it must entail making a decision one way or the other, resulting in acting or not acting. *Third*, it must be a clearly recognizable, discrete act, not an act that is vague, unclear, or unrecognizable. *Fourth*, it must be nonroutine, that is, one has to make a decision as to whether or not to do it—it can't be something that is done automatically, like tying one's shoelaces. And *last*, it must be the sort of action where the actions of others are relevant to that of one's own; more specifically, it must be an act where the cost or benefit of doing something or not doing it *is dependent on how many others make a similar or different choice.* Some examples of such situations include strikes, leaving a social occasion, migration to another area, rumor, voting, and the diffusion of an innovation. Clearly, the theory applies to far more than collective behavior as we've defined it, although it focuses on one specific *aspect* of collective participation.

One assumption of the threshold model is that the greater the number of people who engage in a given action, the lower the cost of one's participation in it. (Although at some point, this relationship begins to reverse itself, as we'll see.) Again, cost isn't just monetary, but cost of any kind: getting arrested, suffering social embarrassment, eating terrible food, having other people think you're a fool, marrying the wrong person, getting stuck with a product that breaks down. The threshold model assumes people are rational; that is, they make choices that maximize their benefit and minimize their cost. One of the factors that influences their calculation of cost and benefit in making a certain decision is their sense of how many other people have already made that decision. *Independent of their own personal preferences*, people are likely to feel that risk is lower and gain is greater in doing something that other people are also doing.

Take a couple's decision to enter a restaurant. One evening, they decide to go to a place called "Sam's." At 7:00 P.M., they look in the window and realize there is no one in the restaurant. This does not inspire much confidence in the quality of the restaurant, and so they decide to pass it by and eat in another one. But what if one couple had been inside? Would they have eaten at Sam's? Would their chance of eating there have risen with two couples? Four? If it had been half filled? Completely filled? Chances are, if they are a lot like most people in this respect, their likelihood of entering would have risen to the point where all of the tables had been filled except one. This maximizes their confidence in the restaurant and minimizes the likelihood of waiting. After that point, the longer the line, the more their inclination to enter would decline. However, some very trendy folks might think a long line indicates the restaurant is excellent, and they'll put up with a long wait. But how long? An hour? Two? Four? The point is, with each one of us, our inclination to enter the establishment is contingent on how many people are already in it, although exactly where we draw the line and decide to enter is somewhat different from person to person. For most of us, our inclination to participate in a given form of behavior rises as the participation of others rises, although at some point, there is a drop-off, where too much participation discourages us.

Each person, the model holds, has a somewhat different threshold for a given action. Again, one couple will enter the restaurant even if no one is inside, another will enter if one is inside, a third will do so only if it is half full, another only if it is three-quarters full, and so on. So, a couple with a zero threshold walks by at 7:00 P.M., they walk in and sit down; at 7:05 P.M., a couple with a one-couple threshold walks by, looks in, sees the first couple inside, and they walk in and sit down; at 7:10 P.M., a couple with a two-couple threshold looks in and enters; and so on. Gradually, the restaurant fills up. But notice: If the couple with a zero threshold had decided not to eat out that night, *no one* would have entered the restaurant! It would have been completely empty, even though there would have been a large number of couples who wanted to eat there that night—although only under the right threshold circumstances.

Does this model work for collective behavior phenomena? Let's take a riot. Clearly, joining a riot entails more difficult and complex decisions than entering a restaurant, but threshold theorists argue that the principle is the same. In a given crowd, we have a number of individuals who are differentially inclined to participate in a given riot. They require different levels of safety before entering a riot; the greater the number of people who riot, the "safer" it will seem. And they know that if a certain number of others participate in the riot, it is more likely to be successful. Thus, one person joins in only if a lot of others riot, that is, the likelihood of succeeding in achieving the rioter's demands is high, while another will join if only a few do so, that is, knowing that this likelihood is lower. Thus, each person has a different threshold for joining the riot. The threshold is the proportion or number of people assembled that each person would have to see rioting first before joining in. Dedicated revolutionaries, who want to overthrow the existing political system at any cost, would have a rioting threshold of zero; that is, they may riot even if no one else does. They could be called the "instigators." Less hard-core radicals, let's say, have a rioting threshold of 100 people. This threshold builds up to the point of conservatives, who won't riot under any circumstances (the threshold at which they would riot is so high that they would *never* riot).

Thus, if a full range of people, each with his or her own threshold, is present at a given assemblage, the riot may very well come off. Person A (the revolutionary) has a threshold of zero; person B's threshold is one—he'll riot if A does; C's threshold is two; D's is three, and so on. So, in a given crowd situation, if we have A through Z in the crowd, we have a full-scale riot on our hands. Now, let's imagine almost exactly the same crowd, but in this case, A is missing. What happens? A doesn't riot, because he isn't there. That means that B doesn't riot, because his threshold isn't attained, which means that C didn't riot, and so on down the line—which means that there's no riot! In the two different hypothetical gatherings we've looked at, in terms of the individual composition of the crowd, we have two almost identical crowds. And yet, in one, a riot took place, and in the second, nothing at all happened. In other words, we cannot assume that we can predict collective behavior from individual characteristics. People in a given social situation are influenced by the nature of that situation; it is an independent causal agent in their behavior. Only very slight changes in crowd composition can influence its dynamics, that is, the collective behavior its members engage in. Of course, as threshold theorists agree, many factors influence the workings of threshold processes, including the presence of friends at the gathering in question and the accuracy with which they perceive the behavior of others.

One important implication of the threshold model ought to be mentioned. It offers a very different model from that of the emergent norm perspective. Turner and Killian (1987) say that people engage in collective behavior because the situation demands that they revise their notions of what is the right thing to do. People have *redefined* their conception of right and wrong as a result of being in certain ambiguous or conflicting situations. Turner and Killian insist that people act on the basis of their norms, even if their normative structure is revised.

In contrast, the threshold model says that norms and actions exist in somewhat separate realms. People can still hold certain norms but do something quite different. In other words, it isn't possible to predict action from norms; the norms people hold are not the only factor influencing their behavior. The threshold model is purely behavioral, and says nothing about what the actor thinks is the right thing to do. It may be regarded as the wrong thing to do *in the abstract*, but the right thing to do *in a particular situation*. To a threshold theorist, we do not have to posit "emerging" norms in a collective behavior situation; in fact, we do not have to posit norms at all. In a given situation, what people believe to be right may simply not operate, may seem irrelevant, may be nullified, or may contradict the felt demands of a situation at the moment. For example, you and I may agree that every Wednesday night we should eat Italian food, which is Sam's specialty, but if no one is there when we get there, and our threshold is that four tables must be full, we are simply not going to eat there, regardless of our norm about eating Italian food. I may be strongly opposed to the current adminstration or regime, and agree that a violent demonstration would help bring it down, but if I get to a peaceful gathering and no one is violent at all, and I need a threshold of at least a dozen rioting people, I am not going to riot.

The model assumes fairly detailed knowledge on the part of actors of the situations in which they act (or do not act), a condition that is often—indeed, *usually*—not met. And most actors, as we saw in the previous section, are far from being careful calculators of goals and means, and therefore hardly totally rational. Often, the reasons for participation in a given episode of collective behavior aren't clear, and hence, not "cost effective" given the fact that an individual, like everyone else, will receive access to certain ends anyway (Morris and Herring, 1987, p. 159). This is, in any case, an empirical question, one that cannot be assumed in the first place. Moreover, actors do not simply "find" themselves in a given situation in which they can enact collective behavior; for instance, not all crowds are "random samples" of the population at large (Granovetter, 1978, p. 1431), and often, there are normative and motivational reasons why some people, but not others, are in a given crowd situation. People are available for crowd behavior for a variety of reasons. Besides, how is the threshold of different individuals calculated? How determined? What caused it? The theory doesn't say.

The model seems elegant. In theory, we could grant that the world could work in the way that the threshold model predicts. But *does* it? Or even better, *has* it? While the threshold model makes a certain amount of theoretical sense, does it make empirical sense? Do we have enough information about enough crowds or other gatherings to say with confidence that the threshold model explains collective behavior outcomes? When we have a limited number of people, whose behavioral threshold we know, acting in fairly specific circumstances, it is likely that we could predict what is going to happen. But very *rarely* do we know the thresholds of potential actors, and very rarely will the thresholds of the assembled alone be the crucial factors in influencing outcomes.

In fact, the world is a much *messier* place than the model seems to indicate. We can grant that an individual's likelihood of participating in collective behavior is influenced by the participation of others—indeed, that is the field of collective behavior's central assumption. We can grant that numbers have a great deal to do with this. We can grant that there's such a thing as a threshold. That each person's threshold is a bit different, and that the chances of someone's engaging in a given episode of collective behavior has something to do with the presence, and therefore the *sequencing*, of the behavior of others. And that the added-up characteristics of individuals in a collectivity cannot predict that collectivity's likelihood of acting a certain way.

After all of this is granted, can we look at a given episode of collective behavior and better understand what happened? For some, yes; for many others, no. Do we understand the demonstrations in Tiananmen Square during the Spring of 1989 better with the threshold model? Or the civil disturbances of the 1960s in the United States? The anti-Vietnam War demonstrations of the 1960s? The 1979 demonstration at the Shoreham nuclear facility, which we'll look at in Part 5? The riots and demonstrations in Seoul, South Korea in 1987, which led to an electoral democracy? We suspect that thresholds were operating in all of these examples, but the model doesn't explain any more than that. In most cases, we don't have enough information. Moreover, it is obvious that many more factors are at work aside from and in addition to the operation of thresholds. In short, it is possible that the threshold model goes a bit too far from the direction of elegance, and a bit astray of real-world grit and grime and sloppy complexity. It is a model that works better on paper than in real life. Again, we can agree that thresholds influence collective behavior in principle without insisting that the threshold model predicts many—or any—actual, concrete instances of collective behavior. It is a model we can keep in mind when looking at collective behavior phenomena while, at the same time, realizing that it is inadequate to explain much of what takes place.

THE SOCIAL BEHAVIORAL/INTERACTIONIST (SBI) THEORY____

The social behavioral/interactionst or SBI perspective (McPhail and Miller, 1973; Miller, 1985, pp. 40-51; McPhail, 1991, 1992) focuses on *behavior in gatherings*, which overlaps with, but is not identical to, collective behavior. Proponents of this school, as we saw, have expanded the concept of collective behavior so broadly as to include all social interaction (McPhail, 1991, pp. 158ff), but, at the same time, it is only overt behavior that is focused on. In John Lofland's words, SBI represents "a species of behaviorism in which the study of collective behavior is merely the study of human coordination" (1985, p. 40). In the view of most observers, myself included, many gatherings are *not* sites of collective behavior (most casual and conventional crowds, for example), and much collective behavior does not take place in gatherings of any size (the behavior of most masses and publics, for example). Still, the behavior that takes place in *some* gatherings is collective behavior, and *some* collective behavior takes place in large gatherings.

The social behavioral/interactionist approach examines "*assembling processes, behavior within gatherings*, and *crowd dispersal*," or the "*organization of convergent activity*" (Miller, 1985, pp. 40, 41). By extension, it considers more dispersed phenomena such as "campaigns," "waves," and "trends" (McPhail, 1991, pp. 176ff), but, in fact, researchers following this school have focused their attention exclusively on crowds and other compact gatherings and collectivities. People assemble in response to "assembling instructions," that is, instructions for response supplied by participants and others, and "immediate cues to conduct" (Miller, 1985, pp. 41, 42). There are two major factors that determine whether individuals assemble. The first is "availability," that is, the presence or absence of "competing demands from family, job, or other social relationships" (McPhail and Miller, 1973, p. 726). The second is the time and space distance the individual is from the assemblage, plus the frequency of the assembling instructions, that is, how often they are repeated. The greater the time and distance someone is from the event, the more competition there is from competing activities (McPhail and Miller, 1973, p. 726).

SBI emphasizes three factors relevant to crowd behavior. First, with emergent norm theory, it stresses the *heterogeneity* of the behavior of the crowd; in most gatherings, all of the members of a crowd are not focused on a single object or phenomenon (Miller, 1985, p. 46). Second, there are two features relevant to the immediate gathering that influence crowd behavior: the *physical setting* within which the crowd acts and *crowd-management practices* that the relevant authorities follow. For example, crowd panic resulting in spectator deaths is more likely in an enclosed stadium or theater, where the crowd is packed in together and cannot escape, than in an outdoor venue, where people have the chance to disperse. Likewise, when the authorities attempt an unrealistic crackdown on crowd behavior, or fail to act at the appropriate time, collective behavior may be encouraged.

A good example of the role of assembling processes can be seen when we contrast the explanations that contagion and convergence theories offer for civil disturbances versus that put forth by the SBI perspective. Contagion theory would say that in a civil disturbance, as in all crowd behavior, collective fervor is contagious; the excitement of a few will touch off the excitement of the many. Convergence theory would say that civil disturbances, like all crowd actions, are caused because troublemakers or radicals have come together to cause trouble or encourage protest or revolution.

But the social behavioral/interactionist approach would say that these approaches ignore some major features of the situation within which those who take part must act. What time of the day did the disturbance start? The more people that are out on the street, the greater the likelihood that disorder will break out; most disturbances take place after work or during weekends. Did a potentially precipitating event take place in view of relevant parties; for instance, was a Black suspect roughed up by the police in full view of his or her neighbors and peers, or in an alleyway far from the gaze of the community? Who is available to take part in the disturbance? SBI would say that the outbreak of a collective disturbance is influenced as much by the individual's *availability* to take part as his or her attitudes toward what it might accomplish. For instance, the fact that most participants in the civil disturbances in the 1960s were young, single, Black males led some to suggest that these outbreaks were the product of the impetuosity, daring, disenchantment, and alienation of the participants. But the SBI perspective would emphasize that young, single, Black males, "minimally involved in scheduled social relationships with their competing claims on time, are simply more available for participation" (McPhail and Miller, 1973, p. 726).

And lastly, the SBI approach focuses on how crowd phenomena come to an end, that is, what causes "the dispersal of gatherings" (Miller, 1985, p. 47). As with assembling, again, instructions for dispersal, both those that are known in advance and those that are disseminated on the spot, influence the break-up of gatherings. Exactly when some gatherings begin and end is not clear, however. Sometimes, authorities—the police, for instance—force crowds to disperse. Even in emergency or disaster situations, crowd members tend to follow widely accepted rules for dispersal; it is only when their physical surroundings do not permit orderly withdrawal that panic may occur—and even then, individual panic rarely aggravates the seriousness of the situation (Miller, 1985, pp. 47–50).

One SBI theorist (McPhail, 1991, pp. 191ff) proceeded from these entirely reasonable observations to a mechanistic "sociocybernetic" explanation of collective action, based on a computer analogy, in which all "control systems—human and electromechanical—share several features in common" (p.198). It is too early to speculate on the potential contribution of this particular application of SBI theory. Still, at present, the "sociocybernetic" theory is an idiosyncratic and extremely specialized approach within an already fairly specialized approach. And since it is lacking in the subjective, experiential dimension that informs much current research and writing, it is therefore likely to be inherently unsatisfying to most collective behavior researchers. Moreover, it is probably without application in much of the field. However, perhaps time will prove this conclusion wrong!

In all, the social behavioral/interactionist approach is more a *perspective* than a *theory.* That is, it focuses more on the importance of a specific set of factors that are important in collective behavior than on explaining why it takes place. It is clear that some of these factors are critical; it is also clear that they do not operate in a great deal of collective behavior. In directing our attention to important processes and variables, SBI makes a valuable contribution to collective behavior. Still, it is a specialized approach rather than a general theory. It can be used when the opportunity arises and ignored when it does not.

THE RESOURCE MOBILIZATION PERSPECTIVE ⎯⎯⎯⎯⎯⎯

The last theory or perspective we'll look at in this chapter is called the *resource mobilization perspective* (McCarthy and Zald, 1973; Zald and McCarthy, 1987). Resource mobilization focuses exclusively on social movements and social movement organizations; it examines practically none of the more spontaneous and less organized collective behavior phenomena we'll look at in Parts 2 and 3 of this book. Consequently, we won't be dealing with resource mobilization theory in detail until Part 5. At the same time, it will be relevant from time to time throughout this book, and so a brief mention of it at this point is in order.

The central idea of resource mobilization theory is that social movements arise *not* because of society-wide strain or breakdown or because of the fact that certain segments of a society are objectively deprived, exploited, frustrated, or oppressed. Social conditions relating specifically to strain or deprivation have very little to do with why social movements are generated and sustained; there is nearly always enough strain and deprivation everywhere to supply support for a movement (Zald and McCarthy, 1987, p. 18). Every society on earth generates the objective conditions for grievance and discontent and in all of them, they could be used to mobilize a following into a social movement organization. In other words, the "raw material" for a mass movement exists nearly all of the time and practically everywhere. Why do social movement organizations spring up at some times and in some places but not in others?

Resource mobilization argues that the true explanatory factor in the genesis and maintenance of social movements is *the way that discontent is mobilized by leaders.* The capacity of movement leaders to translate the beliefs and ideas of a constituency into an organizational network is what creates and sustains successful social movements. A *core group of sophisticated strategists* (Turner and Killian, 1987, p. 234) is what counts here, a cadre of talented, skilled *entrepreneurs.* Organizational talent and skill represents one possible resource relevant to social movements; so do money and connections with the rich and powerful—anything that can get a segment of society working on an issue that is important to them.

As we'll see in Chapter 10, resource mobilization theory has been criticized on a variety of grounds. It focuses too narrowly on the characteristics of the leadership of social movements and not enough on their ordinary, rank-and-file members. It underplays the grievances that members of a society have, and fails to understand the relationship between grievances and movement mobilization (McAdam, 1982, pp. 23–35). In my view, its assumption of the rationality of social movements and movement participants is unnecessary and often empirically incorrect. It also underplays the spontaneity and the impulsive, expressive and emotional quality of movement participants' actions. It also exaggerates the gulf between social movement activity and collective behavior, rather than seeing the two as shading off into one another. Like most perspectives, resource mobilization is a valuable but limited, and often overly ambitious, perspective that works better for some movement processes than for others and for some social movements and movement organizations than for others. As such, it deserves our close attention; we'll examine it in detail in Chapter 10.

SUMMARY

Eight perspectives have been discussed in an effort to understand collective behavior phenomena. Four of them are general: contagion, convergence, emergent norm, and value-added. Four are more specifically focused on some aspects or types of collective behavior but not others: the gaming or rational choice model, the threshold model, the social behavioral/interactionist (SBI) model, and the resource mobilization perspective.

Contagion theory (or the transformation hypothesis) argues that, under certain circumstances, the presence of others generates collective excitement and therefore episodes of collective behavior, usually of an emotional, irrational, and often violent nature.

Convergence theory (or the predisposition hypothesis) argues that when like-minded individuals with a "predisposition" or tendency to engage in certain kinds of collective behavior come together (or "converge"), it is likely to take place.

Emergent norm theory argues that collective behavior represents not so much a violation of already-held norms by its enactors as a *redefinition* of what is considered right in a normatively ambiguous situation.

The *value-added theory* argues that collective behavior occurs when, and only when, six preconditions are met: structural conduciveness, structural strain, generalized beliefs, precipitating factors, mobilization for action, and the operation of social control.

The *gaming* or *rational choice* model argues that people carefully calculate how certain means will attain their valued goals, and engage in collective behavior—or refuse to do so—as a result of the outcome of this calcuation.

The *threshold model* argues that people engage in collective behavior to the extent that they perceive that others are doing so; each person has a specific threshold that influences that decision—for some, only a few others must participate for them to do so, while for others, many must do so to entice them to follow.

SBI or the *social behavioral/interactionist model* focuses on the assembling processes of crowds, the behavior that is enacted within gatherings, and crowd dispersal. Its focus is what gets people together and what they do when they are together.

And lastly, the *resource mobilization perspective* argues that social movements emerge and are successful to the extent that a sophisticated leadership can mobilize the discontent in a given constituency; it focuses on variables such as power, money, organizational ability, the use of the mass media, the cooptation of (and by) elites, the actions of agencies of social control, goals, and the achievement of goals.

The lesson we learn from an examination of theories of collective behavior is that no single perspective applies to any and all collective behavior phenomena. All are limited in their scope and, as a general theory, all are flawed. Each is completely or largely irrelevant to some forms or aspects of collective behavior. Indeed, the earliest of these theories—contagion and convergence—must be very carefully qualified to be relevant in any way to any forms of collective behavior at all. The job of the creative student of collective behavior is to understand *when, where, why, how, to what extent*, and *under what circumstances* each applies.

Blackout Looting, New York City, July 1977

As a result of a power failure upstate, the lights went out in all boroughs of New York City at 9:35 P.M. on July 13th, 1977. In contrast to the blackout which took place in New York in 1965, the looting in 1977 was vast and extensive. In some places, looting began almost as soon as it got dark. Brother Ramzas, a community leader and owner of Muslim Jewelry on Utica Avenue in Brooklyn, arrived at his establishment at 9:45 P.M. to find the gates ripped off and looters pouring out of the store, its shelves stripped bare of merchandise. The owner of Discount Liquors on Fulton Street in Bedford-Stuyvesant said that the looting began five to ten minutes after the blackout began. "It was almost like they came out of the air," he said (Curvin and Porter, 1979, p. 3). In the Bronx, police commanders and community workers put the starting time of the looting at 15 to 20 minutes after the lights went out, just enough time for a substantial number of people to realize that power wasn't going to be restored quickly. The first word that the looting was taking place reached police headquarters at 10 o'clock. Within 20 minutes of the outage, someone drove a car through the iron gates of a sporting goods store on Broadway and Decatur in Brooklyn; a crowd swarmed in, assaulted the owner, cleaned out the merchandise, and set the store on fire. The great New York City blackout looting of 1977 had begun in earnest.

Several important features of the looting should be mentioned. First, it took place almost exclusively in minority neighborhoods; very few stores in predominantly white neighborhoods were looted. Second, looters, for the most part, did not distinguish between white- and Black-owned stores; it was the merchandise that the establishment sold that determined whether or not it was looted. Third, there were very few racial or political overtones to the looting; it was, for most participants, an apolitical incident. And lastly, the incident was "basically a welfare disturbance" (p. 21), that is, a way that poor or economically struggling people managed to acquire "items to fulfill personal needs or to sell to make money." In this instance, the priority of the looters "was obviously direct material gain" (p. 22).

Perhaps the most interesting aspect of the 1977 looting was that it fell more or less neatly into three stages. During Stage I, the first hour to hour and a half of the blackout, the looting was overwhelmingly performed by what can only be called criminal types. They were young minority men, a majority of whom were 20 to 30 years old, with an extensive arrest record (over 80 percent had been arrested before), who lived by means of various hustles and illegal dealings, including theft. They needed no blackout to engage in crime in their everyday lives, but the power outage did give them another opportunity to get away with crime. At this stage, there was "virtually no law enforcement" (p. 5), that is, practically no police on the street at the time. In effect, these looting initiators controlled the streets, even to the extent of keeping others out of stores until they had cleaned out the most valuable merchandise. Items that could be readily resold were the ones that were stolen at this stage—liquor, jewelry, cars and auto parts, electronic equipment, and steaks and other expensive grocery items. Clearly, the initiators provided an example for later looters to follow.

It became obvious to many residents of minority neighborhoods that the police were not out in force and that most of the looters were not getting caught. Stage II of the looting began around midnight and lasted until roughly three in the morning. Over 40 percent of the looters in Stage II were age 16 to 20, mostly male, many of whom were alienated, unemployed or sporadically employed, educational dropouts, and about two-thirds of whom had been arrested before. They were less "criminally-inclined" than Stage I looters, at least they were less likely to engage in serious criminal behavior. To put things another way, their serious criminal involvement was in the budding stage. While they did not initiate the looting, they were willing to follow the example of more daring looters who had led the way and had gotten away with their crimes without getting caught. The most popular item that was stolen during Stage II was sneakers. Said one police officer, "If you had sneakers [in your store] that night . . ., you were in big trouble." The shop of "The Sneaker King," on Willis Avenue in the South Bronx, consisted of four stores, linked together, all filled, from floor to ceiling, with sneakers. "In a brief orgy of sneaker acquisition that night, the looters quickly cleaned him out" (p. 24).

Stage III, which stretched until the early afternoon of July 14th, was made up of an altogether different looter, a more or less cross-section of the minority community. This looter was likely to have a family, a job, and community ties; a high proportion of Stage III looters were females. In comparison with the other two stages, Stage III looters tended to be more law-abiding, stable, and respectable. These looters were attracted to taking goods from stores because they saw that many others were doing it, and that few were getting caught. The Stage III looter "allowed himself to be swept up by the feeling in the street and submitted to the strong social pressure to join in the stealing" (p. 12). Said one Stage III looter, a married man with a respectable job, "Things started flying out [of the store], and I happened to get my hands full of the stuff. And I was standing on the corner talking, when suddenly a police car pulls up, and they got me." When apprehended, he had ten pairs of women's slacks and seven blouses (p. 15).

Clearly, some of the perspectives discussed in this chapter are relevant to one or another of these three stages, others are relevant to a different stage, and still others are completely irrelevant. *Resource mobilization* theory is irrelevant to this incident since it deals exclusively with organized social movements, and the looting was distinctly disorganized, at least on a formal level. *Convergence theory* best explains the Stage I looter; these are men whose way of life is crime, who needed no special opportunity to engage in theft. Their prior characteristics explain why they did it; the blackout only provided a "cloak of darkness." *Contagion theory* plays no role here; these young men were not influenced by any emotion even remotely like collective fervor. They were cool, calculating, and motivated solely by the urge to make a buck. *Threshold theory*, too, plays no role in Stage I, since these looters acted with a zero threshold. While some of their stealing was a form of collective behavior, much of it was individual and parallel behavior. Insofar as collectives of some sort were involved in the stealing, they tended to be small teams or gangs rather than crowds or other types of substantial gatherings. The chances are, theories of deviance and crime explain Stage I looters as much as theories of collective behavior.

Stage II looters are clearly marked to some degree by *contagion*— by then, a collective fervor or euphoria had taken hold; the excitement of seeing Stage I looters get away with crime motivated younger offenders to take part in the looting. But Stage II looters were not strangers to crime, either; they could be called "budding" criminals (two-thirds had been arrested before). Thus, *convergence theory* has to be consulted as well in understanding why they did what they did; their prior characteristics had something to do with their looting. Moreover, we see in Stage II looters individuals who are influenced by a *threshold*—a far lower threshold than for those who acted in Stage III, but a threshold nonetheless.

In Stage III, *convergence theory* is totally irrelevant, since looters by this time represented something of a cross-section of the entire minority community—males, females, employed, unemployed, those with and without an arrest record. *Contagion theory* plays a role in explaining the events of Stage III looters. Indeed, it is perhaps a more potent factor now, since far more people are seized by the collective fervor; "stable poor and working-class members of the community . . . were caught up by the near hysteria in the streets" (p. 7). And *emergent norm theory* clearly plays an explanatory role at this point, for many of them explain what they did in terms of a redefinition of conventional norms. Said one Stage III looter: "There's a wallet on the floor and some money sticking out of it, and nobody's going to see you take it. That's what it was like, the same situation. I saw an opportunity and took advantage of it. . . . I would never, like, do any stickups or mug someone. . . . I just took a chance. I don't know anyone who's gotten anywhere and didn't take a chance. Rockefellers and the Gettys—you know what their fathers were all about? Their fathers were murderers and thieves. They took a chance. They just got over" (p. 16). And clearly, *threshold theory* offers some explanatory power here, too, for the many people who looted in Stage III had thresholds that were far higher than looters in the earlier stages.

The *rational calculus model?* Well, the Stage I looters stole the most valuable items when the risk of arrest was extremely low; that is, they maximized their gain and minimized their cost. Stage III looters stole very little of value, and their risk of arrest was extremely high. In fact, most of the arrests during the blackout took place in Stage III. News of the merchandise that was stolen and the ineffective presence of the police in Stage I and, to some extent, Stage II, led Stage III looters to believe that they wouldn't be caught, that is, that their reward would be high, and their cost would be low. In fact, they were wrong. Are we therefore to say that Stage I looters were rational while Stage III looters weren't? The rational calculus model doesn't explain the differences between the stages of the looting.

The *value-added approach* seems to address many of the features of the blackout looting. *Structural conduciveness* is present—for instance, the existence of retail stores in a materialistic society. *Structural strain*, likewise, is present in this case; many minority neighborhoods are poor, and a substantial proportion of their residents feel resentment about not having the standard of living that prevails in white areas. Certain *generalized beliefs* are key here, too, for residents in minority neighborhoods believe (correctly, it turns out) that stores in their communities tend to charge more for merchandise than do those in white neighorhoods. (It must be emphasized that very few of the blackout looters explained their participation in political terms, however.) The *precipitating factor* here was the blackout itself, a powerful incentive for the looting to commence. *Mobilization for action* took place, as we saw, by the example set by Stage I looters. And the *operation of social control* (in this case, the key stage) it was almost completely absent, paving the way for the belief that no one would be arrested. While the value-added approach does not address the whys and wherefores of the different stages of the looting, it does at least address the looting that took place in a general fashion.

Lastly, the *SBI perspective*, likewise, addresses some aspects of the looting. Assembling instructions were plain and simple: Some people are acquiring merchandise at very little risk to themselves—let's go out and do the same thing! The availability of large numbers of looters was assured by the time that the blackout began at 9:35 P.M. However, in contrast to what the social behavioral/interactionist theory would predict, a cross-section of individuals who were available at that time did not join in; only those who made crime a way of life did so. Time and space considerations were important, for the stores that were hit were close to home; those that required an investment of time and travel were not looted. (Of course, there were other considerations here, too; looters knew that stores in more affluent white areas would be more heavily guarded, and that community support would be absent in them.) The activity that was engaged in was the stimulus for the assembly; people got together specifically for the purpose of looting. And dispersal took place, for the most part, when it was clear that large numbers of looters were being arrested.

In sum, then, some of the perspectives or theories of collective behavior address the incident of looting that took place in New York City in 1977 and some do not. Some address one or another of the stages of the looting, while other theories address a different stage. None of these approaches analyze all of the important aspects of the looting. It should be clear that an *eclectic* or *theoretically diverse* approach is necessary to explain collective behavior phenomena—an approach that borrows a little of one theory and a little of another. No large-scale, complex instance of collective behavior can possibly be explained, in its entirety, by a single approach. It is for this reason that, throughout this book, an eclectic approach to the study of collective behavior phenomena will be adopted.

References

Allport, Floyd. 1924. *Social Psychology*. Cambridge, Mass.: Houghton Mifflin.

Aveni, Adrian F. 1977. "The Not So Lonely Crowd: Friendship Groups in Collective Behavior." *Sociometry*, 40 (March): 96–99.

Berk, Richard A. 1974a. *Collective Behavior*. Dubuque, Iowa: William C. Brown.

Berk, Richard A. 1974b. "A Gaming Approach to Crowd Behavior." *American Sociological Review*, 39 (June): 355–373.

Billig, Michael, et al. 1988. *Ideological Dilemmas: A Social Psychology of Everyday Thinking*. London: Sage.

Blumer, Herbert. 1939. "Collective Behavior." In Robert E. Park (ed.), *Outline of the Principles of Sociology* (1st ed.), pp. 221–279. New York: Barnes & Noble.

Blumer, Herbert. 1969. "Collective Behavior." In Alfred McClung Lee (ed.), *Principles of Sociology* (3rd ed), pp. 67–120. New York: Barnes & Noble.

Bolce, Louis. 1982. "Why People Riot." *Policy Review*, no.22 (Fall): 119–140.

Cantril, Hadley. 1941. *The Psychology of Social Movements*. New York: John Wiley & Sons.

Crosette, Barbara. 1989. "Tibetan's Tale: Unrest, Explosion, Crackdown." *The New York Times* (April 13): A15.

Curvin, Robert, and Bruce Porter. 1979. *Blackout Looting! New York City, July 13, 1977*. New York: Garnder Press.

Dollard, John, et al. 1939. *Frustration and Aggression*. New Haven, Conn.: Yale University Press.

Gorman, Christine. 1989. "The Fall and Fall of Argentina." *Time* (June 12): 47.

Gould, Stephen Jay. 1984. *Hen's Teeth and Horse's Toes: Further Relections in Natural History*. New York: W. W. Norton.

Granovetter, Mark. 1978. "Threshold Models of Collective Behavior." *American Journal of Sociology*, 83 (May): 1420–1443.

Hazleton, Leslie. 1989a. *England, Bloody England*. New York: Altantic Monthly Press.

Hazleton, Leslie. 1989b. "British Soccer—The Deadly Game." *The New York Times Magazine* (May 7): 40, 66–69.

Hines, Terence. 1988. *Pseudoscience and the Paranormal: A Critical Examination of the Evidence.* Buffalo, N.Y.: Prometheus Books.

Killian, Lewis M. 1980. "Theory of Collective Behavior: The Mainstream Revisited." In Hubert M. Blalock, Jr. (ed.), *Sociological Theory and Research: A Critical Appraisal*, pp. 258–274. New York: Free Press.

Kogon, Nathan, and Michael A. Wallach. 1967. "Effects of Physical Separation of Group Members Upon Group Risk-Taking." *Human Relations*, 20 (February): 41–48.

LeBon, Gustave. 1982. *The Crowd: A Study of the Popular Mind* (originally published in 1895). Marietta, Georgia: Larlin.

Lebovics, Herman. 1988. *The Alliance of Iron and Wheat in the Third French Republic 1860–1914: Origins of the New Conservativism.* Baton Rouge: Louisiana University Press.

Lewis, Jerry M. 1972. "A Study of the Kent State Incident Using Smelser's Theory of Collective Behavior." *Sociological Inquiry*, 42 (2): 87–96.

Lieber, Arnold L. 1978. *The Lunar Effect: Biological Tides and Human Emotions*, Garden City, N.Y.: Doubleday.

Lofland, John. 1985. *Protest: Studies of Collective Behavior and Social Movements.* New Brunswick, N.J.: Transaction Books.

Mack, John. 1983. "Inside Sing Sing: An Inmate Chronicles the Revolt." *The Village Voice* (February 8): 1, 9–11.

Mackay, Charles. 1932. *Extraordinary Popular Delusions and the Madness of Crowds* (1st ed. originally published in 1841, 2nd ed., 1852). New York: L. C. Page.

McAdam, Doug. 1982. *Political Process and the Development of Black Insurgency, 1930–1970.* Chicago: University of Chicago Press.

McCarthy, John D., and Mayer N. Zald. 1973. *The Trend of Social Movements in America: Professionalism and Resource Mobilization.* Morristown, N.J.: General Learning Press.

McPhail, Clark. 1971. "Civil Disorder Participation: A Critical Examination of Recent Research." *American Sociological Review*, 36 (December): 1058-1073.

McPhail, Clark. 1991. *The Myth of the Madding Crowd.* New York: Aldine de Gruyter.

McPhail, Clark. 1992. *Acting Together: The Organization of Crowds.* New York: Aldine de Gruyter.

McPhail, Clark, and David L. Miller. 1973. "The Assembling Process: A Theoretical and Empirical Examination." *American Sociological Review*, 38 (December): 721–735.

Merton, Robert K. 1960. "The Ambivalences of LeBon's *The Crowd*." Introduction to Gustave LeBon, *The Crowd: A Study of the Popular Mind*. New York: Viking/Compass.

Miller, David L. 1985. *Introduction to Collective Behavior*. Belmont, Calif.: Wadsworth.

Morris, Aldon, and Cedric Herring. 1987. "Theory and Research in Social Movements: A Critical Review." In Samuel Long (ed.), *Political Behavior Annual*. pp. 137–198. Norwood, N.J.: Ablex.

Park, Robert E. 1972. *The Crowd and the Public and Other Essays* (principal essay originally published in 1904). Chicago: University of Chicago Press.

Park, Robert E., and Ernest W. Burgess. 1921. *Introduction to the Science of Sociology*. Chicago: University of Chicago Press.

Perry, Joseph, and Meredith D. Pugh. 1978. *Collective Behavior: Response to Social Stress*. St. Paul, Minn.: West.

Quarantelli, Enrico L., and Russell R. Dynes. 1970. "Property Norms and Looting: Their Patterns in Community Crises." *Phylon*, 31 (Summer): 168–182.

Rudé, George. 1959. *The Crowd in the French Revolution*. Oxford, England: Clarendon Press.

Rule, James B. 1989. "Rationality and Non-Rationality in Militant Collective Actions." *Sociological Theory*, 7 (Fall): 145–160.

Sherif, Muzafer. 1936. *The Psychology of Social Norms*. New York: Harper.

Sherif, Muzafer, and O.J. Harvey. 1952. "A Study of Ego Functioning: The Elimination of Stable Anchorages in Individual and Group Situations." *Sociometry*, 15 (August–November): 272–305.

Smelser, Neil. 1962. *Theory of Collective Behavior*. New York: Free Press.

Sullivan, Thomas J. 1977. "The 'Critical Mass' in Crowd Behavior: Crowd Size, Contagion and the Evolution of Riots." *Humbolt Journal of Social Relations*, 4 (Spring/Summer): 46–59.

Talbott, Strobe. 1989. "Defiance." *Time* (June 19): 10–13.

Turner, Ralph H. 1964. "Collective Behavior." In Robert E.L. Farris (ed.), *Handbook of Modern Sociology*, pp. 382–425. Chicago: Rand McNally.

Turner, Ralph H., and Lewis M. Killian. 1957. *Collective Behavior.* Englewood Cliffs, N.J.: Prentice-Hall.

Turner, Ralph H., and Lewis M. Killian. 1972. *Collective Behavior* (2nd ed.). Englewood Cliffs, N.J.: Prentice-Hall.

Turner, Ralph H., and Lewis M. Killian. 1987. *Collective Behavior* (3rd ed.). Englewood Cliffs, N.J.: Prentice-Hall.

Zald, Mayer N., and John D. McCarthy (eds.). 1987. *Social Movements in Organizational Society: Collected Essays.* New Brunswick, N.J.: Transaction Books.

Zygmunt, Joseph F. 1986. "Collective Behavior as a Phase of Social Life: Blumer's Emergent Views and Their Implications." *Research in Social Movements, Conflicts and Change,* 9: 25–46.

PART TWO

INTRODUCTION TO BEHAVIOR IN COMPACT COLLECTIVITIES

When people act in compact collectivities, gatherings, or *crowds*, they behave quite differently from the way they behave in diffuse collectivities, or masses and publics. The generation, dynamics, and demise of crowd behavior are very different from those of mass or public behavior. Different types of behavior take place in each of them: Riots, demonstrations, protests, ecstatic visions and miracles, joyful celebrations—all of these, for the most part, are born and acted out within a crowd setting, and it is the crowd that gives each behavior its distinctive shape and form. Likewise, myths, legends, folktales, collective delusions, paranormal beliefs, gossip and rumor, fads, fashion, and crazes—these unfold on the much larger canvas of the diffuse collectivity, that is, the mass and the public. Again, the fact that participants are spread out makes some of these collective behavior phenomena possible and gives some their special flavor.

Disasters cannot be clearly located in compact or diffuse collectivities; they are something of a transitional type. Some disasters are fairly localized and hit fairly tightly assembled collectivities, while others may befall individuals who are fairly widely scattered and dispersed over a wide area. Because they are so diverse and difficult to classify, we'll discuss them in Part 3.

Some observers are uncomfortable with the term "crowd," arguing that there are "long-standing misconceptions" associated with the concept—the "illusion of unanimity," the view that crowds act in a unisequential fashion; that they act in a certain direction indefinitely; that their behavior is "simple if not simplistic"; and that they frequently engage in competition, conflict, and violence (McPhail, 1991, pp. 162–163). The term "gathering," some say, contains no such connotations and should be used in place of "crowd." In my view, such a substitution is unnecessary. One of the functions of this discussion will be to dispel misconceptions; I imply none of them in using the term "crowd." I will use the term "gathering" or "fairly large gathering" as more or less synonymous with "crowd." I will assume that the reader is intelligent enough to cast off misconceptions about the crowd as they are refuted. The term "crowd" is too useful and too widely used to discard; in fact, the same critic who prefers the term "gathering" has entitled his next book, *Acting Together: The Social Organization of Crowds* (McPhail, 1992).

Throughout this chapter we'll follow the scheme, originally spelled out by Blumer (1939, 1969) and discussed in Chapter 1, that distinguished *casual, conventional, expressive*, and *acting* crowds. *Casual crowds* are assemblages of people who happen to be in the same place at the same time; an example is the collectivities that gather regularly in areas in large cities, such as in Times Square or in lower Fifth Avenue in New York City. *Conventional crowds* are groups of people that attend certain events and pretty much obey the rules of proper behavior—the audience at the Metropolitan Opera, for instance, or at a neighborhood theater to watch a movie. *Expressive crowds* are collectivities that gather mainly for the purpose of expressing an emotion—a political rally, for example, or a protest demonstration. *Acting crowds* are groups of people who gather to *do* something, such as a lynch mob or a revolutionary crowd. As I said in Chapter 1, this classification is not airtight; many crowds are a composite of two or more of these types and contain a mix of people in several different categories.

Crowds: What comes to mind when you hear or read this word? What does a collectivity of people have to do, be, or have, to qualify as a crowd? If you're like most people, a crowd needs to have at least three qualities: It must be of a certain *size;* it must be fairly *dense*, that is, people must be fairly closely packed together; and its members must be fairly *contiguous* or *continuous*, that is, they can't be separated by barriers or physical space.

How many people are necessary for an assemblage or gathering to qualify as a crowd? There has to be a fairly sizable number at the lower end, otherwise no one will call it a crowd. Obviously, three people don't make up a crowd. What about ten? Or 50? Or 100? There is no precise line we can draw and say, on this side we have a crowd, on that side we don't. Some observers argue that crowds should be hall-sized, that is, "too big for a room" (Brown, 1954, p. 837), let's say, more than a few hundred. Still, this limit can't be stipulated with any real precision.

Does a point come at the *upper* end when there are *too* many people to call a collectivity a crowd? Some claim that all of the members of a crowd should be able to interact or communicate—by shouting, for instance—with all of the other members face-to-face (Brown, 1954, p. 837). Thus, if the assemblage is too large, this face-to-face process of communication can't take place. But at what point is this limitation reached? Again, no one can say with any measure of exactitude. Is a football stadium filled with 80,000 people a crowd? Hardly anyone would say no. In 1984, 1.5 million protesters demanding democratic elections gathered in the Praça da Sé in São Paulo in Brazil; was this gathering too large to be called a crowd? As with the lower limit, it's probably best to leave the upper limit open and simply say that the size of a gathering has *something* to do with how a crowd is defined and with the behavior of its members, but no precise line regarding size can be drawn.

The same applies to *density*. If people are scattered around in a given area, let's say, if there is far more area with no people than there is area containing people, it's hard to call it a crowd, even if there are a lot of people there. It's reasonable to assume that density has something to do with the behavior of a gathering's members, but, again, it is likely that this relationship is complex and far from unilinear. It is possible that, other things being equal, the more compact a gathering, the more influence the behavior and mood its members have on a given individual; the more dispersed it is, the less this is the case. But back to definitions: If many people are packed together very densely, with little or no space between them, observers are very likely to call this assemblage a crowd. But again, while density has to be considered in defining a crowd, we can't stipulate its degree with precision. Some observers (Turner and Killian, 1987, pp. 136–137) refer to masses and publics as "diffuse crowds"; in them, people are so scattered that they aren't in the same place at the same time. To my way of thinking, "crowd" isn't the best way of describing this sort of collectivity. It's a crowd only in the metaphorical (or, in Gabriel Tarde's term, "spiritual") sense, not in the concrete or literal sense. It is a diffuse collectivity, not a real crowd.

Crowds have to be fairly *continuous*; if the crowd's continuity is broken by empty space or barriers, we refer to the discontinuous assemblages as *separate* crowds or a number of more or less *disconnected* crowds. To qualify as a crowd, there must be some sort of physical continuity to it, some sort of physical unity, a kind of "metaphorical skin" around it, so to speak.

It's hard to argue with these three criteria—size, density, and continuity. But what about the social and psychological characteristics that many observers identify with crowds, such as solidarity, a common mood or goal, intensity, coordination, identity? Are these characteristics necessary to define a crowd? As we saw, at least as far back as LeBon almost 100 years ago, scholars have made a distinction between a crowd as a mere assemblage of people in the same place at the same time and a gathering whose members possess a common mental state that binds them together into a real collectivity; LeBon called the latter an "organized" or "psychological" crowd (1982, pp. 1ff).

Some observers choose not to call gatherings that lack such unifying attributes crowds. I prefer to argue that such attributes are matters of degree; some gatherings lack them altogether, others possess them to a certain degree, and still others are powerfully marked by them. For most purposes, a mere assemblage of people—a casual crowd—is not studied as a type or locus of collective behavior; the same holds for the conforming or conventional crowd. Our only interest as a student of collective behavior in casual and conventional crowds is the circumstances that would transform them into true loci of collective behavior, that is, into expressive and acting crowds. (Notice that *assembling processes*, most of which are relevant to casual and conventional crowds, as collective behavior are discussed by Miller, 1985; McPhail and Miller, 1973; and McPhail, 1991, and 1992; this view is not shared by the majority of the field, however.) Thus, while such qualities as cohesion and a common mood influence crowd behavior, they are matters of degree and cannot be used to define what a crowd is in the first place. Perhaps it's better to say that crowds that possess them act differently from crowds that don't.

As we've seen, the actions of the casual and conventional crowd are not usually regarded as within the province of collective behavior; such crowds tend to be normative and traditional and their behavior more or less predictable. Of course, certain conditions can transform a casual or a conventional crowd *into* an expressive or an acting—in short, an unconventional—crowd. For example, a sporting event, with tens of thousands of spectators present, can start as a loud, boisterous, but basically law-abiding—that is, an expressive—crowd. But, because of a combination of emotional intensity and a triggering event, such as a bad call by an official, the crowd can become an acting crowd with fans rushing out onto the field, tearing up the stadium, and fighting one another. In fact, most sporting events are marginal or half-way between conventional and expressive crowds; most of the time decorum is followed, despite the great expression of emotion. Only extremely rarely—considering the huge number of sporting events that take place each year around the world—some members of such crowds, usually only a small proportion, become an acting, violent crowd. Certain sports, such as professional wrestling (if it can be called a sport) draw more expressive crowds, while others, such as polo, draw more conventional crowds. No sport, to my knowledge, draws a crowd a significant segment of which is so highly motivated to act violently that they do so under any and all circumstances.

A college football rally designed to whip up excitement and support the home team can be called an expressive crowd. And yet, it has many qualities that place it outside the realm of collective behavior. It is planned and organized, not spontaneous; it has leaders and something of a hierarchy: football players, cheerleaders, and fraternity leaders wield more influence than outcastes, social marginals, "creeps," "losers," "lames," and "nobodies." Its course and outcome are fairly predictable, that is, people yell and scream for a time and then go home (though occasionally one may get out of hand). It is held regularly, usually the night before a football game. Perhaps the only two ways a football rally would differ from everyday, conventional behavior is the *level of emotional intensity* and fact that it is somewhat *out of the ordinary*, not entirely routine. The point is, many gatherings have one foot in conventional and one in collective behavior, or one foot in one type of crowd and one foot in another. Again, Blumer's original four-type classification of crowds is not airtight, although it is fairly useful for most gatherings.

A recent contribution to the literature on collective behavior put forth by sociologist John Lofland (1981, pp. 418–419, 1985, pp. 35–88) divides collectivities according to where they stand on the following two dimensions: whether they are *compact* or *dispersed collectivities*, that is, crowds or publics, and whether the dominant emotion expressed or felt is *fear, hostility*, or *joy*. (Dispersed collectivities are discussed in Part 4.) This typology yields the six types of collectivities presented in the following table.

	Dominant Emotion		
	Fear	**Hostility**	**Joy**
Crowd:	stampede	riot	victory celebration
	panic	lynching	revivalist meeting
Mass:	mass hysteria	mass rioting	fads
	false dangers	mass vilification	crazes

Source: Adapted from Lofland, 1981, pp. 418–419; 1985, pp. 35ff.

Most examinations of crowds by researchers in the field of collective behavior in recent years have focused on those whose members express negative emotions, either hostility and rage—such as riots, protests, demonstrations, disorders of some sort—or fear, as in disasters. In one textbook (Perry and Pugh, 1978, pp. 43ff), only violent crowds and disasters (along with social movements) are discussed as examples of collective behavior. There is nearly nothing in recent literature in the field on crowds whose members express *positive* emotions—joy and ecstasy, for example. This was not always so. In the early days of the subject, in the 1920s and 1930s, ecstasy, particularly religious ecstasy, figured more heavily in the study of collective behavior. (See, for example, LaPierre's chapter on "Revelous Behavior," 1938, pp. 462–487.) Now, that focus has almost entirely disappeared. Lofland suggests that we bring joy and ecstasy back into the study of collective behavior and elevate them to a prominent place. I agree.

In the chapters that follow, a wide range of emotions that grip crowd members, or at least some of the members of certain crowds, will be covered. We'll look at *riots*, that is, crowds that express hostility; *ecstatic crowds*, and *miracles*. *Disasters*, which strike collectivities (some compact, some less compact, but rarely true masses or publics) and generate fear in their members, will be discussed in Part 3.

Something has to be said about crowd *characteristics* and *dynamics*. What makes crowds different from other collectivities? What forms of behavior do crowds permit, generate, and sustain? Why do certain actions take place in crowds and not in more dispersed collectivities? What is it that is unique about crowds? The field of collective behavior has generated a number of key generalizations about compact collectivities.

First, as we've already seen, *crowds are very rarely completely unified.* In all crowds, there is some diversity, although, clearly, different crowds stand at different positions along this homogeneity-diversity continuum. In some crowds, a number of people can be seen with a central focus or activity (for instance, shouting or watching a specific action), while others can be seen with a different focus or activity (talking to one another, looking away, looking bored, being quiet, and so on). We should not assume that, simply because a specific crowd does something dramatic or unusual, all members of that crowd are directly involved or participating in the activity in question. In all crowds for almost any given activity there are usually onlookers, spectators, witnesses, critics, skeptics, hecklers, reporters, or exploiters. For instance, in many riots the number of individuals who engage in destructive behavior is typically quite small; many individuals are simply standing around watching the action. In short, we should not fall victim to the "myth of crowd unity" or "the illusion of unanimity."

It must be emphasized, however, that, even though many or most members of a given crowd are not engaged in a specific action or set of actions (say, violence), *the more striking and significant that action is* the more likely it is that observers will classify the crowd according to that action. It may not be very important that "only" one out of ten members in a gathering of 100,000 are attacking and killing some of its other members, since 10,000 individuals engaged in such striking, significant actions generates a great deal of violence! It is crucial to make this clear because some recent observers are meticulously concerned with how gatherings may be classified on the basis of exactly who is doing what in them (McPhail, 1991, 1992).

Second, in nearly all crowds, *members tend to be in friendship groups.* Crowd members are rarely collections of isolated, atomized individuals in a sea of other isolated, atomized individuals. Crowd members are rarely "by themselves"; they are nearly always with one or more friends (Aveni, 1977). Moreover, the fact that crowds tend to be assemblages of friends has an impact on crowd behavior (Granovetter, 1978, pp. 1428–1433); people tend, for instance, to be more susceptible to social influence if they are with others whose opinions they care about than if they are among strangers. Any examination of crowd behavior that leaves the factor of friendships out of the picture is not only incomplete, but seriously misleading. The classic or traditional view of crowd members as anonymous and therefore lacking in accountability is clearly false.

Third, *the physical and temporal setting within which crowds form can influence their behavior* (Wright, 1978, pp. 38ff; Miller, 1985, pp. 43ff). Crowds can be broken up by physical barriers; brought together by large, open spaces; facilitated by streets; impeded by buildings; halted by closed gates; and panicked by too-few exits. Did the relevant stimulus or crowd assembly take place during the day or at night? During the workday? During the lunch hour? After work? On weekends? In front of a large number of witnesses or a few? On a university campus? In the street? At a rock concert? All of these factors can, and do, influence what gatherings or crowds do.

Fourth, *the convergence of substantial numbers of certain "kinds of people" can influence the behavior of crowds of which they are members.* Who can doubt that the presence of large numbers of people who engage in certain kinds of behavior in their everyday lives can influence whether behavior of that type is likely to happen in the crowd? Can we seriously expect wrestling fans to be as quiet as the members of an audience watching a polo match? Such an expectation would be not only foolish, it would be wrong in nearly every empirical instance we examined. At the same time, who can doubt that the predisposition of some members of a crowd to act in a certain way cannot, by itself, explain what that crowd does? While "convergence" factors can influence crowd behavior they do not determine what crowds do in any precise or predictable fashion. They are, as we saw in Chapter 2, only one piece of a very large puzzle. While it has been fashionable of late to entirely dismiss predisposition factors, *for certain types of gatherings,* they explain a great deal. (Just as they explain little or nothing for other types.)

Fifth, *the actions of social control agencies,* when they take place, *not only influence crowd behavior but may, in themselves, be seen as forms of collective behavior.* In a sense, often the *cause,* or at least one of the causes, of the collective behavior that takes place is the action of the police. The killing of four and the wounding of nine Kent State University students in 1970 by the National Guard was a form of collective behavior in response to another form of collective behavior, a political protest; moreover, it effectively put an end to the protest the Guard were called out to control. Social control cannot be thought of as a form of behavior that always and necessarily stands *in opposition to* collective behavior. In fact, social control is sometimes *a form of* collective behavior. What were vigilante actions but an extralegal, extra-institutional form of social control in the name of law and order that amount-ed to a special type of collective behavior (Turner and Killian, 1987, pp. 122–123)? When the police get out of control and attack the members of an unruly, boisterous crowd, what are they doing except engaging in a police *riot* (Stark, 1972)? Social control is often, although not always, densely intertwined with collective behavior (Smelser, 1962, pp. 261–269).

Sixth, *crowd size* is a key factor in influencing crowd behavior; however, the relationship between crowd size and crowd behavior is complex rather than unidirectional. As a general rule, the larger the number of individuals in a crowd who are already engaged in a given form of behavior, the greater the likelihood that a specific individual in that crowd will engage in that same behavior. However, the greater the number of individuals in a crowd, the more difficult it will be to stimulate *all* or *most* members of that crowd to action, that is, the greater the number of individuals who will depart from crowd unanimity. Of course, for certain actions, crowd unanimity or near unanimity may not be necessary; a minority can engage in an action while a majority watches. For other actions, the fact that some members depart behaviorally from that which others do or want to do may *itself* generate col-lective behavior—for instance, fights may break out between factions in a crowd. And at some point, the gathering may be so large that face-to-face communication between a substantial proportion of the members of the crowd breaks down, thereby inhibiting collective action. In short, group size influences collective behavior, but in complex, difficult-to-predict ways.

Many forms of collective behavior take place in compact collectivities, and their generation, dynamics, and decline are influenced by that fact. How-ever, the many crowd collective behavior phenomena have their own dis-tinctive shapes and characteristics and should be discussed separately. Riots and protests are two of the more commonly discussed crowd phenomena; ecstatic crowds and miracles, although less often discussed forms of collec-tive behavior, are interesting enough to warrant discussion. Let's look at some of the many examples of crowd collective behavior phenomena.

References

Aveni, Adrian F. 1977. "The Not-So-Lonely Crowd: Friendship Groups in Collective Behavior." *Sociometry*, 40 (March): 96–99.

Blumer, Herbert. 1939. "Collective Behavior." In Robert E. Park (ed.), *Outline of the Principles of Sociology* (1st ed.). New York: Barnes & Noble, pp. 221–279.

Blumer, Herbert. 1969. "Collective Behavior." In Alfred McClung Lee (ed.), *Principles of Sociology* (3rd ed), pp. 67–120. New York: Barnes & Noble.

Brown, Roger W. 1954. "Mass Phenomena." In Gardner Linzey (ed.), *Handbook of Social Psychology* (vol.2), pp. 833–876. New York: Free Press.

Granovetter, Mark. 1978. "Threshold Models of Collective Behavior." *American Journal of Sociology*, 83 (May): 1420–1443.

LaPiere, Richard T. 1938. *Collective Behavior*. New York: McGraw-Hill.

LeBon, Gustave. 1982. *The Crowd: A Study of the Popular Mind* (originally published in 1895). Marietta, Georgia: Larlin.

Lofland, John. 1981. "Collective Behavior: The Elementary Forms." In Morris Rosenberg and Ralph H. Turner (eds.), *Social Psychology: Sociological Perspectives*, pp. 411–446. New York: Basic Books.

Lofland, John. 1985. Protest: *Studies of Collective Behavior and Social Movements*. New Brunswick, N.J.: Transaction Books.

McPhail, Clark. 1991. *The Myth of the Madding Crowd*. New York: Aldine de Gruyter.

McPhail, Clark. 1992. *Acting Together: The Organization of Crowds*. New York: Aldine de Gruyter.

McPhail, Clark, and David L. Miller. 1973. "The Assembling Process: A Theoretical and Empirical Examination." *American Sociological Review*, 38 (December): 721–735.

Miller, David L. 1985. *Introduction to Collective Behavior*. Belmont, Calif.: Wadsworth.

Perry, Joseph, and Meredith D. Pugh. 1978. *Collective Behavior: Response to Social Stress*. St. Paul, Minn.: West.

Smelser, Neil J. 1962. *Theory of Collective Behavior*. New York: Free Press.

Stark, Rodney. 1972. *Police Riots: Collective Violence and Law Enforcement*. Belmont, Calif.: Wadsworth.

Turner, Ralph H., and Lewis M. Killian. 1987. *Collective Behavior* (3rd ed.). Englewood Cliffs, N.J.: Prentice-Hall.

Wright, Sam. 1978. *Crowds and Riots: A Study in Social Organization*. Newbury Park, Calif.: Sage.

Account: From Conventional to Expressive to Acting Crowd

A few years ago, I took an undergraduate course with a professor who had a reputation for being an especially difficult grader. It became the most dreaded course in our department; for many majors, it was the only course that prevented them from graduating. Nearly 500 students took the course that year; I was one of two undergraduate representatives. Past exams were on file at the department, so a number of us prepared for the final exam by going to the office and getting hold of past exams. We wrote out our answers and went to the teaching assistant to get confirmation, then we got the correct answers for the questions we couldn't answer. Then all of the questions and answers were circulated among all of the students in the course.

The exam was divided into two parts—essay and multiple choice. As soon as we began taking it we realized that a substantial proportion of the questions on the final had already been asked in past exams. As a result, many of us felt good while taking the final; we felt confident that we had done extremely well.

About ten days after the exam, before the class had received their grades, the other student representative and I were called into the professor's office. He seemed very angry. He told us our performance on the exam was far too high; in fact, it was unprecedented. He said he suspected that students had been seated too close to one another and, judging by how well they had done, that they had cheated by copying each others' papers. We tried to explain that we had studied very hard for this exam, and that it was not our fault he had asked questions from prior exams. He was very stubborn and maintained that the exam did not reflect our knowledge or ability. He said that all the multiple-choice questions would be discounted and that grades would be calculated exclusively on the basis of the essay portion of the exam. None of our arguments swayed him in the least. Finally, he asked us for our approval of his edict. We said we could not do that without first consulting the other students in the course.

In the next class, at which the professor was not present, the other student rep and I presented his proposal. There was a lively discussion, the upshot being that the members of the class refused to accept any retroactive changes by the professor. They had taken the exam and they wanted the results to stand as they were, based on both the essay and the multiple-choice questions. Some students said that the cheaters should be punished if there was any proof of cheating; but, in fact, there was no such proof. The class concluded that they shouldn't be punished simply because they had done so well. A couple of students even said that they would institute a lawsuit against the professor if he stood by his ruling. We went back to the professor and communicated the students' reactions to his edict. He was adamant and insisted that his position was logical and reasonable. He agreed to tell the students about his decision himself.

At the next class, the professor explained his position to the students. Things began very quietly, almost pleasantly. But soon students began expressing their displeasure and interrupting his speech. I tried to calm them down and asked them to behave politely. When he was through he was flooded with questions, some specific and practical, some provocative and angry; again, one student threatened legal action. Finally, the professor said that, whether we agreed or not, he was going to discount the results of all the multiple-choice questions.

At that point, suddenly and spontaneously, a huge roar, sounding like "WOOOOOHHHHHH!", emanated from the class, and hundreds of students rose up out of their seats. Students began yelling that they would not let the professor leave the room until he backed off from his position and allowed the results of the exam to stand. There was a great deal of milling and screaming, and matters looked as is they were getting out of control. I got very nervous that the professor might get hurt, so several friends and I stood around him, pushing and shoving our way through the crowd. As we escorted him out of the lecture hall, hundreds of students milled around, standing in our way, shouting, accusing, threatening; trying to get through them was almost like running a gauntlet. But we kept shoving until we finally managed to get him out of the lecture hall and into the corridor, then up one flight of stairs, where the dean's office was located. Still, students continued to block our way and scream and argue about the exam; they stood in the hallway outside the office by the hundreds. The professor immediately went into the dean's office. By this time some of the students had burst out of the lecture hall and ran to all of the outside exits in the building and locked the entire building, stating that they would not let anyone in or out until the professor relented and counted all portions of the exam.

The chair of the department was called at her home; she came, and the students, recognizing her, let her into the building. She conferred with the dean about what to do. Shortly thereafter, the other undergraduate rep and I were called into the dean's office and we were told that the results of the entire exam would be counted. We had won! The professor was there, in the room, looking very upset. In retaliation he informed us that he would not give anyone in the class a recommendation. We went back to the students and told them of the dean's decision, at which time, the gathering dissipated rapidly. The whole incident took about two or three hours.

(From the author's files. For a similar, but artificial, event, see Clark McPhail, "Student Walkout: An Examination of Elementary Collective Behavior," *Social Problems,* 16 [Spring 1969]: 441–455.)

CHAPTER
3

COLLECTIVE VIOLENCE: RIOTS

W hen crowds get together they occasionally engage in collective violence—disturbances, hostile outbursts, or *riots*. What are riots like? What causes them? How does the field of collective behavior look at the phenomenon of hostile outbursts? Let's look at a few examples.

SANTA FE, NEW MEXICO, 1980

In the early morning hours of February 2, 1980, after some hasty planning and the consumption of a quantity of home-brewed alcohol, several inmates of the Penitentiary of New Mexico in Santa Fe overpowered four guards. They soon captured eight other guards stationed at other locations in the prison and discovered an unlocked door, an open security gate, keys to various doors and gates, and several blowtorches. Within short order, hundreds of prisoners went on a rampage, killing 33 fellow inmates (of whom a dozen were first tortured and mutilated), beating or raping roughly 200; and beating, stabbing, or sodomizing seven of the 12 guards who had been taken hostage. None of the guards were killed. The rioters seemed to have no clear political objective; the victims included several suspected "snitches," a child rapist, some mentally disordered inmates whose screaming kept other prisoners awake at night, and prisoners with whom the rioters had had a past conflict or grudge. Several of the inmates who were killed were simply vulnerable individuals whose deaths would not result in retaliation. In fact, most of the killings were little more than an effort to establish a reputation for violence; apparently, in prison, the more individuals one kills, and the more brutally one kills them, the more power one has among inmates in the penitentiary (Colvin, 1982).

In comparison with many prison riots, such as Attica in New York State in 1971, the inmates in the 1980 New Mexico disorder lacked solidarity and political focus. A group of inmates who were involved in a class action suit against the penitentiary "made a futile attempt to organize the disturbance into a collective protest" (Colvin, 1982, p. 459), submitting a list of demands to authorities. But this group was unable to control the hostages or the rioters, and their communication with the prison administration was constantly interrupted and contradicted by other inmates. While all observers agreed that the prison conditions, as well as the authority structure, of the Penitentiary of New Mexico had been disintegrating for some five years prior to the riot and that, during this time, inmates had begun feeling increasingly deprived, frustrated, and angry, the riot itself directly addressed neither the prison's conditions nor the inmates' feelings about them. The penitentiary was retaken 36 hours after the guards had been captured; hundreds of inmates had ingested doses of barbiturates, stolen from the prison's pharmacy, and were in no mood for resistance. It had been the bloodiest, most violent prison riot in the history of the United States (Useem, 1985).

ASTOR PLACE, NEW YORK CITY, 1849

On three separate nights in May 1849, several riots took place in Astor Place in New York City outside a theater called the Opera House. In the riots, at least 22 people were killed and over 150 were seriously wounded or injured. What caused these riots? Incredible as it might seem, they were touched off by the appearance of the British actor William Charles Macready on the stage of the Opera House in William Shakespeare's play, *Macbeth*. In order to understand how a bloody riot could break out over a specific actor playing a part in a play, it is necessary to elaborate the details of the social and historical circumstances of the time.

William Charles Macready was not merely an actor, he was a symbol. He and an American actor named Edwin Forrest, perhaps America's most well-known Shakespearian actor at the time, had developed an intense and heated rivalry. The actors "took to answering each other's accusations and jealous outbursts in the press" (Buckley, 1984, p. 9). The two attracted followers, partisans, and claques of supporters. Although Macready's supporters tended to be more restrained, Forrest's fans would heckle, hiss, and boo Macready's performances, often throwing rotten eggs, fruit, and vegetables at him. Once, in Cincinnati, a sheep's carcass was thrown onto the stage as Macready was playing *Hamlet*. Obviously this was a great deal more than an ordinary rivalry between two actors; if this had been the whole story, it is unlikely that the Astor Place riots would have broken out.

Something of an artistic revolution was taking place in the United States between 1820 and 1860. Theater audiences specifically, and the market for art and culture generally, were becoming less elitist and upper-middle class, and more democratic and working class. Art and culture were reaching and becoming adopted by the masses, who were beginning to have their influence on them. This was especially true of the theater. The split between Macready's and Forrest's fans reflected this change: Macready's supporters tended to be bourgeois, elite, upper-middle class, and well-educated. They loved everything British and anything they considered refined, genteel, and cultured. In contrast, Forrest's fans tended to be working class, nationalistic Americans, contemptuous of everything English and whatever smacked of snobbishness and elitism. Moreover, the style of each actor reflected this same split: Macready's acting style was seen as scholarly, intellectual, cerebral, and true to the written text, while Forrest's was more intuitive, untrained, athletic, physical, and melodramatic. Macready called Forrest a "thick-headed, thick-legged brute." On the other hand, to Forrest's followers, he seemed to personify everything that was distinctively American. His voice was likened to Niagara Falls; his thighs were said to have been "carved out of the American forest." He was said to look to nature, not to books, for his inspiration. And so the battle lines were drawn.

After one particular performance, during which Macready had been awarded such an abundance of rotten fruit, vegetables, and eggs that he was driven off the stage, he vowed never again to appear in a play in the United States. But a letter published in the *New York Herald* implored him to accept a role in New York. It was signed by "some of the most powerful mercantile, legal, and intellectual figures in the city." The petition was placed on the desk of the mayor of New York. At the same time, a leaflet was distributed by a group calling itself the "American Committee," which asked its readers the following question: "Workingmen—Shall Americans or English rule?" The leaflet claimed that some Englishmen "threatened all Americans who shall dare to express their opinion this night at the English aristocratic opera house! We advocate no violence," it stated, "but a free expression of opinion to all public men! Workingmen! Freemen! Stand by your lawful rights!" In this highly charged atmosphere, the mayor was asked to approve Macready's performance. The governor of New York State and the general of the national militia, fearing trouble, objected, but they were overruled. The mayor mobilized 350 troops, 150 in the theater itself, the rest either outside or near the hotel where Macready was staying or near the homes of several prominent citizens who were responsible for Macready's booking (Buckley, 1984).

At 6:00 P.M., the police took possession of the Opera House and the surrounding area. Although all ticketholders were supposed to have been admitted, some 200, who said that they had tickets, were not allowed in; they remained outside, waving their tickets and loudly objecting to their exclusion. Soon, a crowd, roughly 1,000 strong, joined them and began claiming that they too were ticketholders, insisting that they had been refused entry because they were not members of the "gentry." At 7:30 P.M. the performance began; the theater was "by no means full." The police brooked no disturbance; anyone acting unruly was promptly carted off to a holding pen in the basement of the Opera House. By 8:00 P.M., the crowd outside had increased severalfold. They began throwing rocks and breaking down the front door of the theater. At 8:45 P.M., troop reinforcements were called in, which only inflamed the crowd; before long, members of the crowd began taunting the soldiers to fire. A few hundred jittery soldiers faced an angry mob of nearly 10,000 outraged, angry citizens. At first, the troops fired over the heads of the crowd; when that failed to calm them down, they began shooting directly into it. Immediately, the crowd cleared out of the area; 18 dead lay on the street and four later died of their wounds. (One historian [Moody, 1958] claims that 31 people died in the riot.) Although more riots followed for several days thereafter, none was as lethal as the one that took place on the first night. Incredibly, New York witnessed a tragic and bloody dispute that resulted in the deaths of 22 people over an actor's right to perform Macbeth.

It's interesting to compare the professions of the men (they were all men) who were killed and wounded in the riot, as well as those who were arrested during and immediately after the riots, with those who signed the petition imploring Macready to appear in New York. The men who were killed, wounded, or arrested were overwhelmingly working class—sailors, butchers, sailmakers, carpenters, plumbers, servants, machinists, and common laborers. In contrast, those who signed the petition were made up of various businessmen and merchants, 22 lawyers, one banker, a ship owner, five editors, two physicians, and three well-known authors, including Herman Melville and Washington Irving (Levine, 1988, pp. 64, 65). What the riot revealed was a challenge by the members of the working class culture to the cultural dominance of the upper-middle class; it heralded the entry of the so-called common man into the public sphere of politics, print, art, and the theater. The exclusive right of the rich and the educated to dominate these arenas was being challenged. New artistic forms and expressions began to emerge "from below," so to speak. No longer was there a shared and monopolized understanding of culture and what it meant; instead, there emerged a "host of different cultural forms catering to more specialized audiences" (Buckley, 1984, p. 645). In a sense, the Astor Place riots of 1849 represented the beginning of a mass popular culture in the United States, with the working classes influencing and directing cultural expression through an expression of their own tastes (Buckley, 1984; Levine, 1988).

DETROIT, 1984

On October 14, 1984, the Detroit Tigers beat the San Diego Padres 8 to 4 in the fifth and final game of the World Series at Tiger Stadium. Downtown Detroit "erupted in a triumphant celebration." Fans hurled beer bottles, showering the streets with glass, exploded fireworks, which could be heard for miles around, and set off smoke bombs. A crowd of about 40 people surrounded a police car and set it on fire, sending a column of gray smoke over the stadium's right field wall; they also set a taxicab ablaze. Inside the stadium, the moment the game ended, hundreds of fans rushed onto the field and tore up chunks of sod between home plate and the pitcher's mound. One man sold two chunks outside the stadium for $20 apiece; another said that he'd keep a two-foot piece in his freezer. A teenager broke both wrists leaping from the bleachers. About 20 people were treated in nearby Southwest General Hospital, mainly for head injuries "sustained from flying beer bottles" (Barron, 1984).

WHAT IS A RIOT?

The term "riot" is used loosely by most people. There are two myths or stereotypes that are widely held about what riots are and who participates in them. The first may be called the traditional or conservative stereotype; it tends to be held by the man and woman on the street. To the conservative, "riot" is a pejorative term to refer to a violent, large-scale disorder, usually of an illegitimate, irrational, uncontrolled, and highly emotional nature. Rioters are "the dregs of society," common criminals who simply run amuck in a frenzy of destruction. During the disorders that took place in the Watts Neighborhood of Los Angeles, the mayor and the police chief branded the rioters as "hoodlums" who belonged to "the criminal element." (As reported in *The New York Times*, August 13, 1965, p. 26; August 14, 1965, p. 8, and September 14, 1965, p. 22; Bolce, 1982, also presents a version of this myth.) This may be called the "mad dog" or "riffraff" stereotype of the rioter; one observer dubs it the "scum of the earth" theory of civil violence (Rule, 1988, pp. 174, 242).

The second myth or stereotype about riots has been held by radicals and conflict-oriented sociologists and social critics; it is that riots are, by their very nature, political—a protest against injustice, oppression, and exploitation (Geschwender, 1968; Skolnick et al., 1969; Feagin and Hahn, 1973). This may be called the "noble protester" stereotype of the rioter.

Riots: The Reality. In truth, riots may be motivated by political or non-political motives; they may protest existing conditions or not; they may be at least partly planned or completely spontaneous, at least partly organized or completely uncoordinated, purposive or not; they may reflect the views of radicals, liberals, conservatives, or reactionaries—or have no clear-cut views at all. They may crush the weak or the strong, the just or the unjust, the exploited or the exploiters. They may uphold or destroy traditional values. They may be supported by existing political authorities, put down by existing political authorities, or both supported and put down at the same time. Riots may even have been instigated by representatives of official agencies of social control, acting as if they were participants in minority social movements who are, in other words, agent provocateurs or informants (Marx, 1974). A riot may escalate from a demonstration, or it may begin by the police attempting to *crush* a demonstration. *Intrinsically*, riots stand at no particular place along the ideological or political spectrum. Rioters could be "mad dogs," "riffraff," and criminals; they could be "noble protesters," revolutionaries, and insurrectionists; or they could fit almost any conceivable description, depending on the riot and the rioter. Of course, riots and rioters are *more likely* to be or do certain things than others, as we'll see in this chapter.

Moreover, the term "riot" is a catch-all phrase to describe an event, or a set of events, that hides a great deal of the complexity that exists in the real world. All individuals who take part in a specific riot do not have the same motive when they act; in fact, an individual rarely engages in a single action for one motive alone. For some riots we can, of course, refer to a *dominant*, modal, or *most common* motive, but very rarely do all the people who take part in a given action engage in it for the same reason. As we saw in the New Mexico prison riot of 1980, some inmates rioted because they wanted to improve the conditions that existed in the prison, while others rioted simply because they wanted to kill someone in order to earn a fearsome reputation.

Defining a Riot.   Now that we are no longer burdened by the prevailing myths and stereotypes about riots, we again ask the question, "What is a riot?" One definition defines a riot as *relatively spontaneous group violence* (Marx, 1972, p. 50). This definition adds the criterion that a riot must also be "contrary to traditional norms" but, many riots actually *support* traditional norms—at least, the norms of a certain tradition. For instance, a riot that occurred in Mecca in 1987 was intended to support the Shi'ite tradition of Iran. Many riots take place because events or factions have challenged the traditions of another faction, and rioters engage in violence because they want things to return to the way they were in the past. In Brazil in 1874–1875, demonstrations and riots broke out as a result of the "Quebra-Quilo" ("smash the kilos") revolt, which was designed to uphold peasant tradition and autonomy from the government by promoting nonpayment of taxes, destruction of the newly instituted metric system, and the burning of official records (Barman, 1977). Clearly, opposition to traditional norms cannot be a criterion of a riot.

In the end, we are left with three criteria that define a riot. *First*, there must be some level of violence and destruction, even if what is destroyed is property and not human life. *Second*, it must be the action of a fairly sizable group of people and not just a few individuals, although exactly how many individuals it must be has to be left open. And *third*, it must be fairly spontaneous and unplanned, although a small number of individuals can instigate a riot by rousing a larger number of people to action. It is difficult to call "Kristallnacht," the murder of Jews and the destruction of Jewish property that took place in November 1938 in Germany, a riot, since it was at least partially planned beforehand by certain segments of the the the Nazi hierarchy (although it was opposed by others). Many "supposed" riots in totalitarian countries are in fact carefully coordinated, choreographed semiofficial events made to look like the spontaneous, righteous will of the people.

Demonstrations Vs. Riots.   This definition of riots creates a distinction, often difficult to make in real life, but valid in most cases and in principle as well, between *demonstrations* and *riots*. There are at least two important distinctions between them. First, demonstrations do not necessarily include the element of violence and destruction, while riots always do. If there's no violence, what a crowd does cannot be called a riot. If violence does break out, it is no longer simply a demonstration, but a riot as well—a violent demonstration, but a riot to be sure.

Second, demonstrations are almost always planned, almost always held as the result of a decision made by the members of an organization, almost always hierarchically coordinated by leaders, and almost always designed to achieve a specific end. In contrast, riots are relatively spontaneous; are not directly led by anyone, although usually indirectly led, by example, by a small number of initiators; and may or may not be driven by the motive to achieve a concrete goal. Even where planning for a riot is made in advance by the leaders of an organization, a demonstration does not necessarily turn into a riot. Riots do not occur because a small number of individuals decide that they will engage in violence, or because a number of participants in a demonstration are committed to engaging in it. By their very nature there is a measure of spontaneity in all riots. Even incipient riots may be quelled by authorities under the right circumstances. Of course, some demonstrations that are preplanned to become riots actually *do* turn violent, as we can verify by reading the headlines in our local newspapers.

The Monolithic Conception of Riots.   In approaching hostile outbursts, we should not fall victim to what has been called the "monolithic conception of riots" (McPhail, 1971), that is, that riots are a phenomenon with clear-cut, clearly-recognizable features whose reality all observers will agree upon. Remember, "riot" is a conception, a label, not a concrete reality. What some people will call a riot, others will call a disturbance, a disorder, an outburst, a criminal action, a revolution, an uprising, an act of heroism, or an expression of joy. Moreover, rioting is not a continuous action, with a discrete beginning, middle, and end; during a specific time period, the violence that takes place may occur sporadically, with dramatic fluctuations, waxing and waning with each hour. Also, everyone present at an event that is called a riot is not engaged in violent behavior; some are watching, some are encouraging the rioters, some are restraining them, some are restraining or attacking firefighters or the police, some are protecting their own property, and so on. In fact, a large crowd can gather to watch a small group of individuals inflict a great deal of damage, and the press will call it a riot. It is important to emphasize that most riots have a very complex character (Miller, 1985, pp. 230–231).

Riot: A Pejorative Term?   Even though the term "riot" is often used in a negative sense, no pejorative connotations whatsoever are intended. Use of the term in this text is devoid of any and all evaluative meaning. It is meant to define a "relatively large-scale, relatively spontaneous collective violence." In the 1960s, some observers objected to the term "riot" to describe ghetto and civil disturbances, feeling that this implied a criticism of the events, branding them, by implication, criminal or irrational. When a certain action is called a "riot," criticism, either explicit or implicit, is not intended. Here—if nowhere else—the term has a completely objective meaning.

The Rarity of Riots. As stated in the very first sentence of this chapter, riots *occasionally* occur when people gather in substantial numbers. It must be stressed that, contrary to the position suggested by the contagion perspective of LeBon and others, collective violence is *extremely rare*. This is not to say that many riots haven't taken place in the history of the world, or that they haven't been influential! It is possible that *millions* of large-scale collective disturbances have broken out since humans began to gather in the same place at the same time in crowds of any considerable size. But, considering the vastly greater number of gatherings that have been relatively peaceful, violent outbreaks have been exceedingly atypical—in all likelihood, a minuscule fraction of one percent of all large-scale gatherings. Thus, the important questions should not be, "Why do riots take place?" or, "Why are riots so common?" Rather, considering the volatility of human emotions and the immense amount of conflict that takes place between individuals and categories and groups in any society—some more than others, of course—the question should be, *"Why is collective violence so infrequent?"* It is every bit as important to investigate the forces inhibiting riots as it is to look at those that encourage them. For, judging by the rarity of riots, such forces must be extremely influential.

TYPES OF RIOTS

To say that riots stem from a variety of motives is not to say that there is no point in classifying them into types. Although riots are of almost every conceivable type, some types are more common than others. With respect to the most commonly held or dominant goal or purpose that rioters have in mind, there are four types of riots: *purposive, symbolic, revelous,* and *issueless*. Again, all riots are to some degree "mixed" in that not all rioters have exactly the same motive in mind when they act; still, we assume that, for a given riot, participants are more likely to be moved by certain motivations than by others.

Purposive Riots. Purposive riots are those where a substantial proportion of the participants have a fairly specific goal in mind when they engage in their destructive acts. Rioters disrupt the labor process in order to achieve higher wages or better working conditions. They burn down buildings to get the government to divert more money into their neighborhood; overturn and burn police cars to put an end to police brutality; attack, beat, or kill members of another race to keep them out of their community or to keep them in their "place"; kill or lynch a suspect in a crime to avenge a felt wrong; and destroy government property or records to put an end to an unjust war. In a purposive riot, collective violence is a form of protest; participants engage in what the English historian Eric Hobsbawm called "collective bargaining by riot" (1959, p. 54). To the extent that revolutions have a measure of spontaneity, they provide an excellent example of purposive riots. At the same time, revolutions tend to be the planned, organized product of social movements; hence, social movements will be examined in detail in Part 5.

Symbolic Riots.   A symbolic riot is one in which the action is not intended to achieve a specific goal but that, directly or indirectly, protests conditions or circumstances or gives voice to a particular view or group. The Astor Place riots of 1849 fall into this category. Participants were not trying to achieve any concrete goal; what they had in mind was more complex and indirect. More was at stake than simply achieving something concrete and specific. If one had asked the Astor Place rioters what they were doing, they may have said that they were trying to prevent Macready from appearing on the stage of the Opera House. But it was more than that—as many rioters may have told you if you had been able to talk to them long enough. The downfall of Macready and the triumph of Forrest represented something to these men such as their dignity and respect and their growing influence in public affairs and the arts. Motives such as these lay behind the Astor Place riots. Many riots, then, are expressive and symbolic rather than purposive; they represent a "displacement of anger onto an accessible target" (Marx, 1972, p. 55).

Revelous Riots.   A revelous riot is one where rioters engage in violence as a kind of celebration that has gotten out of control; for many individuals and groups, there is an intimate connection between celebration and violence (Marx, 1972, pp. 57–58). All celebrations contain an element of spontaneity and wild abandon, to be sure, although in all, spontaneity is always to some degree restrained, and in all, there are some rules, however broad. It is very rarely the case that literally "anything goes." Examples of revelous behavior include New Year's Eve, celebrations following a home team victory or warfare victory, evangelical and religious ecstasy, festivals, orgies, and Mardi Gras and carnaval. However, not all celebrations turn into riots; it is when one becomes violent that we have a revelous or ecstatic riot. The announcement of Japan's surrender to American military forces in 1945 ending World War II touched off violent acts on the streets of San Francisco. Eleven deaths and over 1,000 injuries were reported; uncalculated damage was done to property; and countless women were raped, seemingly at random (Rule, 1988, p. 189). The rather minor riot, entailing a small amount of property damage and only 20 injuries, that took place after Detroit won the World Series in 1984 provides a good although modest example of a revelous riot. It is entirely likely, curiously enough, that *supporters* of the victorious side or team are more likely to engage in post-contest violence than is true of the *defeated* side or team. We'll look at ecstatic crowds in Chapter 4.

Issueless Riots.   Issueless riots (Marx, 1972) are those that entail an outburst of violence with no clear or dominant motive, goal, or direction. In some, the motives of the participants are so individualistic or mixed that ideology and politics take a back seat in determining the action, for example, the New Mexico prison riot of 1980. In others, mass violence was touched off simply because the police went on strike, formal social control was absent; no one risked arrest by engaging in criminal behavior. Following a police strike in Liverpool in 1919, there was "orgy of destruction"; as a result of a police strike in that same year in Boston, "the mob ruled the streets." In 1969 in Montreal, again, when the police walked out, looting, vandalism, and arson followed. In Swedish cities in 1970, mass violence occurred again after a police walk out (Marx, 1972, pp. 56, 57). Thus, it would be a mistake to assume that all rioters, or even most rioters in all cases of collective violence, have a concrete goal, purpose, or motive in mind when they act. Some riots, in short, are, from the political or ideological point of view, "issueless."

EXPLAINING COLLECTIVE VIOLENCE

We've already encountered some of the earliest thinking on why riots occur. In Chapter 2 we saw that Gustave LeBon believed that when people assemble in crowds and develop "mental unity" they often behave emotionally, irrationally, and violently. LeBon was part of a fairly large school of thinkers who held a similar negative, gloomy, irrational view of crowd behavior. This largely European "irrationalist" school influenced several American sociologists, including Robert Park (1864–1944), who studied in Germany at the turn of the 19th century and wrote the influential *The Crowd and the Public* (reprinted 1972). Park, in turn, influenced Herbert Blumer (1900–1987), one of his students who, as we saw, held a largely negative and irrational view of crowds and collective behavior in general. The central view of LeBon and the other irrationalists was that, not only was the crowd an unreasoning, destructive mob, but its behavior was both a product of and further generated a *breakdown in social control.* Collective violence occurs because the social order is disintegrating, because society's social fabric is unraveling. Not only did LeBon see only pathological causes of crowd actions, but (although he qualified this a bit) he also saw only pathological consequences. Crowds are exclusively, or almost exclusively, destructive; they are, for the most part, incapable of noble, creative, constructive acts. Park went a few steps further in his qualification; although crowd violence is an expression of the disintegration of the social order, it sometimes ushers in a new social order.

The classic view of collective violence as emanating largely from pathological conditions or causes resonates in today's writing on the subject. Are riots caused by societal breakdown? By pathological conditions? By pathological individual characteristics? Are episodes of collective violence irrational; that is, do they serve the very values and goals that rioters themselves seek? Can riots be seen as a clash of interpretations or world views—a conflict between factions in power who wish to see the status quo preserved and those who wish to overturn major aspects of society, by force if necessary?

That is, is it possible to refer to "the social order" at all? Perhaps what the irrationalists like LeBon saw as "the social order" was a preservation of the privileges of a small elite. In other words, riots may not be so much an unraveling of the social order as one social order challenging another. On the other
hand, can riots be analyzed in such political terms? As we've seen, many,
probably most, episodes of collective violence do *not* challenge or threaten
the status quo. Is it possible to generalize about collective violence at all?

Riots are to some degree unpredictable affairs. Each is a consequence of
a historically unique and unprecedented set of circumstances. The very spontaneity that is part of our definition of a riot makes it impossible to say when
and where one will explode next. At the same time riots are not random
affairs; they are more likely to take place under certain social conditions than
under others and to be engaged in by some members of society more than
by others.

Some observers (for instance, Barron, 1984) claimed that the violence that
took place in Detroit after the 1984 World Series occurred, in part, because
Detroit had not won a championship in 16 years and the unemployment rate
for the city that year was 15 percent. Yet, there are 26 teams in the major
leagues. If winning the World Series were evenly divided among all of the
teams in the majors each one would win only once every 26 years. Does that
mean we should predict that a riot should take place each time each team
wins, that is, every year? Some of the older teams have not won a championship in over half a century, and several of the newer teams have never
won. Will their city's residents inevitably riot when and if their teams win?
Riots have not occurred in cities whose baseball teams have won the World
Series and whose unemployment rate has been high. Clearly, the factors of
how long ago a team last won the Series and its city's unemployment rate do
not go very far in explaining why rioting took place in Detroit in 1984, or in
any other World Series city in other years.

In 1980, extensive rioting exploded in the Black neighborhoods of Miami
after the announcement that five white police officers were acquitted of murdering a Black man in their custody. A number of factors contributed to this
outburst of collective violence, including deteriorating police–minority relations, a stagnant economic picture, and competition between the Black and
Cuban communities (Ladner et al., 1981). Without minimizing the crucial
importance of these factors for Miami in 1980, they have been duplicated in
other cities during the 1980s without collective violence. Blacks in East St.
Louis are far poorer than they are in Miami. In New York City, more than a
dozen extremely ugly, major, widely publicized encounters between African-
Americans and the police have stained the political landscape during the
course of the 1980s. Various kinds of complex inter-ethnic rivalry exists in
most major cities in America—again, all of these have existed elsewhere
without producing major outbreaks of collective violence. Perhaps in Miami
it was the *combination* of these circumstances. Still, it is easier to analyze
why rioting broke out *after the fact* than it is to predict when and where it is
going to happen *before* it actually does. While no one would doubt that a

variety of factors and variables are related in some way to the outbreak of collective violence, the complexity of this kind of behavior prevents observers from explaining it in anything like a definitive fashion.

Who could have predicted the episodes of protest and, in some instances, collective violence that took place in Islamic nations around the world in 1989 with the appearance of *The Satanic Verses*, a novel by the Indian-born, Muslim-raised author, Salman Rushdie, which was interpreted by fundamentalists as blasphemous and an affront to Islam?

Why did the appearance of William Charles Macready result in a riot in New York City in 1849, while his roles in other American cities brought forth little more than boos and a shower of rotten fruit and vegetables? The societal conditions that contributed to the Astor Place riots certainly existed elsewhere—why New York and nowhere else?

While experts admit that the prison conditions and the authority structure of the New Mexico penitentiary had been deteriorating for some five years prior to the 1980 riot (Colvin, 1982; Useem, 1985), they have been as bad or worse in other prisons at other times without riots breaking out.

In short, the many conditions that have been associated with the outbreak of collective violence at particular times and in particular places may be seen as *potentiating* factors. They do not determine riots so much as they *facilitate* them. None of them can be said to be necessary; none can be said to be sufficient. In combination, they make them more likely. But they have been present when and where riots haven't occurred and absent when and where riots did take place. We must abandon a rigidly causal or deterministic approach to collective violence; riots *are* related to social and individual factors—but not in any mechanistic, one-to-one fashion. What factors or variables can be said to be related to outbreaks of collective violence?

Two sets of factors or variables have been isolated by researchers. The first set, representing a more traditional or old-fashioned approach, is made up of the factors relating to the individual rioter; this type of approach asks the question, *"Who riots?"* Some of these theories simply look at individual characteristics without bothering to understand the influence of the society or social contexts in which the individual is located, while others locate the individual *in* specific settings. The second set of theories, representing a more recent development, asks about the *social conditions that influence collective violence.*

WHO RIOTS?

At least as far back as LeBon, for more than a century, observers of collective violence have been speculating about whether some individuals are more likely to engage in rioting than others. Who riots? And why? To the extent that we focus on individualistic explanations of rioting, we adopt the *convergence* approach discussed in Chapter 2. People riot, convergence theory says, because they are the *kinds of people* who are riot prone—they have the characteristics that would lead them to riot and they have a tendency or a *propensity* to engage in rioting behavior. Some observers are extremely critical of all individualistic or convergence explanations of collective violence (Ladner et al., 1981, p. 173), assuming that they automatically uphold the "riffraff" or "scum of the earth" stereotype. In fact, to say that some types of individuals are more likely to engage in hostile outbursts is not the same thing as saying that all rioters are the "dregs of society." In fact, *in principle*, an individualistic explanation could show that rioters are *not* "criminal types," but in many ways *superior* to nonrioters—more politically astute, sophisticated, aware, better educated, and more knowledgeable, for instance. But, as with all explantions, remember that individualistic theories only focus on one set of factors at a time, that is, the characteristics of rioters versus nonrioters. All of the other possible causes of rioting are taken for granted; they are separate factors and require a separate examination.

First, as to proportions. In a given riot, *how many* people engage in a given episode of collective violence? Clearly, it varies according to the riot. The mini-riot that broke out in Detroit after the Tigers won the World Series in 1984 involved only a few hundred people, no more than 1,000, which is a minuscule fraction of the population of the city of Detroit, even a small proportion of the fans who were in Tiger Stadium during the last, decisive game. The riot that exploded in the New Mexico state penitentiary in 1980 involved nearly all of the inmates there, either as perpetrators or victims. The civil disturbances in minority communities in the 1960s were participated in by roughly 12 to 15 percent of the affected neighborhoods. In the riot that took place in 1980 in Miami, roughly a quarter of the Black population participated (Ladner et al., 1981, pp. 187–188). Of course, "participation" covers the entire waterfront, from setting fire to cars and buildings, to encouraging others to act, to attempting to prevent others from rioting to protecting one's own property. The point should be clear; the proportion of a relevant community participating in a given episode of collective violence varies according to the specific episode in question, from a minuscule percentage to a substantial minority to, if the community is small enough, nearly everyone.

We should not be surprised that finding relationships between individual characteristics and rioting *in general* is likely to be an uncertain exercise since there are so many *different kinds* of collective violence. Why should we expect individuals who engage in revelous and essentially apolitical riots to be the same sorts of persons who engage in purposive and distinctly political forms of collective behavior? In fact, if we do find such commonalities, they should be more surprising than expected. Nonetheless, at least four different types of individual variables or factors have been explored as relevant to the likelihood of engaging in rioting behavior. First, factors that relate to *being available* for engaging in rioting; second, those that are related to engaging in *unconventional behavior*; third, those that relate to *attitudes and beliefs* that are *directly* relevant to the issue that the riot addresses; and fourth, those that relate to *socioeconomic status*, specifically, education and employment versus unemployment.

The Social Behavioral/Interactionist (SBI) Approach. As we saw in Chapter 2, the SBI approach emphasizes the *availability* factor in engaging in collective violence. It is the only individual factor approach that is not a variation of "convergence" theory. Having free time and having relatively few social obligations and commitments are correlated with engaging in rioting (McPhail, 1971; Miller, 1985, pp. 232–233; McPhail, 1992). For instance, rioters are far more likely to be single than married and to have no children than to have children. It's difficult to take part in a riot with a baby strapped to one's back. (Although one may take part in a more or less peaceful demonstration.) It's difficult to go out on the street and engage in crowd violence if one has to have dinner on the table at 6:30 P.M. Certain activities are restricted if people are counting on you to do certain things and to be at a certain place at a certain time. This is not to say that it's impossible, only that such obligations make participation more difficult and therefore less likely. The same applies to occupational involvement. Riots are more likely to take place during weekends than during the week and after 5 o'clock in the evening than before. Why? Because, at these times, most people have fewer binding social obligations. Riots that take place during the typical work week are more likely to be participated in by individuals who do not have occupational involvements. Again, while individual availability does not explain rioting behavior it may make it more likely, under certain fairly specific circumstances.

Unconventionality. To many observers who are sympathetic to rioting—at least, rioting for *certain* goals or motives—pinpointing the dimension of unconventionality seems to make the claim that rioters are more "criminally inclined" than individuals who don't riot. It borders dangerously, they feel, on the "riffraff" theory that was so popular in the 1960s, and that conservatives today still seem to favor. Moreover, this viewpoint seems to say that people don't riot because of unjust conditions, but because of individual characteristics, moreover, because of "bad," undesirable, or pathological characteristics. In truth, we can focus on individual differences, even those that have to do with the likelihood of engaging in deviant or criminal activities, without implying that social conditions don't count. The fact is, some people *are* more daring, more willing to flout convention and the authorities, and more likely to take risks and engage in dangerous behavior than others. It would be foolish to pretend that people have an equal likelihood of breaking the law, even if that entails engaging in behavior that represents a protest against existing conditions.

Differences in the likelihood of engaging in unorthodox, nontraditional behavior explain, in part, why men are far more likely to riot than are women. (Just as they are more likely to engage in a wide range of unconventional and illegal behaviors; in fact, other things being equal, the more unconventional the activity, the greater the male edge among those who participate in it.) The factor of unconventionality also helps explain why the young are more likely to riot than the old, the unmarried more than the married, the unemployed more than the employed, racial minorities more than members of the majority, urban residents more than rural dwellers, and so on. As with the factor of availability, unconventionality does not take us very far in explaining why people engage in collective violence; still, its role cannot be ignored. In most comparisons of rioters versus nonrioters, rioters are more likely to have been involved with the law—to have been previously arrested, for example—than nonrioters (Ladner et al., 1981, p. 190).

Attitudes and Beliefs. Attitudinal and belief factors are also related to engaging in collective hostile outbursts, although less powerfully than we might expect. McPhail (1971) examined 287 separate relationships between predicted predisposition to riot and actual riot participation in the 1960s. Of these relationships, 268 or 93 percent were either statistically insignificant or were extremely weak. Of the 79 attitudinal variables examined, only six were of a moderate level of significance. One of these, negative attitudes toward the police, may have been a product of participating in a riot, and therefore started by being mistreated by the police—in other words, a result rather than a cause of riot participation (McPhail, 1971, p. 1067; Miller, 1985, p. 233).

Still, for many riots that have direct political relevance, there is some connection with ideology and participation; the link cannot be entirely discounted. One study (Caplan and Paige, 1968) found that participants in the Detroit and Newark ghetto riots of 1967 were more likely than nonparticipants to say that the country is not "worth fighting for" (53 versus 28 percent), "sometimes I hate whites" (72 versus 50 percent), affluent Blacks "are just as bad" as whites in not helping the Black community (51 versus 35 percent), and Blacks are smarter than whites (53 versus 26 percent). Overall, rioters held a more radical, militant, and even angry ideological position. While a politically relevant ideological difference is not always found when riot participants are compared with nonparticipants—in fact, it is surprising how rarely it is—the political and ideological factor cannot be dismissed as crucial in *some* episodes of collective violence, especially of a purposive nature.

Socioeconomic Status. The last individualistic variable that has been examined as relevant to the propensity to engage in hostile outbursts is socioeconomic status (SES), especially education and employment. As we saw earlier, the "riffraff" hypothesis argues that rioters engage in collective violence because they are unemployed (or underemployed), and poorly educated. On the contrary, most studies of Black rioters (Ladner et al., 1981, p. 190; Caplan and Paige, 1968, pp. 17–18), find that the rioter is not only somewhat educated, but he is in fact likely to be somewhat *better* educated than the nonrioter. Differences in employment status generally show a somewhat higher rate of unemployment for riot participants than nonparticipants. Combined with the educational picture, this suggests that racial minorities are more likely to engage in politically oriented collective violence when their educational attainment significantly outstrips their occupational achievement. However, it is very unlikely that socioeconomic factors relate in the same way to nonpurposive, nonpolitical riots as they do to episodes of purposive, political collective violence.

Overall, individualistic variables do not take us very far in explaining riot participation. Some of them help us understand an individual's potential for engaging in acts of collective violence, and some do not. Common sense tells us that the main reason that someone engages in a certain kind of behavior are due to his or her individual characteristics; in this case, common sense is wrong. There is much more to the picture of collective violence than the influence of individual characteristics.

SOCIAL CONDITIONS
_____ THAT INFLUENCE COLLECTIVE VIOLENCE _____

Social conditions that encourage, generate, or influence riots have been studied in addition to individual characteristics. Are some societies, communities, or social settings more riot prone than others? Do certain social conditions generate the conditions for collective violence? Is rioting a socially patterned event? Or is collective violence a random affair, just as likely to break out here as anywhere else? Clearly, there are different types of riots and just as clearly, different types of societal explanations can be called for to account for them. It would be foolish to expect a single theory to explain collective violence of all kinds. At the same time, it is possible that some societal conditions and processes are common to a wide range of riots. Several key societal conditions have been pinpointed as possible causes for collective violence. Over the years, the approaches or theories on riots that have attracted the most attention are the *stress* or *breakdown perspective;* the *relative deprivation theory;* the *political perspective;* and, once again, *SBI,* or the *social behavioral/interactionist model,* focusing on the societal rather than the individual level.

The Stress or Breakdown Perspective. The stress or breakdown perspective is certainly the most commonsensical of the four explanations. The man and woman on the street are most likely to come up with some version of stress or breakdown theory in attempting to account for riots on the societal level. Does the evidence support this explanation? The New Mexico prison riot of 1980 was due in large part to a breakdown in prison conditions (Colvin, 1982; Useem, 1985) and not to the mobilization of political resources among inmates and inmate leaders. During the 1970s, the New Mexico State Penitentiary changed "from a relatively benign and well-run institution to one that was harsh, abusive, [and] painfully boring. . . . The riot was a product of the termination of inmate programs, crowding, idleness, and a generally poorly-administered prison system." Further, there is no evidence that the riot took place because of an increase in inmate resources of solidarity, "which resource-mobilization theorists say must precede collective action" (Useem, 1985, p. 685).

During the 1960s, a very large number of hostile outbursts took place, a substantial proportion of them in response to the assassination of Rev. Martin

Luther King in April, 1968. The overwhelming majority of these incidents occurred in the Black community, and were widely interpreted to represent a protest against minority oppression. One study (Downes, 1968) examined 239 incidents of collective violence that spanned the period from 1964 to 1968. During 523 days during which rioting took place, nearly 50,000 individuals were arrested, nearly 8,000 were injured or wounded, and 191 were killed. During the middle three years of this period, it has been conservatively estimated, $210 million worth of property damage was incurred, with over $500 million in economic losses. A full reckoning of the entire period, measured in today's dollars, would run well into the billions. Taken as a whole, the 1960s represented the period of America's "most serious domestic violence in this century" (Caplan and Paige, 1968, p. 21).

What caused these racial disturbances? What generated collective violence in the Black community? Were there differences among cities in the propensity of their Black populations to engage in rioting? Early research (Downes, 1968) suggested that cities with a low educational level, a low median family income, a high unemployment rate, poor and unsound housing, and a municipal government that was unresponsive to the needs of its residents, tended to be those in which riots, as well as the most severe riots, took place in the Black communities in the 1960s; cities with higher levels of education, higher incomes, adequate housing, and a responsive government, tended to be those in which riots did not occur, or, if they did, they occurred at a significantly lower level of severity.

Later research (Spilerman, 1970, 1971, 1976) questioned these conclusions, not so much because these differences among cities were not correlated with the outbreak of collective behavior but because they were not the crucial or causal factors here. In fact, the *only* variable that influenced the likelihood that a city experienced racial disturbances in the 1960s was the size of its Black population. If a city had a substantial number of Blacks, then riots, and severe riots, took place there in the 1960s. If a city had few Blacks, either riots did not take place or those that did were small and insignificant. *All* of the other factors (education, income, unemployment, housing, and city government) were of secondary importance. Explanations of the riots "must be sought in frustrations which carried nationwide salience" (Spilerman, 1976, p. 789). Blacks saw collective violence taking place all over the country on the TV news, immediately recognized it as a protest against oppressive conditions, and saw themselves as facing much the same deprivation the disturbances seemed to express. In short, many Black viewers *identified* with what and whom they saw in stories about rioting in the media. This identification with the television reporting of these events "contributed in a fundamental way to the creation of a black solidarity that would transcend the boundaries of community" (Spilerman, 1976, p. 790).

Thus, the crucial community factors here are not the education, income, employment, housing, and government of a city, but rather, the size of a city's Black population *because that influences all of the other factors.* As a consequence of racism and discrimination, Blacks tend to have substantially lower levels of education, income, employment, live in more inadequate housing, and are more likely to live in cities with unresponsive municipal governments; Blacks typically recognize this, and tend to be favorable toward a collective recognition of this fact. The outbreaks of the 1960s highlighted this fact, and Blacks who lived in communities with a substantial Black population were simply more likely to initiate, or join, acts of collective violence than Blacks living in communities with a smaller "critical mass" of Black residents. At that time, the only thing that influenced the incidence and severity of racial disorders was the size of the African-American population; being Black carried such overwhelming subjective importance that nothing else mattered very much.

Of course, this explanation does not address the timing of the disturbances or the fact that the riots took place in the 1960s and, with very few exceptions, that they did not take place in the 1970s and 1980s. Still, it does explain a particular type of collective violence that took place at a particular point in time. Clearly, racial inequality is a type of "stress"; if it increases over time, it is a kind of "breakdown." To the extent that it is a major cause of a major type of rioting, the stress and breakdown approach has explanatory power.

Lang and Lang (1961, pp. 125–135) describe and analyze four cases of collective violence—the lynching of a fascist collaborator that took place in Rome in 1944; a violent demonstration by street vendors in Shanghai in 1946; fighting that took place when veterans and other American patriots attacked a group of union members and radicals attending a concert given by Paul Robeson, Black singer and actor and Soviet sympathizer, in Peekskill, New York in 1949; and a riot in Montreal in 1955 that erupted when a hockey player, Maurice Richard, was suspended by the National Hockey League president for engaging in violence on the ice. In all cases, the cause of the riot was closely associated with *a breakdown of traditional societal structures* and *the generation of widespread anxiety and discontent.* In short, social change brings dislocation, upheaval, and turmoil that, in turn, generate into action a population ripe for collective violence.

When a society changes radically and drastically, the social, economic, and political structures undergo a transformation. Some of this change may be undesired, may bring anger and frustration rather than satisfaction. Conventional conditions and practices no longer exist. What members of a society once did is no longer possible; who they were has been stripped away; where they can go has been rendered inaccessible. A person of dignity and respect may now be ignored or treated with disrespect; what was once valued has become irrelevant or is looked down upon. Social change has a way of tearing away anchorages and foundations and making previously inconceivable behavior possible, likely, or even welcome and attractive.

One year, the people in a society are materially comfortable; the next year, inflation has destroyed their ability to purchase basic necessities. One year, there's peace; the next year, a foreign power invades their homeland. At one time, everyone is living in a tribal village; less than a generation later,

Can personal and social upheaval explain participation in riots and violent demonstrations? In 1949, a largely blue-collar crowd, many of whom were World War II veterans, attacked concert-goers attending a performance by Paul Robeson, Black activist and supporter of the Soviet Union.

they all abandon their village because they are starving and move to a huge city. One year, everyone is a small, independent farmer; a decade later, everyone is working for subsistence wages for a boss. One year, the people in an area pay no taxes to anyone; the next year, they have to hand over half their incomes to pay their taxes. One year, they receive water without having to pay for it; the next year, they have to pay for what they had always received for free. One year, their cattle or sheep can graze in a collective field; the next year, the field is fenced off, their livestock can't graze, and they have to sell them off. These are some of the changes that can and have taken place in human history that have caused upheavals in people's lives that have generated riots and other violent outbursts. Under conditions such as these, we don't have to look to the characteristics of specific individuals to understand why they find collective violence attractive. In these cases, something is happening to the society generally; society is experiencing a breakdown.

The discontent that people feel need not be based solely on economic frustration. In Italy and Shanghai, just after World War II ended, the termination of warfare did not bring about anything like a measureably more comfortable society; instead, new and previously unforeseen problems emerged. Whatever existed in the way of security and old routines evaporated. Old norms were no longer valid; many citizens were fearful. Foreign armies came and went, and others moved in. Migration destroyed what was once a stable social and cultural life. Groups that hadn't had contact with one another for thousands of years found themselves interacting frequently. Sometimes, positions in life were reversed, with previous top dogs on the bottom and underdogs in command. Hopes for a vastly better post-war life filled everyone's minds—dreams of enough food on the table, a gain in social prestige, and political reform—and were dashed. Social convention and social ties were dissolved. Skills that were once used and considered important were devalued. A feeling that all authorities were liars and frauds ran rampant through the population. Conventional, institutionalized channels of expression and action no longer operated. In short, social unrest was rife in Rome and Shanghai at the end of World War II. Is it any wonder that large-scale crowd mobilizations erupted in those cities at that time?

While sociopolitical and economic instability, group conflict, and frustrated expectations—in short, "breakdown"—certainly play a role in the receptivity of the members of a society to engage in collective violence, we still must fall back on the fact that all four of the riots described by the Langs (see p. 124), and, for that matter, all riots that have ever taken place are historically unique, due to the immediate concrete circumstances of the time. In each of the Langs' cases, there is a background of social dislocation and disruption. At the same time, collective violence has not occurred in many, if not most, other times and places where similar disruption has taken place. Thus, we have to face the fact that violence is triggered by circumstances that are, to a certain degree, historically specific. Any attempt to devise grand theories about riots that ignores this basic fact will inevitably founder on the shoals of concrete reality. General conditions provide a background or a foundation for hostile outbursts. But what generally launches the riot into existence is the events that are unique to each one. In short, in order to understand what causes collective violence we have to steep ourselves in the details of history, culture, and social structure to know what took place and why.

It is, in fact, remarkable how *often* riots break out in societies with relatively *little* breakdown and stress and, contrarily, how *rarely* they occur in societies with *a great deal* of breakdown and stress. It is enough to note that, in the United States, Black incomes rose between the end of World War II (1945) and 1973, a period when civil disturbances were extremely common, and have remained stagnant since then, when riots became very rare. While misery, even changes in a society's level of misery, has *something* to do with collective disturbances, this factor only sets the stage for them. Many other factors are necessary for an adequate explanation.

Relative Deprivation Theory. The relative deprivation theory is both an individualistic and a societal explanation because it attempts to understand collective violence as the outcome of certain kinds of individuals who are produced by certain kinds of societies and societal conditions. The relative deprivation perspective (Davies, 1962, 1969; Gurr, 1970) argues that people will feel deprived not because they are objectively and absolutely deprived, but because they feel deprived *in comparison with* others around them or with their own past circumstances. When they feel deprived, they will be more likely to engage in some form of collective violence, especially a revolution, to improve existing conditions. One variety of this theory is called *the theory of rising expectations*, which holds that improving objective conditions generates subjective expectations of further improvement. As conditions improve, people quickly get used to the improvement and take it for granted. The faster things improve, the faster the desire for more improvement rises. If a temporary setback deteriorates conditions, or merely prevents them from rising or rising as fast as they had been rising, widespread dissatisfaction sets the stage for protest, collective violence, and revolution.

Actually, a few, but only a very few, instances of collective violence or revolution are illuminated by this model. History notes countless uprisings in which relative deprivation has been entirely absent. Moreover, the theory does not address the issue of what happens once the populace, or a segment of the populace, has been prepared for collective violence; it simply assumes that widespread discontent is sufficient to generate it. How does the populace become organized to mount a mass protest? What kinds of leaders are most effective in mobilizing mass discontent into protest, violence, and revolution? What stages do such actions go through? How do governments defuse, coopt, or crush such uprisings? These questions have to be addressed if one is interested in the issue of collective protest, violence, and revolution. They are precisely the kinds of question that the relative deprivation theory ignores. It takes such issues for granted; it leaves deprived and discontented individuals dangling without an effective *vehicle* for expressing their deprivation and discontent.

The Political Perspective.   The political perspective toward collective violence, associated with Charles Tilly (1978; Tilly, Tilly, and Tilly, 1975) and his followers, shares some of the same basic assumptions held by resource mobilization, which was discussed briefly in Chapter 1 and will be discussed in detail in Chapter 10. It argues the following four points.

First, *collective violence cannot be clearly demarcated from nonviolence.* Indeed, the two shade off into one another. Many ordinary, everyday, relatively routine social interaction is conflictual. Many activities provide the setting for competition between groups—strikes, protests, demonstrations, even ordinary meetings. Under most circumstances, they do not break out into overt violence. However, under certain specific conditions, such activities may turn violent. Collective violence is not unusual, freakish, abnormal, or pathological behavior that is isolated from mainstream activities. Violence is rooted in and is intrinsic to ordinary social relations between competing factions in any society (Tilly, 1972).

Second, the political approach argues that *participation in collective violence is not a product of rootlessness, alienation, anomie, or an estrangement from social institutions.* Indeed, the approach argues, the matter is precisely the other way around: It is the individuals who are *most* attached to certain key social and cultural institutions who are *most* likely to engage in certain types of collective violence. Examining a key uprising, the European revolutions of 1848, Tilly writes, "most of the insurgents had formed substantial attachments to one or another of the city's subgroups, had undergone a fairly extensive socialization to the city's way of life, and had perhaps simultaneously received a political indoctrination" (1963, p. 34; cited in Rule, 1988, p. 174). For emphasis, he adds, "Maybe attachments to some kinds of groups facilitates rebellion; maybe intensive political socialization normally preceded participation in insurrection" (p. 35). Clearly, this approach is a far cry from—indeed, takes almost precisely the opposite position of—the "riffraff" theory spelled out above.

Third, *collective violence is rational and intentional; it is one means that members of a group use to attain a valued end or goal.* Rioters tend to have something in mind they wish to achieve when they engage in acts of destruction—these are not irrational, emotional, random outbursts. Participants in collective violence weigh costs and benefits before they decide to act; when they do act, they are taking certain risks in the hope of making specific gains (1978, p. 99). In this view, collective violence most decidedly does *not* take place among people with "nothing to lose." Instead, it is most likely to occur when people forsee that they have a great deal to *gain* by engaging in it. Of course, as we saw with the gaming or rational calculus school in Chapter 2, actors may not have complete or accurate information when they act. The political school of thinking is aware of the fact that some episodes of collective violence are not politically motivated—witness some of the outbursts detailed above. On the other hand, such apolitical, revelous, or issueless violent episodes rarely have the kind of impact that politically motivated riots have. Hence, it is the latter that demand an explanation. When we look at the engine of social change—the factors and forces that have a historical impact—it is the politically motivated, not the apolitical, riots that feature prominently. Moreover, apolitical violence does not exhibit much variation from one decade to the next, whereas political violence is tightly related to struggles for power (1978, pp. 181–182).

A fourth major point made by the political approach is that *collective violence represents a struggle for power among contending social factions.* Violence is generated by the clash between the interests of subgroups in the population. More specifically, violence often represents an attempt to acquire power by factions that had been previously excluded or the effort by those in power to crush such an attempt (Tilly, 1974, 1979). Strikes by workers typically represent more than a demand for higher wages and better working conditions; they also represent a demand for more legitimate power in national politics and less power by industrialists. Wars, likewise, are rarely conflicts over specific, concrete issues; more often, they represent attempts by one nation to usurp another's international influence. Collective action often results in *transfers of power* from one group, faction, or interest to another. Revolutions provide the most obvious set of examples: The French revolution transferred power from the monarchy and the aristocracy to the bourgeoisie; the Russian revolution destroyed the Czar and his family, cast out the aristocracy, and placed power in the hands of the Bolsheviks. Clashes between labor and the police, usually acting on behalf of the interests of management, legitimized the labor movement and labor unions, and yielded more power to labor and less to the capitalist class.

Like most theories of collective violence, the political model works better for some examples than for others. In fact, much of Tilly's work represents a careful selection of historical cases that fit his model best. It is entirely possible that, contrary to his assertion (1978, pp. 181–182), *most* instances of riots and other collective violence are *not* politically motivated. It is difficult to read specific, concrete political goals into the civil disturbances that exploded in minority communities in the 1960s; they seem more a righteous, spontaneous outburst of collective rage at existing conditions than the effort to attain concrete political objectives. In 1984, following the assassination of India's president Indira Gandhi by her Sikh bodyguards, thousands of Sikhs were set upon, beaten, and killed by Hindus all over India (Gupte, 1985). In what way can this fit into Tilly's model? (Rule, 1988, pp. 197, 198). The revelous riots that follow victory in war or sporting events hardly seem legitimate candidates for the political approach. Of course, political meaning and intent can be *read into* any and all such events after the fact, but few observers need take such an exercise seriously. At the same time, Tilly has made a major contribution by focusing on an extremely crucial and often neglected factor in the genesis of collective violence.

The Social Behaviorial/Interactionist (SBI) Model. The SBI model of collective violence (McPhail, 1971; Snyder, 1979; Miller, 1985, pp. 249–250; McPhail, 1992) argues that riots occur in an "immediate interactional environment" (McPhail, 1971, p. 1072), that is, where crowds gather. Some cities provide a "greater likelihood than others for assembling processes" and, as a consequence, for collective violence as well (Miller, 1985, p. 249). Factors such as population density, racial segregation, the location of street intersections, the types of residential dwellings, the presence or absence of barriers to street-level communication (highways, railroads, rivers, and so on), and, of course, the availability of variables such as employment and vacations, and the impact of work schedules play a major role in drawing crowds and generating an environment that potentiate riots. Some racial ghettos "are more riot prone than others," not because their residents feel more discontent than others, but because they "have significantly greater numbers of police–citizen contacts that can be easily observed by ghetto residents." These communities have a larger number of people who are "on the streets" with "nothing to do" (Miller, 1985, p. 250; Snyder, 1979). Of course, this approach takes all other factors for granted and focuses on only one set of variables. Assembling is a necessary but not sufficient condition for collective violence to take place. Riots rarely break out in a concert hall, even though a large number of people are assembled because the people there simply do not feel the frustration and discontent that would impel them to engage in collective violence.

RIOTS AND RUMOR

The majority of rumors circulate among fairly dispersed collectivities; hence, a discussion of the subject belongs in Part 4 (see Chapter 7) rather than in this part of the book, which focuses on crowds. Still, rumor does circulate among compact collectivities as well and, more specifically, before, during, and after riots; thus, some discussion of the rumor process is called for here.

Rumor is usually present in riots—often before, usually during, and nearly always afterwards. When riots take place between hostile groups in a society—for instance, racial and ethnic groups—rumors typically trigger or at least exacerbate them. It must be emphasized that by itself, a rumor cannot cause a collective disorder; "it merely helps prepare the way for violence," operating in concert or along with a number of other factors (Knopf, 1975, p. 153). Rumors fly especially thick and fast when they are generated by a "hostile belief system" (p. 154). Rumors crystallize the perceptions that members of each group have of the group toward which they feel hostile. They are "concrete representations" held by members of each respective category or group. They dramatize these beliefs, give them flesh-and-blood material substance. They are real-life enactments or embodiments of these hostile beliefs. They confirm or offer proof that these beliefs are valid; they show that they are "rooted in objective reality," that is to say, really true (p. 159).

In addition, rumors also *intensify* hostile beliefs (Knopf, 1975, pp. 160ff); that is, an event is exaggerated when it makes the already-held beliefs *seem tame by comparison.* The behavior of an adversary group "is magnified and seen as extraordinary, beyond the pale of expected norms" (p. 160). Paranoid fantasies and atrocity stories play a major role in rumors told before, during, or after riots that manifest group hostilities. During times that such hostilties break out into the open, rumors are a measure or indicator of them. They announce to all who would listen: "You see, I may hate group X and believe that its members are capable of cruel, vicious behavior toward us, but look—this story shows that they are *even worse* than what I believe about them!" In addition, rumors provide instant recognition of the "good guys" and the "bad guys," and instant affiliation with one side of the conflict. In short, rumors reflecting intergroup hostility provide *morality tales*, complete with a plot, characters, a message, and sometimes even a call for action.

The racial disturbances of the 1960s offer a fertile setting for countless examples of race-related rumors that reflected intergroup hostility (Knopf, 1975). At that time, many whites believed that Blacks were "naturally" violent, conspiring to undermine the system on which the country was based, and did not know their "rightful place" in society. Such beliefs encouraged, for example, a rumor that circulated late in July 1967 that some 8,000 armed Blacks were poised to attack the peaceful city of Cedar Rapids, Iowa, which jammed the switchboards of the local newspaper and the police precincts, and generated long lines of white customers at sporting goods stores waiting to purchase guns and ammunition (p. 152).

On the opposite side of the conflict, many Blacks believed that whites were "naturally" violent, that drastic change was necessary to change American society, that the police were unusually brutal toward Blacks, that white institutions were designed to oppress African-Americans, and that whites were conspiring to deny Blacks their rightful place in society. These beliefs gave birth, for example, to a rumor in October 1968 that soul singer James Brown had been shot to death by a white man, which touched off widespread rioting in Washington, D.C. (p. 152). In each case, the rumor was completely untrue, but both were plausible to members of the respective group, even when told in the total absence of evidence, because of the hostile beliefs that they held toward the other racial category. In short, rumors play an important role in riots, especially when they are a manifestation of intergroup hostility. Such rumors nearly always express and give life to that hostility, and, if they do have an impact, nearly always ignite or exacerbate riots of an intergroup character.

_____Two Riots That Didn't Happen_____

For every episode of serious collective violence that breaks out, there are hundreds that, for one reason or another, do not break out. Many crowds seem to have all the prerequisites for an explosion, but, somehow, the excitement is never translated into action. The crowd is there, the hostility is mobilized, but no riot takes place. One problem with attempting to explore the causes of crowd violence is that nonriots are very rarely studied; many researchers feel, why look at something that _didn't_ happen? How can we understand what generates collective behavior when we never look at negative cases? This methodological limitation puts something of a roadblock in our path to a complete understanding of riots.

Certainly the reasons why individuals have gathered into a crowd in the first place is crucial here; it is related to the likelihood that they will act on directives or triggering events leading to collective violence. If a crowd has assembled because most of them support such an action in advance, then it is more likely to happen—it isn't certain, only more likely to happen. And if such potential actors are surrounded by too many individuals who are resistant to directives favorable to acting out collective behavior, then likewise, it is less likely to happen. If, in the milling process, when crowd members are sounding one another out for possible lines of action, and suggestions to act are thrown out, and are met by indifference or disagreement, diluted by naysayers, then collective violence is unlikely to happen. We need something of a _critical mass_ of individuals who are positively inclined toward rioting for a group outbreak to take place. In short, the convergence perspective cannot be dismissed; clearly, the characteristics and inclination of a crowd's members makes a difference in whether or not collective violence is likely to break out.

THE MACARTHUR DAY PARADE, 1951 _____

A good example of a riot that didn't happen is provided by the return of General Douglas MacArthur from the Korean War to a hero's welcome in Chicago in 1951 (Lang and Lang, 1961, pp. 146–148). MacArthur, a World War II hero, was the commanding general of the American forces in the Korean War. In 1951, after the battle lines had shifted back and forth several times, MacArthur revealed, in a letter read to the United States Congress, that he planned a massive invasion of North Korea. This plan had not been cleared or authorized by Harry S Truman, who, as President, was comman-der-in-chief of the armed forces. It seemed to Truman that MacArthur was going over his head and appealing directly to the American people. He labeled this an act of insubordination, and he immediately dismissed MacArthur as commander-in-chief of the allied forces in Korea.

This action generated a great deal of resentment among American con-servatives, who saw MacArthur as a hero and a martyr, and who saw MacArthur's action justified, indeed, even necessary to "contain commu-nism." Two observers at the time said, "It is doubtful that there has ever been in this country so violent and spontaneous a discharge of political passion as that provoked by the President's dismissal of the General and by the Gen-eral's dramatic return from his voluntary, patriotic exile" (Rovere and Schlesinger, 1951, p. 5). Even allowing for exaggeration here, we can assume that many Americans were upset by the firing. It seemed that Truman was "going soft" on communism, that he was aiding and abetting the enemy, and refusing to unleash the power of American military might in order to crush the Communist menace. There was talk of impeachment of the president; ral-lies and protests arose in support of MacArthur.

It was in this atmosphere that a parade was scheduled in Chicago for the general upon his return from Korea, a ticker tape welcome back to the Unit-ed States. Provocative and inflammatory pro-MacArthur and anti-Truman arti-cles appeared in Chicago's newspapers daily for some time before the event. Would the parade spontaneously break into a riot? A protest? A demonstra-tion of some kind? MacArthur certainly could have marshalled that kind of response—in the right place at the right time, with the right crowd. Why didn't it happen in Chicago? There were strong MacArthur supporters there, but also a large number of ordinary citizens, who had come simply to see a parade. Many in the crowd didn't feel strongly about his dismissal in political terms. When MacArthur passed, the crowd strained to see him; there was mild and sporadic cheering. There were no hysterical or wildly enthusiastic reactions. "Normal reserve among the spectators never allowed [strong] pro-MacArthur support to develop" (Lang and Lang, 1961, p. 147).

The following interchange illustrates the kind of give-and-take interaction in the milling process that squelches, rather than encourages, a riot. One man, about 25 years old, ventured to remark, "Boy, if the Republicans were smart, they would put up MacArthur for president. In fact they should try to have an election right now; he would be sure to get in. . . . The people always feel sorry for the underdog, and it wasn't nice the way Truman fired him. I bet he would get elected easily—Don't you?" This was said to no one in particular. A well-dressed Black man about the same age as the MacArthur supporter said, "Let's forget about politics and enjoy the parade." At which point about five people in the vicinity chimed in, "Yes, forget about politics and enjoy the parade." The young man persisted. "I think he would get in if the Republicans played it right." No one answered him or made a comment about his remark. By this time, everyone in the crowd was straining to see if MacArthur's procession was coming by (Lang and Lang, 1961, p. 147).

Why didn't the interchange escalate? Why didn't some sort of collective behavior develop in this crowd? The fact is, the majority of the members of the crowd simply had no taste for disorder. People came to the parade bent on watching the parade. The majority of the crowd was not angry at anyone. It was a happy holiday crowd; many had gotten the day off from school or work to attend the parade, and they wanted to have a good time. (Which is why the SBI perspective is inadequate: It isn't the simple fact of assembling that makes for collective disorder—it is *who is assembled*, and *under what conditions*, that makes it possible or likely.) It did not seem like a day that was suitable for revenge on behalf of a deposed hero. Even President Truman had defused the situation by giving MacArthur a hero's welcome upon his return. Crowd members were far from unanimous in their view that something had to be done to protest the general's dismissal. Ironically, a protest would have taken away from the dignity of the occasion, and would have seemed to taint the occasion designed to honor the man. And so, collective violence never developed.

LABOR DAY WEEKEND, MARLBORO, MARYLAND, 1965

A second riot that didn't happen took place in 1965 in Upper Marlboro, Maryland, a semi-rural, semi-suburban area near Washington, D.C. A national motorcycle race, as well as several other motorcycle-related events, were scheduled for the Labor Day weekend in and around the community; a well-publicized riot had taken place only weeks before at an earlier race in New Hampshire. Shortly after the New Hampshire riot, three motorcyclists claiming to be Hell's Angels had been arrested in Upper Marlboro for disorderly conduct. When they were released, they threatened to return during Labor Day and "tear up the county." Rumors circulated about a motorcyclist "invasion and destruction" of the community that "were persistent and proliferating." Two social scientists who worked for the federal government (Shellow and Roemer, 1966) conferred with the police and other local officials about the upcoming motorcycle races. They turned down a proposal to cancel the event, deciding instead to work to minimize the possibility that it would turn violent.

Reasoning that many riots are generated because factions polarize the crowd into "them" and "us," outsiders and insiders, visitors and locals, the social scientists worked with the police and local motorcycle groups to dispel stereotypes, to air grievances, and to emphasize the importance of good judgment and caution in exercising, and being subject to, social control. In addition, they urged that adequate camping facilities be provided for the spectators who were to attend the races over the long weekend. When the date arrived, however, a group that had agreed to provide those facilities reneged on its promise, and so motorcyclists began camping in a field near the race track. While this technically entailed trespassing, the police wisely decided to ignore it; to evict a "noisy, potentially troublesome group" would have threatened the peace. The area was monitored by the county's 45-man, anti-riot Civil Disturbance Unit.

By the first day of the weekend, hundreds of motorcyclists were squatting in the field sporting "Hell's Angels," "Pagans," or "The Gooses" jackets. Many wore their hair at shoulder length, and some sported nose rings, gold earrings, swastikas, and, in one case, a Halloween wig. A substantial quantity of beer, wine, and hard liquor was consumed. Meanwhile, tourists, campers, and curiosity seekers formed a crescent around the camp, ogling the bikers or simply engaging in their own recreational activities. An impromptu dragstrip had been set up, and motorcycles roared through the field, criss-crossing and, in most cases, narrowly escaping collision. Accidents began to occur, and finally, a fight broke out between a "short-haired local" and "a very wobbly Pagan." The local punched the biker unconscious. "The victor had the poor taste and bad judgment to sit triumphantly astride the hood of a truck, waving his beer can in bravado challenge" (Shellow and Roemer, 1966, p. 228). The Pagans and their allies decided to charge the locals en masse.

Luckily, at that moment, a drunken biker ran his motorcycle into a rut and fell; his mishap was noticed by the police on the highway, who immediately dispatched an ambulance and five cruisers. This immediate show of force, along with the sight of the vehicles' flashing lights, forced the would-be combatants to retreat and reconsider. Potential troublemakers "got the message that there was a large force of police nearby, ready for action at a moment's notice" (Shellow and Roemer, 1966, p. 229).

Then, 20 bikers decided to replenish their beer supply at a nearby bar. Entering, they began to "throw their weight around in the bar and threaten the owner." Again, at the right moment, a sergeant and another officer entered the bar and the group quieted down. Three cyclists moved to the window to assess the size of the force accompanying the two officers, perhaps reasoning that 20 against two weren't bad odds at all to start a fight. However, four cruisers were parked outside, enough officers to give the bikers pause. The sergeant began with, "I hope you all are behaving yourselves." Seeing a motorcycle chain worn loosely around one biker's waist, and recalling a meeting with one of the social scientists working to defuse the weekend, who told the officers that a chain worn in that fashion is usually used as a weapon, the sergeant asked, "What's that chain for?" The biker replied that he locked his motorcycle with it. The sergeant then said, "Well, aren't you afraid someone'll steal your motor, not being locked up and all? You better come with me while we put that chain on right, son." The group immediately tensed, but the young man complied with the sergeant's request. After the group left, the bar was closed prematurely for the weekend.

All weekend, near-triggering events continued to take place. At 2:00 P.M. on Sunday, a fire was started on a railroad caboose on a siding next to the field. The fire was extinguished, and no attempt was made to find the arsonists. An hour later, a crane was started up on an adjacent construction site, and tools were stolen from its cab. At 4:30 P.M., a young man set fire to his dilapidated old car and, with a friend straddling the hood, drove it onto the drag strip and jumped free. The car rammed a motorcycle and the rider and the cyclist both suffered broken legs. A fire engine came and put out the blaze, a police officer assisted the injured, and the ambulance soon arrived to take them to the hospital.

At 6:00 P.M., a fight broke out between bikers and locals over the possession of a starting flag; ten Civil Disturbance Unit officers arrived immediately. The fact that they were visible in full riot regalia, including helmets, gas masks, clubs, and shotguns, helped cool things down. A half-hour later, the flagman and a delegation from his motorcycle club pleaded with the police to clear the field of bikers; if the police didn't protect them, he said, they would bring in their own weapons. At 7:00 P.M., a number of motorcyclists ran to their machines to get iron bars, chains, and other weapons. The entire Civil Disturbance Unit came out into the field and took position; the Inspector drawled out over the bullhorn, "All right men, you've had your fun, now it's time to go home" (Shellow and Roemer, 1966, p. 230). The crowd dispersed. There were several minor incidents soon thereafter—ten bikers broke the windows of the bar that had been closed down, and another ten were arrested for harrassing customers at a local filling station—but by Monday, it was clear that the threat of a riot had passed.

What prevented the riot? It is clear that the police were working in a hostile, threatening, and potentially explosive situation. Many of the members of the crowds that gathered around the Labor Day weekend events wanted nothing more than to engage in violent, brawling behavior. Participants clearly were "people who need and seek the stimulation of collective action, excitement, and violence. Without it, they become depressed and demoralized." They can be seen as "mob seekers and mob creators" (Shellow and Roemer, 1966, p. 231). If we relied solely on the perspective of convergence theory, we would have predicted at least one serious riot that weekend. But none broke out. Why?

At least four factors are responsible. First, the police combined a show of strength with demonstrations of fairness and neutrality. The police did not harass or antagonize; minor violations were ignored, and more serious ones were dealt with firmly. Second, the police decided to ignore the camping and drag racing that took place on private property and to intervene only when violence clearly threatened others. This contained potential troublemakers, kept them occupied, and minimized conflict with other groups. Third, information was constantly gathered and disseminated, both before and during the events. And fourth, plain, old-fashioned good luck was in their favor. As we can see by the history of collective violence all over the world and throughout history, other gatherings are not so fortunate.

Does the experience at Upper Marlboro, Maryland in 1965 mean that riots can always be prevented with good police work? Of course not; in other situations, police intervention one way or the other makes no difference in the outcome. Does this mean that the social, political, and economic conditions underlying many riots are of no consequence and can be ignored, that what counts is the quality of the control of rioters? This would be an absurd and erroneous conclusion; underlying conditions, the coming together of a substantial number of certain kinds of individuals, triggering events, and social control all contribute to the outcome of a given gathering. But these events do show that police work in dealing with rioters can often inhibit a riot where one is brewing *or*, potentially, generate a riot where none would otherwise have taken place. The factor of social control cannot be ignored in the picture of collective violence.

SUMMARY

The term "riot" is used loosely by most people; more specifically, it contains a negative, pejorative connotation; it is an illegitimate act of collective violence engaged in by social undesirables. Here, we intend no negative meaning when we use the term. To the field of collective behavior, a riot is simply a relatively large-scale, relatively unplanned act of collective violence. Some riots may be planned by a small minority, but if there is no mass receptivity to engage in it in the first place, such planning could not touch off collective violence.

There is a variety of types of collective violence; indeed, there is a variety of classifications of these types. Four types of riots seem common: purposive, symbolic, revelous, and issueless. A *purposive riot* is one in which a substantial proportion of the participants have a fairly specific goal in mind when engaging in destructive acts. A *symbolic riot* is one in which a broader, more indirect goal motivates many of the participants, one which gives voice to a view or a group rather than attempts to achieve a specific, concrete goal or objective. A *revelous riot* is one that represents a celebration that has gotten out of hand. *Issueless riots* are ones in which no clear reason or motive predominates among the participants; often, they occur simply because social control is absent or has broken down.

A variety of theories has been offered to explain collective violence. Some explain why specific individuals or categories of individuals riot, while others focus on social conditions that tend to be related to the occurrence of collective violence. While unique factors tend to be at work in every riot, and hence, no single explanation can account for riots in general, still, some general forces or factors do seem to be operating at many times and in many places. General factors can be seen as potentiating, rather than causal, in nature.

There are at least four individualistic theories of rioting. The SBI or social behavioral/interactionist approach says that riots occur when a large number of people are *available* to engage in collective violence. Second, approaches that focus on unconventionality see riots as caused by individuals who have a general propensity to engage in criminal, deviant, or otherwise unconventional behavior. Third, some observers claim that individuals with attitudes and beliefs directly related to the issue expressed by the riot are more likely to participate than is true of similarly situated individuals who do not riot. And fourth, some researchers argue that socioeconomic status (SES) is related to participation in collective violence: Lower SES individuals are more likely to riot than higher SES individuals.

Another set of factors that have been isolated as causes of collective violence are societal rather than individual in nature. The stress or breakdown perspective holds that people engage in acts of collective violence to the extent that the society, or a specific segment of it, is unstable and disintegrating and that there is widespread anxiety and discontent. Relative deprivation holds that it is not absolute discontent that causes collective violence but *relative* discontent: People compare themselves with their past situation, or with the situation of others, and express their discontent in rioting. The political perspective argues that most instances of collective violence represent purposive, rational demands by politically excluded groups for power in the government. And the SBI perspective focuses on both the avilability of individuals to engage in collective violence but also social and situation factors that encourage assembling processes and therefore facilitate riots.

Rioting is frequently accompanied by rumors, and vice versa, since both are fueled by the hostile beliefs that members of one group have toward another group. The role that rumors play in riots illustrate several collective behavior processes.

Most studies of collective violence focus on riots that *did* happen. Negative cases—riots that *didn't* happen—can be instructive because they show that, often, the differences between a riot and a near-riot are a set of accidental, fortuitous factors or events. Two riots that didn't happen are the MacArthur Day parade in Chicago in 1951 and the invasion by a gang of motorcyclists of a small suburban town in Maryland in 1965. We learn as much from these cases as we do from those that did take place. Each type of case illuminates the dynamics of collective behavior.

References

Barman, Roderick J. 1977. "The Brazilian Peasantry Reexamined: The Implications of the Quebra-Quilo Revolt, 1874–1875." *Hispanic American Historical Review*, 57 (3): 401–424.

Barron, James. 1984. "Detroit Rejoices at Tigers' Victory." *The New York Times* (October 15): A1, C4.

Bolce, Louis. 1982. "Why People Riot." *Policy Review*, no. 22: 119–140.

Buckley, Peter George. 1984. *To the Opera House: Culture and Society in New York City, 1820–1860.* PhD Dissertation, Department of History, State University of New York at Stony Brook.

Caplan, Nathan S., and Jeffery M. Paige. 1968. "A Study of Ghetto Rioters." *Scientific American*, 219 (August): 15–21.

Colvin, Mark. 1982. "The 1980 New Mexico Prison Riot." *Social Problems*, 29 (June): 449–463.

Davies, James C. 1962. "A Theory of Revolution." *American Sociological Review*, 27 (February): 5–19.

Davies, James C. 1969. "The J-Curve of Rising and Declining Satisfaction as a Cause of Some Great Revolutions and a Continued Rebellion." In Hugh Davis Graham and Ted Robert Gurr (eds.), *Violence in America: Historical and Comparative Perspectives*, pp. 690–730. New York: Bantam Books.

Downes, Bryan T. 1968. "Social and Political Characteristics of Riot Cities: A Comparative Study." *Social Science Quarterly*, 49 (December): 504–520.

Feagin, Joe R., and Harlan Hahn. 1973. *Ghetto Revolts: The Politics of Violence in American Cities.* New York: Macmillan.

Geschwender, James A. 1968. "Civil Rights Protest and Riots: A Disappearing Distinction." *Social Science Quarterly*, 49 (December): 474–484.

Gupte, Pranay. 1985. *Vengeance: India After the Assassination of Indira Gandhi.* New York: W.W. Norton.

Gurr, Ted Robert. 1970. *Why Men Rebel.* Princeton, N.J.: Princeton University Press.

Hobsbawm, Eric. 1959. *Primitive Rebels.* New York: W.W. Norton.

Knopf, Terry Ann. 1975. *Rumors, Race, and Riots.* New Brunswick, N.J.: Transaction Books.

Ladner, Robert A., et al. 1981. "The Miami Riots of 1980: Antecedent Conditions, Community Responses and Participant Characteristics." *Research in Social Movements, Conflict and Change*, 4: 171–214.

Lang, Kurt, and Gladys Engel Lang. 1961. *Collective Dynamics.* New York: Thomas Y. Crowell.

Levine, Lawrence W. 1988. *Highbrow Lowbrow: The Emergence of Cultural Hierarchy in America.* Cambridge, Mass.: Harvard University Press.

Marx, Gary T. 1972. "Issueless Riots." In James F. Short, Jr., and Marvin E. Wolfgang (eds.). *Collective Violence*, pp. 47–59. Chicago: Aldine/Atherton.

Marx, Gary T. 1974. "Thoughts on a Neglected Category of Social Movement Participation: The Agent Provocateur and the Informant." *American Journal of Sociology*, 80 (September): 402–442.

McPhail, Clark. 1971. "Civil Disorder Participation: A Critical Examination of Recent Research." *American Sociological Review*, 36 (December): 1058–1073.

McPhail, Clark. 1992. *Acting Together: The Organization of Crowds.* New York: Aldine de Gruyter.

Miller, David L. 1985. *Introduction to Collective Behavior.* Belmont, Calif.: Wadsworth.

Moody, Richard. 1958. *The Astor Place Riots.* Bloomington: Indiana University Press.

Park, Robert. 1972. *The Crowd and the Public and Other Essays* (Principal essay originally published in 1904). Chicago: University of Chicago Press.

Rovere, Richard H., and Arthur M. Schlesinger, Jr. 1951. *The General and the President.* New York: Farrar, Strauss & Young.

Rule, James B. 1988. *Theories of Civil Violence.* Berkeley: University of California Press.

Shellow, Robert, and Derek V. Roemer. 1966. "The Riot That Didn't Happen." *Social Problems*, 14 (Fall): 221–233.

Skolnick, Jerome H., et al. 1969. *The Politics of Protest.* New York: Simon & Schuster.

Snyder, David. 1979. "Collective Behavior Processes: Implications for Disaggregated Theory and Research." *Research in Social Movements, Conflict and Change*, 2: 35–61.

Spilerman, Seymour. 1970. "The Causes of Racial Disturbances: A Comparison of Alternative Explanations." *American Sociological Review*, 35 (August): 627–649.

Spilerman, Seymour. 1971. "The Causes of Racial Disturbances: Tests of an Explanation." *American Sociological Review*, 36 (June): 427–442.

Spilerman, Seymour. 1976. "Structural Characteristics and the Severity of Racial Disorders." *American Sociological Review*, 41 (October): 771-793.

Tilly, Charles. 1963. "Queries on Social Change and Political Upheaval in France." Unpublished Manuscript.

Tilly, Charles. 1972. "The Modernization of Political Conflict in France." In Edward B. Harvey (ed.), *Perspectives on Modernization: Essays in Memory of Ian Weinberg*, pp. 50–95. Toronto: University of Toronto Press.

Tilly, Charles. 1974. "Town and Country in Revolution." In John Wilson Lewis (ed.), *Peasant Rebellion and Communist Revolution in Asia*, pp. 271–302. Stanford, Calif.: Stanford University Press.

Tilly, Charles. 1978. *From Mobilization to Revolution.* Reading, Mass.: Addison-Wesley.

Tilly, Charles. 1979. "Repertoires of Contention in America and Britain, 1750–1830." In Mayer N. Zald and John D. McCarthy (eds.), *The Dynamics of Social Movements: Resource Mobilization, Social Control, and Tactics*, pp. 126–155. Cambridge, Mass.: Winthrop.

Tilly, Charles, Louise Tilly, and Richard Tilly. 1975. *The Rebellious Century, 1830–1930.* Cambridge, Mass.: Harvard University Press.

Useem, Bert. 1985. "Disorganization and the New Mexico Prison Riot of 1980." *American Sociological Review*, 50 (October): 677–688.

CHAPTER

4

ECSTATIC CROWDS AND MIRACLES

The church is packed with people; the minister preaches a hellfire-and-brimstone sermon; the audience sings, sways, dances, claps, and shouts enthusiastic encouragement. A dozen members begin babbling in unknown tongues; several leave their seats, enter into a trance and shake, twitch, and fall on the floor, screaming.

The university's football team wins the big game; the main street bordering the town is cordoned off, and a crowd of hundreds of thousands of people gather, seemingly almost out of thin air. Everyone is shouting and screaming, hugging one another, and jumping up and down. Uncountable cans of beer appear and are drunk almost without restraint. Although everyone seems to be having a good time, dozens of police officers, scattered around the fringes of the gathering, eye the crowd warily for signs of trouble.

A poor woman, whose husband has been sick in bed for a year with a debilitating, incurable disease, lights candles in a Catholic church for the hundredth time, kneels, and prays. She looks at the statue of the Virgin Mary with imploring, supplicating eyes. Suddenly, she spots moisture coalescing beneath the Virgin's eyes. Are they tears? Is the Virgin crying in sympathy for the woman's plight? Has she witnessed a miracle? She tells her friends, and within a week, the church is crowded with 200 worshippers, all of them looking at the statue, yearning for another appearance of the miracle she witnessed, praying for a solution to their worldly cares.

These gatherings are examples of *miraculous* and *ecstatic crowds*. The word "ecstasy" stems from the ancient Greek (*ex-stasis*) and refers to a state of being "out of" or transported "away from" one's ordinary, everyday state of being. In certain times and places, some individuals are gripped with the feeling that "something unusual is happening." Lofland prefers the term "joyful" to ecstatic, but either way, the "attitude of everyday life is to some degree suspended; the frame of ordinary reality, the taken-for-granted world" is set aside (Lofland, 1982, 1985, p. 37). As John Lofland reminds us (1982, 1985, pp. 87–88), although ecstatic or joyful crowds have been studied in the past, recent students of collective behavior have, for the most part, ignored them. (But see Turner and Killian, 1987, pp. 97–98.) There is, in the field, something of a "fear that [a] discussion of emotions" will conjure up the specter of the discredited irrationalistic theories of LeBon, Freud, and Herbert Blumer (Loftland; 1985, p. 87). Contemporary theories that focus entirely on behavior (the social behavioral/interactionist approach, for instance) pretty much ignore the role that powerful emotions play in influencing or controlling crowd members' actions. Although some see such a view as "heretical" (p. 87), it is time, Lofland says, to look at such gatherings and understand their dynamics and just how they fit in and articulate with collective behavior.

The object or focus of such intense emotions is seen by those who express them in reverential, religious, sacred, or semi-religious, semi-sacred terms, with a feeling that borders on awe. He, she, or it is "out of the ordinary," beyond the everyday. Even if such an object is as profane as a rock or movie star or an athlete, he or she is invested with supernormal qualities. Here, we are in the realm of the *charismatic*—the sphere of "the gift of the spirit" (Weber, 1968, pp. 1,111ff). Many such expressions are incited by religious figures, such as the Virgin Mary, religious revivals, or religious states or feelings. There are also secular occasions that generate expressions of joy and ecstasy, such as carnaval. Regardless of the focus of such joyous, ecstatic feelings, the expression of joy and ecstasy in a crowd setting has a common thread that permits us to look at it as a single entity or phenomenon.

The perception or experience of *miraculous visions* shares important qualities with ecstatic crowd expressions (Lofland, 1981, p. 440). A crowd anticipating a vision tends to be reverential rather than joyous, "the quiet worshipful coming together of people to give homage to what is defined as the cosmic and to make requests of the cosmic" (p. 440). The same "out of the ordinary" and beyond the everyday feeling (that feeling of stupendous specialness), the same investment of an object with sacred attributes, the same charismatic quality of the revered object, the same intense focus of attention, the same heightened emotion, the same joyous, rapturous delight—these states grip the members of a crowd witnessing, or about to witness, a miracle. There is no doubt that miracles have characteristics in common with ecstatic crowds, and therefore belong in any general study of collective behavior.

_____WHAT ARE ECSTATIC CROWDS?_____

Émile Durkheim (1858–1917), an early, pioneering sociologist, describes in his classic book, _The Elementary Forms of the Religious Life_ (1915), the "collective effervescence" of the Australian religious ceremonies; in fact, Durkheim believed that religion itself was "born out of this effervescence" (p. viii). In the Australian corrobboree, a sacred, festive religious gathering, the participant "easily loses control of himself." He is carried away with "transports of enthusiasm . . ., running here and there like a madman, giving himself up to all sorts of immoderate movements, crying, shrieking, rolling in the dust, throwing it in every direction, biting himself, brandishing his arms in a furious manner." When the corrobboree takes place, with tribal members assembled, "a sort of electricity is formed by their collecting which quickly transports them to an extraordinary degree of exaltation. Every sentiment expressed finds a place without resistance in all minds, which are open to outside impressions; each re-echoes the others, and is re-echoed by the others. The initial impulse thus proceeds, growing as it goes, as an avalanche grows in advance." Such active passions, Durkheim writes, "so free from all control could not fail to burst out. . . . This effervescence often reaches such a point that it causes unheard-of actions. The passions released are of such an impetuosity that they can be restrained by nothing. They are so far removed from their ordinary conditions of life . . . that they must set themselves outside of and above their ordinary morals. . . . They produce such a violent super-excitation of the whole physical and mental life that it cannot be supported very long: the actor taking the principal part finally falls exhausted on the ground" (pp. 215–216). Allowing for the fact that Durkheim's description is not first-hand, but based on anthropological reports, and allowing, too, for the fact that Durkheim may have been overly influenced by LeBon here, nonetheless, we see that religious ceremonies in some cultures express ecstatic states to an extraordinarily uninhibited degree.

Highly emotional states and trances, in which the dominant mood is positive, joyous, rapturous, even frenzied, are common in a number of cultures throughout the world. In Bali, an island in Indonesia, falling into a trancelike state during certain ceremonies is a customary practice. Again, although it is the custom to do so in Bali, tradition does not determine with precision who will fall into a trance or what that person in a trance will do during a given episode, or how long the trance will last. During trance, the Balinese "perform all sorts of spectacular activities—biting off the heads of live chickens, stabbing themselves with daggers, throwing themselves wildly about, speaking with tongues, performing miraculous feats of equilibration, mimicking sexual intercourse, eating feces, and so on—rather more easily and much more suddenly than most of us fall asleep" (Geertz, 1973, p. 36). In such ceremonies, 50 or 60 people may fall into such a trance, "emerging anywhere from five minutes to several hours later, totally unaware of what they have been doing and convinced, despite the amnesia, that they have had the most extraordinary and deeply satisfying experience a man [or a woman] can have" (p. 36).

In the Western world, in both the religious and the secular spheres, such ecstatic expressions of emotion are less common, and they tend to be less intense when they do occur. Nonetheless, there are traditions in North America and Western Europe that encourage the expression of highly emotional ecstatic states. As we'll see, in several religious contexts, such as some sects and cults, and in evangelical revival meetings, ecstatic crowds have played a prominent role. On the secular side, some entertainers have appeared from time to time who have generated joyous, rapturous hysteria in their fans: for example, Frank Sinatra in the 1940s, Elvis Presley in the 1950s, the Beatles in the 1960s; more contemporaneously, New Kids on the Block, Two Live Crew, and Run DMC. Fans have shrieked, swooned, and literally fainted with excitement. They were clearly in a state of mind that fell outside the ordinary, everyday mental set; these fans were in ecstasy, out of their heads with passion and joy. An examination of film or video footage of these events shows that nearly all of those who seemed to be totally and utterly emotionally transported to another emotional plane were teenage girls. Moreover, those who reached this extreme end of the emotional continuum usually made up a minority of the crowd. In some political settings (Nazi Germany comes most readily to mind), Western society has generated wildly ecstatic crowds. Clearly, expressing a heightened positive emotional state at what might be called extraordinary, extranormative levels is not unknown in the modern, industrial West. However, it does tend to be more common in non-Western societies.

Too often, recent researchers of collective behavior have focused entirely on the negative side of crowds, the fear and hostility that crowds sometimes express, on the violence they commit. In contrast, a crowd gathering may express "collective joys"—"delight, gaiety, pleasure, jubilation, merriment, and bliss" (Lofland, 1981, p. 435). While much joy is expressed in small, especially two-person, groups, a great deal of it is manifested in crowds, and to that extent, may be examined by the field of collective behavior. Expressions of such joyous states include "hand clapping, dancing, singing, foot stomping, and cheering." At higher levels of intensity, they include "screaming, body shaking, glazed eyes, tranced demeanor, and fainting" (p. 436). By definition, the ecstatic state is "beyond reason and self-control"; it expresses "overwhelming emotion, especially rapturous delight," "intense emotional excitement," and "a state of exaltation" (p. 438). Not all the members of a given crowd need exhibit such expressions for us to label the assembly an "ecstatic" crowd, but a substantial proportion should—again, as with all definitions dealing with the social world, the exact line at which this can be drawn is a bit arbitrary.

There are, of course, *degrees* of collective ecstasy (Lofland, 1981, pp. 436ff; 1982; 1985, pp. 72–73); nonetheless, they all have similar features that bear investigating. How are these degrees or levels exhibited? How do we know that one crowd is more ecstatic, aroused, or joyful than another? First, there is variation in the "amount of motor activity" combined with the expression of a joyful or ecstatic emotion. The more vigorous and agitated the actions of the members of a crowd, the more ecstatic it is. Second, the higher the proportion of members displaying such high levels of motor activity, the more confident we are that we are looking at an ecstatic crowd. Third, the more that a *definition* of unusualness, sacredness, out-of-the-ordinariness is read into the gathering, the more ecstatic it is. Fourth, the more spontaneous, the more of a "surprise," the more *emergent* the actions, the more ecstatic it is. And last, the longer the action lasts, the more we have our hands on an ecstatic crowd (Lofland, 1985, pp. 72–73). Thus, while collective ecstasy or joy is a matter of degree, we usually know an ecstatic crowd when we see one.

For decades, the field of collective behavior has been trying to live down its reputation of focusing on irrational, emotionally charged behavior. Every few years, a sociologist rises up and states that collective behavior is no more irrational or emotionally charged than ordinary, everyday, conventional behavior. (For the latest such effort, see McPhail, 1991, 1992.) The "specter of LeBon" (Wenger, 1987, p. 215) still haunts the field, inasmuch as its practitioners find it necessary to refute some of this early theorist's more extreme statements about the supposed irrationality and emotionality of the crowd. I've already emphasized in Chapter 1 that the quality of irrationality probably plays no greater role in collective behavior than it does in more traditional behavior. But emotionality may be a slightly different matter. *While collective behavior is not necessarily highly emotional, most highly emotional group behavior is collective behavior.* It is difficult to think of many examples of emotionally charged group behavior that are *not* instances of collective behavior. The fact is, extreme emotional states rarely grow out of convention and tradition alone. Although highly emotional states may be *an aspect of* tradition in many cultures of the world, tradition alone does not spell out exactly how those states manifest themselves. To put things a bit differently, there is an element of spontaneity in all highly charged emotional states.

RITUAL VERSUS SPONTANEOUS ECSTASY

Some aspects of emotional, ecstatic states are tightly programmed and may be as predictable as the movement of the hands on a clock. We all know, for example, that during a ceremony in certain religions devotees will fall into a trance; the trance state is a standard fixture of religious expression, for example, in the Brazilian sects of *candomblé, umbanda, macumba,* and *batuque* (Landes, 1947; Leacock and Leacock, 1972; Birman, 1983). In this sense, then, trance in these traditions is not a pure type of collective behavior. But to the extent that, in a given culture, what the participants feel or do in the trance, or in any highly emotional state associated with specific ceremonies or activities, is *not* predictable or programmed, it can be said to be a clear-cut instance of collective behavior. However, given the fact that extreme emotional states felt in a group setting tend to be highly volatile and difficult to control, it should come as no surprise that they usually fall within the field of collective behavior.

McDaniel, in her study of ecstatic religion in Bengal, distinguishes between *ritual* and *spontaneous* ecstasy (1989, pp. 17–20), a distinction, she argues, that exists not only within the Indian religious tradition, but in Chinese Zen Buddhism and Christianity as well. Ritual ecstasy "conforms completely to doctrine, with ecstatic vision arising from expectation and imitation of previous models. It is regulated behavior, according to rule, following tradition and religious practices, emphasizing purity and obedience to authority. Ecstasy is similar among different practitioners, who take identical paths to an identical goal." A state regarded as "madness" would be "a failure of discipline, a break in concentration, a wrong word in the ritual" (p. 19). On the other hand, spontaneous ritual "is individual, different for different people"; it is "innate," coming to the individual "without effort." The person is "overcome by passion for a god, or possessed, or in a trance. Such a state is not limited by textual rules. Its emphasis is on mystery and intuition, the limits of its conscious will" (p. 19). Clearly, then, the more preprogrammed the emotion and the behavior, the less the field of collective behavior has to say about it. The less institutionalized and the more of a "surprise" it is, the more emergent and spontaneous it is (Lofland, 1985, pp. 72–73), the more it conforms to a "pure" type of collective behavior.

Clearly, in looking at the difference between "spontaneous" and "ritual" ecstasy, we have to distinguish between the reactions of the leaders of a crowd and those of the members of the crowd itself. Some crowd rituals are preplanned in great detail, but the responses of the members of the crowd to these rituals may be both genuine and spontaneous. Certainly Nazi political rallies must be included among the most spectacular—and frightening—examples of ecstatic crowds in human history. Although carefully staged, they generated a genuine, uncontrived, and extremely powerful emotional response from their audiences. In planning and executing these rallies, Adolph Hitler, Nazi leader and Chancellor of Germany (1933–1945) was acutely conscious of the principle of contagion. In his book, *Mein Kampf* ("My Struggle"), he remarks:

> When from his little workshop or big factory in which he [the individual] feels very small, he steps for the first time into a mass meeting and has thousands of people of the same opinion around him . . . he is swept away by three or four thousand others into the mighty effect of suggestive intoxication and enthusiasm, when the visible success and agreement of thousands confirm to him the rightness of the new doctrine [Nazism] and for the first time arouse doubt in the truth of his previous conviction—then he himself has succumbed to magic influence of mass . . . suggestion. The will, the longing, and also the power of thousands are accumulated in every individual. The man who enters such a meeting doubting and waver-

ing leaves it inwardly reinforced: he has become a link in the community.

While "always contrived and never spontaneous," Hitler's speeches were described by the faithful as "spellbinding." His audiences marched home "shoulder to shoulder . . . singing patriotic songs and shouting anti-Semitic slogans—their prejudices confirmed, their hopes rekindled by a man who identified himself with their fears and aspirations and in a masterful fashion promised to realize their deepest desires" (Carr, 1978, p. 5). Said Otto Strasser, an early Nazi who later defected, "His words go like an arrow to their target, he touches each private wound on the raw, liberating the unconscious, exposing its innermost aspirations, telling it what it most wants to hear" (1940, p. 65). What seemed to non-Germans (and to Germans of a democratic persuasion), and to nearly all contemporary observers, as little more than "empty gibberish" was, somehow, enormously moving to many Germans at the time. During the rallies, especially during Hitler's speeches, audiences felt as if they were "under the spell of a deep prayer" (Sinclair, 1938, p. 583). Said one of Hitler's early supporters

> My heart was pounding with curiosity and anticipation, I was awaiting the appearance of our Hitler from my seat in the crowded auditorium. A storm of jubilation rising from afar, from the street and moving into the lobby, announced the coming of the *Fuebrer*. And then suddenly the auditorium went wild, as he strode resolutely . . . to the rostrum. When the speech came to an end, I could not see out of my eyes any more. There were tears in my eyes, my throat was all tight from crying. A liberating scream of the purest enthusiasm discharged the unbearable tension as the auditorium rocked with applause. I looked around discreetly and noticed that others, too, men and women and young fellows, were as deeply moved as I. They also wiped tears from their eyes. Deafened and with an enormous sense of joy I stormed into the street. At last I was no longer alone. There were people around me who felt the same as I, who were looking at each other in joyful rapture, as if they were all one family or a brotherhood . . . and happy community where everyone could read in the others' eyes a solemn oath of loyalty. . . . This experience I had again and again during the course of the following years, and my feeling became ever stronger and deeper (Merkle, 1975, pp. 105–106).

Clearly, there are strong parallels between Nazi rallies and "revivalist gatherings of the old-fashioned bible-thumping variety, full of fire and brimstone. . . . There was the same infectious enthusiasm, the same electrically charged atmosphere, the same extraordinary credulity and the same intensity of feeling welding speaker and audience in a mystical union" (Carr, 1978, p. 5).

Religion and Ecstatic Crowds: The Limits of Contagion

As we might expect, religion provides the source for many instances of ecstatic crowds. At a weekend retreat sponsored by the Presbyterian church not long ago, an unusual episode of collective behavior broke out. Some 40 university students, along with a few working people of college age, attended the weekend retreat. Throughout Friday and during the day on Saturday, events "progressed according to plan," with the usual hymn singing, sermons, and Bible study. On Saturday night, an event known as the "fellowship of the burning heart" took place. It is a "well-established" and "fairly routinized affair," with people getting up and speaking, giving testimony about the benefits of prayer, Bible reading, and the like. "It is a very business-like arrangement with relatively little emotion involved." The "church extrovert" led a chorus of songs, "just as he had for years." An assistant pastor spoke briefly, led a prayer, and asked if "anyone felt led to give a brief testimony." The first few "were of the orthodox variety" (Hamilton, 1987, p. 24).

At that point, a young woman arose. She had been a member of the church for some time, and was regarded as one of the most attractive and popular of those who were present. She very rarely said anything at meetings such as this one. That night she said that, during the afternoon and again at the evening prayer meeting, "the Lord had spoken" to her "in a very real way." She hoped that God would give her the strength "to say what was upon" her heart. Amidst sobs, she said that, although she had been a member of the church for some time and had always regarded herself a Christian, she "never really knew Christ." As a result of the hardness of her heart and her selfishness, she said, she had "prevented Christ" from entering her life. Now, in front of her friends, she wanted to "confess Christ as my personal savior for I now know for the first time in my life what it really means to be born again" (p. 24).

As she spoke, the mood of the gathering shifted abruptly from "token reverence" to "absolute silence." As she spoke, people either stared at the ground or buried their heads in their hands. The silence following her testimony was broken by the assistant pastor, who said, "The Lord bless you." What followed was an outpouring of emotional testimony and confessional. "One after another individuals would arise, confessing everything from cheating on exams to fornication, each apparently outdoing the preceding in describing the intensity of his [or her] sinfulness" (p. 24). Most were delivered in "sobbing, choking voices." During these testimonies, about three-quarters of those present slipped to their knees in prayer. (Normally, Presbyterians, like other evangelical Protestants, never kneel in prayer, "so that this kneeling represented a considerable deviation from the usual Calvinist simplicity.") These testimonies continued for an hour and a half, each one lasting about 10 to 15 minutes (pp. 24–25).

Then, a young man who was studying for the ministry arose and stated that he believed that the testimonies were "in conflict with our Protestant heritage" and hindered rather than encouraged "our Christian development." Many of the things that were said there that night, he argued, "might better have been said in private prayer to our Lord rather than through public confession." This statement was followed by a protracted period of silence, which was broken when the assistant pastor said, "Let us pray." In his prayer, he said "the Lord speaks to his children in diverse ways." At which point, the meeting broke up. As the members of the group walked back to their quarters, the statement, "Well, the Lord's presence was certainly felt tonight," was overheard (Hamilton, 1987, p. 25).

Several things are noteworthy about this event. First, it was unplanned, relatively spontaneous, and extrainstitutional; it was outside what usually takes place, and is regarded as acceptable, during a Presbyterian religious retreat.

Second, what happened was clearly a group product; the example provided by the first young woman who gave her emotional testimony stimulated others to do so and, in fact, charged the group as a whole with a feeling of collective excitement. In short, there was a "contagion of religious excitement" (Turner and Killian, 1987, p. 25). However, there are clearly limits to contagion, because the intensified mood did not grip everyone nor was approved by everyone—including the ministry student who spoke out against the proceedings and the author of the account (Hamilton, 1987).

Third, for some, there was a "rapid formation of a norm that defined a certain type of behavior"—religious expressiveness and excitement—"as appropriate to the situation" (p. 25). What was previously regarded as unacceptable in the gathering of that crowd, came to be seen as acceptable. In short, *emergent norm* theory is relevant here. However, once again, the revised norm did not meet with universal approval.

And fourth, there may have been a process of convergence operating here. It is possible that individuals who were prone to, and who had previously experienced, religious excitement in gatherings were specifically those who experienced it at the retreat, while those who had always found such overtness of expression unacceptable also did so there. However, as with contagion, convergence has its limits, since the young woman who was first to offer her emotion-filled testimony very rarely spoke out at meetings.

In short, gatherings charged with intense religious fervor may provide an excellent setting in which to examine the dynamics of collective behavior.

A Religious Leader Is Buried

In June, 1989, Ayatollah Rudollah Khomenei, the Islamic cleric who led the uprising that overthrew the Shah of Iran, Mohammed Reza Pahlavi, and who dominated Iran for a decade, died and was buried. His funeral procession, which lasted for two days, was an extraordinarily emotional affair, and provides a good example of an ecstatic crowd.

The number of mourners in attendance was estimated at some

three million. So huge and emotional was the crowd, so anxious were its members to push forward and be near their leader, that the funeral was delayed more than five hours; in fact, at one point, authorities feared that the cleric's burial would have to be put off for another day.

The mourning was described as "frenzied." On the first day, eight people were trampled to death in the procession. "We have lost our father!" mourners chanted at one point. "This nation, what will we do without you?" "Over and over again, all day long, the mourners beat themselves on the head and chest," in accordance with the funeral ritual of the cleric's Shi'ite sect. "Fire hoses played over the crowds to cool them down." Khomenei's coffin, transferred to an army helicopter because the truck carrying it could not get through the crowd, was seized by the crowd and pulled from the craft. His body was yanked out of its coffin by the surging, "nearly hysterical" crowd, desperate to touch it and its shroud, and was carried off. Soldiers "pushed and wrestled, finally firing warning shots, to get the body back." Even as soldiers managed to get the body into the helicopter, the crowd swarmed over the craft, and dragged it back down as it attempted to take off. "People love him too much to let him go," said one mourner.

Another "mad scene of pushing and shoving" followed the helicopter's landing at the burial site "as the body was moved toward the grave." Custom in Iran dictates that bodies should be buried in a grave only in a shroud and without a coffin. The top of the coffin was ripped off, carried away, and "wrenched to pieces" by the crowd. Two hours after the cleric's burial, "vast crowds still stretched around his grave, slamming both hands against their heads in grief."

"O martyr!" cried the announcer on state television, breaking into tears (Kifner, 1989).

TYPES OF ECSTATIC CROWDS

Three types of ecstatic crowds will be discussed here: revival meetings, sporting events, and carnaval.

REVIVAL MEETINGS

One of the more spectacular settings in which religious ecstasy is expressed by and in a crowd is the snake-handling cult that emerged in the South in the late 1940s and early 1950s. In the Bible, Mark 14, Verse 17 contains the line, "They shall take up serpents." Although other biblical texts contain lines that counsel against snake handling, this one has been interpreted by some as encouraging the practice. During its ceremonies, poi-

The burial of Ayatollah Ruholla Khomenei in 1989 was described as "frenzied." Here, mourners fight to touch the Ayatollah's body.

sonous snakes, representing Satan, are grasped, passed from one person to another, and stroked; snakes' heads are brushed against the faces of members of the audience—all of this as a test of religious faith. While this is going on, some members of the audience are "shaking" and "jerking their heads and bodies around wildly"; some perform "a vivacious dance" and speak in "unknown tongues"; some stand "trance-eyed," "their eyes closed and their mouths open"; and some are "dazed," are "sobbing and crying out" while others are "shouting and singing" (LaBarre, 1969, pp. 6–9).

The Southern snake-handling cult was short lived and, even in its heyday, never widespread. On the other hand, the ecstatic crowds that gather for evangelical Christian services, sermons, and meetings persist to this day, have a long tradition, and number in the tens of millions people. The root *evangel* stems from the ancient Greek; it means "good news." Evangelical Christianity stresses the importance of personal conversion; direct, emotional religious experience; enthusiastic congregational response; the expiation of sin through public testimony and ceremonial participation; and the strong, personal presence of Jesus Christ in religious ceremony. Most evangelical Christians believe in the Second Coming of Christ in a quite literal, concrete, and imminent way. Well-known evangelical ministers include Billy Graham, Jimmy Swaggart, Jerry Fallwell, and Jim Bakker. Within evangelism, there is a tradition that argues that religious faith must be renewed from time to time through *revivals*. For many, religious practice has become a stale, routine, meaningless rote ritual; former believers have fallen away from the church; secularism has eroded righteous faith. Today's evangelists have retained something of the style of the old-time revivalists, although the style of revivalism has tempered and moderated with time and a more secular audience whose members live less isolated, more complex lives.

Revival meetings took place throughout the 19th, and into the 20th, century. Even today, although less flamboyant and expressive than in the past, revival meetings are extremely emotional and represent excellent examples of collective behavior. All revival meetings have a dual character—positive and negative. On the one hand, their leaders denounce sin; such meetings share in some of the qualities of the hostile crowd (Lofland, 1985, pp. 42, 54–63), and they stimulate audience fears. Thus, these gatherings take on elements of the fearful crowd (pp. 42, 46–53). But they also display the opposite or positive side as well—in fact, a successful revival meeting sends an audience away uplifted and full of joy. In short, the best revival meetings are examples of the ecstatic crowd.

Mainstream Christianity has never been entirely comfortable with revivalism. It sees the emotionalism generated by revival meetings as unstable, bringing forth many souls who profess to be "born again," whose commitment is shallow and temporary. Carol Flake, a former evangelical Christian, dubs revival meetings "praying with fire" and "pep rallies of the soul." She quotes several 19th century ministers skeptical of the revivalist tradition who say that revival meetings are like a brush fire a farmer uses to clear his land; if kept under control, it can hasten the harvest, but if it gets out of control, it can burn down the barn. They warn of the "extravagance of disorder" and the "semi-barbarism" that can result from "the release of pent-up passions in a revival meeting" (Flake, 1984, p. 30).

Revival meetings possess the following eight qualities. First, they are *emotional*. The emotion expressed by speaker and audience member alike can often be overpowering, sometimes obliterating their intellect. Said one individual at a New York camp meeting; "Bretheren, I feel—I feel—I feel—I feel—I feel—I can't tell you how I feel, but O I feel! I feel!" (Pratt, 1920, p. 184). All revivalist preachers recognize that they must first excite strong emotions before they can win converts, and all good revivalist preachers are successful in that aim. Again, this emotionalism has tempered somewhat in our secular age, but heightened emotion is inherent in all revivalism.

Second, there is a great deal of active *audience participation*. Members of the audience sing, clap their hands, shout encouragement ("Amen, brother!" "Praise the Lord!"), stamp their feet, jump up and down, cheer, and sometimes even faint. Compared with the more restrained, liturgical tradition of Catholics and mainstream Protestants, in evangelism generally and in the revival tradition specifically, emotional expression is given a free reign. Revival meetings are perfect illustrations of a group in which the leader interacts with and stimulates members of the audience to give expression to their deepest feelings, thereby stimulating the crowd as a whole to do so.

Third, the sermon is delivered in a *dramatic* and *vivid* fashion. The gestures and tone of voice of the preacher are far more important than the content of his or her words. Sermons are part entertainment, part theater. Of Billy Sunday (1863–1935), one of the most famous and influential evangelical preachers of all time, it was said, "He could make twenty thousand persons follow his address and keep their eyes fastened on him from beginning to end. He did this in part with his voice, a peculiarly rasping and hoarse voice but one which was capable of a wide range of expression. . . . He spoke at the rate of three thousand words per minute, but his sentences were short and simple, and he acted out every word he uttered. . . . Like any experienced showman he knew how to draw laughter or applause, how to wait for it, and when to repeat a line or vary it slightly a second time in order to wring the full response from it." The drama of his performance "was heightened by his pounding the pulpit, standing on a chair, swinging a chair over his head, sliding, jumping, falling, staggering, whirling, and even doing handsprings" (McLoughlin, 1959, p. 426). Even today, and even on television, evangelism is watched for its "sheer entertainment value"; it is "a damned good show" (Packard, 1988, p. 226).

Fourth, the ceremony of the revival meeting is—or rather, must seem to be—*completely spontaneous*, even if the same sermon has been delivered a hundred times before. Everything that takes place must seem to be "innate," issuing directly from the soul, inspired by God, unrehearsed, charismatic (a "gift of the spirit"), as if it descended from the heavens.

Fifth, logic and fact are entirely secondary in the revival meeting; what counts is *faith*. Doubt and reason are put aside; what is important is making the members of the audience want to believe in the message with all their hearts, making them feel that they ought to believe. "To doubt would be disloyal, to falter would be sin." Such a faith "produces seeming miracles and regularly accomplishes the impossible." It "stops the mouths of lions, quenches the violence of fire, and endures without complaint the unheralded drudgery of the common day" (Pratt, 1920, pp. 190, 191). Most revivalists rail against the intellect as inhibitory to faith; they preach a life of certitude (Packard, 1988, p. 154).

Sixth, in the sermon, the world is painted in *black-or-white* terms. Billy Sunday reduced his doctrine to ten simple words: "With Christ you are saved, without him you are lost." His theology represented a simple choice of heaven or hell: "You are going to live forever in heaven or you are going to live forever in hell. There's no other place—just the two. It is for you to decide. It's up to you and you must decide now" (McLoughlin, 1959, p. 409). Satan is evil, God is good; what counts is recognizing which is which and making the right choice—nothing else whatsoever matters in life. All subtlety, complexity, and qualifications are seen as nit-picking, and detract from the central message.

Seventh, the audience must be *terrified by the wrath of God*. Entertaining "anecdotes and theatrics" are "not enough." To change people "from selfishness to benevolence, from complacency to conviction," it is often "necessary to threaten or even frighten them." Said Charles Grandison Finney (1792–1875), one of the most successful of America's 19th century revivalists, sinners are wicked and disobedient children who must see "the rod uplifted" before they will submit. "Look, look, see the millions of wretches biting and gnawing their tongues as they lift up their scalding heads from the burning lake [of hell]. . . . Hear them groan amidst the fiery billows as they lash and lash and lash their burning shores" (McLoughlin, 1959, p. 89). This "hellfire-and-brimstone" approach to preaching has certainly declined in popularity over time, but, compared with other religious traditions, revivalism has always, and will always, include an element of threat and an appeal to fear and terror.

And eighth, *the joy of salvation* is offered. Even the worst of sinners are told, "God loves you, and you may be saved." Everyone in the audience is told that they can walk down that "sawdust trail," testify for Christ, be "born again," and achieve enternal salvation. The climax of any revival meeting is the call for converts. Ultimately, the success of all revival meetings is measured by the number of converts won and the amount of money contributed. Preaching is good if it wins souls and bad if it does not (McLoughlin, 1959, p. 87). Everything in the revival ceremony—the arousal of strong emotion, collective enthusiasm, audience participation, the preacher's theatrics, the hellfire-and-brimstone sermon—is directed toward a single aim: winning souls. However, all too often, revivalists remind themselves, sinners seem to think that getting emotionally aroused at a meeting and declaring for Christ is enough. Religious conviction must carry over into the rest of their lives; converts may fall back into a life of sin after the revivalist has moved on to a new community. The charisma of the revival meeting must be routinized into everyday patterns of worship. In other words, collective behavior must be coverted into conventional, everyday, institutionalized behavior.

SPORTING EVENTS

The fans gathered at a sporting event display elements of the ecstatic crowd; but, at the same time, they also exhibit some features that are very different. For many fans, athletic contests are intensely exciting; they engage their emotions profoundly and extravagantly. The most dramatic moments of a game are often an "out of one's head" experience for spectators, generating a wildly cheering and screaming mob. Janet Lever's book on Brazilian soccer, titled *Soccer Madness* (1983), includes a photograph of a female fan so transported with ecstasy that she fainted. It can hardly be doubted that sporting events house one variety of the ecstatic crowd.

Why are athletic contests so exciting to spectators? Why is the emotional involvement of fans often so intense that we are forced to see sports crowds as a form of the ecstatic crowd? There are many factors, of course. Most athletic contests are (potentially at least) intrinsically dramatic, and no elaborate sociological or psychological explanations need be invoked to explain fan ecstasy or even enthusiasm. At the same time, put a sports enthusiast in a stadium in which unfamilar teams compete at an unfamiliar sport and the chances are, he or she will find the experience less than gripping. Thus, more than the intrinsic nature of sports is at work here.

Some observers argue that the egocentric bias is what fuels the excitement and ecstasy often observed among fans of sporting events (Cialdini, 1984, pp. 191–199), that is, people find sporting events exciting because, in a sense, they see themselves on the playing field. As a general rule, people "strive to link themselves to positive events and separate themselves from negative events—even when they have not caused the events" (p. 191). Thus, a fan would feel personally diminished "by a hometown defeat" and personally "enhanced by a hometown victory" (p. 194). By identifying strongly with the home team, in effect, we are saying that when the home team wins, *we* win, and thereby demonstrate our personal superiority; when the home team loses, *we* lose, and thereby admit our personal inferiority. We want to "bask in reflected glory" if the home team wins and "attempt to avoid being darkened by the shadow" of defeat when it loses. At prominent football universities, students are significantly more likely to wear home school shirts the Monday after a victory than is true if their team loses; moreover, the bigger the margin of victory, the more such shirts are worn (pp. 194–195). When a home team wins, fans refer to the team as "we"; when it loses, they refer to it as "they" (p. 196).

No wonder sports spectators become so involved with sporting events: The home team is quite literally a representation of the fan! When a spectator screams at a play, he or she is actually screaming for himself or herself out there! The fan's ego is on the line: If the team loses, the fan feels inferior; if it wins, he or she feels good about himself or herself. A lot is riding on the outcome of the game. There are, however, ways in which the emotions of the crowd at sporting events are quite different from the positive emotion of the ecstatic crowd. Perhaps the most prominent is the instability of the mood of the crowd at an athletic contest. As we've already seen (Hazleton, 1989a, 1989b; Barron, 1984), sports crowds often turn violent; as a general rule, the more ecstatic fans are, the greater the likelihood they could become angry and violent.

The anthropologist Felicitas Goodman interviews a Mexican soccer fan who explains this duality of mood in sporting events as follows.

> When you watch a soccer game, it is like good and evil being played out. You believe in your own team, it can do nothing wrong. The bad guys are the other team. You go to a game because everybody goes. But once you are there, everything changes. The flags are waving, and there is a lot of color, a lot of green. Your favorite team is on one side, they look so good in their uniforms. The other team is there, too . . ., but you don't pay too much attention to them. They play the national anthem. In school you had to learn it, and probably you didn't care for it. But now it sounds great and everybody sings along.

The other team's national anthem is played too, but that doesn't sound impressive at all.

When the match starts, you want your team to win, and no matter what they do, everything is always right. Whether they kick a field goal, or just dribble, it doesn't matter. It's so beautiful, you've never seen anything like that before. But when the other team does the same thing, it looks terrible, it doesn't have the same class.

You start shouting and screaming, and you can shout obscenities, nobody knows what it is you're shouting. Everyone does the same thing, and you never realize that you are shouting that much until when the game is over and you calm down, then you realize that your throat is hurting. Maybe two or three days later you still can't talk because your throat is really sore.

At some point you get the feeling that you don't care what happens to you. If there were violence, I could get involved because I don't perceive things clearly anymore. All you know is that you want to do something. If something were to trigger a riot, I would want to participate. Everyone is one unit, you don't have any responsibility. . . .

You want your team to win so badly that if the Devil were to exist and would arrive at that point and ask you for your soul in exchange for your team winning, you wouldn't give it a second thought. You would say yes, whatever that might mean. Your body goes into contortions, you want your team to win so badly. Then when it loses, you simply can't stand it. I feel real low, terrible, for days. When it wins, you are happy (Goodman, 1988, pp. 162–163).

Sporting events, Goodman argues, are a "secular ritual" and actually represent "giant exorcisms," confrontations that cease to be vicarious contests to the fans and end up being a genuine, personal experience. They "bring out crowds and arouse passions" to cast out the feelings generated by the intense pressure cooker atmosphere of contemporary urban life (p. 163). In short, the ecstatic, "out of their heads" mood of sports fans is nearly always fueled by the conditions of their everyday lives. In January 1991, 40 fans were killed in a riot at a soccer match in South Africa after an unpopular call by an official. The riot did not burst forth out of nowhere, but was inflamed by recent events, as well as the social conditions that prevail today in South Africa. Just the day before, 35 mourners were massacred at a funeral in a nearby township, thereby generating a mood of tension, anxiety, anger, and fear (Wren, 1991). Clearly, sports offer an arena in which intense passion is aroused, fans feel directly and personally involved, and violence is never very far away.

Once again, we should remind ourselves not to fall victim to the "illusion of unanimity." Not all fans are equally intense in their focus and emotional expression. Snow, Zurcher, and Peters (1981) demonstrate that crowds in victory celebrations are diverse rather than monolithic, and act in a variety of ways. In fact, this is so much the case that we should think in terms of different *segments* or *categories* within a given crowd—or, even better, *different smaller crowds* within a large assemblage of people, which may engage in "disparate behaviors" (p. 28). Moreover, there is social interaction between and among these categories and a social presentation by the members of certain categories to one or more of the others. In some, the assembled come to define specific actions as appropriate as a result of their interaction with the other categories. For instance, celebrants may consider the impact their behavior is having on *bystander crowds* and even more farflung *bystander publics* who monitor, evaluate, and even influence the former's behavior. Often, if celebrants become too unruly or destructive, bystanders, whether in the immediate vicininty or in the public at large, can provide feedback to them which will put a damper on their enthusiasm (Snow, Zurcher, and Peters, 1981). Once again, neither convergence nor contagion theory offers an adequate or complete analysis of victory celebrations following a sporting event. While in such crowds, celebrants may be more unrestrained than in their everyday lives, yet their behavior is never unchecked, totally spontaneous, or wholly outside institutional and normative commitments and entanglements.

CARNAVAL[1]

Brazil's carnaval offers a good example of an occasion that generates joyous, revelous crowds.[2] Carnaval has qualities that put it at least partly within the realm of collective behavior; many of the feelings and expressions of ecstatic states are in evidence during carnaval. Nonetheless, it is not a pure type of collective behavior. Since it occurs regularly, parts of it are fairly well organized, even institutionalized; there are rules, and its gaity can, to some degree, be predicted. In fact, one feature of the festive occasion known as carnaval that has emerged in recent years is what can be called *the routinization of carnaval*, which I'll explain shortly. Still, carnaval is characterized by a certain measure of spontaneity and strong emotion and, hence, has one foot planted in the realm of collective behavior.

Carnaval is a period of festivity in many Catholic countries around the world. Its roots extend back to the fertility rites of pre-Christian Egypt, Greece, and, especially, the Roman Saturnalia or orgiastic festivals for the god Saturn. Today, carnaval is celebrated just before Lent; more specifically, it begins the weekend before Ash Wednesday and ends on the first day of Lent, that is, Ash Wednesday itself. In the United States, it is celebrated main-

---

[1]The Portuguese spelling, *carnaval,* is used rather than its English counterpart, *carnival.*

[2]The following account is based on Critchfield, 1978; DaMatta, 1978, 1981, 1984; and the author's personal observations.

ly in two locales: One, in New Orleans, in the form of Mardi Gras ("fat Tuesday," or Shrove Tuesday), and two, in communities with a substantial number of Caribbean residents. (The celebration called *carnivale*, celebrated in some Italian-American communities, is a considerably quieter and more toned-down version of its Latin cousins.)

In Brazil, carnaval is celebrated enthusiastically with festivities, parties, dances, and parades. The atmosphere is gay, revelous, spontaneous, and fun. Although one might get the impression that "anything goes" during carnaval, clearly, some behaviors are regarded as deviant, such as violence and stealing. (They are more common during carnaval than they are during the rest of the year, and more common in some cities than in others, but they are still unacceptable behaviors. Critchfield, 1978, suggests that this may not be entirely true for Salvador, however.) The point is, the range of permitted behavior during carnaval is much wider than is true of all other times during the year. It is said that *carnavalization does not have a text* (DaMatta, 1981, pp. 95–97). In other words, what happens during carnaval is something you make up as you go along; it is, by its very nature, relatively spontaneous and ruleless.

Much of the activity during carnaval entails dancing in the street to a pulsating samba beat. There is dancing, shouting, laughing, singing, and general cavorting about. Drums throb, lights flash, and confetti is thrown into the air. It is a body and psychic experience that takes you outside your rational self; it is compulsive and ecstatic. Critchfield describes the street crowd during carnaval in Brazil as "a human mass of bobbing heads and raised flailing arms, a raging mob, mindless, plunging, twisting, stamping, twirling forward, its path a swarm of seething, panting bodies. . . . Mists of confetti drift down from the roofs and balconies, falling on heads like snow. . . . Someone is tossed high into the air by his companions and lands with shouts, bounding back into the mass. . . . The drums beat faster and faster until it seems thunder is rising from the pavement. The dancers break loose, their eyes flashing, faces filled with laughter, their four limbs whirling about them as they speed up their rhythm, defying equilibrium. . . . Nothing stops the mob, dancing, pushing and shoving forward with flailing fists and whirling bodies." It is, he says, a "mindless eruption of joy," a "bursting free" (1978, pp. 53, 54).

Carnaval has several important qualities that set it apart from everyday life. The first is that it is *distinctly unserious.* It is play, recreation, pure pleasure, spontaneity, hedonism; it extends outside the boundaries of the workaday world. What happens during carnaval should have no real-life, material consequences; one is allowed to forget the demands of the everyday world. Death, poverty, hunger, taxes—these are suspended for a time, or even made fun of. The point is to have a good time. Second, carnaval is a *fantasy*; in fact, the Portuguese word for costume is *fantasia.* Much of the real world is turned on its head during carnaval; in many ways, it is the opposite of everyday life. During carnaval, the streets, which during the year belong to cars—that is to say, to the middle classes who are able to afford cars—belong to "the people," that is, to the lower and working classes. Women, who are ordinarily regarded in this Latin country as inferior, become the "center of the world"; the world of carnaval is a "feminized" world (DaMatta, 1981, pp. 53–55, 45ff). Poor Blacks, usually at the bottom of the economic and political heap in Brazil, are the main focus of attention, at least during the most important parades. Poor people can dress up as kings and queens; rich people may dress in the costume of a bum, a derelict, or a clown.

In Brazil, there are two kinds of carnaval—street carnavals and club carnavals (DaMatta, 1978, pp. 70ff; 1981, pp. 35–43). Street carnavals are open to anyone without distinction; everyone in the vicinity may take part. People may or may not wear costumes, walk out onto the street, take part, begin dancing, have a good time, and be the equal of anyone else there. Here, there is no real audience, no distinction between a participant and an observer. Street carnavals are social levelers; social distinctions that rule at other times become irrelevant. In contrast, club carnavals cost money; are closed except to members only; and have elitist, "aristocratic" tendencies. Only the affluent and socially prestigious may join and participate. Street carnavals are what everyone—tourist and ordinary Brazilian citizen alike—sees and associates with the phenomenon of carnaval. Street carnavals imply *decontrol* and "massification"; club carnavals imply *control* and "authoritarianism" (DaMatta, 1978, p. 70). Street carnavals take place out in the open; club carnavals take place in private, behind closed doors, in a hall or a building; they are organized and "run" by someone in authority.

Street celebrations during carnaval in certain poor neighborhoods have become so well-known, the costumes of their participants so magnificent, their dances so skilled and elaborate, that these previously spontaneous neighborhood gatherings have organized into associations or "schools" (*escolas de samba*), which vie with one other during an annual competition. In Rio, where the best and most famous schools are located, there is a huge, nationally televised contest among the top-ranked categories of these schools. In 1983, a multimillion-dollar, quarter-mile long facility called the "Sambadrome" was built specifically for the contest. During carnaval, hundreds of thousands of people pack the Sambadrome to watch the nearly 24-hour contest, held on two consecutive nights starting at 8:00 P.M. and running each night into the early morning hours. In addition, a national television audience of tens of millions of Brazilians also watch the event. One club will win and achieve prestige and honor much like that of winning the Super Bowl or the World Series in the United States, and one club will be knocked out of the front rank of the top 15 samba schools, to be replaced by a school that was previously in a lower category. Scoring is conducted by a panel of experts; it is extremely detailed and based on a series of specific criteria— song, theme, costumes, floats, dancing, and so on. The contest entails a march or parade by the members of each of the top-ranked *escolas de samba* to the beat of a popular song, written especially for the occasion and released months before.

Actually, "marching" isn't a very good term for what the members of these samba schools do; North American marches and parades are much more tightly organized than the Brazilian march, parade, or, in Portuguese, *desfile*.

In Brazilian parades, participants do not march; they swirl, prance, dance, samba, strut, and "boogy." Although carefully choreographed and synchronized, it is organized in a looser, more spirited, more free-flowing, and less tightly coordinated fashion than is true of North American parades. Each school has roughly a thousand members, dancing to the beat of its own percussion section, some 300 members strong. Members wear elaborately coordinated costumes and they march in sections, called *blocos*. Each school depicts a theme—such as the seven deadly sins, soccer through history, or the contributions that Bahia, a state in Brazil, has made to the country's culture. In addition to the marchers, huge, elaborate, magnificent floats, or *allegorias* are pushed along in the parade by members. (Motorized floats are not allowed.) A member may spend a month's salary on a costume; a school may spend half a million dollars or more competing in the contest. Each top-ranked school receives a sum of money from the Brazilian government—not nearly enough to cover its cost—and private patrons support the schools as well (the most generous of such patrons are the men who run the country's illegal lottery).

Thus, what began as more or less open, spontaneous street carnavals in poor neighborhoods has turned into a highly elaborate, highly organized, and highly institutionalized affair. Clearly, in this case, the spontaneity has disappeared; the joy is somewhat artificial and staged (especially in Rio, where the institutionalization of carnaval has reached its pinnacle, it is difficult to call these spectacles collective behavior). Of course, there are still street carnavals in poor neighborhoods in Rio that do have this spontaneous, ecstatic quality, just as there is sand-lot baseball in the United States in addition to the World Series. And in smaller cities, of course, street carnaval is spirited, impulsive, uninhibited, and spontaneous (Critchfield, 1978). But the most visible representative of Brazil's carnaval is anything but spontaneous: There is a rigid distinction between participants and audience; the passive audience is huge; and every aspect of a school's performance is recorded for posterity and carefully evaluated (down to the tiniest detail) by experts. Any misstep by a participant can mean the difference between winning and losing, between remaining in the top rank and being relegated to a lower category. There is an immense organization of labor: the performance of each school (including costumes), the percussion section, the members of each *bloco*, the men who pull the floats. In short, what was once spontaneous, free-flowing fun has become a routinized, institutionalized performance; what was once collective behavior has become traditional, conventional, and normative.

What Are Miracles?

Although miracles are often witnessed or eagerly awaited by crowds, not all the processes that contribute to seeing miracles grow out of crowd dynamics. Receptive audiences make it possible for certain individuals who are members of such a crowd to see a miracle, but there are individual processes operating as well. Not everyone exposed to what the others around them see as a miraculous stimulus actually see a miracle. Individual members of an audience must be *open* to the idea of miracles occurring, must believe that they are possible, that God (or whatever supernatural force they believe in) manifests himself (or herself or itself) in extraordinary, overt actions in the material world. The inception of a miraculous event is often experienced not in a crowd setting but by a single individual or small group of individuals, who conveys that experience to others. At that point, the miracle becomes as much a public phenomenon as compact collectivities. In fact, as Lofland (1985, p. 37) says, "The attitude of everyday life is probably suspended most frequently by individuals or by very small groups rather than by collectivities of significant size." Thus, the individual perception of a miracle, outside a group setting, is often a *building block* for its collective perception, including the crowd.

Late one summer evening, Rita Ratchen, 58, resident of a small town in Ohio, grandmother, devout Catholic, and independent businesswoman, was driving along Route 12 when her gaze fell on the side of a soybean oil storage tank. "Oh, my Lord, my God!" she exclaimed, crossing her arms over her heart. Nearly driving off the road in excitement, she required a few seconds to compose herself. Ms. Ratchen decided not to report her vision to anyone; "I didn't want to be put away," she said. After four days, however, she finally relented and drove her best friend to the spot, parked the car on the shoulder of the road, and pointed to the tank. Her friend "saw it immediately." Said Ms. Ratchen, "Oh boy, two kooks now!" The next night, they showed the image to another friend. Over the next week, word spread through the community "like prairie fire." One night there were a dozen cars parked near the tank; the next night, 20; soon there were 150. One resident said that one night, there were so many parked cars, it took an hour and a half to drive two miles past the spot. A lot of people were seeing the same thing that Rita Ratchen had seen a just a few days before.

The storage tank had been painted a yellowish-orange, but the tank had rusted in spots, so that portions of it were a brownish-orange color; if one looked at it a certain way, one could make out the figure of a man in a robe, arms outstretched, standing next to a child. To a viewer with a traditional Christian background, the image appeared to be a vision of Jesus. Some who saw it took its appearance as a kind of miracle.

The local newspaper was contacted about the vision. At first, the editor was skeptical, but finally, he ran the story: "Image of Christ Reported West of Town." (It should be said that the image was so faint that the editor had to hire an artist to sketch an outline on the photograph accompanying his story so that it could be seen by the paper's readers.) Soon thereafter, the news agency Reuters picked up the news, and before long, the image had generated "a stampede." A photographer sold hundreds of photographs of the image at $2 apiece; "I'm getting calls from all over the United States," he said. Local entrepreneurs sold thousands of coffee mugs and T-shirts with "I Saw The Image" printed on them. A restaurant down the road from the tank jumped in business volume from 53rd place in a 55-restaurant chain to third place. After several weeks, the local newspaper was criticized for letting the story fall out of the news; the editor explained that he couldn't think of anything more to say about the tank. "I'm imaged to death," he said. "We shot it from the air. We shot it in the daytime. We shot it at night. What else can I do?" The tank owner threatened to paint over the image; a "save the tank" movement immediately sprang up. The faithful simply didn't want to let go of the image or the story.

In summing up her feelings about the image, Rita Ratchen, who saw it first, said: "I see it as a natural phenomenon. . . . It is caused by the lights and the rust, but I believe that the Lord permitted it to happen. Just as I believe the Lord permits things to happen in our lives, even illness, in order to bring us closer together." Perhaps anticipating criticism of her view, she added, "Besides, if they took me to the nut house now, they'd have to take thousands with me" (Jaynes, 1986, p. 14).

The reactions of some to the image that was seen in Ohio are a form of "extrainstitutional" behavior; they are outside the everyday, the routine, the normative. People living in a rational, sophisticated, highly educated society are not "supposed" to see an image of Jesus in patterns of paint and rust on the side of a soybean oil storage tank. In addition, miracles often run counter to institutionalized structures; they may challenge the power of entrenched authorities, transferring legitimacy from a certain hierarchy, like the church, to some very humble people. (Unless that hierarchy is clever enough to coopt, legitimate, use, and exploit those reactions to its own advantage.) Say two sociologists with reference to a particular miracle that took place in Puerto Rico: "Could it be that the response of the crowd was in part a reaction against the church hierarchy; that here each man [and woman] found himself [or herself] on an equal footing with all others in his [or her] relation to the Divinity; and that the words coming out of the mouths of babes was [*sic*] seen and felt directly and immediately as more deeply commanding of fervor and belief?" (Tumin and Feldman, 1955, p. 136).

The reactions of those who see miracles are usually spontaneous rather than preprogrammed; they cannot be predicted from the condition of the physical world itself. In miracles, mass culture is "at its height: democratic, spontaneous, uninhibited, emotionally gratifying" (Tumin and Feldman, 1955, pp. 136–137). What happens, we must ask, in that instant between the sight of a particular image or the occurrence of a certain event and public reaction to it? Some viewers saw the image on the tank, and some didn't. What translates the image, or an event, *into* a miracle? Seeing a vision of Jesus on the tank was, to a large degree, socially and individually *patterned*, that is, was influenced by social and individual background characteristics: For instance, Catholics were more likely to see the vision than non-Catholics; believers, in general, more so than nonbelievers. And, after one person saw the vision and pointed it out to others, many more people began to see it. The vision was, in short, truly *collective*. Lastly, miracles often take place, or are validated, in crowds—and thus, everything we've said so far about the dynamics of crowds generally applies to miracles specifically. In fact, miracles provide an almost perfect example of collective behavior. It is unfortunate that they have not been studied more by the field.

RELIGIOUS MIRACLES:
_____ SCIENCE AND THE LAWS OF NATURE _____

As students of collective behavior, there are three basic positions we could adopt with respect to the literal, concrete occurrence of miracles. The first is the position of the *believer;* that is, that the miracles happened or, at least, *some* of them literally and concretely happened. The second is the position of the *disbeliever;* that is, that the miracles *didn't* happen—in fact, *couldn't* have happened. And the third is that of the *agnostic;* that is, that it doesn't much matter whether the miracles happened or not—the *perception*, the social patterning, and the consequences of miracles are what count and need to be explained.

The first or the believer position, that they happened, does not require an explanation of why they are seen; people see miracles because they literally and concretely occurred. In a given miraculous event, they simply saw what was "out there" in the material world, much as they would see a cloud, a tree, a car driving by. A miracle is "there for all to see," or at least, there for the faithful to see. Far from needing to explain why people see miracles, believers argue, what is problematic is why certain people *don't* see miracles and don't *believe* the stories of those who do. There are few, if any, experts in the field of collective behavior who hold this position.

The second or disbeliever position, that miracles did not literally and concretely occur, demands an explanation of *why they are perceived.* To the disbeliever, the most important thing about miracles is that they are false; what the disbeliever wants to do is to *disprove* miraculous claims. *Debunking* is the disbeliever's primary interest. If they did not take place, why were they seen? How can someone see something that isn't really there? It is the *departure* of such a perception from reality, their contradiction with what science knows to be true, that makes such a phenomenon interesting. Miracles are by their very nature scientifically *impossible*, the disbeliever would say; our job is to debunk them so that no one will believe that they happened. Disbelievers feel there is something different, unusual, and, in all likelihood, pathological with someone who believes in miracles.

In some ways, the third or agnostic position is a great deal like the second or disbeliever point of view in that both agree that *the perception of miracles needs to be explained.* To both, miracles are not simply a set of events or physical stimuli that everyone, or everyone who is receptive, would perceive "out there" in the real world as a readily observable physical reality. At the same time, to the agnostic, the literal occurrence of a miracle is a secondary, almost irrelevant question. The theological question of whether they are real or were guided by the hand of God does not interest the agnostic. What is important is that they *were* seen and believed by some and that they *do* play a significant part in their lives. Such visions may be culturally patterned and are not a sign of pathology. Some people see things a certain way because such an interpetation dovetails with their backgrounds and the lives of the people with whom they interact in comfortable, gratifying ways. Furthermore, such people use their vision to strengthen their beliefs, and they act in such a way that those beliefs are verified. They communicate it to others, finding a community of the faithful who also use the image to reinforce their faith; this collective validation further strengthens it. Thus, some students and researchers do not go around proving *or* disproving the authenticity of miracles. They try to understand how they got started, who believes in them (as well as who doesn't) and how that belief influences or reinforces the lives of believers, both on the individual and the collective level.

Still, the question of how people come to see something that really "isn't there" cannot be ignored. The concrete, literal reality of miracles cannot be sidestepped. How are miraculous visions seen? The chances are, both the disbeliever and the agnostic positions would agree on this process. It happens in the following fashion. People respond in a certain way to *ambiguous physical stimuli* in their environment; they use what they see as *raw material* out of which to construct a certain vision. They "see" Jesus on a storage tank because they have learned that God manifests himself in physical form. Someone who did not grow up in a Christian tradition and who does not believe that God creates such physical forms would just see blotchy colors on the side of the soybean oil storage tank. The fact is, the form of Jesus *just wasn't there*; it was *read into* phenomena that occurred naturally by people who were *disposed* to see it.

In looking at the perception of miracles, it is necessary to make a crucial distinction between two types of miracles proposed by performers and believers: *violation* and *contingency miracles* (McCarron, 1987). A violation miracle is one that clearly violates or deviates from the laws of nature; given what science knows to be true, they *could not* have happened. Violation miracles are *event-oriented*; that is, anyone questioning their validity questions the occurrence of the events that supposedly happened. In contrast, a contingency miracle is *interpretation-oriented*; here, the events are not questioned but interpreted in a certain way. Contingency miracles are regarded by believers as miraculous because they *interpret* them that way. Contingency miracles *could have* happened within the laws of science, but they are improbable. If blotches of colors looking something like Jesus appear on the side of a storage tank, this is a contingency miracle; if Jesus himself were to appear in the sky, his arms outstretched, in full view of a large crowd, that would be a violation miracle. If a lost dog, whose return was prayed for, returned home, that is a contingency miracle; only the believer will interpret it *as* a miracle. On the other hand, if a dog suddenly changed into a deceased and longed-for relative, that would be a violation miracle. A lame person walking would represent a contingency miracle; a person with no legs growing new ones would be a violation miracle. As we might expect, in today's sophisticated and scientifically trained society, religious figures who claim to perform miracles, and believers who accept what they say as true, refer almost exclusively to contingency miracles. In contrast, in the Bible, nearly all the miracles that are claimed are violation miracles (McCarron, 1987).

Clearly, then, in miraculous claims, it is not "what's out there" that counts. It is rarely the case nowadays that a miracle is claimed that clearly violates natural law. Instead, events occur that are interpreted a certain way—one way by the believer and a different way by the disbeliever or agnostic. In other words, *reality is socially constructed.* The process by which miracles come into existence is called "the social construction of reality" (Berger and Luckmann, 1966). People do not build an account or version of reality as a direct consequence of what's "out there" in the material world, but as a result of what they believe to be true, what "passes for knowledge" in certain social circles. "Multiple realities" exist in the same physical world. What a devoted Catholic will see as tears on the face of the Virgin Mary or the form of Jesus on the surface of a structure, a scientist will see as a natural phenomenon put there by accident. Many believers will argue that, *even if* such a phenomenon were to have an immediate natural cause, it must be explained ultimately by the guiding hand of God. Thus, the same physical reality is "socially constructed" in radically different ways. Again, the material world is simply raw material out of which to *construct* or *verify* a particular view of how things work, the way things are. Although, perhaps it has more relevance in the study of miracles, the concept of the social construction of reality is one of the more important and influential in the entire field of collective behavior; it is fundamental to the study of rumor and gossip, urban legends and collective delusions, and the study of social movements as well. We should keep it in mind throughout our investigation of collective behavior.

To the student of collective behavior, what is referred to as a miracle is a divine or supernatural *interpretation* of a phenomenon that exists or took place in the material world. This phenomenon may be an image; a dream; even a smell interpreted to have divine significance; or an event, interpreted to have happened as a result of divine intervention. Manifestations of miracles, that is, the physical appearance of the phenomenon that signifies the miracles to believers, are typically *culturally ambiguous.* This means they may be interpreted in a variety of ways according to one's social and cultural background. The faithful may see them as a sign that a miracle is taking place, while the skeptic, agnostic, or disbeliever may see them as having no religious significance and attribute their appearance to strictly physical and natural causes. There is no ready or straightforward explanation for the physical event outside of the culturally provided interpretation. Miracles do not announce themselves to all as miracles; something is happening, but we may not be certain exactly what it is. Moisture on the face of the statue of the Virgin Mary, again, is a phenomenon that has to be interpreted. What is important to us is how certain events or phenomena are interpreted, how they are experienced, especially within a compact collectivity, and what social and personal consequences they have.

The Miracle at Sabana Grande

On April 25, 1953, the Virgin Mary appeared to seven children near their school, by a well, on a hillside, near a small village called Sabana Grande in Puerto Rico (Tumin and Feldman, 1955). Mary appeared to them almost continuously for seven days thereafter, and she promised to reappear at 11:00 A.M. on May 25th at the original spot. It is possible that the children were perpetrating a hoax, since important details of their stories conflicted, and several claimed that Mary appeared to some of them, but not to others. No matter; word of the vision spread like wildfire. They told their teacher, and eventually everyone in the area knew about it. At first, the newspapers and radio stations were hesitant to report the sighting; eventually, they took up the miracle with real enthusiasm and reported it as news. The mayor of a nearby town became something of a publicity agent and a promoter, arranging to have an altar built at the site of the vision. He organized the children to lead crowds in a religious procession and in group prayer, he directed the collection of money from the pilgrims, and, on the day of the predicted reappearance of Mary, he transmitted the wishes of the children to the crowd.

The organized Catholic Church hierarchy opposed the miracle, claiming that it did not possess the necessary criteria of an authentic miracle. This created a rift between the clergy and the Church hierarchy on the one hand, and their flock of believers on the other. If anything, rather than dampening enthusiasm for the miracle, the Church's opposition seemed to stimulate even more interest in it. And, as with the events at Joaseiro (see page 172), once the media took up the cause, publicity of the event stretched far beyond the boundaries of the local area. On the day of the predicted reappearance of the Virgin, in two leading Puerto Rican newspapers, one-quarter of all their news space and two-thirds of all their photo space were devoted to the miracle. One radio station began broadcasting on-the-spot interviews about the miracle beginning May 4th, nine days after the children reported their vision, and continued to broadcast them until the 28th, four days after the Virgin was supposed to reappear. Clearly, Sabana Grande was an important news story in Puerto Rico.

By 11:00 A.M. on May 25th, about 150,000 people had assembled on the hillsides at the site of the miracle. They came from all over Puerto Rico, from the Dominican Republic, Haiti, Cuba, Miami, and even New York. As the hour approached, the tension in the crowd grew almost palpable. Rain began to fall, and many pilgrims took out their umbrellas—until one of the children commanded that no umbrellas should be opened. In the 15 minutes before the vision was to appear, various people reported seeing different visions. Mary was silhouetted in the clouds. Rings of color appeared around the sun, people who had been sick for years suddenly felt well, the rain appeared in colors off the garments of the children. Finally, just after 11:00 A.M., a cry went up that the Virgin, dressed in black, was walking down a hillside toward the well. It took some persuasion to convince some members of the crowd that this was not the Virgin Mary but only an old woman dressed in black. Then, another cry rang out that the Virgin, this time dressed in white, was walking up another hillside. This one turned out to be no more than an old man in a white shirt.

Some readers might say, "If there's a crowd of people there, how could anyone question whether or not there was a miracle; after all, can't everyone see more or less the same thing?" The truth of the matter is that, if people are strongly prepared to see something that doesn't exist, the evidence that it takes to convince them that things are that way need be slim to nonexistent. As we saw in the classic experiments by the social psychologist Muzafer Sherif (1936; Sherif and Harvey, 1952), discussed in Chapter 2 (see page 62), the more ambiguous the evidence in the physical world, the more influenced we are by individual expectations and social influence. Miracles do not appear in so solid and clear-cut a form as a 100-foot high Jesus coming out of the clouds with arms outstretched. Miracles are physically ambiguous events; the physical cues that are presented to viewers have to be socially and culturally interpreted. Different viewers see different things in the physical world; material reality does not appear to all people as identical. When a variety of people see something in the world, a collective interpretation as to what was seen is hammered out through interaction with others.

If only those who saw the Virgin Mary in the appearance of the old woman in the black dress or the old man in the white shirt had been present in that crowd, we might have had another miracle on our hands! But, as it turned out, there were enough people in the crowd who saw what was concretely and literally there to prevent this from happening. We have 150,000 people, hoping for a miracle, gathered on a hillside near a small village in Puerto Rico. For hours, people watched the skies, the trees, the hills—to no avail. Try as they might, there was simply no raw material in their surroundings to interpret a miracle to the satisfaction of those who had assembled there. By 5:00 P.M., the crowd began to desert the area.

It would seem to make sense that the failure of the Virgin Mary to appear would have been seen by all who were assembled as a failed prophecy. It might even have indicated that Mary had not appeared to the children in the first place. While there is no doubt that that is how some who came to see a miracle thought, Mary's failure to reappear did not deter the truly faithful. In fact, people continued to come to the hillside site for some time afterwards. For a year, 200 came every day on weekdays, and 3,000 came every Sunday. They poured water from the well over afflicted parts of their bodies, and filled up bottles of water to bring home for medicinal purposes. They took artifacts from the site, including leaves from a nearby mango tree; donated money to the altar that was built on the site; and signed their names in the guest register (see also Shepherd, 1987).

A team of sociologists (Tumin and Feldman, 1955) interviewed a sample of the pilgrims who gathered at Sabana Grande. All but two believed in the authenticity of the original miracle. Over half came to the site to get relief from an illness, either for themselves or for others at home; the rest had various religious motives for coming. Hardly anyone came simply because they were curious. The major reason for coming—illness—points to a failure of a traditional, normative, institutionalized structure, in this case, medicine. Many of the worshippers who came to the site had illnesses that were regarded as incurable by naturalistic medicine. Physicians tried and failed to cure diseases that seemed to be incurable to modern medicine. At this point, paranormal, supernatural medicine took over.

Medicine is one of the few areas of human life where experts (in this case physicians) literally give up on their patients. They are doomed to suffer or die when, the doctors say, nothing can be done for them. Yet, here is a living human being doomed to live a life of disability, poisoned by incurable disease, condemned to die, whom the medical profession has abandoned. It seems only natural, indeed, almost inevitable, that if one has been raised within a tradition that accepts the reality of miracles, if one has little education and hardly any scientific training, if one is poor, if one holds an ideology that says anything is possible and that God works in mysterious ways, one may believe that a miraculous cure can blossom out of the visitation of a divine figure such as the Virgin Mary (Tumin and Feldman, 1955).

The Amazing Randi Unmasks Reverend Popoff

Some miracles are conscious hoaxes, or at least semiconscious hoaxes. That is, the individuals who witness or perform them don't altogether believe in their authenticity. They are perpetrated on a credulous audience whose members are highly motivated to believe in them. One category of such hoaxes is made up of faith healing. Faith healers perform what some regard as miracles. They supposedly heal the sick, make the lame walk, the blind see, and the deaf hear. Modern science and medicine reject the validity of faith healers, of course. Still, we should not dismiss faith healing quite so lightly. It is, to begin with, a form of collective behavior; its spontaneity inheres not so much in what the faith healer is doing, but how his or her ministrations are reacted to. And, interestingly, although there is a measure of fraud in all faith healers, there are at least three factors in naturalistic medicine that make faith healing seem to work upon occasion.

The first is *the placebo effect.* A certain proportion of patients will feel significantly better simply because of the medical intervention itself, even if that treatment is, in strictly medical terms, completely ineffective. For instance, if patients who are in pain are given an inert substance and told it is a painkiller, the level of pain that some feel will be substantially reduced.

Second, *optimism* can have real medical benefits. Patients who believe that their treatment will make them better are more likely to be cured than those who are more skeptical; moreover, physicians who believe in the effectiveness of their own treatment are more likely to cure their patients than those who are more skeptical.

And third, most diseases *cure themselves* because most cases are not particularly serious. In fact, even in cases of a serious illness, often, there is a temporary, or even a permanent, remission. Many diseases shift in seriousness over time, with the patient feeling better for a month or two, and worse for a time, and some even spontaneously heal themselves for reasons that are not fully understood.

In short, because someone who is subject to the ministrations of a faith healer feels better, or even if the symptoms of his or her disease disappear altogether, does not mean that there is anything unique or distinctive about what the faith healer is doing. And not everything that the faith healer is doing is fraudulent or totally different from what physicians are doing; a measure of faith plays a role in traditional medicine, too. Nonetheless, most of what faith healers do is a fraud; most of their "cures" are nonexistent. And most would not allow a close, systematic, empirical scrutiny of the results of their work.

Reverend Peter Popoff was a Christian faith healer whose television show was broadcast over 50 stations around the country until he was unmasked by James Randi, magician and skeptic of the paranormal, known professionally as "The Amazing Randi." Here's how the Rev. Popoff worked his miracles one drizzly April Sunday in 1986.

"Be sensitive to the flow of the Holy Spirit. Amen," he says. "I tell you God is letting his spirit work here to get you ready for the miracle that you need. Amen, amen. Hallelujah, halle—" Popoff suddenly breaks off, as if inspired. "Who is Lizzie Vincent?" A cry comes up from the audience, and a wheelchair is pushed toward Popoff. Lizzie Vincent is a gray-haired Black woman wearing gold-framed glasses and a blue flowered dress. "Glory to God. Come on out here," says Popoff. "Is it 3381 Monterey? Is that your house number?" She nods, unsurprised. He always knows the address. "The Lord's angels are all around you, you're going to see the Lord give you an overhaul job." "Thank you, Jesus!" cries Lizzie Vincent. "And I'll tell you, you're going to get up and put some of these teenagers to shame." The crowd applauds wildly. "You're going to have so much energy—oooooh!" he gasps into the microphone. Popoff touches her knees and takes hold of her hand. "Glory be to God! How long has this arthritis been this bad?" Mrs. Vincent replies, "I fell in '73 and I've been having trouble with my knees ever since, and the doctor said I had rheumatoid arthritis, a very bad case" (Tierney, 1987, p. 53).

"Did you hear that," Popoff asks the crowd, "she fell in '73, and the doctor said she had rheumatoid arthritis." He strokes her arm. "I just believe that Dr. Jesus is going to touch you right now, right—NOW! THERE IT IS!" he shouts, and he jerks forward to slap his palm onto her forehead. Her head falls back, her arms reach up, and Popoff holds the microphone to her as she shrieks, "Thank you, Jesus!" "Stand up, hallelujah," says Popoff, lifting her out of the chair. Haltingly, she takes a step, and the crowd roars. "Glory to God, let's go, let's go, hallelulah, just keep going," shouts Popoff as she keeps walking. In an aside to his assistant, Popoff says, "Bring her wheelchair." By the time Mrs. Vincent reaches the other side of the auditorium, her wheelchair is waiting. "Turn around now and just push that thing back," says Popoff, and, as she begins pushing, he plops himself down into it. "Push me now, Lizzie," he shouts as she wheels him back across the front. The camera is rolling, the organ has piped up, and Popoff is chanting: "Hallelujah, hallelujah, hallelujah, let's clap your hands." The crowd breaks into thunderous applause (Tierney, 1987, pp. 53–54).

Did Popoff really perform a miracle? In front of an audience of 2,000 people, he has just correctly picked out a woman's name; her address; her ailment; and, by touching her, has gotten her up out of a wheelchair and walking across the room. He has convinced the people in the audience that they have just witnessed a miracle. If it wasn't a miracle, how did Rev. Popoff do it? In this case, we have a clear-cut fraud on our hands. As the audience filed into the auditorium, each person filled out a form, giving their name, address, and ailment. Mrs. Vincent had walked into the building on her own two feet, and so Popoff's assistants knew that she could walk. They asked if she would like to sit in a wheelchair, and waited for her name to be called out so that they could wheel her onto the stage. Meanwhile, Mrs. Popoff was in a trailer outside the auditorium, watching the rally on closed circuit TV. Mr. Popoff had a radio receiver in his ear, disguised to look like a hearing aid. (Of course, some might ask, if he has a hearing problem, why can't he cure himself?) Popoff's wife read the names, addresses, and ailments to her husband over the radio receiver—all of which was being monitored by James Randi over a short wave radio.

A true believer could say that it was God who was sending these messages, and God just happened to sound a lot like Mrs. Popoff. So the Randi team sent in someone with a fake ailment—Don Henvick, alias Bernice Manicoff. Henvick is a 260-pound mailman, who was dressed in a woman's dress for the occasion. Before he went in, he was interviewed by Popoff's assistants, to whom he claimed he had uterine cancer. During Popoff's routine, he called out Henvick's alias, identified his fake ailment, and went through the faithhealing ritual. "Dr. Jesus is going to burn all those cancer cells out of your body," Popoff announced to the audience, followed by wild applause. Suddenly, Popoff's wife spotted Henvick as an impostor, and said to her husband over the shortwave: "That's a woman? That's not a woman. . . . Hey, isn't that the guy who was in Anaheim? Pete, that's the man who was in Anaheim you said had arthritis." (Randi used Henvick twice before in attempting to unmask Popoff.) But Henvick, milking his impersonation for all it was worth, continued to run back and forth on the stage. The story of Popoff's fraudulent miracles was presented soon after on national television on the Johnny Carson show, and within a few months, Popoff went off the air and contributions to his crusades dropped by more than 80 percent. He has appeared before small audiences since then, but on a big-time commercial basis, Randi put Popoff out of business.

The day after the rally, in Detroit, the author who covered the Popoff-Randi story (Tierney, 1987) visited Mrs. Vincent. "I feel better," she said, "but I wouldn't expect myself to be very well. I wouldn't expect the Lord to just—well, you know." Still, she was sure something had happened when Popoff touched her. "It's a different feeling you can't explain—a different feeling that comes through your body." As to why she was put in a wheelchair when she could walk, or how Popoff knew her name and ailment—these questions didn't interest her. She watched the Carson show with the author. (Carson, a former magician, seemed visibly outraged by Popoff's fraud.) None of this made an impression on Mrs. Vincent; she said that she didn't believe any of it. "If I contradict what these people are doing," she said, "I'm contradicting the Bible."

The writer also interviewed another of Popoff's supporters who had a different reaction, Mrs. Abel, an 84-year-old woman with arthritis. After the exposé, she became skeptical. She wrote to the faith healer once more for medical help, and he responded by asking for money—claiming that something wonderful was about to happen. As it turned out, the wonderful thing that happened to her was that part of her foot had to be amputated. So, she threw Popoff's letters in the trash. Did Mrs. Abel decide that traditional medicine was doing the best it could for her, and that all faith healers were perpetrating a hoax and a fraud upon vulnerable, needy, and gullible people such as herself? No, she simply transferred her faith to another religious healer named Father DiOrio. When told that James Randi had denounced Father DiOrio, too, she said, "I think Father DiOrio is different. When you see him on television, it's like electricity going through people's bodies. And he doesn't write all the time asking for money. The only time I hear from him is when I send him a few dollars. And he sends me a thank-you note with a prayer. I'd like to keep receiving those notes from him," she explained. The notes continued, but not long after, Mrs. Abel died (Tierney, 1987, p. 58).

THE VIRGIN MARY MAKES AN APPEARANCE IN TEXAS

One Monday night in 1988, ten parishioners gathered in St. John Neumann Church in Lubbock, Texas. Their pastor, Monsignor Joseph James, had just returned from a pilgrimage to Yugoslavia, where six youths reported seeing daily visions of the Virgin Mary for seven years. At one point, the worshippers began to smell the distinct scent of roses. Said one, "We all felt the strong presence of the Blessed Mother. . . . We fell to our knees praising God." A few days later, another parishioner awoke to what she says was a message from Mary; she wrote it down. It said: "Go and tell your priest and tell your bishop that Mary your Mother has come to give a message. That they should spread her word throughout radio, throughout television, throughout the pulpit, throughout the world . . ., to come and say the rosary with me on Monday nights." The parishioner continued to receive such messages every Monday night for several months; when she was out of town, two other worshippers received them in her place (Belkin, 1988).

To the faithful, these manifestations indicated a divine presence and constituted miracles. Each succeeding Monday brought a larger crowd to the church—by the end of July, an average of 2,000 people appeared each Monday. In August, during the Feast of the Assumption, the celebration of Mary's ascension into heaven, some 12,000 gathered on the lawn outside the small church facing a rooftop altar that had been built for the occasion. Some said that their ailments had been healed. Dozens announced that their silver rosaries had turned to gold. One man said that he saw a vision of a flock of doves flying in formation over the church. A woman said that she had heard that the crown of the church's statue of Mary was seen spinning on top of her head. During the mass said at the Feast of the Assumption, shortly before dusk, the sun broke through the clouds. Shrieks went up from the crowd; some cried, some prayed, and some pointed toward the clouds. Others said that they saw Jesus in the clouds, some saw Mary, and some saw heaven's gates. Church deacons took testimony from individuals who had seen visions and apparitions, and collected film from those who said that they had taken pictures of images of various divine manifestations. The monsignor planned to use this evidence to convince the Vatican that miracles had indeed taken place in Lubbock (Belkin, 1988).

The local bishop was skeptical. "I take a cautious attitude about the . . . messages," he said. "I neither encourage people to participate nor discourage them. The church has always been cautious about judgments of this sort." Charles Mahone, a professor of clinical psychology at Lubbock's Texas Tech, was even more dubious. "I think this would come under the heading of mass hysteria," he explained. "If people are brought together by some strong wish or hope, the situation is ripe for that wish to take concrete form, for people to see things and experience things because they want to, not because the things are there." Meanwhile, the faithful who come to St. John Neumann Church remain convinced that Mary makes regular visitations to them in Lubbock, Texas (Belkin, 1988).

Miracles as Collective Behavior

There are several lessons to be learned about the dynamics and processes of collective behavior from these events. First of all, the acceptance of miracles is socially and culturally patterned. While we might think of the appearance of miracles as a completely spontaneous, quirky, unpredictable, freakish event, it is clear that belief in them is neither random nor beyond our understanding. Two sets of individuals, facing more or less the same evidence, come to exactly the opposite conclusions. In 1889, a miracle—the oozing of blood from the mouth of a lay nun during communion—occurred in Joaseiro, a tiny hamlet in Brazil. The event was believed to be miraculous by the Catholic laity and by most local priests, but was rejected as inauthentic by the Catholic hierarchy (Della Cava, 1970). What appeared on the surface to be a totally spontaneous phenomenon, issuing forth from simple faith, was dependent on a number of crucial sociological factors, variables, and forces. Belief in the miracle was patterned by education, level of affluence or poverty, region of residence, country of birth (Brazilian versus foreign), and rank in the Catholic hierarchy.

At the same time, it is the very seeming spontaneity of miracles, their democratic and grass-roots dynamics, the fact that they are uncontrollable by an ecclesiastical hierarchy, that makes them so threatening. When feelings bubble up in people that are not preprogrammed—feelings that operate outside norms, dogma, and orthodox belief and which cannot be contained by organizational dictates—those who have a stake in keeping things the way they are, are threatened. When a hierarchy or chain of command is threatened by loyalties that transcend and challenge that hierarchy, it faces instability. For instance, the people of Joaseiro said that they didn't care if the Pope himself declared the miracles illegitimate—they knew better. The authority of the Pope, the very authority of the Church itself, was being challenged. Faith in the miracles transcended faith in the legitimately constituted Church. Surely that had to be—and was—of concern to the Catholic hierarchy. In effect, a new and different hierarchy was created, one not based on traditional rules, bureaucracy, or an organizational structure, but on an absolutely unshakable faith in the reality of a series of miracles that were experienced by a barely literate, barely educated launderess and a lay nun, while a humble parish priest administered communion. All the sacred learning of all of the doctors of the Church, the authorities in Rio and Rome and all over the world, could not shake the faith of the believers of Joaseiro (Della Cava, 1970).

Here we see a perfect illustration of collective behavior. Belief in a non-normative, extrainstitutional interpretation of reality can actually threaten a social order and threaten the privileges and the authority of those at the top of a powerful hierarchy. The authority of the miracles was spontaneous and therefore *unstable*. Miraculous manifestations of the divinity are imbued with what Max Weber called *charisma* (1968, pp. 1,111ff)—the "gift of the spirit." Charisma draws authority from sources other than those accepted by the hierarchy and, thus, challenges the legitimacy of the hierarchy. Unless a hierarchy can harness, contain, and coopt that spontaneous feeling, it has the potential for introducing instability in the social order. By its very nature, collective behavior can threaten the status quo, tradition, and existing social structure.

Of course, most forms of collective behavior do not have this potential. No matter how much the phenomenon of "streaking" may have upset some puritans and prudes, there was no possibility that it would threaten the stability of American society in the 1970s. It may have been a more-or-less spontaneous phenomenon, it may have represented a sphere of behavior over which established authority—adults, parents, college administrators— had no control, it may even have generated an informal hierarchy of its own, but it was not a truly subversive activity, as anyone would admit.

On the other hand, if certain other forms of collective behavior were to become truly widespread, they would have the potential for subverting the existing social, political, or economic structures. Belief in "paranormal" phenomena undermines rational, scientific thinking. Belief in occult phenomena undermines traditional religious faith. Adhering to the dogma and practices of ultra-right, supernationalistic, racist political groups undermines adherence to democratic principles. If enough people put their money into faddish "get rich quick" schemes, such as the pyramid scam, the established monetary system would be thrown into turmoil. If people put their medical or psychological fate into the hands of therapeutic quacks, or followed fad or quack dietary plans, it's possible that their health would be affected and traditional Western medicine would be undermined. In Germany during the 1920s and 1930s, millions of Germans followed a charismatic, racist politician named Adolph Hitler, and tens of millions of people died in the holocaust of World War II. Thus, while many forms of collective behavior do or can have little or no substantial social impact, many others have the potential for transforming society, for good or ill.

One crucial aspect of collective behavior is how its many forms are linked up with the rest of the social structure, how, in other words, they impact upon the society. The miracle of Joaseiro generated a conflict that, in turn, gave birth to a social movement, neither of which abated until the death, at the age of 94, of the priest who originally administered the communion to the lay nun (Della Cava, 1970). What the events in Joaseiro show is that collective behavior is not behavior that is removed from the rest of society's institutions. Rather, much of it is intimately intertwined with a society's social structure and its culture. Some forms of collective behavior so challenge and threaten the status quo that, once they become widespread, what once was unthinkable becomes widespread, even generating the basis for a new institutional order. When they erupt in a society and take hold, things can never be the same again; at times, and in certain places, collective behavior becomes an agent of social change. For that reason alone, it deserves serious attention.

SUMMARY

Miracles and ecstatic crowds represent a type of collective behavior. In both, audiences are outside their ordinary, everyday reality; their attitudes range from reverential to joyous, but in all, charisma—"the gift of the spirit"—plays a major role. In both, members hold a feeling of stupendous specialness toward the revered object. Ecstatic crowds are common in cultures around the world. Although less common in Western society than in most, they may be found in sporting events, in the worship of the members of certain sects and cults, in responses to some public figures, and in some political settings.

Strong emotion, often neglected in contemporary studies of collective behavior, is a prominent feature of ecstatic crowds, although its intensity, like the quality of spontaneity, is a matter of degree. In many groups, rituals that generate ecstasy are programmed and planned out in advance. Nonetheless, the ecstasy felt by many members of an audience is often genuine and spontaneous. Disturbing though they were, Nazi party rallies provide a good example of this principle. Contagion plays a major role in all ecstatic crowds, although in religious ritual, as elsewhere, contagion has its limits.

Revival meetings, although toned down considerably from their heyday some generations ago, offer an excellent example of ecstatic crowds. The key to revivalism is the institutionalization of charisma—converting ecstacy into conventional, everyday, institutionalized observance. Sporting events offer a secular look at ecstatic crowds. It is possible that egocentrism—seeing oneself as elevated by the victory and degraded by the defeat of one's chosen team—plays a central role in the fans' excitement during a sporting event. Brazilian carnaval is a good example of how an activity that began as a spontaneous and grass-roots event became routinized and institutionalized, with one foot in collective behavior and one foot in conventional, organized behavior. Carnaval offers a temporary release from the crushing problems in an elitist, racist, sexist, and extremely poor society.

Miracles represent another instance of ecstatic crowds, although the dominant emotion is more central than joyful. Miracles are perceived as a result of a process known as the social construction of reality: A miraculous interpretation is "read into" ambiguous physical stimuli by audiences already inclined to that interpretation. In most case, what is seen provides *raw material* for the miraculous interpetation of unusual but possible events or phenomena. Occasionally, a conscious fraud is perpetrated upon a gullible audience, with the supposed miracle-maker staging events through clever tricks.

References

Barron, James. 1984. "Detroit Rejoices at Tigers' Victory." *The New York Times* (October 15): A1, C4.

Belkin, Lisa. 1988. "Reports of Miracles Draw Throngs." *The New York Times* (August 17): A14.

Berger, Peter L., and Thomas Luckmann. 1966. *The Social Construction of Reality.* Garden City, N.Y.: Doubleday.

Birman, Patricia. 1983. *O Que É Umbanda.* São Paulo: Editora Brasilense.

Carr, William. 1978. *Hitler: A Study in Personality and Politics.* New York: St. Martin's Press.

Cialdini, Robert B. 1984. *Influence: How and Why People Agree to Things.* New York: William Morrow.

Critchfield, Richard. 1978. "Wild at the Carnival." *Human Behavior* (February): 53–57.

DaMatta, Roberto. 1978. *Carnavais, Malandros, e Herois: Para Uma Sociologia Do Dilema Braziliero.* Rio de Janeiro: Zahar Editores.

DaMatta, Roberto. 1981. *Universo do Carnaval: Imagens e Reflexões.* Rio de Janeiro: Edições Pinakotheke.

DaMatta, Roberto. 1984. "Carnival in Multiple Planes." In John J. MacAloon (ed.), *Rite, Drama, Spectacle, Festival*, pp. 210–258. Philadelphia: ISHI.

Della Cava, Ralph. 1970. *Miracle at Joaseiro.* New York: Columbia University Press.

Durkheim, Émile. 1915. *The Elementary Forms of the Religious Life* (trans. Joseph Ward Swain). London: George Allen & Unwin.

Flake, Carol. 1984. *Redemptorama: Culture, Politics, and the New Evangelicalism.* New York: Penguin Books.

Geertz, Clifford. 1973. *The Interpretation of Cultures.* New York: Basic Books.

Goodman, Felicitas D. 1988. *Ecstasy, Ritual, and Alternate Reality: Religion in a Pluralistic World.* Bloomington: Indiana University Press.

Hamilton, Robert W. 1987. "Weekend Retreat." In Ralph H. Turner and Lewis M. Killian, *Collective Behavior* (3rd ed.), pp. 23–25. Englewood Cliffs, N.J.: Prentice-Hall.

Hazleton, Leslie. 1989a. *England, Bloody England.* New York: Atlantic Monthly Press.

Hazleton, Leslie. 1989b. "British Soccer—The Deadly Game." *The New York Times Magazine* (May 7): 40, 66–69.

Jaynes, Gregory. 1986. "In Ohio: A Vision West of Town." *Time* (September 29): 8, 14.

Kifner, John. 1989. "Amid Frenzy, Iranians Bury the Ayatollah." *The New York Times* (June 7): A1, A7.

LaBarre, Weston. 1969. *They Shall Take Up Serpents.* New York: Schocken Books.

Landes, Ruth. 1947. *The City of Women.* New York: Macmillan.

Leacock, Seth, and Ruth Leacock. 1972. *Spirits of the Deep: Drugs, Mediums, and Trance in a Brazilian City.* New York: Doubleday Natural History Press/American Museum of Natural History.

Lever, Janet. 1983. *Soccer Madness.* Chicago: University of Chicago Press.

Lofland, John. 1981. "Collective Behavior: The Elementary Forms." In Morris Rosenberg and Ralph H. Turner (eds.), *Social Psychol-*

ogy: Sociological Perspectives. pp. 411–446. New York: Basic Books.

Lofland, John. 1982. "Crowd Joys." *Urban Life*, 10 (January): 355–381.

Lofland, John, 1985. *Protest: Studies of Collective Behavior and Social Movements.* New Brunswick, N.J.: Transaction Books.

McCarron, Gary. 1987. "Lost Dogs and Financial Healing: Deconstructing Televangelist Miracles." In Marshall Fishwick and Ray B. Browne (eds.), *The God Pumpers: Religion in the Electronic Age*, pp. 19-32. Bowling Green, Ohio: Bowling Green State University Popular Press.

McDaniel, June. 1989. *The Madness of the Saints: Ecstatic Religion in Bengal.* Chicago: University of Chicago Press.

McLoughlin, William G., Jr. 1959. *Modern Revivalism: Charles Grandison Finney to Billy Graham.* New York: Ronald Press.

McPhail, Clark. 1991. *The Myth of the Madding Crowd.* New York: Aldine de Gruyter.

McPhail, Clark. 1992. *Acting Together: The Organization of Crowds.* New York: Aldine de Gruyter.

Merkle, Peter H. 1975. *Political Violence Under the Swastika: 581 Early Nazis.* Princeton, N.J.: Princeton University Press.

Packard, William. 1988. *Evangelism in America: From Tents to TV.* New York: Paragon House.

Pratt, James Bissett. 1920. *The Religious Consciousness: A Psychological Study.* New York: Macmillan.

Shepherd, Gordon. 1987. "The Social Construction of a Religious Prophecy." *Sociological Inquiry*, 57 (Fall): 394–414.

Sherif, Muzafer. 1936. *The Psychology of Social Norms.* New York: Harper.

Sherif, Muzafer, and O.J. Harvey. 1952. "A Study of Ego Functioning: The Elimination of Stable Anchorages in Individual and Group Situations." *Sociometry*, 15 (August–November): 272–305.

Sinclair, Thornton. 1938. "The Nazi Party Rally at Nuremberg." *Public Opinion Quarterly*, 2 (October): 570–583.

Snow, David A., Louis A. Zurcher, and Robert Peters. 1981. "Victory Celebrations as Theater: A Dramaturgical Approach to Crowd Behavior." *Symbolic Interaction*, 4 (Spring): 21–42.

Strasser, Otto. 1940. *Hitler and I* (trans. Gwenda David and Eric Mosbacher). London: Jonathan Cape.

Tierney, John. 1987. "Fleecing the Flock." *Discover* (November): 51–58.

Tumin, Melvin M., and Arnold S. Feldman. 1955. "The Miracle at Sabana Grande." *Public Opinion Quarterly*, 19 (Summer): 124–139.

Turner, Ralph H., and Lewis M. Killian. 1987. *Collective Behavior* (3rd ed.). Englewood Cliffs, N.J.: Prentice-Hall.

Weber, Max. 1968. *Economy and Society: An Outline of Interpretive Sociology* (Guenther Roth et al., trans.; Guenther Roth and Claus Wittich, eds.). New York: Bedminster Press.

Wenger, Dennis E. 1987. "Collective Behavior and Disaster Research." In Russell R. Dynes, Bruna DeMarchi, and Carlo Pelanda (eds.), *Sociology of Disasters: Contributions of Sociology to Disaster Research*, pp. 213–237. Milan, Italy: Franco Angeli.

Wren, Christopher S. 1991. "40 Are Killed and 50 Injured as Fans Riot at a South African Soccer Match." *The New York Times* (January 14): A3.

PART THREE

INTRODUCTION TO DISASTERS

C rowds are compact collectivities, a fairly substantial number of people in the same place at the same time. *Publics* are diffuse collectivities, a large number of people scattered around a country who are focused on a single issue. The nature of these collectivities influences the kinds of behavior that takes place in them. For instance, the immediacy of the crowd makes riots and ecstatic celebrations possible; the more-or-less stable composition of publics make phenomena such as legends and fashion possible.

Disasters do not fall clearly into either type of gathering. Some disasters, such as airplane crashes, take place in crowd-sized gatherings. Others, such as earthquakes and hurricanes, are scattered over a public-sized collectivity. Disaster can hit a single gathering, a neighborhood, a community, areas within a state, an entire state, substantial regions within a country, an entire country, or several countries. Consequently, their dynamics differ from those of both the crowd and the public; at the low end, they are like crowds, while at the high end, they are like publics. Hence, they have to be examined as belonging to a separate conceptual category.

A disaster presents a threatened population with novel problems, puts them in situations they have probably never faced, threatens them with danger they may never have even contemplated—problems, situations, and danger that call for innovative, impromptu, on-the-spot responses. Above all, what happens in disasters cannot be anticipated in detail. It is a surprise experience *par excellence*. Even with some measure of surprise reduced by scientific forecasting and effective pre- and post-disaster action by relevant organizations and bureaucracies, disasters can never be wholly tamed. It is their very nature to generate unpredictable chaos in the lives of humans. So, what happens when disaster strikes?

The image of the behavior that takes place in disasters that is generally conveyed in the media, and that held by much of the public, adheres to the age-old contagion and convergence models. Much of the public believes that, when disaster threatens, people become panicky and overreact; they flee in terror, often pushing others aside in their headlong flight. And, sensing the panic around them, their motto is, "Every man or woman for himself or herself!" Most people also believe that if they run fast enough, are smart enough, or push enough people aside, they will be able to save their own lives, regardless of the severity of the threat they face. Moreover, much of the public believes that shady people tend to converge on a disaster site to exploit the victims in one way or another—to loot stores and burglarize homes, for instance.

The reason why disaster behavior is studied in a course on collective behavior is precisely because this image is inaccurate. More specifically, people tend *not* to engage in the wild, selfish, individualistic, exploitative behavior described by the myth. Disaster victims must be spontaneous in their responses to threat, it is true, but they rarely come up with these responses on their own. Disasters take place in social contexts. People tend to confer with others about the appropriate line of action. They weigh alternatives, consider consequences, and come up with socially and collectively reasoned solutions.

181

Disasters create disruption and havoc in the lives of the people living in the stricken area. More economically developed nations usually have the resources to deal with the impact of natural disasters, and the dislocation they cause tends to be short-lived.

In the distant past, the focus on disaster behavior was on what *individual victims* did under conditions of extreme threat and emergency, and how they managed to recover from such a traumatic experience. Today, the focus is far more likely to be what *organizations* do before, during, and after the disaster. So, instead of asking how an individual copes with disaster—even an individual integrated into social networks—contemporary research is more likely to ask how communities and organizations cope with a disaster. How do agencies cooperate to rebuild a community? For instance, how does the Red Cross deal with local agencies to more effectively deliver its resources to the community? This makes the analysis structural rather than individualistic, but it also tends to underplay the degree of spontaneity that takes place and the emotion that is felt and expressed, while emphasizing the predictability, rationality, and purposiveness of disaster-related behavior. These are concerns that are not part of the classic collective behavior tradition. It should be clear, then, that, while some disaster researchers regard themselves as collective behavior specialists, many do not. Like the field of social movements, a large portion of disaster research is being redefined out of the field of collective behavior.

How do we know what we know about disaster behavior? In order to understand what people do and don't do when faced with a mass emergency, we have to look at the first-hand empirical research conducted on such behavior. We are interested not in "armchair" speculation about what seems to "make sense" from the perspective of popular, taken-for-granted, widely-held assumptions, but what real people do in real situations, or what they are likely to do, given what they say their priorities are. Far from releasing us from the responsibility of using concepts and theories, our emphasis on the primacy of empirical evidence demands that we integrate evidence into concepts and theories and that we test concepts and theories with empirical evidence. A gap should not exist between the two; instead, they have a mutual or dialectical relationship. Facts enable us to determine the validity of concepts and theories, while concepts and theories enable us to search for relevant and meaningful evidence.

Below, we have two documents on disaster. The first is a personal, first-hand account of one individual's experience with a recent disaster—the California earthquake of 1989. This account will give us a flavor of what it is like to live through a disaster. And the second document is a fairly detailed description of how disaster research is conducted, more specifically, how the Disaster Research Center at the University of Delaware studies the phenomenon of disaster. This inside look as disaster research is likely to be instructive.

Account: The California Earthquake of 1989

The following letter was written by a physician in her thirties to her friends. It details her and her family's reaction to being in San Francisco when the 1989 California earthquake struck. Her account illustrates several important generalizations about how people react to and experience disasters.

About the earthquake—it occurred at 5:04 in the afternoon and I was in the kitchen trying to keep my daughter away from the garbage pail. . . . Suddenly, there was a rolling and swaying motion typical of an earthquake. (We just had a smaller one in May that woke us from our sleep, so there was no question in my mind what was happening.) I picked the baby up, covered her head, and went to a part of the house where there are a lot of door frames, which is what they say to do. We are on the ground floor and I could feel the three stories on top of us swaying. I felt sure the top of the building would break off and the walls would start coming in at me at any second. I kept balance by leaning against a door frame and kept turning around, looking this way and that, hoping I could jump away from whichever wall collapsed first.

Fortunately, the swaying soon stopped. I could hear people out on the street crying and yelling. I found a vase and some pictures in one room of our apartment that had fallen and broken, but that was the only damage. Some loose wood fell into our walkway from the roof, and an old-fashioned curved window broke in the Victorian-era apartment next door. My brother and husband were working in the neighborhood, about a mile away, in a friend's photography studio; my father was at home alone. We all tried to call each other at once. The electricity was totally out, but the phones were off and on, so when we did get busy signals, we didn't know if that meant the person on the other end was calling or if it was a phone malfunction. Finally, we all found out we were fine, and that there had been no significant damage in our neighborhood, which is old and built on rock. The foundations of all our houses are brick; it is only the flexibility of the wood-frame structures, and their location, and the fact that this earthquake was a 7 and not an 8 [on the Richter scale] that saved everyone.

We weren't too worried about my mother, being under the delusion that she was in our area of this city. Actually, she was driving with a friend and her daughter to see the sunset through the Marina district, which, as it turns out, was the neighborhood that was hardest hit by the quake. She showed up 45 minutes later, looking pale. She said that they first noticed a problem when the car began rocking as if one after another tire was blowing out. Then they noticed sidewalks buckling upwards and "exploding," with geysers of water bursting through them. Then they noticed the smell of gas because of all the gas lines that were severed. Finally, they realized it must be an earthquake. Through the rear window, they saw an apartment building sink into the ground. They left the area quickly; traffic lights were not working, but people were polite. They had been on the exact block where the worst damage occurred.

Later, we found out that houses four blocks from us have been condemned because they were built on a filled-in lake. (Any landfill turns to liquid when the earth shakes.) No one we know was hurt on the Bay Bridge or on freeways. Luckily, there were surprisingly few deaths, considering how the media terrified everybody who had anyone they cared about in San Francisco. We are being told that this was not the "big one."

We all felt exhausted and afraid to go anywhere for weeks afterwards. I didn't realize what was going on until the psychiatrists at work gave a conference on "post traumatic stress syndrome." It is stupid to stay here and wait for "the big one." I have not been to a movie since the quake [a month ago] and am very careful about going on freeways. I think carefully about each building I go into. Things are just now starting to get a little easier in this respect. I am grateful that we don't own our own house. The multiple aftershocks served to reinforce our state of somewhat helpless vigilance. The damage, other than being worse in landfilled areas and little in areas with rock under them, really was haphazard to a large extent, and not entirely based on how close one was to the fault. So, although we are physically fine, a normal existence seems a much more fragile thing these days.

Dissecting Disasters[1]

At 1:08 A.M. on Monday, Nov. 28, the first tornadoes touched down in Wake County, N.C. Before dawn four people were dead, 157 people were injured and 850 people were left homeless across north Raleigh and parts of eastern North Carolina. The tornadoes left at least $100 million worth of damage in their wake.

At the first word of a disaster, University of Delaware research teams head out. They arrived immediately after earthquakes in Mexico City, Athens and Tehran. They were there as survivors struggled through flood waters and mud when the Vaiont Dam overflowed in Longarone, Italy. They studied community response to a typhoon in Japan, a flash flood in Canada and brush fires in Australia.

This time, the research team doesn't have far to go. Less than 18 hours after the tornadoes touched down, three university graduate research assistants are in Raleigh, prepared to study the response of area emergency medical workers in this latest disaster.

How communities prepare for, respond to and recover from disasters is the focus of research at the University's Disaster Research Center (DRC), the only center for quick-response disaster studies in the United States.

A few days after the tornadoes, everything appears completely normal. The "miracle mile" of neon-lit chain restaurants and motels found in the suburbs of any major city is operating a full tilt. Not a bulb appears broken, not a golden arch bent.

But, on the right, is a gas station with plywood covering its windows. No lights on there. And, on the left, is a city-block-

[1]Anderson, 1988–1989, pp. 16–24.

sized pile of rubble that used to be a K-Mart. At this, the start of the Christmas shopping season, barricades skirt the perimeter, yellow police-boundary tape flaps in the wind, signs admonish people to "Keep Out." And giant arc lights illuminate the orange interior now open to the weather, seen over piles of debris and through twisted girders that used to support the roof.

First established in 1963 at Ohio State University, the center moved to Delaware in 1985. Before its founding, most social science studies focused on the behavior of individual disaster *victims*. Almost no one paid attention to a disaster community's emergency organizations, even though those groups generally determine how well a community copes with a crisis.

So the DRC took as its research focus police and fire departments, Civil Defense offices, The Red Cross and Salvation Army, hospitals, utilities and other agencies that respond to large-scale community emergencies.

To study the response of these groups to disaster, the center uses "firehouse research." Its field research teams arrive on the scene within a few hours after a disaster is reported. When a natural disaster, such as a flood, is imminent, a DRC team can arrive at the site beforehand.

"At the time the center was started, there was no permanent [research center] in the social and behavioral sciences where people were standing around waiting to run out and study disasters," Enrico Quantarelli, director and one of the founders of the center, explains.

Since the center was established, research teams have made more than 500 field trips to the sites of floods, hurricanes, earthquakes and other disasters.

Emotions run high. There's surprise and gratitude that only four people have been killed. But even one death is too many, and two of the dead are children. Community groups organize to provide food, clothing and shelter for the hundreds who lost their homes. One woman sets out to meet an unusual, but important, need—finding and caring for lost pets until they're reunited with their owners. Strangers help strangers and neighbors get to know each other, digging through destroyed homes for personal treasures that can never be replaced. The mayor of Raleigh declares the following Sunday a day of thanksgiving that more people weren't hurt or killed.

Cynthia Arcoraci, Catherine Simile and Bruce Crawford make up this particular DRC team, working under a grant from the Federal Emergency Management Administration. Simile, of Ft. Collins, Colo., is a doctoral student. Arcoraci, of Alexandria, Va., and Crawford, of

Wilmington, Del., are working on their master's degrees. In the middle of a city where the inhabitants are working their way through relief, sorrow and anger, these three must collect cold, hard data.

Because they're studying emergency medical response, the students don't talk to victims—the people who crawled out from under the piles of wood and tile that used to be their homes. Instead, they interview hospital emergency room nurses, ambulance corps volunteers and representatives of agencies that coordinate emergency medical response.

Though they seek only factual information, which often is backed up with written records, they find that the highly charged emotional atmosphere surrounding the disaster helps them gather information. Everyone, even those whose lives weren't directly touched, feels a little traumatized. Everyone wants to talk about that night—where they were, what they did. A month later, when formal reports are written, their memories will be a little less vivid.

But in the days immediately following the disaster, detailed and sometimes hours-long interviews allow the three researchers to fill notebook after notebook with information. How many ambulance runs were made? How many injuries were treated? What mistakes were made? What worked particularly well? By the time Arcoraci, Simile and Crawford leave Raleigh—72 hours after their arrival—they have contacted 10 hospitals, nine volunteer ambulance organizations, one city-paid ambulance crew and two coordinating agencies. Telephone calls from the DRC in the following weeks reach those who weren't available at the time and allow for double-checking of data.

Most of the community is undamaged. Tornadoes hit with uneven destruction, destroying one home while leaving the house next door intact. But that Monday night is the primary, the only topic of conversation. Those behind the counter in stores near the demolished K-Mart seem almost offended when congratulated on their apparent good luck at escaping damages. "No," they argue, "we lost" . . . something: A shipment parked out back on the loading dock, waiting to be unpacked, a car, windshield smashed by flying debris. Everyone insists they are part of the story.

The DRC has several goals, Quarantelli says. "The basic one is simply to come to some sort of knowledge and understanding of what actually happens. . . . The initial disaster researchers found that popular conceptions, official expectations and the public view of disasters was fundamentally incorrect—[these have] come to be known as the disaster 'myths.' When the center was established, we decided we wanted a clear and accurate picture of what goes on. At that level, its basic goal is simply a ground-clearing and knowledge-establishing kind of activity," he explains.

"The second goal is centered on the fact that the people at the center are fundamentally social and behavioral scientists. There is no such discipline a 'disasterology,' nor are there 'disasterologists.' So, many of them see this as an opportunity to learn what goes on in disasters," Quarantelli says. "If you study human beings or societies or organizations under stress, that presumably gives you a much better understanding of the fundamentals of the phenomena.

"The third goal is the one that, in some respects, leads to most of the funding of the center," he notes. "The people who fund the center, usually government agencies, are interested in what can be learned so as to either change the planning for, or the response to, disasters. In other words, that is the practical pay-off in terms of the studies: How to improve whatever it is that's looked at."

The winds, estimated at over 200 miles per hour at the height of the storms, left their mark on nature as well as on businesses and homes. In one stand of 300 pines, every tree larger than a few inches in diameter is neatly snapped off about six feet above the ground. And the trees all tilt at the same strange angle, as if some giant had crushed them from above. Wrapped around some of the trees, like huge gray ribbons, are sheets of metal, blown from nearby construction sites. In residential areas, the bent trees and shrubs sport soft tufts of pink and white, like some crazy imitation snow spread over miles as an early holiday decoration. It's insulation, ripped from between walls and under roofs by the wind.

Twenty-three people staff the Disaster Research Center. Beside support personnel, graduate students and Quarantelli, the staff includes co-directors, Russell Dynes, professor and chairperson, and Dennis Wenger, both of the Department of Sociology.

Frequently there are several studies running concurrently at the center. The research project that took the three graduate students to Raleigh in November also sent research teams to large public events, to study how medical emergencies can be handled in huge crowds. Another study, just getting underway, looks at "lifelines": the water, gas, telephone and electric lines that sustain a city.

Initially, center researchers primarily studied natural disasters like tornadoes, earthquakes and floods. Over the years, they also began to study technological disasters, like a train derailment and phosphorus spill in Ohio, a plane crash in California and the 1979 nuclear accident at Three Mile Island in Pennsylvania.

The Disaster Research Center has studied a wide range of disaster-related problems, including the delivery of mental health services during disasters, mass evacuation, mass media and disasters, panic "flight" behavior, the function and structure of emergency operations centers, rumor-control centers during disasters, the role of volunteers, disaster subcultures and the images of human behavior in disaster movies.

The side wall of the huge warehouse is missing, exposing an incredible jumble of metal shelving and cardboard boxes. It was a Mack truck dealership, its shelves and boxes held thousands of truck parts, neatly categorized and filed. Now, the parts that are salvageable are being hauled away. What is striking is the sight of a truck resting on its side—on top of another truck. Like a Tonka Toy, the tornado lifted it up in the air and flipped it over and dropped it onto the second truck.

DRC staff members serve as consultants to many states, more than 20 nations and the United Nations on disaster and emergency planning. There are frequently visitors at the center, which boasts a resource library of more than 20,500 items—the largest collection of publications in the world on the human and social aspects of disasters. Many visitors come from outside the United States, reflecting the center's international status.

"Last year, for example," Dynes says, "we had a Canadian scholar with us all year, on his sabbatical, working on risk communications. We had a Belgian lawyer here during the summer working on emergency preparedness."

A conference in 1972 of Japanese and American social scientists fostered continuing contacts among them. A number of the Japanese scientists, in fact, have spent anywhere from a week to a year at the center.

"We've also worked with the Japanese in a cooperative project on the media in comparable disasters in that country and the United States," Dynes continued. "We've done a similar thing recently with Italian social scientists."

Dynes says the center now is planning a research project with the People's Republic of China. It will study two communities in China and two in the United States in terms of their earthquake preparedness and mitigation—the efforts after a quake to prevent recurring damage. Center researchers are working on a similar project with Taiwan examining risk perception and emergency preparation. Joint projects with India and France also are being discussed. Dynes is now in Bangkok on a Fulbright scholarship, working at the Asian Disaster Preparedness Center. There he teaches students from China, Vietnam, and Sri Lanka.

The young man had crawled out from under the pile of wall-board, wood, bricks and shingles that had recently been an

apartment in a three-storey building. How long did it take for the tornado to rip apart his home? "Fifteen seconds . . . and it felt like two hours," he says. Asked when the cleanup would start, when he could start retrieving something of his from the rubble, he laughs. "You don't understand," he says. "It's gone. Everything's gone. I won't get anything of mine out of this mess. But, it's okay, because I'm alive." And, he means it.

"It's very clear . . . that the disaster business, which has always been frighteningly good, will be even better, unfortunately, in the future," Wenger says. "The picture's very clear. We're going to have bigger and more and worse disasters than we've ever had in the past."

Wenger's not unduly pessimistic. As populations grow more dense, future disasters will affect more people. For example, the most massive earthquake in the United States took place in the 1800s in the Midwest, according to Wenger. The New Madrid Quake, as it's known, was so severe that the Mississippi River flowed north for two weeks. But the area was almost unpopulated at the time.

"Now," Wenger says, "an earthquake of the same magnitude in that locale would have, perhaps, catastrophic effects because it would affect the metropolitan areas [from] St. Louis, down to Memphis and up to Cincinnati. Nothing's changed with respect to the ground; nothing's changed with respect to the fault. The changes have been social."

Technological advances also endanger us, Wenger warns.

"Any community, for example, that has a major highway or a railroad track running through it faces the daily possibility of a catastrophic event through a toxic release, a hazardous materials accident," Wenger says. "Some estimates are that approximately one in every 10 trucks on the highways carry hazardous materials, and approximately one in every 20 cars is carrying materials that can potentially kill."

The cars pull in and stop near the fence erected around the K-Mart to keep looters out. People park for a few minutes and just stare at the wreckage of the store. Most people sit quietly. Then they pull away. The stream of cars never seems to stop. Even after midnight, the cars come filing through, stopping for a moment and then leaving. Just as everyone slows to look at automobile accidents, it seems everyone wants to see first-hand what devastation looks like.

People in a disaster area are curious about the damage done by a tornado or flood. But research done at the center shows they're also, generally speaking, supportive, hard-working and eager to help their neighbors.

"There's an image," Wenger says, "that people will not perform their official duties during a disaster because of concern for their families, that people will abandon their jobs and that there will be a shortage of personnel to do necessary work, such as staffing hospitals and emergency centers.

"The problem is exactly the opposite in disasters," he says. "Organizations don't have a shortage of personnel; there are usually many more people than are needed to do the job."

Emergency-related organizations, like police and fire departments and hospitals, are usually 24-hour operations. That means three shifts of people are available.

"A typical pattern is that, at the time of a disaster, these people are either called in or, even more often, simply go to work because they think they'll be needed. The difficulty is an overabundance of people."

It's not only the emergency workers who come to the aid of disaster victims, Wenger says, it's also the victims themselves.

"Who do you think rescues the victims? The other victims. Who are the first people to start to clear the streets? The victims. Who are the first individuals to begin assessing damages? They do all the essential tasks."

References

Anderson, Mary. 1988–1989. "Dissecting Disasters." *University of Delaware Magazine,* 1 (Winter): 16–24.

CHAPTER
5

DISASTERS: I

You are watching the 6:00 P.M. news on television. The weather forecaster states that a hurricane is 400 miles away, and predicts it will hit
your community in two days. It is described as massive; officials strongly recommend that all residents evacuate the area. What do you do? Do you board
up the windows of your house, throw a few necessities in your car, and drive
off to the nearest emergency shelter? Do you call friends and relatives in your
community to ask them what they intend to do? Do you call friends and relatives outside the area and ask if you can stay with them for the duration of
the storm? Do you wait a few hours, or another day, to make sure the weather forecaster's prediction is correct? Do you figure the storm's impact really
couldn't be all that bad, and decide to wait it out in your own home? Whatever you decide to do, it is likely to be influenced by what others do or tell
you, and it is unlikely to be a simple product of institutionalized norms and
values; it is likely, in other words, to be a form of collective behavior.

Your apartment building is ablaze. Fire engines are outside, and fire
fighters have entered the building, but you're not sure where they are. The
walls are too hot to touch. You are on the 12th floor; it is too far to jump. If
you stay in the apartment, you will die in the blaze. You go into the hallway;
it is thick with smoke. Although you hear other people coughing and yelling,
you can't see anyone because of the smoke. Again, what do you do? Where
do you go? How do you ensure your survival? What are the others doing to
make sure they'll live through the fire?

Behavior in disasters is a good example of the "emergent" or spontaneous
quality of collective behavior. Most of us do not *expect* to be hit by a disaster;
we do not have a plan to deal with one if we are. Even if we are vaguely aware

193

of what to do and what not to do during some of the more common disasters, hardly anyone can imagine what to do in case of the less common ones. For example, we all know, in case of fire, that we should close the windows and the doors, drop to the floor, help small children, and get out of the building as quickly as possible. In areas often hit by earthquakes, we know that we should stay in dooorways or, if we can, get out of buildings; in areas hit by tornados, we know that we should try to stay underground. Still, there are many other types of disasters that could devastate a community. Moreover, we only know the broad outlines of what we should do with respect to the ones we know a little about. In a real-life case of an emergency, unanticipated limitations and contingencies make many of the things we ought to do impossible. In short, disasters are a perfect situation in which spontaneous, innovative, non-normative behavior is not only likely, but often necessary for survival.

Most Americans are unaware of how devastating disasters can be in many regions of the world. Each year, worldwide, the population equivalent to a city of 250,000 dies in disaster (Burton, Kates, and White, 1978, p. 4). In some countries, a single disaster will more than wipe out the economic gains of more than a decade (Eckholm, 1984, p. C2). Each year, disasters cause disruption in the lives of tens of millions of people. Moreover, most experts agree that, although tumultuous natural events remain more or less constant, the death toll in natural disasters is on the rise (Eckholm, 1984; Green, 1977, pp. 23–27; Burton, Kates, and White, 1978, pp. 2–4). It is our job to understand how and why.

WHAT IS A DISASTER?

The word "disaster" is taken from both Latin and Greek and it means "bad star," "an unfavorable aspect of a star or planet," that is, a bad omen, a calamitous event, a misfortune. Most people use the term "disaster" fairly loosely; if your home team loses an important game, if someone spills soup on your clothes, or if you do poorly on an exam, you might refer to such an experience as a "disaster." Researchers who study disasters, however, use the term in a more restricted sense. In the field of collective behavior, a disaster must cause a great deal of damage and many people must be affected. Most often, disasters are measured in loss of human life; the greater the number of people killed, the more serious the disaster. If two people are killed in an automobile accident, that is a tragedy for them and their families but it is not a disaster; if 500 people are killed in an airplane accident, that is a disaster. Property damage, too, is often used as a measure of a disaster's impact. If one family's house is destroyed by a fire, that is a calamity for them, but it isn't a disaster; if a hurricane or a tornado destroys 10 percent of the buildings in a town or a community, that is a disaster. Property loss in disasters is measured in the millions of dollars, even the billions.

Recently, a third measure of the seriousness of disasters has begun to be used—damage to the environment. If an oil spill pollutes a body of water, it may cause no immediate loss of human life or direct destruction to anyone's personal property, but wildlife may be destroyed on a vast scale and the natural environment may be imperiled. In 1989, an oil tanker, the Exxon Valdez, ran aground in Prince William Sound near Valdez, Alaska; over 10 million gallons of oil gushed out of a gash in the ship's hull. Exxon spent $1.2 billion to take steps to clean up the mess, and a federal court decided that the company must pay a billion dollars in damages; numerous lawsuits remain to be settled. The oil pollution killed tens of thousands of birds, including over 100 bald eagles, thousands of sea otters, and uncountable numbers of other species. It inflicted incalculable damage to the land and the water in the vicinity. Certainly all of us would agree that the Exxon Valdez oil spill was a disaster, even though no one died and no structures were damaged.

The damage disasters cause is a matter of degree, not an either-or proposition. The earthquake that devastated northern Iran in 1990 killed 40,000 people and caused billions of dollars in property damage. The leakage of a toxic gas from a Union Carbide chemical plant in Bhopal, India, in 1984 killed over 3,500 people and injured nearly a quarter of a million; a New Delhi court ordered Union Carbide to pay out nearly half a billion dollars to the victims and their families in compensation (Hazarika, 1989). In 1987, a forest fire destroyed three million acres of timber, valued at $4 billion, in Manchuria (Salisbury, 1989); it is estimated that between nine and 15 million acres burned on the Siberian side of the border in the same fire, but, so far Soviet authorities have refused to release information on the impact of the blaze. On March 27, 1977, two Boeing 747s, one operated by Pan American and the other by KLM, collided at the airport at Tenerife in the Canary Islands; 582 passengers and crew members were killed. These events are disasters by anyone's definition. Most disasters are not nearly so catastrophic, however. Exactly where a damaging event ceases to be simply a personal tragedy for a few and begins to be a disaster for a society as a whole cannot be determined with any precision. As long as we recognize that disasters must entail substantial property or ecological damage or loss of human life—and that this is a dimension or matter of degree—we are on firm ground.

The J-Curve of Disasters. As a general rule, and as with many phenomena in human life, the amount of harm that damaging events inflict can be plotted on what is called a J-curve. A J-curve describes a certain kind of relationship between two dimensions, in this case, the amount of damage and the number of cases at each level of damage. There are many cases of damaging events in which there is very little damage; as the level of damage increases, the number of events that inflict that much damage decreases. For instance, there have been many thousands of accidents in which one person was killed, a smaller number in which two were killed, fewer still in which three were killed, and so on. Only eight civilian airline accidents in history killed between 200 and 300 people, only three killed between 300 and 400, and only two killed over 400, both of which, in fact, resulted in over 500 deaths (Table 5-1). A J-curve for the relationship between the extent of harm

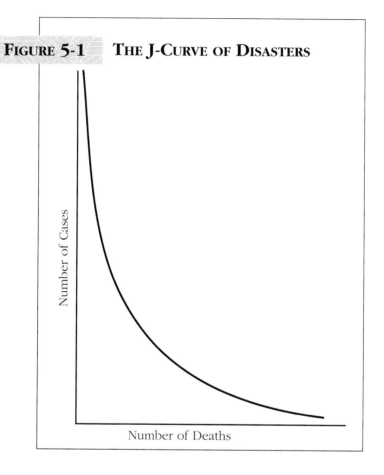

FIGURE 5-1 **THE J-CURVE OF DISASTERS**

Number of Cases

Number of Deaths

that a given damaging event causes and the number of cases of events that cause that much damage would look like the J-curve presented in Figure 5-1.

Usually, when many people are killed, much property is damaged, and the natural environment is devastated on a widespread scale, some disruption or stress is caused in or introduced into a society or a segment of it (Perry and Pugh, 1978, pp. 82–83). A disaster is something that must be coped with or dealt with; it calls for a large-scale organizational response to deal with the problems and difficulties it introduces. The loss of human life calls for steps to be taken to tend to the survivors; damage to property calls for efforts at rebuilding; poisoning the environment produces demands in some quarters for a cleanup. Disasters cry out for action—before, during, and especially after. A period of adjustment and restructuring is necessary for a society or a community to rebuild and recover.

Disasters: Disorganization or Organization?   A personal tragedy, such as the death of a loved one, has a devastating impact on one or more persons' lives, but it rarely has an impact on the social structure as a whole. The

TABLE 5-1 **WORST AIR CRASHES ON RECORD**

Date	Location	Fatalities
March 1977	Canary Islands	582
August 1985	Japan	520
March 1974	Paris, France	346
June 1985	Coast of Ireland	329
August 1980	Saudi Arabia	301
July 1988	Persian Gulf	290
May 1979	Chicago	275
December 1988	Scotland	270
September 1983	Soviet Air Space	269
July 1991	Saudi Arabia	261
November 1979	Antarctica	257
May 1991	Thailand	223
December 1985	Newfoundland	256
January 1978	India	213
December 1974	Sri Lanka	191
August 1975	Morocco	188
May 1987	Poland	183
November 1978	Sri Lanka	183
November 1983	Spain	183

(*Source.* Associated Press and *The New York Times,* September 24, 1989, p. 35, with additions.)

social fabric is not torn, the community is not disabled, the society is not disrupted. With a mass disaster, a community's social life is affected. It should be emphasized—and this has been a major theme of recent research in the field—that, under certain conditions, the organizational response that overcomes the disruption that the disaster presents may actually *strengthen* and *affirm* the social structure. Thus, rather than introducing *disorganization*, a disaster may actually reintroduce social *organization*. Still, all disasters present a challenge that must be overcome, and not all social structures rise to that challenge. (For example, disasters in poorer countries tend to be more devastating than those in more affluent ones, that is, those with greater organizational and material resources.) The disruption, stress, or tension that disasters cause or present to a social order make them interesting to the sociologist of collective behavior.

Disasters as Unscheduled Events. Disasters have been described as "unscheduled events" (Perry and Pugh, 1978, p. 83). While some disasters—for example, tornados and floods—can be predicted, the predictions that are made are not always accurate, the time lag is rarely more than a few days, and the full extent of the devastation cannot be known until the event passes. Moreover, many, perhaps most, disasters are completely unpredictable. This unpredictability of the events that cause disasters, and the unpredictability of the behavior of people who are caught up in them, make the study of disaster behavior a form of collective behavior and make it interesting to researchers studying this phenomenon. If everything in a disaster, down to the tiniest detail, were completely predictable, it wouldn't be very interesting—and it wouldn't be a form of collective behavior.

What Is a Disaster? A Summary.   Disasters, then, have the following characteristics: They are defined by the *extent* of their damage, the *disruption* or *challenge* they generate or present to the social order, and the relative *unpredictability* of their arrival. Their unpredictability implies a fourth characteristic: They are *sudden, or "rapid onset," single-event phenomena.* Disaster researchers typically do not look at phenomena that are continuous and ongoing, that stretch out over a period of time—several months, a year, a decade. (Although the *impact* of a disaster can last for centuries, of course.) The long-term pollution of a country's air and water may be disastrous to human life and to the environment, but it is not usually conceptualized as a disaster by experts. The cancer that smoking tobacco cigarettes causes is a medical catastrophe, but it is not a disaster as the field has defined it. (The Black Death, or Plague, which took place in Europe and Asia in the 1300s, and may have killed half the population in the affected areas, had some features of a disaster, but it is rarely treated in the literature as such.) Because some damaging events are sudden, single-event phenomena, people react to and deal with them in ways that are quite different from those that last a much longer period of time. Longer-lasting physical catastrophes can be dealt with in a more planned, organized, and institutionalized fashion. (Or can be ignored with fewer social—but just as many physical—consequences.) Wars, which have killed more people than any of the disasters discussed in this book, are rarely looked at as a disaster in the senses discussed. When I discuss disasters in this chapter, they will be short-term, sudden events.

Natural Vs. Technological Disasters.   There are many different kinds of disasters, many different causes of the sudden, large-scale loss of life and destruction to property and the environment. However, if all the different ways disasters could occur were to be classified, only two broad categories would emerge. The first category is made up of *natural disasters*, or "acts of God." These include monsoons and floods, hurricanes (on the East coast) or typhoons (in the Pacific), tropical cyclones, tidal waves or tsunamis, tornados or "twisters," blizzards, hailstorms, many forest fires, earthquakes, avalanches, landslides, mud slides, sandstorms, and volcanic eruptions (Table 5-2). The second category includes the many possible *technological accidents*. These include nuclear radiation, airline crashes, train wrecks, ship sinkings, chemical leaks, fires in buildings, and explosions. (This classification is not air-tight, of course, and some disasters may have elements of both categories.) While

TABLE 5-2 SELECTED NATURAL DISASTERS OF THE 20TH CENTURY

Year	Event	Location	Death Toll
1900	Hurricane	USA (Texas)	6,000
1902	Volcanic Eruption	Martinique	29,000
1902	Volcanic Eruption	Guatemala	6,000
1906	Earthquake/Fire	USA (California)	1,500
1906	Typhoon	Hong Kong	10,000
1906	Earthquake	Chile	20,000
1908	Earthquake	Italy	83,000
1911	Volcanic Eruption	Philippines	1,300
1915	Earthquake	Italy	30,000
1916	Landslide	Italy, Austria	10,000
1919	Volcanic Eruption	Indonesia	5,200
1920	Earthquake	China	100,000
1923	Earthquake	Japan	100,000
1927	Earthquake	China	100,000
1928	Hurricane/Flood	Caribbean, USA	2,000
1932	Earthquake	China	70,000
1933	Tsunami	Japan	3,000
1935	Earthquake	India	30,000
1939	Earthquake/Tsunami	Chile	30,000
1939	Earthquake	Turkey	30,000
1949	Flood	China	57,000
1949	Earthquake/Landslide	USSR	12,000–20,000
1951	Volcanic Eruption	New Guinea	2,900
1954	Flood	China	40,000
1959	Typhoon	Japan	4,600
1960	Earthquake	Morocco	12,000
1962	Earthquake	Iran	12,000
1962	Landslide	Peru	5,000
1963	Cyclone	Bangladesh	22,000
1963	Landslide	Italy	2,000
1965	Earthquake	USA (Alaska)	131
1965	Cyclone	Bangladesh	17,000
1965	Cyclone	Bangladesh	30,000
1965	Cyclone	Bangladesh	10,000
1968	Earthquake	Iran	12,000
1970	Earthquake/Landslide	Peru	70,000
1970	Cyclone	Bangladesh	300,000–500,000
1971	Cyclone	India	10,000–25,000
1976	Earthquake	Guatemala	24,000
1976	Earthquake	China	200,000–800,000
1977	Cyclone	India	20,000
1978	Earthquake	Iran	25,000
1985	Cyclone	Bangladesh	10,000
1985	Volcanic Eruption	Colombia	22,000
1988	Earthquake	Armenia	25,000
1989	Earthquake	USA (California)	62
1990	Earthquake	Iran	40,000
1991	Cyclone	Bangladesh	125,000–200,000

(*Sources*: National Research Council, U.S. National Academy of Sciences, U.S. National Academy of Engineering, 1990; adapted from *The New York Times*, June 22, 1990, p. A10.

victims of each category may be equally devastated, there are important consequences, particularly psychological, of having been victimized by one or the other type (Baum, 1988; Baum, Fleming, and Davidson, 1983). Three additional points are in order.

Violent Natural Phenomena Vs. Disasters.   First, violent natural phenomena, such as earthquakes and tornados, are not, *in and of themselves*, human disasters or even intrinsically bad—although they often are. The earth—in fact, the entire universe—is dynamic, always in flux, eternally changing; the forces that launch violent natural phenomena are simply strong, sudden triggers for change. It is only when humans, and that which humans value, get in the path of these upheavals that we have a disaster on our hands. A huge natural upheaval can occur very far from human habitation and cause no damage whatsoever; a relatively small natural phenomenon in a densely populated area could cause a great deal. As we'll see, humans often are forced to live in areas that are routinely threatened by natural upheavals. When one occurs, many lives are—tragically but, given sufficient resources, preventably—lost.

Disasters and Human Habitation.   Second, human habitation often *exacerbates* or even *creates* the destructive impact of natural upheavals. When humans cut down the trees in an area, flooding is facilitated; when they destroy a coral atoll barrier, a cyclone will devastate an island more severely; over farming and over grazing will destroy the grassland in an area, permitting sandstorms to wipe out the fertile land that remains. Mud slides and avalanches are often triggered by human activity in a physically precarious, vulnerable area. As we'll see, the humanly-made impoundment at Buffalo Creek created a lake of water and slag which, in turn, made a flood possible (Erikson, 1976, pp. 24–27). Ground surface collapses are often not natural events at all, but caused by unregulated human geological activity, such as coal mining (Whittow, 1979, pp. 178ff). Thus, many disasters are "acts of humans" as much as "acts of God" (Wijkman and Timberlake, 1988).

Planning for Disasters.   And third—the flip side of the second point—is that humans can often reduce the death toll through planning, evacuation, and rescue. In 1980, a previously inactive volcano, Mount St. Helens, located in Washington State, erupted, conveying destruction as far as 60 miles away, precipitating landslides, mudflows, wildfires, and floods; volcanic ash fell over a 40,000 square mile area, and economic losses were estimated at close to a billion dollars. However, since geologists had been able to predict the blast, permitting authorities and local residents to plan for it, only 62 lives were lost. One of the major thrusts of contemporary research on disasters is limiting the damage, especially the death toll, through informed, timely planning, organization, and intervention.

The Social Impact of Disasters.   Clearly, here, our interest is not in the "triggering event" of disasters, that is, the natural cataclysm itself except insofar as it is relevant to and impacts upon human behavior). As social scientists, we are primarily interested in "the impact of disasters on humans, on property, on institutions" (Ebert, 1988, p. xi). More specifically, students of collective behavior are interested in behavior *before, during*, and *after* disasters, and they are interested in the behavior of both the many *officials* whose job it is to minimize and cope with the damage the agent causes, and the many *citizens* who are threatened and assaulted by that agent. As we've already seen briefly, and as we'll see in more detail, the human response to disasters is partly planned out and partly spontaneous and emergent. In other words, behavior in disasters has one foot in collective behavior and one foot outside the field. Exactly *how, why*, and *to what extent* do natural upheavals influence and impact human behavior generally and spontaneous, noninstitutionalized behavior specifically? How do people *act in* and *experience* disasters? How do they cope with them? How do officials deal with them? How is the plight of disaster victims seen by the general public? By officials? And how does this influence how they are treated? These are some of the issues we'll be dealing with in this and the next chapter.

_____ THINKING ABOUT DISASTERS _____

As we might expect, LeBon's view of the barbaric, hysterical nature of the crowd heavily influenced the earliest writings on human behavior in disasters; in fact, "the spector of LeBon," according to one expert, "still haunts much lay thinking" on this subject (Wenger, 1987, p. 215). Blumer's contributions, which stressed the contagion inherent in circular reactions, likewise argued that crowd behavior, and, by extension, behavior during disasters, was likely to become unthinking and highly charged emotionally. Convergence theory, too, added to mythical thinking about disasters; again, by extension, theorists adopting the convergence view argued that individuals with certain preexisting tendencies were likely to flock to a disaster site and act in a uniform fashion—mainly to loot and exploit the victimized. In short, theoretical work on collective behavior generally, and about disasters specifically, done prior to the 1950s, seriously distorted the phenomenon it focused on. It emphasized the individualism, emotionality, irrationality, and homogeneity of disaster behavior (Wenger, 1987, p. 218).

Beginning in the 1950s, systematic empirical work was conducted on disaster-related behavior (Marks and Fritz, 1954; Form and Nosow, 1958). The results of these early investigations "challenged traditional views of collective behavior," finding "very little support for the perspective that contagion, convergence, and homogeneous anti-social behavior were the essence of disaster response" (Wenger, 1987, p. 219). Beginning in the late 1960s and the early 1970s, research and writings on disasters began focusing on *organizational responses* to disasters (Barton, 1969; Dynes, 1970; Brouillette and Quarantelli, 1971). How do communities and agencies cope with disaster? Does a disaster generate interagency cooperation? How are the resources of the relevant organizations related to disaster-coping outcomes? Do disasters tend to generate social organizations and social movements? Can communities and organizations more effectively prepare themselves for disasters? These are some recent questions that the field of disaster research is asking (Stallings and Quarantelli, 1985). In other words, the field is moving *away* from looking at disaster-related behavior as a form of collective behavior, and *toward* looking at it as a form of institutional, organizational behavior. There is a parallel here with the study of social movements, which, likewise, are now seen by the "resource mobilization" perspective, discussed in Chapter 1, and to be discussed in more detail in Part 4, as a form of organizational behavior (Zald and McCarthy, 1987). In fact, some researchers are seeing disaster-related behavior *as* a form of social movement activity (Walsh, 1984; Walsh and Warland, 1983). In short, the study of both disasters and social movements is being redefined out of the traditional scope of the field of collective behavior.

___ The Role of Organizations in Disasters ___

In recent years, disasters have been studied from the point of view of formal organizations, that is, how such organizations overcome the challenges that disasters pose for a community or a society. To the extent that this is true, recent disaster research falls outside the scope of collective behavior. On the other hand, to the extent that disasters are never completely predictable and pose challenges that require organizations to innovate and engage in impromptu, spontaneous behavior, collective behavior is highly relevant to the study of disasters. In order to appreciate this recent focus in the field, it is first necessary to set the stage by describing how sociologists look at groups, both primary and secondary, informal and formal.

Human Groups

All groups can be classified by the extent to which the social interactions that takes place within them are largely *primary* or *secondary*.

Primary Interaction. Primary social interaction is informal, emotional, intimate, mainly face-to-face, broad in scope, of intrinsic value—valued as an end in itself rather than a means to an end—and particularistic, that is, instances in which people relate to one another as individuals rather than as representatives of broad categories. Friendship groups, families, street gangs, and two lovers provide examples of groups in which the principal interaction taking place is primary in nature; such groups may be referred to as primary groups.

Secondary Interaction. On the other hand, *secondary* social relations are those that are formal, emotionally neutral, both indirect and face-to-face, segmental or narrow in scope, practical, expedient, purposive, instrumental—where people relate to one another mainly as a means to an end—and universalistic, that is, in which people relate to one another mainly as representatives of a given category. Groups whose members relate to one another in a secondary fashion include formal organizations or bureaucracies such as General Motors, the United States Army, and the Red Cross. Such groups are usually referred to as secondary groups. Of course, not all social interaction in any group is entirely of one type; within secondary organizations, there are pockets of informal interaction, such as in friendship groups in the army or among factory workers. Group relations are "more or less" primary, not absolutely so, or "more or less" secondary; in secondary groups, formal social interaction predominates.

Formal Organizations. Formal organizations represent the most secondary of all secondary groups. They represent a territory in which social interaction is characterized by emotional neutrality and narrow, universal rules. A formal organization is a group that has been instituted deliberately to achieve specific goals and whose members' activities are systematically integrated to achieve them. The hallmarks of the formal organization are a high degree of rationality; the deliberate setting of goals; the institutionalization of means to achieve those goals; and a high degree of organization or coordination among its members, usually achieved by a hierarchical structure, or chain of command, in which it is always clear who can give orders to whom. Most formal organizations are bureaucracies. Of all formal organizations, bureaucracies are the most rational, the most hierarchical. In addition, they provide careers for their employees. Some formal organizations are not bureaucracies—for instance, many voluntary associations, like Parent Teacher Associations—because they are not large, have no hierarchies or chains of command, and they do not provide jobs or careers for their members.

DISASTERS AND FORMAL ORGANIZATIONS

For at least a generation, mainstream research on disasters has focused largely on the role of formal organizations in coping with disasters—before, during, and after they take place. One of the principal functions of a formal organization is to maximize the achievement of a given goal by maximizing preparedness and minimizing surprises. To that extent, much of what the field of disaster research studies lies outside the traditional realm of the field of collective behavior. On the other hand, to the extent that surprises, including spontaneity, can never be completely eliminated, especially in disasters, disaster research will always have one foot firmly planted in the field of collective behavior. In fact, Brouillette and Quarantelli (1971) argue that, precisely for this reason, the original formulation of the bureaucracy, by Max Weber (1864–1920), is inadequate to understand bureaucracies in a disaster situation. Bureaucracies demand routinization, predictability, standardization, and institutionalization, while, in contrast, disasters demand that organizations that deal with them be adaptable, flexible, spontaneous, resourceful, capable of impromptu behavior. In fact, the organizations that face and overcome the challenges presented by disasters must engage in "de-bureaucratization" so that they may quickly develop new organizational structures to perform new organizational tasks (Brouillette and Quarantelli, 1971). This dilemma, tension, or contrast between the bureaucratic structure and tasks of classic formal organizations and the "de-bureaucratized" structure and tasks of disaster organizations has been a major theme—perhaps *the* major theme—in recent disaster literature.

According to the typology developed by Russell Dynes (1970, 1978), disaster-related organizations may require *change* or *no change* in their *structure* or their *task* when dealing with a disaster. This generates four types of organizations: those that require no change in either task or structure; those that require no change in task, but a change in structure; those that require no change in structure, but a change in task; and those that require a change in both task and structure. Dynes refers to these types of disaster-related organizations as: *established, expanding, extending,* and *emergent organizations.*

Established Disaster-Related Organizations. *Established disaster-related organizations* are those whose function already includes coping with emergencies and smaller-scale disasters, even before a full-scale disaster strikes. That is, events very much like disasters are the organization's regular, routine task; in a disaster, such organizations simply do what they normally do, only on a larger scale. They do not have to take on new tasks, and the structure that is already in place is adequate to meet the challenge the disaster poses. A good example is a community's fire department. During their everyday activities, they fight fires and other emergencies; during a large-scale disaster, they do much the same thing. And during a disaster, much like all the other times, there is a clear-cut structure with a well-known chain of command: a battalion commander gives orders to a precinct captain, who gives orders to an ordinary firefighter who, in turn, has authority over most ordinary citizens. If large-scale disasters did not exist, established organizations would still exist because smaller-scale emergencies, such as fires, will always plague human life.

Expanding Disaster-Related Organizations. The second type of organization is the *expanding disaster-related organization.* Its main job is to cope with disasters, too, so the disaster generates no change in task. On the other hand, when a disaster strikes, they must vastly expand their size and transform their structure so that they can conduct the business at hand; suddenly, many individuals must come "on board" to do a job which they anticipated and for which they were trained. Expanding organizations do not carry out disaster-related operations on an everyday, day-to-day basis. Instead, they maintain a state of preparedness—they are always at the ready for when disaster strikes. The Red Cross is a good example of the expanding disaster-related organization. Such an organization can only exist if it is supported by a large number of volunteers (along with a much smaller core staff of professionals); it is not economically feasible for large numbers of individuals to train, prepare, and wait for disasters that come along very rarely. Unlike the established organizations, disasters, for the expanding organization, are their very reason for existence; if there were no disasters, these organizations would not exist.

Extending Disaster-Related Organizations. *Extending disaster-related organizations* represent a type whose structure is unchanged by a disaster, in that existing personnel carry out the required tasks, but the nature of their tasks are vastly altered. Extending organizations spend nearly all of their time normally engaged in other than disaster-related activities; most of what they do in a disaster is unfamilar to them. They help out—and are expected by others to help out—when disaster strikes, but disasters are not their reason for being. If disasters did not exist, they would be identical to they way they usually are. A construction company represents a good example of the extending organization. During a disaster, builders will often place their equipment at the disposal of the community, truck drivers will take stranded residents to a safer location, operators of earth moving equipment will build temporary dams against flooding, and so on. At the same time, the disaster does not alter their organizational structure; the same owners, managers, and employees help out and coordinate with one another in much the same way as they do normally.

Emergent Disaster-Related Organizations. The last type of organization is the *emergent disaster-related organization,* for whom the disaster changes both task and structure. Unlike the other three, this type is not a formal organization at all, although it often takes on some of their characteristics, such as chain of command, specialization of tasks and roles, and a clear-cut conception of membership. Emergent organizations spring up almost spontaneously before, during, and after disasters and are usually based on social networks that already exist, such as those based on neighborhood and community residence and membership in a family, work group, or group of friends. These disaster-related groups or organizations are "ephemeral and temporary" (Killian, 1952; Zurcher, 1968); they spring up when the community is threatened, and usually dissolve when the threat has been overcome (although, occasionally, emergent organizations are institutionalized into more long-term structures). The informal community and neighborhood rescue and work crews that spring up during and after a disaster are good examples of the emergent organization.

Disaster Myths

As with collective behavior in general (Couch, 1968), there are several myths about behavior during disasters that are widely held by the public (Quarantelli, 1960; Quarantelli and Dynes, 1972; Wenger et al., 1975; Anderson, 1988–1989a, 1988–1989b). These myths tend to be perpetuated in the media and, when the public reads or hears them, or sees them on television news, few people who are not actually in the disasters being reported about know that they are false. They impede an understanding of what disaster victims go through, and may even impede efforts to help disaster victims. Understanding *why* they are false helps us understand the nature and dynamics of collective behavior generally.

Perhaps the "master" myth, the one that generalizes nearly all of the more specific ones, is the myth of *exaggeration*—the attempt to portray the impact of a given disaster as significantly more devastating than it actually is. The media do this, much of the public does this, although, interestingly, disaster victims generally do not. It is clear why the impact of disasters is exaggerated in the media: It creates the illusion of a more important story than is actually the case. When the public talks about a disaster, likewise, exaggeration stresses the fact that they are discussing something very important. For instance, during an earthquake in Alaska, the original estimate of the total number of fatalities was 1,000; soon thereafter, Chicago newspapers reported 500 dead; in Seattle, the papers said that 300 had died; in Anchorage papers, it was 100. The actual number who were killed in Anchorage by the earthquake was seven (Quarantelli and Dynes, 1972, p. 70), and in Alaska as a whole, 131. Nearly all of the other disaster myths center around the theme of exaggeration, in one way or another. Eleven of the most widely-held disaster myths are: panic, individual behavior, the illusion of control, evacuation, convergence, emergency shelters, passive dependency, disaster trauma, looting, martial law, and misconceptions about the constraints of the physical setting.

Panic. Blumer's contagion perspective, as well as the stereotype most people hold, would predict that during disasters most people engage in irrational, panic-stricken behavior that not only threatens their own lives but the lives of others as well. Like the proverbial drowning man, people in disasters become so terrified that they are literally incapable of doing anything to survive—indeed, they act in such a way that they guarantee their own demise. In a blind, hysterical flight to escape danger, they stampede headlong in a random direction, without regard for others, to their own deaths; this might be called the "grip of terror" view (Miller, 1985, pp. 175–179). During Hurricane Carla, which hit the Gulf coast communities of Texas and Louisiana, a half million people were evacuated from their homes; the evacuation was orderly, and no one was killed in it. Nonetheless, several newspapers ran the headline: "More than 100,000 Persons Flee in Near Panic" (Quarantelli and Dynes, 1972, p. 70). Reporting "panic" indicates that the hurricane was a terrifying experience for many, and therefore an important and interesting story.

All research on the subject demonstrates that the view that widespread panic occurs during most disasters is completely mythical (Quarantelli, 1960, pp. 68ff; Quarantelli and Dynes, 1972, pp. 67–68; Wenger, 1987, p. 225; Wenger et al., 1975, pp. 34–35). This is not to say that no one has ever panicked during a disaster, or that mass panic has never occurred. Nonetheless, panic behavior during disasters is "incredibly rare," says Dennis Wenger, codirector of the Disaster Research Center, which is located at the University of Delaware (Anderson, 1988–1989b, p. 20); you can "count on your fingers the number of verified cases of panic that occurred in the United States since 1900 and still have fingers left over for rings." The vast majority of people who are trapped in a disaster situation engage in adaptive, survival-oriented behavior, and, when they are able, they tend to help others who are in greater need. During disasters, people tend to be remarkably composed, realistic, and problem-solving oriented about physical dangers. Panic usually takes place only under very restricted conditions, specifically, the "perception of immediate danger, limited escape routes, the perception that escape routes are open, but closing, and a lack of communication about the current situation" (Wenger, 1987, p. 225).

As an aside, it is interesting to note that mass panic often figures in fictional and news portrayals of ongoing or predicted disasters. A common belief among individuals who imagine that unidentified flying objects (UFOs) are extraterrestrial creatures visiting Earth is that high-level officials know but refuse to release information about them for fear of mass panic among the population. In the film, *2001*, a space crew discovers a black monolith buried beneath the surface of the moon by members of an intelligent civilization, but the authorities refuse to communicate this to the public, again, because it is felt that mass panic and "social disorganization" would ensue. In the 1970s, in Sweden, a fictional news bulletin announced a leak of radioactive material from a nuclear plant in Barseback. The mass media reported that mass panic had occurred, whereas, in fact, panic reactions were practically nonexistent (Rosengren et al., 1979). Even the extent of the panic that was supposed to have occurred in reaction to the famous 1938 "War of the Worlds" broadcast was grossly exaggerated by the media, making the mass panic stories about the broadcast "a wonderful example of a cultural myth" (Anderson, 1988–1989b, p. 21). In Woody Allen's movie, *Radio Days* (1987), a couple is parked in a deserted spot near a beach in Brooklyn in 1938. When "The War of the Worlds" broadcast comes on the radio, the man immediately jumps out of the car and runs off into the night fog. *Miracle Mile* (1989) fictionalizes the panic that follows a rumor—true, as it turns out—of an impending nuclear attack on Los Angeles; vehicular gridlock, car crashes, and machine-gunnings ensue on a mass scale. Depictions such as these keep belief in disaster myths such as this one alive and influential.

Individual Behavior.   In line with the "grip of terror" image of people's behavior during disasters is the view that such behavior is totally individualistic, with each person acting to save himself or herself, uninfluenced by the behavior or the reactions of others. The myth of individual behavior is the myth that, during disasters, behavior tends to be *parallel* in nature, that is, atomistic and noninteractional, that people are engaging in *mass* behavior (Wenger, 1987, pp. 214, 224). On the contrary, human behavior in disasters is collective—that is to say, *social*—behavior. When people are hit by disasters, they act, react to others, and interact with one another; they hardly ever launch off on a line of action without taking others into account. (If they do, in all likelihood, they are alone!) As the early experiments by Muzafer Sherif (1936; Sherif and Harvey, 1952) showed, when people are unsure as to what they should do, they tend to be more likely to rely on others to provide cues to appropriate behavior. This generalization applies with even greater force during disasters than it does for ordinary, everyday behavior.

The Illusion of Control. This belief (not widely referred to in the disaster literature) is a myth about the *potential for control* that individuals who are faced with danger actually have. Most people have a very distorted notion of what can be done in a disaster; they believe that most people panic, but *they* wouldn't, that most people are trapped or engage in self-destructive behavior, but *they* wouldn't. It comforts us to know that if someone dies in a disaster, they didn't exactly deserve it, but perhaps they didn't do everything they could have to save themselves. We want to think that *we* wouldn't have gone down in the disaster, *we* would have done something different to save ourselves. The realization that there is absolutely nothing that could have been done to save the victims is a terrifying thought. We live in an optimistic, interventionist culture, one whose members believe that there is a direct relationship between effort and outcome; we live, in other words, in a "just world" (Lerner, 1980). The thought that the world is *not* just, that blind, stupid accidents determine whether some people live or die, is incompatible with the view that if we work hard enough, we can overcome anything.

In many ways, the myth of the illusion of control seems to contradict some of the other disaster myths, particularly the "master myth" of exaggeration. After all, if I could have overcome the danger, how serious could it have been? In fact, this myth addresses not the seriousness of the danger of a given disaster, but two biases most people hold—first, most people tend to overestimate their own competence at a given activity, and second, they tend to overestimate the degree to which competence is related to a given result or outcome. There is a great deal of research in the field of social psychology on these issues; the first is related to what's called *the egocentric bias* (Ross and Sicoly, 1979; Zuckerman et al., 1983), and the second is related to *the just world hypothesis* (Lerner, 1980; Langer, 1975). Unfortunately, these concepts have not been systematically linked either to collective behavior or to behavior in disasters.

A good example of the principle of the illusion of control is the view, aided and abetted by depictions in film and television dramas, that many of us hold about the nature of fires. As Frank Field, former weather forecaster for the New York City CBS News, pointed out in his 1988 series, "Plan to Get Out Alive," the stereotypical and mythical image of fires is that all it takes to save one's own life and the lives of others is a little courage and effort. What does a movie or a TV fire look like? Inside a burning building, you can see the flames; everything is brightly lit. The room is intensely hot, although just bearably so. There's a lot of smoke, although by covering your mouth, you can get some air if you fight hard enough; you cough a lot, that's all. (Also, people in dramatic renditions of fires rarely drop to the floor and crawl along, because, if they did, the audience wouldn't be able to see them very well.) That's a movie or a TV fire. It is dramatic, but it has no correspondence whatsoever to a real-life fire.

In a real fire, you can't see anything; you can't see the room, you can't see the flames, you can't see anyone. Everything is black with smoke; you stumble around in pitch darkness. Second, there's no air. Within seconds, a fully-engaged fire consumes all the oxygen in the room. You can hold your breath for a couple minutes, although, chances are, you're excited and exerting yourself, so you'll have even less time than this. If you try to breathe, you'll take in smoke, causing great pain to your lungs. The fact is, if you're not out of there within two minutes, you're dead. And third, it's much hotter than we can possibly imagine. It's not just hot—everything is literally burning up! It's not just burning a few feet away, where the walls are in flames; the air is so hot, *you'll* go up in flames! The room is between 500 and 1,000 degrees Fahrenheit; you are roasted to death as you stand there! You can't do anything, you can't save anyone's life, you have no time to get out—you are dead. So, when people see news reports on TV or read accounts of fires in newspapers, they tend to hold a totally inadequate notion of what happened. They have a distorted view of what the victims could have done to save themselves and others; they typically imagine that *they* could have done more to survive or to help others. They are suffering from "the illusion of control."

Evacuation.   The evacuation myth holds that, during a disaster or, when an impending disaster, such as a tornado or a hurricane, is announced, most people wisely evacuate the area (Wenger et al., 1975, p. 36). In fact, only a small minority of the residents of an ongoing or upcoming disaster evacuate. People show a "great reluctance . . . to withdraw" from the familiar surroundings of their communities, their relatives and friends, their homes (Quarantelli, 1960, p. 69). Here, we have an example of institutional norms— obey the authorities, they know best about what's safest for you; evacuate the area, which are ignored, circumvented, or contradicted by people's spontaneous, emergent, informal, collective behavior (Quarantelli, 1980). The media image of a disaster is not complete without hordes of victims, a few possessions in their cars, or, better yet on their backs, streaming out of the stricken area. In reality, it takes a great deal of danger to dislodge people from their communities. Research shows that, unless an area is totally incapacitated (for example, if a flood swamps a community), or unless residents are forced by civil or military authorities to leave, rarely does more than a quarter of the population evacuate (Quarantelli, 1960, pp. 69–70).

Quarantelli (1960, p. 70) cites the classic example of Bootle, England, during the Second World War. The city was bombed "nightly for a week." Sixty percent of the dwelling structures were damaged at least twice, and only 10 percent "escaped serious damage." All community facilities were shattered; the roads were impassable, gas mains were torn apart, water was difficult to obtain, public services were practically nonexistent, and getting food was chancy business, and yet, one-quarter of the residents "remained to sleep in their homes throughout the raids." Outsiders imagine that being *in* a given disaster situation is highly stressful, which is true, but they do not picture how stressful being *away* from one's own home during a disaster will be for most people. And, in fact, with very few exceptions, staying put is a fairly rational decision. Just to be on the safe side, authorities tend to be overly cautious about ordering an evacuation. It is an extremely rare disaster that proves to be fatal for even a minute fraction of the resident population.

The refusal of the residents of a stricken area to evacuate is related to at least three other factors aside from their rational assessment of the disaster's impact. They are psychological in origin, and so sociologists do not usually examine their influence. The first, which we've already come across, is "just world" thinking; many people think, if I am virtuous and good (and who does not think that they are?), nothing really bad can happen to me; bad things only happen to those who deserve it. Therefore, this disaster can't hurt me. The second, which we've already encountered, is *egocentrism*; many people think, I'll avoid getting hurt in a disaster, even though others won't, because I'm smarter, cleverer, stronger, and faster than they are. And the third is *denial*, what psychologists call "the feeling of personal immunity" (Wolfenstein, 1957, p. 18). Imagining that one will be killed or injured by a catastrophe is painful, uncomfortable, and something to be avoided. Denying the danger, believing that one is immune from it, is a common means of avoiding such thoughts.

Convergence.   Convergence isn't so much a myth most people hold about disasters as it is a *consequence* of such a myth. "Convergence" refers to the supplies and assistance that "converge" on the disaster area. (Obviously, this is a different type of convergence than that which was discussed earlier in this chapter and in Chapter 2, that is, the convergence of certain types of individuals in crowds or to a stricken community. [see pages 58 and 201].) When disaster strikes an area, outsiders usually send in food and clothing; why they do this is not clear. In fact, there is usually enough clothing to clothe everyone in the affected community and usually enough food, although distribution of the latter is sometimes a problem (Fritz and Mathewson, 1957; Wenger et al., 1975, p. 38). Typically, "tons of unneeded, unwanted, unusable clothing will pour into disaster areas. In many ways, that becomes a disaster. No one knows what to do with all the stuff that arrives," says Dennis Wenger, codirector of the Disaster Research Center (Anderson, 1988–1989b, p. 21). This period of convergence does not last forever, however; as we'll see, when the publicity of the disaster declines, the convergence of assistance usually vanishes along with it.

In September 1989, Hurricane Hugo struck the South Carolina coastline. Nearly 1,000 people were killed, 5,300 houses were demolished and 73,000 severely damaged, 75% of the state's timber was destroyed—valued at a billion dollars—and the damage to its agriculture, mainly peach and pecan trees and fields of cotton, tobacco, and vegetables, was incalculable. More than half the state's counties were declared federal disaster areas. Supplies donated by Americans all over the country began pouring into the affected areas at such a massive volume that sorting them out became a major, time-consuming job for volunteer relief workers. In a single day, a convoy of 38 trucks filed into a tiny fishing village of 500 residents. The problem was less the volume of supplies that were donated than their nature. What was needed most,

Disasters often place an immense burden on the communities they strike and demand that residents be innovative and creative in their responses to them. Here, Avianca Flight 52 crashes in a small suburban community near New York City. Thirty-seven fire and ambulance companies and more than 700 police officers responded, generating an on-the-site overload of assistance resources and personnel.

said Charleston County's director of planning and public affairs, was "heavy equipment, non-perishable food, generators, chain saws, and money. . . . What we don't need are clothes. We have lots of clothes" (Schneider, 1989).

On January 25th, on its approach to John F. Kennedy Airport, Avianca Flight 52 ran out of fuel and slammed into the ground at Cove Neck, an affluent, heavily-wooded Long Island community. Seventy-three passengers were killed, and there were 86 survivors. The volume of rescue vehicles that arrived on the scene was so great that the roadways became gridlocked, and ambulances leaving with injured survivors found it extremely difficult to get to local hospitals. Roadblocks were set up, and many vehicles had to drive over median strips to get to their destinations; "near anarchy" erupted on the roads. In addition, hundreds of curious people skirted the roadblocks on foot and tramped through the woods to get a look at the crash sight. Three hundred reporters descended on the scene, many calling in their stories on their cellular phones, which jammed up the telephone circuits, thereby making rescue-related calls all but impossible (Rather, 1990). Clearly, because of the *convergence* of too many people on a disaster site, rescue work is often a difficult proposition.

Emergency Shelters. A good news story of a major disaster is not complete without scenes of hundreds of victims huddled together in a public shelter; it combines the elements of need, altruism, and working together to overcome a problem. In fact, though much of the public believes that shelters are widely used during an emergency (Wenger et al., 1975, p. 37), the vast majority of the people who leave their homes do not go to shelters. Shelters are usually too far away, too inconvenient, and very uncomfortable. Most people prefer to rely on friends and relatives, even acquaintances, not disaster organizations.

During the Second World War, nearly one and one-half million Londoners were bombed out of their homes, and yet, only one in seven "passed through the official rest centers" that had been provided. In a tornado that hit Worcester, Massachussetts, 10,000 people were made homeless, and yet, only 50 people chose to be housed by the public authorities. In a flood in southern Texas, out of over 5,000 homeless people, only 350 chose to stay in mass public shelters. Out of over 50,000 people evacuated from their homes in a California flood, less than one in five stayed in shelters. In fact, public shelters are "the last source that people turn to for help when seeking to cope with crisis-created problems" (Quarantelli, 1960, p. 74; Rosow, 1977). As with the evacuation myth, the emergency shelter myth makes the mistake of *underestimating* people's love for the familiar and *overestimating* their tendency to follow directives from authorities.

Passive Dependency. The view that disaster victims are stricken, passive, dependent creatures whose behavior can be controlled by the authorities in a crisis situation is often held both by the authorities themselves and by much of the general public. Behavior during disasters is collective behavior, which is why we are looking at it in this chapter. This means that, to a significant degree, it is spontaneous and unpredictable. It is not a simple outgrowth of the formal norms of institutions and organizations, but emerges in the dynamics of person-to-person interaction. When the authorities announce that they want the victims of a given disaster to do something, they do not passively comply. They consider what they are doing, get together and talk with other victims, and arrive at an agreeable line of action. There is, in other words, a great deal of unplanned, impromptu behavior among those who are affected by a disaster. Said one official after a flood in New York State, "These darn people going off and doing things for themselves are just making a mess of things. We can't send them off the right way and keep proper track of them" (Quarantelli, 1960, p. 75). Of course, the "right way" to an official may not be the "right way" to a disaster victim. Public representatives often fail to understand that people are not inanimate objects that can be manipulated in conformity with official needs; instead, they almost always make decisions based on their own needs.

World War II films often show Londoners crowded into subway tunnels during a bombing. This is an accurate image; the shelters were widely used for this purpose. What is not generally known is that, initially, the government *banned* the use of subway stations as overnight shelters from air raids. It was only after people continued to use them that the official directive was cancelled. During a tidal wave in California, officials ordered the downtown area evacuated; the population complied with the order—but only to go to the beach to watch the tidal wave! (Quarantelli, 1960, pp. 76, 77). After a tornado in Kansas, relief workers were concerned about preventing further injury and death from severed power lines, broken glass, and twisted wreckage. Announcements were made on the media for people to stay in their homes, but "people came en masse to the disaster area." It seemed, said one survivor, that everyone wanted to get a look at the devastated part of town. The roads were "full of cars that were stopped and people were out taking pictures and looking at the wreckage." These sightseers "were, in effect, tourists of disaster" (Taylor, Zurcher, and Key, 1970, pp. 13, 14). In short, "When people feel that they have a legitimate reason for non-compliance, the issuance of an order has no more effect than the existence of unpopular laws against gambling preventing such activities. Disaster situations in themselves do not necessarily make people more pliable to direct organizational control than they ordinarily are" (Quarantelli, 1960, p. 76).

Disaster Trauma.   Disaster victims are often portrayed as dazed, shocked, traumatized, and unable to care for themselves. Trauma and shock are characteristic of a small minority of disaster victims—in the more serious disasters, perhaps one in 10, and this state rarely lasts more than a few minutes (Quarantelli, 1960, p. 73; Quarantelli and Dynes, 1972, p. 68; Anderson, 1988–1989b, p. 21; Wenger et al., 1975, p. 36). There are important exceptions, of course (Erikson, 1976; Gleser, Green, and Winget, 1981; Stern, 1977), as we'll see later on in more detail, but they occur under highly specific conditions. Extreme trauma tends to be very unusual. What is so impressive about disaster victims is how clear-headed, practical, resilient, and altruistic they are. Reporting many cases of stunned, highly traumatized victims exaggerates the seriousness of the disaster and creates the impression of a bigger, more important story than is actually the case. Thus, the media are unlikely to discontinue the practice, and as a consequence, the public is likely to go on believing this myth.

Looting.   The belief that looting is common during disasters is a widely-held myth; in fact, looting during natural disasters is quite rare (Quarantelli and Dynes, 1972, p. 69; Anderson, 1988–1989b, p. 21; Wenger, 1987, p. 232–233; Wenger et al., 1975, p. 35). This is not to say that it never occurs—only that is is infrequent and atypical. The crime rate actually *declines* during disasters—the exact opposite of what most people think. An interesting contrast can be made between looting during disasters and looting during civil disturbances, or so-called "race riots." During disasters, looting has little or no community support, it is rare, those who do loot tend to be outsiders, and they do so individually. During civil disturbances, looting has a great deal of community support, it is common, those who engage in it tend to be mainly from the community, and it is done in groups or collectivities of people (Quarantelli and Dynes, 1970). In short, looting during disasters may be criminal and deviant behavior, but typically, it is parallel, not collective behavior. On the other hand, looting during civil disturbances represents a genuine form of collective behavior.

Still, the image of looting during disasters persists, partly because it is news when it does happen, partly because people are shocked when it happens in the first place—after all, victimizing victims does not sit well with most of us—partly because the police and officials want to appear to be taking steps to prevent a potential problem (even though that problem doesn't actually exist), and partly because behavior *that looks* like looting often does take place—such as someone using equipment that he or she doesn't own to save lives, or survivors picking through the rubble of their homes for salvageable possessions (Quarantelli and Dynes, 1972; Anderson, 1988-1989b, p. 21).

A Contrary Case: Looting in St. Croix

In September 1989, Hurricane Hugo hit the Caribbean Islands with a special ferocity. On St. Croix, one of the Virgin Islands, three people died, 700 were injured, and three-quarters of the houses were destroyed or severely damaged. Four days after Hugo, relief supplies had still not arrived, and there was no running water, electricity, or telephone service; there was little food, and the local hospital, badly damaged, was closed. Three days after Hugo hit, President Bush declared the Virgin Islands a disaster area.

The looting of stores and burglarizing of homes in the hurricane's aftermath was extensive and widespread. "People are going nuts around here," said one eyewitness. "It's an area totally out of control . . . at the point of mass panic." There are, reports said, "mobs running up and down streets . . . looting stores, walking down the street carrying TV sets and refrigerators, helping themselves to store stocks and going right into private homes" (Fireman, 1989, pp. 3, 36). As with the New York City blackout looting, it engaged a broad cross-section of the island's population, including "grandmothers with toddlers, pregnant women, and men of all ages." The thieves "took their time selecting merchandise and made little effort to conceal what they were doing. When a news photographer approached, one woman was so unfazed that she ran to get her grandson so he could be in the picture too." While some of the looters were hungry people "picking over groceries that were about to rot anyway," much of what was stolen consisted of unnecessary items, like cans of paint, T-shirts, slide projectors, and sneakers. Observers reported police officers and National Guardsmen assisting looters. Said one resident of North Carolina, "I saw National Guardsmen reaching into the windows and handing jewelry and stuff to people. It was like it was their gift to the people" (Schmalz, 1989a, p. A22). Another witness reported seeing police cars "loaded to the gills with loot" (Fireman, 1989, p. 3). (Officials claimed that they may have been impostors, since uniforms and official vehicles were among the merchandise stolen.) Some claimed that they had seen store owners telling people to come in and take what they wanted so that they could claim a 100 percent loss on their insurance.

Why did looting take place on St. Croix and practically nowhere else in the Caribbean? (Some—far less extensive—looting was reported in St. Thomas and Puerto Rico.) Why did this community depart from the general pattern? Clearly, there are exceptions to any pattern; no general explanation can fully account for a single case or event. Each case exhibits some features and factors that may be somewhat different from elsewhere, but nonetheless subject to generalizations. Moreover, as we saw in earlier chapters, the dynamics of collective behavior in a given event are often volatile and subject to concrete, situational forces that can encourage or inhibit further, more dramatic behavior—a crowd leader emerges, rises up, and takes the initiative to act; a police officer assaults a citizen; the path of a crowd is blocked; local citizens patrol an area and call for calm; it rains on a given day; a rumor circulates. Thus, generalizing about why looting took place in one community but in no others is likely to be a tricky proposition.

While it is possible that the difference may have been immediate, situational, and accidental, many observers believe that there are several factors that made St. Croix somewhat different from other, superficially similar Caribbean communities: its crime rate, the depth of its poverty, the sharpness of its class and racial tensions, its isolation from governmental authority, and the fact that social control was lacking during much of the looting.

Crime in St. Croix is significantly higher than it is on St. Thomas, the capital of the Virgin Islands, and three times as high as the national average. Officials admit that crack use is subtantially higher on St. Croix than in most other Caribbean islands. One factor possibly influencing the behavior following this particular disaster was the fact that the hurricane so badly destroyed the island's prison that a number of inmates escaped. (Exactly how this impacted on the looting that took place on the island has not been studied empirically, however.)

St. Croix is three-quarters Black; most Blacks on the island hold low-paying, menial jobs. There are few Black-owned businesses. In contrast, whites own nearly all of the businesses, and they tend to hire whites from the mainland instead of local Blacks. Unemployment is unofficially estimated at 30 percent, nearly all of it Black. Resentment against whites runs high on the island. The federal government is felt by many to be the government of and for white people.

Said Ann Brittin, an anthropologist who has studied the Virgin Islands: "I'm not surprised about the looting. . . . When you look at the isolation, the crime already there, the low wages, the fact that Blacks cannot afford to rent or buy a house, it was bound to happen." Charles Fisher, an editor at *The St. Croix Avis*, the only Black-owned paper in the Virgin Islands, said, "This is a class fight. The rich guys come down from New York or wherever and build a hotel, but they can't be bothered to build a hurricane shelter or a playground." Larry Birns, director of the Council on Hemispheric Affairs, a Washington-based research group, said, "St. Croix has been a Watts or a Harlem in the waiting. The United States is not good at being a colonial power. . . . St. Croix is treated as backwoods. It has few paved roads, poor schools, poor medical care. If it wasn't the hurricane that touched things off, it would have been something else" (Schmalz, 1989b).

There is some feeling on the island that St. Thomas, the Virgin Islands' main tourist attraction, receives the lion's share of federal assistance while St. Croix is neglected. It is 37 miles away, and many residents feel that its government is distant and irrelevant to their lives.

In sum, many of the same factors that prevail in a civil disturbance—polarization of classes and races, resentment by residents of a given community against the class in power, a category who owns most of the local shops, business enterprises, real estate—also seemed to prevail in St. Croix at the time of the looting. In contrast, many of the factors making for community solidarity during a disaster seemed to be absent.

Finally, after all of the background factors are pinpointed and discussed, the fact remains that, when many National Guard troops and police officers failed to report for duty the day after the hurricane, "that reinforced the feeling of many [residents of St. Croix] that there was no authority" on the island (Schmalz, 1989b). Said a mainland government spokesperson three days after Hugo hit, a landing party went ashore to attempt to make contact with civil authorities on the island, but could find none. "We are still looking for a governing authority and we haven't found anyone yet" (Fireman, 1989).

Although looting did take place in St. Croix following Hurricane Hugo, such behavior is unusual and atypical and seems to occur as a consequence of a fairly specific convergence of background and immediate circumstances. Much of the field of disaster research ignores disaster looting; it deserves more attention, and it is entirely possible that it will become more common and widespread as these factors converge more frequently.

Martial Law. When martial law is declared, the military rules; our ordinary, everyday rights, guaranteed by the Constitution, are suspended. You could be arrested on no specific charge, held for an indefinite period of time without bail, your freedom of speech no longer exists, and you could be ordered to stay off the streets for any reason. Declaring martial law is an extremely serious step for a government to take. Contrary to what much of the public believes, martial law has *never* been declared in the United States (Quarantelli and Dynes, 1972, p. 69; Wenger et al., 1975, p. 35). It has taken place in some other countries where the authorities felt that law and order broke down entirely, for instance, by the Chinese government in Tibet in 1989. Many people imagine that martial law has been declared when the National Guard is called in to assist in an emergency or when a curfew has been ordered (Anderson, 1988–1989b, p. 21). The National Guard is often called in to assist during disasters (and other emergencies as well, such as civil disorders), and curfews are not infrequently ordered, but neither means that martial law has been declared.

Physical Setting.   People who are not in a disaster have only a sketchy idea of how constraining the physical setting of a disaster is. The myth here is that most people tend to underplay the importance of physical setting and emphasize the importance of individual enterprise. In fact, the major determinant of people's behavior in disasters is the physical circumstances of the disaster itself. For the most part, people engage in adaptive behavior when faced with a disaster; however, most disasters do permit some mobility, choice, and room for action. In contrast, some disasters are so totally devastating, and the physical conditions so limiting and brutal, that adaptive behavior—indeed, behavior of almost any kind—is virtually impossible. Headlong flight may be the only avenue possible. Again, people do not panic because they tend to be hysterical when faced with disaster conditions. They usually panic because there is no way out of certain death, or because they see a way out that is quickly disappearing. In other words, to speak or write of the kinds of behavior people engage in during disasters without referring to the physical setting of those disasters is to spout nonsense. It is impossible to understand human behavior in disasters without discussing what sort of behavior is physically possible.

Miller (1985, pp. 179–183) has summarized some of the objective factors or "immediate circumstances" related to multifatality disasters, specifically those caused by the evacuation of a crowd from a dangerous area or situation. The first is *overcrowding*; "drastic overcrowding precedes most multifatality evacuations" (p. 180). When proprietors pack too many people into an enclosed area, the potential for a disaster in case of an emergency—for example, a fire—is heightened. The second is a *limited time for dispersal*; some rapidly spreading fires engulf buildings in short order and often the fire has spread for some time before it is discovered. If a building is not equipped with automatic sprinklers, the problem is further compounded. *Instructions for dispersal* may inhibit or, if they are inadequate or misleading, contribute to the severity of a disaster. The prompt, appropriate notification of an emergency can sometimes make a difference between life and death for many occupants or residents of a disaster area. *The availability of exits* is a fourth physical factor related to whether disasters take place. If enough are not available, or if some are blocked off, or if the occupants of a room or a building aren't aware of where they are, trampling deaths could occur. And last, *sensory interference* could contribute to a disaster—for example, background noise, darkness, and the spread of smoke (pp. 182–183). In short, multifatality disasters tend to "result not from panic but from largely unavoidable circumstances. . . . Few if any stampede panics have occurred in uncrowded buildings where occupants faced a threat that allowed reasonable time for dispersal and otherwise posed little threat to life and limb" (Miller, 1985, p. 183).

Disasters: Belief and Reality

A sample of about 350 of the residents of a county in Delaware was asked about their beliefs concerning disasters (Wenger et al., 1975, pp. 38ff). There is no reason to believe that their responses are significantly different from residents of other areas of the country. As can be seen from Table 7-1 above, the public strongly believes in the disaster myths discussed in this chapter. Well over eight respondents in ten (84 percent) believe that "the panic of people fleeing from the danger area" is a major problem for officials. Only a small minority (28 percent) believe that looting "rarely" occurs in a disaster, while the majority (65 percent) disagree. A minority (17 percent) believe that martial law has never been instituted in the United States; a majority (60 percent) disagree. About half (51 percent) believe that the crime rate rises during a disaster. Eight in ten (80 percent) believe that most people evacuate an area when a disaster is announced. Nearly three-quarters (74 percent) believe that victims are usually in a state of shock just after a disaster. And over half (55 percent) believe that the mass media portray the seriousness of disasters accurately. In other words, a majority of the public is wrong in their beliefs about *every single aspect* of disasters that was asked about! (Wenger et al., 1975, pp. 38ff.)

TABLE 5-3

PUBLIC BELIEFS ABOUT DISASTERS

	Agree	Undecided	Disagree
Panic[a]	84	6	10
Looting[b]	28	8	65
Martial Law[c]	17	23	60
Crime Rate[d]	51	14	35
Evacuation[e]	80	6	14
Disaster Shock[f]	74	7	19
News[g]	55	10	36

[a]"A major problem community officials confront when faced with a natural disaster is controlling the panic of people fleeing from the danger area."

[b] "Looting rarely occurs after the impact of natural disasters."
[c] "Martial law has never been instituted in a disaster area in the United States."
[d] "The crime rate of a community usually rises after it has experienced a natural disaster."
[e] "When warned of an impending disaster, people are willing to cooperate and evacuate the area."
[f] "Immediately following the impact of a disaster, the disaster victims are in a state of shock and unable to cope with the situation by themselves."
[g] "The news media accurately portray the amount of devastation resulting from a natural disaster."

SUMMARY

Disasters represent a site or setting within which emergent, spontaneous, noninstitutionalized behavior often takes place. The field defines a disaster as a relatively sudden, unscheduled, one-time event that causes a great deal of property or ecological damage, or large-scale loss of life, and substantial disruption or stress among residents in the stricken area. As a general rule, there are many events that cause little damage and the loss of few lives, and very few that cause a great deal; tracing the relationship between seriousness and frequency produces what is known as the J-curve. Disasters may be divided into those that are natural and those that are technological in origin; researchers find that survivors of each type react very differently.

The earliest views of disaster-related behavior emphasized its individualism, emotionality, irrationality, and homogeneity. LeBon's and Blumer's contagion perspective, which would predict that people tend to act in an unthinking, emotionally charged, even barbaric fashion during a disaster, is totally inadequate to describe or predict real-life disaster behavior. Likewise, the convergence perspective, which would argue that people are likely to converge on a disaster to exploit the situation for personal gain, is inaccurate. In fact, much of the public holds a number of misleading or empirically false myths about disaster-related behavior.

Beginning in the 1950s, empirical research replaced speculation on the subject. It found that, for the most part, during disasters, people do not panic; tend to behave in a social and collective, rather than in an individualistic, fashion; often do not evacuate a threatened area and prefer to wait out the threat; very rarely converge on an area to exploit victims, but *do* converge to help out—often in an excessive and inappropriate fashion; rarely make use of public community emergency shelters; rarely become stricken, stunned, passive, dependent, or traumatized but, rather, in concert with others, often take the initiative and take control of the situation; rarely (although sometimes) loot; in addition, contrary to the stereotype most people hold, martial law has never been declared in the United States.

Unlike the commonly-held stereotype, people's responses to a disaster threat are typically adaptive. The very rare panicky reactions that do take place are nearly always a response to a very specific type of situation, that is, when people realize that there is no way out of certain death, or because they see a way out that is quickly disappearing. Thus, to refer to behavior in a disaster without referring to the nature of its immediate physical setting is nonsensical. Most multifatality disasters, for example, occur because there is overcrowding, a limited time for dispersal, inadequate or misleading instructions for dispersal, insufficient availability of exits, and/or extreme sensory interference.

References

References to Chapter 5 may be found interspersed with the Chapter 6 references (see page 245).

CHAPTER
6

DISASTERS: II

I n this chapter, we will discuss to six additional aspects of disasters. In Chapter 5, I emphasized the huge gulf between popular stereotypes and the reality as revealed by detailed, systematic research. I extend that point by examining a careful, detailed, systematic, empirical case study of a disaster, a stampede that took place at The Who concert at Riverfront Stadium in Cincinnati in 1979. Second, I suggest that the optimistic view held by many disaster researchers that emergency workers generally do their jobs when called upon to do so may not be entirely warranted. Some evidence points to the fact that this may not be the case, that there are serious "limits to altruism." Third, I look at the contrast between the intial cooperation that communities experience during and immediately after a calamity hits and the conflict that tends to develop in the reconstruction period. A devastating earthquake that destroyed the town of Yungay, Peru, illustrates this principle stikingly. Fourth, I examine the process by which we identify with disaster victims. Do we empathize with their plight in direct proportion to the degree of suffering they experience? I suggest that another factor may be at work here—something called egocentrism, which is perhaps the basis of all ethnocentrism. Fifth, the Buffalo Creek disaster provides a look at the large-scale destruction of a community that gives us a more pessimistic view of the impact of disasters than that which generally prevails in the literature. And sixth, are there systematic difference in the ways that members of different societies experience disasters? Are some disasters more, or less, serious according to the type of society they strike? Are some societies more capable of dealing with the problems that disasters pose?

A CASE STUDY OF A STAMPEDE: THE WHO CONCERT, 1979

One commonly cited event in multifatality disasters is the *stampede*. In a stampede, a large number of people are said to have been trampled to death as a result of one of two causes. The first cause of trampling can be called the *fearful panic*; a crowd, seized by the "grip of terror," hurls itself blindly and selfishly toward what they think is safety, oblivious to or uncaring of the presence and movement of others. This is a "headlong rush *away* from something" (Smelser, 1962, p. 170). The second is the *acquisitive panic*; people are trampled because they are in a mad, headlong rush to acquire something they value, stampeding over someone's body to get it, uncaring that others are dying. Here we have a craze, or the headlong rush "*toward* something" (Smelser, 1962, p. 170).

On December 3, 1979, 11 young people were crushed to death while trying to enter Riverfront Coliseum in Cincinnati to go to a concert by the British rock group, The Who. In the media, the deaths were attributed to a "stampede" of one or the other type. A highly respected, nationally syndicated newspaper columnist, Mike Royko, said that the crowd was made up of barbarians "who stomped 11 persons to death after having numbed their brains on weed, chemicals, and Southern Comfort." A local editor wrote of the "uncaring tread of the surging crowd." The "magnetizing effect" of rock music was blamed; "mob psychology" was said to have taken over; a psychologist claimed that the "amorphous personality" of the crowd ruled that day (quoted in Johnson, 1987, p. 362).

In fact, not one of these forces was at work at The Who concert in Riverfront Coliseum. The crowd waiting to enter was tightly packed together at the doors; many had been waiting for six hours. Members of the crowd began to sway to and fro, creating a "wave" effect. When the doors were opened, about 25 people near the front of the crowd fell down, and those immediately behind them were pushed by the surge onto the group that had fallen. Far from uncaringly trampling them, a number of patrons attempted to form a protective cordon around those who fell; some were helped to their feet by those who were standing. However, those further away from the doors were unaware that others had fallen, and so continued to surge forward. The crowd moved into the lobby, filling it up. To regulate the flow of the crowd, security guards closed the outside doors, thereby exacerbating the problem. There was no panic in the crowd, and no surging forward to grab the best seats.

Far from acting selfishly, one police officer said the members of the crowd "were the most helpful people that I've ever known. . . . Everybody I saw was helping everybody else. At some point in the crowd, people could not help them. It's not that they didn't want to. They were physically unable to" (Johnson, 1987, p. 367). In many instances, those attempting to help found that the only people who could hear were also unable to move or do anything else. Said one young person in the crowd, "People in the crowd 10 feet back didn't know it was happening. Their cries were impossible to hear above the roar of the crowd. . . . I screamed with all my strength that I was standing on someone. I couldn't move. I could only scream" (p. 368). In short, though The Who concert stampede has been described, among other things, as an acquisitive panic, with people killing one another to get to the best seats, in fact, the people in the front of the crowd were trying to get to the doors to get away from the crush. And there was no fearful panic, either; the tramplings did not take place as a result of a blind, terrified headlong rush, but because communication among individuals in different parts of the crowd, and between members of the crowd and some security personnel, was impossible.

Some of the coliseum personnel, again, cut off from crucial information about the dynamics of the crowd, defined the pushing and shoving they saw in terms of an acquisitive mob. One patron realized what was happening, and tried to open up more doors to ease the crush; but an usher grabbed him and shoved him back in line and said "either get in line or get back out." He pleaded with the usher, explaining that "people are getting hurt, people are down," to no avail. Another patron pleaded to be let in because of the crush, but understood that officials might not believe her pleas because they "might have heard it before and figured it was just people pretending or whatever, just to try to get in early" (Johnson, 1987, p. 370). In other words, there were divergent definitions of the situation, according to where people were in the crowd, both physically and organizationally. Security guards were more likely to define the pushing and shoving as selfish, acquisitive behavior; they had seen this before at rock concerts, and made the assumption that it was more of the same. In fact, the definition that they brought to the situation contributed to the danger, while the definition that members of the crowd brought to the situation was not regarded as legitimate by the coliseum personnel because their behavior was defined as selfish.

In short, inaccurate stereotypes were operating at that rock concert in Cincinnati, stereotypes that may very well have contributed to the death toll. One of these stereotypes is the "convergence" view that adolescents, especially those attending a rock concert, are crazed, irrational, destructive, and potentially violent. The second is the "contagion" view that crowds generate intense emotion and mass panic. And the third is that an "acquisitive panic" can easily occur when people get together, are faced with something they want, and have to compete with others to get it. Not one of these stereotypes even remotely explains what happened in this instance. It is often the case that the view we have of a given event may be totally transformed when we learn more about it. In thinking about disasters, crowd phenomena, and collective behavior in general, what we need is more facts, and not preconceptions, ideological biases, and stereotypes.

The Limits of Altruism: Role Conflicts in Disasters

Most research on disaster shows that survivors and relief workers tend to help victims in greater need than themselves. The evidence points to the fact that, in the face of a disaster, when someone is in a position to help those in desperate need, he or she typically does so. In short, most of us are fairly *altruistic* during disasters. However, stated this simply, these generalizations seem to be an overly optimistic view of the matter. Is it possible that some dislocations are too severe, that some communities do not recover? Is it possible that, under certain circumstances, most people have not helped out in an emergency? The fact is, helping others takes place under a specific set of circumstances and the *refusal* to help others, likewise, occurs for certain reasons. In other words, altruistic behavior (like selfish behavior) is *socially patterned*. As Perry and Pugh point out (1978, p. 124), there are "limits to altruism." The generalizations about disaster altruism probably apply only under special circumstances. In fact, much research in situations *different* from disasters shows that under ordinary, everyday circumstances, most people are not very helpful to others (Latané and Darley, 1968). This is in part because they believe that helping out is the responsibility of a number of people and, consequently, no one helps. Acting during many disasters is uncomplicated; one acts or one does not act, one helps or one does not help, others are around to help out or they are not. However, often, in everyday life, the decision as to whether or not to help may be complicated by a number of difficult considerations.

For example, what if assisting the public in a disaster means neglecting one's own family, possibly placing them in mortal danger? How do most people act in such circumstances? *Multiple group memberships* may limit one's behavior in a disaster; role conflicts may make heroism a difficult enterprise. Under most circumstances, there is no conflict among our various group memberships; we tend not to be "cross pressured" most of the time. Most of us, for example, can leave our work concerns at the job and our family concerns at home. But occasionally, there are role and status conflicts and strains that have to be resolved (Goode, 1960a, 1960b, 1973, pp. 97–120; Merton, 1957, 368–384). In a disaster, there may be *conflicting loyalties* among rescue workers that limit their ability to help the community at large. In a study of community response to four disasters—tornadoes and explosions—Killian (1952) found that conflicts may arise between family obligations and work roles. Most of the individuals who were interviewed in the study resolved the dilemma in favor of loyalty to the family; much of the confusion, disorder, and disorganization common in the initial phases of a disaster are a consequence of the rush of people attempting to find and rejoin their families. The exceptional individuals who acted heroically tended either to have no conflicting family obligations or could act in such a way that they could save their families and help the community simultaneously (Killian, 1952).

This is fairly typical of most people's behavior in disaster situations. The fact is, most of us would help the people we are closest to first; the public comes later. Only after you are sure that no one in your family is in imminent danger do you feel the obligation to help individuals with whom you have a less intimate relationship. In other words, altruistic behavior takes place to the extent that engaging in it does not endanger one's own life or the lives of one's loved ones. If too much sacrifice is called for to help strangers or even neighbors and acquaintances, most people will not make it. The less it costs in human sacrifice to engage in altruistic behavior, the greater the likelihood that one will engage in it. Thus, to characterize people's behavior during disasters with a blanket term, the term "altruistic" is misleading; it is altruistic up to a point, when helping does not entail too much sacrifice. Only the very rare person will risk life and limb, and endanger his or her loved ones, to help the public. These rare people are called heroes, and are accorded special honor (or, occasionally, are thought of as fools). Often, in fact, heroes are simply people with few social obligations to intimates.

Even during difficult and chaotic conditions such as disasters we all act out what might be called a *hierarchy of values*. Our behavior displays a kind of informal ranking system that represents a weighing of what is important to each one of us. We are more likely to save a loved one than a stranger because we value them more. We are more likely to help friends and neighbors than we are to drive 100 miles away to help the residents of another town. We are more likely to help our compatriots than to help those we regard as foreigners. As a general rule, the closer people are to us—personally, geographically, culturally, and socially—the more we will make an effort to help them during an emergency. This applies to disaster workers no less than to ordinary citizens.

In the 1970s, the Long Island Lighting Company (LILCO) built a nuclear plant on Long Island's north shore, at Shoreham, to supply the growing power needs of the island's residents. Representatives of LILCO had to appear before various state and federal licencing boards to receive approval to go on line. (The fact is, the licensing was never granted, the plant has never opened, and its completed multibillion-dollar structure sits idle, a testament to administrative folly.) One of the conditions the company had to satisfy was one of safety: In the event of a nuclear accident, could the area within a 10-mile radius of the plant be evacuated quickly? Both LILCO and local citizen's groups opposed to the opening of the plant commissioned reports favorable to their position, and both sides made extensive use of the collective behavior and disaster literature in their arguments.

Stephen Cole, a sociologist, conducted three surveys of key rescue workers—one survey of nearly all the school bus drivers in the potentially affected area, and two surveys of nearly all the volunteer fire fighters in the potentially affected area—to determine whether and to what extent they would perform their duties during a nuclear disaster at LILCO's Shoreham plant. The study was summarized in testimony given before a federal licensing board (Cole, Turner, and Barton, 1988). He concluded that a significant number would be so torn by their conflcting role obligations that they would be unable to do so, and that this would seriously hamper the evacuation of residents from the evacuation zone. The Cole study goes far beyond the simple assertion that rescue workers "will" or "will not" perform their obligation to assist the community during an emergency. It systematically specifies the circumstances under which they are more, or less, likely to do so.

Two-thirds of the school bus drivers (69 percent) said that the first thing they would do in case of an accident at LILCO's Shoreham plant would be to "make sure that my family was safely out of the evacuation zone." Eighty-six percent of the bus drivers *agreed* with the statement that, in the event of a nuclear emergency, it would be the obligation of everyone to first look after the health and safety of their families; 74 percent *disagreed* with the statement, in the event of a nuclear emergency, a school bus driver must place duty to drive a bus over duty to family. The responses of the fire fighters were similar in some ways, but different in others. In case of a nuclear accident, 16 percent of the firefighters said they would first report to the fire house; nine percent said they would check on their families and report without delay to the fire house; four percent said they would check on their families and, unless their spouses asked them to leave the evacuation zone, would report "relatively promptly" to the fire house; nine percent said they'd stay at home with their families; 51 percent said they'd leave the evacuation zone with their familes; three percent said they'd do something else that would make it difficult or impossible to perform their duties; and seven percent weren't sure what they would do. Combining categories four, five, and six shows that 64 percent of the fire fighters said that, during a Shoreham nuclear emergency, *they would engage in behavior that would make it difficult or impossible to perform their fire fighting function* (Cole, Turner, and Barton, 1988, pp. 53–54).

Judging from these responses, a substantial number of emergency workers would be so role-conflicted that they would choose to attend to the safety of their families before their emergency tasks. However, the Cole report emphasizes the fact that not all emergency workers are equally "at risk" to abandon their jobs during a disaster, and not all disasters are equally as likely to result in emergency workers abandoning their jobs. There are systematic differences here that need to be looked at.

School bus drivers may be especially likely to abandon their jobs because they "are not trained emergency workers and do not, in the normal course of their duties, perform emergency functions." School bus driving "is not an emergency role; the drivers have not volunteered for emergency service, or for the potentially dangerous activity of driving through a potentially contaminated area" (pp. 21–22). As a result, "their level of commitment to driving a bus during an emergency is low compared with their commitments to protect their families" (p. 22). *Volunteer* fire fighters, likewise, may exhibit a relatively low level of commitment compared with *professional* fire fighters, which may explain the high proportion of those who are unlikely to report to the fire house during a nuclear power plant emergency.

A second dimension relevant to the likelihood of relief workers abandoning their post during an emergency is whether the disaster is natural or technological in origin. In natural disasters, there is no concrete "enemy," only the devastation caused by nature against which the community struggles. A disaster of this sort is likely to generate a high level of community cohesion. A nuclear accident is not seen as natural but technological, with the community blaming the incompetence of a corporation; in the case of a nuclear accident at Shoreham, the community would blame LILCO. "It is possible that many people may feel their own emergency responsibilities lessened because the accident is plainly the fault of the power company that built and runs the nuclear plant. In an emergency the only organization which would expect school bus drivers to drive the school buses is LILCO" (p. 23).

In addition, disasters vary in the *duration* of their threat, the *range* or *extent* of the impact area, and the degree to which the threat is visible (pp. 32–33). Tornadoes and earthquakes are over quickly; their duration is brief. In contrast, the threat posed by a serious radiological accident at a nuclear power plant is likely to last a very long time. In a tornado, the impact area tends to be narrow, but after hurricanes, floods, earthquakes, and radiological emergencies, it is usually broad. And during most disasters, the threat is highly visible, but, without special equipment, radiation leakage is invisible. When the threat posed by a given emergency or disaster is technological, lasts a long time, affects a widespread impact area, and is invisible, disaster workers are more likely to put family obligations above those of relief tasks than is true of disasters that are natural in origin, last a brief period of time, impact a narrow area, and are highly visible. And lastly, if the emergency worker's family lives *outside* the devastated area, he or she is more likely to tend to relief duties; if they live *within* the affected area, he or she is more likely to abandon those duties and tend to their safety.

Clearly, then, altruism has its limits. The behavior of emergency workers is not guided by altruism alone, or even the obligations of their jobs. There are a number of factors that make it more, or less, likely that they will report to work and do their duty of helping those in need during a disaster. Members of the community do not automatically pitch in and help out. There are systematic forces compelling them do so so, and others that push them away from helping out. Only by understanding the nature of our multiple obligations, the concrete nature of each specific emergency, and how the two interlink, are we able to understand altruistic behavior during disasters.

——— DISASTER VS. POSTDISASTER BEHAVIOR ———

Most researchers note a "dualistic response" to the "sudden, severe stress" brought on by natural calamities (Quarantelli and Dynes, 1976, p. 139). During the *emergency period*, that is, during and shortly after the calamity strikes, the emergence of conflict is relatively rare; the community is cohesive, and people pull together to help one another. (As we just saw, there are limits on this process, however.) In contrast, the post-emergency, or *recovery* period is marked by considerable conflict among the various factions involved. Why are people "saints" at one time and "sinners" at another? What accounts for this dramatic reversal of people's behavior in disasters? As we've seen again and again, the characteristics of people often influence their behavior less than the situations they are in. What situations do disasters and post-disaster recovery force people into that would account for this turnaround?

THE DISASTER PHASE

During natural disasters (unlike technological accidents), there are a number of factors that make it very likely that communities will be marked by an absence of conflict (Quarantelli and Dynes, 1976, pp. 141–144). To begin with, natural disasters involve an *external threat*, not a human agent. Solidarity is generated because the community is threatened *as a whole;* differences among community members are minimized because they all face the same threat equally. Second, the threatening agent can usually be "perceived and specified" (p. 142). The threat of *social* problems is not always clear; the nature of the problem, the responsible agent, the solution—all these things can be debated endlessly, and usually are. However, with a natural disaster, the agent is clear and unambiguous—a tornado bearing down on the community, an earthquake shaking the ground beneath its feet, a flood threatening to wash it away. Third, there usually is a high *consensus* on priorities in natural disaster situations; nearly everyone knows what has to be done—save the children, get the boats to stranded residents, get the injured to area hospitals. The saving of lives takes precedence over everything else (p. 142); selfish, particularistic interests have a low priority at this point.

Fourth, the natural disaster faces the community with "community-wide problems that need to be solved quickly" (p. 142). The reasons *why* things have to be done, and immediately, are usually obvious; no conflicting interpretations intrude. This woman has to be pulled out from under that pile of debris, this baby has to be given artificial respiration, this man has to have the cuts on his face bandaged up. When problems are "immediate and imperative" (p. 142) the conflicts over how to solve them are minimal. Fifth, disasters "lead to a focusing of attention on the present" (p. 142). During most times, people are preoccuped with the past, the present, *and* the future, and often differ with others as to their interpreation. However, when disaster strikes, past grievances and attachments and plans for the future take a back seat; we have to do something, and we have to do it right now is the watchword in an emergency situation. Sixth, *social distinctions are leveled* in a disaster situation. Natural disasters "democratize" social life (p. 143); social distinctions are minimized. Danger, loss, and suffering "become a public phenomenon" (p. 143). Last, disasters usually "strengthen community identification" (p. 143). All those who have had the experience "are brought together in a very powerful psychological sense by their common participation in such a dramatic event" (p. 143). And participation in activities for the "good" of the community is maximized.

It is clear to see therefore that the emergency period tends to be one of relative harmony, cooperation, altruism, and cohesion. This is not completely the case, of course, as we've seen over and over again. At the same time, *compared with the post-disaster period,* during an emergency and soon thereafter, people usually pull together and help one another out. Something happens from disaster to recovery; what is it?

DEMARCATING THE DISASTER FROM THE POST-DISASTER PERIOD

To begin with, how do we demarcate the disaster from the post-disaster period? The latter does not begin the moment the storm has passed, the lava from the volcano stops flowing, or the earth has stopped shaking. Even when these events take place, a true crisis still exists because lives are still at immediate risk. The emergency period may last 36 hours, or two days, or four or five, depending on the community and the nature of the natural calamity. How do we know when it has passed? We usually know it when most of the community has ceased to focus on disaster-related problems and has begun to focus on more long-range matters—reconstruction and otherwise. When people go back to work and "move back to normal dress patterns," we know we are in the recovery period, when people once again begin to engage in "activities considered unnecessary during the emergency period" (p. 145). Banking, teaching, the sale and purchase of luxury items, watching movies—these and thousands of other activities are not necessary, and usually do not continue, during a serious disaster; in the recovery period, they do. Of course, the emergency does not end for all segments of the community at the same time; fire fighters, the police, construction workers, repairpersons of telephone lines are still at work repairing the damage the disaster has caused long after the rest of the community has returned to normal.

POST-DISASTER: THE RECOVERY PERIOD

What forces generate conflict in the recovery period? How does a cohesive community become riddled with conflict? And what is it, exactly, that a community fights over? There are two major axes of conflict: *assigning blame* and *allocating resources* (p. 146).

The assignment of blame usually occurs in technological accidents; in fact, many of the forces that generate cohesion during a natural disaster are missing in a humanly created disaster. However, under certain conditions, blame can be assigned even in the case of some "acts of God." This usually happens in disasters where there is some time for warning, such as hurricanes and floods (p. 146). Did the National Weather Service predict the hurricane? Were the right probabilities assigned? Did it give a sufficiently long warning time? Was the magnitude of the storm assessed accurately? Did civil defense and the police forces in the area act adequately and decisively? Was the evacuation conducted in a responsible fashion? These are the kinds of finger-pointing questions that are asked that could become sources of conflict in certain post-disaster communities.

Far more common as a source of conflict is *the allocation of resources for rehabilitation* (p. 146). As we pointed out earlier, the convergence of resources and personnel onto a disaster site (which sometimes even impedes giving victims assistance) is the rule. In the period immediately after the disaster, these resources are often allocated freely, with "no questions asked," "no strings attached," with bureaucratic niceties suspended; people are given help because they need it. However, in the restoration period, formal, bureaucratic issues become important; to a community struggling to rebuild, such issues seem "heartless." Government agencies ask questions "which in another context would be routine, but now appear as prying. Local agencies find that state, regional, and federal organizations no longer seem willing to cut the 'red tape'; if anything, procedures appear to be more complicated, complex, detailed, and time-consuming than seemingly similar pre-disaster activities" (Quarantelli and Dynes, 1976, p. 147). Hostility may develop toward outside agencies because they do not appear to be sufficiently sensitive to the disaster victims' suffering. Residents will want the control of the allocation of funding to be placed in their own hands, not in the hands of outsiders.

Who gets what becomes extremely important in the recovery period. At some point, the resources that once poured into the community in seemingly endless abundance begin to dry up; the outside world has become less concerned with the disaster-stricken community now that the crisis appears to be over. Agencies compete among themselves for resources, often attempting to "grab" whatever is left of the dwindling pool of money and supplies donated by the world outside. Segments of the community present themselves as having been more victimized than others, and therefore as more deserving of the recovery resources. Accusations may be made (some, although not necessarily all, justified) concerning discrimination against less powerful groups, such as Blacks and the poor, in the allocation of relief.

A CASE STUDY: YUNGAY, PERU, 1970

Few disasters typify the principle of a low level of conflict during the emergency period and a high level during the recovery period more strikingly than the avalanche that struck the village of Yungay, Peru. On May 31, 1970, an earthquake shook the coastal and Andean areas of north-central Peru. It registered a 7.7 on the Richter scale, and "unleashed such devastation that it has been referred to as the worst natural disaster in the history of the western hemisphere" (Oliver-Smith, 1979, p. 41). About 70,000 people lost their lives in the earthquake and its aftermath. More than 4,000 of them were inhabitants of the town of Yungay, nestled below the peaks of the Andes mountain range.

In Yungay, the quake shook the ground for 45 seconds, reducing most of its adobe buildings to rubble and sending showers of roof tiles onto the street. Some of the residents sought refuge in the church, the town's largest building; others ran out into the central plaza, attempting to avoid the falling tiles; a few ran to cemetery hill, the only high ground near the center of town. The earthquake had shaken loose a gigantic slab of ice and rock nearly half a mile square from the face of the mountain looming above the town. This slab slid, then dropped nearly a mile straight down, finally hurtling toward the valley at 300 miles per hour, carrying with it earth and boulders standing in its path. Eyewitnesses report seeing a wall of debris as high as a 10-story building come crashing down upon the town. Four minutes after the earthquake stopped shaking the ground, all that was left of the town was four palm trees, a small band of survivors at the cemetery huddled at the base of a statue of Jesus, and 200 terrified children and a few adults in the half-destroyed stadium—who had been there watching a circus. Covering the town was an immense mass of dull grey, viscous mud, interrupted by chunks of ice . . . and huge granite boulders" (Oliver-Smith, 1979, pp. 42–43). The total volume of ice, mud, and rock that had descended on the town and its immediate environs was estimated to be about 50 million cubic yards. Nearly 95 percent of the town's residents were killed in the avalanche.

A ghastly silence, broken only by the rumble of the avalanche as it proceeded down the valley "to further destruction," followed the death of Yungay. Within minutes, most of the survivors began tending to the wounded and searching for the trapped and buried who were still alive. As night began to fall, committees were formed to find food, obtain water, build shelter, and care for the wounded. All roads to the valley had been destroyed, and the cloud of dust stirred up by the avalanche was so dense and massive that an aerial view of the region was not possible for nearly four days.

Cooperation both among the surviving townspeople and between them and the residents of the suburban communties and outlying rural areas was considerable. "The crisis had an immediate status-leveling effect. . . . A sense of brotherhood, cutting across both class and ethnic lines, prevailed as Indian and *Mestizo* [of mixed Indian and Spanish descent], lower and upper class, collaborated in the collective effort to obtain immediate necessities" (Oliver-Smith, 1979, pp. 44–45). There was a "heightened spirit of unity and common identity." "We are all brothers," was the characteristic phrase heard at this time. "People implicitly felt the need for unity and cooperation of all the people if they were to solve the problems which faced them in the immediate aftermath" of the avalanche. Every individual "faced problems which would not be solved by the individual alone. In fact, since virtually all individuals faced the problems of shelter, warmth, clothing and food, they became community wide problems with solutions backed by community consensus and effort" (p. 45). Concepts of private property "literally disappeared" immediately after the impact, and everything was shared according to need.

However, within two or three days, even before the helicopters arrived, this cooperation began to break down; increasingly in the post-disaster period, conflict asserted itself. The survivors of the town and the residents of the outlying areas gathered in encampments in such large numbers that considerable quantities of food became necessary to feed everyone. At one point, a violent confrontation took place when a surviving politician ordered the slaughter of a steer whose owner was not only alive and present but who had not granted his permission. With this incident, the period of immediate post-impact solidarity came to an end (p. 45).

Conflict split the community in a variety of ways. To begin with, in the camps, the urban survivors of the avalanche (only a few hundred), began to be outnumbered by the rural refugees, who were victims only of the earthquake (several thousand). Thus, everyone acquired a disaster identity—an "in-group, out-group perception in terms of suffering and deservedness of aid" (p. 45). Urban survivors saw themselves as more deserving of aid, because they lost "everything" in the avalanche; they asserted there were impostors who pretended to live in the town so that they could receive more assistance, but who really lived in the countryside.

Second, highland Peru is very stratified, and class and ethnic distinctions were made as soon as outside assistance began to arrive at the encampments. The middle class *Mestizo* townspeople regarded themselves worthier of more aid than the poor rural Indians. Townspeople began saying, "The Indians never had anything to begin with, so why should they get help now?" One urban survivor said: "The Indians are those that are benefiting most from the aid. We, the decent people of Yungay, are only about 100 people. The rest are all Indians. They ought to give more to us. . . . The Indians have everything they need, and besides, they are accustomed to live as they do" (Oliver-Smith, 1979, p. 46). In fact, egalitarian aid was considered hostile to the interests of the previously more favored middle class; poor Indians who received assistance were considered undeserving, and the aid they received, dishonest. At the same time, survivors of humbler origins regarded assistance received by the middle-class *Mestizo* townsfolk as a result of graft and unfair influence. "We are not equal!" became a commonly repeated phrase in the camps. The conflict between contending factions over who deserved what grew to even greater intensity when the government began building temporary structures to house the refugees.

Finally, conflict erupted over the issue of where the new town was to be built. The government wanted it to be built in a safer location next to a town a few miles away; the survivors wanted it to be built as close to its old location as possible. Soon after the government's intention became known, signs sprouted up along the road leading to the camp, which read: "Yungay Stays Here!" and "Yungay is Reborn Here!" Yungay survivors saw the government as insensitive to their needs. Community leaders even brought the dead into the conflict, exhorting the survivors with words like these: "The glorious tradition of Yungay must be carried on here . . . or the dead shall have been betrayed. It is our duty as survivors to realize the continuity of Yungay here!" (p. 49). Resistance to be government's relocation plan spread from urban survivors to rural dwellers, "forming an almost monolithic block of opposition to the government relocation plans" (p. 49). The government, in pushing its relocation plan, became the new enemy, the new adversary, the new disaster. Eventually, the government backed down and allowed the new Yungay, Yungay Norte, to be built near the original town's location.

One of the most important lessons we can learn from the avalanche at Yungay is that the cooperative, collective spirit that is usually generated during and immediately after a disaster dissipates fairly quickly, often to be replaced by competition, conflict, and even hostility.

EGOCENTRISM:
＿＿＿ EMPATHIZING WITH DISASTER VICTIMS ＿＿＿

The willingness of relief workers to help disaster victims is strongly related to the closeness they feel to them. The more we identify with victims the more empathy and sympathy we have, and the more we are willing to help them. "Sympathetic identification" with disaster victims is "usually based on shared characteristics" (Perry and Pugh, 1978, p. 124; Barton, 1969, pp. 203ff). *Egocentrism*, as we've seen, is the degree to which we see the world as revolving around ourselves. We tend to see our own characteristics as desirable and measure others by the degree to which they measure up to our own. Egocentrism is a strong ingredient in ethnocentrism—seeing the groups to which we belong as more central and intrinsically desirable than others, the standard by which all other groups are judged. Many experts believe that *egocentrism drives ethnocentrism*, that is, people overevaluate the groups to which they belong because they want to see themselves in a positive light. (See, for instance, Cialdini, 1984, pp. 191–199). This principle is extremely important in looking at disasters—specifically, in understanding when the public in a given society will empathize or identify with the victims of a given disaster.

Here is a fairly simple way of testing this. The amount of space—that is, column-inches—in a newspaper that is devoted to a given disaster story (or any story, for that matter) is related to the similarity in social and cultural characteristics between the newspaper's readers and those of the disaster victims. It is reasonable to assume that the size and detail of a story, that is, the amount of space devoted to it is related to the amount of public interest in it—or, at least, to the editors' *estimate* of that interest. Further, it is reasonable to assume that the newsworthiness of a story is related to the body count: The greater the number of deaths, other things being equal, the bigger the story. But, of course, "other things" are hardly ever equal. (For instance, a strong earthquake disrupts roads, water and gas mains, and electrical lines, while an airplane crash does not.) How many deaths would have to take place in Bangladesh for a disaster story to rate the same number of column-inches as a story about an accident in New Jersey or Colorado that took three lives? Thirty? A hundred? For that matter, since this also operates on the regional level, how many deaths would have to take place in Colorado for a New Jersey newspaper to devote as much space as it did on an accident that took three lives in New Jersey? (Or vice versa?) This is, once again, a manifestation of the egocentric bias: We tend to pay closer attention to and have more interest in whatever is geographically, socially, and culturally closer to us than that which is further away (Chovnick, 1990).

An interesting affirmation of this principle is the fact that the residents of Charleston, West Virginia, the site of a Union Carbide plant that manufactures the same chemical that killed the residents of Bhopal, India, paid more attention to and retained more crucial information about the Bhopal disaster—such as the death count, the name of the corporate owner, and the health hazards of the chemical responsible—than did the residents of an area not threatened by hazardous pollution (Wilkins, 1987). Residents of Charleston were able to identify with the victims of the Bhopal disaster to the extent that they shared an important characteristic with them—their mutual vulnerability to the same threat.

One of the biggest stories of 1989 was the earthquake that hit California in October. It preempted regularly scheduled broadcasting on the three major television networks and remained a page one story in most newspapers for weeks afterwards. While property damage was extensive, it resulted in only 62 deaths. One hundred and eighty-one articles were published in *The New York Times* (using this one newspaper as an index for media attention in general) entirely or partly on the California quake. Just a year before, an earthquake hit Armenia. It caused 25,000 deaths, and generated 74 articles in the *Times*. (There are several million Americans of Armenian descent.) An earthquake that killed 40,000 Iranians in 1990 resulted in 19 articles in *The New York Times*. Thus, relative to the number killed, the California earthquake attracted 380,000 times more media attention than the Iranian one, and about 60,000 times more attention than the Armenian quake. The relative attention we pay to disasters, and our relative ability to empathize with their victims, according to our closeness to those victims, is one of the more remarkable generalizations we could possibly make about disaster phenomena.

If egocentrism influences the attention we pay to disaster stories in the media, then why was so much attention paid to the nuclear disaster that took place in Chernobyl in the Soviet Union? The actual number of on-the-spot deaths, or those that occurred within a few days, totalled "only" 250 (*Newsday*, November 9, 1989, p. 13)—a tragedy for the victims and their families, but as disasters go, not at the high end as measured by the total human toll. And yet, it was one of the biggest stories of 1986. After all, if most people tend to pay more attention to what's nearest to them, and the Soviet Union is far away, with a political system that is seen by most Americans as alien and unacceptable, then why was there so much attention—so much *media* attention—paid to the Chernobyl nuclear accident? There are several reasons.

To begin with, the meltdown was kept a secret by Soviet authorities for several days. Swedish technicians began noticing abnormally high levels of radiation in the vicinity, which was finally pinpointed to airborn radiation coming from the Ukraine, 1,500 miles to the south and east. The secret out,

The explosion in the Chernobyl nuclear facility, in the Soviet Union in April 1986, was one of the most catastrophic technological disasters of all time; its effects are being felt to this day. Here, a worker checks on the level of radiation inside the shattered plant.

12 hours later a newscaster on Moscow television delivered a terse, four-sentence statement about "an accident" at the Chernobyl plant. The long silence about so serious and deadly a matter touched off international rage about the incident, and generated far more attention to it as a consequence. Second, several early reports coming out of the disaster site exaggerated the number of immediate deaths. An anonymous source, a resident of Kiev, who "has never proved to be unreliable," according to a United Press International foreign editor, claimed that 80 people "died immediately and some 2,000 people died on the way to hospitals." A Dutch radio ham picked up a broadcast originating from the Chernobyl area which referred to "many hundreds dead and wounded" (Greenwald et al., 1986, p. 40). Both these reports were grossly exaggerated, but these huge overestimates fueled public interest in the disaster. Important though the Chernobyl meltdown story was, early on, it seemed like an even more important story than it proved to be. And third, the number of *indirect* deaths over the long run—people who will contract one or another of various diseases and die prematurely over the course of their lives as a result of exposure to nuclear contamination—may eventually total in the tens of thousands, possibly even in the hundreds of thousands.

But fourth, and this is probably the most important reason why the American public was so interested in the Chernobyl meltdown: Much of the concern in the American media about the accident at Chernobyl focused around the issue of whether it could happen here. Thus, the concern was at least partly egocentric, because many people reasoned that, if it happened there, it could also happen here. Experts were called upon to state that the Chernobyl plant was obsolete, faulty, and dangerous, while the American nuclear plants are modern and safe; therefore, there's no need to worry. The absence of a protective containment structure, the lax safety measures in Soviet nuclear plants, and Chernobyl's use of graphite instead of water as a coolant, were all pointed to as contributing to the disaster. This goes back to the "just world" fallacy I discussed earlier. Cherbobyl, the reasoning goes, wasn't a random event, it wasn't a complete accident. It happened for a reason— obsolescence—that doesn't apply to *our* nuclear plants. In a sense, the Soviets got what they deserved; Chernobyl was an accident waiting to happen. On the other hand, *we* don't have to worry about such a serious accident happening here because our plants aren't out-of-date or defective. Said White House Spokesman Larry Speakes, with reference to American atomic plants, "Ours are quite different from the Soviet system and have a number of redundant safety systems built in." James Moore, a vice president for power systems at Westinghouse agreed, "The Soviets have racked up an open car going 100 miles an hour. We drive 30 miles an hour in a tank. We take the conservative approach" (Greenwald et al., 1986, 43, 52).

Interestingly, the same reasoning took place, in reverse, prior to Chernobyl. During 1985, the American movie, *Silkwood*, about a worker who publicizes the dangerous conditions in a nuclear materials plant, was playing in Havana. The communist hierarchy feared that the film would convey to the public the idea that all nuclear facilities, including those in Cuba and other socialist countries, are unsafe, which would generate some of the same antinuclear sentiment that exists in the United States and Western Europe. During the film's run, an article appeared in the Cuban Communist Party newspaper, *Granma*, which stated that nuclear plants in the United States and other capitalist countries are unsafe, but *not* those in socialist countries. Under capitalism, the article stated, the business elite doesn't care about the welfare of the workers or the people, whereas in socialist countries, the government, which runs the plants, cares deeply about the safety and the welfare of the workers and the people. Nuclear energy is unsafe only under capitalism; such contamination as that which happened in *Silkwood*, the *Granma* article stated, couldn't happen in a socialist country—a somewhat ironic observation in view of the Chernobyl disaster that took place a few months later.

BUFFALO CREEK: AN EXCEPTION TO THE RULE

The prevailing view of behavior during disasters in the research literature is that most people tend to act collectively, actively, responsibly, and often altruistically—although often contrary to official directives—and hardly ever suffer long-term catastrophic effects. During disasters, communities typically organize, pull together, utilize their resources, face the challenge the disaster has laid down, and overcome whatever difficulties it introduces. Disasters reveal and activate community and organizational resources. Far from being defeated by disasters, most communities emerge stronger and more cohesive than before. This is not alwasy true, however.

One thoroughly documented American disaster took place in a community called Buffalo Creek, West Virginia, in 1972 (Erikson, 1976; Gleser, Green, and Winget, 1981; Stern, 1977). It is interesting because, in many ways, what happened there was contrary to most of the widely-accepted findings in the disaster literature. This does not mean that those findings are wrong, only that they apply specifically to certain kinds of disasters—*typical* disasters. In many ways, Buffalo Creek was not a typical disaster, at least, not for the United States. Its physical impact, especially relative to the size of the community, was much greater than that of most disasters; in fact, it devastated the area and its people much more thoroughly and catastrophically than is usually the case. The disasters that have been studied in the literature have typically been much less extreme than is true with Buffalo Creek. And so, it would be instructive to look at Buffalo Creek to understand what can happen in a really devastating disaster.

THE BUFFALO CREEK DISASTER: WHAT HAPPENED?_____

At one minute before 8:00 A.M. on the 26th of February, 1972, a dam holding a 20-acre, 40-foot deep lake of water and sludge collapsed; the liquid rolled downhill through a narrow valley, washing away "everything in its path" (Erikson, 1976). When the water subsided, 125 bodies were recovered—seven missing persons were never found—and 4,000 people out of a total of 5,000 residents were left homeless. Three bodies of young children of identical size were recovered; they had to be placed in anonymous graves because they were too battered to identify. "The story is that they were headless." In terms of its total impact relative to the size of the community, the flood was almost incalculably devastating. Buffalo Creek was not a simple disaster; it was a catastrophe. How could an event of such damaging proportions have happened in the modern age?

Although usually referred to as a flood, it was not even, strictly speaking, a natural disaster. To explain what happened, it is necessary to explain the physical setting of the area. Buffalo Creek is a mountain hollow in West Virginia, at the bottom of which is a creek bed, which flows into the Guyandotte River. Before the disaster, 16 villages stretched along the hollow for a distance of some 17 miles. The hollow is a very narrow strip of land, only about 60 to 100 yards wide, just wide enough to accommodate the creek bed itself, a road, a railroad track, and a row or two of houses. Each village had little more than a few churches, a few stores, a post office, and a few hundred houses. The area was totally dependent on coal for a living; nearly everyone in Buffalo Creek was economically dependent on the Pittstown Corporation-

The failure of a slag heap empoundment at a Pittston Corporation-Buffalo Mining Company plant to hold 132 million gallons of water in an artificial lake destroyed 17 communities and washed away the way of life of thousands of Buffalo Creek residents.

Buffalo Mining Company. They earned a decent, although modest, wage, probably a bit below the national average but, given the low cost of living in Appalachia, their wages provided a livable, comfortable, and secure lifestyle. In 1972, Buffalo Creek was not a poverty-stricken community.

At the top of the hollow, referred to as Middle Fork, stood a pile of slag. Slag is waste from the coal mines that is dumped wherever it is convenient for the coal company to do so. Wet, it looks like black mud or sludge. About 1,000 tons of slag was being deposited on the heap every day. In effect, the slag heap served as a gigantic dam. Actually, there were three dams that the coal company called "impoundments"; they were structures of timber and cinder blocks. The dams held back a million tons of waste. The heap was nearly 60 feet high and nearly 500 feet wide and nearly 500 feet front to back. It trapped some 130 million gallons of water—a lake some 20 acres in size and 40 feet deep. The whole thing, water and slag together, was described as being "like a pool of gravy in a mound of mashed potato" (Caudill, 1972, p. 16).

The days preceding February 26th were wet and rainy. Inspections revealed that the level of the water atop the heap was dangerously high, and the surrounding formation was dangerously soft. Rumors spread about the condition of the dams, and a few residents closest to it moved to higher ground. A few minutes before 8:00 A.M. on the 26th of February, a heavy equipment operator inspected the surface of the dam, saw it was mushy, and drove off in his car, honking the horn, warning passersby of the danger. At 7:59 A.M., the dam gave way and the water and sludge came rolling down the valley. An engineer described it as a "mud wave"; one eyewitness called it "rolling lava." It was a literal wall of water and sludge and debris. Said a resident, "It just looked like a black mountain going down that hollow" (Erikson, 1976, pp. 28, 32). It shot through the ravine, destroying and carrying away everything that stood in its way. It carried away trucks and trailers and cars and houses and telephone poles and trees as if they had been toys; it literally scraped the ground bare. After the water and sludge roared by, explosions from ruptured gas and electricity lines followed. And then the hollow was deathly silent. Within three hours, the water was gone.

The survivors, most of whom managed to scramble a few feet up the hollow, returned to where they had once lived, dazed, looking for missing relatives, picking through the rubble, and trying to comprehend the enormity of what had happened before their very eyes. Said one survivor, "There wasn't anything to do but just sit there. We looked out over that dark hollow down there and it just looked so lonesome. It just looked like it was God forsaken. Dark. That was the lonesomest, saddest place that anybody ever looked at" (Erikson, 1976, p. 42). After the cleanup, the valley looked like a long, black gash, devastated beyond all recognition. Most of the residents stayed on in the area, with relatives or in shelters. Housing and Urban Development (HUD), a federal agency, set up 13 trailer camps, more or less at random, housing about 2,500 residents, allowing them to stay rent-free for a year. But the project cost a great deal more than had been originally estimated, and the residents had many complaints about the set up—the trailers were located without respect to community ties, they were hot in the summer and cold in the winter, and the residents had no privacy. "We are all like animals in a cage," said one resident bitterly. "We are closed in like a pack of sardines. . . . I feel like I'm in jail" (Erikson, 1976, pp. 152, 151).

COLLECTIVE TRAUMA

After the flood, it became clear to everyone in Buffalo Creek that the disaster was the coal company's fault; residents engaged the services of a law firm to conduct a lawsuit to seek compensation for them. A sociologist, Kai Erikson, was hired to assess the sociological damage that the flood inflicted upon the life of the community. Erikson argued that the residents of Buffalo Creek suffered both *individual* and *collective* trauma as a result of the disaster. What he meant by individual trauma was more or less what each of us understands by the term. Of the survivors of the Buffalo Creek flood who were examined by psychiatrists a year and a half after the disaster, "a grim 93 percent were found to be suffering from an identifiable emotional disorder." In all, "the sheer volume of pathology is horrifying" (Erikson, 1976, pp. 156,

157). Confusion, despair, and a sense of hopelessness emerged in the survivors' efforts to cope with their lives. The experience of the flood was so devastating to most of them that, in all likelihood, they will never recover from it. Near-total demoralization seems to characterize the lives of most residents. Said one survivor, "As for myself, every time I go to Buffalo Creek I start to cry because it is like visiting a graveyard. I left there crying after the flood . . . and I wake up all through the night crying. I can see the water from the dam destroying my house, clothing, furniture, cars. We lost everything we had saved all our lives in a very few minutes. I can see my friends drowning in the water and asking for help. I will never be the same person again" (p. 157).

But Erikson went far beyond the simple assertion that the individual residents of Buffalo Creek were traumatized by their experience of the disaster. In fact, the flood was far more than the sum of thousands of individual losses. In the flood, a community was devastated; it was *communality* that was destroyed, and all that it entailed. The 16 villages that made up Buffalo Creek made up a tight-knit network of communities characterized by a great deal of intimacy and closeness. Suddenly, all that was torn apart. Said one resident, "We was like one big family. . . . If someone was hurt, everybody was concerned, everybody. If somebody lost a member of their family, they was always there. Everybody was around bringing you something to eat, trying to help" (p. 188). Collective trauma refers to "a blow to the basic tissues of social life that damages the bonds attaching people together and impairs the sense of community." It is "a gradual realization that the community no longer exists as an effective source of support and that an important part of the self has disappeared." People who once had that support "learn that they are isolated and alone, wholly dependent upon their own individual resources" (p. 154). Survivors characterize Buffalo Creek today in answers that are "crisp and to the point." "It is almost like a ghost town now." "It has changed from the community of paradise to Death Valley." "It's like a graveyard, that's what. A cemetery" (p. 195).

WHY WAS BUFFALO CREEK DIFFERENT?

The research literature has portrayed the impact of disasters in fairly optimistic terms; most of the time, most survivors recover fairly quickly—indeed, many feel better about themselves and their lives after having weathered a catastrophe. Wallace (1956, p. 127) refers to a "stage of euphoria" that sweeps over survivors after a disaster. Prince (1920) refers to a "city of comrades," Kutak (1938), a "democracy of distress." Fritz (1961), a "community of sufferers," Wolfenstein (1957), a "post-disaster utopia," and Barton (1969), an "altruistic community." Erikson found that "nothing of the sort seems to have occurred on Buffalo Creek, even for a moment" (p. 201). The question is, why?

There are several factors at work here. To begin with, the clean-up was conducted and controlled not by members of the community but by outsiders. On the one hand, survivors felt beholden to strangers, and on the other, they had no control over what was happening to their lives. Second, Buffalo Creek was not a natural disaster, it was a technological catastrophe, which is likely to have more serious and long-term negative effects on survivors (Baum, 1988; Baum, Fleming, and Davidson, 1983). The blame was laid squarely at the feet of the Pittston Corporation for casually permitting a dangerous condition—the slag heap—to build up and threaten the lives of the residents. Their negligence undermined the residents' previous feeling that Pittston executives cared about them and were a part of their community. They felt betrayed, which added to their psychic and social devastation (Gleser, Green, and Winget, 1981, p. 149).

Third, the flood was *all-encompassing* in its impact; that is, the proportion of the community it affected was nearly total. As we saw, some 80 percent of the 16 villages of Buffalo Creek were made homeless. Everyone in the community knew someone who died in the flood—a friend, a relative, a neighbor. Few disasters are so catastrophic; even when as many people die in one as in Buffalo Creek, it usually touches only portions of the community—neighborhoods, pockets of residents, families here and there. It is hardly ever the case that all, or nearly all, residents of a community are devastated by a disaster. And last, while the physical and social displacement of survivors after most disasters is temporary, in Buffalo Creek, not only were nearly all residents displaced, they were displaced permanently; their "former environment" was totally destroyed, never to be rebuilt (Gleser, Green, and Winget, 1981, p. 148). The breadth, the extent, and the permanence of the displacement and the devastation at Buffalo Creek were quite unlike the vast majority of disasters. The impact of the flood was simply too catastrophic for most residents to cope with.

One manifestation the survivors' psychic trauma took was in their dreams. One resident's nightmares expressed an "alienation from others" as "a form of death, a grim rehearsal for that final act of separation." He said, "In the dream there is a big crowd at the funeral—the whole family is watching. I'm being buried. I'm scared to death. I'm trying to tell them I'm alive but they don't pay no attention. They act like I'm completely dead, but I'm trying to holler to them that I'm alive. They cover me up and let me down, but I can see dirt on me. I'm panicked and scared. I become violent trying to push my way through the dirt. . . . I think I'll suffocate if I don't fight my way out. . . . I'm trying to shout that I'm alive" (Erikson, 1976, pp. 243–244).

A Comparative Look at Disasters

In 1988, an earthquake hit Armenia; it registered 6.9 on the Richter scale. In 1989, another struck California; it was slightly stronger—registering a 7.1. Both occurred in heavily populated areas; if anything, the California quake's epicenter was closer to somewhat denser concentrations of habitation. In the Armenian quake, as we've already seen, 25,000 people died; in California's, only 62 (Browne, 1988; Taubman, 1988). In 1990, an earthquake struck northern Iran; it killed 40,000 people. More people died in that one disaster in Iran than died in all the disasters that took place in the United States during the entire 20th century! Perhaps the most famous earthquake of all time, the San Francisco earthquake of 1906, measured 8.3 on the Richter scale—a quake of stupendous magnitude; it killed only 451 people. (About a thousand San Franciscans died in the subsequent fire caused by the quake.) In 1976, a 7.5 earthquake struck China, and killed between 200,000 (the official estimate) and 800,000 (most experts' estimate). In 1971 a 6.4 earthquake hit the San Fernando region of California, in which seven million people live; 58 people were killed. A year later, a 6.2 quake struck Managua, Nicaragua; it killed 6,000 of the city's 400,000 people. In 1970, a tropical cyclone lashed the shores of Bangladesh and flooded nearly the entire costal area of the country; nearly half a million died in the devastation. In 1991, another cyclone killed nearly 200,000 people. The storms were only two of the worst of dozens in the past generation or so, each one of which routinely causes tens of thousands of deaths. In the United States, the number of hurricanes or typhoons that have caused more than a thousand deaths in the 20th century can be counted on the fingers of one hand, and the most destructive of them, which hit the coast of Texas, occurred in 1900.

No one who looks at the figures on disaster deaths can fail to be astonished by the enormous disparity between the more versus the less economically developed countries of the world. Invariably, when a natural upheaval strikes a heavily populated region of a poor, Third World Country, many people die; when a comparable one hits an affluent, industrialized country, relatively few perish. Why this disparity? In fact, even more specifically, it is "the poorest people in the poorest countries who are most vulnerable to injury [and death] in natural disasters" (Eckholm, 1984, p. C2). Again, why? What is it about being poor in a poor, economically developing country that places one at greater risk for disaster, injury, and death?

It will not be surprising to learn that the two bugaboos from Chapter 2, contagion and convergence, do not play a role here. The differences we observe between the economically developed and the less economically developed world are not due to panicky behavior of the victims during disasters or the background characteristics of the affected population. There are many reasons for the death toll disparity, but among them, three stand out. One is economic and architectural, the quality of construction; a second is economic and ecological, where people live; and the third is economic and social structural, the nature of post-disaster rehabilitation.

WHY THE DISPARITY?

Different kinds of construction place a population in different kinds of risks, depending on the nature of the calamity; for instance, an earthquake would place the residents of a certain type of building at considerable risk, but a flood might not. However, the importance of construction in disasters is best illustrated by what happens in earthquakes. In an earthquake, most victims die as a result of the collapse of a building in which the residents are crushed to death. And the simple fact is, some buildings are built to withstand the tremors of earthquakes, and others are not. Most buildings in much of the non-industrialized world (along with those in Eastern Europe) were not built to withstand the assault of nature's upheavals. The safer and sturdier the building, the more it costs to construct. In poorer countries, contractors rarely have the requisite capital, purchasers can rarely afford the added costs, and laws and ordinances requiring safer construction either do not exist or, if they do, are routinely skirted. Ironically, small, one-story buildings made of wood and other traditional materials are actually relatively safe in an earthquake; it is the multi-story concrete buildings in the Third World and Eastern Europe that are most often responsible for huge fatailities (Browne, 1988).

CONSTRUCTION

There are at least four construction techniques that are usually observed in the industrialized world, one or more of which are very often ignored in the less industrialized world—*connectivity, foundation pilings, reinforced concrete,* and *"clean load paths."* First, connectivity refers to the firm connections of all components, especially beams and columns supporting the floors and walls of a structure with each other and with the ground. In poorer countries, the components of a building are often simply placed together, unconnected, in slabs. In a quake, they collapse into a "pancake" or fly apart. Second, safe buildings are those that are built on pilings driven solidly into the ground, into rock if possible. Buildings that are simply placed on the ground without a foundation—built much more cheaply—have no support and can collapse much more easily. Third, concrete reinforced with steel rods is far less vulnerable to collapse; unreinforced masonry is common throughout the Third World and Eastern Europe, and is more likely to buckle and break apart under stress. And fourth, even where these features are built in, the safest buildings are those that are engineered to incorporate "clean load paths," that is, vertical beams or columns supporting a building's floors and walls that transmit their loads straight down to the ground rather than sideways (Browne, 1988).

As we all know, construction shortcuts, cheating, and corrupt noncompliance with building ordinances are widespread in the industrialized world, and spontaneous building collapses, even without seismic activity, are not unheard of. At the same time, these practices are many times more common throughout the less fully economically developed regions of the world, which is why we see such a high death toll in them. Said Charles Scawthorn, a structural engineer and expert on the effects of eathquakes on buildings: "The ways in which governments and people can protect themselves are limited, but should be pursued with all speed. Many lives hang in the balance" (Browne, 1988, p. 4).

WHERE PEOPLE LIVE

A second, and equally vital, reason why it is the poorest people in the poorest countries who are most vulnerable to disasters is *where they live.* Poverty forces people to live in disaster-prone areas while, at the same time, the total population in these areas is increasing all the time. Increasingly, prime farmland is becoming scarce, large farms are becoming mechanized, and peasants are being forced off their traditional lands. As a result, rural familes "are being forced to scratch a living in drought-prone areas, in flood plains, and on steep hillsides where the risk of landslides is high." In addition, millions upon millions of former rural dwellers flock to the cities of Third World countries, building "substandard housing on the only plots available—on the sides of ravines, along known geological fault lines, and in low-lying areas." In nearly all populous Third World countries, near large cities, shantytowns have sprung up "without planning or sanitation, transportation, health services, and other infrastructures. . . . The results are populous communities vulnerable to disasters" (Green, 1977, p. 17). In addition, "the degradation of forests, pastures, and soils has led to increases in the frequency of floods and droughtlike conditions" (Eckholm, 1984, p. C2). Unless ecologically sound practices are followed and housing for poor people in poor countries is built in safe areas, the death toll from disasters will continue to mount.

THE OFFICIAL RESPONSE

And the third major factor that influences the number of fatalities in a calamity is the nature of the response by the public and by officials. More affluent countries simply have many more resources to deal with the effect of disasters—more physicians, medical supplies, ambulances, nearby hospitals, earth-moving equipment, helicopters, boats, generators, chainsaws, and, of course, money. In poorer countries, fewer personnel using less sophisticated devices track the onset of natural calamities, and hence, officials and the public tend to be less prepared for them. And, in disasters, although wealthier nations tend to be donor countries and poorer ones, recipient countries, often, the former's inability to identify with the plight of the latter limits their contribution to the relief effort. Only $300,000 was raised in the United States in private donations for the victims of the 1990 Iranian earthquake, clearly a response by Americans to Iran's anti-American stance. More generally, many wealthier countries resent the view of poorer ones that disaster relief is a human right which should be received without having to beg for it. Many of the poorer countries of the world are marked by armed conflict which makes it difficult and sometimes impossible for relief workers to get through to victims and survivors. Some poorer governments are too proud to admit to the world that they need outside assistance, some minimize the extent of the damage in order not to frighten away the tourist business, and some are apprehensive that disaster assistance will bring foreign journalists, who will look around for even more problems. And, although sometimes unfounded or exaggerated, charges that corruption and theft are rife in disaster relief cannot be dismissed.

SUMMARY

This chapter made six points. First, a close, detailed look at the trampling deaths of 11 teenagers at The Who concert at Riverfront Stadium in Cincinnati in 1979 shows us that the images the media present of such events and their reality are often wildly discrepant. Second, evidence suggests that the conflicting role demands on rescue workers are such that some of them are unlikely to help out in the event of a disaster. Third, while there is typically a great deal of community cooperation during the emergency period of a disaster, this all too often dissipates, to be replaced with competition, conflict, and even hostility. Fourth, egocentrism and ethnocentrism often make it difficult for many of us to identify strongly with the plight of disaster victims. Fifth, the devastating impact of the flood that destroyed the community of Buffalo Creek, West Virginia, reminds us that the community recovery from a disaster does not always take place. And sixth, the death toll of disasters tends to be markedly higher in poorer, less industrialized countries than in more affluent, more highly industrialized ones.

References

Anderson, Mary. 1988–1989a. "Dissecting Disasters." *University of Delaware Magazine*, 1 (Winter): 16–24.

Anderson, Mary. 1988-1989b. "Dispelling Disaster Myths." *University of Delaware Magazine*, 1 (Winter): 20–21.

Associated Press and *The New York Times* (September 24, 1989): 35.

Barton, Allan H. 1969. *Communities in Disaster: A Sociological Analysis of Collective Stress Situations.* Garden City, N.Y.: Doubleday.

Baum, Andrew. 1988. "Disasters, Natural and Otherwise." *Psychology Today* (April): 57–60.

Baum, Andrew, Raymond Fleming, and Laura M. Davidson. 1983. "Natural Disasters and Technological Catastrophe." *Environment and Behavior*, 15 (May): 333–354.

Brouillette, John R., and Enrico L. Quarantelli. 1971. "Types of Patterned Variation in Bureaucratic Adaptations to Organizational Stress." *Sociological Inquiry*, 41 (1): 39–46.

Browne, Malcom W. 1988. "Quake-Proof Technology Little Help to Armenians." *The New York Times* (December 17): 1, 4.

Burton, Ian, Robert W. Kates, and Gilbert F. White. 1978. *The Environment as Hazard*. New York: Oxford University Press.

Caudill, Harry M. 1972. "Buffalo Creek Aftermath." *Saturday Review* (August 26): 16–17.

Chovnick, Steven. 1990. "Selective Attention Bias: Media Coverage of Airplane Disasters." Unpublished paper, State University of New York at Stony Brook.

Cialdini, Robert B. 1984. *Influence: How and Why People Agree to Things*. New York: William Morrow.

Cole, Stephen, Ralph H. Turner, and Allen H. Barton. 1988. "Role Conflict of School Bus Drivers." United States of America Nuclear Regulatory Commission, Before the Atomic Safety and Licensing Board, In the Matter of Long Island Lighting Company (Shoreham Nuclear Power Station, Unit 1), Docket No, 50-322-OL-3 (Emergency Planning), April 8.

Couch, Carl J. 1968. "Collective Behavior: An Examination of Some Stereotypes." *Social Problems*, 15 (Winter): 310–322.

Dynes, Russell R. 1970. *Organized Behavior in Disaster*. Lexington, Mass.: D.C. Heath.

Dynes, Russell R. 1978. "Interorganizational Relations in Communities Under Stress." In Enrico Quarantelli (ed.), *Disasters: Theory and Research*, pp. 49–65. Newbury Park, Calif.: Sage.

Ebert, Charles H.V. 1988. *Disasters: Violence of Nature and Threats by Man*. Dubuque, Iowa: Kendall/Hunt.

Eckholm, Erik. 1984. "Fatal Disasters on the Rise." *The New York Times* (July 31): C1, C2.

Erikson, Kai T. 1976. *Everything in Its Path: Destruction of Community in the Buffalo Creek Flood*. New York: Simon & Schuster.

Fireman, Ken. 1989. "Disorder After Hugo." *Newsday* (September 21): 3, 36.

Form, William H., and Sigmund Nosow, with Gregory P. Stone and Charles M. Westie. 1958. *Community in Disaster*. New York: Harper & Brothers.

Fritz, Charles E. 1961. "Disaster." In Robert K. Merton and Robert A. Nisbet (eds.), *Contemporary Social Problems*, pp. 651–694. New York: Harcourt Brace.

Fritz, Charles E., and J.H. Mathewson. 1957. *Convergence Behavior in Disasters.* Washington, D.C.: National Academy of Sciences/National Research Council.

Gleser, Goldine C., Bonnie L. Green, and Carolyn Winget. 1981. *Prolonged Psychosocial Effects of Disaster: A Study of Buffalo Creek.* New York: Academic Press.

Goode, William J. 1960a. "A Theory of Role Strain." *American Sociological Review,* 25 (August): 483–496.

Goode, William J. 1960b. "Norm Commitment and Conformity to Role-Status Obligations." *American Journal of Sociology,* 66 (November): 246–258.

Goode, William J. 1973. *Explorations in Social Theory.* New York: Oxford University Press.

Green, Stephen. 1977. *International Disaster Relief: Toward a Responsive System.* New York: McGraw-Hill.

Greenwald, John, et al. 1986. "Deadly Meltdown." *Time* (May 12): 39–44ff.

Hazarika, Sanjoy. 1989. "Bhopal Payments Set at $470 Million for Union Carbide." *The New York Times* (February 15): A1, D3.

Johnson, Norris R. 1987. "Panic at 'The Who Concert Stampede': An Empirical Assessment." *Social Problems,* 34 (October): 362–373.

Killian, Lewis M. 1952. "The Significance of Multi-Group Membership in Disaster." *American Journal of Sociology,* 57 (January): 309–314.

Kutak, Robert I. 1938. "Sociology of Crises: The Louisville Flood of 1937." *Social Forces,* 17 (1): 66–72.

Langer, Ellen J. 1975. "The Illusion of Control." *Journal of Personality and Social Psychology,* 32 (2): 311–328.

Latane, Bibb, and John M. Darley. 1968. *The Unresponsive Bystander: Why Doesn't He Help?* New York: Appleton-Century-Crofts.

Lerner, Melvin J. 1980. *The Belief in a Just World: A Fundamental Delusion.* New York: Plenum Press.

Marks, Eli S., and Charles E. Fritz. 1954. "The NORC Studies in Human Behavior in Disaster." *Journal of Social Issues,* 10 (1): 26–41.

Merton, Robert K. 1957. *Social Theory and Social Structure* (rev. ed.). New York: Free Press.

Miller, David T. 1985. *Introduction to Collective Behavior.* Belmont, Calif.: Wadsworth.

National Research Council, U.S. National Academy of Sciences, U.S. National Academy of Engineering, *Confronting Natural Disasters: An International Decade for Natural Hazard Reduction,* Washington, D.C.: National Academy Press, 1987.

The New York Times (June 22, 1990): A10. "250 Deaths at Chernobyl."

Oliver-Smith, Anthony. 1979. "Post Disaster Consensus and Conflict in a Traditional Society: The 1970 Avalanche of Yungay, Peru." *Mass Emergencies,* 4 (1): 39–52.

Perry, Joseph B., Jr., and Meredith D. Pugh. 1978. *Collective Behavior: Response to Stress.* St. Paul: West.

Prince, Samuel Henry. 1920. *Catastrophe and Social Change, Based Upon a Study of the Halifax Disaster.* New York: Columbia University Press.

Quarantelli, Enrico L. 1960. "Images of Withdrawal Behavior in Disasters: Some Basic Misconceptions." *Social Problems,* 8 (Summer): 68–79.

Quarantelli, Enrico L. 1980. *Evacuation Behavior and Problems: Findings and Implications from the Research Literature.* Columbus, Ohio: Disaster Research Center.

Quarantelli, Enrico L., and Russell R. Dynes. 1972. "When Disaster Strikes (It Isn't Much Like What You've Heard & Read About)." *Psychology Today* (February): 67–70.

Quarantelli, Enrico L., and Russell R. Dynes. 1976. "Community Conflict: Its Absence and Its Presence in Natural Disasters." *Mass Emergencies,* 1 (3): 139–152.

Rather, John. 1990. "Response to Jet Crash May Bring Reappraisal." *The New York Times* (February 11): 6LI.

Rosengren, Karl Erik, Peter Arvidson, and Dahn Sturesson. 1979. "The Barsebak 'Panic': A Radio Programme as a Negative Summary Event." *Acta Sociologica,* 57 (4): 309–321.

Rosow, Irving. 1977. *Authority in Natural Disasters: Four Tornado Communities in 1953.* Columbus, Ohio: Disaster Research Center.

Ross, Michael, and Fiore Sicoly. 1979. "Egocentric Biases in Availability and Attribution." *Journal of Personality and Social Psychology,* 37 (2): 322–336.

Salisbury, Harrison E. 1989. *The Great Black Dragon Fire: A Chinese Inferno.* Boston: Little, Brown.

Schmalz, Jeffrey. 1989a. "Troops Find an Island Torn By Looting and Devastation." *The New York Times* (September 22): A1, A22.

Schmalz, Jeffrey. 1989b. "Roots of Looting on St. Croix Lie in Racial and Class Tension." The New York Times (September 26): B8.

Schneider, Keith. 1989. "A New Flood Swamps Charleston: Help. " *The New York Times* (October 2): A12.

Sherif, Muzafer. 1936. *The Psychology of Social Norms.* New York: Harper.

Sherif, Muzafer, and O.J. Harvey. 1952. "A Study of Ego Functioning: The Elimination of Stable Anchorages in Individual and Group Situations." *Sociometry,* 15 (August–November): 272–305.

Smelser, Neil J. 1962. *Theory of Collective Behavior.* New York: Free Press.

Stern, Gerald M. 1977. *The Buffalo Creek Disaster.* New York: Vintage Books.

Taubman, Philip. 1988. "Rescue Effort Straining Soviet Economy." *The New York Times* (December 14): A8.

Taylor, James B., Louis A. Zurcher, and William H. Key. 1970. *Tornado: A Community Responds to Disaster.* Seattle: University of Washington Press.

"250 Deaths at Chernobyl." *Newsday* (November 9, 1989): 13.

Wallace, Anthony F.C. 1956. *Tornado in Worcester.* Washington, D.C.: National Academy of Sciences-National Research Council.

Walsh, Edward J. 1984. "Local Community Vs. National Industry: The TMI and Santa Barbara Protests Compared." *International Journal of Mass Emergencies and Disasters,* 2 (March): 147–163.

Walsh, Edward J., and Rex H. Warland. 1983. "Social Movement Involvement in the Wake of a Nuclear Accident: Activists and Free Riders in the TMI Area." *American Sociological Review,* 48 (December): 764–780.

Wenger, Dennis E. 1987. "Collective Behavior and Disaster Research." In Russell R. Dynes, Bruna DeMarchi, and Carlo Pelanda (eds.), *Sociology of Disasters: Contribution of Sociology to Disaster Research,* pp. 213–237. Milan, Italy: Franco Angeli.

Wenger, Dennis E., James D. Dykes, Thomas D. Sebok, and Joan L. Neff. 1975. "It's a Matter of Myths: An Empirical Examination of Individual Insight into Disaster Response." *Mass Emergencies,* 1 (October): 33–46.

Whittow, John. 1979. *Disasters: The Anatomy of Environmental Hazards.* Athens: University of Georgia Press.

Wijkman, Anders, and Lloyd Timberlake. 1988. *Natural Disasters: Acts of God or Acts of Man?* Santa Cruz, Calif.: New Society Publishers.

Wilkins, Lee. 1987. *Shared Vulnerability: The Media and American Perceptions of the Bhopal Disaster.* Westport, Conn.: Greenwood Press.

Wolfenstein, Martha. 1957. *Disaster: A Psychological Essay.* Glencoe, Ill.: Free Press.

Zald, Mayer N., and John D. McCarthy. 1987. *Social Movements in Organizational Society: Collected Essays.* New Brunswick, N.J.: Transaction Books.

Zuckerman, Miron, et al. 1983. "The Egocentric Bias: Seeing Oneself as Cause and Target of Others' Behavior." *Journal of Personality,* 51 (December): 621–630.

Zurcher, Louis A. 1968. "Social-Psychological Functions of Ephemeral Roles: A Disaster Work Crew." *Human Organization,* 27 (Winter): 281–297.

PART FOUR

INTRODUCTION TO DIFFUSE COLLECTIVITIES

Masses and publics are unlike crowds (and groups of people called upon to deal with disasters) in a number of key respects. As with crowds—or compact collectivities—*diffuse collectivities,* or *masses* and *publics,* have specific traits that encourage or make certain social behavior and dynamics more likely. What are the characteristics of a public? It has two defining qualities: First, it is a collectivity of individuals who are focused on or interested in a given issue or engaged in a form of behavior, and second, it is geographically dispersed. The fact that people who are focused on a specific issue are spread out across a society or a country, but engage in social interaction in small, usually intimate groupings, means that their behavior relevant to that issue is going to follow certain patterns and regularities. It is necessary to spell out some of the crucial characteristics of masses and publics so that we may understand what they are likely—and unlikely—to do. Of course, for the purpose of the field of collective behavior, we are not interested in just any and all dispersed collectivities—only those that are engaged in, or may engage in, collective behavior. The overwhelming majority of most publics enact more or less exclusively traditional, conventional, institutional behavior; they are not a focus of the field of collective behavior.

As was said in Chapter 1, in past generations, the concept of the "mass" had a strongly pejorative connotation. Much was made at one time of the thesis that the United States is a "mass" society, a nation of atomized, rootless individuals who passively consume the mass media, but who do not interact with one another about its content, or influence it in any way (Kornhauser, 1959; Rosenberg and White, 1957). While these social critics were right in arguing that the media create a public, they were wrong in their understanding of how the mass media work. A mass or public exposed to the media is not passive; no one receives or accepts messages emating from the media, and very few people are exposed to them in isolation. Today, hardly anyone believes the "mass media" thesis—that is, publics as atomized and passive—and hence, the concept of the "mass" as it was originally formulated has fallen into disuse. In fact, in a recent introductory sociology textbook, the term "mass public" is used (Kornblum, 1988, p. 595; 1991), indicating that the concepts are often used as more or less equivalent. I will *not* use the concept of the "mass" in its original sense of a large number of scattered, isolated, atomized individuals. To me, "mass" and "public" can be used more or less interchangeably. They refer to a large number of geographically dispersed individuals who are interested in or focused on a particular issue, problem, or phenomenon.

As with crowds, there is no exact lower limit on the size of a diffuse collectivity. Certainly a few dozen, or even a few hundred, people scattered around the country cannot be referred to as a mass or a public. Publics are usually much larger than crowds, but exactly how much larger, again, cannot be defined with much precision. A mass need not be the entire population of a country, nor even all of its adults—in fact, it hardly ever is. Nearly all issues generate interest and activity in only a portion of the population—rarely a majority, sometimes half, or a tenth, or even a fraction of one percent. There is, for example, a public that is made up of individuals who are interested in Elvis Presley. They visit Graceland, his home in Nashville, collect Elvis memorabilia, talk to others about him (usually in reverential tones), read about him, criticize articles and books that seem critical of his life, form fan clubs, lobby to make his birthday a national holiday, make claims that they have seen him recently in the flesh or have talked to him in their prayers, and so on. This public comprises a fraction of one percent of the American population (the Elvis phenomenon attracts followers from other countries as well), but it is a public nonetheless. Of course, most publics are much larger, such as the voting public, the television public, or the public that is interested in the state of the economy.

A key difference between a diffuse and a compact collectivity is that, although expressive and acting crowds generally assemble for a reason, individuals of all crowds are members of a crowd *simply by virtue of their physical location alone*, whereas membership in a mass or a public is defined not by simple physical or geographical location, but by *interest in a given issue.* Anyone who is *in* a given crowd is a member *of* that crowd, even if they do not engage in the collective behavior enacted by the majority. On the other hand, if you pay attention to or vote in a given election, you are part of a voting public; if you watch television, you are part of a TV public; if you talk to others about the economy, you are part of a public concerned with the state of the economy. Again, none of these is determined by physical location, as is true of the crowd. Publics and masses are dispersed *within* a physically and geographically dispersed population. Of course, some publics are determined at least *in part* by geographical location—for instance, the readership of *New York* magazine tends to be located in and around New York City— but physical location is not a *definition* of the public or the mass in the same way that it is for the crowd. Of course, as we've already seen, everyone is a member of several publics simultaneously, a quality emphasized by Gabriel Tarde nearly a century ago (1969, originally published 1901). This quality imparts a special dynamic to publics not shared by the compact collectivity.

Diffuse collectivities need possess no particular level of density, they may be thickly or thinly scattered about the countryside—again, unlike the crowd. They need possess no particular level of continuity or contiguousness, again, unlike the crowd. The reason for this is the fact that in a crowd, communication is face-to-face, and takes place as a result of seeing and hearing others with one's own eyes and ears. For this to happen, it is necessary for people to be packed together fairly closely. If people are scattered about too thinly, or if there are physical discontinuities in crowds, people cannot communicate with one another on a face-to-face basis. With dispersed collectivities, this is a different matter. When people are scattered about, they can communicate with one another in small clusters of people; all of the members of a public need not hear or see what every other member is saying or doing.

And they can communicate in a variety of ways—by telephone, letter, Fax machine, computer linkup, as well as through second-, third-, or fourth-hand talk in a gossip or rumor network.

With a mass or a public, unlike the crowd, there need be no particular *assembling processes*, no mechanisms that bring large numbers of people together in the same place at the same time, because publics *need not assemble to exist*. There are processes of interaction and communication, of course, but, again, physical proximity is *not* a characteristic of the dispersed collectivity, hence, they need not assemble to begin with. They may (and in all likelihood, do) assemble in tiny groups of intimates, or they may communicate in other ways, as we saw. Assembly is *not* a defining characteristic of publics.

Members of publics vary with respect to their *degree of involvement and interest* in a given issue. With a certain issue, the degree of involvement of different members of a diffuse collectivity can be represented by a large circle with increasingly smaller concentric circles inside of it, much like an archery target. They have, in other words, a "core" membership, represented by the innermost circle, which is made up of individuals who are the most active and intensely involved with a given issue; increasingly less involved members, represented by the circles outside the inner one; and a fairly large "periphery" membership of casually involved individuals, represented by the outermost circle. For instance, for the UFO (unidentified flying object) public, the "core" segment is made up of individuals who are members of UFO clubs, go to UFO meetings and conventions, drive around the countryside looking for UFOs, give speeches and talks on the subject, write for and subscribe to UFO journals, and so on. The peripheral or casual member of the UFO public simply has an opinion on the subject, occasionally reads an article or talks to others about it, but does not engage in any of the activities that define a more active participant. The exact degree of involvement in a given issue that defines membership in the relevant public cannot, again, be determined with any degree of precision, but *some* measure of involvement in it is necessary to define someone as a member of that collectivity.

Lofland (1981, 1985, pp. 35–70) examined the "elementary forms" of collective behavior—the expression of fear, hostility, and joy in both crowds and masses. The expression of fear in a mass situation provides the locus of a number of examples of collective behavior. Lofland (1981, p. 421) emphasizes that, most of the time, collective fears are expressed not in crowds but in more diffuse collectivities. The fear felt by a crowd can be communicated much more quickly—a few seconds, a few minutes—than is true in a more diffuse collectivity. A mass is more likely to react to a "slow, space-and-time dispersed trend," whereas a crowd can also react to a sudden, immediate danger as well (p. 422), such as an armed police column or an oncoming flood, a tornado, or a hurricane. The fears to which masses and publics are likely to react are often of a social and economic nature, such as the fear of crime, deteriorating race relations, inflation, and so on.

The fears that publics and masses feel and express can stem from an accurate assessment of "true dangers" or from imaginary or "false dangers" (p. 422). As we might expect, it is impossible to determine with a great deal of precision whether a danger is accurate, or "true," on the one hand, or imaginary, or "false," on the other. Some observers claim that an accurate assessment of the nature of concrete reality cannot be made at all. (Although the same individuals make such assessments all the time, both in their everyday lives and in their scholarly work.) Indeed, experts are often mistaken about the chances that a given danger will materialize. For instance, in the mid-to-late 1970s, public health officials announced the imminence of a particular strain of influenza, the swine flu. If the entire American population did not receive innoculations against it, they warned, an influenza epidemic would break out. As it turned out, the swine flu never infected a substantial number of Americans; the experts were simply wrong about the magnitude of the danger the virus posed to the American population. At the same time, some fears *are* a great deal more grounded in evidence than others are; some are clearly baseless and others are just as clearly based on a fairly accurate and valid reading of the facts. Because, in some cases, it isn't possible to assess the true magnitude of certain dangers does not mean that the distinction between "true" and "false" dangers is always invalid.

It might be expected that the field of collective behavior ignores fears of "true" danger, and focuses entirely on fears of "false" danger. After all, what's so interesting about widespread fear over something that presents a clear and present danger? It seems terribly logical and commonsensical; why do we need to explain why people feel fearful about something that really and truly threatens them? This assumption is false; in fact, sociologists of collective behavior have studied "true" fears as much as "false" ones. It is not nearly so logical and commonsensical to study true fears as it might seem, because even true fears have to start somewhere. Indeed, the widespread fear of "true" dangers wax and wane over the years, often quite out of proportion to their objective threat. The definition or "discovery" of a social problem is a sociological process, and not a simple reflection of the presence of objective danger (Cohen, 1972; Ben-Yehuda, 1986; Best, 1989; Gentry, 1988). This is such an important topic that we'll be looking at it in more detail in the section on social movements.

In any case, the collective behavior literature is replete with collective fears of "false" dangers, such as the following six examples.

1. In the 1950s, the residents of the Pacific northwest thought that an inexplicable force was pitting the windshields of their cars. The pitting turned out to be a combination of the effects of airborne pollution as a result of the use of bituminous coal and ordinary road wear and damage (Medalia and Larsen, 1958).

2. In the 1960s, a number of factory workers imagined that they were being bitten by a bug of some kind; investigators were unable to discover a physical cause for the symptoms (Kerckhoff and Back, 1968; Kirckhoff, Back, and Miller, 1965).

3. In the 1970s, in the Midwest and Rocky Mountain states, it was

widely believed that cattle were being killed and ritually slaughtered by mysterious agents; it turned out that they died a natural death and were partially eaten by animal scavengers (Rorvick, 1980; Stewart, 1980; Kagan and Summers, 1984).

4. In the 1980s, fundamentalist Christians believed that Proctor and Gamble, a soap and household products manufacturer, contributed 10 percent of its profits to the Church of Satan, and that its logo, the face of the man in the moon on a field of 13 stars, was proof of this connection (Esposito and Rosnow, 1983; Fine, 1990, pp. 136–140; Koenig, 1985, pp. 39–54; Brunvand, 1984, pp. 169–186). The fear was of course completely groundless, although Proctor and Gamble, unable to put a halt to the false rumors, dropped its well-known trademark, which had been in use for nearly a century (Anonymous, 1985).

5. In 1990, toll booth attendants in New York City fell ill on the job to a mysterious, undiagnosable, and possibly psychogenic disease (Golden, 1990).

6. Throughout the 1980s and into the 1990s, all over the English-speaking world, hundreds of thousands of people, mainly fundamentalist Christians, became extremely concerned that a large and highly organized group of satanists was kidnapping (and breeding) tens of thousands of children, sexually molesting them, and murdering them in sacrificial rituals (Victor, 1989, 1990a, 1990b; Richardson, Best, and Bromley, 1991; Alexander, 1990; Thompson, King, and Anette, 1990; Hicks, 1991). No solid evidence has ever been found to support this claim.

In each of these cases, a large number of people felt a certain measure of fear about an agent that, the evidence suggests, was nonexistent or imaginary.

It must be emphasized that the collective fear of a "false" danger—often referred to as "mass hysteria"—is a great deal less common than is widely believed. The fear generated by the "War of the Worlds" radio broadcast in 1938 was substantially exaggerated by the media. Miller (1985, pp. 98–119) goes so far as to argue that mass hysteria is next to nonexistent. Certainly, if mass hysteria is defined as a strong fear of a false danger that grips the majority of a relevant population *and results in some kind of mobilization*, such as flight, then Miller is correct. However, if we look at mass fear based on a false danger that grips *a substantial proportion* of a relevant population—although not necessarily a majority—and does *not* necessitate mobilization, such as flight, then the phenomenon has occurred many times in human history (Sirois, 1974). Not all widespread fears are necessarily based on the sober assessment of a clear and present danger; some arise as a consequence of cultural forces that may result in unfounded beliefs, such as the fundamentalists' fear of the influence of Satan.

Bartholomew (1990) makes a persuasive case for abandoning the term "mass hysteria" and substituting "collective exaggerated emotions." The label *mass hysteria* is pejorative and evaluative; the observer puts forth the claim that it is an abnormal, pathological, or disease entity. In fact, practically none of the individuals discussed as falling victim to this syndrome manifests any signs of mental illness, other than the unusual behavior itself. Moreover, by applying the label "mass hysteria" to such episodes, the observer further makes the claim that they all have a universal, transcultural, common thread that can be located and explained, usually stress of some kind. In fact, no such universal factors have been found, and those that are located in a specific instance are identified only post hoc, or after the fact. In fact, a careful examination of episodes of collective exaggerated emotions show that they make a great deal of sense *within a given cultural or subcultural context*. Referring to them as episodes of "mass hysteria" represents an ethnocentric bias that is inappropriate in a course on collective behavior (Bartholomew, 1990).

Hostilities, too, are expressed in masses and publics, as well as in crowds. However, most of the collective behavior in which hostility is expressed that has been studied by the field has been crowd behavior, such as riots, and not the behavior of more diffuse collectivities. In fact, as Lofland states (1981, p. 434), there has been very little speculation—let alone empirical research—concerning the expression of mass hostility. Still, when people live in conditions they define as undesirable, they often single out a target defined as the enemy toward which the expression of hostility is encouraged (Klapp, 1971). The mass and crowd denunciations that took place in Iran and Iraq in the 1980s and early 1990s (most of which were staged, not spontaneous) provide good examples of mass vilification. The expression of hostility toward certain racial and ethnic groups sometimes breaks out of its traditional, normative mold and enters the realm of collective behavior. The continual reappearance of belief in the authenticity of the "Protocols of the Elders of Zion," a document forged, probably by the Russian secret police, at the turn of the century, which supposedly revealed a Jewish conspiracy to dominate the world, provides a good example of the expression of hostility on a mass, although minority, basis. Endorsement of the "Protocols" as evidence that Jews are evil and that anti-Semitism is valid has cropped up in Germany in the 1920s (Hitler used it as a basis for his book, *Mein Kampf*), after World War II in South America among Nazi immigrants, and today in the Middle East, and, of all places, in Japan (Johnson, 1987).

Expressions of mass joy provide examples for a large number of collective behavior phenomena. It is possible that the term "joy" is a bit strong for some of the phenomena that illustrate Lofland's typology (1981, pp. 441–445)—notably, fads, fashion, and crazes—but all represent a strong positive feeling about something that expresses itself in behavior of some sort. Collective joy may also be expressed in a diffuse collectivity in *mass migrations, rushes* and *booms*, such as gold rushes, land booms, and certain periods of intense, frenzied financial speculation, and *mass celebrations*, such as the end of World War II or the overthrow of an unpopular dictator. We'll examine some of these mass collective behavior phenomena in the chapters that follow.

References

Alexander, David. 1990. "Giving the Devil More than His Due." *The Humanist* (March/April): 5–14, 34.

Anonymous. 1985. "P & G Drops Logo from Its Packages: Satan Rumors Are Blamed." *The New York Times* (April 25): D1.

Bartholomew, Robert E. 1990. "Ethnocentricity and the Social Construction of 'Mass Hysteria.'" *Culture, Medicine and Psychiatry*, 14 (December): 455–494.

Ben-Yehuda, Nachman. 1986. "The Sociology of Moral Panics: Toward a New Synthesis." *The Sociological Quarterly*, 27 (4): 495–513.

Best, Joel (ed.). 1989. *Images of Issues: Typifying Contemporary Social Problems*. New York: Aldine de Gruyter.

Brunvand, Jan Harold. 1984. *The Choking Doberman and Other "New" Urban Legends*. New York: W.W. Norton.

Cohen, Stanley. 1972. *Folk Devils and Moral Panics*. London: Macgibbon & Kee.

Esposito, James L., and Ralph L. Rosnow. 1983. "Corporate Rumors: How They Start and How to Stop Them." *Management Review*, 72 (April): 44–49.

Fine, Gary Alan. 1990. "Among Those Dark Satanic Mills: Rumors of Kooks, Cults, and Corporations." *Southern Folklore*, 47 (1): 133–146.

Gentry, Cynthia. 1988. "The Social Construction of Abducted Children as a Social Problem." *Sociological Inquiry*, 58 (4): 413–425.

Golden, Tim. 1990. "Toll Workers' Illness: All in Their Minds?" *The New York Times* (March 12): B1, B4.

Hicks, Robert D. 1991. *In Pursuit of Satan: The Police and the Occult*. Buffalo: Prometheus Books.

Johnson, George. 1987. "The Infamous 'Protocols of the Elders of Zion' Endures." *The New York Times* (July 26): 6E.

Kagan, Daniel, and Ian Summers. 1984. *Mute Evidence*. New York: Bantam Books.

Kerckhoff, Alan C., and Kurt W. Back. 1968. *The June Bug: A Study of Hysterical Contagion*. New York: Appleton-Century-Crofts.

Kerckhoff, Alan C., Kurt W. Back, and Norman Miller. 1965. "Socio-metric Patterns in Hysterical Contagion." *Sociometry*, 28 (1): 2–15.

Klapp, Orrin E. 1971. *Social Types: Process, Structure, and Ethos.* San Diego: Aegis Publishing.

Koenig, Frederick. 1985. *Rumor in the Marketplace: The Social Psychology of Commercial Hearsay.* Dover, Mass.: Auburn House.

Kornblum, William. 1988. *Sociology in a Changing World.* New York: Holt, Rinehart & Winston.

Kornblum, William. 1991. *Sociology in a Changing World* (2nd ed.). New York: Holt, Rinehart & Winston.

Kornhauser, William. 1959. *The Politics of Mass Society.* New York: Free Press.

Lofland, John. 1981. "Collective Behavior: The Elementary Forms." In Morris Rosenberg and Ralph H. Turner (eds.), *Social Psychology: Sociological Perspectives*, pp. 411–446. New York: Basic Books.

Lofland, John. 1985. *Protest: Studies of Collective Behavior and Social Movements.* New Brunswick, N.J.: Transaction Books.

Medalia, Nahum Z., and Otto N. Larsen. 1958. "Diffusion and Belief in a Collective Delusion: The Seattle Windshield Pitting Epidemic." *American Sociological Review*, 23 (April): 180–186.

Miller, David L. 1985. *Introduction to Collective Behavior.* Belmont, Calif.: Wadsworth.

Richardson, James T., Joel Best, and David Bromley (eds.). 1991. *The Satanism Scare.* New York: Aldine de Gruyter.

Rorvick, David. 1980. "Cattle Mutilations: The Truth at Last." *Penthouse* (September): 121–122, 142–143.

Rosenberg, Bernard, and David Manning White (eds.). 1957. *Mass Culture.* Glencoe, Ill.: Free Press.

Sirois, Francois. 1974. *Epidemic Hysteria.* Copenhagen: Munskgaard.

Stewart, James R. 1980. "Collective Delusion: A Comparison of Believers and Skeptics." Unpublished Paper Delivered Before the Midwest Sociological Society, Milwaukee, Wisc., April 3.

Tarde, Gabriel. 1969. (Principal essay published in 1901.) *Gabriel Tarde on Communication and Social Influence.* (Terry N. Clark, ed.) Chicago: University of Chicago Press.

Thompson, Bill, Alison King, and Jason Anette. 1990. "Snuff, Sex, and Satan: Contemporary Legends and Moral Politics." Paper Presented to the International Society for the Study of Urban Legends, Sheffield, England.

Victor, Jeffrey S. 1989. "A Rumor-Panic About a Dangerous Satanic Cult in Western New York." *New York Folklore*, 15 (1–2): 23–49.

Victor, Jeffery S. 1990a. "Satanic Cult Legends as Contemporary Legend." *Western Folklore*, 49 (January): 51–81.

Victor, Jeffrey S. 1990b. "The Spread of Satanic-Cult Rumors." *Skeptical Inquirer*, 14 (Spring): 287–291.

CHAPTER

7

RUMOR AND GOSSIP

R umor and gossip are universal. They exist in all societies and, as far
as can be determined, they have existed at all times; one observer
calls rumor "the oldest form of mass media" (Kapferer, 1990, p. 1). We are all
exposed to rumor and gossip; no one can escape—they are everywhere. It is
possible that every human being on earth (with the exception of autistic persons, who communicate with no one) has engaged in the process of gossiping and telling and listening to rumors. Says one anthropologist, "Every single day, and for a large part of each day, most of us are engaged in gossip"
(Gluckman, 1963, p. 308). Enough research has been conducted on the subject, mainly by sociologists, psychologists, and anthropologists, for us to be
able to make some generalizations about how gossip and rumor work. How
and why do rumors get started? What is talked about in rumor? In gossip?
How do gossip and rumor differ? Why does one rumor die out and another
continue for years, generations, even centuries? Who passes on rumors and
who doesn't—who tells and who "dead-ends" a rumor? Who gets gossiped
about—and who doesn't? What social conditions maximize rumormongering?
Which ones minimize it? What functions does gossip serve for society? These
are some of the questions we'll be looking at in this chapter.

Rumor is both a *process* and a *product*; that is, it is both a *mechanism* that
pervades collective behavior and an *example* of collective behavior. As a process, rumor takes place before, during, and after riots, ecstatic crowds, and
disasters. It helps propagate myths, legends, mass delusions, fads, fashion,
and crazes. It can affect—both accelerate and retard—the genesis, growth,
and demise of social movements. As a process, its influence could be studied
in each and every chapter of this book. However, this would be inconvenient

and repetitious, and so, for the sake of expositional flow, we'll look at the subject of this chapter as a separate and distinct entity. We've already seen how rumor works in riots; now let's see how it works in general. Gossip is every bit as pervasive as rumor, and can have all of these effects as well; however, as we'll see shortly, unlike rumor, it is defined not by the process by which it is propagated, but exclusively by its content.

Earlier, we saw that disasters take place among gatherings that range in size from compact to diffuse collectivities, from crowds to publics. In this respect, rumor and gossip, likewise, are a bit difficult to place. Gossip and rumors are transmitted among collectivities whose size and degree of compactness/diffuseness also range from crowds to publics. For gossip and rumors to be transmitted in publics, however, they have to be of general interest to a fairly wide spectrum of people, as we'll see. In contrast, gossip and rumors about the details of the lives of a small circle of friends rarely travel much beyond that local circle unless, of course, there is something remarkable about their lives. As has been pointed out (Buckner, 1965, pp. 56, 63–65), the dynamics of rumor in collectivities with a stable, close-knit group structure are very different from those in which the group structure is more diffuse.

WHAT ARE RUMOR AND GOSSIP?

We've all heard and told rumors—but what *is* a rumor? Do we know one when we hear one? Do we even know one when we've *told* one? Gossip is often discussed in the same breath as rumor. What's the difference between rumor and gossip? They are related, but not identical, concepts. Both are forms of communication, but not all forms of communication are gossip or rumor.

RUMOR

The first and most distinctive defining characteristic of rumor is that it is a story that is *unsubstantiated* and *unauthenticated;* it is told *without reliable factual documentation.* By definition, a story that is factually substantiated is not a rumor. Before it was known by the public that Rock Hudson had contracted AIDS, it was widely rumored that he had the disease. Most people who told the rumor were going on very superficial and unreliable indicators—he was known by many to be a homosexual, he had lost a great deal of weight, and many felt that he looked ill. At this point, the story was still a rumor. However, when the news that he had checked into a French hospital for treatment for the disease appeared in the media, the allegation that Rock Hudson had AIDS was no longer a rumor; it was reliably authenticated and, at that point, it acquired the status of a fact. Rumor is *by definition* unsubstantiated; when a statement is substantiated, it is no longer a rumor. In short, rumor is *hearsay* (Rosnow and Fine, 1976). Another way of saying this is that rumors tend to be *theory-driven* rather than *fact-driven* (Rosnow, 1988,

p. 15). That is, rumors are believed and passed on not because of the weight of the evidence presented when they are told, but because of the expectations that tellers hold that they are true in the first place. In short, rumor is defined by a *lack of evidence* supporting a statement or story, not by its falsity. A given rumor may turn out to be true or false; what counts is that it is told without factual foundation.

At least one observer (McPhail, 1991, p. 106) questions whether this prevailing definition of rumor is valid—although he proposes no definition of his own. Further (p. 92), he claims, the prevailing conceptualization of rumor may not even designate a unique or distinctive phenomenon. As to whether these comments are of any theoretical or empirical value remains to be seen. It is conceivable (but unlikely) that hundreds of social scientists are investigating a phenomenon that does not exist in the first place! However, these researchers do not operate under the behaviorist rule that, if something can't be measured with meticulous precision, it is not real. It should not come as a surprise that an approach that is disturbed by subjectivistic phenomena would find the prevailing definition of rumor troubling.

GOSSIP

In contrast, gossip may be substantiated *or* unsubstantiated, factually verified or not; it is not defined by its factual foundation. One may tell stories about someone else that are known to be true, based on reliably documented facts; by definition, such stories cannot be rumors—they are gossip. If one person says to another, "Isn't it dreadful the way John and Jane carry on!", that would be gossip, not rumor, since presumably both know about the couple's relationship, and both teller and listener probably already know that each agrees with respect to its scandalousness. Contrary to the stereotype, most of the stories that appear in gossip columns have been factually substantiated—some haven't, but most have (Levine and Arluke, 1987, pp. 63ff). An article, complete with photographs, about a celebrity sunbathing nude on an isolated beach would be factually substantiated—and therefore not rumor—but it *would* be gossip. Thus, a lack of factual substantiation is *not* part of the definition of what gossip is, as it is with rumor. This leads us to our second distinction.

RUMOR VS. GOSSIP

Rumor may be personal *or* impersonal. The topic of the rumor is unimportant. In contrast, gossip, by its very nature, is *personal*. An unsubstantiated, false statement about a dam bursting would be rumor, not gossip, because gossip is *always* personal, and *always* about people and their doings. If a statement is about impersonal matters, by definition, it *cannot* be an example of gossip. Rumor covers the entire spectrum, from personal to impersonal; gossip, in contrast, is, by its very nature, solely and exclusively about personal matters. People love stories about the doings of others; gossip is made up of those personal, usually interesting stories about what others are doing.

In short, rumor is defined by the *process* by which it is passed on, that is, it lacks sufficient evidence; whereas gossip is defined by its *content* or its *topic*, that is, it is personal in nature (Levine and Arluke, 1987, p. 42; Fine, 1985, p. 223). Of course, rumor and gossip overlap a great deal: Much rumor is also gossip, and much gossip is also rumor. But a great deal of rumor is not gossip, and a great deal of gossip is not rumor. Some instances of story telling are clearly rumor and not gossip, some instances are clearly gossip and not rumor, and some are both. The two "represent overlapping, but not identical, sets of discourse" (Fine, 1985, p. 223).

WHY ARE RUMOR AND GOSSIP COLLECTIVE BEHAVIOR?

What makes rumor and gossip forms of collective behavior? They have three key characteristics that qualify them for attention by the field. First, they represent the product of a *collective* endeavor; they are generated in the give-and-take of social interaction. Second, they are attempts to "fill in the gaps" in an information vacuum; that is, they are made up of more or less *spontaneous*, more or less *extemporaneous*, statements that arise under certain social conditions. And third, they are *extrainstitutional*, nonnormative, and somewhat unconventional in nature. Mainstream values and norms frown on rumor and gossip. They have no value in court; they are discouraged in the media, at least, as "hard" news (purveyors of gossip and society news rank at the bottom of journalism's prestige hierarchy); they are excluded from the educational system, at least in principle; and a good military strategist would not launch a major offensive based exclusively on hearsay. In short, "rumor is [based on] non-normative evidence. Someone who repeats a rumor is transmitting suspect evidence" (Rosnow and Fine, 1976, p. 11). Says a journalist about gossip, "Accuracy is not as highly prized in gossip as on the news pages. Columnists expect to be wrong fairly frequently. . . . If a gossip columnist has the essence of a story right, he or she often doesn't mind that many of the details are in error, a situation that would make most reporters flinch." Says Jerry Nachman, editor of the New York *Post,* "[gossip] exists in a netherworld where the traditional tests that would hold in the rest of the newspaper get flexed a bit. . . . The normal rules of journalism don't apply here" (Henry, 1990, p. 51).

And yet, gossip and rumor are the lifeblood of any society's communication system, as pervasive as the air we breathe. If we had to rely solely on the information conveyed by the conventional institutions, we would be deprived of some of the most interesting and valuable statements we hear. The "aboveboard" institutions reject gossip and rumor, but we all crave and need them; they are "deviant in an ideal level even while being useful and conforming in practice" (Rosnow and Fine, 1976, p. 11). Exactly *why* we crave and need them demonstrates the fact that they are, indeed, examples of collective behavior.

CONTEMPORARY LEGENDS VS. RUMOR

Many stories are told without factual foundation about people or events that represent a very special and distinct type of rumor. Although they are often called rumors (Morgan and Tucker, 1984, 1987), they are so different from ordinary rumors that they have a special name; they are called *legends* or, if they are modern, *contemporary* or *urban legends* (Brunvand, 1980, 1981, 1984, 1986, 1989). They differ from the ordinary, everyday garden variety of rumors in that they are about abstract, general, or *cartoon* people and events; that is, it doesn't much matter who the people in the stories are—almost anyone with a few key characteristics will do. In contrast, the everyday rumor is nearly always about *specific people* and *specific events;* that is, just *who* or *what* the story is about is one of its crucial aspects. In contrast, in the legend, the people in the stories have a readily *substitutable* quality. For instance, when rumors circulated about Rock Hudson and Liberace having AIDS, the fact that it was *these* specific celebrities who had the disease was absolutely crucial; no one else could have substituted for them. If there's a rumor about a dam bursting and water rushing toward us, it is important that a *specific* dam burst and that the water is rushing specifically toward *us*. In short, "In contrast to a legend, a rumor usually dwells on topical content" (Rosnow and Fine, 1976, p. 11). While legends are stories that people tell without authentication and, hence, technically qualify as rumors, experts usually put them in a separate category since they are so different and distinct.

With legends, the specifics of the story are very much in the background. Many urban legends are about celebrities; however, almost any celebrity will do as the subject of the story, or any celebrity with one or more key characteristics. For instance, in the 1970s, a story circulated that anyone could use Burt Reynolds' credit card to make an unlimited number of free long-distance calls (Morgan and Tucker, 1984, p. 90). Here, it wasn't important that the credit card was held by Burt Reynolds; any wealthy celebrity would have done just as well. It could have been Johnny Carson; in fact, the same story *did* circulate about Johnny Carson, too. The story has practically the same impact either way; again, it is an abstract, cartoon story with readily substitutable subjects. I prefer to call such stories legends, and not rumors. With rumors, in contrast, the details and the specifics of the story, including who they are about, are crucial, indeed, absolutely central.

A second important difference between the everyday rumor on the one hand and the legend on the other is a consequence of the former's topicality and concreteness: Rumors about specific people and events tend to have a fairly brief life span, whereas legends may never die out; they keep reappearing again and again, in somewhat different guises, over the years. With most rumors, evidence verifies or refutes the story, people tire of telling it, it becomes irrelevant, or it simply dissipates. "Although rumors born of myth [or legend] have the potential for rebirth, the average rumor, once activated or reborn, has a relatively brief life span. . . . Most rumors are born, have a period of prominence, and then disappear" (Rosnow and Fine, 1976, p. 44).

This is not always true, however. If a story is important enough, and key information is lacking, the rumor conveying it can circulate for some time. President John F. Kennedy was assassinated in November 1963, and rumors still circulate about the particulars of his death to this day. Did Lee Harvey Oswald really kill Kennedy? Were there others in on the plot—was there a *conspiracy* to kill the president? Was Jack Ruby, the man who killed Oswald, part of the conspiracy? Likewise, President Kennedy's younger brother, Senator Edward M. Kennedy, drove off a bridge on Chappaquiddick Island in Massachussetts in July 1969, and his companion, Mary Jo Kopechne, age 28, drowned in the accident. Today, more than two decades later, people still pass on rumors about the incident. Both these events were of such importance, and so many crucial questions about them still remain unanswered, that stories circulate to "fill in the gaps" where authenticated information is lacking.

An even more long-standing rumor claims that Catherine II ("Catherine The Great"), Tsarina of Russia from 1762 to 1796, died while having sexual intercourse with a horse; supposedly, the animal, hoisted up on ropes and a pulley above her, fell and crushed her to death. The tale is, of course, completely untrue, although, so credible to some individuals that the authors of several recent books felt compelled to refute the charge (Alexander, 1989, pp. 332–335; Morgan and Tucker, 1984, pp. 81–82). A pornographic novel, with the subtitle "The Carnal Confessions of Catherine the Great," which appeared in 1984, had as its central theme the horse story. Still, ordinary rumors generally do have a briefer life span than legends. We'll look at legends in the next chapter. As with gossip, some rumor may shade off into legend, and vice versa. There isn't any clear-cut or sharp difference between them; in practice, it is often difficult to distinguish between them.

COLLECTIVE DELUSIONS

A second distinct and important type of rumor is one that is clearly false, and yet is often told and widely believed; it is referred to as a *collective delusion*. Not all collective delusions originate as rumors—many are simply part of a society's traditional culture—but many do. Collective delusions abound in history, and exist in nearly every area of human life. Some are classics of the collective behavior literature; they include the Seattle windshield pitting incident (Medalia and Larsen, 1958), the cattle mutilation mystery (Rorvik, 1980; Stewart, 1980; Kagan and Summers, 1984), the June bug epidemic (Kerckhoff and Back, 1968; Kerckhoff, Back, and Miller, 1965), the link between the Proctor and Gamble corporation and satanism (Anonymous, 1985; Koenig, 1985, pp. 39–54; Fine, 1990), and the "phantom anesthetist" of Mattoon (Johnson, 1945). We'll examine collective delusions, along with legends and myths, in Chapter 8.

CHARACTERISTICS OF RUMOR AND GOSSIP

At one time, rumor was defined as *word-of-mouth* or even *face-to-face* communication (Allport and Postman, 1947, p. ix; Buckner, 1965, p. 55).

However, it must be emphasized that, today, the mass media are a major source of communication, and they often pass on relatively unverified, unsubstantiated statements. Such stories are recognized by reporters as unconventional, even deviant, news, and the profession of journalism usually frowns on repeating them in print and in the broadcast media. Nonetheless, in the absence of "hard" evidence reporters often resort to using such items because of the pressure they feel in "getting the story out," especially because of the competition that exists among them to be first with an important story. Novelist and essayist Norman Mailer calls a printed rumor, or an assertion based on no evidence that is passed on as news or fact, a *factoid*, "facts which have no existence before appearing in a magazine or newspapers" (Mailer, 1973, p. 18).

It must be emphasized that, contrary to public opinion and a great deal that has been written on this subject, informal, face-to-face communication among intimates is nearly always more convincing than messages that appear in the mass media. When they discuss the subject in the abstract, most people exaggerate the influence of the media and underplay the influence of personal contact, but in real life, it is personal contact that actually wins the influence contest, hands down. Which are you more likely to believe and be influenced by if they differ—a news account of an event, based on eyewitness reports, or an account related to you by a close friend, again, who was an eyewitness to the event? The friend says, commenting on a news account, "That's wrong; I was there; here's how it really happened." Most people are far more likely to believe the friend's account than the media's. Of course, the mass media do not terminate their influence by relating an account to their listening, watching, or reading audience. In fact, people who are exposed to the media often relate news to their friends, which means that television, radio, and magazines and newspapers usually have a *dual* influence—both impersonal (directly) and personal (indirectly). Thus, in studying rumor and gossip, we must focus on both face-to-face or word-of-mouth communication and the impersonal communications that are directly transmitted by the mass media.

Both rumor and gossip have an overwhelmingly negative image in the public mind; whenever a story is referred to as a rumor or as gossip, most people automatically assume that it is nasty, vicious, and invidious. This is not necessarily the case. Studies of the content of both rumor and gossip have shown that people tell stories about one another that cover the entire spectrum, from very positive to very negative, and everything in between. Two researchers placed students in a lounge where other students congregated and talked; for eight weeks, these students eavesdropped on the nearly 200 conversations they could hear, and coded them as to their content. Over a quarter (27 percent) of the overheard gossip was clearly negative, the same proportion was clearly positive, and the rest was mixed (Levin and Arluke, 1985). Clearly, the stories that circulate about the doings of other people are not necessarily negative. Does the same hold for published gossip?

It might seem, offhand, that the contents of the gossip columns—certain

A major form of gossip may be found in supermarket tabloids. While some of their articles are consciously fabricated, most are based on unverified, undocumented stories from questionable sources. Moreover, even the fabricated stories themselves create a flurry of gossip among the public that reads them.

celebrity magazines and newspapers, such as *People*, the *National Enquirer*, and the *Star*, and the gossip or "society" columns of local newspapers—are mainly negative, but, again, this is mistaken. In fact, unlike spoken gossip, which ranges from good to bad, published celebrity gossip tends to be overwhelmingly either neutral or positive. Even the relatively few negative items rarely describe violations of "the major norms of society. . . . For at least the last forty years, syndicated columnists have focused on folkways, not mores, on eccentricity rather than evil." The more seriously damaging facts about celebrities tend to be avoided by the pages of gossip magazines, newspapers, and columns (Levin and Arluke, 1987, p. 71). Of course, scurrilously nasty gossip does appear and is often hungrily consumed (for instance, Kelley, 1991); it tends to be the exception rather than the rule, however. In short, the stereotype of rumor and gossip as being largely or overwhelmingly negative and pejorative is fallacious; it is as positive as negative, and is more likely to be neutral or mixed than either. After all, if published gossip were consistently negative, the gossip-mongering press would find future access to their subjects closed off. Certain celebrities will not talk to reporters who have given them bad press, and so, if they do, they have "burned their bridges" with those celebrities. At least one major gossip columnist "sanitizes her scoops in order to retain her unparalleled access" to what is sometimes called "higher society" (Gross, 1988, p. 41). In any case, since negative gossip sticks in people's minds more than the positive variety, most of the public thinks that rumor and gossip are mainly negative.

Many media and entertainment figures court publicity at the same time as they denounce it. Why? Even if mainly negative, gossip demonstrates the one essential truth about its subject: *Only people who are the focus of attention attract gossip.* The higher the status of the individual, the greater the likelihood that he or she will become the subject of gossip. To many prestigious celebrities, there is no such thing as bad publicity, because gossip, however malicious, keeps them in the public eye and reassures them, their agents, and their audience that they still matter, that they are newsworthy and therefore important. Unless there is something otherwise remarkable about them, no one gossips about individuals toward whom they are indifferent and consider unimportant. Gossip is a measure of subjective significance. Even hostility expresses concern by the gossiper for the subject, and therefore the latter's consequence to the former.

Another stereotype of rumor and gossip is that it is *trivial;* again, this is largely false. While some of the topics dealt with in rumor and gossip do seem distinctly trivial, this is not an essential or defining quality of either. Rumor and gossip have made or destroyed careers, overthrown leaders, generated riots and even fueled revolutions, put the rich and powerful to shame, decided the outcome of military conflicts, elevated the humble to positions of authority and respect, earned millions for the fortunate and lost millions for the unfortunate, and destroyed or created enduring relationships. Rumor and gossip about seemingly trivial events may have a profound social impact that goes far beyond their content. Rumor and gossip cannot be dismissed as trivial; they are an important type of human communication that is often, although not always, about important matters. Rumor and gossip often, although not always, have important consequences. They deserve to be studied in a serious, systematic fashion.

THE FUNCTIONS OF GOSSIP: AN ANTHROPOLOGICAL PERSPECTIVE

A great deal of research has been conducted by anthropologists on the social and individual functions of gossip in small, preindustrial societies. (Anthropologists are more likely to study gossip than rumor.) A functionalist line of thinking argues that social institutions and activities that are as widespread and long-standing as gossip must survive because they *do* something for the participants and the society as a whole. As we've already seen, people "in all places and at all times" have been intensely interested in gossip; it is, as far as we know, a cultural and historical universal (Gluckman, 1963, p. 313). Any phenomenon that is everywhere as culturally entrenched as gossip must serve some very strong universal positive functions. What are some of them?

Integration of the Group or Community.   Gossip is an expression or affirmation of group or community solidarity. Belonging to a gossip circle or network asserts that one is "in the know" about the subject of the gossip and what is relevant and important about that subject. When two people gossip about a third person, they affirm that they belong to the same social circle. When an outsider unacquainted with the subject attempts to join the conversation, for him or her, the gossip seems boring, trivial, without topical importance, and usually, for that reason, the gossip ceases (unless the gossipers intentionally wish to freeze the outsider out of the conversation, to remind him or her that he or she does not "belong" in their social circle; or unless the activities described are truly remarkable, which is rare, and in which case, the talk in question transcends mere gossip). Teller and listener must know, or at least know about, the subject. Thus, being incorporated into a gossip network, and being able to understand and pass it on, indicates group membership, and strengthens group solidarity. Gossip is a sign of trust between people; it designates that the listener is part of the same group or community the teller belongs to (Levin and Arluke, 1987, p. 24). In a sense, then, "gossiping is a duty of membership in the group" (Gluckman, 1963, p. 313). Gossip networks constitute, and reaffirm, an *invisible neighborhood* (Levin and Arluke, 1987, pp. 79, 192), even if the subjects are celebrities, the gossipers, writers for supermarket tabloids, and the listeners (in this case, readers), the anonymous public.

Elizabeth Colson (1953) described the Makah, a very small Indian tribe threatened with assimilation living in the northwest corner of Washington State. Their gossip was extremely invidious, criticizing tribal members with respect to their ancestry, position in the class structure, adherence to tradition and tribal custom, and gift-giving practices. Such put-downs might seem to be divisive to the tribe; but, in fact, they had the opposite effect. Even in the most vicious gossip, the Makah are demonstrating their right to be Makah and challenging others to demonstrate their right as well. By gossiping about others concerning matters that only a fellow tribal member could understand and appreciate, tellers, listeners, and the subject were all simultaneously being incorporated into a "war of scandal" from which outsiders were excluded. "Scandalizing is one of the principal means by which the group's separateness is expressed, even though it is also the principal manner in which internal struggles are fought" (Gluckman, 1963, p. 312). In a sense, then, groups and communities may be united through the expression of their hostility. Gossip reminds everyone involved that they, unlike outsiders, belong to the group or community who can understand and appreciate it. Consequently, gossip "is part of the very blood and tissue of . . . community life" (p. 308); it is "the glue that binds individuals together" (Levin and Arluke, 1987, p. 25).

Affirmation of the Moral Code.   Gossip is a means of social control; it reminds everyone of what's right—and wrong. In fact, gossip "is one of the strongest sanctions found in group living. . . . Reputations and lives have often been ruined by gossip, and the threat of public disapproval as expressed in gossip holds many persons within the cultural rules of his [or her] society. Ostracism from one's group is one of the greatest fears of all mankind and is one of the strongest sanctions against non-conformity" (Stirling, 1956, p. 267). Denunciation of an action, and the subject, affirms the moral virtue of teller and listener; in scandalizing, the subject becomes a negative role model. Gossip has the capacity "to discredit, isolate, or even prevent nonconventional behavior" (Rosnow and Georgouli, 1985, p. 72). In a small town in the midwest in the 1940s, an anthropologist writes, "The religious control of morals operates mainly through gossip and the fear of gossip. People report, suspect, laugh at, and condemn the pecadilloes of others, and walk and behave carefully to avoid being caught in any trifling missteps of their own" (West, 1945, p. 162). "Socially, the victim of gossip may be ostracized, ignored, and ridiculed. In some cultures, this takes the form of nasty nicknames, mocking songs, practical jokes, nightly attacks, or insulting remarks" (Levin and Arluke, 1987, pp. 126–127). Even positive gossip is evaluative; it may be a morality play in which virtue triumphs over evil, reminding those in the gossip community of what the correct behavior is.

There are limits to the power of gossip as a means of social control, especially in a large, complex, urban, industrial society. In such societies, people are more mobile than they are in small, traditional, preindustrial societies; if people become the target of damaging gossip, they can move from one geographical location, where they are known, to another, where they are unknown. In addition, many communities are composed of a variety of social circles, and denigrating gossip about the members of one of them may not hurt the members of a different one. Nonetheless, gossip still retains some of its power to control behavior and mold it to certain moral standards, especially in certain "close-knit ethnic enclaves." In addition, malicious gossip "about a particular employee can reduce chances for raises and promotions" and can "follow a victim from job to job." If the target of gossip moves, there is always the possibility of "discovery" of one's former status "by gossip-mongers in the new community" (Levin and Arluke, 1987, pp. 129–130).

Gossip has a second moral function as well: *It introduces abstract morality to the everyday world.* "Moral norms are abstract. To decide whether some particular, concrete, unanalyzed [that is, previously unfamiliar] action is forbidden, tolerated, encouraged, or required, principles must be applied to the case" (Sabini and Silver, 1982, p. 100). One can learn rules of morality in the abstract, but how does one know *whether* and *how* what one has learned applies in the particular case one confronts? For instance, everyone has been taught not to bother one's neighbors—for instance, playing loud music or revving up a motorcycle engine late at night—and trained to recognize the exceptions. But what if the rules one has learned don't quite apply to the real-life cases one encounters? Should the parents of a sick, crying baby be told to keep the noise down? What if it continues every night for a month, or six months, or two years? Should a student studying for exams inform his or her neighbors that their normal noise is especially bothersome at this time?

What if a pianist continues practicing for an important upcoming recital well into the night—until midnight, for instance? Or 2:00 A.M.? Or 6:00 A.M.? The function of gossip in cases like these is to sound out others in your group, culture, or society with respect to an action's morality. In gossip, you have encountered, or will encounter, specific, concrete examples of cases like this one and found out what's right and wrong. "Gossip, then, is one method . . . actors have to externalize, dramatize, and embody their moral perceptions" (Sabini and Silver, 1982, p. 102).

Competition Between Groups. In all societies with two or more conflicting groups or categories, gossip embodies, sharpens, and conveys that conflict. In a Trinidadian community studied by the anthropologist Melville Herskovits (1947), the local Christian minister was gossiped about for supposedly being responsible for the arrest of members of a sect called the Shouters because they had drawn members of his congregation away from the church. Likewise, prominent lay members of a Christian church were accused in gossip of leading the police to a Shouter's meeting. Here, the function of the gossip for two rival groups—one made up of wealthier, traditional, established Christians, and the second, of religiously and politically unconventional individuals from a lower socioeconomic position who felt discriminated against—is obvious. Gossip gives vent to grievances against rival factions; it reminds the teller and the listener of the virtue of their own faction.

On a Hopi reservation in Arizona studied by an anthropologist (Cox, 1970), the tribe is divided into two factions—the traditionalists, who want to adhere to the old tribal customs, and the "progressives," who favor more assimilation, the adoption of more European practices, and the acquisition of more American services and material possessions. Traditionalists oppose drilling for gas and oil, building permanent roads, and installing electric power lines, and their gossip blames the recent droughts and defiling of sacred shrines on the inappropriate use of Hopi lands as contrary to "warnings from the Great Spirit" (Cox, 1970, p. 90). The Council, dominated by progressives, are sell-outs, they say, who seek an alliance with white government power. One village with five resident whites is condemned by the traditionalists for being a "Whiteman's town." Progressives are, they say, "materialistic and irreligious upstarts who are toadies to the Indian Service [a federal agency] and to Whites" (p. 95). Traditionalist leaders claimed that members of the Council sold some of the reservation to oil companies and are themselves getting rich from these deals (p. 92). They do not acknowledge the legitimacy of the Council and refuse to admit that it represents the tribe. On the other hand, the progressives see the traditionalists as obstacles to tribal prosperity. In gossip, they accuse traditionalist priests of using malevolent magic in their rituals—in one case, a ritual involving human sacrifice—and brand them with their own stigmatizing names, including "so-called Traditionalist" and "commie" (in English). They claim that by refusing to negotiate with the government, traditionalists will end up losing all Hopi land to the whites. Here, gossip seems not to contribute to social unity at all.

Rather, "Hopi factions compete, through their gossip, for public support." Each faction tries to stigmatize the other, thereby weakening its rivals' political power and strengthening its own. Clearly, then, gossip sharpens boundary lines between groups, and both manifests and intensifies group conflict. This is, in fact, one of its most important social functions.

Enables Social Comparison.   Gossip "is initiated to learn what behaviors, achievements, or transgressions are acceptable or reasonable" (Suls, 1977, p. 165). One of the reasons why people gossip, and one of the reasons why gossip is so widespread around the world, and has survived for so long, is that individuals and groups use it as a way of determining if they "measure up" to others, a means of evaluating oneself and one's peers relative to others. Given its covert nature, it is possible to make these comparisons in private; one wants the information, but a public comparison would be embarrassing and humiliating—suppose one does not, in fact, "measure up," that they learn that the other party is superior? Gossip is the ideal vehicle for making this kind of comparison.

A great deal of gossip about celebrities, for instance, shows an audience that they really aren't all that different from their heroes. Gossip may demonstrate that, since the high-and-mighty have "made it," perhaps they, the ordinary man and woman in the street, can make it as well. Celebrities provide us with levels of aspiration for our own behavior. Even negative gossip about celebrities may turn an "unapproachable idol into a flesh-and-blood human being with frailties just like the rest of us" (Levin and Arluke, 1987, p. 32). In addition, such comparisons tell us that, in spite of the fame and fortune of many celebrities, they are not always happy, which can be comforting when one finally realizes that one will never enter those lofty ranks. "See, life at the top isn't what it's cracked up to be, now is it?" (p. 37). In contrast, gossip about individuals or groups who are clearly "immoral" or "inferior" will serve to "enhance our own feelings of respectability and self-worth. By comparison with their illegal, illicit, immoral activities, we can feel some satisfaction with ourselves" (p. 34). Clearly, then, comparison and evaluation are crucial functions of gossip. And just as clearly, gossip cannot be studied apart from what it does for those who engage in it, and for the group, community, and society as a whole.

A CLASSIC RUMOR

One way of understanding how rumors get started and what functions they serve both individually and socially is to describe several concrete examples. One that has been examined in the literature on rumor in some detail is the "death" of Beatle Paul McCartney in 1969. In addition to being a rumor, it has elements of a contemporary legend as well, a phenomenon we'll look at in the next chapter. However, to the extent that it was crucial that the details of the rumor applied specifically and uniquely to Paul McCartney, this story was more a rumor than a legend.

The origin of the rumor claiming that Paul McCartney was dead is in dispute; music magazine *Rolling Stone* claims that an article appeared in *Northern Star*, a student newspaper published at Northern Illinois University, as early as September, 1969, with the title "Clues Hint at Possible Beatle Death." But the rumor did not attain continuity until two events occurred. The first: On October 12, 1969, a Detroit disc jockey received a call on the air from a young man who identified himself only as Tom, who discussed two unusual and obscure messages hidden in Beatles' songs. He discovered the first message in the song "Revolution 9," which is on the so-called *White Album*. If the passage "Number nine, number nine, number nine" is played backwards, Tom said, it sounds like "Turn me on, dead man." And the second message was found in the song "Strawberry Fields Forever," a cut that appears on the album, *Magical Mystery Tour;* if background noises are filtered out, a voice can be heard saying, "I buried Paul!".

The second event occurred two days after the call to the Detroit disc jockey, when an article by Fred LaBour appeared in the *Michigan Daily*, the student newspaper of the University of Michigan. Ostensibly a review of the Beatles' album *Abbey Road*, the piece put forth the claim that McCartney had been killed in an automobile accident three years before; his place had been taken by a double who resembled him. The article was accompanied by a photograph of a decapitated head whose face looked like McCartney's. As with the mysterious caller Tom, LaBour said that he had discovered some hidden evidence to support his thesis, although his could be found on the album covers rather than in the songs. The bottom of the album cover of *Sgt. Pepper* depicts a grave; yellow flowers form a shape that resembles both the letter P and Paul's guitar. Inside the album cover, Paul is wearing an arm patch with the initials O.P.D., meaning "officially pronounced dead." He is also wearing a medal, indicating that he died a hero's death. On the back of the album cover, the other three Beatles are facing forward, but Paul is facing backward. On the cover of *Abbey Road*, John Lennon is dressed in a white suit, clearly a minister's garb, George Harrison is dressed as a gravedigger, Ringo Starr is in an undertaker's outfit, and Paul is barefoot—the way corpses are sometimes buried in England. They are leaving a cemetery. The license plate of a car parked by the side of the road in the photograph reads "28 IF," indicating the age that McCartney would have been at the time *if* he had lived!

Following the publication of this article, the rumor quickly "caught fire. It whipped across the country, fueled by innuendos and ambiguities. . . . Soon, countless additional oddities began to be reported as the story rapidly disseminated. New meanings were attributed to things that seemed perfectly innocent and insignificant before the rumor appeared" (Rosnow and Fine, 1976, p. 16). For instance, on the *Magical Mystery Tour* album, a photograph depicts John, George, and Ringo sporting red carnations, but Paul has a *black* one. A story circulated to the effect that if a Beatles' album were placed in water, the apple logo would turn blood red. And the deeper meaning of the walrus came under heavy scrutiny: The animal is supposedly a Norse, or perhaps an Eskimo, symbol of death; or, alternatively, presumably the ancient

Greek word for "corpse" is walrus. In "I Am the Walrus," it is Paul—or his double—who sings, "I am the walrus," and in "Glass Onion," which appears on the *White Album*, Lennon sings: "Well, here's another clue for all, the Walrus *was* Paul."

The newspaper photograph of the look-alike decapitated head was, of course, a hoax, as was the report of the accident. In fact, absolutely no credible evidence whatsoever existed that supported the contention that Paul had died. (It is possible that the Beatles planted clues to that effect—even though they explicitly denied that they had.) The oddities put forth as evidence backing up that claim were spawned of an overactive imagination interpreting what was undoubtedly a series of simple coincidences. "But whatever the explanation, they soon became the foundation for a fantasy that swept across American adolescent society" (Rosnow and Fine, 1974, p. 67). Why did this fantastic rumor achieve such widespread dissemination? Why was the story told and retold so often by such a substantial number of people? Why was such incredibly flimsy evidence used to support this story?

A number of factors, processes, and dynamics have been used to explain the McCartney death rumor. Some of them focus on general societal conditions, some on the nature of the rumor itself or on the Beatles, while others look at the characteristics of those who told the story.

The Entertainment Value.   Regardless of whether it was true or not, the story was undoubtedly entertaining. In fact, most people who heard it didn't believe that it was true (Rosnow and Fine, 1974, p. 68). But it did "provide a fascinating subject for conversation" (Suczek, 1972, p. 72). "It was 'fun' hunting for clues and talking about the mystery with friends. The rumor flourished for many of the same reasons that mysteries are so popular" (Rosnow and Fine, 1974, p. 68).

The Credibility Gap.   It is important that the story was initiated in and endorsed by student and "underground" radio stations and newspapers. The 1960s was a time of increasing distrust of the official version of reality, especially with respect to such subjects as the war in Vietnam, drugs, sex, and rock and roll. Many adolescents and young adults felt that the alternative media and their own rumor network could be counted on to counteract the lies of the mainstream media (Rosnow and Fine, 1976, pp. 17–18).

Its Mythical Appeal.   "The untimely death of a beautiful youth who is subsequently transformed into or revealed to be a god is a recurrent mythical theme. . . . The legends of Osiris, Adonis, Dionysis, and Jesus have all conformed, in some major way, to this pattern. It may be that the McCartney rumor represented an aborted attempt to re-create such a myth" (Suczek, 1972, p. 72).

The Seeming Plausibility of a Stand-In.   The idea of a "double" being passed off as a prominent figure might seem to be fantastic and implausible to most hard-headed, evidence-demanding skeptics, but it is an idea that has provided the theme for a substantial number of rumors, as well as the basis for many fictional plots. Stories have circulated about the use of doubles for Adolph Hitler, Franklin Delano Roosevelt, Winston Churchill, Napoleon, John F. Kennedy, and Mao Zedong (Suczek, 1972, p. 75; Rosnow and Fine, 1974, p. 68). A film was made titled *I Was Monty's Double* (1958), based on the claim of a man who said that, to confuse the enemy, he was a stand-in for British general Field Marshal Bernard Montgomery during the Second World War. In fact, in the 1960s, artist Andy Warhol *did* send out a double to handle some of his speaking engagements, and in the 1980s and 1990s, if the reports on this are accurate, Saddam Hussein, president of Iraq, had a double to make public appearances and even speeches in his place to confuse his opponents. (In June 1991, one of Stalin's doubles or "understudies" died; the event merited enough attention that the man received an obituary in *The New York Times*.)

Status Seeking.   Rumors represent a kind of exchange—where information is valuable, it is given to the listener and, in exchange, greater status or esteem is given to the teller. In the Paul McCartney story, the fact that the information that was passed on was fanciful exemplifies an unsuccessful attempt to garner esteem, since research shows that the tellers of this story were less popular, dated less, and socialized with their friends less, than was true of individuals who did not pass on the rumor (Rosnow and Fine, 1974, p. 67).

What the Paul McCartney rumor shows, more than anything else, is the problematic nature of the evidence that is frequently used to document rumors. A statement is accepted as true "when it is consistent with one's frame of reference. Information is processed in light of the assumptions one holds about the nature of the world, for knowledge is culturally determined. What is truth to one person may be part of a massive conspiracy to another" (Rosnow and Fine, 1976, p. 18). Extremely flimsy evidence will prove, as well as extremely strong evidence will fail to disprove, an assertion if one believes strongly enough in it in advance. Further, it shows that a rumor may be told without being believed by a majority of even its tellers. And last, it illustrates the fact that rumors are not spread in a random fashion. Rather, rumors follow fairly clear sociological lines; for instance, they tend to be told by a relevant social audience—in this case, teenagers—and often, when one is especially implausible, they are more likely to be passed on by socially marginal individuals.

AN EARLY PERSPECTIVE ON RUMOR: ALLPORT AND POSTMAN

One of the earliest systematic studies of rumor was conducted by two psychologists, Gordon Allport and Leo Postman (1947). It was initiated as a means of combatting rumors about troop movements in World War II (pp. 1ff). The phrase, "Loose lips sink ships," emerged out of that concern; that is, if rumors about what the Allied forces were doing or were about to do were to reach enemy ears, the war effort could have been sabotaged. There are three aspects to the Allport-Postman perspective on rumor. The first is their "basic law of rumor"; that is, their theory of why rumors circulate. The second is intertwined with their "law," and represents the outcome of the process explained by it; that is, the final content of rumors—what happens to the substance of a rumor after it has been told and retold by a number of parties. And the third is the experiment they devised to study rumor transmission.

ALLPORT AND POSTMAN'S BASIC LAW OF RUMOR

Allport and Postman's basic "law" of rumor is that rumor arises to the extent that the subject of a story is *important* to the teller and the listener and to the extent that the facts of the story are "shrouded in some kind of *ambiguity*" (p. 33). Rumors emerge to explain important yet confusing and ambiguous situations where information is lacking. Rumors, Allport and Postman argue, relieve the tension of uncertainty; they reduce the anxiety of not knowing crucial facts about the subjects of the rumor. Where a topic is unimportant to a given audience, rumors are unlikely to be told about it. Where the facts are well known about a given topic, again, rumors are unlikely to be told about it. The ideal "hot house" environment for rumors is a situation where importance and ambiguity are maximized. Rumor is an excellent case of the generation of collective behavior in an ambiguous situation, and conforms closely to the classic experiments by Sherif (1936; Sherif and Harvey, 1952) on the autokinetic effect, which we looked at in Chapter 2 (see page 62).

Allport and Postman's experiment on rumor was designed much like the children's game of "telephone." They began their research by gathering together an audience made up of a group of people from a college class or a forum, out of which six or seven volunteers were selected. They were told that they must listen carefully to a story they would be told, and repeat what they had heard "as exactly as possible." They were then sent from the room. One subject was shown a picture on a screen, a line drawing of a certain scene—a battle scene, a street scene, and a subway scene; he or she was asked to relate some 20 details about it to the second subject, who was called back into the room, but seated where he or she couldn't see the picture. After the story about what was depicted in the drawing had been related, the first subject, the original "eyewitness," returned to the audience, and the third subject came in and sat down next to the second subject, who then related what he or she had heard from the first subject. This was repeated until all of the subjects had heard the description of what was supposed to have been depicted in the picture. Subjects were not allowed to ask questions, interrupt, or ask for clarification or detail.

From the results of this experiment, Allport and Postman concluded that *rumor tends to be highly inaccurate.* More specifically, three things happen to stories as they pass through the rumor mill.

Leveling. The first thing that happens is *leveling* or simplification: In the Allport-Postman research, about 70 percent of the details in the stories that were passed on through five or six transmissions were eliminated or forgotten. "As rumor travels, it tends to grow shorter, more concise, more easily grasped and told. In successive versions fewer words are used and fewer details are mentioned" (p. 75).

Sharpening.   The second thing that happens to stories as they run through the rumor mill is *sharpening*. Details were not dropped randomly; certain aspects of the stories were retained and others were eliminated. There was a selective attention to certain detail. The key word here is *salience*, that is, subjective importance. Any topics that were highly emotionally charged, such as racial issues, tended to be retained. If the characters in a story were engaged in active behavior of some sort—running, jumping, falling, hitting— that detail tended to be retained. If they were engaged in highly striking, unusual, novel, or odd behavior, again, that was retained.

Assimilation.   Third, *assimilation* took place in the rumor process. The details that were passed on tended to contribute to a central theme, motif, or expectation, while those that were dropped were less likely to contribute to that theme or expectation. Sometimes, when the original details did not support an expectation or central theme, details were fabricated or transposed appropriately. For instance, among white tellers, about half the time, a story about a white man holding a razor was changed into a *Black* man holding a razor (p. 111).

ALLPORT AND POSTMAN'S EXPERIMENT ON RUMOR

Allport and Postman's approach to rumor has been widely criticized by the two generations of researchers who have written about the subject since their original, pioneering effort. Of all aspects of their approach, the experiment they conducted has come under the most intense fire. There are at least two problems with their experiment. The first problem is that it was set up so that there was no interaction, no reciprocity, no give-and-take—as there actually is in real life. In reality, we *do* interrupt, ask questions, request more detail. Allport and Postman's research did not permit subjects to engage in this fundamental interactional process, which made their experiment extremely unrealistic; this restriction also maximized and exaggerated the likelihood of distortion. In real life, if we don't hear or understand a message, we ask the teller to repeat it. In the Allport-Postman "telephone" experiments, there was no checking, cross-checking, verification, or repeating.

The second problem with these early experiments is that rumor was passed along in a *linear* or *serial* fashion. One person told a second, who told a third, and so on. Here, there were only tellers and listeners. In contrast, in real life, we talk in *networks* or webs, not in a straight line: One person tells another something, the first may tell three others, one of them may actually go back and retell the story to the original teller, a second may tell no one, and the third may tell 20 people. Rumors spread out more like a fan than a straight line. Again, the Allport-Postman experiment was an extremely unrealistic test of what happens in real life.

ALLPORT AND POSTMAN: AN ASSESSMENT

In addition to the methodological problems with their experiment, many critics have pointed to the fact that Allport and Postman's experiment has little if anything to do with their basic "law" of rumor. To repeat, rumoring is maximized under conditions of great importance and ambiguity; it is minimized under conditions of little importance and ambiguity. Although the hypothesis itself seems sound, their experiment really has nothing to do with it. How is the experiment related to the factors of importance and ambiguity? Perhaps if one can't hear the whispered message of the teller, it does become rather ambiguous—again, only because of the way the experiment is set up; that is, in a noninteractional way. Allport and Postman did nothing to establish the importance of a given topic to their subjects and next to nothing to establish its ambiguity to them. In short, their research bears practically no relationship whatsoever to the theory they proposed.

Another problem with the Allport-Postman model of rumor is that the basic "motives in rumor mongering" they propose are psychological, indeed, pathological in origin; they have nothing to do with gathering information or finding out what is really going on. In fact, these psychological processes *by their very nature* make for the distorted nature of rumor. Allport and Postman believed that rumor served to "*relieve, justify*, and *explain* underlying emotional tension . . . by providing a verbal outlet that gives relief" (pp. 36, 38). Rumors are a means of verifying or projecting biases and anxieties onto the world. The bad conduct of others becomes a reasonable explanation for one's own negative feelings.

For instance, people love sex scandals (p. 178). This usually is because they feel uneasy about their own sexual urges. Telling tales about the misconduct of others makes one feel better about one's own guilty feelings. In this case, no one has the slightest bit of interest in establishing what the facts of the case are; all that matters is that one has dug up dirt on others to alleviate one's feelings about one's own dirt. Telling atrocity stories about the enemy during wartime justifies holding almost inhumanly hostile feelings toward them. Passing on rumors about the doings of members of other racial and ethnic groups, likewise, eases one's conscience about having prejudiced attitudes toward them and makes these attitudes seem justified. It is these distorted or pathological psychological processes that made for distorted rumor messages. Given why rumormongering takes place, in Allport and Postman's eyes, it could hardly be otherwise.

It must be emphasized that, while contemporary observers are somewhat critical of a number of aspects of Allport and Postman's model of rumor transmission, some elements have been verified; for instance, importance and ambiguity remain central to the field of rumor studies. At least as important is the fact that everyone in the field respects their pioneering effort. They were among the very first researchers to study the dynamics of rumor in a systematic, empirical fashion. It is on the shoulders of such trailblazing efforts that later, more adequate, work was done.

Tamotsu Shibutani: Improvised News

A somewhat later approach was adopted by sociologist Tamotsu Shibutani, who coined the term "improvised news" to characterize rumor (1966). To Shibutani, rumor is a *substitute* for news; it replaces news when established or institutionalized channels of communication have broken down, or are silent or unreliable concerning events of importance. For Shibutani, rumor is an effort at *collective problem solving*; it allows people to cope with the uncertainties of life (Rosnow and Fine, 1976, pp. 30, 12). Notice that the *absolute* supply of news need not be small for rumoring to flourish; in fact, it is highly likely that rumor "flies thickest when news is most *plentiful*" (Allport and Postman, 1946–1947, p. 501). The media can even *create* a rumor in the first place. The absolute quantity of news available concerning a given topic is not the point here; it is the *discrepancy* between what is reliably reported and known with certainty and what the public wants to know. Where people want to know more about something than they feel they know, they will circulate rumors about that subject.

Real Life vs. Experiments

Shibutani began thinking about the rumor process in four real-life "unsettled contexts": first, as a Japanese-American living in San Francisco right after the bombing of Pearl Harbor; second, as one of some 112,000 Japanese-Americans who were sent to and confined in relocation camps during World War II; third, as a soldier in that war; and fourth, as a member of the United States occupation of postwar Japan. In each of these settings, events were taking place of importance to all concerned, and channels of communication were disrupted, undermined, censored, or blocked; in each, rumors flew thick and fast. In other words, Shibutani began studying rumor in real-life, naturalistic situations, not in laboratory settings. He later examined some 60 case studies of rumor, again, in naturalistic settings. Although experiments can often tell us a great deal about how the real world works, they can do so only if they are sufficiently realistic and lifelike, if their conditions approximate those of the real world. If they are so artificial as to be significantly different, then we will be misled if we attempt to generalize experimental findings to the world around us. The problem with Allport and Postman's research on rumor was not that it was based on experiments, but that their experiments were quite unlike the way rumor is transmitted in reality. In any case, that flaw did not exist in Shibutani's research on rumor, because he used the real-life case study method.

Shibutani's Hypothesis: Supply and Demand

To Shibutani, rumor is a form of communication through which people attempt to construct a meaningful interpretation of a threatening or ambiguous situation. His "law" (he calls it a hypothesis) of rumor is, "*If the demand for news in a public exceeds the supply made available through institutional channels, rumor construction is likely to occur"* (p. 57). "The greater the *unsatisfied* demand for news, the more likely it is that rumors will develop. Demand for news, furthermore, is positively associated with intensity of collective excitement, and both depend upon the felt importance of the event to the public" (p. 58). Although this hypothesis sounds a great deal like Allport and Postman's "basic law," since it contains the two crucial elements of importance and ambiguity, it is really quite different, as we'll see.

What conditions maximize ambiguity? Shibutani provided concrete situations in which ambiguity was heightened. During wartime, during disasters, or in a totalitarian government where censorship is routinely practiced and accurate news does not exist, or whenever secrets are kept from the public concerning subjects that people care about, rumor is common. Of course, there are areas of social life in which there is literally no institutionalized news, where verbal reports are the only source of information, such as what is happening among your friends and acquaintances. Here, of course, gossip and rumor have to be relied on quite heavily. Importance, Shibutani's second major explanatory variable, can also be established empirically. It must be emphasized, however, that importance is subjective in character, not objective; it is whatever people think or feel is important. In the vast scheme of things, whether or not a certain celebrity couple is about to get divorced is of no consequence whatsoever, but if the public is *interested* in the question—and the supply of information about it is sparse—rumors will circulate about it.

INDIVIDUAL CHARACTERISTICS VS. SOCIAL CONTEXTS _____

Notice that, even though the two theories sound somewhat similar, the dynamics of rumormongering in Shibutani's model are significantly different from those in Allport and Postman's. There are three main differences between these two models, each of which grows out of the fact that Allport and Postman are psychologists and Shibutani is a sociologist. To begin with, Allport and Postman emphasize *individual characteristics* that make for rumor transmission—factors such as personal fears, insecurities, feelings of inadequacy, and guilt feelings. In contrast, Shibutani stresses *social situations or contexts* that maximize rumor, circumstances or settings in which people are likely to "fill in the gaps" concerning subjects they discuss. His "basic unit of analysis" is not individual characteristics, but the *ambiguous situation*; rumors cannot be understood "apart from the social contexts in which they arise (1966, pp. 23, 24).

SHIBUTANI'S MODEL OF THE RUMORING PROCESS _____

A second difference between the two models of rumor transmission is indicated in their respective methods: Allport and Postman's experiment indicates a *linear* and *serial* model of rumor transmission, while Shibutani's naturalistic case study approach implies an *interactional* model. In Allport and Postman's experiment, A tells B, B tells C, C tells D, and so on down the line.

There is no possibility of reversing the process, no chance of feedback or interaction, of any party talking to any other except for the one next in line. In contrast, in Shibutani's model, A can relate a rumor to a dozen parties, all of those parties can ask A questions, and can come back later and retell the rumor in a different form, and any one of them can also tell the rumor to dozens of others. In Shibutani's model, there is a give-and-take dynamic that is absent from Allport and Postman's.

SHIBUTANI: RUMOR AS AN EXTENSION OF EVERYDAY LIFE ___

The third difference between the two models is that, while Allport and Postman see rumor as not only *inaccurate* and *distorted* but *pathological* as well, Shibutani sees rumor as *an extension of everyday life*. He underplays the differences between them and emphasizes their similarities. To Shibutani, many of the same dynamics that occur in the rumor process also take place in ordinary, conventional settings. Shibutani argued that where the unsatisfied demand for news is moderate, and the degree of interest or excitement about a given subject likewise is moderate, people generally engage in some form of *critical deliberation*; they check assertions and verify the reliability of the sources. However, when unsatisfied demand for news is great, and the subjective excitement and interest in a given subject is great, rumor is more spontaneous and extemporaneous. Here, rumors are more likely to be accepted at face value from almost any source. However, this is fairly rare, Shibutani believes. The more common situation is where listeners retain some measure of critical deliberation. In contrast, Allport and Postman do not treat importance and ambiguity as dimensions, but as all-or-nothing affairs. Their model seems to say that people lose all critical ability when confronted with a rumor. In contrast, Shibutani argues that, in the process of rumor transmission, people typically retain some critical ability. We tend to be suggestible only to the extent that the statements we hear do not violate the views or standards that we accept in everyday life.

SHIBUTANI ON RUMOR: AN ASSESSMENT_____

Just as Allport and Postman focused too much on the *irrational* side of rumor, Shibutani probably overemphasized its *rational* and *cognitive* side. He stressed that rumors are an effort to make sense out of a confusing, ambiguous—and important—topic, but, in reality, "making sense" does not always mean seeking accurate information or generating details in the absence of accurate information. In fact, the rules for verifying the veracity of statements vary according to who the listener and teller are; what is believable to one party will not be believable to another. Our social location and prior beliefs shape what we regard as true, and often, as Allport and Postman say, there are systematic reasons why distortion takes place.

For instance, rumors about racial conflicts often circulate according to the race of the audience. A horrifying rumor (also an urban legend) with a strong racial slant cropped up in Detroit during the late 1960s, only months after several devastating racial riots took place there. It was rumored that a mother took her young boy to a department store for a shopping expedition, where he went into a public lavatory; there, a man attacked and castrated the boy. Whenever the story was told by a white person, the boy was always white and his attacker, Black. Whenever the story was told by a Black person, the boy was Black and his attacker was white (Rosenthal, 1971). Of course, the event never took place; it is, in fact, a legend with quite ancient roots, but that did not stop people from telling and believing it. (It should be stated that the rumor is not as utterly lacking in plausibility among Blacks as might seem at first; after all, the castration and lynching of Blacks by whites in the South during the generation prior to the rumor did take place in not inconsiderable numbers. The tale's plausibility among whites is a different matter, however.) Again, rumor tends to follow social lines; it is patterned according to group membership.

In this and many other instances, rumor goes considerably beyond a quest for information where it is unobtainable. Rumor often represents an effort on the part of tellers to demonstrate the validity of their general view of the world, to show that they, and the groups to which they belong, are virtuous, while their enemies are wicked and unfair. While all rumors are not necessarily false, it is also true that *not all rumors represent a quest for verified information.* Indeed, the last thing that many people who tell rumors want is verified information; the "reality testing" Shibutani posits as central to rumor transmission (pp. 148–155) may not influence many rumor tellers and listeners. Much of the time, rumoring is a distinctly "irrational" process. Often, rumor affirms in-group membership, virtue, and victimization, and out-group exploitation and wickedness.

Shibutani also failed to notice the many other motivations and functions that rumor serves aside from that of seeking information. (Fine and Rosnow, 1978, and Stirling, 1956, note some of them with respect to gossip.) Clearly, some, like the Paul McCartney rumor, have entertainment value. While most unverified entertaining stories qualify as gossip, they are also rumors as well. We love to hear tales of the eccentricities and foibles of others. The fact that they are unverified—and given their nature, it is almost inevitable that they be unverified—only adds to their allure. Many rumors are told to bestow status on the teller. (Although this tactic may backfire, as we saw with the "Paul is dead" rumor.) If you tell a story to someone else, it supposedly shows that you are in the know, privileged to have access to inside information. Rumor also circulates because tellers and listeners feel powerless to do something constructive about their lives. Imaginative stories, especially those denigrating individuals in power or those demonstrating that the restrictions of their lives can be overcome, give them a sense of power and control. Many rumors are morality tales, exemplified by the castration stories that circulated in Detroit in the late 1960s; they say we are virtuous and victimized, while our enemy is evil. Some rumors are prescriptive; they call for a certain type of action or response. A rumor about a "crack" den in the neighborhood, for example, might be a cry of outrage, a demand for police assistance, and a call for community action. Some are also proscriptive; they say not to do a certain thing. For instance, stories about a teenage girl who was raped while hitchhiking that circulate among teenage girls convey the not-so-hidden message: Don't hitchhike! Thus, though information seeking is often involved in telling and listening to rumors, it is not the only motivation or function at work here.

A CONTEMPORARY PERSPECTIVE ON RUMOR

A great deal of research has been conducted on rumor since these early, classic studies were done. Rosnow (1988, 1991) has integrated a variety of sociological and psychological findings to put together a contemporary perspective on the rumor process. He calls it a *contextualist* approach because rumors can be understood only "within a specific context of expectations and assumptions." The generation and transmission of rumors "is a process of explanation, an attempt to make sense" out of current events; rumor "extracts meaning from, and gives meaning to, the context in which it is situated." Certain experiential contexts "invite" or "allow" rumors to flourish (1988, pp. 13, 14, 16). What are these contexts? More specifically, what factors or conditions influence rumor generation and transmission? Four are most influential: *importance* or *involvement, uncertainty* or *ambiguity, anxiety,* and *credulity* (Rosnow, 1988, 1991).

Importance or Involvement. As a general rule, a story about a situation that is felt to be inconsequential in its implications is "not a source of suspicion or speculation." Rumors about unimportant events are less likely to be transmitted, and are more likely to be dead-ended when they are told, than rumors about events that are felt to have important consequences or "outcome—relevant involvement," both good and bad (Rosnow, 1988, p. 23; 1991, pp. 484, 485). People tend to be egocentric in their rumor-mongering; they tell tales about things that are *relevant* to their lives. Here, the views of the classics are confirmed; as Allport and Postman say, "an American citizen is not likely to spread rumors concerning the market price for camels in Afghanistan because the subject has no importance for him" or her (1946–1947, p. 502). Other things being equal, the more subjectively important and relevant the topic is for an audience, the greater the likelihood that rumors will be told about it. The less important the subject is regarded, the less the individual is personally involved in it, the lower that likelihood is.

Rumor and gossip circulate about topics that are felt to be important to people's lives. Thus, some contexts, situations, or subjects within or about which rumor and gossip are highly likely to circulate include: wartime (Posonby, 1928; Allport and Lepkin, 1945; Caplow, 1947; Nkpa, 1975, 1977), disasters (Larsen, 1954; Sinha, 1952; Prasad, 1935), the stock market (Rose, 1951; Shiller, 1984, 1989; Smith, Suchanek, and Williams, 1988; Rice, 1988), politics and political figures (Seymour-Ure, 1982; Festinger et al., 1948; Damore, 1988), the lives of celebrities (Levin and Kimmel, 1977; Levine and Arluke, 1987; Gross, 1988; Suczek, 1972; Henry, 1990), mass produced products and corporations that manufacture and distribute these products (Solomon, 1984; Brunvand, 1981, pp. 81–92; Brunvand, 1984, pp. 103–107, 118–127; Koenig, 1985), the expulsion and deportation of groups from a country (Adams and Bristow, 1979), organizational and occupational settings (Esposito and Rosnow, 1983), race and racial tension (Rosenthal, 1971; Knopf, 1975; Kerner et al., 1968, *passim*), an especially sensationalistic crime (Rosnow and Fine, 1976, pp. 55–56), and the doings of friends and intimates (Haviland, 1977; Suls, 1977; Cox, 1970; Gluckman, 1963). It seems almost intuitively obvious that people tend to talk about what seems most relevant to their lives. Again, remember, here we are talking about *subjective* importance. In the grand scheme of things—that is to say, objectively—what celebrities are doing makes no difference whatsoever to most people, but it is subjectively important to the public, and therefore of importance to them.

Uncertainty.   For the most part, rumor contexts are those that are *problematic*, that is, about which not enough is known, or which present a puzzle or problem. Thus, the second crucial "rumorogenic" (Rosnow and Fine, 1976, pp. 22ff) factor is *uncertainty*, which corresponds fairly closely to Allport and Postman's and Shibutani's dimension of ambiguity. However, ambiguity implies an objective condition of the world, whereas uncertainty incorporates a subjective element; that is, *how ambiguity is experienced*. A topic must not only be important; people must be uncertain about the causes and consequences and about information concerning the causes and consequences of a given condition. Rosnow defines uncertainty as "a belief or intellectual state produced by doubt, such as when events are unstable, capricious, or problematical" (1988, p. 20; 1980). Rumor thrives on doubt.

During a war, for example, the public wants to know more than the media can report. Is our side winning or losing? What's the death toll—on both sides? Is our government releasing accurate information about the war? Has the enemy committed atrocities against our troops? Are elements at home profiting from the suffering of the rest of us? The troops, too, want to know more about what is happening and what will happen to them than the military is able to tell them. Where are we being shipped? What's it like there? What are our chances of being killed? Are we being treated fairly? What's happening at home? Is everybody supporting the war effort? When will the war be over? These are all questions that people want answered. They address issues that are ambiguous, and about which they feel unsettled, uncomfortable, and uncertain. To the extent that this is true, rumors are likely to circulate to help supply answers to them.

Anxiety.   The third factor that feeds the rumor process is a state of anxiety, a dimension that was missing or assumed in Allport and Postman's and in Shibutani's models. Anxiety may be defined as "a negative affective state produced by apprehension about an impending, potentially negative, outcome" (Rosnow, 1988, p. 20). To some degree, anxiety is a more or less inevitable outcome of the combination of importance and uncertainty, but even under the same objective contexts, people vary with respect to how much anxiety they feel. That is, anxiety has two dimensions: *individual* and *structural.* Experimental studies have shown that, under the same conditions, highly anxious individuals are more likely to pass on rumors than calmer, less anxious individuals (Anthony, 1973; Jaeger, Anthony, and Rosnow, 1980). However, feeling anxiety is more than a personal or individual variable; certain structural conditions make for higher levels of anxiety than others. As a general rule, the more threatening and anxiety-provoking a given condition or situation, the more likely it is to give rise to rumors.

For instance, during the 1960s, just before and during racial rioting, the tenser a community became with respect to race, the faster and thicker rumors flew about that subject (Knopf, 1975). In 1972, noncitizen Asians were expelled from Uganda by Idi Amin. Their property was confiscated, they were forced to leave a country they had lived in for all or much of their lives, and many were searched or arrested. While the actual numbers of beatings, rapes, and killings were relatively small, the rumors about such events were rampant in the Asian communities of Uganda; many Asians claimed to have fled from "a living hell" (Adams and Bristow, 1979). During the civil war in Nigeria in the late 1960s, because food supplies were uncertain, there were outbreaks of malnutrition and stillbirths caused by the malnutrition. During this time, rumors ran rampant that the food sent by the British was poisoned, which was causing the medical pathologies that were observed (Nkpa, 1977). In the stock market, where the price of stocks in the future is always a puzzle and, depending on whether they go up or down, can make or wipe out vast fortunes, interpretations, speculations, and rumor will flourish to ease the tension (Rose, 1951; Kimmel and Keefer, 1991; Kleinfeld, 1984; Koenig, 1985, pp. 149–161). There doesn't seem to be any doubt that situations that maximize feelings of apprehensiveness also maximize rumormongering.

In short, "rumor flies on fear" (Goleman, 1991). As a general rule, according to Allan J. Kimmel, a psychologist investigating the rumor process, the more frightened people are by a rumor they hear, the greater the likelihood they will repeat it. Such rumormongering may serve a personal motive, says Dr. Kimmel; the anxious teller hopes that the listener will challenge the rumor they repeat with a contradictory fact, thereby assuaging his or her fears. Often, however, the listener believes the rumor, and the teller's fears intensify (Goleman, 1991, p. C5).

Credulity.   The fourth dimension that fosters rumormongering is credulity, that is, "belief or trust in the rumor" (Rosnow, 1988, p. 20) Rumors are accepted and passed on to the extent that they are believable. For rumors to be transmitted there must be a *suspension of disbelief* (p. 15); rumors must *seem to be true.* Again, as with the dimension of anxiety, there are two dimensions here: a personal or individual dimension and a structural or situational one. Some individuals are simply more credulous than others are, and some situations make rumors seem to be more true than others.

If some people are very knowledgeable about, and have had a great deal of experience with, the specific subject of the rumor, they are likely to be extremely skeptical concerning clearly false statements. They are not likely to be credulous; in fact, they are likely to be highly skeptical. In other words, they will approach these rumors with a *critical set* (Buckner, 1965, pp. 55–56). Clearly, knowledgeability and experience diminish credulity and increase the likelihood of a critical set. In addition, knowledge about situations *very much like* that of the topic of the rumor will also diminish credulity and maximize the chances of adopting a critical set. For instance, if someone has had a great deal of firsthand acquaintance with past elections, he or she is less likely to place much stock in election-eve rumors attempting to slander a given candidate (p. 56). If a given rumor arises within "a stable interactional system," that is, a group of people who continue to interact with one another over a period of time, a rumor about one of their members is likely to be checked and cross-checked. Again, a critical set is likely to be adopted, and credulity is likely to be low (p. 56). Skepticism and a critical set are the enemies of rumor.

The *uncritical* set—high credulity and a high likelihood of passing on a rumor—is also a personal or a situational variable, and is fostered by some of the following conditions: ignorance and lack of knowledge, either about the specific situation being discussed or situations like it; a low level of education; a high level of anxiety, urgency, tension, and insecurity; a close "fit" between the rumor and expectations or a need for it to be true; and a disruption of stable systems of interaction (Buckner, 1965, pp. 57–58). Certain individuals who possess one or more of these characteristics are more likely to pass on rumors in a given situation than are those who do not possess them. Likewise, certain situations that foster these conditions, or certain people among whom the rumor arises, will experience a great deal of rumor-mongering. In short, the greater the credulity and the lower the likelihood of a critical set, the greater the likelihood that rumors will arise and be transmitted. If people believe almost anything they hear, or believe what they hear about a given subject, they are very likely to pass on what they hear as true. Credulity is an intimate friend of rumor.

THE MANIPULATION OF RUMOR

Claims of the conscious manipulation of rumor are a standard fixture in controversies between two contending parties. For instance, during an election, when the public begins talking about the evil deeds enacted by one candidate, his or her spokespersons will claim that the other side is guilty of a "whispering campaign" of planting malicious rumors. Such accusations are sometimes true, although my guess is that they are far more often false than true. In introducing the subject in the beginning of this chapter, I mentioned that rumor is largely, although not entirely, a spontaneous affair; it is difficult to plant a successful rumor, although some classic cases are part of the literature. There are at least two obstacles faced by parties launching a "whispering campaign" to foster their own ends, or to undermine those of their enemies.

To begin with, a number of carefully conducted studies (Sinha, 1952; Back

290 · CHAPTER 7 · *Rumor and Gossip*

et al., 1950; Festinger, Schachter, and Back, 1950) have shown that, for the most part, "a rumor may be successfully manufactured only under the same conditions under which it would develop spontaneously. . . . Formulation of messages requires special ingenuity; they must fall within the limits of plausibility and also reflect the current mood" (Shibutani, 1966, p. 199). In other experiments, when material was released that was not plausible to subjects, it was simply not believed and not passed on (Schall, Levy, and Tressell, 1950). To imagine that any rumor planted among any audience by any party to achieve its own ends will be widely believed and transmitted to the point where those ends will be achieved is naive; social dynamics simply do not work that way.

A second problem with planting rumors lays in "controlling rumor content after the transaction gets under way. Like mobs, rumors are difficult to keep in check. They form spontaneously, and the line of development depends on fortuitous events, momentary emotional reactions of those who happen to be on the scene, and the particular interests of those who make up the public" (Shibutani, 1966, p. 197). A rumor may be coopted by the public, or segments of the public, to its own ends, and sometimes against the interests of the original propagator of the rumor. For example, in 1958, in a multipronged effort to overthrow Indonesian president Achmed Sukarno, who, American officials felt, was becoming too close with Communist factions in that country, the United States government launched a "whispering campaign." To discredit Sukarno, U.S. representatives unofficially distributed a film of him having sex with prostitutes. This effort backfired, however, because the film was interpreted by much of the public and by Sukarno himself as a demonstration of his virility; instead of discrediting him, the campaign actually strengthened his rule.

A good example of the view that self-serving, manufactured rumors are common or, at least, not difficult to propagate, can be seen in one segment of the popular television series, *LA Law*. A Mexican-American lawyer, played by Jimmy Smits, represents a small Mexican brewery, "Quintana," whose once-popular product has declined precipitously in sales and whose owners are on the verge of bankruptcy. It seems that the representatives of a large American competitor, which had unsuccessfully attempted to purchase the smaller firm, had begun a rumor to the effect that Quintana's employees were urinating in the shipments of beer sent to the United States—hence, its decline in sales. This television program was fiction, of course. In real life, the same rumor was told about Corona Beer, an actual product imported from Mexico. However, there is no indication that competitors began or spread the rumor, although it is possible the salespersons of a large distributor that did not handle Corona "spread it vigorously" (Fine, 1989, pp. 159–160).

In the 1930s, Chesterfield was in a seemingly similar position; a rumor was afoot that a leper worked in its plant and was contaminating its cigarettes with his disease. Ligget & Meyers, the owner of Chesterfield, hired detectives to track down its source, and offered $1,000 to the first 25 people who could give evidence that would lead to the party who planted it. Fully expecting that the rumor would be traced back to the executives of one of its competitors, the company issued the following statement, "We do not object to legitimate competition, but cowardly attacks of this sort have no place in American business or American life." The effort ended in failure, of course; Ligget & Meyers never did track down the origin of the rumor, and no one collected the reward. Rumors that a product sold to the public is being contaminated arise spontaneously and have existed for at least a century and, thus, nearly all the time, no conspiracy theory concerning who started it is necessary (Morgan and Tucker, 1984, p. 14; Koenig, 1985, pp. 89–102).

Nonetheless, at times, the conscious, self-serving manipulation of rumor has been successful, although "there is some question of whether the accomplishment was by accident or design" (Shibutani, 1966, p. 186). A few areas in which rumors have been planted by a particular party to achieve a specific end include: election campaigns, the world of business, and international intrigue.

ELECTION CAMPAIGNS

Perhaps the most widely publicized example of the effort to create and disseminate rumors to discredit political opponents took place during the 1972 presidential campaign; it was a series of actions commonly referred to as "Watergate," after the building in which the Democratic National Headquarters was located. The Committee to Re-elect the President (CREEP) was engaged in a series of "dirty tricks" to help Republican Richard Nixon's campaign and hurt the campaigns of his Democratic rivals, Senators Edmund Muskie, Henry Jackson, George McGovern, and Hubert Humphrey, who were vying for the nomination. In Florida, during the primary, CREEP sent out copies of a forged letter on Citizens for Muskie stationery to the effect that Jackson had fathered an illegitimate child and had been arrested on a charge of homosexuality. The letter also stated that Humphrey, with a prostitute in the car, had been arrested for drunk driving after hitting two cars and a mailbox. In California, CREEP sent out a press release on Humphrey stationery claiming that Shirley Chisholm, a highly respected Black member of the House of Representatives, had spent a year in a mental institution; Humphrey's initials were forged at the bottom of the letter.

While some of the "dirty tricks" employed by CREEP generated little or no talk and had no impact—indeed, some even backfired—the campaign as a whole, most contemporary political strategists agree, did achieve its stated ends; that is, to hurt the Democratic candidates and to help President Nixon. Muskie's campaign manager said that these illegal, unethical tactics "took a toll in the form of diverting our resources, changing our schedules, altering our political approaches, and being thrown on the defensive." Said McGovern's campaign manager, referring to the Democratic rivals, "we were no longer opponents; we had become enemies and I think largely as a result of this activity" (Lukas, 1976, pp. 157–158, 165, 164, 166). Of course, in the long run, Nixon was hurt very badly by these tactics because, when these and other illegal dealings were revealed to the press and the public, he was forced to resign his presidency.

The World of Business

A spectacular example of planted rumors in the business world took place in the late 1980s. In 1983, American Express ("Don't leave home without it") purchased one of two major banking operations owned by international billionaire banker, Edmond Safra, who remained active in the firm's affairs. But Safra, a Lebanese-born Brazilian national, was not happy with what he felt was the stifling bureaucracy that ruled at American Express; in 1984, he left the firm to attend to his other corporation. Safra took some 20 high-level executives with him and, some at American Express suspected, some valued customers as well; in addition, sources claimed, when the banker left, important files and software programs disappeared. All-in-all, the failed business marriage left a feeling of resentment among many American Express managers. The corporation hired several private detectives to shadow Safra's employees.

Starting in 1986, and continuing into 1988, articles appeared in newspapers and magazines all over the world claiming that Safra was engaged in a wide range of illegal and unethical activities. A *New York Times* article charged that Safra's bank supplied the United States national security advisor with a plane on his secret mission to Iran, which was part of a series of illegal actions by American government operatives that led to the Iran-Contra scandal. An Italian magazine published a story that Safra was involved in a drug-smuggling operation. A French newspaper article, and later one in Peru, then one in Mexico, claimed that Safra's banks laundered drug money. A French weekly asserted that the billionaire had business dealings with the Mafia, and that one of his bankers had been killed by Colombian drug dealers in Panama. Although these stories were later retracted, the accusations left a lingering doubt on the part of some members of the banking community that they could be true.

It turns out that not one of these charges was true. Safra hired his own team of detectives and retained an aggressive criminal lawyer to track down the source of the rumors; the investigation led directly to the board rooms of American Express. Safra's lawyer, Stanley Arkin, published an article in a law journal summarizing the findings of his investigation. "Spreading false and malicious rumor or flat-out lies," he said, "may well amount to criminal fraud." American Express, he charged, was guilty of "dirty tricks . . . reminiscent of Watergate." Executives at American Express, fearful that Safra and Arkin were planning serious legal action, decided to admit their guilt. The chairman of the firm, James Robinson, sent a letter to Safra admitting American Express' part in the rumormongering, and apologizing for it: "certain persons acting on behalf of American Express began an unauthorized and shameful effort to use the media to malign you," he stated. "I want to apologize to you and your organization. . . . I appreciate . . . how painful it must have been for you to endure these baseless attacks." American Express agreed to pay $8 million to four charities named by Safra, $4 million as "an apology" and $4 million as "an expression of goodwill" (Taylor, 1989).

INTERNATIONAL INTRIGUE

International intrigue provides some of the most noteworthy and numerous examples of the attempt to disseminate rumor for self-serving ends. Some of the efforts of government agencies can be classifed as *propaganda*. The term is usually restricted to statements issued by a particular government that are false. However, most experts use the term to refer to *any* communication that attempts to achieve the goal of the propagandist—whether that communication is true or false. Of course, not all propaganda is successful, but if the propagandist is especially clever and insightful, it may produce belief among some people in its target population and result in widespread rumor transmission and changes in behavior. Experts distinguish between at least two different types of propaganda. (It is unfortunate that the terms that are used have a pejorative racial connotation.) "White" propaganda is overt, a communication whose source is correctly identified, and not necessarily false; an example would be the Voice of America beamed throughout Eastern Europe. "Black" propaganda, in contrast, is covert, a communication whose source is falsely given, in which "lies, fabrications, and deceptions" are spread (Jowett and O'Donnell, 1986, p. 18). Another term for "black" propaganda is *disinformation*, which is "a carefully constructed false message leaked into an opponent's communication system to deceive the decision-making elite or the public" (Bittman, 1985, p. 49).

Agents of both the American CIA (Central Intelligence Agency) and the Soviet KGB (in English, the Committee of State Security) have been actively involved in efforts to disseminate propaganda, both of the "white" and "black" varieties. Much propaganda can be classified as hearsay and therefore rumor, although a great deal of it is fabricated and therefore not believed by the teller. In any case, some of it has been successful in generating harmful rumors and beliefs both in target populations and among political leaders of the other side. In 1975–1976, a CIA chief stationed in Angola put out a story that Cuban soldiers had raped several local teenage girls, were captured by U.S.-backed rebel forces, put on trial, and executed; the story was complete with photographs of the trial, the execution, and the young women who supposedly had been raped. The whole thing was a hoax, of course; Cuban soldiers had conducted themselves in Angola in an eminently peaceful fashion (Poelchau, 1981, p. 38). In 1986, the CIA released forged documents that indicated that dissent was rife in the Libyan military; that there was, in fact, an "underground" in the Libyan army; that Libyan dissidents had met with Soviet officials; that the Soviet Union was plotting a coup against Col. Muammar Quaddafi; and that the United States government was planning extensive raids against Libya (Woodward, 1987, pp. 472ff). Here, once again, disinformation reared its ugly head, and it caused the international diplomatic community to speculate about whether these charges were true.

The KGB, not to be outdone by its American counterpart, has released false statements—disinformation—of its own, sometimes generating a landslide of rumor that helped to achieve Soviet aims. In 1956 in Hungary, when a popular uprising threatened to overthrow the Soviet-backed Communist regime, Russian tanks were sent in to crush the rebellion. A broadcast, which called itself Radio Free Hungary, begged for U.S. intervention, described Soviet atrocities "in hideous detail, and the Russians were cursed and denounced in every transmission." In reality, the radio station did not exist; it was "actually a totally brilliant fake operated by the KGB to embarrass the United States." There was no chance of an American military intervention, and the Soviets knew it. Since statements had been broadcast over Radio Free Europe to the effect that the U.S. would support a popular uprising in Hungary, the effect of the fake pleas over Radio Free Hungary was to dramatize that the United States could not be relied upon to help a country in revolt. The broadcast was so convincing that even the CIA was taken in by the ruse (Jowett and O'Donnell, 1986, p. 18).

Rumor Summary. Most people love to hear a good conspiracy story about how the rich and powerful are manipulating their lives. If they can control society's major institutions, doesn't it seem reasonable that they control the rumor mill as well? Representatives of the major social institutions do plant rumors to achieve specific, often self-interested, ends, and these efforts often do pay off; but the number of unsuccessful rumor plants—those that are not passed on and that do not achieve their desired effect—are far more numerous than those that are successful. Conditions must be exactly right for a rumor to be spread, and individuals in power can rarely control most of the more crucial conditions that maximize rumormongering. Moreover, in some contexts, rumors fly so thick and fast, on the basis of such skimpy information, and the advantage to those who initiate them to have others believe and act on them is so obvious, that they are often discounted as fast as they are told. Said one stock market trader about Wall Street rumors, "There are just too many whacky stories for me to care" (Kleinfeld, 1984, p. 133). Still, the conscious planting and manipulation of rumors by individuals in positions of power is a major category of rumor; it cannot be ignored. The relatively few rumors of this type that do take root and become transmitted typically have a far greater impact than most run-of-the-mill, grassroots rumors about friends, celebrities, and consumer products. It is no surprise that we should pay close attention to rumors that issue from politicians, diplomats, and other highly placed government officials, the military brass, corporation executives, public relations specialists, advertisers, and stock market traders. It is in their best interests, and the interests of the institutions they control, to lie, and often, the impact of these lies is contrary to the interests of the public.

SUMMARY

Rumor is both a process and a product, that is, it is both transmitted in a certain way, and it is a certain kind of story. By definition, rumor is unsubstantiated, a story that is told without factual documentation. In contrast, gossip may be substantiated or unsubstantiated. Gossip is defined by its content: It is always personal in nature. In contrast, rumor may be personal or impersonal. Gossip and rumor are forms of collective behavior: They are group products, they are spontaneous and extemporaneous, they are attempts to "fill in the gaps" in an informational vacuum, and they are extrainsitutional or nonnormative forms of communication. Legends are a special kind of rumor; they are about abstract, general, cartoon, readily substitutable people or events, while the ordinary garden-variety rumor, although often false, is about specific, concrete people and events. Most rumors have a brief life span, whereas legends, in one guise or another, last for years, decades, sometimes centuries. Collective delusions are transmitted via rumor, but, again, are so distinct as to warrant a separate discussion. Rumor and gossip are transmitted both face-to-face, word-of-mouth, and by means of the mass media. Rumor and gossip are not necessarily negative or trivial.

Anthropologists have isolated a number of functions of gossip for the individual and for society—social integration, social control, group conflict and the maintenance of group boundaries, and social comparison.

A classic rumor (which is also an urban legend) that was examined in detail, in order to understand how rumors get started and what functions they serve, was the "death" of Beatle Paul McCartney in 1969. Although based on extremely flimsy evidence, it was believed by some tellers and listeners.

One of the first systematic efforts to study rumor was undertaken by psychologists Allport and Postman in the 1940s. They devised an experiment similar to the children's game of "telephone," postulating a basic "law" of rumor, that rumor arises and is transmitted to the extent that the subject is important and the facts of a story are shrouded in ambiguity. They argued that rumor tends to be highly inaccurate, with leveling (or simplification), sharpening (focusing on crucial details), and assimilating (organizing the story around a central theme) taking place. Rumor serves individual functions and is largely an irrational phenomenon.

Sociologist Tamotsu Shibutani criticized Allport and Postman's approach, arguing that their experiment was unrealistic. Rumor takes place in an interactional setting, not in a straight line, and spreads out like a fan, in a network. Far from serving exclusively individual motives, it tends to arise in certain social or collective situations. If the demand for news exceeds the supply, rumor tends to take place; rumor is "improvised news." Rumor is an extension of everyday life and is not an unusual or pathological process.

Ralph Rosnow, a social psychologist, has isolated four central factors or conditions that contemporary researchers agree influence the transmission of rumor: topical importance, uncertainty or ambiguity, personal anxiety, and credulity.

It has long been asserted that false rumors can be planted to achieve the rumor initiator's goals. While there are spectacular examples of this happening, it is less often true than falsely claimed. It is difficult to fabricate, then circulate rumors, that do not resonate with what is regarded as already believable in a society, community, or group. Moreover, once started, rumors may get out of control and subvert the initiator's goal. Still, this process takes place often enough to pay attention to it and understand how and why it succeeds when it does.

References

Adams, Bert N., and Mike Bristow. 1979. "Ugandan Asian Expulsion Experiences: Rumour and Reality." *Journal of Asian and African Studies*, 14 (3–4): 191–203.

Alexander, John T. 1989. *Catherine the Great: Life and Legend*. New York: Oxford University Press.

Allport, Floyd H., and Milton Lepkin. 1945. "Wartime Rumors of Waste and Special Privilege: Why Some People Believe in Them." *Journal of Abnormal and Social Psychology*, 40 (January): 3–36.

Allport, Gordon W., and Leo Postman. 1946–1947. "An Analysis of Rumor." *Public Opinion Quarterly*, 10 (Winter): 501–517.

Allport, Gordon W., and Leo Postman. 1947. *The Psychology of Rumor*. New York: Henry Holt.

Anonymous. 1985. "P&G Drops Logo from Its Packages: Satan Rumors Are Blamed." *The New York Times* (April 25): D1, D8.

Anthony, Susan. 1973. "Anxiety and Rumor." *Journal of Social Psychology*, 89 (February): 91–98.

Back, Kurt, et al. 1950. "The Methodology of Studying Rumor Transmission." *Human Relations*, 3 (3): 307–312.

Bittman, Ladislav. 1985. *The KGB and Soviet Disinformation: An Insider's View*. McLean, Va.: Pergamon-Brassey's International Defense Publishers.

Brunvand, Jan Harold. 1980. "Urban Legends: Folklore for Today." *Psychology Today* (June): 50–62.

Brunvand, Jan Harold. 1981. *The Vanishing Hitchhiker: American Urban Legends and Their Meaning*. New York: W.W. Norton.

Brunvand, Jan Harold. 1984. *The Choking Doberman and Other "New" Urban Legends*. New York: W.W. Norton.

Brunvand, Jan Harold. 1986. *The Mexican Pet: More "New" Urban Legends and Some Old Favorites*. New York: W.W. Norton.

Brunvand, Jan Harold. 1989. *Curses! Broiled Again! The Hottest Urban Legends Going*. New York: W.W. Norton.

Buckner, H. Taylor. 1965. "A Theory of Rumor Transmission." *Public Opinion Quarterly*, 29 (Spring): 54–70.

Caplow, Theodore. 1947. "Rumors in War." *Social Forces*, 25 (March): 298–302.

Colson, Elizabeth. 1953. *Makah Indians*. Minneapolis: University of Minnesota Press.

Cox, Bruce A. 1970. "What Is Hopi Gossip About? Information Management and Hopi Factions." *Man*, New Series, 5 (1): 88–98.

Damore, Leo. 1988. *Senatorial Privilege: The Chappaquiddick Cover-Up*. Washington: Regnery Gateway.

Esposito, James L., and Ralph L. Rosnow. 1983. "Corporate Rumors: How They Start and How to Stop Them." *Management Review*, 72 (April): 44–49.

Festinger, Leon, et al. 1948. "A Study of a Rumor: Its Origin and Spread." *Human Relations*, 1 (August): 464–486.

Festinger, Leon, Stanley Schachter, and Kurt Back. 1950. *Social Pressures in Informal Groups*. New York: Harper.

Fine, Gary Alan. 1985. "Rumors and Gossiping." In Teun A. Van Dijk (ed.), *Handbook of Discourse Analysis: Discourse and Dialogue*, pp. 223–237. London: Academic Press.

Fine, Gary Alan. 1989. "Mercantile Legends and the World Economy: Dangerous Imports from the Third World." *Western Folklore*, 48 (April): 169–177.

Fine, Gary Alan. 1990. "Among Those Dark Satanic Mills: Rumors of Kooks, Cults, and Corporations." *Southern Folklore*, 47 (1): 133–146.

Fine, Gary Alan, and Ralph L. Rosnow. 1978. "Gossip, Gossipers, Gossiping." *Personality and Social Psychology Bulletin*, 4 (Winter): 161–168.

Gluckman, Max. 1963. "Gossip and Scandal." *Current Anthropology*, 4 (June): 307–316.

Goleman, Daniel. 1991. "Anatomy of Rumor: It Flies on Fear." *The New York Times* (June 4): C1, C5.

Gross, Michael. 1988. "Inside Gossip." *New York* (May 9): 41–47.

Haviland, John Beard. 1977. "Gossip as Competition in Zinacantan." *Journal of Communication*, 27 (1): 186–191.

Henry, William A., III. 1990. "Pssst . . . Did You Hear About?" *Time* (March 5): 46–51.

Herskovits, Melville J. 1947. *Trinidad Village*. New York: Alfred Knopf.

Jaeger, Marianne E., Susan Anthony, and Ralph L. Rosnow. 1980. "Who Hears What from Whom and with What Effect: A Study of Rumor." *Personality and Social Psychology Bulletin*, 6 (3): 473–478.

Johnson, Donald M. 1945. "The Phantom Anesthetist of Mattoon: A Field Study of Mass Hysteria." *Journal of Abnormal and Social Psychology*, 40 (2): 175–186.

Jowett, Garth S., and Victoria O'Donnell. 1986. *Propaganda and Persuasion*. Newbury Park, Calif.: Sage.

Kagan, Daniel, and Ian Summers. 1984. *Mute Evidence*. New York: Bantam Books.

Kapferer, Jean-Noël. 1990. *Rumors: Uses, Interpretations, and Images* (Bruce Fink, trans.). New Brunswick, N.J.: Transaction.

Kelley, Kitty. 1991. *Nancy Reagan: The Unauthorized Biography*. New York: Simon & Schuster.

Kerckhoff, Alan C., and Kurt W. Back. 1968. *The June Bug: A Study of Hysterical Contagion*. New York: Appleton-Century-Crofts.

Kerckhoff, Alan C., Kurt W. Back, and Norman Miller. 1965. "Sociometric Patterns in Hysterical Contagion." *Sociometry*, 28 (1): 2–15.

Kerner, Otto, et al. 1968. *Report of the National Advisory Commission on Civil Disorders*. New York: Bantam Books.

Kimmel, Allan J., and Robert Keefer. 1991. "Psychological Correlates of the Transmission and Acceptance of Rumors about AIDS." *Journal of Applied Social Psychology*, 21 (19): 1608–1628.

Kleinfeld, Sonny. 1984. *The Traders*. New York: Holt, Rinehart & Winston.

Knopf, Terry Ann. 1975. *Rumors, Race, and Riots*. New Brunswick, N.J.: Transaction Books.

Koenig, Frederick. 1985. *Rumor in the Marketplace: The Social Psychology of Commercial Hearsay*. Dover, Mass.: Auburn House.

Larsen, Otto N. 1954. "Rumors in a Disaster." *Journal of Communication*, 4 (Winter): 111–123.

Levin, Jack, and Arnold Arluke. 1985. "An Exploratory Analysis of Sex Differences in Gossip." *Sex Roles*, 12 (3/4): 281–285.

Levin, Jack, and Arnold Arluke. 1987. *Gossip: The Inside Scoop*. New York: Plenum Press.

Levin, Jack, and Allan J. Kimmel. 1977. "Gossip Columns: Media Small Talk." *Journal of Communication*, 27 (Winter): 169–175.

Lukas, J. Anthony. 1976. *Nightmare: The Underside of the Nixon Years.* New York: Viking Press.

Mailer, Norman. 1973. *Marilyn, a Biography.* New York: Grosset & Dunlap.

McPhail, Clark. 1991. *The Myth of the Madding Crowd.* New York: Aldine de Gruyter.

Medalia, Nahum, and Otto N. Larsen. 1958. "Diffusion and Belief in a Collective Delusion: The Seattle Windshield Pitting Epidemic." *American Sociological Review*, 23 (April): 180–186.

Morgan, Hal, and Kerry Tucker. 1984. *Rumor!* Middlesex, England: Penguin Books.

Morgan, Hal, and Kerry Tucker. 1987. *More Rumor!* New York: Penguin Books.

Morin, Edgar. 1971. *Rumour in Orleans* (Peter Green, trans.). New York: Pantheon Books.

Nkpa, Nwokocha K.U. 1975. "Rumor Mongering in War Time." *Journal of Social Psychology*, 96 (June): 27–35.

Nkpa, Nwokocha K.U. 1977. "Rumors of Mass Poisoning in Biafra." *Public Opinion Quarterly*, 41 (Fall): 332–346.

Peterson, Warren A., and Noel P. Gist. 1951. "Rumor and Public Opinion." *American Journal of Sociology*, 47 (September): 159–167.

Poelchau, Warner (ed.). 1981. *White Paper, Whitewash: Interviews with Philip Agee on the CIA and El Salvador.* New York: Deep Cover Books.

Posonby, Arthur. 1928. *Falsehood in War-Time.* New York: Dutton.

Prasad, J. 1935. "The Psychology of Rumor: A Study Relating to the Great Indian Earthquake of 1934." *The British Journal of Psychology*, 26 (July): 1–15.

Rice, Berkeley. 1988. "Boom and Doom on Wall Street." *Psychology Today* (April): 51–54.

Rorvik, David. 1980. "Cattle Mutilations: The Truth at Last." *Penthouse* (September): 121–122, 142–143.

Rose, Arnold M. 1951. "Rumor in the Stock Market." *Public Opinion Quarterly*, 15 (Fall): 461–486.

Rosenthal, Marilynn. 1971. "Where Rumor Raged." *Transaction*, 8 (February): 34–43.

Rosnow, Ralph L. 1980. "Psychology of Rumor Reconsidered." *Psychological Bulletin*, 87 (3): 578–591.

Rosnow, Ralph L. 1988. "Rumor as Communication: A Contextualist Approach." *Journal of Communication*, 38 (Winter): 12–28.

Rosnow, Ralph L. 1991. "Inside Rumor: A Personal Journey." *American Psychologist*, 46 (May): 484–496.

Rosnow, Ralph L., and Gary Alan Fine. 1974. "Inside Rumors." *Human Behavior*, 3 (April): 64–68.

Rosnow, Ralph L., and Gary Alan Fine. 1976. *Rumor and Gossip: The Social Psychology of Hearsay.* New York: Elsevier.

Rosnow, Ralph L., and Marianthi Georgouli. 1985. "'Killed by Idle Gossip': The Psychology of Small Talk." In Bernard Rubin (ed.), *When Information Counts: Grading the Media*, pp. 59–73. Lexington, Mass.: D.C. Heath/Lexington Books.

Sabini, John, and Maury Silver. 1982. "A Plea for Gossip." In *Moralities and Everyday Life*, pp. 89–106. New York: Oxford University Press.

Schall, Herbert M., Bernard Levy, and M.E. Tresselt, 1950. "A Sociometric Approach to Rumor." *Journal of Social Psychology*, 31 (2): 121–129.

Seymour-Urie, Colin. 1982. "Rumour and Politics." *Politics*, 17 (2): 1–9.

Sherif, Muzafer. 1936. *The Psychology of Social Norms.* New York: Harper.

Sherif, Muzafer, and O.J. Harvey. 1952. "A Study of Ego Functioning: The Elimination of Stable Anchorages in Individual and Group Situations." *Sociometry*, 15 (August–November): 272–305.

Shibutani, Tamotsu. 1966. *Improvised News: A Sociological Study of Rumor.* Indianapolis, Ind.: Bobbs-Merrill.

Shiller, Robert J. 1984. "Stock Prices and Social Dynamics." *Brookings Papers on Economic Activity*, 2: 457–510.

Shiller, Robert J. 1989. "Fashion, Fads, and Bubbles in Financial Markets." In *Market Volatility*, pp. 56–68. Cambridge, Mass.: MIT Press.

Sinha, Durganand. 1952. "Behaviour in a Catastrophic Situation: A Psychological Study of Reports and Rumours." *British Journal of Psychology*, 43 (July): 200–209.

Smith, Vernon L., Gerry L. Suchanek, and Arlington W. Williams. 1988. "Bubbles, Crashes, and Endogamous Expectations in Experimental Spot Asset Markets." *Econometrica*, 56 (5): 1119–1151.

Solomon, Jolie B. 1984. "Proctor & Gamble Fights New Rumors Of Link to Satanism." *The Wall Street Journal* (November 8): 1, 18.

Stewart, James R. 1980. "Collective Delusion: A Comparison of Believers and Skeptics." Unpublished Paper Delivered Before the Midwest Sociological Society, Milwaukee, April 3.

Stirling, Rebecca Birch. 1956. "Some Psychological Mechanisms Operative in Gossip." *Social Forces*, 34 (March): 262–267.

Suczek, Barbara. 1972. "The Curious Case of the 'Death' of Paul McCartney." *Urban Life and Culture*, 1 (April): 61–76.

Suls, Jerry M. 1977. "Gossip as Social Comparison." *Journal of Communication*, 27 (Winter): 164–168.

Taylor, John. 1989. "Bank Shot." *New York* (September 18): 42–47.

West, James. 1945. *Plainsville, U.S.A.* New York: Columbia University Press.

Woodward, Bob. 1987. *Veil: The Secret Wars of the CIA, 1981–1987.* New York: Simon & Schuster.

CHAPTER
8

CONTEMPORARY LEGENDS AND COLLECTIVE DELUSIONS

On September 5, 1967, a horse named "Snippy" failed to show up for his daily watering at the corral of the King Ranch, near Alamosa, Colorado. The next day, a search party discovered the dead horse, whose flesh, from the shoulders up, had been neatly removed, leaving the skull and shoulder bones entirely exposed. A Denver pathologist was quoted as saying that neither predators nor a knife could have performed the bizarre mutilation. News accounts claimed that Snippy's internal organs, blood, and brain fluid were missing. Not content with one mystery, some observers added another: They blamed extraterrestrial activity (or UFOs) for the unfortunate horse's demise. A wave of sensationalistic publicity brought thousands of visitors to the King Ranch for months afterward. Later, the United States Central Intelligence Agency, the CIA (Sanders, 1976, 1977), and satanic cults were blamed for the incident. From 1967 to the late 1970s, some 10,000 incidents of horses and cows mutilated "with surgical precision" were reported to authorities in the Midwest, the South, and the Rocky Mountain states.

In 1979, the First Judicial District Attorney's office of Santa Fe, New Mexico, submitted a grant application to the federal government that read: "After the death, the animal's rectum and sex organs are removed in a mutilation case with a precision many investigators believe could be accomplished only with a sophisticated instrument, such as a laser beam. . . . Strong evidence exists that the cattle are killed elsewhere, then flown by aircraft to the spot where they are found, and dropped to the ground" (quoted in Rorvik, 1980, p. 121). Headlines in local newspapers and magazines read: "Did Poor Horse Poke His Head Inside Radioactive Saucer?" "UFOs Linked to Weird Animal Mutilations," "Is It the Work of a Witches' Cult, Space Aliens, or the CIA?," "Doctor Says Cattle Mutilations May Switch to Human Victims," "Veterinarian Says Flying Objects, Cattle Mutilations May Be Related," "Mutilators Psychotic" (Rorvik, 1980; Stewart, 1977, 1980). A study conducted in the mid-1970s of a sample of adults living in South Dakota revealed that just under half (44 percent) believed that the animals had been done in by mysterious agents: cultists, psychotics, UFOs, or the CIA. The rest either had no opinion or were skeptics, believing there was a naturalistic explanation for what happened to them (Stewart, 1980).

Finally, in 1979, Herb Marshall, a curious and enterprising sheriff of Washington County, rigged up an experiment. Two of his officers hid in the bushes for 30 straight hours, observing a calf that had died of natural causes. At night, they watched through a Starlight Scope, which enables the viewer to see in the dark. "At the end of those 30 hours," Sheriff Marshall said, "we had us a classic case, a carcass that looked exactly like most of the others that were reported to us. Its tongue was gone, one of its eyes was missing, its anus had been cored out, the whole thing." How had it happened? "First we observed what any pathologist will tell you happens whan an animal dies. The tongue protrudes and lies right there on the ground; the anus . . . sticks out. . . . Then the predators and scavengers come along and eat the parts that protrude, the soft, easy-to-get-at parts: the tongue, the genitals, the udder if it's a female. Then as the animal gets colder, the tongue, or what's left of it, retracts back into the mouth so it looks like it was cut off way down deep. The anus retracts, too, and gives the appearance it's been operated on, especially after the blowflies have finished with it" (Rorvik, 1980, p. 142). In addition to the blowflies, Sheriff Marshall's officqers witnessed scavanging forays upon the dead calf's body by a skunk, some buzzards, and a stray dog—"all of which enjoyed a good meal" (p. 142). The cattle mutilation mystery turned out to be explained by entirely natural causes; those who believed otherwise fell victim to a mass or *collective delusion* (Stewart, 1977; Kagan and Summers, 1984)

One evening, a teenage couple parked at a local "lover's lane." The boy turned the radio on to a station playing soft, romantic music, and they began kissing and hugging. Suddenly, a news flash interrupted the music and announced the escape of a homicidal maniac, imprisoned for rape and robbery, who wore a metal hook in place of his right hand. The girl became very frightened and begged her date to take her home; the boy wanted to stay and continue necking. They argued, but the girl insisted, and so, annoyed, the boy drove off hurriedly. Arriving at his date's house, he walked around to the passenger side of the car—and there, hanging on the door handle, was a metal hook (Brunvand, 1981, pp. 47–52).

A man suspected his wife of having an affair. Employed as a cement truck driver, he drove home in his cement truck, got out, saw an unfamilar car, a Cadillac, in his driveway, and snuck around the house, hoping to find his wife in a compromising situation with her lover. Peeking through a window, he spied her sitting in the kitchen talking in a friendly manner with a strange, well-dressed man. "That does it!" he said to himself. He backed the truck up next to the Cadillac, lowered a window, shoved the cement chute inside, and emptied a load of cement into the car, filling it completely. Satisfied, he drove back to work. Returning home after work, his wife greeted him at the door, and informed him—surprise!—that she had just bought a brand-new Cadillac for his birthday, and there it was, sitting in the driveway! (Brunvand, 1981, pp. 125–132).

Three well-dressed, obviously affluent, middle-aged women visiting New York City were in the elevator of an expensive hotel. A large, muscular Black man got in, leading a Doberman on a leash. The elevator door closed. "Sit!" the man commanded, and the three women slumped to the floor. Apologetically, the man explained to the women that he wanted his dog to sit, not them. Getting up, the sheepish women told him that they were from out of town and new to the ways of New York. They timidly asked him if he knew of a good restaurant in town. He recommended one, and they followed his suggestion. After the meal, they asked for the check, but the waiter explained that it was paid by Reggie Jackson—the man they had met on the elevator (Brunvand, 1984, pp. 18–28).

These three stories—"The Hook," "The Solid Cement Cadillac," and "The Elevator Incident"—have all been told as true events by a substantial number of individuals around the country recently or in the not-too-distant past, and yet, all are unlikely to have happened. They are examples of contemporary or urban legends. The details of contemporary legends are not impossible, only unlikely. However, even those that literally, concretely occurred are *far rarer* than the number of tales about them. For instance, Fine (1979) was able to locate 45 court cases in which the Coca-Cola bottling company was sued by a customer who discovered a dead mouse in a bottle of Coke. (This does not count the instances which did not lead to a court case.) At the same time, the tale has been told so often that one would think the experience had been shared by millions, not dozens, of Coke purchasers!

WHAT ARE CONTEMPORARY LEGENDS _____ AND COLLECTIVE DELUSIONS?_____

In the last chapter, I contrasted rumor and gossip with a related phenomenon called the *legend*. To be more precise, because the legends we'll focus on are contemporary, they are called *modern, contemporary,* or *urban legends* (Brunvand, 1981, 1984, 1986, 1989). Contemporary legends are strikingly different from fairy tales, which are fantastic happenings set in a far-away time or land. In contrast, modern legends (some of which have ancient roots) supposedly happened recently or deal with newly-emerging threats, and they took place in the physical or social setting of the person telling the tale. Some contemporay legends contain a moral, personal, or political message: Something must be done about this, and it must be done now! Legends resonate with the life circumstances of the people who tell and hear them. Some legends arise, circulate for a while, die out, lie dormant, and arise again. Some appeal so strongly to persistent themes in many people's lives that they possess a certain ever-present *latency* to crop up again and recirculate. Why they burst forth depends partly on local circumstances and partly on broader national and cultural factors.

To understand the distinction between rumor and gossip on the one hand and contemporary legends on the other, it is necessary to separate the *process* or *mechanism* by which rumor and gossip are conveyed from their *content.* Legends are hearsay; that is, they are transmitted without proper factual foundation. In that respect, they are identical to rumor. On the other hand, their *content* is somewhat different from the everyday garden variety of rumor. Nearly all ordinary rumors are about specific people and specific events; just what or who the story is about is one of rumor's most crucial aspects. In contrast, while legends *seem* to be about specific people and events, in reality, they have an abstract, general, or *cartoon* quality; that is, it doesn't much matter exactly who the people in the stories are—nearly anyone with one or two important characteristics will do. In the legend, the subjects of the stories are readily substitutable for others with those same characteristics.

For instance, the credit card story—an urban legend—mentioned in Chapter 7 has been told about both Burt Reynolds and Johnny Carson. The key element here is that the subject of the story is rich and famous, not exactly who he is. The story about the Black man, the dog, and the suburban matrons, also a legend, again, has been told about a number of African-American athletes aside from Reggie Jackson, including "Magic" Johnson, O.J. Simpson, "Mean" Joe Green, and Wilt Chamberlain. With respect to the subject's identity, all that counts in the story is that the man be famous, large, athletic, and Black. (In fact, the same story has been told about Lionel Ritchie, a not-especially large or muscular African-American popular singer, indicating that, perhaps, all that counts is that the subject be famous and Black!) Of course, the line between everyday rumor and urban legends is not sharp or clear-cut; some stories may qualify as both—for instance, the rumor that circulated in the 1980s that Proctor and Gamble supported the Church of Satan. Nonetheless, in principle, they may be distinguished.

A second type of assertion that is told without factual documentation—and therefore technically qualifies as a rumor—is also so distinct as to merit a separate discussion: the *collective delusion.* As its name indicates, the collective delusion is *belief in a story that is clearly false and yet is told as true and is widely believed.* As I said in the previous chapter, not all collective delusions originate spontaneously as rumors—many are part of a society's traditional culture—but many do. Collective delusions are common throughout history and exist in practically every area of human life. The belief that

Jews are involved in a conspiracy to rule the world is a collective delusion that crops up every few decades and can be found in societies all over the world (Johnson, 1987). A few collective delusions that have a more recent origin, and will probably not reoccur, include the Seattle windshield pitting incident (Medalia and Larsen, 1958), the June bug epidemic (Kerckhoff and Back, 1968; Kerckhoff, Back, and Miller, 1965), and the "phantom anesthetist" of Mattoon (Johnson, 1945). Note that it is not necessary for the majority of a society or population to believe a given assertion for a collective delusion to exist—only a substantial proportion. For instance, according to a 1989 CBS News poll, seven percent of all Americans agree with the statement, "Elvis Presley may still be alive," an extremely unlikely state of affairs. While the proportion is low, the belief involves a very large number of individuals, and thus, it qualifies as collective in nature.

It must be emphasized that what the sociologist refers to as a collective delusion is distinctly different from what the psychiatrist and the clinical and abnormal psychologist call a delusion. For the latter, delusions are "idiocyncratic beliefs, utterly lacking in social validation" (Oltmanns, 1988, p. 4); such beliefs are "not held by the majority of people in the culture concerned. If a belief is held by most people, no matter how illogical it is and no matter how much it flies in the face of evidence, then it tends to be regarded as nondelusional" (Maher, 1988, p. 333). To the psychiatrist and the psychologist, a delusion is an *individually devised* belief; to the sociologist, a delusion that is individually devised and individually held is *not* a social or cultural product and *not* an example of collective behavior. The fact that group influences operate in the acceptance of such beliefs, and that they are widely accepted—even if not by a majority—is what makes them sociological phenomena. Further, it must be emphasized that absolutely *no* implication of psychopathology is intended when we refer to certain beliefs as delusions; most of the individuals who hold them are perfectly normal. There is nothing psychotic, sick, or abnormal about these people. They are your friends, classmates, roommates, neighbors, perhaps even your relatives—in fact, possibly even you yourself! A major theme running throughout this chapter—indeed, throughout this entire book—is that some rather unremarkable people can believe and do some rather remarkable things, and there are some basic and unremarkable sociological reasons for this.

Legends and collective delusion overlap with, but are conceptually distinct from, *parananormal beliefs*. In principle, legends and delusions *could be true but aren't*. From the point of view of mainstream science, most are theoretically possible, although, in many instances, extremely unlikely. (Of course, later information may render them *next to impossible;* thus, it is only in hindsight that we could refer to them as paranormal beliefs.) A crazed man *could have* jumped out of the bushes somewhere in Illinois in the 1940s and gassed innocent passersby; some sort of a biting insect *could have* infected dozens of factory workers in the South in the early 1960s; the fall-out from atomic tests in the Pacific *could have* pitted automobile windshields in the Seattle area in the 1950s; members of a satanic cult, or the CIA, *could have* mutilated cattle in the Rocky Mountain states in the 1970s. (If extraterrestrials did it, that's another story.) In contrast, as we'll see in Chapter 9, paranormal beliefs are, for all practical purposes, all but impossible, given what we know about how the material world works. Most modern legends are similar to contingency miracles, discussed in Chapter 4, while paranormal beliefs are similar to violation miracles.

To put things another way, *paranormal beliefs would force us to rethink and recast scientific theories as they currently exist,* while the discovery that certain beliefs we now think are myths, delusions, and legends would *not* require such a radical restructuring of our thinking about the real world. For instance, if unidentified flying objects (UFOs) turn out to be extraterrestrial aircraft, scientists would have to discard or at least thoroughly revise the view that objects cannot travel at speeds approaching the speed of light. On the other hand, if Jesse James and Billy "The Kid" are revealed to be a great deal more decent and humane than historians think, this finding would not have such profound or broad implications for our view of the nature of the world in general. Another way of saying this is that, as a rule, *paranormal beliefs stand on a broader theoretical base* than legend and collective delusion; the latter tend to be more historically specific and concrete. In addition, paranormal beliefs tend to refer to the workings of the natural and physical world, while myths and legends usually refer to the social world, to the world of human behavior. (Even the behavior of psychics depends on physical, psychological, and natural laws.)

Still, there is a great deal of overlap here. Given what we know about the social categories in question, *it is impossible that* the Jews are engaged in a conspiracy to rule the world; McDonald's puts earthworms in their "Big Macs"; Proctor & Gamble supports the Church of Satan; and bandits all over the world are as decent, humane, heroic, and kindly as many accounts of their behavior claim—yet, these assertions are considered legends and collective delusion, not paranormal beliefs. It is important to keep in mind that the line between legend and collective delusion, on the one hand, and paranormal beliefs on the other, is not clear or sharp. These two realms overlap a great deal, and some specific beliefs may be examples of both simultaneously. In fact, some—a minority of—contemporary legends and delusions do contain a supernatural element. Many folklorists believe that paranormal beliefs (such as UFO abductions) are held because of their folkloric and legend-like qualities (Degh, 1977; Ellis, 1988; Rojcewicz, 1987, 1988; Hufford, 1982).

Although some urban legends and collective delusions are stories about a one-time, one-place event or phenomenon, many of them are stories that keep reappearing in a somewhat different form again and again in locations around the country and even all over the world. The tales told in legends are stereotypical, they have a standard dramatic form (they adhere to a fairly fixed formula), and they contain a fairly simple plot and readily recognizable characters. They are a kind of "folk soap opera" in miniature, and thus, have a widespread and almost timeless appeal. For instance, the story about "The Vanishing Hitchhiker" (Brunvand, 1981, pp. 24–40; see the boxed insert

In 1909, Jesus Malverde, a Mexican bandit, was hanged. Regarded by local peasants as another Robin Hood who shared his take with the exploited poor, he became a legendary figure. Here a visitor worships at his shrine.

page 311) represents a roadside ghost story that has been told at least as far back as the 19th century, modernized in the 1930s to take account of the widespread use of the car, and told as far away as Korea. Stories of snake, octopus, or worm eggs being ingested by a person by drinking from a body of water, hatching, then growing to adulthood in the person's stomach, only to emerge under horrifying circumstances, is part of a genre of "bosom serpent" folk legends that have been told in most of the countries of Europe since ancient times (Brunvand, 1984, pp. 107–112). Aspects of this theme often figure in science fiction and horror films, such as *Alien* (1979) and *Invasion of the Body Snatchers* (1956, 1978).

What makes widely-told and believed legends and delusions a form of collective behavior? Like rumor and gossip, they have an unauthorized, unofficial, subterranean quality. Like rumor and gossip, they arise more or less spontaneously, they are told with great frequency and intensity at a particular time, and they subside for a while, often, to be reborn in a somewhat different guise at another time in another place. It is not their falsity alone that qualifies them as collective behavior; indeed, all societies perpetuate myths—that is, factually incorrect beliefs. To the extent that such myths become incorporated into a culture's approved belief system, they are no longer a form of collective behavior.

For instance, the myth of George Washington as a young boy chopping down a cherry tree ("I cannot tell a lie") has been told to generation after generation of American school children in spite of its apocryphal character. It is not an example of collective behavior because it has become an institutionalized myth. It originated with a single individual, Parson Mason Locke Weems (1759–1825) in a single book, *The Life and Memorable Actions of George Washington* (1800)—ironically, a lie that was told for the purpose of teaching children to tell the truth. Myths such as this are too stable and too traditional to be a form of collective behavior. In contrast, contemporary urban legends and mass delusions are dynamic, evanescent, extrainstitutional phenomena. They arise, often independently in different locations. They are transmitted, they become transformed with each telling, they are constantly in flux, and they die down or out, often, only to be reborn and flourish again. They are, in short, excellent examples of collective behavior.

Six Classic Urban Legends

Below, I summarize six "classic" modern legends. They are stories that have been told as true in different locales around the United States for at least a decade; some are a half-century old. They are believed by most (although not necessarily all) tellers and a great many listeners. The stories below are only the "bare bones" of the tales as they are told, and are missing local details and variants. One quality of the contemporary legend is its spontaneity, that is, each time it is told, it is a little different. Here, in each story, only the major stable elements remain.

"THE BOYFRIEND'S DEATH"

A teenage couple is driving to a party when they run out of gas. The boy tells the girl that he's going to get some gas, and he'll return shortly. "Lock the doors and don't open them for anyone," he warns her, "you never know what kind of a maniac might come by." Well, some time goes by, and the girl hears a scraping on the roof of the car—"scrape, scrape, scrape." She becomes very frightened, and huddles in the car. An hour goes by, then two, then three. The scraping continues all night—"scrape, scrape, scrape." By now, the girl is scared to death. But she dozes off, and awakens when the sun comes up. A police officer is at the window with a horrified look on his face; his patrol car is parked nearby. He indicates to the girl that she should get out of the car, which she does. "Come with me," he says, *"and don't look back!"* But she does, and sees her boyfriend, hanging by a rope from a tree branch, his shoes scraping against the roof of the car (Brunvand, 1981, pp. 5–10).

"THE PHILANDERER'S PORSCHE"

A man in California saw an ad in a paper for an "almost new" Porsche—for $50. He rushed to the address to look at the car. The woman who answered the door verified the price of the car. Looking at it, he could discern no defect. He took it for a drive around the block, and still, it seemed fine. He handed the woman the money, and she gave him the necessary papers. But he had to know the answer to the mystery, and so, he asked her why she was selling it for such a ridiculously low price. Her answer was simple: "My husband ran off with his secretary a few days ago and he left a note instructing me to sell the car and send him the money. Well, that's what I'm doing!" (Brunvand, 1981, pp. 22–24).

"THE POISON DRESS"

A young woman was invited to a dance. For the occasion, she purchased an elegant dress from a local department store. During the dance, she began feeling dizzy, and her escort noticed an odor emanating from the dress. She went into the women's room, took off the dress, and examined it, but there appeared to be nothing wrong with it, so she put it back on and returned to the dance. Throughout the evening, she contineued to feel faint, and the odor remained. Her escort decided to take her home and call a doctor, but she died before he got there. An autopsy was performed on her, which revealed that she had formaldehyde in her bloodstream, which caused her blood to stop flowing. An investigation revealed that the dress she bought had originally been purchased and was worn by a corpse, but it was returned to the store and resold to the young woman. When she wore it, the formaldehyde entered through her open pores, and killed her (Brunvand, 1984, pp. 112–114).

"THE SNAKE IN THE BLANKET"

A woman shops in a local bargain center that imports products from all over the world, including the Far East. She picks up a blanket from a counter and begins examining it, running her hands over the material to check out its quality. Suddenly, she feels a prick on her arm. Thinking it is a pin, she goes home, but feels sick, and decides to go to a hospital. Shortly thereafter, she dies. It turns out that the blanket she was examining, which was imported from Hong Kong, had harbored a nest of snake eggs, which had hatched. One had bit her (Brunvand, 1981, pp. 160–171; Fine, 1989, pp. 154–156).

"THE VANISHING HITCHHIKER"

A man is driving along a road when he sees a young woman hitchhiking; he stops and she gets in, but insists on sitting in the back seat. She asks to be taken to a house a few miles down the road. When they arrive at her destination, he stops the car, turns around, only to find that she has vanished—except that she leaves her sweater behind.

The man knocks on the door of the house to return the sweater, and a woman answers the door. When the man explains what happened, the woman takes the sweater sadly, and tells him that her daughter has been dead for over a year—killed in an automobile accident at the very spot he picked her up—and that this is the third time she has made an earthly appearance (Brunvand, 1981, pp. 24–40).

"THE DEATH CAR"

A man answers an ad for an almost-new Buick for $200. He is told that the car is so inexpensive because the car's previous owner committed suicide in it, and his body wasn't discovered until months afterward, and "they just can't get the smell of death out of it" (Brunvand, 1981, pp. 20–22; Dickson and Goulden, 1983, pp. 133–134; Morgan and Tucker, 1987, p. 198).

FOUR CLASSIC COLLECTIVE DELUSIONS

The four cases discussed below—the "War of the Worlds" radio broadcast, the "Phantom Anesthetist of Mattoon," the "Seattle Windshield Pitting Epidemic," and the "June Bug Epidemic"—have been variously referred to as instances of mass hysteria, hysterical contagion, and mass panic. These terms imply three components on the part of a population, a segment of a population, or a substantial proportion of a population: (1) a mistaken *belief* about threatening events or their cause; (2) emotional *excitement* or *arousal* about these events; and (3) some sort of *mobilization*, that is, engaging in behavior to deal with these threatening events. It is not difficult to show that very few, if any, cases—including these that follow—qualify as examples of mass hysteria if these three stringent criteria are applied (Miller, 1985, pp. 98ff.). At the same time, if we broaden the notion of mobilization to include not only mass flight from a supposed threat, but a range of other activities as well—such as protests, rallies, marches, speeches, social movement activity, even giving or attending seminars and writing and publishing articles and books—then mobilization in response to a mistaken belief is extremely common in human history. I conclude this chapter with one example of this phenomenon, the current panic over satanism among some fundamentalist Christians.

However, if we were to focus exclusively on the *belief* component (Stewart, 1984)—that is, they are examples of widespread mistaken beliefs about a supposed threat of some sort—it is clear that they *do* qualify as instances of mass or collective delusions. Moreover, they are clear-cut examples of collective behavior: In each case, concern about, and belief in, a given phenomenon arose fairly suddenly, increased in intensity, peaked at a given point in time, and declined after that fairly quickly. In one instance, the entire trajectory took place in a matter of hours; in another, within less than a week; in a third, slightly more than a week; and in the fourth, the time span was a bit less than a month. (In this, these four cases differ from the cattle mutilation mystery, which stretched out over a dozen years.) In my view, we should not "throw the baby out with the bathwater"; that is, reject these cases as examples of collective behavior. Clearly, they fit as one type (collective delusion), even though they do not fit as another (mass hysteria). While relatively few people in a given area may engage in headlong flight in response to a perceived threat, a much higher proportion may have opinions that the threat *exists*. (And many may engage in behavior other than flight to deal with the putative threat.) For instance, Miller (1985, pp. 103, 111) claims the fact that less than one percent of the affected population *reported* cattle mutilations shows that it was not a true case of mass hysteria, which may be true. At the same time, 44 percent believed that the cattle were done in by mysterious agents (Stewart, 1977, 1980), which shows that, if the phenomenon was not a valid case of mass hysteria, it was one of collective delusion.

THE WAR OF THE WORLDS RADIO BROADCAST

The most famous case of collective delusion of all time—also, mistakenly, often referred to as a case of mass hysteria—is *The War of the Worlds* radio broadcast, which took place on the evening of October 20, 1938. In 1898, H.G. Wells published a science fiction novel, set in England, titled *The War of the Worlds*, which was about a Martian invasion of Earth. A key element in the novel was that fear and panic gripped the population in response to the threat of the invading Martians. Four decades later, the young actor and director, Orson Welles (no relation to the novelist, H.G. Wells), broadcast a radio play based on the novel under the auspices of the Mercury Theater; in the Welles version, the Martians landed in New Jersey.

From the point of view of collective behavior, the most remarkable thing about this broadcast was the fact that a substantial proportion of the listening audience—estimated at 28 percent, or 1.7 million of the total of six million listeners—believed that the drama was a news story of an actual Martian invasion. Of this 1.7 million, 70 percent (or 1.2 million listeners) became "frightened or disturbed" (Cantril, 1940, pp. 56, 58). In the words of the psychologist who studied the response to the radio play, "Thousands of Americans became panic-stricken. . . . Probably never before have so many people in all walks of life and in all parts of the country become so suddenly and so intensely disturbed as they did on this night. . . . Long before the broadcast had ended, people all over the United States were praying, crying, fleeing frantically to escape death from the Martians. Some ran to rescue loved ones. Others telephoned farewells or warnings, hurried to inform neighbors, sought information from newspaper or radio stations, summoned ambulances and police cars" (Cantril, 1940, pp. vii, 47). Said the 23-year-old Welles—no doubt tongue in cheek—while surrounded by reporters after the broadcast, "I'm extremely surprised to learn that a story, which has become familiar to children through the medium of comic strips and many succeed-ing novels and adventure stories, should have had such an immediate and profound effect upon radio listeners" (Klass, 1988, p. 48).

From today's perspective, it is clear that the degree of the panic described by commentators at the time—including the author of the research report that studied it—was greatly exaggerated. Very few people actually *did* anything in response to the broadcast, such as drove off in a panic or hid in a cellar. Even those that did, for the most part, engaged in quite reasonable behavior. One young man drove to be with his girlfriend, another to his family, a third to a parish priest; none drove away from where they thought the Martians were. Cantril (pp. 59–60) claims that the increase in the volume of telephone calls (in Northern New Jersey, a 39 percent increase during the hour of the broadcast, 25 percent during the following hour, less substantial increases elsewhere) indicates hysteria on the part of the callers. In fact, most of the calls represent-ed entirely reasonable reactions to the program: thanking the station for an interesting show; condemning the station for putting on such a scary, realistic show; calling friends and relatives to talk about the show. Even the calls that were based on a belief in the Martian invasion were similar to the kinds of reactions that people display during a disaster (Miller, 1985, pp. 107–108)—questions about where the caller could donate blood, when the National Guard would be mobilized, and whether casuality lists were available, were noted. It is clear that whatever the public reaction to *The War of the Worlds* radio broadcast was, it did not qualify as an instance of mass hysteria.

On the other hand, to convince nearly two million listeners that a radio drama about an invasion from Mars was an actual news broadcast has to be regarded as a remarkable achievement. What we have here is an example of a *collective delusion*—that is, a belief on the part of a substantial proportion of the listening audience that they faced a threat from an unlikely, improba-ble source. How was it possible for so many listeners to believe that the Earth was being invaded by Martians? While many commentators at the time depicted the believers as foolish, gullible, stupid, and hysterical, there were several factors that encouraged the mistaken belief.

First, most listeners tuned in too late to hear the one-minute announce-ment at the beginning of the program that the broadcast was a drama and not a news program about an actual event. From then until the end of the pro-gram, there were no other such announcements, except for a station break in the middle of the broadcast (which could easily have been missed in the excitement, or misinterpreted); there were no commercial breaks during the entire show.

Second, the program was revolutionary in its realism. Unusual for a drama at the time, it made use of the documentary technique. The first half of the show used an "open format" in which simulated news bulletins and on-the-scene reports repeatedly broke into what seemed to be routine programming, such as weather reports and dance music. In these simulated news flashes, it made use of static, microphone feedback, and background sounds of police sirens, the voices of milling, frightened, panicky, spectators—all routine in

In 1938, 23-year-old Orson Welles caused widespread panic in the northeastern United States by broadcasting a radio play based on H.G. Wells's novel, The War of the Worlds, *about an invasion from Mars. Some 1.7 million of the broadcast's audience thought that they really were listening to an attack by Martians.*

television dramas nowadays, but unusual in 1938. The actor who played the on-the-scene newscaster describing the monsters emerging from the space capsule spent hours studying the broadcast of an announcer reporting a then-recent actual disaster—the explosion of the zeppelin Hindenburg in May of 1937 in Lakehurst, New Jersey—and was inspired by his emotional, tearful account. The build-up of the drama, from the supposed "gas eruptions" on the surface of Mars, to the "seismograph registered shock of almost earth-quake intensity" near Princeton, New Jersey, to the interview with the farmer on whose property the space capsule landed, to the emergence of the Martians and their destruction of humans on the scene—including the death of the announcer—was constructed with cunning brilliance. The attack of the Martians was followed by the announcement, "Ladies and gentlemen, due to circumstances beyond our control, we are unable to continue the broadcast. . . . Evidently there's something wrong with our field transmission." This was extremely unusual for the time and convinced many listeners that the

Martian attack was real. In addition, the broadcast made use of the names of real places, which (as we'll see with urban legends) gave the broadcast an air of authenticity. In all, taken as drama, the broadcast was so well done that it is entirely plausible that it was taken by many listeners to be a depiction of real events. Said contemporary science fiction writer Paol Anderson, "It was very well done, *very, very* realistically done" (Klass, 1988, p. 48).

Third, a major reason why the broadcast caused so many listeners to believe it depicted an actual attack was "war jitters." The international crisis was deepening by the day, and many Americans expected war imminently (ten months after the broadcast, Nazi Germany invaded Poland, and World War II began). A higher proportion of listeners who believed the broadcast was about real events were concerned about the approaching war than was true of those who correctly interpreted it as drama. In fact, a substantial proportion of listeners became confused and thought that the events in the news flashes depicted a German or Japanese attack (Cantril, 1940, p. 160).

In short, there were some very good reasons for believing that the broadcast could have been depicting real events; we need not categorize listeners who were taken in as gullible or hysterical. Rather than condemn them, it seems wiser to try to understand how such a belief could have been so widespread. While it was mistaken, it was quite reasonable at the time. As students of collective behavior, it is our job to understand the origin of spontaneous, extrainstitional belief and behavior, however mistaken they might be. Whether or not the degree of panic that the broadcast touched off was exaggerated and sensationalized, reaction to *The War of the Worlds* radio broadcast is an instance of collective behavior. Said Douglas Forrester, who formed an organization to celebrate the 50th anniversary of the broadcast and its aftermath, "What happened that night was really an international event, a rich piece of Americana that deserves recognition. . . . It's one of *the* events of social psychology." Mr. Forrester's committee to commemorate the event has commissioned a bronze monument depicting a space ship, with Orson Welles at a microphone, and a family huddled around a radio, listening to *The War of the Worlds* broadcast. The inscription reads: "One million people believed it" (Barron, 1988).

THE PHANTOM ANESTHETIST OF MATTOON

On September 1st, 1944, in Mattoon, a small city in central Illinois, a woman had a friend call the police and tell them that she and her daughter had been gassed. The police came, but could find no intruder. Two hours later, when the woman's husband walked toward the house, he saw a man running from the window. The police were called again, and again they found no intruder. The next evening the local newspaper ran a front-page headline on the story, titled "Anesthetic Prowler on Loose" (Johnson, 1945, p. 175). This unusual set of events touched off a small wave of similar reports. The next day, two more reports of gassing—individuals waking up feeling sick, coughing, unable to walk—were made to the police. In both cases, they occurred prior to the newspaper story of the first report, but the victims "did not suspect gas until they read the papers [the] next day" (p. 176). Over the next eight days, 22 new cases of gassing attacks were reported by the citizens of Mattoon; in three of these cases, the reports speculated that the family dog was also a victim, "since he did not bark at the intruder" (p. 176). The reports ceased as quickly as they began, for after the 12th of September, no gassing reports were made to the police.

At first, the media took the reports at face value and assumed that a mad prowler was indeed on the loose. Sensationalistic newspaper headlines like "Mad Anesthetist Strikes Again" and "State Hunts Gas Madman" greeted their readers. Soon, the Chicago papers joined in on reporting the story, and eventually news services papers all over the world carried it; even *Time* and *Newsweek* reported the gassing incident. The first paragraph of one story read, "Mattoon's 'mad anesthetist' apparently took a respite from his maniacal forays Thursday night and while many terror stricken people were somewhat relieved they were inclined to hold their breath and wonder when and where he might strike next" (Johnson, 1945, p. 180). "Up to this point the reader is treated to an absorbing horror story—with a mysterious marauder whose 'maniacal forays' increase in a fantastic crescendo, a frightful new scientific device for gassing the victims, and a succession of tantalizing clues" (pp. 180–181).

Public reaction was not confined to the 25 or so individuals who claimed to have been gassed. The police wanted to catch the prowler in the act, and rushed to the scene of the crime "before the phone was back on the hook" (p. 177). Despite their efforts, no prowler was apprehended. The citizenry became apprehensive; some refrained from taking their evening stroll, and some were extra careful about locking their doors and windows. On the eleventh, the police commissioner issued a statement to the effect that "roving bands of men and boys should disband" and that guns be put away "because some innocent person may get killed" (p. 177). The number of nongasser prowling complaints to the police jumped significantly during the period of newspaper coverage of the gasser—declining to zero soon after the end of the epidemic—and, in fact, the total number of calls to the police for all reasons increased by a third during this period, and then, again, fell back to their previous level. Clearly, fear—a "mental epidemic"—was "sweeping through Mattoon" (p. 179).

However, by September 11, the tone of the media accounts changed; a hint of skepticism begins to creep into the stories. On the 12th, the phrase "hysteria abates" was used in a headline. The next evening, "a comic twist is given to the affair," when two false alarms turned out to be first a cat and then a doctor who forgot his keys trying to break into his own office. By the 20th, the local newspaper ran an editorial suggesting that much of the excitement "may have been due to hysteria" (p. 181); with that editorial, the story no longer ran in that paper. On the 17th, 18th, and 20th, a Chicago paper ran an interview with a psychiatrist suggesting that hysteria may have been behind the episode. On December 3, the same paper carried a story titled

"The Manhunt for Mr. Nobody." The *Time* and *Newsweek* articles were skeptical, even sarcastic. Within just a bit more than a week, the media shifted from printing positive and sensationalistic articles about the gasser to running articles that claimed that the gasser did not exist, attributing the fear to hysterical excitement, and then they dropped the story altogether.

THE SEATTLE WINDSHIELD PITTING EPIDEMIC

In March 1954, Seattle newspapers began publishing reports of damage to local automobile windshields—at first, to cars in a community 80 miles away, and eventually, to cars in Seattle itself. Windshields were said to be "peppered" or pitted with tiny holes. Speculation as to the cause of the windshield damage ranged widely, but focused largely on radioactive fallout from H-bomb tests in the Pacific earlier that year. Public concern about the holes was both generated, and could be measured, by newspaper coverage of the event. The number of column-inches devoted to the windshield phenomenon in two Seattle newspapers grew from 14 on April 13 to 22 on the 14th to 248 on the 15th. On April 16th, it declined to 210; on the 17th, to 109; on the 18th, to 62; and on the 19th, to 11. From then on, the story no longer received any newspaper attention. Calls to the police regarding pitted windshields, likewise, grew, peaked, declined, and ceased altogether very quickly. In the period between April 14 and the 18th, the police received 242 calls, then 46, then 10, and finally, no calls at all (Medalia and Larsen, 1958).

On the 19th of April, 1954, a survey was conducted of 1,000 residents of Seattle about the pitting incident. Half of the respondents (50 percent) were classified by the researchers as *believers*; that is, they believed that the damage was unusual and was caused by an "unusual physical agent," mostly the H-bomb test. Other causes included cosmic rays, vandalism, meteorites, and chemicals. Only a quarter of the sample (26 percent) were classified as *skeptics*; that is, they doubted that the damage was unusual and that anything other than ordinary road damage caused the pitting. The rest of the respondents were either undecided as to the cause or refused to answer.

In actuality, the windshield damage was not unusual and was not caused by any unusual or unnatural agents. People noticed the pitting—that had always been there—as one newspaper article suggested, because they were looking *at* their windshields for the first time, instead of *through* them. The pits were caused by simple road damage and the presence of bituminous coal in the atmosphere; the extent of the pitting increased with the age and the mileage of the car. Said a scientific panel from the University of Washington's Environmental Research Laboratory, "Although there is a considerable body of testimony from reputable witnesses to the effect that windshields are pitted by some mysterious cause . . ., it has *not* been possible to substantiate a single one of these statements by scientific observation. Actually, the observed facts tend to contradict such statements" (quoted in Medalia and Larsen, 1958, p. 181). The "Seattle windshield epidemic" proved to be an example of a collective delusion.

THE JUNE BUG EPIDEMIC _____

One day in June 1962, the workers in a textile plant located in a small city in the South, began to fall ill. The cause was attributed to "some kind of insect [that] was in a shipment of cloth that arrived from England" (Kerckhoff and Back, 1968, p. 3). In all, 62 workers—three men and 59 women, which represented one percent of all the men in the plant and nine percent of all the women—fell victim to the "bug." More than a dozen were hospitalized for its symptoms, which included severe nausea, numbness, cold sweats, stomach pains, and dizziness.

Two physicians, experts from Atlanta's federal Centers for Disease Control, several entomologists (biologists who are experts on insects), representatives of the plant's insurance company, representatives of a local exterminating company, and an engineer from the State Board of Health conducted a thorough investigation of the plant. The team located one black ant, a housefly, a couple of gnats, a small beetle, and a chigger, none of which could have caused the symptoms described. The experts concluded that the outbreak "was almost exclusively psychogenic in nature. There were probably no more bites at the plant during that week than in any other normal period at the plant" (p. 12). In short, they held, the epidemic was "an almost classic case of . . . 'hysterical contagion'" (p. 12). One Sunday, the plant was thoroughly sprayed by exterminators; on Monday, the workers returned to their jobs. Said one exterminator, "Whatever has been here ain't here now" (p. 7). Nearly all of the reports fell within an 11-day period, and 50 percent of them occurred in two consecutive days (p. 16).

While only six percent of the nearly 1,000 workers in the plant reported having been bitten, the vast majority believed that insects were responsible for the symptoms observed. Less than one worker in ten did not believe, and half of the total believed that *only* insect bites caused the illness. In short, with the "June bug epidemic," we see a contrast or contradiction between the "scientific" definition of the situation—that the evidence does not support bug bites being responsible for the symptoms—and the "social" definition, that is, that bug bites caused the illness to which the workers fell victim (p. 11). Not only did the workers "*believe* in the insect theory; many of them felt they had very impressive evidence of its validity." Said one, "I could see places on their arms and neck where little black bugs had bitten. We could see the bugs hop away. Then I could see the people being carried out" (p. 8). Said another, "I've got two little places on my arm where something bit me. They told us it was our imagination, but I don't think it was. One girl had convulsions so bad we all had to help hold her on the bed. She even foamed at the mouth" (p. 9).

The authors attribute the epidemic to psychological strain and physical fatigue—a speedup at the factory, too much overtime, difficulty in coping between work and caring for children, the strain of having to be the main source of financial support of their families, and not feeling that they could go to their supervisor with a work-related problem. In addition, the contagion fell into two distinct phases. In the first phase, social isolates—"unusual and socially insignificant" women with few friends in the factory—fell ill; they were the ones who started the epidemic. In the second phase, contagion followed "sociometric channels"; that is, women with friends in the plant tended to get sick if their friends got sick. At this point, the pattern became a kind of "crowd response" (p. 115)—a type of collective behavior (Kerckhoff and Back, 1968; Kerckhoff, Back, and Miller, 1965).

THE QUESTION OF FACTUAL TRUTH

To a radical or strict relativist, there is no such thing as a collective delusion, or a delusion of any kind; if you believe it, it's true—for you, at any rate—and if a collective believes it, so much the better. Some folklorists (Degh, 1977; Degh and Vazsonyi, 1976) insist that it is of absolutely no importance that a tale be literally and concretely false for it to be a legend or a folktale; objective or factual falsity should not be a criterion that defines the legend. While contemporary legends need not be defined by their truth value (the mass delusion is, of course, by definition, false), still, to the sociologist, it is important to note that they *tend to be* apocryphal stories; they are *usually* false, spurious, fallacious. Given what we know about how the world works, they are *unlikely* to have taken place. The truth value of legends is an important dimension because it is related to their credibility. While the literal, empirical truth of a statement or a story does not ensure that it will be believed and widely circulated, nor does the falsity of one guarantee that no one will believe it, factual truth is related to its credibility.

To put things a different way, empirical falsity is more *problematic* than empirical truth; we do not have to wonder so much about why empirically true statements or stories are believed and passed on. It is more interesting, sociologically strategic, and revealing that statements that are untrue or improbable are widely circulated. The more fantastic and unlikely the tale, the more powerful the forces impelling the members of a society to believe it must have been for it to have been believed and passed on. We do not wonder why someone believes and tells someone else that George Bush was elected President of the United States in 1988, that an earthquake hit northern California in October 1989, or that the United States landed men on the moon in 1969. The fact that such statements are made and believed would be boring, unproblematic, and commonsensically explained. On the other hand, if stories circulated to the contrary—that Bush's election was a fraud; that, in actuality, no earthquake hit California; that astronauts really didn't land on the moon—we might be very interested in how they got started and why they are believable, considering the fact that there is a great deal of evidence supporting what is widely believed. It is the departure of a given statement from concrete and literal truth that alerts the sociologist to the possibility that important social and psychological processes are at work.

To put the matter another way, many contemporary legends describe events that are themselves, supposedly, embedded in sociological and psychological reality. And we are, after all, social and behavioral scientists; we should have some idea of what is sociologically and psychologically plausible or likely with respect to the behavior described in a story. A contemporary legend is not only an account, interesting as a social and psychological creation, *but a description of reality as well.* It purports to relate events that, supposedly, literally took place. We should be led to ask some key questions when we hear or read one. Given what we know about how the world works, is the story credible? Is it plausible that the events being related actually and literally occurred? Are they even possible? To ignore the dimension of realism makes no more social or psychological sense than reducing their entire reality to a question of facticity or falsity. Each dimension is relevant; neither can be ignored.

In my view, the question of literal truth is crucial, because of an extremely important fact: Not only does a high proportion of the audiences of the stories I've included in this chapter *believe* the stories they've heard, but also, people who believe a given story *are more likely to pass it on* (Goleman, 1991; Rosnow, 1991). If we dismiss the dimension of concrete reality, we would also have to dismiss a question that audiences of both legend and rumor themselves regard as crucial—*is it literally, concretely true?* In my view, declaring this question irrelevant displays contempt for much of the audience of urban legends, an attitude that the sociologist should avoid.

At the same time, it must be emphasized that legends *are not necessarily completely untrue*; many, in fact, probably most, contain at least a grain of truth. Literal, concrete truth cannot be seen as an all-or-nothing affair; there are *degrees* of truth and falsity. Stories may be more or less totally true, substantially or partially true, they may contain a grain of truth, or they may be totally untrue in every detail. My guess is that legends are more likely to fall much closer to the completely untrue than the substantially true end of the continuum. No matter; it is important to keep in mind that truth value is *not* a defining criterion of a legend, and truth comes in degrees, not in black-or-white packages (Degh and Vazsonyi, 1976, 1978).

Take the story that huge, hungry alligators live in the sewers of New York City (Brunvand, 1981, pp. 90–98; Dickson and Goulden, 1983, pp. 1–3; Morgan and Tucker, 1984, pp. 149–153), a legend I heard when I was a graduate student in the early 1960s. It seems that vacationers, returning from Florida with baby alligators, decided they didn't want to keep them as pets and flushed them down their toilets, from whence they were deposited into the city's sewer system, only to grow to full-sized adulthood. Is the story true?

Some aspects of this story are clearly false, and some seem to be at least partially true. A two-foot baby alligator cannot be flushed down a toilet without causing it to become clogged up. If alligators were deposited in the city's sewage system, it would have to be through storm drains or manholes. Second, while there were several reports of alligator sightings in the 1930s (two, in fact, reported in *The New York Times*, in 1932 and 1935), none were made in the 1960s, when the legend proliferated. (The legend was current in the 1960s because of the publication of a popular book on the New York City sewer system in 1959 [Daley, 1959], which contained a chapter on the alligator story.) And third, in 1935, a sewer superintendent, Teddy May, dispatched several assistants into the sewers to check out the validity of the story. A small number of the reptiles were sighted and killed, but they were an average length of only two feet long, not of adult size. So, again, the story is not completely untrue, nor is it completely true. There is a *factual basis* for the alligator story, even though the number and size of the reptiles were exaggerated, the recency of their sightings was made much more current, and the route by which they ended up in the sewers was made more dramatic than it actually was. In short, the alligator-in-the-sewers story is partly true, but it is still a legend.

Another important point to be emphasized about the legend and the mass delusion is that belief, like literal truth, is a continuum. That is, not everyone who listens to, or even who tells, these stories actually believes them completely. As we saw with the cattle mutilation mystery, a minority of the residents of South Dakota (44 percent)—a sizeable minority, considering how amazing the story was—believed that the cattle were done in by mysterious agents. About the same proportion (42 percent) were skeptics and believed that the demise of the animals was probably caused by natural forces; the remainder weren't sure what happened (Stewart, 1980). At the same time, with legend, as with rumor, belief of a story one listens to is an important dimension of the picture; the more that people believe a rumor or a legend, the greater the likelihood that they will pass it on (Jaeger, Anthony, and Rosnow, 1980; Goleman, 1991). Consequently, belief cannot be dismissed as irrelevant.

Two folklorists (Degh and Vazsonyi, 1976) classify "participants in the legend process" into believers, indifferents, skeptics, nonbelievers, and proponents. Members of any of these categories can "participate in the process of legend formation and in the legend transmission." Disbelief or even outright opposition "does not prevent the legend from coming into existence by the legend process and from being passed through the legend conduit" (Degh and Vazsonyi, 1976, p. 117). Even the original creator of the legend "does not need to believe his story. He can add his doubts, his disbelief; he can tell it with a negative sign. The germ wrapped in the shell of incredulity might fall into fertile soil. It might happen that the incredulous proponent passes the rudimentary beginnings of a legend to a firm believer. If the story coincides with the common frame of reference of the man who has the believer's disposition, he will transmit his version with the addition of a positive sign. . . . And so the legend passes through the legend conduit: the continuation is endless as more and more people of diverse personality take part and shape the legend into untraceable variations" (Degh and Vazsonyi, 1976, p. 118). Although legends are more likely to be transmitted by believers than by skeptics, remember, belief and disbelief make up a continuum; not every time a tall tale is told does the teller necessarily believe in its literal truth. At the same time, such tales are *typically* believed, at least in major part, by their tellers. For instance, one common reaction when young people hear "The Hook" (see the boxed insert on page 304) is, "I don't really believe it, but it's pretty scary; I sort of hope it didn't happen" (Brunvand, 1981, p. 50).

It must be emphasized, however, that when I refer to legends and delusions as false, I mean one thing and one thing only: They tend to be false strictly within the empirical framework of the scientific method. Scientific facticity is only one of a number of dimensions of truth and falsity. A given statement may be false scientifically but true in other ways. Consider the 1960s rumor, discussed in Chapter 7, that a white (or Black) boy was abducted and castrated by a Black (or white) man. Considered strictly from an empirical perspective, there is absolutely no evidence that such an event ever took place. Factually, the tale may be regarded as false. But taken from other points of view, the story was, in a sense, true. For instance, the subjective reality of the story, *to many whites*, was that Blacks often commit violence against whites and thus are dangerous and threatening in their presence. *To many Blacks*, the reality of the story was that it confirmed the fact that the United States is a racist society and that whites often commit violence against African-Americans and get away with it. Thus, the castration story may be true *in a very different sense* than the scientific and the empirical sense—that is, it may be *felt* to be true, and may verify the life experience of many listeners and tellers. It is important to stress the point that truth and falsity may be looked at through a variety of perspectives, and each may be appropriate under certain relevant circumstances. However, it is important to keep in mind the particular dimension we are discussing when we refer to a statement's truth or falsity. If we are assessing the truth value of a given legend or story *from a strictly empirical point of view*, we are forced to admit that nearly all are false in most particulars.

Why Legends and Mass Delusions? General Factors

Why should the public tell and believe fantastic tales and apocryphal stories? What is the appeal of urban legends and collective delusions? Aren't we all knowledgeable and intelligent enough in this day and age to squelch them each time they are told to us, to "dead end" them whenever someone tries to convince us they are true events that happened to real people?

It will be noticed at once that collective delusions and, especially, contemporary legends, have some strong parallels with rumors (Mullen, 1972). In fact, because they are stories told without factual documentation, with respect to the *mechanism* by which they are transmitted, legends typically are rumors. (But recall that in terms of *content*, rumors tend to be about specific persons or events, while legends tend to be about general, cartoon characters.) So similar are they that some observers make little or no distinction between rumors and legends; two authors (Morgan and Tucker, 1984, 1987), in fact, title their books on urban legends, *Rumor!* and *More Rumor!*

Given their strong similarities, it should come as no surprise that the same factors that maximize the transmission of rumor also facilitate the transmission of modern legends and collective delusion: *(1) interest, (2) importance, or salience, (3) uncertainty or ambiguity, (4) anxiety, and (5) credulity.* That is, to the extent that a given subject or phenomenon is of subjective importance to a given group or in a given society, legends will tend to proliferate about it; to the extent that aspects or details of that subject or phenomenon are unknown or ambiguous, legends will tend to proliferate about it; to the extent that some individuals are anxious about some aspects of a given subject or phenomenon, legends will tend to proliferate about it; and to the extent that certain individuals are ignorant or gullible about some details of a given subject or phenomenon, they will be more likely to pass on legends about it. While it is likely that the origin of legends may be different from the origin of most rumors, the "transmission, form, and function" of the two seem to be quite similar (Mullen, 1972, p. 98).

Some of the tales told, in what are referred to as contemporary legends, that turn out to be mass delusions and contemporary legends are so fantastic, so totally lacking in objective credibility that, after sober reflection, it is difficult to believe that anyone took them seriously in the first place. Many, perhaps most, contain at least one key element that is so unlikely as to be all but impossible. The "bosom serpent" legends, for instance, mentioned earlier, depend on suspending knowledge that everyone has—that organic objects in the stomach will be digested; eggs, therefore, cannot possibly hatch in anyone's stomach. A dress that once draped a corpse is unlikely to have been returned to a store and resold to another customer, and it is unlikely to have absorbed enough formaldehyde to kill its wearer. A man running away from his wife would, in all probability, take his Porsche and, if he did not, his wife, in all probability, would sell the car and keep the money.

Moreover, many of these stories depend enormously on coincidence: someone being in exactly the right place at exactly the right time. For instance, the "lover's lane" couple had to hear the news flash of the maniac with the hook and drive off at exactly the time he tries to open their car door. (And why didn't he try to open the door with his good hand?) In real life, coincidences happen, of course, but their occurrence is statistically rare; the odds are extremely slim in each case. And lastly, the fact that these stories are supposed to have happened, independently, at different times and places and are retold in different guises should give teller and listener alike pause to question their factual content. Instead, when they hear two different versions, they typically respond by saying, "No, it didn't happen that way; the way it happened was. . . ." All of these factors make us wonder why these stories are told and believed. They cause us to ask, *"Why legends and collective delusions?"*

There are at least seven additional reasons, in addition to those that also propel rumors, as to why contemporary legends and collective delusions originate and circulate. To the extent that a given tale possesses these factors, or a combination of them, they will become modern legends or collective delusions that are widely told: (1) They tell a strong, interesting, dramatic story, (2) they tell a story with a meaningful moral or message, (3) they reflect contemporary fears, (4) they contain a "grain of truth" with respect to what is currently believed, (5) they supply supportive detail or local color, (6) they supply or point to a credible source, and (7) they are circulated by the mass media (Brunvand, 1981, pp. 10–12; Dickson and Goulden, 1983, pp. 128–135; Mullen, 1972). Some of these factors relate mainly to the intrinsic characteristics of the story itself and some to the general characteristics of the society in which they are told (or, to be more specific, to the relevance of these characteristics to the nature of the story).

A Dramatic Story. Interestingly enough, several factors that, objectively speaking, work *against* a story's believability from the objective perspective—for instance, simplicity and coincidence—actually make it more subjectively dramatic and interesting for many listeners, and therefore, to some, *more believable.* For instance, the appeal of "The Hook" rests in part in "the tidiness of the plot. Everything fits. On the other hand, the lack of loose ends would seem to be excellent testimony to the story's near impossibility." The story is too pat and too coincidental. "Too much, too much—but it makes a good story" (Brunvand, 1981, p. 50).

A Moral or Message. Urban legends and collective delusions contain a "meaningful message or moral," that is, they "teach valuable lessons." Their "primary messages are quite clear and straightforward" (Brunvand, 1981, pp. 10, 11). "The Hook" warns teenagers not to park and neck in lonely, isolated places. "The Snake in the Blanket" warns shoppers to be wary of products imported from exotic, faraway, and therefore dangerous locales. Many legends, it should be stressed, contain a xenophobic or racist element, for instance, the product rumor about workers urinating in a certain Mexican beer (Fine, 1989, pp. 159–160). "The Incident in the Elevator" reassures whites that many urban African-Americans are decent human beings. "The Solid Cement Cadillac" warns husbands not to be overly suspicious of their wives. "The Philanderer's Porsche" warns husbands not to abandon their wives and then assume they will act in a completely rational or generous fashion. "The Death Car" warns us not to expect a bargain without some strings attached.

In fact, much of the force of these stories rests in what is called "the belief in a just world" or "the just world hypothesis," which is "a fundamental delusion" (Lerner, 1980; Wachs, 1988, pp. 86–88) that people get pretty much what they deserve in life, that the righteous are rewarded and, more important, the evil or stupid are punished. Legends, in short, dispense "poetic justice," "the undeniable pleasure of getting even" (Brunvand, 1981, pp. 11, 24). The drama that stems from many legends is that the teller or the listener thinks, "Why were they so stupid? I wouldn't have done that; maybe they got what they deserved."

The wife "gets even" in selling her husband's Porsche. The husband's unjustified suspicion of his wife's infidelity was punished by the destruction, at his own hands, of his valuable birthday present—a Cadillac! Shoppers so foolish as to ignore warnings about the dangers of foreign products may suffer the ultimate punishment, death. On a superficial level, "The Bosom Serpent" legend, which has an extremely ancient origin, warns us to avoid contaminated waters. On an even deeper level, the tale warns women (and, emphatically, men as well) of the dangers of impregnation. Although, often, the only punishment the subjects of these stories suffer is fear or embarrassment ("The Hook" and "The Incident in the Elevator"). With many such stories, it is only through the intervention of an alert soul or sheer, blind good luck that they escape an even worse fate. In short, many of the unfortunate events told in urban legends are the result of bad judgment, poor luck, and doing the wrong thing. Time and time again the meanings of these stories are clear: "He should have known better," "She got what she deserved" (Brunvand, 1981, p. 190).

Contemporary Fears. "The Hook" originated in the 1950s when teenagers spent a great deal of time "necking" in cars and worrying about whether it was safe to do so. "The Solid Cement Cadillac" originated and was widely transmitted because many men are concerned about the sexual infidelity of their wives and want to be assured that this fear is groundless. Stories about finding things in or purchasing products from foreign countries corresponds to the fear that many Americans have that these countries are unsafe, threatening, and altogether too seductive for their own good. "The Incident in the Elevator" answers fears that many whites have of urban crime and Black people.

Stories about earthworms in McDonald's hamburgers (Brunvand, 1981, p. 90) or fried rats in Colonel Sanders' fried chicken (Fine, 1980) are generated and sustained because a huge number of Americans eat in fast food restaurants, and very few of us have any idea of the ingredients in their food. The fact that fast food is often called "junk" food implies that its contents are bad for us—and what could be worse than eating worms and rats?

The story—both a rumor and an urban legend—that circulated about Proctor and Gamble's supposed support of a satanic cult answers the concerns that fundamentalist Christians have about the secularization of contemporary society. They denounce homosexuality, abortion, drug use, sexual equality, humanism, liberalism, and the disintegration of the traditional family. So concerned are they about these trends that they fear that they may have their origins in intentional plots or conspiracies. The metaphor "the forces of Satan"—what they see as the origin of this corruption and decadence—takes on a literal meaning in the form of an actual, concrete satanic cult. And a company that sports a logo that seems to smack of occultism becomes the target of these bizarre speculations.

Stories about the bizarre and tragic things that babysitters do (for example, baking babies in the oven) reflect parents' concerns about leaving their children in the care of people they don't know well enough. Tales about someone doing something wrong with a microwave oven (exploding a small dog, for instance) reflect our fear of new, unfamiliar, and potentially dangerous technology. Urban legends exploit the fear that many people have that danger is lurking around every corner. Their stories make that fear a seeming reality.

A Grain of Conventional Truth. However false, conventional beliefs provide the foundation for the credibility that urban legends possess for some listeners. Outlandishly amazing stories—those that violate our sense of how the world works—are rarely believable to most of us; however, stories that possess a few key commonsensical details or elements become far more persuasive. For instance, "The Death Car" originated with a true story: In 1938, in a small town in Michigan, a man did commit suicide in his car, a distinctively styled 1929 Ford, and his body wasn't discovered for three months (Brunvand, 1981, p. 20; Dorson, 1959, pp. 250–252). Indeed, the tale is so believable that it made the rounds in England after 1951 as "The Ineradicable Blood-Stain" (Sanderson, 1969, p. 250). Of course, beyond the existence of the car itself, the rest is fancy: There was no "ineradicable" bloodstain, and no incredibly low price. But many people would love to believe that such bargains exist if only they keep their eyes and ears open, and to them, the "smell of death" that "they just can't get out" seems a likely explanation for the amazingly low price. One folklorist reports that the tale was so believable during its heyday in Lansing, Michigan, that "Buick dealers were flooded with calls about the non-existent smelly car" (Brunvand, 1981, p. 22; Dorson, 1959). While legends must "make sense" to many listeners, they make sense *only within a certain conventional framework*; they need not make a great deal of sense to someone who is being hardheaded, factually oriented, and objective.

Supportive Local Detail.   Stories are credible to the extent that they contain "a semblance of seemingly supportive specific detail" (Dickson and Goulden, 1983, p. 130). "Most legends give concrete detail which grounds them in reality; place names are mentioned, names of people are given and details of setting are described" (Mullen, 1972, p. 99). The way the legends are summarized in the boxed insert (see page 309) is misleading in that they do not supply local color; "anchoring" stories to specific locations and specific individuals gives them their believability. A coat imported from Hong Kong and costing a specific amount is purchased at a specific store at a specific shopping mall; a woman is bitten by a snake and taken to a specific hospital and dies; the story is hushed up but the sister of an intern working in the hospital where the woman died tells a specific reporter on a specific newspaper, who is told by his boss to keep the whole thing quiet. Stories like this thrive on such detail; the more details about familiar locales a story contains, the more credible it will be. Of course, this may also work against the story, since anyone who is at least half-way enterprising can check out the veracity of the story by asking people knowledgeable about these locales. Luckily for the survival of such stories, few people ever care to verify them, and so they continue to be told and believed.

A Credible Source.   Stories take on credibility to the extent that a specific source is named: a newspaper reporter, a scientist, a physician, a lawyer, a government official. The best source of all is, of course, the eyewitness or the person to whom the experience happened. Lacking that, the source that is invoked is simply the person who transmitted the story, who is, supposedly, only one person away from the eyewitness. In a very high proportion of urban legends, the source is a "friend of a friend," the "foaf" for short. Many tellers are convinced that they can track down the ultimate source of the story they tell, that is, the person to whom the events happened. When asked more closely about the events in question, "It usually turns out instead that they only heard them from other friends; and so it went through legions of friends and relatives beyond counting who had always *heard of* but have never *seen*" or *experienced* the events or phenomena in question (Brunvand, 1984, pp. 50–51). The fact is, most people are not very careful about passing on stories that sound interesting, and they rarely think very hard about where the story comes from. So common is the "foaf" in propagating contemporary folklore that a newsletter dedicated to news about "contemporary legend research" is entitled *Foaftale News*.

The Mass Media.   Another common source of many contemporary legends is the mass media; in fact, much of what is communicated in the news contains folkloric or legend-like qualities (Bird, 1976; Baker, 1976; Degh and Vazsonyi, 1979). A famous example of this is the spurious history of the installation of the first bathtub in the White House by President Millard Fillmore in January 1851. The story was made up by journalist H.L Mencken in an article published in New York's *Evening Mail* on December 29, 1917. The story was taken seriously and the hoax was passed on in numerous articles and books thereafter. In the *Chicago Tribune*, and again in the *Boston Herald* in 1926, Mencken confessed that he had made the whole thing up. However, his retraction did nothing to stem the tide of repetitions of the legend. It has been cited countless times as true—in articles and in newspapers all over the country; in 1966 on Johnny Carson's "The Tonight Show"; in 1976 by three network television anchormen Harry Reasoner, Roger Mudd, and John Chancellor; and, incredibly, even in a book of history, *The Americans: The Democratic Experience*, by one-time director of the Library of Congress, Daniel Boorstin (1973). The jacket of a book, *Presidential Anecdotes* (Boller, 1981), depicts a smiling Millard Fillmore sitting in a bathtub, smoking a cigar. Once an interesting, dramatic story is launched by the media, it becomes extremely difficult to put an end to it, even after countless factual refutations.

Like the "foaf," citing the media as a source takes on credibility; it validates a story passed on by tellers. "I read it in the paper" is shortened by folklorists to "rip"—"read in the paper." Just as when the person whose friend's friend had the experience, the friend cannot be tracked down; also, the person who 'read it in the paper' never has the clipping in hand or the exact reference available" (Brunvand, 1984, p. 52).

There is, in short, a set of contradictory qualities that legends and mass delusions must possess. "On the one hand we want our factual lore to inspire awe, and at the same time we wish to have the most fantastic tales include at least a hint of a rational explanation." Urban legends "gratify our desire to know about and try to understand bizarre, frightening, and potentially dangerous or embarrassing events that may have happened" (Brunvand, 1981, p. 12). In short, legends infuse the mundane, the everyday, and the prosaic with shock, amazement, and wonderment.

In attempting to understand how legends are generated and sustained, it is necessary to realize that, for many people, certain assertions about events that take place are simply more credible than others. Many people find fiction—that is, what is not true—more believable than the facts; they are more likely to believe certain versions of events than others. To them, fiction is better than fact; the truth is often harder to swallow and more difficult to assimilate. Truth is usually more complex and more qualified; it rarely fits clearly or neatly into what many of us take to be true. Moreover, truth—that is, events as they literally and concretely unfolded—is almost always less interesting than fiction.

There is a saying, "Truth is stranger than fiction," which is, of course, completely fallacious if examined carefully. What is usually meant by the statement is that *some* truth is stranger than *some* fiction. But the strangest truth is never as strange as the strangest fiction. It can't be. Fiction is bound by no rules whatsoever except those of drama and audience response, whereas fact is bound by certain rules of causality and logic. In fact, in many ways, the rules of drama and those of fact are almost entirely contradictory: Often, what's true is boring, and what's fascinating and amazing is untrue. Truth is sometimes strange *because* it is truth, that is, literally and concretely true; because it is bound by the rules and constraints of the real world, we are amazed that it can be so strange. But this is very different from saying that it is *stranger* than fiction. The "strangeness" of fact and fiction are judged by entirely different standards. To put things a different way, imagine that a given book, which you thought was a literally true account of concrete events, was in fact a novel—a work of fiction. Would it seem less (or more) remarkable? Most people would find it less so. Richard de Mille (1980, pp. 17–18) opines that Carlos Castaneda's "Don Juan" works were fobbed off as nonfiction rather than announced as the fiction they actually are because they were *remarkable* as judged by the standards of fact (if what was described literally happened, the books were amazing), but *unremarkable* by the stricter standards of fiction. "Readers love a true adventure even if badly told" (de Mille, 1980, p. 18).

People who feel strongly about a given issue, or those who are in a highly emotionally charged situation, rarely wish to examine all sides of an issue, to weigh the pros and cons and arrive at a reasoned conclusion. They want their views verified by the facts of the real world. Almost anything that takes place will become a stimulus, a cue, or evidence to verify their views. Recall the castration rumor that circulated in Detroit in the late 1960s (Rosenthal, 1971). If this rumor was told among Blacks, the victim was always Black and his attacker was white; if it was told among whites, the victim was white and the attacker, Black. As we know, there was no castration of any boy, Black or white, and no attacker, again, Black or white. This tale—as much a rumor as an urban legend—is so appealing as an affirmation of the evil intentions of racial and ethnic groups other than one's own during periods of turmoil and conflict that it has been told in hundreds of different locations at different times.

In fact, in one form or another, the story of the castration or mutilation of a boy of one racial or ethnic group by a member of another goes back at least as far as the fifth century A.D. Earlier variants of the legend had it that ancient Romans were sacrificed by Christians (Ellis, 1983) and, later, that Christian boys were sacrificially mutilated by Jews (Ridley, 1967). If a story is circulated about a highly unusual event, it is entirely possible that that story is true; on the other hand, if the same or a very similar story crops up again and again in many different locations and at different times, it not only seems extremely unlikely that it took place in the literal sense, but it is also extremely likely that the story arose because it answers some need or function in the relations between hostile or rival groups in a society. In other words, it is "a tale told too often" (Ridley, 1967).

The same was true of the rumor that touched off the race riots in Detroit in 1943 (Lee and Humphrey, 1968): If it was Blacks who were spreading the rumor, it was a pregnant Black woman who was thrown off a bridge by a mob of angry whites; if it was spread among whites, it was a pregnant white woman who was thrown off a bridge by a mob of Blacks. Both versions were false from the strictly factual point of view, but both expressed the extant fears and anxieties of whites and African-Americans toward members of the other racial category. Members of each racial group felt resentment against members of the other race and were prepared to believe almost any manner of nasty rumor about the other, however flimsy the evidence. In truth, not every event in the real world is going to cooperate in verifying the beliefs we hold or predelections we have about how things take place. But these beliefs and predelections do help explain how myths and legends are transmitted.

WHY LEGENDS AND MASS DELUSIONS? INDIVIDUAL FACTORS

It has become fashionable to debunk earlier collective behavior research that showed that certain kinds of people are more likely to pass on clearly false rumors, propagate legends, and fall victim to mass hysteria. (See Miller, 1985, pp. 98–99, 110–111 for an example.) Such research, some claim, often makes the individuals involved "seem stupid, gullible, and dangerous" (Miller, 1985, p. 98). While such objections may have some merit—indeed, responsible social researchers should respect their subjects, informants, and respondents, and never use their data to denigrate them—the fact remains that certain individuals or categories of individuals *are* more likely to believe and pass on certain assertions as true, and some of these assertions *are* extremely unlikely to be factually correct. However laudible it may be to defend "the man and woman in the street," some of the beliefs they hold may not be empirically valid, and it *is* a legitimate goal of social science to understand how and why erroneous beliefs are held and transmitted. On the other hand, we should not fall victim to the fallacy that claims that experts are infallible and always know more than the ordinary person. Indeed, experts are often wrong in their judgments about the workings of the world, as any glance at the history of the past century so plainly shows (Cerf and Navasky, 1984).

Most of the broad, general cultural factors that encourage legends and delusions do not address individual differences in believing and passing on such stories. Even though certain anxieties and fears may be current and widespread in a given society, not everyone shares those fears, and thus, they may not find the stories that reflect these fears relevant or believable. Fear fuels the dissemination of both urban legends and rumor, but fear is an individual *and* a structural variable. Individuals in whom a given story arouses a great deal of fear and anxiety are more likely to *believe* it and *pass it on* than those who are not made fearful by it. It is possible that stories are told in part to *allay* fears, because the teller wishes to have their particulars *refuted* by the listener. Yet, when listeners hear and believe the story, the fears of tellers *escalate* rather than diminish (Goleman, 1991). Thus, fear can be both encouraged by a given situation and it can vary from individual to another in the same situation. This applies to most characteristics that influence the dissemination of both legend and rumor (Kimmel and Keefer, 1991).

As we saw earlier, only seven percent of the American population believes that Elvis Presley may still be alive, and 44 percent of the population of South Dakota believed that mutilated cattle were gone over and done in by unusual agents. It is highly likely in both instances that believers are different from nonbelievers. In short, legends are not circulated randomly with respect to tellers, listeners, and believers.

Why does one person find a given story silly and implausible, while another takes it as gospel and tells it to his or her friends as a real-life event? Individual factors distinguishing believers from nonbelievers may be divided into the following: (1) hearing a legend, (2) finding it interesting or remarkable, (3) believing it as literal truth, and (4) passing it on. These factors may not necessarily be found together in the same person, or the same set of persons. For instance, someone may have a great many friends and hear a great deal of rumor, gossip, and contemporary legend from them; another may have few friends and be a social isolate, hearing relatively few stories from others. But the first person (who *hears* many legends) is a skeptic and does not believe them and so does not pass them on, while the second (who hears relatively *few*) is gullible, believes everything, and passes them all on to the few people he or she knows. On the community level, Medalia and Larsen (1958, p. 186) found that in the Seattle windshield pitting incident, *interest* in the event declined at a time when *belief* that it occurred as a result of unusual forces actually persisted at a high level. Clearly, then, several individual characteristics are related to disseminating contemporary legends, not just one. With that in mind, let us examine some of these characteristics.

Credulity.   Certainly the dimension of *gullibility* or *credulity* versus *critical set* plays a role here (Buckner, 1965; Rosnow, 1988), as it does in rumor. Some people do not probe too deeply into a remarkable and unlikely story they hear, while others, perhaps more knowledgeable about some of the story's crucial details, find it too implausible to be true. Some members, to be frank about it, are simply more likely to believe and, possibly, transmit far-out stories that have little or no factual basis than others.

One researcher (Stewart, 1980) examined the individual characteristics that were related to belief in (but not necessarily transmission of) the cattle mutilation delusion. He divided his sample into *believers*—those who believed, implausibly and, as it turns out, incorrectly, that mysterious agents killed and mutilated cattle and horses—and *skeptics*, those who believed, correctly, that the animals were done in and gone over by natural agents, such as illness and scavengers. Individuals who corresponded to one of these two categories were significantly different in a number of respects.

Media Source. Individuals who regarded radio and TV as their most important source of information during these episodes were more likely to be believers (49 percent) than skeptics (37 percent); individuals who regarded their friends and relatives as their most important source of information were also more likely to be believers (50 percent) than skeptics (39 percent). On the other hand, a preference for written sources of information, such as newspapers, was more characteristic of skeptics; those who prefered newspapers were more likely to be skeptics (49 percent) than believers (37 percent). The print media, flawed as they are, are more likely to present news in a detailed, concretely valid fashion than the broadcast media or the rumors of friends and relatives, which tend to be more sensationalistic.

Age. The very young are more likely to be believers than older individuals; again, in Stewart's study, among respondents age 20 and younger, nearly two-thirds (64 percent) were believers and only a quarter (28 percent) were skeptics, whereas only slightly more than a quarter (28 percent) of those in their 40s were believers and over half (54 percent) were skeptics. The most likely explanation for this relationship "appears to center upon previous knowledge of or contact with phenomena smilar to the discovery of mutilated cattle. Older persons are more likely to have encountered something similar during their life and tend to be more skeptical and undecided about the cause; whereas, younger persons are more likely to lack the critical experiential base and, therefore, tend to accept one of the believers' explanations of cause" (Stewart, 1980, pp. 14–15).

Education and Occupation. There tend to be educational and occupational differences between believers and skeptics. In Stewart's study, four-fifths of individuals with a post-college education or an advanced degree were skeptics (80 percent); only fifteen percent were believers. On the other hand, over half (57 percent) of those with some high school education were believers and only 30 percent were skeptics. (The pattern did not quite hold for individuals with less than a high school education, probably, as we'll see, because most were farmers.) In addition, professionals (41 percent believers, 56 percent skeptics) and farmers (40 percent believers, 52 percent skeptics) were more likely to be skeptical about the explanation of unnatural causes than was true of blue-collar (50 percent believers, 34 percent skeptics) and white-collar workers (44 percent believers, 40 percent skeptics). Farmers (who made up a high proportion of individuals with less than a high school education) were skeptical because of their "knowledge and experience with cattle raising," while respondents with a college education "are likely to voice skepticism because of training in and appreciation for the scientific-naturalistic method of determining cause" (p. 17).

Medalia and Larsen (1958, pp. 184, 185) found much the same dynamic, except that the impact of education was far more pronounced among men than women: Three times as many well-educated men were skeptical about unusual agents pitting Seattle windshields as was true of men with the lowest level of education. In *The War of the Worlds* broadcast, too, education played a major role: Respondents with a grammar school education were twice as likely to believe that the program was news than was true of those with a college education (Cantril, 1940, p. 112). Education was found to be "influential in enabling people to check on the authenticity of the program" (p. 114); better educated respondents "were able to call upon certain standards of judgment which they thought were trustworthy" (p. 116). They were more likely to make internal checks (for instance, that events occurred in the program too rapidly to be real life) or external checks (for instance, looking outside the window or calling friends or the police to determine if what was happening on the radio was really happening in real life).

Personal Relevance.   Another characteristic that is related to the transmission of urban legends is the *personal relevance* of a given legend for the lives of those among whom it is told. Certain legends are more likely to be told to certain individuals, or kinds of individuals. When they hear them, they are more likely to find them interesting and relevant to their lives, and they are more likely to transmit them to others. "The Hook," for instance, is of interest mainly to teenagers—that is, individuals who park and "make out" in cars—and of more relevance for girls, who see the maniac with the hook as far more threatening, than boys. "The Boyfriend's Death," too, holds more fascination for teenage girls, who can picture themselves cowering in the car at night, than boys, who are more likely to be puzzled and annoyed by the date's hanging. Tales about the bizarre behavior of babysitters are mainly of relevance either to teenagers who babysit or parents who rely on the services of babysitters. In the 1960s, I heard an urban legend about "Manhattan Silver," a form of marijuana that was supposed to have grown in New York City's sewers, and was, supposedly, unusually potent. (I did not believe the story, and, in fact, it turned out to be erroneous.) It was likely to be relevant only to marijuana users. (Or, in my case, to someone who was doing research on marijuana users.) Anti-Semites are more likely to believe stories demonstrating the cunning and avarice of Jews (such as the famous "Protocols of the Elders of Zion") than are individuals who do not hold prejudiced views of the Jewish people. Racists love and tell stories that show Blacks in a negative light.

A story that originated in Europe and became popular in the United States in the 1960s, "The Runaway Grandmother," exemplifies the importance of personal relevance. It seems that a family, accompanied by their elderly grandmother, is on vacation. During the trip, the grandmother dies; they strap her body to the roof of the car and return home. On their way, the family stops off at a restaurant for a bite to eat. When they get back to the car, they discover it has been stripped of its contents, including the body. They tell the police, and return home. Time goes by, and the body is never recovered. Meanwhile, the family discovers they cannot collect grandmother's insurance or inherit her estate because of the absence of the body.

This story, a modern geriatric tale, is more relevant to the lives of individuals who have to deal with the question of what to do with their elderly parents than those who do not have to worry about this question. "In the legend, a family cannot even go on its once-a-year annual vacation without being plagued by grandmother." The unwelcome presence of grandmother "transforms family pleasure into nightmare. . . . The psychological purpose of the legend is . . . to get rid of grandmother." But then, "there is one striking unpleasant consequence of grandmother's death: what to do with the body?" The guilt conjured up by such a fantasy is assuaged by the theft of the body. The family need not feel guilty about wishing her dead: "the legend kills off grandmother and eliminates the body with a minimum of guilt." But not so fast! The legend seems to say that you don't get to enjoy the fruits of your wish-fulfillment because, as a result of your getting rid of the old lady, you can't inherit her money. Even though "the primary wish of getting rid of grandmother is fulfilled," still, she "is a burden whether she is alive or dead" (Dundes, 1971, pp. 33–36). Again, personal relevance plays a role here in that the legend is likely to be interesting to, and, one would predict, told by individuals who have the responsibility of caring for their elderly parents and who experience this as a burden in their lives.

MASS PANIC AND COLLECTIVE HYSTERIA: DO THEY EXIST?

In Woody Allen's film, *Radio Days* (1987), a couple is out on a date, parked in an isolated spot. It is October 30, 1938. Orson Welles' *The War of the Worlds* is playing on the radio. A Martian invasion of Earth is announced. Suddenly, the man jumps out of the car and runs off into the night in terror. While this scene is meant to be amusing, it exemplifies the view that the media and much of the public have of common reactions to a disastrous threat, real or imagined: fear, panic, hysteria, and terror. The fact that the threat is fictional makes such reactions even more dramatic and memorable.

In fact, these reactions are markedly atypical. As we saw in real disasters, most people "keep their cool" when faced with danger, and very few engage in terror-stricken, life-threatening behavior in response to that threat. It is remarkable, even when assessing people's behavior in disasters in which many lives are lost, how rare panic actually is. People tend to panic, as we saw from the disaster literature, only when their lives are in immediate, imminent danger and no escape route is available, or one is available but is quickly disappearing. As we saw, the classics of the "mass panic" or "mass hysteria" literature (Cantril, 1940; Johnson, 1945; Medalia and Larsen, 1958; Kerckhoff, Back, and Miller, 1965; Kerckhoff and Back, 1968) more properly exemplify cases of collective delusion in that a sizable proportion of the affected population—in some cases, a majority, in others, a substantial minority—believe that a nonexistent agent is threatening their health or their lives. To believe something that is not true is one thing; to engage in hysterical, panicky, terror-stricken behavior as a result is quite another. If we apply the three criteria stipulated by Miller (1985, pp. 98ff), mentioned above—a mistaken belief, emotional excitement, and mobilization in a substantial proportion of the population—mass hysteria is so rare as to be practically nonexistent.

On November 13, 1973, a Swedish radio station broadcasted a fictitious 11-minute news bulletin about a nuclear accident at a power station in Baresbäck, in southern Sweden. As with *The War of the Worlds* radio broadcast, the producers of the show used the documentary method; by all accounts, it seemed realistic. And as with the Welles broadcast, the media carried stories of widespread panic and hysteria in the area. Newspaper and television accounts of the panic claimed that the telephone lines to police stations, fire stations, and the mass media were jammed, that people formed long lines to get into air raid shelters, that people collected their valuables, piled into their cars, and caused traffic jams on the highways. The panic picture was never seriously questioned; it was taken for granted in later discussions of the broadcast and reactions to it. The producers of the broadcast were condemned as irresponsible by the media, by opinion makers, by politicians, and by much of the public.

A month after the broadcast, a team of sociologists (Rosengren, Arvidson, and Sturesson, 1975) interviewed a sample of local residents to determine their responses. Roughly 20 percent of the adult population in the area had heard the program; about half of those who listened did not realize that it was fictional, and, of those who misunderstood, about 70 percent were "frightened or disturbed." No one in the sample of 1,000 respondents phoned the police, the media, or the authorities, and not a single respondent exhibited panic flight of any kind. Roughly one percent of the population in the affected area did anything at all in response to the broacast; in most cases, it was simply to contact friends, neighbors, or relatives. (Two telephone exchanges were jammed for a brief period of time.) There was no escape panic at all, and there were no traffic jams on Sweden's highways as a result of the program. The major variable influencing whether the listeners misunderstood the nature of the broadcast was tuning in too late to hear the program's initial explanation that it was fictional in character. In short, the picture of widespread panic was not only exaggerated but, in some cases, was invented altogether.

In many ways, the important story about the Baresback incident was not the panic behavior of the public, which ranged from mild to nonexistent, but the sensationalistic behavior of the media. The broadcast took place too soon before prime time news for television reporters to cover the story adequately and conscientiously and then meet their newscast deadline. As a result, they did an extremely superficial job, based mainly on a few atypical cases and the reporters' conjecture of what the public's reaction *was likely to be*. And once TV's inaccurate story sank into the public's mind, that became the dominant reality for anyone who thought about or discussed the incident. Two telephone exchanges jammed for a short period of time, through the media's exaggeration, became telephone exchanges all over southern Sweden jammed for a very long period of time. One or two people getting into their cars and driving home to make sure their families were safe, became a massive traffic jam on highways for scores of miles around. Seven percent of the population of the area feeling "frightened or disturbed" magically turned into millions of people feeling terror stricken and hysterical.

The Baresback "panic" became a *summary event*; that is, it became a staged or pseudo-event that focused attention on a given issue, in this case, the dangers of nuclear energy. "Paradoxically, the originators of the programme succeeded by failing. There was, at last, a certain revitalization of the debate on nuclear energy. It was a healthy debate . . ., but its foundations were somewhat shaky; a fictitious disaster, a fabricated panic. . . . The disaster and the panic [however], were defined as real, and consequently they had real effects" (Rosengren, Arvidson, and Sturesson, 1975, p. 321).

In short, mass hysteria and mass panic are extremely unusual events and take place under extremely unusual circumstances. Reports of them should be regarded with a strong measure of healthy skepticism. Panic is far more common in fiction and, unfortunately, in news stories about disasters or supposed disasters in real life. In a film released in 1989, *Miracle Mile*, a rumor about an impending nuclear attack (which later turns out to be true) causes widespread panic in Los Angeles. Everyone is seized in the grip of terror; the center of the city is gridlocked with cars, which smash into one another and into plate glass windows; citizens machine gun one another in the street. In *2001*, a science fiction film (1969), authorities do not inform the public about a black monolith discovered on the moon for fear of widespread social disorganization. If any lesson is to be learned from this chapter, it is this: People often hold silly, clearly erroneous beliefs, but they are far less likely to *act* on them, and very, very rarely do they completely lose their critical capacity, take leave of their senses, panic, and rush headlong away from seeming danger, causing chaos, havoc, and anarchy, endangering their lives, the lives of others, and the viability of communities and entire societies as well. Such behavior belongs in fiction; it has no place in factual accounts of the real world. It is even possible that we should rename the phenomenon, as Bartholomew suggests (1990); since "mass hysteria is pejorative, connoting a pathology of some kind, perhaps "collective exaggerated emotions" is a less evaluative term. In any case, it plays a more substantial role in our imagination than in real life.

A CURRENT LEGEND: SATANISM AND CHILD MURDER

Beginning in the early 1980s, and especially after 1984, a tale has been told on a national scale that qualifies as a contemporary legend, a collective delusion, a moral panic, and, when told among believers, a rumor panic as well (Victor, 1989, 1990, 1991; Jenkins and Maier-Katkin, 1990; Thompson, King, and Anetts, 1990; Richardson, Best, and Bromley, 1991). It seems that a nationwide (and even international) conspiracy of satanists is kidnapping (and breeding) children in order to use them in satanic rituals, which includes sexually molesting, torturing, mutilating, and then murdering them. Most or at least a significant proportion of cases of missing children, sexual molestations, and child pornography, the legend claims, have a satanic connection. Geraldo Rivera, a popular talk show host, summed up the legend when he opened one of his many shows on satanism with the following words: "Satanic cults! Every hour, every day, their ranks are growing. Estimates are there are one million satanists in this country. The majority of them are linked in a highly organized, very secret network. From small towns to large cities, they've attracted police and FBI attention to their satanist ritual child abuse, child pornography, and grisly satanic murder. The odds are this is happening in your town." ("Devil Worship: Exposing Satan's Underground," NBC television documentary, October 25, 1988).

These practices are taking place on a vast scale, these observers claim. Some 50,000 to 60,000 (even up to two million, some estimates have it) children are being murdered *each year* in satanic rituals. This conspiracy is being covered up at the local and national level because of ignorance, fear, and complicity on the part of authorities. Police officials, teachers and day-care workers, newspaper editors, and even judges and politicians are part of the conspiracy, this legend proclaims. Evidence of satanic ritual child murders is all around us, its supporters aver. Satanists use animals as sacrifices before murdering their human victims; the dead, mutilated bodies of animals may be found in communities all across the country, they argue. Tens, perhaps hundreds, of thousands of children are missing each year, and no one is doing anything about it. Sexual molestations, satanic rituals, and animal sacrifices are taking place on a routine basis in day-care centers from coast to coast, and, again, officials are silent. Accounts by dozens of cult "survivors," detailing their childhood participation in satanic rituals, have been given on such talk shows and news programs as "Geraldo," "Oprah," "20/20," and "Sally Jesse Raphael." Dozens of books demonstrating the link between satanism and child murders have been published in the 1980s and 1990s and have received widespread attention. Who could doubt such convincing evidence?

As we've already seen, the ritual sacrifice of children by evil outsiders is a tale with roots extending back in history at least a millenium and a half. In ancient Rome, during the time of the early Christians, ironically, Christians were said to be kidnapping Roman children and murdering them in their unholy rituals (Ellis, 1983). In the Middle Ages, Jews were said to perform blood sacrifices on Christian boys (Ridley, 1967). The fact that a nearly identical story crops up independently a number of times, as we saw with the many other urban legends, does not necessarily or automatically mean that the story is false. However, it does force us to wonder whether it might have been similar historical and cultural circumstances that made the story plausible to some members of a society—or the fact that it tells a gripping, dramatic tale—rather than the story representing an accurate rendering of literal concrete events.

Evidence.   It should be said at once that, as with the historical stories of the ritual sacrifice of children by evil agents, the contemporary version of the tale has not received evidentiary corroboration of any kind. No solid physical evidence, or, in fact, evidence of any kind of any of these claims has ever been offered to support the satanism-child sacrifice link. Circles of satanists *do* exist, of course, several extremely tiny cults with a total national membership of no more than a thousand, not counting scattered satanic "dabblers" unconnected to any organized cult. (Actually, at least in its stated policy, the Church of Satan specifically forbids its members to abuse children, drugs, and animals.) And children *are* sexually molested, of course; roughly one in six to one in seven American children have been sexually molested at least once by their 18th birthday (Russell, 1986, p. 10; Finkelhor, 1979, p. 53). However, these molestations very, very rarely take place in day-care centers; most often, they are committed by relatives, neighbors, or older friends. And child pornography rings *do* exist, of course, but evidence of their link with satanism has never surfaced. And all of the numbers on missing children and child murders cited by the advocates of the satanism claim are almost literally impossible. The official yearly number of criminal homicides—the total number of murders of all people from all sources—in the United States given by the FBI is roughly 20,000. The Justice Department estimates that less than 600 children are kidnapped by strangers each year in the United States; over the past five years, less than 500 are still reported as missing. In contrast about 2,000 children are murdered by their parents each year. Not a single satanist-child murder claim has been borne out by the facts.

Characteristics of Believers.   However, the most interesting feature of the satanism story to students and researchers of collective behavior is not its concrete falsity. At the same time, the fact that it departs *so radically* from the facts should lead us to ask why and how it arose, circulates, and is believed. The social settings in which this modern legend circulates—especially when contrasted with those circles where it has no currency at all—tell us a great deal about its appeal to the former. More specifically, we should be able to apply some of what we learned in Chapter 8 on gossip and rumor. As we saw there, rumormongering is most likely to take place under conditions of maximum anxiety and ambiguity among people who are likely to be highly gullible.

In which social circles are we more likely to find these characteristics? Believers of the satanism tale are almost exclusively fundamentalist Christians, overwhelmingly live in rural areas or small towns, and tend to have relatively low levels of education (Victor, 1989, 1990, 1991). The story typically takes root in areas that are hardest hit by an economic recession; it is most likely to be believed and circulated by individuals who have experienced a serious erosion of traditional values in recent years, especially those pertaining specifically to the family (Victor, 1989; Bromley, 1991). The characteristics and ideology of believers in the satanism tale give us a powerful clue in understanding why such a story has currency nowadays. It is the life circumstances of certain individuals and categories of individuals that make the satanism claims "culturally plausible" (Bromley, 1991). It should be emphasized in the most forceful terms possible that *not all or even most* small-town fundamentalist Christians believe the satanism-child murder legend. However, each factor mentioned by the current research increases the likelihood that a given individual will do so.

Literal Reality Vs. Metaphor.   To us, the satanism story may be taken not so much as a literal description of concrete phenomena that exist and events that are taking place in the world—which is, of course, how they are taken by its believers—but as a *metaphor*, a tale that represents, stands in for, or *symbolizes* an actual state of affairs. That is, "the satanism claims may be *metaphorically true* even if *empirically false*" (Bromley, 1991; my emphasis). To individuals with a certain kind of background living in certain life circumstances, the legend *appears to be* true because of events that are *really* happening that, to them, *very much represent events that happen in the story.* People are receptive to legends to the extent that the story they hear and tell resonates with their preconceptions and their notion of the way things are. *Indisputable evidence* tells some relatively uneducated, blue-collar rural and small town fundamentalist Christians that the satanism legend is true. The myth explains a great deal about things they *know* are true. In other words, certain assertions about satanist happenings will be "relatively unaffected by the lack of evidence" (Bromley, 1991) because a very *different* form of evidence will be taken as supporting those assertions. And it will be the ideology and life circumstances of such individuals that will convince them that evidence that *doesn't* satisfy most other individuals will convince *them* that they are true.

Subversion Myths.   The first and most important fact about the satanism legend is that it is a *subversion myth* (Bromley, 1987, 1991; Victor, 1991). It is a story that explains to members of certain social circles why things are going wrong, why their way of life is being undermined or subverted, and who and what is responsible for the decay of what they most value; it also explains who has introduced practices they regard as an abomination. Subversion myths (some of which may be at least partly true) *demonologize* certain individuals or categories of individuals, holding them responsible for the evil that has rained down recently on the heads of the righteous—that is, these individuals have been characterized as metaphorical devils. These individuals are depicted as subversives—"the embodiment of ultimate evil" (Bromley, 1991). Such individuals typically are scapegoats for the troubles of the members of the social circles who propagate such myths.

Institutional Crisis.   The second crucial aspect of the satanism story is that members of certain segments in American society are facing what Bromley (1991) calls an *institutional crisis.* That is, events are sweeping over them that make previous desirable traditions and practices difficult, untenable, or impossible. In nearly all social change there are winners and losers. Over the course of the 20th century, and especially since the end of World War II (1945), many traditional institutions have been eroded or undermined. Families have gotten smaller and there has been a decline in domesticity, a loss of family control, prestige, and power; government and business have gained in power and size; religion has become less influential, less integral to American culture, and itself markedly secularized. In the eyes of many traditionalists, there has been a virtual explosion of drug use, pornography, teenage sex, abortion, violence, crime, and delinquency, and non- and anti-Christian cults. Many traditionalists feel that they are witnessing the death throes of a once-viable and worthwhile way of life that stood at the center of their existence.

More specifically, the recent, immense growth of several practices or institutions convince many fundamentalist Christians that the satanism tale must be true.

Abortion.   Perhaps the most prominent among them is the legalization and growing legitimacy of abortion. In a way, *if we grant some basic fundamentalist Christian assumptions,* children *are* being slaughtered in extremely large numbers in the United States each year. If we agree that the fetus is a full human being, a child in the same way that an infant is, then it follows that abortion represents the murder of children on a very large scale. Since 1973, when abortion was fully legalized in the United States (see Chapter 11 on a social movement that has attempted to overturn legal abortion), nearly a million abortions have been performed each year—a total of between 15 and 20 million during this period. Legal abortion can be seen as the triumph of a kind of conspiracy of secular humanists—who are seen as being in league with Satan—who have managed to wield their influence over God-loving and God-fearing Christians. In this sense, children *are* being slaughtered by "the forces of Satan"—not literally, of course, but metaphorically. To the fundamentalist Christian, it is a very small step from the metaphor to the concrete reality, from believing that abortions are legally performed by physicians on women who voluntarily request the operation, to believing that children are being kidnapped or bred by an organization of satanists for the purpose of unholy ritual slaughter. In short, abortion is a "concession to the Devil *little less overt* than an actual ritual sacrifice" (Jenkins and Maier-Katkin, 1990, p. 18; my emphasis).

Women Working. Another trouble recent change has wrought has been in the area of women working. In the past 40 years, the proportion of women with preschool children who are employed outside the home increased by nearly five times, from 12 percent in 1950 to nearly 60 percent in 1990. To the traditionist, this development is a catastrophe. A woman's place is in the home, caring for her young children, teaching them traditional values. By taking a job, the woman is neglecting her most important function and exposing her children—and herself—to danger. To a fundamentalist Christian mother with old-fashioned values, being forced to work because of difficult economic circumstances represents the triumph of evil over good; of secularism over religious values; and of having to give up power and autonomy to an alien, uncaring, godless world. To the religious right, the trend toward an abandonment of women's traditional role as homemaker in favor of a job outside the home can only erode the strength of traditional Bible religion, and strengthen the hand of modernism and secularism—tools of corruption in the hands of Satan.

Day Care. Almost as important as the legalization of abortion is the recent explosion of children in day cares. The decay of the family is nowhere as evident as in the proliferation of day-care centers for preschool children. Instead of remaining home with their mothers, children are now being cared for and raised by strangers. Half of all preschool children are being cared for during a significant period during the day by someone other than their parents. Who are these people? Where do they come from? What are they doing with our children? What are they teaching them? What are their beliefs? Can we trust them? Such fears are likely to breed insecurity, powerlessness, paranoia, a suspicion that one's loved ones are being hurt and corrupted, and a receptivity to subversion myths. By emphasizing the fact that satanic ritual abuse is widespread, traditionalists are invoking a metaphor to demonstrate that day-care centers are "an extremely dangerous place for the young" (Jenkins and Meier-Katkin, 1990, p. 17).

Atrocity Tales. The satanism legend represents an example of an *atrocity tale*—a real or imaginary event that is intended to evoke moral outrage and generate action against the alleged perpetrators (Bromley, Shupe, and Ventimiglia, 1979, p. 43). Atrocity tales are routinely disseminated by social movements whose aim is to galvanize support for their cause. Such stories describe *extreme,* rather than more routine, examples, aspects, or practices. Ironically, to gather support for the *typical* conditions they oppose, social movements must invoke *atypical* ones. For instance, it is not enough for opponents of pornography to criticize the centerfolds in *Playboy.* Indeed, "soft-core"—which a very substantial proportion of Americans are not particularly troubled by—is the most common form of pornography. In order to generate public support to attack, restrict, or outlaw pornography, activists must convince the public that truly offensive pornography is the norm toward which all pornography is tending, or, at the very least, is more common than it actually is, or is thought to be. Thus, the assertion that "snuff" films, in which women are actually murdered on camera, are a common fixture of pornographic fare, or are to be expected, given the very nature of, and appeal of, pornography. The "snuff" film thus serves as an "atrocity tale" for antipornography activists (Thompson, King, and Anetts, 1990). Atrocity tales supply concrete evidence to the unconcerned, the uncommitted, and the fence-sitters that outrage and activism are justified and necessary, documentation that the outlook of the activist is a correct one. Activists need not be so cynical as to peddle a tale they know is untrue; many atrocity tales are actually believed to be typical or characteristic by those propagating them.

In a like fashion, stories about the satanic ritual slaughter of innocent children serve as "atrocity tales" for Christian fundamentalists. It is not enough to argue that American society has become secular, irreligious, and humanistic. Any audience listening to such a statement is likely to respond with, "So what else is new?" The satanic legend offers a dramatic and extreme realization of the fears of religious traditionalists. It provides a concrete reason for the fundamentalist's opposition to secular humanism, documentation of the fruit of contemporary developments. It declares, "You see what happens when godless secularism is permitted to fester?" And it purports to describe in graphic terms what most of us would regard as just about the worst thing that could possibly happen: The unpunished murder of our children. Such an appeal, if true, cannot fail to galvanize outrage, a call to action, and, in some circles, support for the fundamentalist Christian cause. The fact that no solid evidence exists to support such claims makes it impossible for most individuals not located in rural or small town, blue-collar, relatively uneducated, fundamentalist Christian social circles to accept the legend.

SUMMARY

Legends are hearsay—stories told without sufficient factual documentation—and so, by their mechanism, they are technically rumors. On the other hand, their content is so different from the ordinary, garden-variety rumor that they belong to a separate category altogether. While ordinary rumors are about concrete people and events, legends are about abstract, general, or cartoon people and events. Collective delusions are also rumors in their lack of factual documentation, but, again, somewhat different in content. The collective delusion is the belief in a story that is clearly false yet is told as true and is widely believed. Paranormal beliefs, another variety of rumor-like tale, challenges conventional science. Contemporary legends and mass delusions are dynamic, evanescent, extrainstitutional phenomena and are therefore forms of collective behavior. Over the years, some have been studied and have taken on a "classic" quality—for instance, modern legends, such as "The Boyfriend's Death" and "The Philanderer's Porsche," and collective delusions, such as "*The War of the Worlds* Radio Broadcast," "The Phantom Anesthetist of Mattoon," and "The Seattle Windshield Pitting Incident."

Some folklorists regard the question of factual truth as irrelevant to the study of legends. Sociologically, this is not entirely the case, since untrue stories are likely to be transmitted and believed in a somewhat different fashion than those that are true.

Researchers have isolated a number of factors that encourage the transmission (and belief) of modern legends and mass delusions. Certainly some of the same factors that operate in the transmission of rumor operate here as well—interest, salience, uncertainty or ambiguity, and credulity. In addition, the factors of a dramatic story, a moral or message, contemporary fears, a grain of conventional truth, supportive local detail, a credible source, and the mass media are influential. The belief in contemporary legends is tightly tied in to the desire to believe a good story, especially one that verifies the values one's group holds dearly.

Individuals vary in the likelihood that they will believe in and/or transmit a legend. Researchers have isolated four such individual factors: critical set versus credulity, age, education, and the personal relevance of the tale for people's lives.

Nearly all accounts of mass or collective panic, with people not only believing a given false story but also mobilizing on a mass basis in fear of its threat, turn out to be wildly exaggerated or false. Like contemporary legends and collective delusions themselves, stories about mass panic are recounted and believed because they tell one hell of a good story!

Perhaps the most striking of all recent contemporary legends—which is, at once, a rumor when told locally, and a collective delusion as well—is the satanism-child sacrifice tale. A very large number of individuals believe that tens of thousands (and perhaps as many as several million) children are being kidnapped (or actually bred for the purpose) each year, forced to take part in satanic rituals, sexually molested, then murdered. They believe a nationwide (and even international) ring of satanists is perpetrating these atrocities, which are being ignored or covered up by the authorities. The story is implausible to most hard-headed observers, and no hard, solid evidence has ever been presented to document it. At the same time, it is plausible in some social circles because of their members' world-view. Satanist stories document the concerns of some small-town fundamentalist Christians about the decay of traditional values and practices, and offer a dramatic appeal to return to those values and practices.

References

Baker, Ronald L. 1976. "The Influence of Mass Culture on Modern Legends." *Southern Folklore Quarterly*, 40 (September–December): 367–376.

Barron, James. 1988. "Fondly Recalling a Martian 'Invasion.'" *The New York Times* (September 16): B1, B3.

Bartholomew, Robert E. 1990. "Ethnocentricity and the Social Construction of 'Mass Hysteria.'" *Culture, Medicine and Psychiatry*, 14 (December): 455–494.

Bird, Donald Allport. 1976. "A Theory for Folklore in Mass Media: Traditional Patterns in the Mass Media." *Southern Folklore Quarterly*, 40 (September–December): 285–305.

Boller, Paul F., Jr. 1981. *Presidential Anecdotes.* New York: Oxford University Press.

Boorstin, Daniel J. 1973. *The Americans: The Democratic Experience.*

Bromley, David G. 1987. "Subversion Mythology and the Social Construction of Social Problems." Paper Presented in November at the Annual Meeting for the Scientific Study of Religion, Lexington, Kentucky.

Bromley, David G. 1991. "Satanism: The New Cult Scare." In James T. Richardson, Joel Best, and David G. Bromley (eds.), *The Satanism Scare,* pp. 49–72. New York: Aldine de Gruyter.

Bromley, David G., Anson D. Shupe, Jr., and J.C. Ventimiglia. 1979. "Atrocity Tales, the Unification Church, and the Social Construction of Evil." *Journal of Communication,* 29 (Summer): 42–53.

Brunvand, Jan Harold. 1981. *The Vanishing Hitchhiker: American Urban Legends and Their Meaning.* New York: W. W. Norton.

Brunvand, Jan Harold. 1984. *The Choking Doberman and Other "New" Urban Legends.* New York: W.W. Norton.

Brunvand, Jan Harold. 1986. *The Mexican Pet: More "New" Urban Legends and Some Old Favorites.* New York: W.W. Norton.

Brunvand, Jan Harold. 1989. *Curses! Broiled Again!* New York: W.W. Norton.

Buckner, H. Taylor. 1965. "A Theory of Rumor Transmission." *Public Opinion Quarterly,* 29 (Spring): 54–70.

Cantril, Hadley. 1940. *The Invasion from Mars.* Princeton, N.J.: Princeton University Press.

Cerf, Christopher, and Victor Navasky. 1984. *The Experts Speak: The Definitive Compendium of Authoritative Misinformation.* New York: Pantheon Book.

Daley, Robert. 1959. *World Beneath the City.* Philadelphia: Lippencott.

Degh, Linda. 1977. "UFO's and How Folklorists Should Look at Them." *Fabula*, 18: 242–248.

Degh, Linda, and Andrew Vazsonyi. 1976. "Legend and Belief." In Dan Ben-Amos (ed.), *Folklore Genres*, pp. 93–123. Austin: University of Texas Press.

Degh, Linda, and Andrew Vazsonyi. 1978. "The Crack on the Red Goblet or Truth and Modern Legend." In Richard M. Dorson (ed.), *Folklore in the Modern World*, pp. 253–272. The Hague: Mouton.

Degh, Linda, and Andrew Vazsonyi. 1979. "Magic for Sale: *Märchen* and Legend in TV Advertising." *Fabula*, 20: 47–68.

de Mille, Richard (ed.). 1980. *The Don Juan Papers: Further Castañeda Controversies*. Santa Barbara, Calif.: Ross-Erikson.

Dickson, Paul, and Joseph C. Goulden. 1983. *There Are Alligators in Our Sewers and Other American Credos*. New York: Delacorte Press.

Dorson, Richard M. 1959. *American Folklore*. Chicago: University of Chicago Press.

Dundes, Alan. 1971. "On the Psychology of Legend." In Wayland D. Hand (ed.), *American Folk Legend: A Symposium*, pp. 21–36. Berkeley: University of California Press.

Ellis, Bill. 1983. "De Legendes Urbis: Modern Legends in Ancient Rome." *Journal of American Folklore*, 96 (2): 200–208.

Ellis, Bill. 1988. "The Varieties of Alien Experience." *The Skeptical Inquirer* (Spring): 263–269.

Fine, Gary Alan. 1979. "Cokelore and Coke Law: Urban Belief Tales and the Problem of Multiple Origins." *Journal of American Folklore*, 92 (366): 477–482.

Fine, Gary Alan. 1980. "The Kentucky Fried Rat: Legends and Modern Society." *Journal of the Folklore Institute*, 17 (May–December): 222-243.

Fine, Gary Alan. 1989. "Mercantile Legends and the World Economy: Dangerous Imports from the Third World." *Western Folklore*, 48 (April): 169–177.

Finkelhor, David. 1979. *Sexually Victimized Children*. New York: Free Press.

Goleman, Daniel. 1991. "Anatomy of a Rumor: It Flies on Fear." *The New York Times*, (June 4): C1, C5.

Hicks, Robert D. *In Pursuit of Satan: The Police and the Occult.* Buffalo: Prometheus Books.

Hufford, David J. 1982. *The Terror That Comes in the Night.* Philadelphia: University of Pennsylvania Press.

Jaeger, Marianne E., Susan Anthony, and Ralph L. Rosnow. 1980. "Who Hears What From Whom and with What Effect: A Study of Rumor." *Personality and Social Psychology Bulletin,* 6 (September): 473–478.

Jenkins, Philip, and Daniel Maier-Katkin. 1990. "Satanism: Myth and Reality in a Contemporary Moral Panic." Paper Delivered Before the 42nd Annual Meeting of the American Society of Criminology, Baltimore.

Johnson, Donald M. 1945. "The Phantom Anesthetist of Mattoon: A Field Study of Mass Hysteria." *Journal of Abnormal and Social Psychology,* 40 (2): 175–186.

Johnson, George. 1987. "The Infamous 'Protocols of Zion' Endures." *The New York Times* (July 26): 6E.

Kagan, Daniel, and Ian Summers. 1984. *Mute Evidence.* New York: Bantam Books.

Kerckhoff, Alan C., and Kurt W. Back. 1968. *The June Bug: A Study of Hysterical Contagion.* New York: Appleton-Century-Crofts.

Kerckhoff, Alan C., Kurt W. Back, and Norman Miller. 1965. "Sociometric Patterns in Hysterical Contagion." *Sociometry,* 28 (1): 2–15.

Kimmel, Allan J., and Robert Keefer. 1991. "Psychological Correlates of the Transmission and Acceptance of Rumors about AIDS." *Journal of Applied Social Psychology,* 21(19): 1608–1628.

Klass, Philip. 1988. "Wells, Welles and the Martians." *The New York Times Book Review* (October 30): 1, 48–49.

Lee, Alfred McClung, and Norman D. Humphrey. 1968. *Race Riot* (Detroit 1943). New York: Octagon Books.

Lerner, Melvin J. 1980. *The Belief in a Just World: A Fundamental Delusion.* New York: Plenum Press.

Maher, Brendan A. 1988. "Delusions as the Product of Normal Cognitions." In Thomas Oltmanns and Brendan A. Maher (eds.), *Delusional Beliefs,* pp. 333–336. New York: Wiley.

Medalia, Nahum, and Otto N. Larsen. 1958. "Diffusion and Belief in a Collective Delusion: The Seattle Windshield Pitting Epidemic." *American Sociological Review,* 23 (April): 180–186.

Miller, David L. 1985. *Introduction to Collective Behavior.* Belmont, Calif.: Wadsworth.

Morgan, Hal, and Kerry Tucker. 1984. *Rumor!* New York: Penguin Books.

Morgan, Hal, and Kerry Tucker. 1987. *More Rumor!* New York: Penguin Books.

Mullen, Patrick B. 1972. "Modern Legend and Rumor Theory." *Journal of the Folklore Institute*, 9: 95–109.

Oltmanns, Thomas F. 1988. "Approaches to the Definition and Study of Delusions." In Thomas F. Oltmanns and Brendan A. Maher (eds.), *Delusional Beliefs*, pp. 3–11. New York: Wiley.

Richardson, James T., Joel Best, and David G. Bromley (eds.). 1991. *The Satanism Scare*. New York: Aldine de Gruyter.

Ridley, Florence H. 1967. "A Tale Told Too Often." *Western Folklore*, 26 (2): 153–156.

Rojcewicz, Peter M. 1987. "The Men in Black Experience and Tradition: Analogues with the Traditional Devil Hypothesis." *Journal of American Folklore*, 100 (April–June): 148–160.

Rojcewicz, Peter M. 1988. "Strange Bedfellows: The Folklore of Other-Sex." *Critique: A Journal Exposing Consensus Reality*, no. 29: 8-12.

Rorvik, David. 1980. "Cattle Mutilations: The Truth at Last." *Penthouse* (September): 121–122, 142–144.

Rosengren, Karl Erik, Peter Arvidson, and Dahn Sturesson. 1975. "The Baresback 'Panic': A Radio Programme as a Negative Summary Event." *Acta Sociologica*, 18 (4): 303–321.

Rosenthal, Marilynn. 1971. "Where Rumor Raged." *Transaction*, 8 (February): 34–43.

Rosnow, Ralph L. 1988. "Rumor as Communication: A Contextualist Approach." *Journal of Communication*, 38 (Winter): 12–28.

Rosnow, Ralph L. 1991. "Inside Rumor: A Personal Journey." *American Psychologist*, 46 (May): 484–496.

Russell, Diana E.H. 1986. *The Secret Trauma: Incest in the Lives of Girls and Women.* New York: Basic Books.

Sanders, Ed. 1976. "The Mutilation Mystery." *Oui* (September): 51–52, 92ff.

Sanders, Ed. 1977. "On the Trail of the Night Surgeons." *Oui* (May): 79–80, 121ff.

Sanderson, Stewart. 1969. "The Folklore of the Motor-Car." *Folklore*, 80: 241–252.

Sirois, Francois. 1974. *Epidemic Hysteria*. Copenhagen: Munskgaard.

Stewart, James R. 1977. "Cattle Mutilations: An Episode of Collective Delusion." *The Zetetic* (Spring/Summer): 55–66.

Stewart, James R. 1980. "Collective Delusion: A Comparison of Believers and Skeptics." Unpublished Paper Delivered April 3 Before the Midwest Sociological Society, Milwaukee.

Stewart, James R. 1984. "On the Nature of Mass Hysteria." Unpublished Paper Delivered Before the Midwest Sociological Society, Chicago.

Thompson, Bill, Alison King, and Jason Anetts. 1990. "Snuff, Sex, and Satan: Contemporary Legends and Moral Politics." Paper Presented to the International Society for the Study of Urban Legends, Sheffield, England.

Victor, Jeffrey S. 1989. "A Rumor-Panic About a Dangerous Satanic Cult in Western New York." *New York Folklore*, 15 (1–2): 23–49.

Victor, Jeffrey S. 1990. "Satanic Cult Legends as Contemporary Legend." *Western Folklore*, 49 (January): 51–81.

Victor, Jeffrey S. 1991. "The Dynamics of Rumor—Panics about Satanic Cults." In James T. Richardson, Joel Best, and David G. Bromley (eds.), *The Satanism Scare,* pp. 221–236. New York: Aldine de Gruyter.

Wachs, Eleanor. 1988. *Crime-Victim Stories: New York City's Urban Folklore*. Bloomington: Indiana University Press.

CHAPTER
9

FAD, FASHION, AND CRAZES

C hange has been more dramatic and substantial in the 20th century than in any other previous 100 years in history in the West during urbanization; the virtual disappearance of the family farm; the decline in family size; the entry of women into the labor market; the expansion of the middle class; the achievement of near-universal education; the extension of the lifespan into old age; the development of mass marketing; and the invention of television, the airplane, the computer, and awesome weapons of destruction—these are just a few changes that have transformed Western society in deep and fundamental ways during the past century.

At the same time, some types of change, while perhaps no less notable, are less consequential and more superficial; they have had a less consequential impact on the other aspects of society. Some changes do not transform society fundamentally; their impact is more superficial. Does it matter in some fundamental or long-term sense that men sport beards or not, that women wear short or mid-length skirts, that purple is "in" or "out," or that one toy versus another is popular? Certainly no one would argue that a change from one of these to the other is going to have the kind of impact on as many other aspects of life that the changes mentioned above have had. The introduction of computers into our lives has transformed the way we think, act, and feel; in contrast, fads, fashion, and most crazes are usually far more limited in their impact. Typically, they have little direct relevance outside their relatively narrow, concrete sphere.

At the same time, fads, fashion, and crazes are intriguing to study for at least three reasons. First, *they reveal general processes at work.* They show that society is a more fluid, dynamic, and less structured phenomenon than some believe. In the adoption of these forms of collective behavior, we are informed about lines of influence; and in miniature, they reveal how social change takes place—or at least can take place. Fads, fashion, and crazes provide a revealing social laboratory for certain important general social processes.

Second, while fads, fashion, and crazes generally do not have a fundamental or wide-ranging impact, they are the *products* of culture and social structure and, hence, reflect what a society is like and is going through at a given point in time. Each society produces its own special types of fads, fashion, and crazes; hence, examining them reveals as much about a given society as its art, its games, its television programs, its advertising.

Third, while fads very rarely have momentous consequences for the society in which they take place, in some ways, fashion sometimes does, and some crazes—a very few—*do* generate important, fundamental, and even lasting changes. No one would question the importance of the multibillion dollar clothing and apparel industry; and temporary infatuations, such as economic manias and religious revivals and persecutions, may transform the society in which they occur utterly and permanently.

Most of us have a fairly clear idea of what fads, fashion, and crazes are. Popularly defined, a *fad* is an activity or product that has two qualities. First, it is *temporary,* that is, it is taken up and dropped fairly quickly, and second, it is trifling or insignificant (it operates or exists in a fairly trivial area of life). The word *fashion* has a wider range of meaning; usually, it applies to a broader range of activities and phenomena than is true of the fad. As it is relevant here, fashion is regarded as a style or custom in a given area, usually dress and manners, that changes over time. And what we usually regard as a *craze* (or a "mania") is a temporary activity that has become obsessively, intensely important to a small group of enthusiasts—for a short period of time, their lives seem totally wrapped up in it. While fads, fashion, and crazes have much in common, they also differ in important respects as well. These phenomena are best illuminated by means of separate discussions.

WHAT ARE FADS?

What do goldfish swallowing, telephone booth stuffing, bungee jumping, piano hacking, Volkswagen swallowing, chain letters, dance marathons, bolo ties, psychedelic art, citizen's band (CB) radios, lava lamps, streaking, the Twist, hula hoops, the turkey trot, bean-bag chairs, coughing ashtrays, Davy Crockett coonskin caps, zootsuits, tie-dyed shirts, pie throwing (or pie "killing"), edible panties, paper clothes, bell-bottom trousers, flagpole sitting, breakdancing, Rubik's Cube, "The Fonz," Dungeons and Dragons, toga parties, droodles, the hunt game, slap bracelets, Teddy Ruxpin, the Watusi, Billy Beer, pop rocks, pet rocks, the Schmoos, 3-D movies, the Twist, subway graffiti, slam dancing, bed racing, Nehru jackets, the Farrah Fawcett look, the Whacky Wallwalker, the hustle, and panty raids have in common?

They all are examples of the fad. According to one definition, fads are "a rapid, sudden, and ephemeral collective adoption of novel behavior which affects only superficial and trivial areas of life" (Gold, 1964, p. 256); according to another definition, they are "an amusing mass involvement defined as of little or no consequence and in which involvement is brief" (Lofland, 1985, p. 68). The "superficial," "trivial," and "no consequence" aspects of the definition *imply* that such involvements will be brief, for, if they have no substance, they cannot last. To label something as "only" a fad is to criticize it as being both insubstantial and temporary. Fads may be *products* (Davy Crockett coonskin hats in the 1950s), *activities* (bungee jumping in the 1980s and 1990s), *words* or *phrases* ("groovy" in the 1960s), or public figures, *characters*, or *heroes* (Henry Winkler as "The Fonz" in the 1970s). In addition, purchasing some types of products usually entails engaging in a specific activity as well—such as purchasing and then using citizen's band (CB) radios, skateboards, or video games—while other products do not, such as lava lamps and psychedelic art. However, whether they are products, activities, words, or public figures, their sudden, sharp rise and fall in popularity marks fads off from ordinary, everyday, more or less conventional activities or products.

Cyclical Fads.   A number of fads existed for some time before their surge in popularity; in fact, some observers believe, fads are not so much invented or born as *rediscovered* (Meyersohn and Katz, 1957, p. 597). So much is this the case that, for many fads, it is impossible to trace their origin, and there is often dispute as to who did what first. (See, for instance, Zetterberg, 1989, on the origin of the frisbee.) Consequently, one may refer to the "multiple origins" of many fads (Aguirre, Quarantelli, and Mendoza, 1988, p. 576). In addition, some fads do not simply disappear once they have ceased to be popular; they may continue to be engaged in or purchased, although at a much lower level than their peak, long after their popularity has waned. What makes an activity or product a fad, however, is its *volatility*—the suddenness of its rise in popularity, the extent of its rise, the extent of its fall in popularity, and the suddenness of this fall. In addition, some fads may recur—they rise and fall, only to rise and fall again—while others may, after their fall, never make another appearance. Still other activities or products experience a sudden rise in popularity, are proclaimed a fad, and become "institutionalized"; that is, they remain fairly popular over a long period of time, even though rarely at the level of their height of popularity. The last type of fad may be called an *institutionalized fad*; examples include frisbees, video games, crossword puzzles, waterbeds, skateboards, miniature golf courses, bicycles, and, in the 1990s, bungee jumping. They are fads only with respect to the suddenness with which they caught on; however, they are not fads with respect to their decline, because they continue to be popular at a fairly high level.

Fads: Freely Chosen, Free of Utilitarian Considerations.   It should be emphasized that not all products or activities that are taken up and/or dropped relatively quickly are necessarily fads. One built-in assumption about the concept is that *people are free to make choices about what to do and buy,* and *these choices are relatively unconstrained by practical considerations.* To say that people are free means that they do not do things because their life circumstances force them to do them. For instance, let's say there is a sudden upsurge in the economy and a rise in a society's standard of living, and its population is now able to purchase automobiles, does so, and then, just as drastically, the economy takes a nosedive and the people become poor, at which point they are forced to sell their cars; in this case, purchasing cars would *not* be regarded as a fad, even though this behavior is volatile, because these people did not freely choose to do what they did.

If one nation wages war against another, and substantial numbers of the members of these societies march off to war, and then, a year or two later, when peace has been declared, they abandon the fighting, the behavior of these soldiers would not be defined as a fad because there is an assumption of some measure of governmental coercion in complying with a military draft. (On the other hand, if everyone is swept up with "war fever," and is enthusiastic about the fighting, perhaps then there is an element of the craze in their behavior.)

Within a very short span of time in the 1960s, Renault sold millions of units of their Dauphine model; then, within an equally short span, purchasers stopped buying the car completely because it was extremely unreliable. Today (in contrast to the VW "beetle," another popular 1960s and 1970s car) hardly any Dauphines may be seen on America's highways. But the Dauphine cannot be regarded as a fad because the public's decision to stop buying it was strictly practical in nature. In short, to qualify as a fad, it is not sufficient that the behavior erupt suddenly and dissipate quickly; the behavior must be, on the surface at least, freely chosen and relatively free from utilitarian considerations.

Fads as a Departure from the Mainstream.   There is one further characteristic of what most people mean when they use the term "fad": It must represent something of a departure from mainstream behavior and conventional products. To most people using the term, fads must be somewhat unusual, a bit "far out," slightly bizarre, even "irrational." It is not the norm—it is regarded as somewhat *odd*—to run past spectators naked, spend $5 on an ordinary rock one could pick up off the ground, cram oneself, along with a dozen others, into a tiny telephone booth, eat live goldfish, sit atop a flagpole for weeks at a time, or cut up an entire Volkswagen microbus and eat the pieces, one by one. While most people admit that fads are fairly harmless, there is a pejorative implication attached to the term that is missing from related concepts, such as fashion. While we need not share in this negative view, it is important that we take note of it.

Fads: A Summary.   To sum up the matter, certain activities and products are taken up or purchased in a pattern that is very different from the norm; this does not mean that their participants or purchasers are sick or abnormal, only that they catch on or are dropped extremely quickly and explosively, in a volatile fashion. Faddish behavior or products are *temporary*—they do not last. Said an extraordinarily unprophetic article published in the late 1920s in *Variety*, the entertainment business's trade magazine, sound movies are "only a fad, say experts"—meaning, they will last only a very short time. Nor are fads, or their followers, "irrational"; as we saw in the first chapter, what seems rational to one observer may be perfectly normal and rational to another. What I mean by a fad is simply that a given activity or product follows a fairly distinct trend: At one time, it did not exist or was extremely rare (although it may have been popular at some time in the distant or even recent past). Suddenly, the fad catches on and becomes extremely popular, seeping into the consciousness of nearly every member of a society—it becomes a noteworthy phenomenon, the "latest thing"; it enjoys a fleeting moment of popularity; and nearly as quickly, it is dropped by most participants or purchasers (although some small number may continue to engage in or purchase it) and becomes passé, out of style, unacceptable for most self-respected individuals to engage in or be associated with. Exactly how brief this boom-and-bust cycle has to be to mark a fad off from a routinely fluctuating, conventional activity or product cannot be determined with any degree of precision. Still, with the great majority of fads, most of us "know one when we see one."

The Unpredictability of Fads.   Fads, like all forms of collective behavior, are largely unpredictable. In contrast, the trend of most conventional activities and products can be predicted in advance—to some extent, at any rate. For instance, we know that, each year in a given society a certain amount of money (more or less) will be spent on apples, oranges, and bananas, that a certain number of automobiles will be purchased, and that a certain proportion of the electorate votes on election day. These numbers change from year to year and even season to season, but their increases and declines are typically not sudden, dramatic, or unpredictable. These and countless other trends, patterns, and tendencies in behavior and spending can be tracked, noted, and predicted in advance—again, within limits. With most such activities or products, there are long-term changes, cycles, and patterns, but typically no sudden, explosive, short-term changes in popularity. We do not expect that, in a single month's time, millions of Americans will begin eating acorns, take up cave exploring as a hobby, decide to sell their houses and purchase land in New Guinea, wear their clothes backwards, or shave their heads completely bald.

_____ FIVE EXAMPLES OF FADS _____

Yet, during much of the history of the industrialized West, people have, suddenly and in large numbers, engaged in certain activities or bought certain products that were rare or unknown before—and, almost as suddenly, discontinued the practice.

Bungee Jumping.   On April Fool's Day, 1979, a group of "tuxedo-wearing, champagne-drinking yo-yos" jumped from a bridge in Bristol, England with elastic bands attached to their ankles. At the time, this practice was, as far as anyone knows, completely unprecedented. Within months, hundreds of daredevils were jumping off bridges, and by the end of the decade, tens of thousands of individuals were bungee jumping (as the activity came to be called), a television commercial (refused by one network but shown on two and eventually withdrawn by both) for athletic shoes depicted the activity, and it had become institutionalized as a full-fledged (although unauthorized and unconventional) sport (Vetter, 1990). In short, we are witnessing a time when "bungee jumping comes of age" (Thigpen, 1991)—an example of an institutionalized fad. It has become so institutionalized that a bungee-jumping attraction may be found at many theme parks throughout the country.

Cabbage Patch Dolls.   In 1983, the Cabbage Patch doll was marketed; it earned about $80 million dollars from June to December of that year. In 1984, sales went through the roof—nearly $550 worth of Cabbage Patch Kids were sold; in 1985, $600 million worth were sold. But in 1986, only $250 million worth were sold and only $125 million in 1987. As a result of its steep decline in sales, Coleco, manufacturers of the doll, lost $111 million in 1986 and $105 million in 1987. In 1988, Coleco filed for bankruptcy (Crudele, 1986; Feder, 1988).

Streaking.   Early in January, 1974, very few people had ever seen, heard of, or engaged in the activity that came to be known as "streaking"—running past spectators completely nude or clad only in socks and shoes and, sometimes, ski masks. By February, literally thousands of individuals had done it, the activity had "become a fad of epidemic proportions," mainly among college students, all over the country (Anderson, 1977, p. 221), and nearly everyone in the United States had heard of it. By March, the behavior had become international; the Eiffel Tower in Paris, St. Peter's Square in Rome, and locations in Taiwan, South Korea, Brazil, and Kenya had been streaked. By May, 1974, the fad had run its course; after that, very few people continued to engage in streaking (Evans and Miller, 1975; Anderson, 1977; Aguirre, Quarantelli, and Mendoza, 1988). Said one undergraduate, "I never really understood why we did it in the first place, and I couldn't say why we're not doing it now" (Marum and Parise, 1984, p. 180).

Pet Rocks.   In 1975, a small, unadorned stone, packaged in a box, was sold as a "Pet Rock." Hundreds of thousands of these items were sold that year at $5 each. Although it did spawn a related product—small rocks with faces painted on them—the pet rock fad lasted only six months; shortly after the Christmas season was over, no one purchased a pet rock (Marum and Parise, 1984, pp. 183–184).

CB Radios.   In 1947, federal regulations permitted the ownership of citizen's band (CB) radios for short-range private communication and, in 1958, for wider public use. From 1947 to 1973, only 850,000 licence applications for CBs were submitted to the Federal Communications Commission, a bit more than 30,000 a year. But in 1973, with the sudden emergence of the gasoline crisis, there were 250,000 applications, 400,000 in 1974, and about a million in 1975. The fad initially caught on because of the need on the part of truckers and drivers to communicate with one another about locating filling stations with available fuel. In 1976, a national 55 mile-an-hour speed limit was enacted; 4.8 million applications were submitted to the FCC, and more than 11 million CB units were sold that year (Kerbo, Marshall, and Holley, 1978, p. 338). But in 1978, the product and the activity had declined in popularity, and by 1980, the CB fad had been declared dead (Keerdoja and Sethi, 1980; Miller, 1985, p. 142; Marum and Parise, 1984, pp. 176–177). Of course, truckers, police officers, taxicab drivers, and emergency paramedic teams still use them in their work, but by the early 1980s, as a recreational activity, purchasing and communicating on a CB was regarded as distinctly passé.

CAUSES AND MECHANISMS FOR FAD BEHAVIOR

Fads are a "seriously understudied" aspect of social life; although "specific discussions" of them abound, "no one has presented a systematic conceptual and theoretical statement about them" (Aguirre, Quarantelli, and Mendoza, 1988, p. 569). What can we say about fads beyond what they are? How and why do they emerge, how and why are they spread, and how and why do they die out?

In the beginning, acceptance of a fad is problematic; that is, the likelihood of its catching on is low, and those fads that have done so had been selected from hundreds or thousands of potential candidates that did not make it. To put the matter a different way, our choices concerning which car to buy are limited to a few dozen models; the decision we make is determined by a fairly small number of key factors, price and practicality included, and a mistake is likely to be costly. With fads, however, our choices are nearly unlimited, the reasons why we adopt fads are vast, and most fads can be picked up and discontinued or discarded without much social, personal, or economic cost. Thus, our capacity to adopt a fad is extremely "open" in comparison with other, more conventional activities and products; our decision is likely to be more impulsive, volatile, and influenced by our social and personal surroundings and circumstances.

There are two more or less distinct mechanisms in the popularity of the fad: first, its initial adoption by a small number of innovators, and second, its *diffusion* to a large number of followers. Who are the innovators? Who first selects a fad that eventually catches on? Why do some activities or products attract a tiny minority but never break out into widespread acceptance? What characterizes the transition, among those that do, from an activity engaged in or a product purchased by an extremely small "statistical" minority to one that attracts a majority, or at least a large segment, of the population? What, in short, is a fad's "life cycle" or "natural history"? Do fads have stages of obscurity, popularity, and death (Meyersohn and Katz, 1957, pp. 596–597, 599)?

The Emergent Norm Theory. The *emergent norm* perspective probably accounts best for the spread of fads: Fads emerge and disseminate because, within certain social and interactional circles, a specific, previously unknown or novel activity or item is defined as acceptable, normative, and even desirable. This "emergent" definition of the situation justifies the fad and articulates its desirability (Turner and Killian, 1987; Aguirre, Quarantelli, and Mendoza, 1988, p. 571). Even though the mass media do spread news of the behavior or item, it is within preexisting intimate, informal, interpersonal groups that most potential participants learn the newly-emerging norm about its desirability. A highly publicized activity or item is not adopted in a particular locale unless it finds favor within specific interpersonal groups. In short, although diffuse crowds (that is, publics, through the media) *facilitate recruitment* into a given faddish activity, participants enact their fad-relevant behavior, and reaffirm the norms that that entails, *within compact crowds,* that is, small, intimate groupings (Aguirre, Quarantelli, and Mendoza, 1988, p. 582; Turner and Killian, 1987, pp. 154–155).

As we might expect, emergent norm theory does not argue that fads represent a radical departure from that which existed previously, that they seriously violate existing behavioral norms. Norms emerge regarding acceptable and unacceptable definitions of behavior; the innovation that the fad represents takes place within "clear normative limits" (Aguirre, Quarantelli, and Mendoza, 1988, p. 582). For instance, "streaking," which took place in 1974, was not unbridled, or uncontrolled, or totally outside conventional norms. Instead, it was constrained by certain existing traditions. For instance, it was taboo to streak in classes where exams were being given, and it was considered wrong or inappropriate to interpret the nudity in streaking as sexual in nature or act on a sexual interpretation of that nudity, since it was seen as a nonsexual event. In short, fads "only go so far" in their movement away from tradition; "they must be perceived as odd, but not too odd" (Aguirre, Quarantelli, and Mendoza, 1988, p. 577). Of course, the emergent norm/interactionist explanation only accounts for the *process* of fad adoption; it does not address its *content*. Why is one specific item taken up on a widespread basis, while another, superficially similar one, is not? The emergent norm perspective cannot, or has not, answered this question. In fact, no theory, whether academic or popular, sociological or psychological, individual or structural, has ever been able to explain successfully or predict the content of fads generally. Indeed, the creator of such an explanation is likely to become rich and famous very quickly!

Society and Culture. A crucial breeding ground for fads is the society and culture in which they emerge. Fads reflect, although imperfectly and in a distorted fashion, the ethic, values, and culture (or *Zeitgeist*) of the society in which they arise (Meyersohn and Katz, 1957, p. 596; Blumer, 1968, p. 343; Blumer, 1969, p. 283). On the broadest level, societies that encourage change, novelty, and newness tend to experience fads. Ken Hakuta ("Dr. Fad"), marketer of the Whacky Wallwalker, a fad that was extremely popular between 1982 and 1987, contrasts American culture with that of his native Japan; the United States, he says, is far more likely to experience fads because it is less structured and people here tend to be more open, more oriented to change, and less self-conscious about looking silly (Bruning, 1989). Another obvious characteristic of a society that encourages fads is the availability of discretionary cash. If a society does not have a money economy, product fads will be unknown or extremely unlikely; if the per capita income of a given society is at the subsistence level, and its people spend all of their available money on simply keeping alive, again, product fads are not likely to proliferate. (Other types of fads are possible, of course.) A capitalist society, in which products are sold to a mass public with a great deal of discretionary income, is a fertile breeding ground for fads.

In addition, as the culture in a given society changes historically, the fads it adopts, likewise, respond to some of these changes. Miniature golf became popular almost instantly in the 1930s, during the Depression. It was an "amusing activity that didn't cost very much," that also allowed Americans "to laugh at the genteel country club way of life (which few could then participate in)" (Marum and Parise, 1984, p. xvi). It is no accident that the 1960s, during a period of much freer political and sexual expression than was true of the previous decade, should have spawned fads that emphasized freedom of sartorial and artistic expression as well, such as tie-dyed shirts and psychedelic art. A central theme of the 1980s Reagan years, some say, was money, profit-making, or, to quote Gordon Gecko, a principal character in the film *Wall Street* (1988), "greed." What better way to express this sentiment than the "preppie" look that became so popular at the time, that is, wearing clothes "that could give the impression of money, tradition and good breeding" (Marum and Parise, 1984, p. xvi)?

Groups and Subcultures.   Just as certain societies and periods of history are more likely to generate fads—and certain *kinds* of fads—than others, likewise, certain categories, groups, or subcultures are more, and others are less, "fadogenic," that is, likely to generate and pick up on fads. Fads are much more likely to take place in groups whose members are less set in their ways; think in terms of a shorter time span and do not have much of a historical memory; and who are less traditional and more open to new experiences, ideas, and ways of doing things. It hardly comes as a surprise that fads tend to arise out of the younger segments of a society—preadolescents, teenagers, and college students—and are far less likely to appeal to the middle-aged and the elderly, who are to a degree almost immune from most fads. Teenage clothing, grooming, music, dancing, and lingo vogues are much more short-lived than comparable styles among adults. Fads serve, in part, as a medium or a basis of identity; consequently, one major motivation underlying fad participation is their function in demarcating teenagers from the adult world. Teenage fads show adolescents that they have a measure of control and choice in their lives; that these fads are theirs and theirs alone; that they live radically different lives from those of their parents; and that they are, in many ways, superior to adults. For most adolescents, fads "serve as a medium of rebellion against the adult world" (Sebald, 1984, p. 257). This applies most strongly to changes in clothing and grooming styles (some of which are called fashions, and others, fads), such as black leather jackets, the zootsuit, the use of pink and black, torn jeans, and unusual hairs styles— such as the "DA" of the 1950s, extremely long hair in the 1960s, the "punk" look of the 1970s, and the 1980s and 1990s vogue of cutting designs into one's hair and scalp. The opposition they arouse in one's parents or in authority figures is clearly part of their appeal.

Freedom Vs. Constraint. As we'll see in more detail in the section on fashion, a major debate in this field centers around the question of freedom versus constraint. Conservatives and other defenders of the status quo argue that, in a capitalist society, people are free to make individual choices, including whether or not to make certain purchases and to engage in certain activities. Critics of capitalism—radicals, Marxists, and "critical" theorists— argue that the capitalist elite limits the choices we make in order to ensure that our behavior either supports, or at least does not threaten, their class interests. To some extent, fad behavior is a bit to the side of this debate, since fads, while they may tweak the nose of the status quo, very rarely, if ever, threaten the interests of the capitalist elite. Still, some fads are economic products (many are not) and, as such, they are part of the capitalist system. Can fads be foisted upon an indifferent public, created out of whole cloth? Is the causal dynamic behind the creation of fads a clever promoter with a scheme to make lots of money? Are fads simply a scheming, calculated creation of capitalist entrepreneurs?

To me, the defenders and the critics of capitalism are engaging in a somewhat empty debate because we do not have an either-or situation here. Some fads are consciously created, while others arise more or less spontaneously. Even those that are economic products—and therefore earn money for the promoter, marketer, manufacturer, and seller—cannot simply be foisted upon an indifferent, uninterested public. To quote a phrase, you can't make something out of nothing. While conscious creation and marketing can make some would-be fads successful, such efforts cannot guarantee their success. Advertising and media attention can only go so far in generating public interest in a product. In short, there is both freedom and constraint in the world of fads. The variety of novelty items is vast, although not, of course, unlimited; advertising and publicity, available largely only to those who have the money to manufacture and market an item, certainly make its success much more likely. Without access to the media, a fad rarely catches on. On the other hand, if large manufacturers were able to guarantee the success of their products through advertising alone, they would always be successful and never lose money on them, and this is clearly not the case.

Many product fads are sold by individuals who stand to profit by their sales. Ken Hakuta ("Dr. Fad"), promoter of the "Whacky Wallwalker," became a millionaire as a result of this one product alone, but he has been unable to duplicate his initial success with other products.

In 1982, Ken Hakuta was a Japanese exporter of ironing board covers and cat food ingredients when his parents sent his children a toy that changed his life; it was a gunky, plastic, 8-legged, octopus-shaped creature that "walked" down a wall when thrown against it. He immediately recognized the sales potential of the toy (his brother, who also received one, merely shrugged and put the thing aside). He purchased the export rights to it, named it the "Whacky Wallwalker," and began exporting it to the United States. After imaginative promotion and some fortunate media exposure, in less than five years, the toy sold 220 million units, and Hakuta himself earned $20 million for his efforts. (He has 80,000 Wallwalkers stored in his basement at the ready for the next emergence of this fad.) Since that time, he has tried, with dozens of products, to create another fad and recapture the popularity of his first venture, so far without success (Bruning, 1989). Clearly, then, the stampede for a fad cannot be generated out of thin air by clever, money-making marketers and promoters. On the other hand, clever marketing and promotion will help make a potentially interested public aware of a product, and make it available to them; such efforts can stimulate the public's interest when the potential exists.

A good example of a product fad that became extremely popular in spite of the fact that its marketer spent no money on advertising or promotion whatsoever is the slap bracelet, a long, thin slat of metal covered with fabric that snaps around the wearer's wrist. Introduced in the summer of 1990, within a few months, Main Street Toy had sold over six million units of the novelty item; in addition, several other companies sold between 10 and 15 million cheaper (and illegal) imitations in the same period. The executives of Main Street Toy, half of them formerly with the bankrupt Coleco Industries, did not want to make the same mistake as they had with the Cabbage Patch doll, and kept overhead costs—including advertising—to a minimum. What counted here in generating the fad was the item's intrinsic appeal and word-of-mouth (Ramirez, 1990). Once again, everyone admits that advertising and other hype can help launch a product fad. On the other hand, some product fads are generated without advertising, while others do not catch on in spite of corporate advertising. With most fads, something is at work beyond mere hype.

INDIVIDUAL FUNCTIONS OF FAD BEHAVIOR

In sociology, *functions* are positive consequences of behavior or a social institution that are often used as the basis for an explanation of why that behavior or that institution exists and survives. At one time, functional explanations were used to explain just about everything. We now know that, by themselves, functions cannot automatically explain the existence or survival of any behavior or institution. Just because something is "good" or profitable for a group of people does not prove that those people created or maintain it. Still, functions represent one piece of evidence that help us understand why people do certain things in the first place and why they continue to do them over a period of time. No one can deny that participating in fads serves certain functions for enthusiasts. Such participation "does" things for people; they feel that it helps their lives in some way—and that's why they engage in it. How can an activity that's so trivial have important functions for individuals?

While fad behavior is generally focused on a relatively trivial or inconsequential activity or product, most fad participants do not define or experience it as trivial or inconsequential. True, very few are likely to regard fad behavior as belonging in the same category of importance as, say, their jobs, marriages, education, or family lives. (Some do, but when their numbers become substantial, we have a craze on our hands, not a fad—a phenomenon we'll look at in the last part of this chapter.) At the same time, fad participation does tend to be seen by participants as "meaningful and consequential to those enacting it" (Aguirre, Quarantelli, and Mendoza, 1988, p. 581); participants define it as at least moderately important—not necessarily crucial or critical to the core of their lives and identities, but of at least moderate importance. It is no contradiction to say that the *focus* of fad behavior (that is, the behavior or the product itself) is trivial while, at the same time, that fad behavior *participation* is meaningful and consequential.

The resolution to the apparent contradiction is that fad behavior is more than the intrinsic qualities of the behavior or the item that is focused on. Participation entails belonging to an informal group and acting out an activity that is symbolic of group membership. Fads typically have a dual character: *cohesion* and *separateness* (Aguirre, Quarantelli, and Mendoza, 1988, p. 577).

By participating in a given activity that is regarded as at least a little bit odd to the cultural mainstream, they are, simultaneously, creating an "in" group (fad participants) and an "out" group (nonfaddists, that is, the rest of the society). Toward the "in" group, they have a certain measure of identity, belonging, positive feeling, even affection; toward the "out" group, they feel distance, alienation, indifference, condescension, even intolerance. To the extent that they reach out to the nonfaddist, it is to proselytize (Turner and Killian, 1987, p. 150).

Group Participation: A Dimension. Of course, this analysis should not be pushed too far; fads vary in the extent to which they attract strong versus weak enthusiasts. Some fads are more "cultish"; that is, they generate sharper in-group/out-group dichotomies than others and enthusiasts that are more intolerant toward the nonfaddist than is true of others. As a general rule, the more similar and the less odd the fad is to mainstream behavior or products, the weaker that dichotomy will be; the more different from and the odder the fad is to the dominant culture, the sharper this division is and the more cultish fad participants will be. Likewise, the more involved the fad enthusiast is in the faddish behavior, the more sharply he or she draws the in-group/out-group line. The act of purchasing and owning, or giving, the Pet Rock in 1975 was *unlikely* to generate strong in-group participation and solidarity; after all, how much can one do with or say about a small stone one has purchased for $5? Streaking generated moderately strong in-group fad identity and participation, which, however, varied somewhat from one locale to another (Aguirre, Quarantelli, and Mendoza, 1988). Generally, when such an identity becomes very strong, sociologists refer to it as a craze, not a fad; for some teens and preteens, the game "Dungeons and Dragons" provided the basis for a strong in-group identity, for seeing the world as sharply divided into enthusiasts and individuals who did not play "Dungeons and Dragons" (Fine, 1983). As a general rule, products that entail or generate no corresponding behavior or activity are very unlikely to create a strong fad identity; fads that are based on an activity or a product that demands a given activity are much more likely to do so.

Individual Functions of Citizen's Band Radios. In the 1970s, when the citizen's band (CB) radio was suddenly purchased and used in numbers some six or seven times greater than was true in previous (and later) decades, it came to be an activity that helped participants "reestablish a sense of *Gemeinschaft*" (Kerbo, Marshall, and Holley, 1978), that is, a close-knit, intimate community with a strong "we" feeling. This was especially important to people who lived in a world they saw as too cold, complex, and impersonal, too lacking in the intense bonds that hold small communities and societies together. CB enthusiasts were provided with a means of counteracting their feelings of social isolation; the CB subculture enabled participants to socialize with others who shared a wide range of interests. By acquiring a CB, adopting a "handle" (a special name used only in CB contexts), communicating with others about meaningful matters while driving around, expanding their sphere of communication manyfold, creating and maintaining friendship networks, keeping up a pool of always-willing conversational participants, joining a CB club, interacting with them outside one's vehicle in part on the basis of their CB involvements—these all generated strong bonds of identity, friendship, intimacy, and *Gemeinschaft*. While it was not a "community" in the classical sense, the CB radio did generate *sociability* for participants (Kerbo, Marshall, and Holley, 1978). In a similar fashion, many fads create the basis for meaningful social interaction, group bonds, and a personal identity.

WHAT IS FASHION?

Fashion, says one writer, is "constantly denigrated" (Wilson, 1987, p. 47). At least three different theoretical traditions have attacked fashion. The first is psychoanalysis. One psychoanalyst (Bergler, 1953) has argued that feminine clothes are a masculine invention created and perpetuated unconsciously by men to assuage their fear of the female body and insecurity about their masculinity; men can undress the woman mentally without having to be put to the test of sexual performance. In addition, this theorist holds, most designers are homosexuals; homosexuals hate women; therefore, they create hideous, monstrous designs to make them look ridiculous and ugly.

A second tradition that has attacked fashion is feminism. Says Susan Brownmiller, "To care about feminine fashion, and to do it well, is to be obsessively involved in inconsequential details on a serious basis. . . . The desperate unending absorption in the drive for a perfect appearance—call it feminine vanity—is the ultimate restriction on freedom of mind" (1984, pp. 51, 80–81).

And the third theoretical tradition that has attacked fashion is Marxism. "Because the origins and rise of fashion were so closely linked with the development of mercantile capitalism, economic explanations of the fashion phenomenon have always been popular. It was easy to believe that the function of fashion stemmed from capitalism's need for perpetual expansion, which encouraged consumption. At its crudest, this kind of explanation assumes that changes in fashion are foisted upon us, especially on women, in a conspiracy to persuade us to consume far more than we 'need' to. Without this disease of 'consumerism' capitalism would collapse" (Wilson, 1987, p. 49).

Fashion: Irrational and Morally Absurd?   These three theories are tied together by the view that fashion is "irrational" and "morally absurd." None even remotely characterizes the reality of fashion. While flawed, the feminist and the Marxist views do contain at least a grain of truth. Clearly, taken to its extreme, an obsession with fashion may result in a flight from the intellect and personal achievement, and, just as clearly, fashion is a money-making, capitalist enterprise, influenced by the rules of a market economy. At the same time, as characterizations of the general reality of fashion, they are largely false. In contrast, the psychoanalytic theory is erroneous in every detail. Today, it is women, not men, who make decisions about fashion and, for the most part, women dress for other women, not for men. Fashion has very little to do with sexual arousal—when men wish to be aroused by pictures of women, they do not look through the pages of fashion magazines, but at pictures of unclad women. And homosexuals do not hate women, they love men, and hideous styles simply do not become popular in the world of fashion. At the same time, while these three critiques have little to recommend themselves as descriptions of the overall reality of fashion, they do represent our society's ambivalent attitude toward the phenomenon.

Promotion Vs. Line Styles. An important issue must be cleared up before we continue. Journalists and other critics and commentators often make fun of the fashion industry because, they argue, it is out of touch with what the public wants to wear; newly introduced styles at fashion shows, they reason, seem impractical, unesthetic, even bizarre and grotesque. The assumption being made here is that these striking, unusual styles are meant to be sold to the general public; when they are not adopted, this provides fresh evidence that the industry is out of touch with the public's taste. This judgment is mistaken, and for a very simple reason. The most unusual and striking styles introduced at fashion shows are typically not intended to sell to the general public—or to anyone else, for that matter. They are meant to make a fashion statement, present an image of the label that introduces them, demonstrate how daring, fresh, and original that label's line is for the new season. We must make a distinction between publicity/promotional clothing, which is introduced to attract attention and is not marketed or sold to the public, and "line" clothes, which are marketed and shipped to retail stores for sale to the public (Bass, 1990). Fred Davis illustrates this point when he quotes a newspaper description of a high fashion show in 1989 that introduced a "chrome and plastic bodice that resembled a speedboat dashboard." At the show, the model wearing the outfit pushed a button in her midriff and "casually extracted an electric cigarette lighter and had herself a smoke." While such a design is likely to create an enormous splash, no woman will ever purchase and wear it; in fact, the speedboat bodice wasn't even available to order at this show (Davis, 1991, pp. 14–15).

Fashion as a Form of Communication. We are told that clothing and fashion represent a "form of communication," a kind of "language," a "code" that conveys intelligible meaning (Lurie, 1981; Barthes, 1983). While this statement is not completely false—it does contain a grain of truth—it is an overly simplistic formulation that must be seriously qualified. All too often, observers and commentators are altogether too hasty in ascribing symbolic meaning to wearing certain styles of clothing. If clothing means something, what exactly does it mean? And to whom? What meaning does the wearer intend? Is there a message in his or her sartorial style? How is his or her clothing interpreted? And among which groups, audiences, cultures, or subcultures? It would be glib to assume we know the answers to these questions simply by looking at clothing beforehand. In fact, the "actual symbolic content" of clothing may elude us for the simple fact that the "clothing-fashion code . . . is heavily context-dependent." In other words, "there is a lot of variability on how its constituent symbols are understood and appreciated by different social strata and taste groupings." What certain clothing styles "mean" varies tremendously, "depending upon the identity of the wearer, the occasion, the place, the company, and even something as vague and transient as the wearer's and viewers' moods." In short, "clothing styles and fashions do not mean the same things to all members of a society at the same time" (Davis, 1985, pp. 17, 18).

Two Meanings of the Word "Fashion." The word "fashion" has two overlapping but, theoretically at least, distinctly different meanings. The more general meaning is the one that overlaps most heavily with fads: fluctuations in styles of manners, grooming, and dress. Here, the terms fad and fashion are almost identical; whether one uses the word "fad" or "fashion" depends on one's preference or the phenomenon one is referring to, *not* to changes in the popularity of what one is referring to. Fads are thought of as taking place in activities and products that are sillier, more trivial, less consequential than is true of fashion and as more distinctly "different" from what most of us do or buy, than is true of fashion. Thus, in this sense, we would usually refer to a bolo tie as a fad, a preppie tie as a fashion; the emergence and disappearance of a Mohawk haircut among American high school and college youths as a fad, wearing short versus long hair during a given decade as a fashion; dying one's hair green or purple as a fad, dying it blonde in one decade and brown in another as a fashion. At the same time, all these examples are based on practices that change from one period of time to another. In this sense, it is not the volatile nature of the behavior that is important—although fads are thought of as shorter-lasting—but the presumed characteristics of the behavior itself, that is, their presumed triviality and departure from mainstream practice. In this general sense, fad and fashion overlap so heavily that the difference between them is a matter of emphasis, it does not lie in their essential character. In this sense, there can be "fashion" in science, medicine, art, philosophy, musical styles, architecture, dance, household decoration, literature. To restate a well-taken point, fashion should not be restricted to adornment, such as clothing, make-up, and grooming (Blumer, 1969, pp. 275-276; Lofland, 1985, p. 66).

There is a second meaning of the term "fashion" that is both more specific and more general: clothing and related adornment and apparel, such as perfume and other cosmetics. Most books and articles that use the word "fashion" in their title refer to the activity and the products of the clothing and apparel industry. In this book, our use of the term is much closer to its first meaning, that is, changes in style in a range of areas; but to the extent that there are fluctuations in the manufacture and wearing of certain clothing and adornment styles, this too is a form of collective behavior. On the other hand, to the extent that aspects of the clothing industry are much like those of stable, institutionalized, conventional industries, what is referred to as fashion is outside the scope of our interests. The fact is, in comparison with more stable industries, the clothing industry is struck by greater-than-average fluctuations in style; this year-to-year fluctuation in clothing styles is what I mean by "fashion" in the clothing industry. Of course, in this sense, there can also be "fashion" in other products—food preferences, for instance, or automobile styling. There is, however, as with the use of the term "fad," the implication that utilitarian considerations do not play a major role in fashion. Thus, most of us do not refer to the recent move to eating more nutritious food as "fashion" (or a "fad"), since we would rather be healthy than unhealthy.

VOLATILITY: FAD VS. FASHION

At the same time, from the point of view of collective behavior, the changes in taste and style that take place in the clothing and cosmetics industry are quite different from those that are usually referred to as fads. This is so because the clothing industry has two qualities that other collective behavior phenomena lack: (1) *a permanent social and economic structure* designed to generate change, and (2) a *routine, cyclical time frame* within which this change is introduced. While there is a $2 to $3 billion "novelty item" industry in the United States which is set up to create, manufacture, market, and sell product fads, this is only one type of fad; it does not encompass fads generally—such as slang, behavior, more useful products, and heroes. Moveover, the "fad" industry is extremely unstable, one whose representatives shift into and out of the novelty item business with a remarkable degree of fluidity. In addition, since novelty items are usually extremely cheap, the public is far freer to purchase, or not purchase, them than is true of most conventional products, clothing included; novelties are far more likely to be impulse items than is true of articles of clothing, and hence, year-to-year ups and downs in their sales are likely to be far more volatile.

In contrast, the $150 billion clothing, cosmetics, and apparel trade is (although unstable by more conventional industry standards) far more stable than the novelty business. In the 1970s, a large number of fashion labels were established as industry leaders—in the United States, Calvin Klein, Bill Blass, Oscar de la Renta, Geoffrey Beene, and Ralph Lauren. These names were at the top of the industry a decade ago, they are at the top now, and they will be at the top a decade or two from now. "In the year 2017, women shopping for designer clothes will find the labels 90 per cent unchanged. Barely a quarter of the first-division fashion emperors will still be alive, but their éclat will have achieved the stature of motor and hotel dynasties" (Coleridge, 1989, p. 278). Over 40 years ago, an article on fashion in women's clothes (Barber and Lobel, 1952) listed a number of magazines that were central to the industry—or major segments of it—such as *Harper's Bazaar* and *Vogue*; although some others have been founded or became prominent since then, and the listing was not intended to be complete in the first place, those same magazines are still central to the fashion industry today. In contrast, it would not be possible to go back four decades and find as stable a list of publications addressed to the novelty trade that still survives nowadays. In short, the networks or social scenes that generate fads fluctuate a great deal, are remarkably unstable, and establish no lasting legacy. In contrast, the fashion world is more stable; it has created an enduring social and economic structure. To that extent, fashion is not a form of collective behavior; to the extent that there is volatility and spontaneity in the buying public's decisions, it is. It is entirely possible that, over time, partly because of economic factors, fashion is becoming less "trendy," more stable, more dependent on "classics," less subject to market volatility and extreme fluctuations in styles (Bass, 1990)—and hence, over time, less and less an example of collective behavior, and more and more a "conventional" industry.

While there is a season for more conventional toys—late fall and early winter, so that they may be purchased in time for Christmas—novelty items are not governed as much by periodicity; they may be, and are, purchased throughout the year. In contrast, the clothing industry has a rigid timetable; there is a fall, spring, winter, and summer "season," and a new line is shown to buyers in time so that it can be ordered and arrive in stores at the appropriate time. Moverover, this timetable is international. Shows for the appropriate season in Paris, New York, and Milan must open at about the same time, but not overlap to the extent that the same buyers and editors of fashion magazines cannot attend all of the most important ones. If a shipment to a large, influential store or shop is a week late, hundreds of thousands of dollars in sales will be lost to a label, and careers can be affected by the loss. In the clothing industry, timing is crucial; in this sense, it is lacking in the spontaneity we associate with many fads. Fashion, unlike fad, can only take place within a highly structured time schedule.

Another way of saying this is that *fashion has one foot in collective behavior and one foot in conventional, institutionalized behavior.* To the extent that fashion is a product of stable social and economic structures, it is not a form of collective behavior; to the extent that it contains an element of spontaneity and unpredictability, it is. A number of other authors have expressed this same ambivalence with respect to fashion's status in the field (Smelser, 1962, pp. 172–173; Lofland, 1985, p. 65). It should be sufficient to say that fashion is somewhat marginal to collective behavior; it represents something of an in-between case—somewhere between collective and stable, conventional behavior—but its study has no intellectual "home" aside from the field of collective behavior (Lofland, 1985, p. 65) and hence, its experts and researchers are the ones who study it.

FASHION: INNOVATION WITHIN STABILITY

Fashion possesses seemingly contradictory qualities: freedom *and* constraint, individuality *and* homogeneity, change *and* stability. To put the matter a different way, what distinguishes fashion is freedom *within* constraint, variation *within* homogeneity, innovation *within* stability (Sapir, 1931, p. 139).

There is a measure of compulsion or constraint in fashion. One is expected, in varying degrees, to be "in fashion," regardless of one's taste—or, at least, not markedly "out of fashion." To put the matter a bit differently, it is expected that one's taste will not stray excessively from the prevailing fashion; the individual who violates this rule is likely to attract ridicule from others. At the same time, the style dictated by a given prevailing fashion is likely to admit of an extremely broad expression. A year's or a season's fashion is rarely so explicit or rigid that every detail of one's wardrobe is dictated by it; each fashion or style permits a fair degree of freedom within the limits it permits. One chooses a style, and this does represent a kind of freedom; but it is a choice within limits, and one knows that one must adhere to these limits.

Fashion expresses one's individuality; one presumably chooses to wear one item of clothing as opposed to another. In putting together one's wardrobe, one may be unaware of the extent to which one is subject to many of the same forces that shape the choices of one's peers. Some of these homogenizing forces come from outside oneself—watching many of the same commercials, for instance—while others are internal, but which, likewise, one shares in common with others, such as one's age, gender, or socioeconomic status. Thus, teenagers can say to themselves, when pulling on a pair of ripped jeans or unlaced sneakers, "It's me," without stopping to think that 10 million other teenagers are doing exactly the same thing. While the style they choose to express themselves does vary from a different style—ripped versus intact jeans, for instance—wearing it does place them in a very large and, in that sense, homogenous category.

Fashion is a seemingly contradictory amalgam of a departure from, and an adherence to, tradition. Clearly, fashion changes from year to year and from decade to decade; what is regarded as fashionable at one time is decidedly out-of-date at a later time. One cannot wear clothes that were fashionable in the 1960s nowadays without seeming a bit foolish. At the same time, while fashion overturns or breaks away from an old tradition, it establishes or adheres to another, a tradition that is no less compulsive than the old. It is innovation, but an innovation based on stability, or at least yearly changes that themselves demand a measure of stability. In short, fashion displays both "historical continuity and modernity." This marks fashion off from the fad. While "new fashions are related to and grow out of their immediate predecessors," fads tend to "have no line of historical continuity; each springs up [more or less] independent of a predecessor and [generally] gives rise to no successor" (Blumer, 1968, pp. 343, 344).

In the words of Edward Sapir:

> Fashion is custom in the guise of departure from custom. Most normal individuals consciously or unconsciously have the itch to break away in some measure from a too literal loyalty to acceptable custom. They are not fundamentally in revolt from

custom but they wish somehow to legitimize their personal deviation without laying themselves open to the charge of insensitiveness to good taste or good manners. Fashion is the discreet solution of the subtle conflict. The slight changes from the established in dress or other forms of behavior seem for the moment to give the victory to the individual, while the fact that one's fellows revolt in the same direction gives one a feeling of adventurous safety. The personal note which is at the hidden core of fashion becomes superpersonalized (1931, p. 140).

The fact is, fashion takes place within the larger structure of custom. Variation from year to year is not complete or revolutionary but subtle and small-scale—variations on a theme, not junking the theme altogether. For instance, in Western society (and much of the rest of the world as well), men wear trousers. Fashion will determine variations within this broad custom, such as the use of certain colors, the presence or absence of cuffs or pegging; it does not represent so great a departure as to abolish pants altogether. Among men, such non-pant clothing styles as kilts, kaftans, and sarongs have simply not caught on in the West to the extent that they represent a serious threat to the sale of pants. On the other hand, occasionally, some fashion styles have become so widely adopted as to represent a departure in custom, and not merely a variation on a larger theme. For instance, in the 1920s, women began to wear trousers in great numbers and, within a short period of time, for some, they became an occasional or even a frequent alternative to wearing skirts and dresses. While they did not replace the more traditional garb, they established a new custom in clothing style, one that was very uncommon before the 20th century. In other words, occasionally, at some point, *fashion becomes custom.*

SYMBOLIZING STATUS: THE "TRICKLE DOWN" THEORY

What is the central dynamic of fashion? Why do clothing styles change from year to year, from decade to decade? What makes beards and long hair acceptable at one time and unacceptable at another? Tie-dyed shirts "in" in the 1960s and "out" in the 1970s? Long skirts seem "right" and "now" in one decade and "hopelessly old-fashioned" in another? Few questions in this field have been as subject to analysis as the issue of the mechanisms of change in the fashion world and, while we now know a great deal about the process, controversy and unanswered questions remain with respect to a number of important aspects.

Fashion as a Status Symbol. Perhaps the most crucial difference between fad and fashion is that, while both represent a means of participating in and announcing a participant's group membership (Lang and Lang, 1961, p. 486), there is a *hierarchical* aspect to fashion that is wholly or partly lacking in fads. Fashion is, probably more than for any other form of collective behavior, a symbol of status. Wearing one style as opposed to another announces to the world that one belongs—in many cases, merely wishes to belong—to a given social class. Clothes affirm class position; in this way, one may say that clothes "make the man"—and the woman.

In 1899, in his *The Theory of the Leisure Class*, economist Thorsten Veblen coined the term "conspicuous consumption" to refer to purchasing and displaying goods, especially clothing, as a means of symbolizing wealth and status. In the evolution from a hunting and gathering economy to farming, which began some 10,000 to 12,000 years ago, an economic surplus, or wealth, was generated. This, in turn, encouraged the emergence of cities, writing, the proliferation of a division of labor, armies, empires, tyrants, and the inheritance of social class which, over time, led to the emergence of the nobility. As the noble class became increasingly wealthy, they came to wear opulent clothing as a means of communicating their station in life, to demarcate themselves from commoners; likewise, in time, wealthy commoners wished to mark themselves off from less affluent commoners, and so on. For thousands of years, fashion was a slow-moving process; styles did not change especially quickly (except when one society came into contact with another), and everyone in a given society simply understood that only aristocrats could afford—and had the right to wear—the clothing they wore as a symbol of their exalted position. In fact, most of the population of ancient agrarian societies were outside the fashion system altogether (Fox-Genovese, 1987, p. 13), and wore, in all likelihood for an entire lifetime, whatever rough-hewn, humble garments they could acquire or fabricate.

Imitating Status Symbols.   But in all agrarian societies with a nobility, there eventually arose a small middle class of traders, merchants, and officials, whose wealth made it possible for them to purchase some of the symbols of the aristocracy. And the more complex the class structure became, the more imitation there was by members of classes just below the ones whose style they wished to emulate. It was only in a society with distinct social classes whose members were sufficiently free financially and culturally to choose their clothing styles and who used clothing styles to emulate higher classes that true fashion emerged, that is, shifting styles in adornment based on status differences.

The fact that members of the wealthier segments of the middle class could purchase clothing as opulent as that of the aristocracy, and the members of the more successful farmers and craftspeople, clothing as fine as that of well-to-do merchants, made it necessary for legislatures to enact what is known as *sumptuary laws*, that is, legislation prohibiting or regulating certain kinds of personal expenditures, especially on food and clothing; such laws often prohibited the members of inferior classes from wearing the clothing or possessing the appurtenances of those of a superior class.

Thus, for example, in 1520, a law was passed by the English Parliament that decreed that servants, common laborers, and farmers whose possessions did not amount to more than 10 pounds in value were prohibited from wearing cloth costing more than two shillings a yard; in addition, all persons below the rank of knight were prohibited from wearing gowns or coats trimmed in velvet. In 1558, during the reign of King Henry VIII, cloth of gold, silver, or satin was denied to all except earls "and all of superior degrees. . . . None shal weare anye sylke [silk]," in a hat, bonnet, nightcap, hose, or shoes, the law decreed, except "the sonne and heyre [heir], or daughter of a knight, or the wyfe of the sayd sonne, [or] a man that . . . is worth two hundred pounds in goods" (Baldwin, 1926, pp. 218, 219).

Fines were levied for such offenses. While these laws were justified on humanitarian grounds—they argued that people should not live beyond their means, thereby becoming impoverished by doing so—it is clear that most of their intent was motivated by the desire to ensure that status be announced by clothing, and that a person of inferior rank not be allowed to pretend to be something better than he or she was, thus cheapening those symbols. Given the frequency of the passage of sumptuary legislation, it is clear that such transgressions were common. To be plain about it, the laws had little or no effect.

Maintaining the Meaning of Status Symbols. How does a more prestigious class maintain its badges of distinction when they are so widely imitated by individuals they see as their inferiors? The answer lies in fashion; that is, in the constant fluctuation in styles of dress, adornment, and behavior. According to sociologist Georg Simmel (1904), fashion arose as a means of distinguishing superior from inferior classes. It is a basic fact of stratified society that upper statuses attempt to demarcate a line between themselves and the less prestigious members of those societies. At the same time, people tend to strive to maximize their status; when a given item or activity symbolizes the status of its bearers, less prestigious individuals seek to possess that item or enact that activity in order to capture that status. But as soon as they do, the status value of that item or activity becomes degraded. "Just as soon as the lower classes begin to copy [the style of the upper classes], thereby crossing the line of demarcation the upper classes have drawn and destroying the uniformity of their coherence, the upper classes turn away from this style and adopt a new one, which in turn differentiates them from the masses; and thus the game goes merrily on" (1957, p. 545). In this way, "the distinguishing insignia of the elite class filter down through the class pyramid. . . . These styles automatically acquire prestige in the eyes of those who wish to emulate the elite group and are copied by them, thus forcing the elite group to devise new distinctive marks of their superior status. Fashion is thus caught up in an incessant and recurrent process of innovation and emulation" (Blumer, 1969, p. 278).

Problems with the "Trickle Down Theory." While Simmel's analysis certainly accurately characterizes much of the dynamic of fashion, it is incomplete and one-sided. It was written at the turn of the 19th century (although it was reprinted over a half-century later), when the fashion world was more closed, clear-cut, and uncontested than it is today. No one questions the hierarchical nature of fashion nowadays; the only question is the exact *nature* of that hierarchy. A major flaw in Simmel's analysis is the fact that there exists not merely one but a large number of fashion hierarchies. Clothes do symbolize status, but just how styles—and the social categories they symbolize—are ranked is a shifting, somewhat pluralistic affair. A style that has high status in one group may have little status in a second one—whose style, in turn, has little status in the first group. The fact is, prestige is not nearly so intimately linked to fashion as Simmel claims. It is possible for many individuals to remain largely outside the system of fashion without losing prestige—for instance, artists, intellectuals, writers, and academics. A great many clothes are "classics," acceptable year after year or even decade after decade; most observers cannot tell if certain garments are one, five, ten, or even 20 years old.

Moreover, the way that style and fashion relate to class and status is far more complex than Simmel's analysis allows. According to the "trickle down" theory of fashion, the style of the upper class is readily identifiable and quickly imitated by the adjacent class; in fact, exactly the opposite is the case. Members of the upper class—"old money," America's equivalent of an aristocracy—pride themselves on their quietly elegant style of consumption, their avoidance of ostentation, glitz, and glamor. (Says one member of the elite, "Glamor is cheap.") Their style is conservative, understated, and their clothes are expensive without seeming to be (Barber and Lobel, 1952). This is a style that is likely to be—and, in fact, actually is—ignored or missed, rather than imitated, by the members of classes adjacent to it. In contrast, it is the newly rich, not the old money families, who support high fashion and the more ostentatious displays of wealth and status. "If you've got it, flaunt it," seems to be their motto. To them, the upper class style seems dowdy, not worthy of imitation. Nearly all the members of the "shiny set," the purchasers of high fashion clothing, earned (usually by marrying) wealth during their lifetimes; almost none inherited substantial wealth from their parents or ancestors (Coleridge, 1989, pp. 54–74). Says *Time* magazine of Ralph Lauren, "Lauren dangles old-money prestige in front of a new-money clientele."

The fact is, not only are hierarchies of style difficult to arrange along a clear-cut hierarchy, even the prestige of the social classes they supposedly symbolize is, too. Which segment of the population has more prestige to the American public—newly rich, multimillion dollar-a-year entertainers, whose style is decidedly glitzy, or the old monied upper class, whose style is, as we saw, low-key, subtle, and understated? Most Americans would pick the former, even though it is the latter whose members appear in the *Social Register*, and whom sociologists regard (and who regard themselves) as belonging to the very top of the stratification ladder. No one doubts that stratification exists and exerts a powerful influence on the members of a society, or that fashion is intimately linked with status. The point is, both social stratification and its symbols are a great deal more complex and pluralistic than the "trickle down" theory admits.

At the same time, fashion does "trickle down" the class structure, but in a far more complicated fashion than the "trickle down" theory argues. Fashion items do not so much "trickle down" as they are *adapted to* the taste and values of the members of each stratum. While the adaptation process does represent a kind of imitation, it is an imitation that results in *gross similarities* but *subtle differences* for each social class it moves into (Barber and Lobel, 1952). A $15,000 dress, a one-of-a-kind original tailored by Geoffrey Beene for Nancy Reagan, will be "knocked off" in a ready-to-wear limited edition by a Seventh Avenue firm and sold in a Fifth Avenue shop for $1,500 to the Westchester wife of a Wall Street lawyer. In the transition, the tailoring will have become more understated and subtle, the colors will be more muted, the effect will be more low key. That same dress will then be copied in a Garment District factory, which will ship thousands of units to shops all over the country and sold in a "femininely pretty" mass edition for $150 to secretaries, nurses, and grade school teachers; the fabric will be less expensive, the tailoring will be sparser, the colors will be less subtle. In the move to each class level, important changes will have been made, adaptations to the taste of occupants of that level, while, at the same time, essential features of the garment will be retained. The adaptations are not based solely on expediency, such as the cost of production and materials; there is a genuine attempt to avoid uniformity and tailor garments to the desires of each class subculture (Barber and Lobel, 1952). Still, the imitations are close enough, once the garment has become mass marketed to less affluent segments of the population, for the consumers of the original, expensive item to feel the need for a new style.

It must be emphasized that, just as fashion "trickles down," it may also "trickle up." It is not unusual for a given item to originate in the lower or working strata and "trickle up" to the middle and upper classes. The most well-known example of an article of clothing that experienced this process is blue jeans or denims, which began as a humble work outfit for miners, farmers, and cowboys, eventually becoming a fashion item for affluent teenagers and young adults (Davis, 1989). "Rap" music, by now no longer a fad, originated in the Black urban ghetto among teenagers from families of modest economic means; it has suffused into young American society at large, and today is listened to by white and Black, poor and affluent alike. The Ralph Lauren label attempts to blend old money chic with elements of a rugged, outdoorsy, Western ethos, in the process, borrowing some items that began in a working-class culture to sell to the new rich and members of the upper-middle class. Clearly, then, fashion does not simply "trickle down." At times, what originates in a lower socioeconomic stratum may become chic and desirable—that is, become the fashion—among those in a higher stratum. Simmel assumed that prestige only worked in one direction, but clearly, fashion is, or has become, more pluralistic than he realized.

FASHION: IMITATION, COERCION, _____ OR INDIVIDUAL CHOICE?_____

As we've already seen, it is clear that the public cannot be stampeded into purchasing novelty items. The industry is strewn with examples of products that were hugely publicized but which nevertheless failed to catch on; items that were popular, declined sharply in popularity, and eventually bankrupted major corporations, or, contrarily, those that seemed to come out of nowhere and became immensely popular. With respect to fads, we have to reject the "conspiracy" theory that fads are foisted off on an indifferent public by scheming, calculating entrepreneurs. But is this true of fashion as well?

Fashion: The Monetary Stakes.   The monetary stakes are much greater, some 50 times greater, in the fashion industry than in the novelty and fad business, and entrepreneurs have far more to lose if a given line fails—and far more to gain if it succeeds. While Ken Hakuta, one of the most successful fad promoters of all time, earned $20 million in five years with his Whacky Wallwalker, the heads of fashion houses are in a different financial league altogether. In 1986—no doubt these figures are substantially higher today— the Ralph Lauren label announced gross sales of $1.3 billion; Calvin Klein, $1.1 billion; Pierre Cardin $2.5 billion; and Georgio Armani, $1 billion. Even the lowest of these sums is higher than the Gross National Products of several entire Central American and African nations (Coleridge, 1989, p. 272). The heads of these firms have personal fortunes that run into the hundreds of millions of dollars; they represent the new, international _designer money._ Clearly, if a capitalist enterprise is able to pressure the public into adopting a given product toward which that public is initially ignorant or indifferent—or to create public interest in it with little more than hype—it is the fashion industry. Perhaps with no other type of commodity is advertising so important, and in no other industry is the aura and mystique that surround a product as crucial relative to the intrinsic quality of the product itself.

Can Fashion Be Foisted on the Public?   No—fashion style _cannot_ be foisted upon the public and become accepted, popular, and sell well. Women (and men) do not slavishly follow the dictates of fashion regardless of whether they like or feel comfortable in a given garment. And simply because a celebrity, or a number of celebrities, adopt or publicize a given style does not guarantee its success. (No one doubts that this helps, however!) When a fashion house heavily touts a certain product, it gains the public's awareness, attention, and perhaps its interest as well. The fact that a line is designed and manufactured by Ralph Lauren or Calvin Klein guarantees that it will fill the shelves of the major and most prestigious stores and shops. But does this guarantee its success as well?

The Miniskirt, 1988.   A good example of the failure of the fashion industry to win over the public with a given product—and the fact that the public

The reintroduction of the miniskirt by the fashion industry late in 1987, accompanied by a huge promotion build-up and great expectations, was a costly marketing failure. It demonstrates that the buying public cannot be stampeded into adopting styles that are not initially acceptable to their taste and way of life.

does not simply purchase any product placed in front of it—took place early in 1988 with the reintroduction of the miniskirt, originally popular in the 1960s. In 1987, fashion designers declared that the short skirt was back in style and that "no woman should even think of covering her knees." Said one designer, "Everyone [in the fashion industry] thought that the customer would say fine and go along with it and we'd have short [skirts] for four years. . . . Short looked so right and so new" (Hall, 1988, p. A1). *Women's Wear Daily*, the fashion trade's most influential magazine, "sustained a rat-tat-tat" of articles extolling the mini; representatives of retail stores "fed the frenzy with breathless reports of the success of short lengths." The hype managed to stimulate sales for a short period of time, perhaps until December 1987. "Then it stopped" (Hall, 1988, p. C8); customers simply stopped buying the short skirt and demanded longer and more varied fashions. Indeed, some deserted clothing stores altogether, deciding to wait another season before purchasing anything. By mid-January, key designers were either introducing a variety of designs with a range of lengths or they simply stopped offering the mini altogether. By spring 1988, the new (or the old, rediscovered) fashion, the miniskirt, was regarded as a disaster. Millions of dollars were lost on the line that dozens of fashion houses had pinned their hopes on for that season. What went wrong?

Short skirts died, many analysts feel, because the industry's designers and manufacturers were out of touch with what their customers wanted; they discovered that the public has a mind of its own and will not purchase just anything that the fashion trade promotes. Today, nearly seven out of ten women work, most spend the majority of their clothing budget on clothes for work, and few can imagine coming to work in a mini. In addition, in 1967, when the original miniskirt was successful, the median age of the American woman was 29; in the late 1980s, it was 33.3, and the older the woman, the less likely she is to wear such frivolous, revealing styles. The fact is, the buying public has become more discriminating and, in a tight economy, more practical and selective. In short, we are in the midst of something of "a fashion revolt" (Kantrowitz et al., 1988). If at one time it was possible to assure the success of a line of clothing with little more than hype, hyperbole, and hoopla—and I suspect this was never the case—this is certainly no longer true. Perhaps now, more than ever before, the fashion industry has to respond to the genuine taste and desires of the buying public.

Fashion as Groping Toward Modernity. While the process of the selection of a given fashion is often likened to a herd of sheep being led in a certain direction by the industry and by key elite figures, in fact, what we actually see is something quite different. Leaders exist in the fashion world, to be sure, but "the leader must . . . be a follower; he [or she] may alter details, but he [or she] cannot either arrest or reverse the process" that has already been set in motion in a particular direction (Bell, 1976, p. 91). In reality, fashion is "set through a process of free selection from among a number of competing models." Designers "are seeking to catch and give expression to . . . the direction of modernity." And buyers for the stores and shops attending fashion shows "are acting as the unwitting agents of a fashion consuming public whose incipient tastes the buyers are seeking to anticipate" (Blumer, 1969, p. 280). The central reality of fashion is "*to be in fashion*"; it is "not the prestige of the elite which makes a design fashionable," but instead, the elite attaches itself to that which is felt to be the emerging fashion. Like everyone else, the elite is *groping toward* modernity, that is, the emerging fashion.

It is their acquaintance with the world of fashion and its developing taste and style that enables the fashion elite to sense where fashion is going; they *anticipate* it, they do not *determine* it. "The prestige of the elite affects but does not control the direction of this incipient taste"; fashion transcends and embraces the prestige of the elite, it is not a product of it (p. 280). "Fashion appears much more as a collective groping for the proximate future than a channeled movement laid down by prestigeful figures" (p. 281). Certain key styles, out of all those that are presented during a given show or season, for some mysterious reason, "click," regardless of their origin or endorsement, and are adopted and become popular; they "click" because they are sensed to represent the fashion statement of the season or period. Leaders are influential in the world of fashion to the extent that they are able to anticipate, and continue to anticipate, developing and future styles. Once they begin to make mistakes and endorse trends that do not catch on, their influence wanes. Their prestige and leadership within the industry only takes them so far; like the athlete, they must continue to perform to remain influential.

In short, as we've seen, the fashion industry must remain in touch with the desires and taste of the public to be successful—or, to put the matter slightly differently, it must be in touch with what the public feels is appropriate *for the immediate future*. In fact, far from being out of touch with the public, as some commentators claim, clothing designers are—and this has been increasingly the case over time—intensely concerned with what styles the public will like and want to wear. Anne Klein, a major New York fashion house, before opening an active wear division in 1989, "first invested in focus group studies before they did anything else. These groups were run to help determine what the customer was looking for in active wear" (Bass, 1990).

FASHION AND GENDER

It is practically impossible to discuss fashion without considering the question of gender. "Fashion is obsessed with gender, defines and redefines the gender boundary" (Wilson, 1987, p. 117). Oddly enough—since gender inequality was more pronounced in earlier periods of history—this was not always the case, at least, not to the extent that it is true nowadays. Until the 18th century, the dress of men and women was not sharply demarcated. In ancient Greece and Rome, both men and women wore togas and sandals. (Although, obviously, in gender-specific contexts, dress was almost necessarily sharply demarcated by sex, for instance, the garb warriors wore when marching off to, fighting, or coming from war, which emphasize the masculine qualities of men.) Historically, in many cultures of the world, both men and women wore facial make-up. In 17th century Europe, both men and women wore lace, frills, feathered hats, ruffles, silk, high-heeled shoes, gloves in an array of different colors, stockings, wigs with ringlets, and perfume (Wilson, 1987, p. 118). Gender-related fashion coincides roughly with industrial capitalism, beginning some time in the 1700s; fashion "became an important instrument in a heightened consciousness of gendered individuality" (Wilson, 1987, p. 120). Beginning with the era of mass production, one could make a fashion statement only as a woman or as a man.

Men Vs. Women, Boys Vs. Girls. At the most superficial level, although the unisex concept has been with us for at least a generation, the simple fact is, men and women must wear different sorts of clothes. Although women may sometimes wear certain male garments—but not others—without eliciting social disapproval, men may not wear women's clothes at all. Moreover, in *most* contexts women must wear distinctly female clothes pretty much all the time. This sexual division begins at birth, stereotypically, with pink outfits and blankets for girls and blue ones for boys. In childhood, this sharp male-female distinction is not nearly as sharp as is true later on. Still, boy's clothes tend to be printed in dark, bold colors with sports, transportation, and wild animal designs, while girl's clothes are more likely to be printed in lighter, typically pastel, colors, with flowers and cute domestic animals. "The suggestion is that the boy will play vigorously and travel over long distances; the girl will stay home and nurture plants and small mammals. Alternatively, these designs may symbolize their wearers: the boy is a cuddly bear or smiling tiger, the girl a flower or a kitten" (Lurie, 1981, p. 214). By adolescence, the male-female dichotomy in clothing has grown to a yawning chasm. Clothing symbolizes, communicates, or announces the wearer's gender status just as, as we saw, it does for status and social class. If one announces that one is a man or a woman and isn't, one's social audiences—the individuals who see one wearing what they regard as sex-inappropriate clothes—will react, in all likelihood, in a negative, punishing fashion. Fashion in clothing tends to reflect the ideal characteristics of men and women at each period of history.

Women Vs. Men in the Fashion Cycle. Not only are male and female fashion in clothes distinctly different, but, almost as important, women are tied into the fashion system far more tightly than men are. Women are evaluated—as women—on the basis of fashion-related criteria much more precisely, harshly, and on a quicker-moving scale, than is true of men. The fashion that is permitted to men is much broader, much more slowly changing, and contains much more latitude, than that of women. Men (although not adolescents, whether male or female) can wear 10- or 20-year-old garments and attract much less notice and criticism than is true with women. What is "in" and "out of" fashion for women is measured on a less flexible scale, one that changes yearly; wearing older clothes is much more likely to attract charges of looking dowdy, out of fashion, out of style. Men are permitted to be immune to fashion in clothes in a way and to a degree that is impossible for most women. A discussion of fashion is primarily a discussion of women's fashion.

Changes in Gender and the Fashion Cycle. The picture is changing, of course, as are the gender roles of men and women generally. During the past decade, there has been a movement toward "feminizing" men's fashion—that is, making men more fashion conscious, quickening the pace of male fashion and fashionableness, blending men's and women's lines, selling men's clothing in women's stores, marketing products to men that were previously sold only to women. There has, in short, been a "growth of a fashion orientation in men's wear" (Bass, 1990). Two causes for the trend present themselves: first, changing gender roles, and second, the targeting of men's fashion as a growth area as a result of the slackening in sales in women's divisions. Thus, while the gender gap in fashion has diminished in recent years, even today, women are under significantly more pressure to be fashion conscious than is true of men.

Nineteenth Century Images of Women.   Early in the nineteenth century, women came to be seen as delicate, helpless, and frail. Women were defined "as something between children and angels: weak, timid, innocent creatures of sensitive nerves and easily alarmed modesty who could only be truly safe and happy under the protection of some man. Physical slightness and fragility were admired. . . . To be pale and delicate, to blush and faint readily and lie about on sofas was ladylike; strength and vigor were the characteristics of vulgar, red-cheeked, thick-waisted servants and factory girls. The more useless and helpless a woman looked, the higher her presumed social status, and the more elegant she was perceived as being" (Lurie, 1981, p. 216). Women's fashion of early nineteenth century Europe and North America, then, emphasized the look of "fragile immaturity"; pale colors and limp, "delicate, easily damaged materials" with "drooping lines" were considered fashionable and were used extensively (p. 216).

The Corset.   Roughly a generation later, a new fashion item was introduced: the corset. This early Victorian costume "not only made women *look* weak and helpless, it made them weak and helpless. The main agent of this debility . . . was the corset" (p. 217). The woman's frame, it was believed at the time, was delicate; her muscles could not support her body without mechanical assistance. "Well-brought up little girls . . . were laced into juvenile versions of the corset as early as three or four. Gradually, but relentlessly, their stays were lengthened, stiffened, and tightened. By the time they reached late adolescence, they were wearing cages of heavy canvas reinforced with whalebone or steel" (p. 217). After a decade or two of wearing such a device, many women were not able to sit or stand unsupported; their internal organs were deformed, their ribs were compressed, and they tired and fainted easily. Overlaying the corset were some ten to 30 pounds of clothing—shifts and chemises, petticoats, bodices, ribbon, beads, a shawl, a metal hoop, and a dress that fell to her ankles. Clearly, a woman attired in this fashion could not run or even walk easily or quickly.

Gender Functions of Women's Clothes.   Such bulky, uncomfortable, even painful outfits served a social function for a male-dominated culture; women were regarded as both the fairer and the weaker sex, not only physically but morally as well. "A lady might be pure and innocent . . ., but this purity and innocence could be preserved only by constant vigilance." Her physical and intellectual movements were restricted and hemmed in on all sides; "she must not attend a university or follow a profession; she must not travel without a chaperone; she must not visit a man's rooms; and she must not see any play or read any book that might inflame her imagination. . . . Even thus guarded, the early-Victorian woman was in constant danger of becoming the victim of man's lust and her own weakness. She needed to be at once supported and confined, in a many-layered, heavily-reinforced costume that would make undressing a difficult and lengthy process" (Lurie, 1981, p. 219).

Changes During the 20th Century.   As Western society, and its definition of femininity, changed, so, too, did its fashion. By the end of World War I (1914–1918), middle-class women were no longer thought of as helpless; they began to attend college, take jobs, travel on their own, date men without a chaperone, and read books that were previously thought to be scandalous. Clothes were still sex-typed, but they did afford women a great deal more freedom than was true of styles just a generation or two earlier. The corset was abolished, multiple layers of undergarments were abandoned, dresses became looser, more flowing, and, almost as significant, slacks, previously worn only by men, became permissible for women. Still, liberation was far from complete. The girdle—a toned-down version of the corset—was worn until about 1960. Stockings and their attachments—clumsy, awkward contraptions—were abandoned only with the introduction of panty hose in the 1960s. Slacks were fully acceptable in informal settings only by the mid-1930s, and in more formal and public settings only by the mid-to-late 1960s. Moreover, certain fashion features continue to emphasize male-female differences—and, simultaneously and significantly, restrict women's movement. High-heeled shoes, for instance, still considered attractive, provocative, and sexually alluring today in many quarters, make the woman's physical mobility difficult, and, like the corset, deform her muscles, which makes it difficult for her to get about both in and out of them.

Fashion Summary.   To the extent that men and women will always be different, the fashions worn by men and women will reflect that difference; to the extent that these differences diminish over time, male and female styles of dress are also likely to converge. In addition, as feminists argue, female fashion is likely to maintain at least an element of "keeping women in their place." On the other hand, fashion is not a simple reflection of the society or the culture within which it operates, and so, many factors will continue to shape it. One constant in the world of fashion is change, and change is central to the study of collective behavior. Luckily, so, too, is a measure of unpredictability, which means that the study of fashion is likely to be undertaken by students of collective behavior for some time to come.

WHAT ARE CRAZES?

The craze, like the fad, represents a relatively spontaneous, noninstitutionalized form of behavior: it is taken up and dropped fairly quickly (it is transient) and, like the fad, most crazes represent a rush toward something their participants believe to be positive or gratifying in nature (Smelser, 1962, p. 170). In these qualities, the fad and the craze are identical. They differ, however, in a number of respects. First, as the term implies, the craze is more intense, more "frenzied" (LaPiere, 1938, p. 190) than the fad. Participants are more preoccupied by the craze—more aspects of their lives are engaged by it. The attention of the participant "is severely restricted" to the craze itself (Turner and Killian, 1987, p. 147) and they are "more or less encompassingly involved" for periods of time (Lofland, 1985, p. 64). Second, since the craze entails more of a commitment, it tends to engage a much smaller number of people than the fad (LaPiere, 1938, p. 190). Clearly, any activity that requires an intense, all-encompassing commitment is likely to attract fewer participants than an activity in which commitment is more superficial and marginal. Third, unlike the fad, some crazes—although they do not themselves endure—have a lasting impact on the society in which they take place.

Stereotype of the Craze.   It should be emphasized that certain popular views of the craze are partly or completely invalid. The terms craze and mania imply "a loss of touch with reality or irrationality, even something close to mass hysteria or insanity" (Kindleberger, 1987, p. 28). In this book, in any course on collective behavior, and in sociology generally, we do *not* endorse such a negative view of the craze. Crazes are likely to be characterized by a heightened, intensified emotion of their participants. They are likely to be nearly all-encompassing for a small number of participants, to be dropped by them after a fairly brief period of time, and to be regarded as unusual, even bizarre by outsiders. But these participants are *not* typically mentally disordered—before, during, or after their participation in the craze—they are not "out of touch with reality" (though they often do ignore more conventional pursuits while in the throes of a craze), and their craze behavior is *not* necessarily irrational. Recall the definition of rationality put forth in Chapter 1: the choice of a reasonable means to attain a valued goal. In the sense that much craze behavior is outside the means-ends scheme altogether, and represents an end in itself, the question of rationality is not even relevant here. In addition, some economic manias may seem like a rational way of making money at the time, and it is only in hindsight that they appear irrational. In other words, some manias may very well be (or may seem to be) a reasonable means of attaining a valued goal, others may not be, while, with still others, participation is *itself* a valued goal. In any case, irrationality is not a defining characteristic of the economic craze.

Crazes: Areas of Life.   Theoretically, crazes can appear in practically any area of life, but, in reality, they have appeared with some degree of regularity in only a few spheres—the economic, the religious, the political, the expressive/estheic (Smelser, 1962, pp. 171–175), and the recreational probably being the most representative. The economic craze, mania, or "boom," is probably the most frequently studied variety of this type of collective behavior. During a short period of time, economic speculation focuses on a particular product or commodity. As a consequence, its price is wildly inflated; soon after, interest declines sharply, panic sets in, its price plummets, and some speculators are financially ruined. In the religious sphere, another oft-studied example of the craze, we have the phenomena of *revivalism, millenarianism,* and *persecution.*

_____ ECONOMIC BOOMS AND BUSTS _____

There has been some debate as to whether wild, frenzied financial speculation leading to extremely irrational decisions—and, occasionally, to such disastrous events such as stock market crashes and economic depression—even exists in the first place. On one side of the debate, some economists argue that the economic irrationality of historical cases of "booms" and "busts" has been greatly exaggerated, and that their dynamics can be explained by traditional and quite rational decisions and forces, given the circumstances (Garber, 1989, 1990; Neal, 1990). On the other side of the question are those who believe that investors are not always entirely rational in their economic decisions, and that, from time to time, "booms" and "busts," some leading to financial crises, are the result of rumor, wild guesses, self-defeating strategies, ignorance, and "mob psychology" or collective behavior (Rice, 1988; Kindleberger, 1987; Shiller, 1989; Smith, Suchanek, and Williams, 1988). Interestingly, it is possible that both sides are correct; that is, that the irrationality of some historical cases *has* been exaggerated *and* that group fervor *has* influenced many extremely poor financial decisions.

Tulipmania.   The economic craze, mania, or "boom," makes such an entertaining story that versions of it have become legendary. All of us have dreams of stumbling upon an investment that seems "too good to be true," one that promises to earn a fantastic amount of money in a short period of time, and make us wealthy beyond our wildest dreams. But, this myth continues, you can't get something for practically nothing; look at what happened to those unfortunate souls who thought they could—they invested in what they thought was a boom, it turned out to be a bust, and they went broke. Perhaps the oldest historically documented version of this myth is referred to as "tulipmania," a speculative boom that took place in the Netherlands between 1634 and 1637. Mackay, writing originally in 1841 (1932, pp. 89–97), claimed that speculation in tulip bulbs was so widespread and all consuming that many Dutch citizens neglected their ordinary jobs, and so frenzied and irrational that prices became astronomical, unrealistic, and wildly out of line with their true value. The market in tulips inevitably collapsed, and a substantial portion of the population of Holland was left impoverished, the country plunged into economic ruin for years afterward. The central message of the tale is that unbridled economic speculation is irrational, harmful, and pathological. In economic matters, people can at times suffer from "mob psychology," become so engrossed in a mania or craze that they lose all reason and invest irrationally, in such a way that they are bound to lose a great deal of money.

Recent historical and economic research has shown that very little of the "tulipmania" story is true (Garber, 1989, 1990). While there was speculation in tulip bulbs in Holland in the 1600s, driving their prices to extraordinary and unprecedented heights, and while a substantial number of Dutch investors did lose money when the speculation subsided, the most interesting and, from the point of view of collective behavior, relevant particulars of the tulipmania story are untrue. There is no evidence whatsoever that the Dutch neglected their more conventional economic activities, such as farming, during the tulip craze, and none to suggest that the collapse of tulip prices precipitated an economic recession, as Mackay claims ("the commerce of the country suffered a severe shock, from which it was many years ere it recovered"). Moreover, the extraordinary prices Mackay cites for tulip bulbs (some of which have been verified by later research) were not an expression of an irrational frenzy, totally out of line with what conventional market forces would produce. For instance, at the height of the speculation, a single tulip bulb sold for a weight of gold equivalent, in today's market, to $50,000; this might in itself seem to represent evidence of frenzied and irrational trading, and Mackay interprets it that way. But even nowadays, in more sober economic times, such prices are not that unusual; for example, in 1987, $480,000 was paid for a small quantity of prototype lily bulbs (Garber, 1989, p. 555). What makes agricultural products like rare tulip and lily bulbs (and, it might be added, stud bulls and race horses) so valuable is that they can continue to reproduce themselves, leading to a huge growth in the quantity of the product. One bulb, over a period of, say, a hundred years, can produce millions of bulbs, a volume worth many times the original investment in the single bulb (Mishkin, 1990). Of course, the more bulbs that are produced, the less valuable is any single bulb—but, at the same time, the greater the total value of all the offspring of that bulb. It is clear to see why the price of individual rare bulbs dropped over time: When they propagated, they were no longer rare.

Stock Market Bubbles.   At the same time, economic booms, crazes, and manias *do* occur. Economists define a "bubble" as a case of intense economic speculation that produces inflated prices that eventually and inevitably collapse, or "burst." Bubbles can take place with any commodity that is bought and sold—real estate, for instance—but the area within which bubbles are said to occur most often is the stock market. Initially in a stock market bubble, investors are attracted to a stock because of factors unrelated to solid economic information. Perhaps an article was published on the stock in *The Wall Street Journal* or *Fortune;* perhaps the chief executive officer of the corporation was seen or photographed talking with the president of the United States; perhaps events relating directly or indirectly to the company's business—war in the Middle East, a flood, unusually bad weather or a crop failure somewhere—may produce a great deal of interest in the stock (Shiller, 1989, p. 60). In addition, like everywhere else, gossip, rumors, tips and hunches run rampant on Wall Street and may play a substantial role in generating bubbles (Rice, 1988, p. 52). Whatever the reason, a great deal of trading in that particular stock suddenly takes place, and its price is driven up to a point that is unrealistic, given the company's assets. "At some point [and for some reason], fear begins to outweigh hope for some investors. With the loss of hope, the bubble suddenly bursts for everyone, since it never had a solid economic base. Once panic sets in, prices plunge. The panic is just as irrational as the enthusiasm that fueled the boom, and prices often fall below a level justified by economic reality" (Rice, 1988, p. 52).

In a set of some 60 experiments in which $10,000 in cash payouts was given to subjects for investment purposes, three economists (Smith, Suchanek, and Williams, 1988) found that "inexperienced subjects never trade consistently near fundamental value, and their trading activities usually generate prices that trace a boom-bust pattern" (p. 24). Moreover, the presence of experienced investors does not eliminate the exaggerated volatility of the market, though it does reduce it. Price "bubbles and crashes can be expected to occur in any securities market where the set of traders is changing frequently, with some traders exiting the marketplace while others are entering to trade" (p. 25). Traders use indicators that are not necessarily related to fundamental value, such as the number of bids for a given commodity as an indicator of its true value, artificially driving up its price (pp. 27, 28). In short, a great deal of investment is based on decisions that do not conform perfectly to strict economic rationality; these decisions often act to produce unrealistically inflated prices for certain commodities, which nearly always decline sharply after a fairly short period of time. This boom-and-bust pattern, often occurring with specific stocks, may also take place with the entire stock market as a whole. In short, economic activity is sometimes characterized by collective behavior.

The Pyramid Game.   One of the most clear-cut examples of the economic craze is the *pyramid game* that appears and disappears in recurrent cycles. In December 1919, Charles (or Carlo) Ponzi discovered that he could make a huge profit by selling notes to customers, who were to redeem them after 45 days at 50 percent interest. This was possible because Ponzi "robbed Peter to pay Paul," that is, he paid the principal and the interest on the early notes with the money coming in from the later ones. This could work only if the number of customers investing in the scheme kept increasing, that is, if more money came in than went out. Eventually, of course, the number of notes would have to level out, and he would have to pay out far more money than came in. This sort of scheme is called the "pyramid scam," and it is illegal; by the time Ponzi was arrested in August, 1920, he had taken in nearly $8 million, and he had only $61 dollars worth of stamps and postal coupons at his place of business—and thousands of customers were clamoring to redeem worthless notes (Dunn, 1975).

Few people take the lessons of history seriously, for the pyramid game continues to resurface in a variety of guises in different places, only, inevitably, to disappear again. It was revived in California—the birthplace of many fads, fashions, and crazes—in 1979 and 1980. In this particular incarnation, the game is a complicated get-rich-quick scheme based on a chart whose bottom level has 32 spaces (each one corresponding to the name of an investor); the level above it has 16 spaces; the next level eight; and the succeeding levels, four, two, and one space, respectively, with the top, above level one, representing the "zero" level. Investors pay $1,000 to enter a pyramid at the bottom; then they must bring in at least two new investors to keep the pyramid growing, who also enter at the bottom. When a level is filled with names, the original investor at that level is moved to the next higher level. Those who make it to the highest level collect $16,000, and a new pyramid is formed. It sounds like a fabulous way to make money—invest $1,000 and collect $16,000! But, once again, it is "robbing Peter to pay Paul"; money isn't being earned as such, it is simply taken out of the pockets of a large number of investors and put into the pockets of a few.

This scheme spread like wildfire in California and, later, to other parts of the country, in the late 1970s and early 1980s, where thousands of Americans were "gripped by a fever that [was] swelling their fantasies" and "encouraging their greed." What attracts so many people to the pyramid game? Mainly the fact "that the money is upfront. You can see it. You can hear the cheers when a new player buys in and hands cash to players who bought in last night. You can watch someone cry as the envelopes pile up in their hands. You can almost smell yourself getting rich." According to one investor, the pyramid game "really took me over. It possessed me. I never went to sleep before 4 A.M., and I lost 12 pounds. I didn't see my wife or kids" (Ager, 1980, pp. 6, 7). What characterized the pyramid was "the religious fervor of its adherents. . . . Pyramid people were obsessed with their new gimmick, and sleeping, eating, and working were sacrifices to the lure of making $16,000—effortlessly" (Klores, 1980, p. 23). In 1980, some bumper stickers in California read: "I Fell Off the Pyramid," "Have You Hugged Your Pyramid Today?," and "You Think You've Got Problems! I'm Still Stuck on Row 32!" Not everyone has $1,000 to invest, of course. Mini-pyramids, specifically tailored to high school budgets, charged a $10 entrance fee, and junior high school students in San Jose, California, "initiated $2 clubs, learning the ropes from their parents or older bothers and sisters" (Olson, 1980, p. 32). The activity continued unabated for several years, despite the efforts of police departments to break up new pyramids. It continued even though winning was a very long shot; since for every $16,000 winner, there had to be 16 investors willing to risk losing $1,000. It continued even though everyone knew that the winner's profits came from the pockets of the losers.

Why did this craze develop? And why was it centered in California? In the first place, such schemes are most likely to emerge during unstable economic periods. People who saw daring speculators and investors earning millions legally, while their own miserable salaries were being eaten away by taxes and inflation, aspired to make a "big score" themselves. The value of property in California skyrocketed in the mid-to-late 1970s—doubling, quadrupling, or more. Real estate investors reaped enormous profits, in some cases becoming wealthy practically overnight. Californians saw other Californians making fortunes while their own financial prospects stagnated. These people were especially attracted to a scheme like the pyramid game. The chance of earning $16,000 on an investment of $1,000 and in the space of a few days was a powerful lure to someone who knew that others were becoming rich through other forms of speculation. Moreover, the winnings, if and when they came, were tax free. Even if you win big at a gambling casino, "they give you a W-2 form right on the spot" (Ager, 1980, p. 5). For some, the game provided a sense of pseudointimacy and closeness—"a warm camaraderie and rallying-round in the face of danger" (Rodseth, 1980, p. 15). Last, the spread of *anomie*—the breakdown of norms and community feeling—may be greatest in a rootless, highly mobile state like California, and this breakdown may have helped create this scheme that did not produce goods or services and made one person's loss another's gain.

RELIGIOUS CRAZES

During all periods of history in all societies, individuals are variably involved in religion—some intensely, some moderately, and some not at all. Likewise, everywhere and at all times, some individuals move into and out of differing levels of religious involvement, while others are more stable in their commitment and activity. So far, we have traditional, institutionalized religious expression, not collective behavior. When does religion become a focus of study by the field of collective behavior? *When new, noninstitutional, nontraditional religion forms emerge and suddenly become popular, or when large numbers of the members of a society, within a given traditional religion, suddenly become seized with a nontraditional, uncharacteristic religious fervor.* Such sudden and temporary religious expressions—religious crazes—have taken hold in certain societies at certain times. Their appearance is not random, but is related to crucial sociological processes.

Religious crazes take a variety of forms. Some represent a *renewal*, with recurrent outbreaks of traditional religious fervor at extraordinary levels of intensity on the part of participants (Rose, 1982, pp. 183–186). Others are *millenial* outbreaks—"episodes in which participants anticipate a sudden and radical transformation of the world" (Rose, 1982, pp. 186–187). Still others take the form of a *persecution* of certain individuals supposedly responsible for evil doings (Rose, 1982, pp. 137ff).

Renewals. America is said to have experienced four religious revivals, renewals, or "awakenings" in its history—roughly, in 1730–1760, 1800–1830, 1890–1920, and, some say, 1960–1990 (McLoughlin, 1978; Rose, 1982, pp. 185–186, 195–196). Each of these awakenings took place during a period of social and cultural crisis.

During the first or "Great Awakening" (1730–1760), itinerant preachers began to crisscross New England on horseback attracting huge crowds of unprecedented size and enthusiasm; the Awakening "spread over the entire New England area like a fire blown to great proportions," both by the itinerants and "by the local ministers inspired to greater evangelical concern by the impact of the revival" (Rossel, 1970). This revival occurred "in a period of cultural uncertainty accompanying rapid frontier expansion and the growth of a commercial-industrial economy" (Rose, 1982, p. 195) as well as the collapse of a medieval and theocratic religious and social structure (Rossel, 1970).

In the "second awakening" (1800–1830), a less "respectable" denomination, Methodism, enjoyed a spectacular number of converts. Churches established Sunday schools, the American Bible Society and the American Tract Society were founded, and the anti-alcohol temperance movement was launched. During this period, the country experienced massive growth, the cities exploded in size, and the massive problems of organizing and governing the new, huge, sprawling nation came into painful focus (Rose, 1982, pp. 195–196).

During the "third awakening" (1890–1920), the social gospel movement— the birth of the church's concern with social problems—was founded and the temperance movement triumphed in the form of national alcohol prohibition. During this period, the disasters of post-Civil War Reconstruction, the rapacious activities of the Robber Barons, and political corruption at every level became evident to all, as was the need for reform.

The "fourth awakening" (1960–1990), some argue, was characterized by a renewed interest in spiritual matters, including a critique of science, technology, and materialism; countercultural activity, including communal living; a recruitment to Eastern religions; and a revitalization of conservative, fundamentalist, and evangelical Christianity (McLoughlin, 1977, pp. 179–216; Rose, 1982, pp. 186, 196; Kelley, 1977). These changes took place in a society in which material superabundance began to seem hollow and unrelated to the traditional virtues of intelligence and hard work. Science and technology were unable to solve society's major social problems and, in fact, created several more serious problems, such as environmental pollution and the threat of thermonuclear warfare. Spirituality, some say, was an inevitable product of such cultural developments.

Millenarianism.   Millenarianism (or millenialism) is the belief that life on earth will be transformed suddenly, imminently, by spiritual intervention, and that humans should prepare the way for the creation of this new spiritual regime. In this scenario, only the faithful will be judged to be righteous, and the wicked shall perish. Probably the most well-known case of millenial fervor is the medieval Crusades, of which there were ten (including the "Children's Crusade") between 1095 and 1291. It was the intention of the crusaders to "wrest the Holy Land from the infidel," that is, the Muslims. The Crusades generated "unprecedented excitement and feverish activity" (Turner and Killian, 1987, p. 1). Their battle cry was "God wills it!" They regarded themselves as "armies of the Lord." Pilgrims believed that the end of the world was at hand, and that, once Jerusalem was captured, Jesus would descend to earth and judge humankind. Many sold their houses, farms, and property and abandoned their jobs and families to march off on a cause whose outcome was extremely uncertain. Many had no idea where Jerusalem was or even what continent it was on; some believed that it lay just beyond their own village. Many crusaders were robbed, beaten, killed, or sold into slavery; the crusaders, in turn, robbed people they encountered, plundered many of the cities they came upon, and slaughtered their inhabitants, who were mainly, but not exclusively, Muslims and Jews. Several million souls lost their lives in the Crusades, and most contemporary historials and theologians—Christian and non-Christian alike—regard them as one of the most disastrous sets of events in the entire history of Christianity.

The Crusades were motivated by a mixture of spiritual and material goals and had a variety of causes—a sudden increase in the population and the prosperity of Western Europe; a desire for territorial expansion, colonies, and the opening of trade routes; the lure of travel and adventure; and the seeming promise of riches for noble and peasant alike. While many crusaders marched off to war with dreams of gold in their pockets, others were genuinely moved by the desire, however misplaced or unrealistic, to recreate a Christian land where Jesus preached. It is possible that, the more unrealistic the goal, the more remarkable the fervor that sustains the quest for it, making the Crusades one of the more astonishing—and distressing—millenial enterprises of all time.

Anthropologists have found that when small, tribal societies were subdued militarily by larger, more powerful and better materially equipped ones, the former often generated millenial or messianic beliefs, that is, beliefs in the coming of a new era, or the rebirth of an old, "golden" age, often accompanied by the prophecy of some sort of a charismatic messiah. These religions are typically nativistic as well: They attempt to revive or regain aspects of a tribal society's original culture after being conquered and dominated by another culture. Among late nineteenth century North American Indians, the Ghost Dance religion, and in 20th New Guinea, the Cargo cult, represent outbreaks of millenial and nativistic fervor. These are examples—as all millenial and nativistic beliefs are—of "crisis cults" (LaBarre, 1971), that is, fervid outbreaks of renewed religious faith and activity brought on by "massive misfortune" in the background of followers and a sense of disillusionment with existing reality. Messianic, nativistic, and millenial movements, cults, and religions serve as an outlet or an expression for a kind of spiritual depression.

The Ghost Dance religion emerged among Western Native Americans at a time when white settlers had appropriated tribal lands and slaughtered the buffalo, and tribal ways had disappeared or were disappearing. A feeling of desolation was widespread among North American Indians, which made them receptive to any message that seemed to offer hope. The Ghost Dance doctrine brought that hope; in it, the invading whites would be destroyed, the buffalo would return, and the old Indian ways would be resurrected. Into this situation of cultural decay and poverty, "the Ghost Dance doctrine shone like a bright light" (Lesser, 1933). This new cult was an adaptive response of a people to intolerable stresses laid upon them by poverty, oppression, and the destruction of a way of life (Wallace, 1965, p. ix; Mooney, 1965). However, since the prophecies concerning coming events were fairly specific and the time frame was fairly immediate, the Ghost Dance could not survive in the lives of its followers for very long. For instance, one tenet in the religion's beliefs was that the holy Ghost Dance shirts that members of the sect fabricated would protect the faithful in battle against the white man's bullets. The failure of this belief must have been bitter and disillusioning.

The return of one's ancestors to right present wrongs is a common theme in nativistic religions. Among natives of New Guinea, in the late nineteenth and early twentieth centuries, a sect arose that was based on the belief that, one day, a Western ship—in more recent versions, an airplane—manned by whites (that is, the natives' own ancestors, who were ghosts, and therefore who were white) will arrive on their shores; in its hold will be "cargo," that is, a great abundance of material goods. At this point, a new order will be ushered in; a new era of prosperity, justice, and equality will arrive. Motivation to participate in the cargo cult came from two sources. First, "antagonism and struggle" against Europeans and their culture, and second, "the arrival of Western goods [and] the awareness of the practical and economic significance of these goods" (Lanternari, 1966, p. 235). The Cargo cult has flared up and died down in various part of New Guinea at different times over the past century. As with the Ghost Dance, however, its predictions are fairly specific and their fulfillment is said to be fairly imminent; while its participants may fervently participate in its ritual and believe in its tenets for a certain period of time, it is difficult to sustain this enthusiasm for longer stretches.

Three basic ingredients that make millenial (or millenarian) religious cults possible are one, some sort of cultural disaster or crisis; two, a prior set of millenial ideas from the original culture; and three, the emergence of a charismatic leader to put together, articulate, and propagate these ideas. In both North America and New Guinea, the indigenous population was conquered, dominated, and exploited by Europeans; their cultural heritage undermined or destroyed; and their traditional livelihood threatened or decimated. With both cultures, beliefs existed concerning the return of dead ancestors to earth who would sweep away the present, corrupt order and reestablish a "golden age." In both, charismatic leaders arose to give voice to these beliefs. The appeal of religious cults based on such ideas, and the fervor with which they were held, should not be surprising. At the same time, such beliefs could not survive for very long, at least in their original form, because they were based on predictions that simply could not come to pass. The Ghost Dance religion died out entirely, or became fused with the more otherworldy thrust of the peyote religion. As late as the 1960s in New Guinea, a "diffuse cargo thinking" was still found and a few "insignificant cults" have been reported recently (Lawrence, 1971, p. 274); but the Cargo cult does not exist in anything like its former glory. All crazes, religious or otherwise, must eventually burn themselves out.

Persecution. The persecution of a religious denomination, some people practicing or thought to practice a certain kind of behavior, a category of human beings, or an imaginary enemy, represents another type of religious craze. Persecutions are different from the other types of crazes in that they do not entail the movement toward something that is regarded as desirable, but an attack against something that is seen as undesirable (Smelser, 1962, p. 170). Still, in many religions, what is positive and what is negative are opposite sides of the same coin, and so, there are strong parallels between "positive" and "negative" crazes. Religious persecutions that become crazes and manias number in the tens of thousands throughout human history and all over the world. Sudden, fervent hostility against the wrongdoing or supposed wrongdoing of a group of individuals is almost an intrinsic aspect of the religions of the world that are built on a powerful sense of the righteousness of their faithful. At times, followers of certain religions have the feeling that "somewhere in the midst of the great society" there is "another society, small and clandestine, which not only threatened the existence of the great society but was also addicted to practices which were felt to be wholly abominable in the literal sense of anti-human." As a consequence, they felt the "urge to purify the world through the annihilation of some category of human beings imagined as agents of corruption and incarnation of evil" (Cohn, 1975, p. xiv).

Perhaps the most famous of all religious crazes involving persecution of an enemy is the Renaissance witchcraze. On the continent of Europe, roughly between 1400 and 1650, hundreds of thousands of people—perhaps as many as a half million—about 85 percent of them women, were judged to have "consorted with the devil," and were put to death. (In contrast, in the witch-hunt that took place in 1692 in Salem, Massachussetts, just 20 people were executed for this supposed crime.) Much of Europe, especially France, Switzerland, and Germany, was buzzing with suspicion, accusations, trials, and the punishment of supposed evildoers. It was in every sense a craze, because, once an accusation was made, there was little the accused could do to protect herself. Children, women, and "entire families were sent to the stake. . . . Entire villages were exterminated. . . . Germany was covered with stakes, where witches were burning alive." Said one inquisitor, "I wish [the witches] had but one body, so that we could burn them all at once, in one fire!" (Ben-Yehuda, 1985, pp. 36, 37).

The causes of the witchcraze were complex and deep-seated, but, in a nutshell, it was generated by a certain kind of perceived threat. Renaissance Europe was emerging from the medieval period, in which a feudal order arranged people into a clear-cut hierarchy and the Church ruled supreme in matters of faith. By the early 1400s, this neatly ordered society was breaking down. Peasants were moving off the estates to take up residence in the cities; trade and commerce were expanding the horizons of the residents of small, formerly isolated villages; manufacturing was stirring in workshops and small factories. Scientific and artistic ideas were coming into conflict with traditional Catholic teaching. Heretics were denouncing and breaking away from the Catholic Church and forming new denominations beyond its control. The Middle Ages were coming apart at the seams; to a traditionalist, something had to be done to restore the moral order.

The witchcraze represented a reaction to these changes, an attempt to "counteract and prevent change and to reestablish traditional religious authority. . . . By persecuting witches, this society, led by the Church, attempted to redefine its moral boundaries" (Ben-Yehuda, 1980, p. 14). Witches were a convenient target since the "opponent had to be widely perceived as a threat to society itself and to the Christian world view. . . . Witches were the only deviants who could be construed as attacking the very core of the social system" (Ben-Yehuda, 1985, pp. 58, 59). The witchcraze was an attempt—a futile and failed one, to be sure—to "prevent the changes that the medieval social order was going through" (Ben-Yehuda, 1985, p. 71). In a sense, then, while the European witch hunt represented an attack on a specific target designated as evil, it was simultaneously an attempt to restore things that were regarded as good and desirable—traditional feudal society and the supremacy of the Catholic Church. In this sense, it is not very different from the other crazes we've looked at, which represented a fervent, headlong rush to acquire or engage in that which took on intense positive value for some people for a brief period of time. By the middle of the seventeenth century, European society had become so secularized that the central idea of the witchcraze—that the basis of all evil was seduction by the devil—was undermined; eventually, "power was taken away from the courts, the inquisitorial machinery was dismantled, and persecution of witches came to an end. . . . A new social order had visibly and triumphantly been created . . ., and the witch-hunt had no purpose whatsoever" (Ben-Yehuda, 1985, p. 70).

SUMMARY

Fads, fashion, and crazes represent a form of social change. At the same time, while some changes—such as industrialization and urbanization—have had a profound and momentous impact, by their very nature, changes broughout about by fads, fashion, and crazes tend to be more superficial and less lasting. At the same time, these phenomena are important to study because they reveal general social processes and reflect cultural conditions at the time they are generated.

Fads are widely regarded as activities or products that are temporary and fleeting and operate or exist in a fairly trivial area of life. Fashion is regarded as a style or a custom in a given area, usually dress and manners, that change substantially over time. A craze or mania is an activity that becomes obsessively, intensely important to a small group of enthusiasts.

Fads are largely unpredictable, far more so that for more conventional products or activities. Why are some activities or products taken up on a mass scale? No theory could possibly predict why specific fads come about and others don't. At the same time, we can discuss factors that make certain fads more likely than others. In spite of their reputation as bizarre behavior, fads nearly always represent only mild departures from conventional norms. As the emergent norm perspective would predict, fads tend to take place within clear normative boundaries. Certain types of societies encourage fads. For instance, product fads usually take place in a capitalist society, usually one in which members do not fear looking silly. Likewise, certain periods of history encourage faddish behavior. Fads tend to attract the young—preadolescents, adolescents, and young adults. Clearly, for these age categories, fads serve important social and individual functions; two include cohesion and separateness.

The view that fashion is irrational, morally absurd, and exploitative is widespread in some intellectual circles. Few such views are able to account for the concrete reality of fashion. Most writing about fashion refers to clothing and related adornment and apparel. Fashion has one foot in conventional, institutionalized behavior and one foot in collective behavior. It is produced within a routine, predictable, cyclical time frame by a permanent social and economic structure. At the same time, it is more shifting and unstable than the world of manufacturing and selling conventional products. Fashion stands somewhere in between the world of selling novelty or fad items and that of more stable industries, such as cars and office equipment. In fashion, the key is *innovation within stability.*

Fashion has been explained by the "trickling down" of high status symbols to less prestigious groups, categories, and classes. Clearly, social class and status play a role in fashion that is far more pronounced than is true for any other forms of collective behavior. Lower status individuals attempt to capture status by adopting the symbols of upper status individuals; when they become widely adopted, they no longer symbolize high status, and upper status individuals abandon them and move on to yet-undiscovered styles. While this view has a grain of truth, it is too simple to explain the dynamics of status. It assumes one clearly recognizable upper status group imitated by a large number of lower status individuals, which is not entirely the case. In addition, fashion may "trickle up" as well as down. Many theories of fashion assume that the public can be stampeded into purchasing nearly any item, no matter how bizarre or how little they may like it originally. This view has little, if any, validity. Recent events show that the public makes rational, considered choices on the basis of its own tastes and lifestyles. The fashion industry anticipates change more than it determines it. Gender is a central factor in fashion: More pressure is put on women to be in fashion than is true for men. The values of each period of history determine the nature of its fashion.

Crazes tend to be more intense and even frenzied, and engage a much smaller number of participants than is true of fad and fashion. Two areas of social life in which crazes are likely to appear are economic activity and religion. Three economic phenomena that manifest craze-like behavior are economic speculation, stock market bubbles, and the pyramid game. Three types of religious crazes are renewals, millenarianism, and persecutions.

References

Ager, Susan. 1980. "What's Beneath the Pyramids: Fear and Fantasy, Greed and Giddy Glee." *Gambling Scene Digest/Newsmagazine* (June): 4–9.

Aguirre, B. E., Enrico L. Quarantelli, and Jorge L. Mendoza. 1988. "The Collective Behavior of Fads: The Characteristics, Effects, and Career of Streaking." *American Sociological Review,* 53 (August): 569–584.

Anderson, William A. 1977. "The Social Organization and Social Control of a Fad." *Urban Life,* 6 (July): 221–240.

Baldwin, Frances Elizabeth. 1926. *Sumptuary Legislation and Personal Regulation in England.* Baltimore: Johns Hopkins Press.

Barber, Bernard, and Lyle S. Lobel. 1952. "Fashion in Women's Clothes and the American Social System." *Social Forces,* 31 (December): 124–131.

Barthes, Roland. 1983. *The Fashion System* (Mattthew Ward and Richard Howard, trans.). New York: Hill & Wang.

Bass, Robert. 1990. Personal communication, December 31.

Bell, Quentin. 1976. *On Human Finery* (2nd ed.). New York: Schocken Books.

Ben-Yehuda, Nachman. 1980. "The European Witch Craze of the 14th to 17th Centuries: A Sociologist's Perspectives." *American Journal of Sociology,* 86 (July): 1–31.

Ben-Yehuda, Nachman. 1985. *Deviance and Moral Boundaries: Witchcraft, the Occult, Science Fiction, Deviant Sciences and Scientists.* Chicago: University of Chicago Press.

Bergler, Edmund. 1953. *Fashion and the Unconscious.* Madison, Conn.: International Universities Press.

Blumer, Herbert. 1968. "Fashion." *International Encyclopedia of the Social Sciences,* pp. 341–345. New York: Macmillan.

Blumer, Herbert. 1969. "Fashion: From Class Differentiation to Collective Selection." *Sociological Quarterly,* 10 (Summer): 275–291.

Brownmiller, Susan. 1984. *Femininity.* New York: Simon & Schuster.

Bruning, Fred. 1989. "Rx for Fun and Profit." *The Newsday Magazine* (December 24): 11, 22–23.

Cohn, Norman. 1975. *Europe's Inner Demons: An Enquiry Inspired by the Great Witch Hunt.* New York: Basic Books.

Coleridge, Nicholas. 1989. *The Fashion Conspiracy: A Remarkable Journey Through the Empires of Fashion.* London: Heinemann-Mandarin.

Crudele, John. 1986. "After the Cabbage Patch Kids." *The New York Times* (August 23): 29, 33.

Davis, Fred. 1985. "Clothing and Fashion as Communication." In Michael R. Solomon (ed.), *The Psychology of Fashion,* pp. 15–27. Lexington, Mass.: Lexington Books.

Davis, Fred. 1989. "Of Maids' Uniforms and Blue Jeans: The Drama of Status Ambivalences in Clothing and Fashion." *Qualitative Sociology,* 12 (Winter): 337–355.

Davis, Fred. 1991. "Herbert Blumer and the Study of Fashion: A Reminiscence and A Critique." *Symbolic Interaction,* 14 (1): 1–21.

Dunn, Donald H. 1975. *Ponzi! The Boston Swindler.* New York: McGraw-Hill.

Evans, Robert R., and Jerry L. L. Miller. 1975. "Barely an End in Sight." In Robert R. Evans (ed.), *Readings in Collective Behavior,* (2nd ed.), pp. 401–417. Chicago: Rand-McNally.

Feder, Barnaby J. 1988. "Coleco Fails to Fend Off Chapter 11." *The New York Times* (July 13): D1, D4.

Fine, Gary Alan. 1983. *Shared Fantasy: Role-Playing Games and Social Worlds.* Chicago: University of Chicago Press.

Fox-Genovese, Elizabeth. 1987. "The Empress's New Clothes: The Politics of Fashion." *Socialist Review,* 17 (January–February): 7–30.

Garber, Peter M. 1989. "Tulipmania." *Journal of Political Economy,* 97 (3): 535–560.

Garber, Peter M. 1990. "Who Put the Mania in the Tulipmania?" In Eugene N. White (ed.), *Crashes and Panics: The Lessons from History,* pp. 3–32. Homewood, Ill.: Dow Jones-Irwin.

Gold, Ray L. 1964. "Fad." In Julius Gould and William L. Kolb (eds.), *A Dictionary of the Social Sciences,* pp. 256–257. New York: Free Press.

Hall, Trish. 1988. "As Women Balk, Fashion Rethinks the Mini." *The New York Times* (March 9): A1, C8.

Kantrowitz, Barbara, et al. 1988. "A Fashion Revolt." *Newsweek* (December 5): 61–64.

Keerdoja, Eileen P., and Patricia J. Sethi. 1980. "CB Couldn't Keep on Truckin'" *Newsweek* (July 21): 12.

Kelley, Dean M. 1977. *Why Conservative Churches Are Growing: A Study in the Sociology of Religion* (2nd ed.). New York: Harper & Row.

Kerbo, Harold R., Kerrie Marshall, and Philip Holley. 1978. "Reestablishing 'Gemeinschaft'? An Examination of the CB Fad," *Urban Life*, 7 (October): 337–358.

Kindleberger, Charles P. 1987. *Manias, Panics, and Crashes: A History of Financial Crises* (rev. ed.). New York: Basic Books.

Klores, Dan. 1980. "The Pyramid Scam Hits Town." *New York* (June 23): 22–25.

Lang, Kurt, and Gladys Engel Lang. 1961. *Collective Dynamics*. New York: Thomas Y. Crowell.

LaBarre, Weston. 1971. "Materials for a History of Studies of Crisis Cults: A Bibliographic Essay." *Current Anthropology*, 12 (1): 3–44.

Lanternari, Vittorio. 1966. *The Religions of the Oppressed: A Study of Modern Messianic Cults* (Lisa Sergio, trans.). New York: Alfred Knopf.

LaPiere, Richard T. 1938. *Collective Behavior*. New York: McGraw-Hill.

Lawrence, Peter. 1971. *Road Belong Cargo*. Manchester, England: Manchester University Press.

Lesser, Alexander. 1933. "Cultural Significance of the Ghost Dance Religion." *American Anthropologist*, 35 (January/March): 108–115.

Lofland, John. 1985. *Protest: Studies of Collective Behavior and Social Movements*. New Brunswick, N. J.: Transaction Books.

Lurie, Alison. 1981. *The Language of Clothes*. New York: Vintage.

Mackay, Charles. 1932. *Extraordinary Popular Delusions and the Madness of Crowds*. New York: L. C. Page.

Marum, Andrew, and Frank Parise. 1984. *Follies and Foibles: A View of 20th Century Fads*. New York: Facts on File.

McLoughlin, William G. 1978. *Revivals, Awakenings, and Reform: An Essay on Social Change in America, 1607–1977*. Chicago: University of Chicago Press.

Meyersohn, Rolf, and Elihu Katz. 1957. "Notes on a Natural History of Fads." *American Journal of Sociology*, 62 (May): 594–601.

Miller, David. 1985. *Introduction to Collective Behavior*. Belmont, Calif.: Wadsworth.

Mishkin, Frederic S. 1990. "Comment on Who Put the Mania in Tulipmania." In Eugene N. White (ed.), *Crashes and Panics: The Lessons From History*, pp. 57–60. Homewood, Ill.: Dow Jones-Irwin.

Mooney, James. 1965. *The Ghost-Dance Religion and the Sioux Outbreak of 1890*. Chicago: University of Chicago Press.

Neal, Larry D. 1990. "How the South Sea Bubble Was Blown Up and Burst: A New Look at Old Data." In Eugene N. White (ed.), *Crashes and Panics: The Lessons From History*, pp. 33–56. Homewood, Ill.: Dow Jones-Irwin.

Olson, Helen. 1980. "How to Make $16,000 Building Pyramids in Your Spare Time." *Gambling Scene Digest/Newsmagazine* (June): 30–32.

Ramirez, Anthony. 1990. "Riding the Fad in Slap Bracelets." *The New York Times* (October 27): 31, 41.

Rice, Berkeley. 1988. "Boom and Doom on Wall Street." *Psychology Today* (April): 50–54.

Rodseth, Bob. 1980. "Pyramid Players: Exponents of the Exponent." *Gambling Scene Digest/Newsmagazine* (June): 14–16.

Rose, Jerry D. 1982. *Outbreaks: The Sociology of Collective Behavior*. New York: Free Press.

Rossel, Robert D. 1970. "The Great Awakening: A Historical Analysis." *American Journal of Sociology*, 75 (May): 907–925.

Sapir, Edward. 1931. "Fashion." *Encyclopaedia of the Social Sciences*, 6: 139–144.

Sebald, Hans. 1984. *Adolescence: A Social Psychological Analysis* (3rd ed.). Englewood Cliffs, N. J.: Prentice-Hall.

Shiller, Robert J. 1989. "Fashions, Fads, and Bubbles in Financial Markets." In Robert J. Shiller, *Market Volatility*, pp. 56–68. Cambridge, Mass.: MIT Press.

Simmel, Georg. 1904. "Fashion." *International Quarterly*, 10 (October): 130–155.

Simmel, Georg. 1957. "Fashion." *American Journal of Sociology*, 62 (May): 541–558.

Smelser, Neil J. 1962. *Theory of Collective Behavior*. New York: Free Press.

Smith, Vernon L., Gerry L. Suchanek, and Arlington W. Williams. 1988. "Stock Market Bubbles." *Finanzmarkt und Portfolio Management*, 2. Jahrgang 1988—Nr.3: 5–32.

Thigpen, David E. 1991. "Bungee Jumping Comes of Age." *Time* (April 15): 50.

Turner, Ralph H., and Lewis M. Killian. 1987. *Collective Behavior* (3rd ed.). Englewood Cliffs, N. J.: Prentice-Hall.

Vetter, Craig. 1990. "Rubber Jump." *Playboy* (September): 98, 100, 160–162.

Wallace, Anthony F. C. 1965. "James Mooney (1861–1921) and the Study of the Ghost-Dance Religion." In James Mooey, *The Ghost-Dance Religion and the Sioux Outbreak of 1890*, pp. v–x. Chicago: University of Chicago Press.

Wilson, Elizabeth. 1987. *Adorned in Dreams: Fashion and Modernity*. Berkeley: University of California Press.

Zetterberg, Stephen I. 1989. "The Pie Tin That Flew Round the World." *The New York Times* (July 26): A22.

PART FIVE

INTRODUCTION TO SOCIAL MOVEMENTS

A fter reading Chapter 1, we already know a few things about social movements. First, we know that they are *organized efforts by a substantial number of people to change, or to resist change, in some major aspect of society.* Second, we know that collective behavior and social movements share several crucial similarities: they are both *dynamic, extrainstitutional,* and *collective.* Third, we know that they are different as well; in contrast to collective behavior, social movements tend to be *longer lasting,* more *organized,* their actions are more *planned out,* they are more likely to *challenge the established order,* and their participants are more *intential* and *goal-oriented.*

And fourth, we know that, over the past generation or so, there has been a shift in the way that social movements and collective behavior have been studied. The older, classical, or *collective behavior approach,* which dominated the field until the early 1970s (McAdam et al., 1988, pp. 695ff), saw social movement participation as a type, form, or aspect of collective behavior. In contrast, the more recent *politico-rational approach,* which has been dominant in the field since the 1970s, stresses the *differences,* not the similarities, between social movements and collective behavior. In addition, this approach emphasizes the similarities between social movement participation and mainstream political and organizational behavior. It emphasizes the question of the outcome of specific movement strategies, especially the attainment of movement goals, and it sees resources, power, social organization, and leadership as a crucial set of factors that determine the attainment of movement goals. These are dimensions that the classical collective behavior approach to the study of social movements usually ignore. The resource mobilization approach argued that the collective behavior approach *simply could not explain* most of the most important things that take place in social movments.

In many ways, the politico-rational approach to the study of social movements sees the relationship between collective behavior and social movements in almost precisely the opposite way that the classic collective behavior school saw it: It emphasizes the differences between the phenomena of collective behavior and social movements. In a sense, it *ignores* and *trivializes* collective behavior while, at the same time, *intellectualizes* and *emphasizes* the phenomenon of social movement participation, both by imputing mainly purposive motives to participants and by stressing its similarity to institutional, organization behavior. One gets the feeling that the politico-rational approach seeks to place as much distance between collective behavior and social movements as possible. Indeed, it seems that its practitioners feel that to draw any parallels between the two phenomena would be to taint social movement activity with the stigma of collective behavior. The politico-rational approach seems to be saying that social movement activity is good, collective behavior is bad; social movement activity is rational, collective behavior is irrational; social movement activity is purposive, collective behavior is purposeless; social movement activity is important, collective behavior is trivial and silly. It seems almost as if the existence of social movements *pre-*

cludes and *negates* the importance of collective behavior. Resource mobilization theorists would like to expel collective behavior from the field of social movements; its observers should "set up shop in some distant geography" (Michael Schwartz, private communication).

In my view, the politico-rational critique of the collective behavior approach offered a corrective to the field. Their studies showed that there was an element of planning, institutionalization, and rationality in all social movement activity, that spontaneity cannot be equated with disorganization, impulsivity, and a lack of structure (Rosenthal and Schwartz, 1989). These are important points. However, in my view, the pendulum has swung too far in the opposite direction. In fact, now, given that the resource mobilization approach has put its social-structural analysis in place in the study of social movements, some of its theorists are now attempting to look at more processible, social-psychological, cultural, and symbolic concepts (Aldon Morris, private communication), suggesting that something of an emerging synthesis between the two approaches may be taking place. Each perspective, taken by itself, is inadequate.

As was discussed in Chapter 1, this book breaks with both approaches; in fact, in a number of ways, it represents a reaction to both the collective behavior and the politico-rational approaches—the traditional view that saw social movements as a form of collective behavior and the newer view that, in effect, has attempted to define the field of collective behavior out of existence. It is not that I believe that the truth lies somewhere in between, it is that, in my view, both views are wrong or at least focus altogether too narrowly on one aspect of the phenomena they investigate. In contrast, I look at the similarities and the differences between collective behavior and social movements, as well as those between social movements and institutionalized organizational behavior, first, *as an empirical question*, and second, *as a continuum, a spectrum*.

Yes, some social movement participation is very much like mainstream political activity—but some of it is not. Yes, a great deal of collective behavior is worlds apart from social movement participation—but much of it is very similar. As I said in Chapter 1, I do not believe that social movement participation can be assumed to be more similar to mainstream political processes than to most forms of collective behavior. This depends on the social movement in question. While social movements can be studied as purposive, goal-directed organizations, this does not mean that, in all cases, that is the *most productive* way of studying them. The two phenomena of social movement activity and collective behavior *shade off into one another;* there are specific social movements that are very much like collective behavior, and specific social movements that are very much like mainstream political organizations. There are important similarities and differences between collective behavior and social movements, just as there are between collective behavior and mainstream organizations. Specific cases of social movements will be far more similar in their spontaneous, emergent, extrainsitutional character to most forms of collective behavior; this is especially true of movements in their initial stages. Likewise, specific cases of social movements will be found to be more similar to behavior in mainstream political organizations than to collective behavior. The similarities and differences between and among these three areas of social life cannot be assumed; they are somewhat different from one social movement to another. (See Marx, 1980, pp. 259ff, for a similar position.)

The politico-rational approach, in its haste to demarcate social movement activity off from collective behavior, in my view, overly emphasizes the rationality, planning, and institutional involvements in social movement activity. While no behavior is completely spontaneous and extrainstitutional, *some behavior is more so than others.* It is important to emphasize that all behavior, whether collective or otherwise, is predicated on participants' involvement in institutional life. However, it is, as I see it, fallacious to infer from this that there is no *dimension* to institutionality. In contrast to both the classical and the politico-rational views, the perspective I adopt in this book would depict the relationship between collective behavior and social movements as a band, spectrum, or a *continuum*, with each case or type shading off into the one next to it. Many social movements share very little in common with many forms of collective behavior, and to look at them as instances of collective behavior would be to ignore their most essential characteristics. On the other hand, many social movements do have a great deal more in common with certain forms of collective behavior than with mainstream organizational behavior; to examine their organization, resources, and leadership to determine (say) the likelihood that their stated goals will be achieved, would be to miss what is most interesting and revealing about them.

Moreover, not only are certain *social movements* more like collective behavior than mainstream political organizations, but also, many *aspects* of social movements can more fruitfully be looked at as forms of collective behavior than as instances of formal organizations. For example, rumor is rife in many contexts—in movements and movement organizations, in corporations, in political parties—and rumor is a collective behavior phenomenon. Riots sometimes (although rarely) figure in the success or failure of certain social movements, and the dynamics of riots falls largely within the scope of the field of collective behavior. Fad and fashion, too, often emerge in the ideology and behavior of some movement activists. For instance, in the 1960s, among Black Power advocates, African dashikis, Afro haircuts, and esoteric handshakes were almost a sign of in-group membership, but they declined in importance, although their efforts to bring about African-American empowerment has not (Aldon Morris, private communication). At the same time, note that rumor, riots, and fads cannot explain what is *most important* about social movement activity, but they may explain *some* of its aspects, which is why the processes of collective behavior cannot be banished to an entirely different field from that of the study of social movements.

Actually, these two approaches—the classical or "collective behavior" and the newer, "politico-rational"—are really studying two quite distinct phenomena. The collective behavior approach wishes to explain social movement *participation*, while the politico-rational approach is looking at a much broader range of phenomena—mainly the *dynamics* of social movements and social movement organizations. The collective behavior approach is entirely "micro" or individual in its focus: How may we explain the individual's behavior? Its attention is centered on how and why certain types of individuals at certain times in certain contexts join social movments, or certain social movements. The "micro" focus is concerned with what the individual is doing, even if that individual is acting within a given structure or organization, and, at least in the past, it often assumed that individual behavior can explain or account for the larger institutional processes. Whether we are looking at individual differences or society-wide characteristics, the variable to be explained here is the behavior of the individual social movement participant. Moreover, the collective behavior approach is not especially interested in the movement after indiiduals have joined it (except insofar as its members engage in further collective behavior, such as rioting). The success of a mass movement is *assumed*, given successful recruitment.

In contrast, the more contemporary politico-rational approach—specifically resource mobilization theory, discussed briefly in Chapter 2 (see page 84) and to be discussed in more detail in Chapter 10 (see page 423)—argues that there is no automatic relationship between mass mobilization and a movement's success (Zald, 1991). Its focus is not exclusively on the individual (or the "micro" level), as that of the collective behavior approach, but is largely on the organization (the middle, or "meso" level of analysis); on relations between organizations (also the "meso" level); and on larger structures called *institutions* (the "macro" level), such as the state and the economy. Thus, instead of *only* asking why certain individuals join social movements (which, however, some resource mobilization theorists do; see Klandermans and Oegema, 1987), the politico-rational approach, working on the "micro," the "meso," *and* the "macro" approach, would ask why certain kinds of organizations succeed while others fail. What is the relationship between leaders and the rank and file in a social movement organization? What societal conditions are likely to generate many social movements and social movement organizations, and which ones are likely to generate a few? How do social movement organizations within a given social movement relate to one another? What is the relationship between the state and social movements? How organizations and institutions (the "meso" and the "macro" levels) act, the politico-rational approach argues, is far more than the total sum of the actions of their individual participants. We cannot know what happens at the organizational and institutional levels simply by knowing what happens at the individual level. Social movements and social movement organizations have a life of their own, a life that must be investigated on their own levels.

What are social movements? How are social movements similar—and different—from collective behavior? How may we study social movements? Which theories of social movements make the most sense? Who participates in social movements? What are social movment organizations like? What types of social movements exist? What factors make for social movement success—and failure? These are some of the important issues we'll be looking at in this section of the book.

A Political Demonstration:
Was It Collective or Organizational Behavior?

In spite of the rain, more than 15,000 people converged on a beach near the Long Island Lighting Company (LILCO) nuclear plant in Shoreham, New York. Their goal: to prevent the plant from going on line. The nuclear accident at Three Mile Island had taken place only two months before, and a clear majority of the residents of the north shore of Long Island opposed the opening of the facility. Protesters, many of them carrying young children in their arms or on their backs, held up signs, heard speeches, chanted slogans, and listened to songs denouncing nuclear power. Volunteers dispensed buttons, T-shirts, food, printed material, and first aid, when needed. The demonstration was peaceful, and an air of goodwill and comraderie dominated the gathering. In addition to the main, legal, demonstration, a small and separate contingent of 600 activists also protested, a few of whom scaled, then knocked down the gate to the plant in an expression of nonviolent civil disobedience. Virtually all of the activist contingent were arrested.

The demonstration was not spontaneous, our principal defining characteristic of collective behavior. It had been planned by a specific organization, the SHAD Alliance (Sound and Hudson Against Atomic Development), with the cooperation of other organizations, months in advance. Transportation to the plant was provided, and most of the protesters came in busses which left from a number of specific, central locations. All of the major details that mounting such a large protest entailed, from increased traffic and the parking problem to possible damage to the town beach, had been worked out in advance with LILCO, Brookhaven town, and local and county police. Even the technically illegal occupation of the plant grounds by the more active "civil disobedience" protesters was discussed in advance with LILCO authorities and the Suffolk County police, who knew more or less what to expect. (Organizers told the activists that they were permitted some on-the-scene innovation, as long as it contributed to anti-nuclear movement goals.) Only the weather, the size of the crowd, and whether each party would behave as agreed, were not known in advance. (I have relied on Goodman, 1989, and my own observations for this account. I participated in the main demonstration; Jonathan Cohen, who took part in the smaller, more activist, demonstration, helped me with the details of that aspect of the event.)

Thus, in the sense that I have defined it, in most of its aspects, the 1979 Shoreham demonstration does not qualify as an instance of collective behavior. As I said, it was not spontaneous. Most of the behavior that was enacted near or on the Shoreham plant grounds had been planned out in advance by the members of a specific organization, the SHAD Alliance, which had (and still has) leaders, supporters, and active participants. Nearly all of the participants at the demonstration had a specific goal in mind in joining it: to prevent the Shoreham nuclear plant from opening. (At this writing, the plant has not gone on line, and, in all likelihood, will never go on line.) While the demonstration itself only lasted a few hours, the organization that sponsored it and the organizations with which it was allied still exist and work against nuclear power. The only elements of the demonstration that were similar to activities that qualify as collective behavior were the fact that it was a less-fully institutionalized or normatively supported activity than mainstream politics, it represented a dynamic element of the culture within which it takes place, and *exactly* what could have happened during the more activist phase of the demonstration was not known in advance. With respect to the last of these points, for example, some of the more militant protestors could have taken more drastic action—attempted to destroy the Shoreham installation, for instance—or the police *could* have been more forceful than they were in their arrests, for instance, by striking the protestors with clubs. In these cases, it is very likely that some form of collective behavior would have erupted.

In short, the anti-nuclear demonstration that took place on a beach in Shoreham, Long Island, on that drizzly day in June, 1979, is *not* a good example of collective behavior. Instead, it qualifies as *social movement activity*, characterized more by the enactment of purposive, goal-directed, organizationally generated plans than by the qualities that define collective behavior. When looking at and thinking about collective behavior and social movement phenomena, we should keep in mind that their similarities and their differences depend on the specific *types* of collective behavior and social movement we are comparing.

References

Goodman, Miriam. 1989. "June 3, 1979: Shoreham's Rainy Day." *The New York Times* (June 4): 20 L.I.

Klandermans, Bert, and Dirk Oegema. 1987. "Potentials, Networks, Motivations, and Barriers: Steps Towards Participation in Social Movements," *American Sociological Review*, 52 (August): 519–531.

Marx, Gary T. 1980. "Conceptual Problems in the Field of Collective Behavior." In Hubert M. Blalock, Jr. (ed.), *Sociological Theory and Research: A Critical Appraisal*, pp. 258–274. New York: Free Press.

McAdam, Doug, John D. McCarthy, and Mayer N. Zald. 1988. "Social Movements." In Neil J. Smelser (ed.), *Handbook of Sociology*, pp. 695–737. Newbury Park, Calif.: Sage.

Rosenthal, Naomi, and Michael Schwartz. 1989. "Spontaneity and Democracy in Social Movements." In Bert Klandermans (ed.), *International Social Movement Research: A Research Annual*, pp. 33–59, vol.2 of *Organizing for Change: Social Movement Organizations in Europe and the United States*. Greenwich, Conn.: JAI Press.

Zald, Mayer N. 1991. "Looking Backward to Look Forward: Reflections on the Past and Future of the Resource Mobilization Research Program." In Aldon Morris and Carol Mueller (eds.), *Frontiers of Social Movement Theory*. New Haven, Conn.: Yale University Press.

CHAPTER
10

SOCIAL MOVEMENTS

A group of women demonstrate outside a Times Square movie theater that is showing a pornographic film depicting violence against women. The demonstrators carry posters, distribute leaflets, and chant slogans. Members of a civil rights organization hold a meeting to discuss the most effective strategy to persuade Black people to vote in an upcoming election. Ecologists drive long spikes into redwood trees to prevent loggers from cutting them down. Animal rights activists break into a university laboratory, open a dozen or so cages, and take out rabbits, rats, and chimpanzees, bring them home, and discuss the most humane means of caring for them. Militant members of an anti-abortion splinter group firebomb an abortion clinic, causing extensive damage and forcing it to close down until repairs are made.

These very different cases are all examples of social movement activity, that is, organized, noninstitutionalized efforts by large numbers of people to change or preserve major aspects of society. Although there are many social movements in the United States and worldwide, actually relatively few people in any society join social movements. Even if huge numbers of people participate in social movements, they make up only a small proportion of the total population. Most people are totally inactive. At the same time, in nearly all of the societies of the world, *some* people *do* band together to bring about change, prevent change, or undo change that has already taken place. Social movements, by their very nature, express *dissatisfaction* with the way things are or with the way, some fear, others want to make them. The participants of social movements think that their own values, needs, goals, or beliefs are being threatened or underrepresented by certain conditions or people, and they want to "set things right." Thus, social movements require three basic

407

conditions to come into being. First, some real, potential, or even imaginary *condition* to which some may object; second, a *subjective feeling* that this condition is undesirable and should be changed; and third, an *organized means* for making this dissatisfaction collective, that is, a social movement *organization.*

In comparison with collective behavior, social movements are more organized; longer lasting; and their participants are more intentional, goal-oriented, and are more likely to seek substantial social change. At the same time, social movements are not a fully institutionalized aspect of the political system. As we saw in Chapter 1, if a social movement becomes incorporated into the governmental structure, it is no longer a social movement. When sociologists refer to social movements as "noninstitutionalized" or "extrainstitutional," they mean that they do not work strictly within the mainstream system; they make use of a wide variety of techniques, including boycotts, protests, demonstrations, and even, occasionally—and this varies from one movement to another—riots, terrorism, and other illegal and often violent means to achieve their ends. Attempting to achieve social change is not a distinctive quality of social movements; social groups that are not social movements also aim to bring about social change. For example, when the federal government passed the Voting Rights Act of 1965, this was not in itself an expression of social movement activity, even though the civil rights movement did put pressure on the government to pass the Act. Oil companies lobby Congress to pass legislation that favors their interests; this is also not an expression of social movement activity because it is institutionalized, it articulates with an aspect of the legally established governmental process.

While social movements may also lobby politicians, they engage in a much wider range of practices than more mainstream political and economic organizations do. As a general rule, social movements lack the power to advance their collective interests in an exclusively normative, institutionalized fashion, such as introducing bills in a legislature or lobbying politicians. "What distinguishes social movements from their institutionalized counterparts is their political situation [that is, their relative lack of direct power in the government] which causes them to rely heavily on a repertoire of disorderly tactics such as strikes, demonstrations, violence, and protest meetings to accomplish political ends" (Morris and Herring, 1987, p. 145). Oil executives never hold demonstrations in the street, stage boycotts, or engage in collective violence to advance their interests. They don't have to; their resources are so massive and their links with government representatives so direct that they can get things done without these less-than-fully institutionalized means. At the same time, "social movements and formal political parties are mirror images because both are political actors pursuing power." Both sets of actors "are propelled by the same political process" (Morris and Herring, 1987, p. 145). Of course, some social movements are so successful that their programs are incorporated into mainstream government policy, as we saw with the federal government's passage of the Voting Rights Act of 1965, a major feature of the program supported by the civil rights movement.

It is important at this point to distinguish between a *social movement* (SM) and a *social movement organization* (SMO). A social movement (SM) is a broad umbrella term for everyone who works for or in relation to a certain cause; some experts even include *potential* members and participants and, even if they are not supporters, *constituents*, that is, people who are or might be helped by the movement. In fact, as we'll see shortly, one perspective on social movements, the "resource mobilization" theory, argues that an extremely wide range of actors are relevant to social movement activity, including bystanders, the media, and the state. There is, in other words, a broad "cast of characters" in the study of social movements (Zurcher and Snow, 1981, pp. 472–477).

A social movement organization (SMO), in contrast, is one of a number of specific groups that fall under the broader umbrella of a given social movement. The women's movement, or women's liberation movement, is a social movement; NOW (the National Organization for Women), WAR (Women Against Rape) and WAP (Women Against Pornography), the National Alliance of Black Feminists, the National Women's Political Caucus (NWPC), and so on, are specific social movement organizations that are part of the women's movement. Some organizations within the same movement cooperate with one another to achieve movement goals, while others compete or even struggle against one another. There may be disagreement as to which specific organizations are part of a given social movement, with members of one sometimes accusing another of subverting movement goals and the members of the second doing the same to the first. Usually, however, different SMOs working for the same social movement will compete for resources but, upon well-publicized occasions, will also cooperate with one another. In any case, we should distinguish between a social movement (SM) and a social movement organization (SMO); the two are by no means identical, and for some purposes, their differences may be as important as their similarities.

Today, in the United States, social movements and social movement organizations abound. It may even be possible that there are as many social movements and specific social movement organizations in America as in the rest of the world combined. Every one of them seeks to achieve one or a set of fairly specific, concrete goals.

1. The environmentalist movement seeks to reduce pollution; to limit corporate activity that damages the Earth's air, forests, and oceans; and to protect endangered species.
2. The Right to Life movement wishes to criminalize and lower the incidence of abortion, which its members regard as murder.
3. The pro-choice movement wants to ensure that abortion remains legal and that every woman who wants to have an abortion (within the legal limit of the first two trimesters of pregnancy) is able to do so.
4. Women Against Rape (WAR) and Women Against Pornography (WAP) seek to criminalize, or to change the laws so that women can sue the makers and distributors of pornography, arguing

that viewing or otherwise consuming pornography violates their rights and causes men to rape women.

5. Aryan Nation, a white supremacist coalition, wants to drive out of the country or to exterminate Jews and nonwhite minorities; to overthrow the federal government; and to institute a racially "pure," decentralized state.

6. The National Organization for Women (NOW) pushes for women's rights and gender equality.

7. The Jewish Defense League (JDL) uses intimidation and violence to eliminate anti-Semitism and acts of discrimination against Jews.

8. The NAACP (National Association for the Advancement of Colored People) seeks to protect the interests of Blacks and other racial minorities.

9. The National Association to Advance Fat Acceptance (NAAFA) aims, as its name implies, to push for the rights of, and to end discrimination against, overweight people.

10. ACT UP, an activist AIDS group, seeks to focus more attention on, and to increase federal funding for, this dreaded disease; to speed up the availability of experimental, less-than-fully tested, drugs to patients; and to ensure humane treatment for AIDS sufferers.

11. Amnesty International aims to eliminate or at least significantly reduce the illegal arrest, torture, and inhumane treatment of political prisoners worldwide.

Literally hundreds of thousands of other movements and organizations are devoted to the effort to achieve their objectives. All represent collective, organized, nonmainstream efforts by individuals to change features of the society in which they operate, to prevent such changes, or even to undo the changes of the past. All are social movements or social movement organizations. Their operation and dynamics will be the subject of this and the next chapter.

___ TYPES OF SOCIAL MOVEMENTS AND SMOS ___

Social movements and social movement organizations (SMOs) can be categorized in a variety of ways. One is the *direction* and *degree* of the changes they seek (Cameron, 1966, pp. 22-24), and the second is the *geographical scope* of the SMOs that make them up (Rosenthal and Schwartz, 1989, pp. 44–46).

Direction and Degree of Change.   First, as to the direction and degree of change they seek: Social movements may be *reactionary, conservative, reformist (or revisionist), revolutionary, escapist (or retreatist), and expressive.* While this typology is not airtight, and there may be some debate as to whether a given movement or group belongs to which category, it does offer a very rough classification of social movement orientation.

Reactionary social movements seek to restore society, or some major part of it, to a former condition or state. Racist organizations, for instance, wish to restore white supremacy in all its former vigor, to return to the days when Blacks were subservient to whites and had even less power and a smaller slice of the economic pie than is true today. Some racist groups even want to banish Blacks from the country altogether. The Moral Majority, now defunct, was another example of a reactionary social movement organization whose members looked fondly to the past; they wished to return to a time when only marital sex was approved, homosexuality was regarded either as a sin or a disease (or both), and abortion was illegal and thus available only to the rich or the desperate.

Conservative movements and SMOs seek to retain the status quo, to fight changes that other movements might propose to bring about. The National Rifle Association (NRA), for instance, organizes to prevent the imposition of controls on handgun ownership. Conservative movements "are most likely to spring up when there is a threat of change, and they are frequently organized to combat the activities of some other movement which is making changes" (Cameron, 1966, p. 23).

Reformist (or revisionist) movements and social movement organizations wish to make partial or moderate changes in the present state of society. In general, they focus on fairly specific, limited, concrete issues or areas (although some of them can be fairly broad): saving whales or baby seals, protecting the environment generally, blocking efforts to build nuclear reactors, promoting equal rights for homosexuals, decriminalizing marijuana, and so on.

Revolutionary movements and SMOs seek major, sweeping, large-scale change. Of course, the line between "reformist" and "revolutionary" movements is not altogether clear. In fact, the same social movement will often contain both reformist and revolutionary factions, wings, or organizations and, even within the same social movement organization, both tendencies may be found. Some members of the women's liberation movement, for example, want society to grant equal occupational rights to women—a major change, to be sure, but essentially a reformist goal; this would include equal pay for equal work, adequate maternity (or paternity) leave, on-the-job protection from sexual harassment and assault, adequate daycare facilities for the children of working parents, and so on.

On the other hand, many feminists argue that these changes cannot come about without a significant and even revolutionary restructuring of sex roles and sexual relations between men and women. Their goals include changing the way men (and women) think and interact: making men feel unashamed of the softer, more vulnerable and emotional (or "feminine") side of their personalities; treating women as full human beings and not simply as exploitable objects; taking on such traditionally women's roles and tasks as housework and childraising; being less competitive, less elitist, and less "macho"; and so on. Some feminists (radical feminist separatists) even argue that the only way women can achieve full power is to separate their lives entirely from men, to live an existence totally without contact with men. (Which actually makes them "escapists" with respect to the larger society rather than "revolutionaries.") Proponents of more sweeping changes argue that merely putting more women in traditionally male jobs would not be an improvement for most women. The distinction between reformist and revolutionary movements and SMOs hinges on *how many areas of society* a movement seeks to change and *how radical* that projected change is. Movements for change can be arranged along a revisionist-revolutionary continuum, with some closer to one end, others toward the opposite end, and still others in the middle.

Escapist or retreatist movements or social movement organizations do not seek to change society at all but to withdraw from it and what they see as its corruption. Marcus Garvey's "Back to Africa" movement was just such a movement. So was Jim Jones's "People's Temple," whose members withdrew into the jungles of South America, only to commit mass suicide several years later. Escapist movements or organizations need not withdraw from society physically; they can withdraw by isolating themselves socially and emotionally, limiting contact with outsiders or nonmembers to a minimum. In fact, the line between escapist movements and some religions is quite fuzzy. Religions, whether escapist or activist, are often "crucibles" of social movements (Zald and McCarthy, 1987, pp. 67–95; Morris, 1984, pp. 4–12, 77–99). Escapist movements are oriented to the change of their individual members and not to the social change of the society in which they live, which is why some experts argue that they are not social movements at all.

Last, expressive movements seek to change the psychic, emotional, internal state of individual members, not the external conditions. Again, many contemporary observers believe that this disqualifies them from the category of social movements altogether. The members of expressive movements believe that society's problems—for instance, hunger, racism, poverty, injustice, drug use, and so on—can be solved simply by changing people's attitudes toward them. For instance, the organization called est (Erhard Seminars Training) began sponsoring the "Hunger Project" in 1977; its supposed aim was to make hunger disappear within two deades, mainly by convincing its members, and sympathetic outsiders, not to feel guilty about the starvation of millions or billions of their fellow human beings. Because guilt is "stupid and counterproductive," eliminating it would eliminate hunger, est leaders declared. The organization released a newsletter that claimed the end of hunger and starvation was just around the corner only a year or so before mass starvation actually broke out in Ethiopia in 1985. (Famine remains in several African countries to this day.) In short, expressive movements seek to express a particular emotion or attitude without taking any concrete steps to change anything. Again, there is considerable debate nowadays as to whether such organizations belong to the category of social movements at all.

Geographical Scope. If we were to classify social movement organizations according to their *geographical scope*, we would have three types of SMOs: *federal movement organizations, local movement organizations, and primary movement groups.*

The *federal movement organization* has a "multigeographical scope"; it is a federated association of a number of local groups. A federal SMO may be city wide—in a large metropolitan area—state wide, nation wide, or even international. What counts is that its members do not all know one another; its entire membership does not and cannot meet at the same time on a face-to-face basis; and it employs a full-time professional staff, usually assisted by part-time unpaid volunteers. A federal SMO has a central headquarters that "coordinates activity in more than one locale," with a number of local organizations "which function quasi-independently of the national body" (Rosenthal and Schwartz, 1989, p. 44). Examples include the NAACP, the National Organization of Women (NOW), and the Women's Christian Temperance Union (WTCU).

The *local movement organization* is, as its name indicates, local in scope. It is usually too small to have a paid professional staff, and its members can all meet at the same time in the same place. Some local movement organizations are a chapter of a larger, federal SMO and some are geared to attack a specific, local issue, such as pollution in a nearby body of water. Even local chapters of a federal SMO typically have autonomy, and they are usually nonbureaucratically and often democratically administered (Rosenthal and Schwartz, 1989, pp. 44–45).

The *primary movement group* represents the lowest level of social movement organization. If, for example, a city-wide tenant's organization represents the *federal* level (that is, a "federation" of geographically-diverse local organizations), a neighborhood tenant's group, the *local* level, the tenants living in one specific building would represent the *primary* level (Lawson, 1983; Rosenthal and Schwartz, 1989, p. 45). The primary level is founded "in informal face-to-face interaction, among people who [know] each other personally." It has a fluid structure, typically a brief life span; its leadership is "diffuse and situational"; and membership, although identifiable, "may be transitory and inconsistent." Primary organizations "have little apparent similarity to formal organizations," and "should be recognized as distinct organizational types" (Rosenthal and Schwartz, 1989, p. 45).

OBJECTIVE CONDITIONS
—————— AND SOCIAL MOVEMENT ACTIVITY ——————

We've learned that subjective discontent over a real or imagined condition is a key factor in the genesis of social movements. But can discontent account for social movements—that is, can variations in discontent explain variations in social movement emergence and participation? Or is discontent a necessary ingredient for social movements, but simply a constant to be found pretty much everywhere? Common sense tells us that the more deprived and miserable people are, the more likely it is that they will form social movements. The commonsensical view that deprivation explains discontent and, hence, activism in social movements, is called the "grassroots," *breakdown, grievance*, or *immiseration* point of view. It is based on an extremely simple assumption: that people form social movements *to the extent that* they are objectively deprived, exploited, miserable, and oppressed—that is, they have a legitimate grievance. In short, when things begin to "break down" in their lives, people begin to organize to get them working again.

Even though, from time to time, some researchers have attempted to resurrect the "breakdown" model (for instance, Useem, 1985), it does not have much currency in the field. As a general explanation for social movement activity, the breakdown or grassroots approach is widely regarded nowadays as wrong. There are simply too many instances in human history where deprived people do *not* rise up and attempt to deal with the problems that make their lives difficult. In addition, there are equally as many cases in which people who lead extremely comfortable lives *do* form social movements to deal with the conditions (to others, seemingly trivial) they find unendurable. In fact, time and time again, we find that the people who have the *most* serious problems, objectively speaking, are *unlikely* to form social movements to deal with them, while those who live in *less* seriously difficult conditions are *more* likely to do so.

For example, if we were to divide American society into two parts on the basis of privilege versus deprivation, it is highly likely that the *most* privileged half would be significantly *more* active in social movements than the *least*. Moreover, many social movements—especially those in affluent nations—are formed by people who manifest no objective deprivation and, in fact, experience no grievance, either, but seek to change conditions *external* to their own lives. Anti-abortion, pro-ecology, and animal rights groups provide ready examples. In short, there is no automatic one-to-one relationship between the *objective conditions* of people's lives and their *subjective feelings* about them, and, likewise, between subjective feelings of discontent and *the mobilization of their social movement activity*. Each step has to be explained; none cannot be assumed. Too often, these dimensions are *not* related in the way that common sense assumes that they are.

The emergence of social movements implies that significant numbers of the members of a society are unhappy about the way things are, and that they wish to change them to what they see as a better way. This is both true and obvious—a truism. A truism is not so much wrong as it is insufficient as an explanation. Most people are unhappy about one thing or another in their lives and wish to change it, but they do not always join or participate in social movements. Moreover, the objective features of people's lives do not necessarily lead to participation in social movements. As we saw, many individuals who are extremely well off are also participants in social movements, and some of the most miserable human beings on Earth will never join a social movement. Black family income in the United States increased by one and one-half times during the decade of the 1960s, and yet, participation in change-oriented African-American movements skyrocketed during this period. In contrast, in the decade between the early 1970s and the early 1980s, Black family incomes did not rise at all in real dollars, and yet, movement activity remained at a very low ebb at this time. India's untouchable population, tens of millions of people whose standard of living is among the lowest on Earth, has no sustained, vigorous social movement to protest or alter its miserable condition. America's middle class—among the most economically privileged of the world's social categories—is probably also among the most active in social movement participation. Clearly, then, objective conditions alone do not determine whether members of a given category or group take part in social movements. Although some measure of objective misery is part of the picture, it is by no means an *explanation* of social movement activity.

One essential ingredient in social movement activity is *hope*—that is, an optimistic feeling that *something can be done* about a given condition that is regarded as undesirable. All over the world, human beings fall sick and die, yet they do not, everywhere, believe that anything can be done to solve the problem of illness. Wars kill soldiers and civilians by the millions—over 100 million humans have been killed in the course of warfare during the twentieth century—but relatively few people in any nation stand up and say, "Let's put an end to warfare." The environment is being systematically despoiled by industrial development and is making many of us sick, indeed, killing us— clearly, an objective condition. Yet not all Americans consider ecological degradation to be a problem that should be controlled, or even a problem at all.

In short, one person's problem is another's fact of life. Undesirable conditions, such as exploitation and oppression, exist everywhere, although in varying degrees, yet social movements do not emerge everywhere. Relatively egalitarian societies may spawn many strong social movements, whereas others that are markedly oppressive may have almost none. Within societies, some exploited groups do not launch social movements against the conditions in which they live, whereas many privileged groups launch them by the score. Objective conditions are *relevant* to the emergence of social movements. However, we cannot take subjective factors—*feelings* of discontent on the part of potential or actual members—for granted. And, even further and perhaps even more crucial, we cannot assume that feelings of discontent will automatically translate into social movement activity. Discontent or grievance cannot explain the formation of social movements, because discontent is extremely widespread, and social movements are only mobilized at certain times and places.

In addition, there are many conditions that are *thought to exist*, regarded in some quarters as a major problem in need of remedy, which have no concrete, objective existence. The condition that is regarded as objectionable or undesirable to some is, in fact, mythical, imaginary—a fantasy. For instance, the members of the "Aryan Nation" movement believe the United States government, which they call "ZOG" (the "Zionist-occupied government") is completely dominated by a Jewish conspiracy, and that Jews, Blacks, and other nonwhite minorities should not be allowed to live in the country at all. In reality, Jews do not dominate the American government, and there is no Jewish or Zionist conspiracy. In short, the Aryan movement is based on a "putative" or *imaginary* condition. The same is true for many social movements. Clearly, then, objective deprivation cannot be an explanation for movements in general, because, for many, no such deprivation exists—in fact, the very objective condition that a given movement is attempting to change may not even exist in the first place. In order to understand the origin and dynamics of social movements, we need to know far more than the objective conditions in which their members live. This factor does not take us very far in explaining social movement participation.

However, even when subjective discontent exists, even when grievances are felt about what is seen as injustice, we still do not have social movements. Subjective discontent is an important step, but it is not the most important or the most problematic or difficult step. Fundamentalist Christians may be unhappy about the teaching of evolution in schools, anti-Semites may feel aggrieved about "too many Jews" in the government, poor people may see their economic plight in life as unjust, animal lovers may hate the slaughter of animals for fur coats, and welfare families may resent the government's intrusion into their lives—at this point, again, social movements do not exist. Something more is necessary.

The central issue in social movement genesis is not objective deprivation; it is not even subjective discontent or grievance. Both objective deprivation and subjective discontent are extremely widespread. The key process here is how discontent "becomes organized and mobilized . . ., the process by which unhappy people find a way of collectively articulating their protest as a demand for [what they see as] social reform . . ., [how] unhappiness [is translated] into successful protest." Throughout history, objective oppression has existed; likewise, throughout history, objective oppression has even led to subjective discontent. Just about everywhere, practically at all times, "there are vast amounts of subjective discontent floating around." It is not objective conditions or even the subjective experience of oppression that represent the key link here; "it is the organizational wherewithal that determines whether people will protest." The real issue, "then, is why, in specific cases where discontent has been strong, those who feel it 'do not mobilize,'" while in other, objectively and subjectively similar cases, they do (Schwartz, 1991). And this is the very issue that the "resource mobilization" theorists focus on. This issue, and the perspective that stresses it, are so important that they will be discussed in the next section.

___ EIGHT PERSPECTIVES ON SOCIAL MOVEMENTS ___

Explanations of social movements and social movement participation have been devised for as long as humans have organized to change the society in which they lived. However, it was only in the last century that these ideas and concepts were applied to the study of social movements generally, rather than specifically to the local one the observer had contact with and was interested in. In fact, it has not been until roughly the last generation or so that the study of social movements has become systematic, sophisticated, and accurate. Of the many explanations of, theories of, or approaches to, social movements, perhaps eight are most important and relevant in a course on collective behavior. They are the irrational group mind theory, Marxism, psychopathology, Max Weber's charisma, the mass society perspective, the Chicago School or the collective behavior approach, Neil Smelser's "value-added" theory, and the resource mobilization theory. These eight are not necessarily contradictory, in the sense that, if one is right, the others must be wrong. In fact, this group represents something of a mixed bag of perspectives on the subject. Three are widely regarded nowadays as invalid and empirically disconfirmed; for all practical purposes, they don't exist as viable theories in the field any longer: the irrational group mind persective, psychopathology, and the mass society approach. They are of almost exclusively historical interest. Three are still held, with serious qualifications, as partially correct theories by some—a declining number of—researchers, but are regarded as largely passé within the field's mainstream: Marxism, the Chicago School, and Smelser's "value-added" theory. Max Weber's charisma is seen as an extremely limited concept, valid for a narrow range of social movement dynamics, but inapplicable for most of what we want to know about the phenomenon. And resource mobilization theory represents the "mainstream" of the field, the locus of the most innovative and "cutting edge" research being done on social movements at this time.

IRRATIONAL GROUP MIND

We have already encountered the irrational group mind theorists, including Gustave LeBon, Charles Mackay, and, on a somewhat more sophisticated level, Robert Park and Herbert Blumer. Adherents of this school assumed that people "go mad in herds." This school argued that, when individuals get together to right a condition they regard as wrong—especially in a crowd—their very mutual presence generates their most primitive, irrational tendencies. Individually, each may have been perfectly rational and reasonable human beings but, collectively, they become a frenzied, unreasoning mob. Nowadays this view has no currency whatsoever. Social movement participation taken as a whole cannot even remotely be characterized by this perspective's view. On the individual or "micro" level, most social movement participants have entirely reasonable and rational goals and seek to achieve them, for the most part, in an entirely reasonable, rational fashion. On the level of the organization (the middle or "meso" level), most social movement organizations obey fairly rational principles, that is, their efforts are designed to achieve concrete goals and, within the limitations of the knowledge of their leaders and members and the limits of available resources, they do strive toward those goals. Far from becoming irrational in group settings, most social movement activists exhibit exactly the opposite tendency—that is, they become more, not less, rational and goal-oriented. Today, the irrational group mind perspective is regarded as invalid; it is little more than a historical relic.

MARXISM

The work of Karl Marx (1818–1883) and his collaborator Friedrich Engels (1820–1895) represented an advance over the commonsensical grassroots approach because it argued that, at a given point in time, the objective condition of being oppressed, exploited, and miserable does not automatically generate social movements. Immiseration has to be combined with another ingredient, Marx argued: *the development of class consciousness.* Individuals who share the experience of being exploited have to be aware of what and who is expoiting them, the fact that others in their social and economic condition share their exploitation, and the steps that have to be taken to destroy the social and economic conditions that continue to exploit them. For example, in Marx's time, rural peasants lived in a state of objective misery and they were exploited by large landowners. But insofar as they were unaware of their mutual exploitation and what they had to do to eliminate it, they were unlikely to organize to form social movements. In Marx's view, rural peasants were no better organized, and had no closer a connection with one another, than a sack of potatoes.

In sharp contrast, factory workers were characterized by the potential for organizing themselves into a social movement. The *contradictions of capitalism* generated the only movement worthy of the name, that is, the labor movement. The owners of the means of production, mainly factory owners, had to exploit workers as much as possible, which led to increasing misery and to class consciousness with other workers which, in turn, made revolution and the overthrow of the capitalist system inevitable. Unlike the rural peasant, factory workers could see with their own eyes the miserable working conditions of their colleagues, and they were massed together at the same time in the same place to complain to one another about them. In addition, over time, their economic condition would deteriorate, Marx and Engels believed, and they would be forced to organize to make their lives livable. Marx did not believe that reformist efforts (such as forming a movement to institute labor unions, which were virtually nonexistent in his day) would do any good. To Marx, it was total revolution or nothing. Marx would have regarded the vast majority of contemporary social movements as a distraction from the true revolutionary task, that is, the destruction of capitalism and the building of socialism.

Although even dedicated contemporary Marxists do not subscribe to Marx's analysis in every detail, it is clear that Marx made a number of major contributions to the study of social movements which, today, are more or less taken for granted. He emphasized the rationality and goal-directedness of movement participation; he stressed the importance of organization and social networks in the genesis and maintenance of social movements; he stressed the fact that the capitalist class will attempt to crush the labor movement and hence, stressed the importance of social control; and he insisted on the fact that certain types of movements arise specifically out of certain types of societies. However, Marx failed to recognize the central importance of movements that are *not* dependent on economic interests, exploitation, or class antagonisms, and movements—reformist movements, for example—

and movements which do *not* aim at, and could never achieve, a true revolution. Marx would have found most contemporary movements—for instance, pro-choice, anti-abortion, animal rights, anti-pornography, anti-drunk driving, survivalist, gay and lesbian—puzzling, irrelevant, unimportant, even silly. It is clear that Marx's focus was entirely too limited. He simply underestimated the power of factors other than social class and the importance of movements other than class-based movements. Still, no one can understand the dynamics of social movements without having at least a nodding acquaintance with the work of Karl Marx.

PSYCHOPATHOLOGY

The psychopathology perspective argues that social movement participants and leaders, or *certain* social movement participants and leaders, are neurotic, psychotic, or psychologically ill; they suffer from unresolved Oedipal conflicts, delusions of grandeur, paranoia, authoritarianism, depression, discontent, anxiety, frustration, anger, hostility, gullibility, fanaticism, selfishness, and/or a very vivid fantasy life (Cantril, 1941; Hoffer, 1951; Adorno et al., 1950; Feuer, 1969; Bettelheim, 1971). In reality, they claim, movement ideology, goals, and activity are irrelevant to participants and leaders; they are a substitute solution, symbolizing the will to power for the participant's tormented psyche. The psychopathology school has received no empirical support whatsoever. Researchers working in the field have realized for some time that it is a dead end. Social movement members or leaders as a whole are not especially characterized by psychopathology or neuroticism. It is entirely possible that, by carefully picking and choosing one's examples, one can find some participants or leaders who do manifest some sort of a psychic disorder. However, no advocate of this position has ever presented an iota of systematic evidence to suggest that this is more likely to be the case than for the population at large, or that any disorder is meaningfully or causally related to social movement participation or leadership. In the study of social movements, this perspective has been totally discredited.

CHARISMA

Max Weber (1864–1920) argued that an "extrordinary quality" surrounds certain leaders; it imparts to them a unique, almost supernatural power over their followers (Weber, 1968, pp. 111–1157). Such individuals often overturn or challenge the institutional order and are capable of legitimating a program or movement they espouse. When such leaders are seized with a mission, they may generate a movement, a revolution, or a new religion or social order. Some charismatic leaders are now regarded as good, others are seen as bad; what unites them is their extraordinary hold over their followers. Jesus, Joan of Arc, Adolf Hitler, Fidel Castro, Ché Guevarra, Mao Zedong, Malcom X, Ho Chi Minh, Josef Stalin, and Martin Luther King, Jr., are good examples of leaders who possessed charisma and exerted influence because of it; they led—in part or totally—as a result of their special "gift of the spirit." The problem with charisma is that it is unstable. When a charismatic leader dies, this magical quality cannot be passed on to anyone else. Who is to be the leader's successor? Often, when such a leader dies, the movement dies with him or her. And, even if a successor is named, he or she is extremely unlikely to have that extremely rare and special gift. How does a movement or a religion capture and transfer that same quality? Chances are, it can't; what it can do is to enshrine the leader's vision into rules—some of which are rules of succession. Leaders who govern by these rules do not generate as much excitement as charismatic leaders, but their reign tends to be far more stable.

By its very nature, charisma is a form of collective behavior; it is emotional, ecstatic, unstable, volatile, demonic, emergent, sacred, unconventional, and extrainstitutional. It is essentially ruleless—or, to be more specific, it represents a rule or order unto itself. It cannot be justified by anything except itself. Charismatic leaders justify their demands not by traditional norms, not by organizational or bureaucratic rules, but by their own extraordinary qualities. "Trust me," these leaders seem to say, and that's the beginning and end of the matter. All the leaders mentioned above said, in effect, "It is written . . ., but I say to you. . . ." To call for evidence or precedent or a norm at that point is irrelevant, improper—indeed, sacrilegious. Charisma is frequently associated with leaders who stimulate crowds to strong emotion or action with their passionate speeches. As we saw, volatile crowd behavior is a form of collective behavior. Hitler's speeches—preserved on film—only call forth puzzlement and anger among contemporary audiences, accustomed as we are to more rational appeals. Yet, in the 1920s, 1930s, and 1940s, they stirred the Germans masses to transports of ecstasy and justified all manner of unspeakable atrocities. It is possible that, without Hitler's charisma, there would have been no Nazi movement, and without the Nazis, no Holocaust, and no Second World War.

What do contemporary observers make of Weber's concept of charisma? Everyone agrees that certain leaders possess this special quality; everyone agrees that certain charismatic leaders can inspire their followers to do their bidding in part because of it; and everyone agrees that, in the genesis of certain movements, the quality of charisma can be influential or even decisive. But as a mechanism for explaining the dynamics of social movements *generally*, the concept of charisma is insufficient. The overwhelming majority of social movements are *not* headed by charismatic leaders; even when one is, the appeal of a charismatic leader does not explain the movement's most important workings. Even so intangible a quality as charisma grows out of a certain cultural setting; it does not strike individuals randomly much as lightning may strike someone standing in an open field.

For instance, it is expected that Black ministers, especially those preaching in the South, will possess the quality of charisma; they are selected for that reason. And a charismatic leader is effective only to the extent that he or she is integrated into a community of potential followers who share his or her vision and are organized and can mobilize resources to achieve his or her program. The reemergence of the civil rights movement in the 1950s and

1960s was dependent not only on key charismatic leaders such as Martin Luther King, Jr., but also on a network of more local leaders and rank-and-file activists who mobilized communities for collective protest (Morris, 1984, pp. 275–286). Most contemporary observers agree that an exclusive focus on Dr. King's charisma—great as it was—detracts from and underplays the efforts and achievements of local leaders and the rank-and-file, committing the fallacy of imagining that history is made exclusively by a very few great leaders. At the same time, it must be recognized that, with Dr. King's assassination, the civil rights organizations with which he was associated "virtually collapsed" (Jenkins, 1986, p. 356). In short, charisma is an important, but extremely limited, concept in the understanding of social movements.

MASS SOCIETY

The mass society approach, which we encountered briefly in Chapter 1, argues that urbanization and industrialization have generated nations of alienated citizens with weak social ties to one another. The modern mass society is accompanied and facilitated by its mass media, which isolates and fragments the public; readers, listeners, and viewers receive messages from the mass media alone, in isolation, but they cannot communicate back to these media sources. The mass society is characterized by "cultural confusion, social heterogeneity, weak cultural integration mechanisms, and a lack of attachments to secondary group structures" (Morris and Herring, 1987, p. 141). It is specifically those individuals in such societies, the mass society perspective argues, who are most socially isolated, rootless, unattached, alienated, and unintegrated into networks of social relationships who are most likely to join movements that aim for sweeping changes (Cantril, 1941; Kornhauser, 1959; Lipset, 1963; Toch, 1965).

Today, we now realize that the mass society approach to social movements is fatally flawed. Contemporary societies are not and never have been mass societies as the concept is defined. All publics are made up of individuals who are integrated into social networks, and even exposure to mass media usually takes place in social settings and typically results in an intensification of social interaction. The rootless, anomic, alienating quality of life in modern, urban society is largely mythical (Fischer, 1984). Moreover, it is the individual who is *most*—not least—deeply imbedded in social networks and relationships who is *most*, not least, likely to participate in social movements. Social movement participation is an *extension* of everyday social interaction, *not* a substitute for it. A good illustration of this principle is the fact that the most militant members of twentieth century Spanish protest movements were deeply integrated into mainstream social institutions in their communities (Logan, 1978). In many ways, as we saw in the discussion of the "political" approach to violence in Chapter 3, certain institutional involvements represent a kind of *socialization* for some rebellious social movements. The mass society perspective toward social movements is no longer taken very seriously in the field.

CHICAGO SCHOOL/COLLECTIVE BEHAVIOR

The Chicago school or the collective behavior perspective toward social movements holds to nine main points. One, as we've seen, social movements are conceptualized as an instance, variety, or *type* of collective behavior. Two, as such, they (along with other types of collective behavior) are a *unique*, emergent, or "sui generis" phenomenon, that is, one with its own characteristics quite unlike those of anything else in the conventional, every-day world. Three, the behavior of social movement participants is seen as spontaneous, nonnormative, and *noninstitutionalized.* Which means that, four, social movement participants' prior institutionalized commitments and normative contraints are regarded as relatively nonbinding and essentially irrelevant, without power to determine their behavior in a social movement context. Compared with other perspectives, the collective behavior approach *minimizes*, even ignores, the institutional memberships and involvements of social movement participants; it does not use such memberships or involve-ments to explain their social movement participation.

Five, while the collective behavior perspective does not argue that social movement participation is irrational, it *does not stress* the factor of rationality in their actions. In fact, six, to the advocates of this approach, the importance of the *goals* that social movement participants seek are not altogether rele-vant as a causal factor in an understanding of their actions because, they argue, participants are forever *redefining* their goals. Actors continually con-struct and reconstruct the meaning of the phenomena in their lives through their interaction with others. As a result, the social organizations and institu-tions in which they are involved are fluid, changeable, constantly in the pro-cess of becoming. In sum, an understanding of social movement goals is not crucial in understanding social movement participants' actions.

Seven, how movements are *organized* is not an important variable to the advocate of the collective behavior approach. Again, since organizations, like all social phenomena, are in a state of flux and change from day to day (Turner and Killian, 1972, p. 252), the fact that different social movements are organized differently is unimportant as an explanation of their participants' behavior. Eight, this approach stresses the genesis or *origin* of social move-ments; once a movement becomes fully organized, institutionalized, and nor-mative, advocates of the collective behavior perspective lose interest in it. And nine, social movement *outcomes*—what they achieve (or don't achieve)—are not a crucial variable to be explained. That is, not only is the perspective not interested in goals as a primary or causal variable, it is also not interested in them as a secondary or "caused" variable. Why do some movements achieve their goals while others do not? The question is not very interesting to this perspective.

The collective behavior approach has been criticized from a variety of perspectives (Morris and Herring, 1987; McAdam, McCarthy, and Zald, 1988; Zald, 1991; Jenkins, 1983). It is no longer dominant in the study of social movements—and, in fact, is widely regarded as passé, essentially irrelevant to most of the field's younger scholars. This is probably not due to the fact that academic fields are characterized by fad and fashion, but to the fact that the collective behavior perspective cannot answer or even address most of the questions and issues now regarded as most pressing in the study of social movements. While, in my estimation, the approach does handle some aspects of collective behavior, it is ill-suited to most social movement phenomena. This is because *most aspects of social movements are not examples of collective behavior.* This perspective was contradictory in its approach; it was altogether too *inclusive* in attempting to define social movements as a type of collective behavior, but, when the time came to examine crucial aspects of social movements (such as planning, goals, outcomes, organization), it suddenly became far too *exclusive*, or narrow in its focus. The critics of the collective behavior approach are right, I think, in what they say about its approach to most aspects of social movements, but wrong in saying that collective behavior processes are entirely irrelevant to social movement activity.

VALUE-ADDED THEORY

We've encountered Neil Smelser's "value-added" theory (1962) before as a general explanation for collective behavior. It attempts to explain collective behavior generally and the genesis of social movements specifically with six key variables: structural conduciveness, strain, generalized beliefs, precipitating factors, mobilization, and social control. For social movements to arise in a given society, each of these variables must be present; when they are all present, social movements will form and social movement activity will break out. For instance, in the emergence of the civil rights movement as well as in specific episodes of civil rights protest, whites control more political power and economic resources than African-Americans (structural conduciveness); this clashes with the basic American value of equality (structural strain); this fact is widely believed to be an injustice about which something ought to be done (generalized beliefs); from time to time, events—such as acts of police brutality—remind Blacks of this fact (precipitating factors); leaders have organized groups to protest these conditions (mobilization for action); and the police are frequently called out to meet such protests, often ineffectively (social control).

Smelser shares three basic assumptions with the collective behavior approach: first, the view that social movements are a form of collective behavior; second, that collective behavior is spontaneous and not fully institutionalized, strictly normative behavior; and third, that all forms of collective behavior, social movements included, can be accounted for by means of a single, coherent explanation.

However, Smelser's theory differs in enough respects to set itself off from the more classical tradition. First, Smelser sees society and social institutions as far more stable and institutionalized than the Chicago sociologists did; he did not resort to the emphasis on fluctuating definitions and interpretations of social phenomena that characterized the collective behavior tradition. Second, Smelser insisted that there is an irrational element in collective behavior and social movements. Beliefs dominant in social movements, he said, can be characterized as "if only" beliefs; that is, *if only* certain conditions could be changed, everything would be wonderful, even perfect. Adherents *short circuit* the causal process; that is, they are unaware of how difficult and complicated it is to make meaningful change, and rely on magical thinking in assuming that their simple solution will do the trick. Social movement activity, like collective behavior generally, "is the action of the impatient" (p. 72). And third, Smelser's value added approach differs from, offers an advance over, and provides a link between, the collective behavior perspective and the more contemporary approach to social movements, which stresses social movement organizations, in its emphasis on the last two of his major variables—*mobilization* and *social control.*

In mobilization for action, Smelser located a key variable that is heavily emphasized in contemporary (especially resource mobilization), perspectives. Leadership, especially that which mobilizes collective participation for action, is crucial here; if it does not exist, or is insufficient, a movement will not arise, and episodes of collective protest will not take place. Scattered individuals facing the same conditions and feeling the same way about them is not enough to generate collective action; they must be organized into a more or less coherent movement, and that takes effective organization and coordination (pp. 296–306, 355–364). In addition, Smelser emphasized the point that specific movement tactics may be more successful than others (pp. 302–305), again, a point that is emphasized in contemporary research on social movements.

Social control, too, was an important structural variable stressed by Smelser's value-added theory (pp. 306–310, 364–379), one, once again, that was underplayed by the collective behaviorists but emphasized by more contemporary theorists. Agencies of social control, such as the police, the courts, and law-making bodies, can determine the fate of social movements; their actions can crush, inhibit, intensify, redirect, or fragment social movement activity, organization, and success. As we saw in Chapter 2, for collective behavior generally, some of Smelser's factors are so broad and vague as to explain both everything and nothing; still, while there are important differences, there is no doubt that Neil Smelser's value-added theory is a precursor to the perspective that is dominant in the field today—*resource mobilization.* In fact, because of its stress on mobilization and social control—largely irrelevant to much of collective behavior but crucial for social movements—it is possible that Smelser's theory offers more as an explanation of social movements than is true for collective behavior generally.

RESOURCE MOBILIZATION

All prior approaches assume a certain measure of *strain* or *deprivation* in the genesis of social movements, all focus on the psychological impact that strain has on individuals, and all downplay political motives and emphasize the importance that social movement participation has in dealing with the

Political protests: social movement activity or collective behavior? Here, a demonstrator attempts to scale a fence surrounding the Long Island Lighting Company in 1979 to prevent the operation of LILCO's Shoreham Nuclear Power Station. While many aspects of the demonstration were planned out in advance, some were more spontaneous.

tensions of that strain (McAdam, 1982, pp. 9–10). Not so with the resource mobilization perspective, which holds the following: (1) that the existence of strain and deprivation *does not* and *cannot* explain social movement because it exists everywhere, in all groups; (2) that social movement participation must be examined at the structural, institutional, and societal levels rather than on the individual level; and (3) that political, not psychological, motives are crucial in explaining social movement participation.

According to resource mobilization theory, social movements rise up in some places at some times and not in other places at other times because some leaders know how to organize, mobilize, and channel the deprivation and dissatisfaction that exists everywhere (Zald and McCarthy, 1979; Zald and McCarthy, 1987; Oberschall, 1973; Morris, 1984; McAdam, 1982; Gamson, 1990). This perspective focuses on variables, such as communication networks, constituency, leadership, time, money, and links with business and government—in short, anything that can be turned to a social movement organization's advantage. Resource mobilization focuses on how collectivities constitute themselves into social movement organizations and how those organizations are related to the success of their efforts. According to two observers, all resource mobilizations share the following basic assumptions: "There is no fundamental difference between movement behavior and institutionalized behavior; movement participants and their actions are rational; social movements pursue interests; movement mobilization occurs through an infrastructure or power base; outcomes of collective action are central, and they are products of strategic choices made by participants; either support or repression by elite groups can affect the outcomes of movements" (Morris and Herring, 1987, p. 157).

A good but extreme example illustrating the resource mobilization approach is the rise and fall of the Italian-American Civil Rights League, an organization founded and directed by Joseph Colombo, at one time the reputed head of one of New York City's most powerful crime syndicates. Colombo's stated aim was to protest the image of Italian-Americans in the mass media and their alleged persecution by the Federal Bureau of Investigation (FBI). Colombo drew some 1,500 contributors to a $125-a-plate dinner in 1970. The League's first "Unity Day" rally drew about 100,000 demonstrators in New York. At Madison Square Garden, Frank Sinatra, along with a large and impressive cast of famous entertainers, raised half-a-million dollars for the League's cause. In 1970, the League's membership had grown to 45,000 (Hills, 1980, p. 91).

Italian-Americans, like members of all ethnic groups, have collective grievances. (Some more than others, it must be said.) But did these "objective" conditions account for the League's instant and enormous success? Let's consider the fate of the Italian-American Civil Rights League. Between 1970 and 1971, the League fell out of favor with the heads of New York's other crime families, who believed that Colombo was attracting too much attention to organized crime and that he was using the League as a means of milking money from an unsuspecting public. The second annual Unity Day rally was sparsely attended—according to some, because the mobs that are alleged to control certain New York labor unions refused to give their workers the day off to attend the rally. At the rally itself, a would-be assassin's bullet left Colombo permanently paralyzed. The hit man, reputedly hired by another crime family, was himself shot to death, and his killer escaped discovery. The Italian-American Civil Rights League soon died in obscurity. In 1970, the League commanded key resources and was a success; a year later, those resources were withdrawn, and it failed. During this time, there was no change in the strain, deprivation, or discontent experienced by Italian-Americans. The only key factor that changed was the resources.

This is an extreme example, since it represents a social movement organization that was little more than a clever scheme by a dishonest leader who exploited the ever-present realities of discontent in a particular American group. Many other social movements, however, do genuinely seek to reform major aspects of society. Consider, for instance, the role played by leaders in mobilizing the Black civil rights movement. That African-Americans suffer from collective injustices and deprivations is an objective fact that can be abundantly documented, and it was even more so in the 1950s, when the civil rights movement began on a mass basis. Blacks also tend to be more dissatisfied with their position in American society than is true of whites—in other words, their *objective* deprivation has been translated into felt or *subjective* deprivation. The next step, mobilizing this discontent, now demands explanation. Beginning in the late 1950s, a series of boycotts and sit-ins broke out in the Southern and border states. Blacks demanded to be served in hitherto all-white stores and restaurants and refused to sit only in the back of public busses. What inspired these protests and demonstrations? What created this powerful social movement, which eventually earned African-American access to public facilities and retail stores all over the country? Deprivation and discontent had existed before this period, but it had not produced an effective mobilization of the African-American public.

One observer (Morris, 1984) argues that the boycotts, sit-ins, and, in effect, the civil rights movement as a whole did not emerge as a spontaneous, sudden, irrational, and extrainstitutionalized outburst of collective behavior, but as a rational, almost inevitable outgrowth of preexisting social structures, commitments, and involvements, which gave the movement resources, organization, leaders, and members. An organizational base—including the African-American church, the center of Black political life in the South; existing civil rights organizations, such as the NAACP and the Southern Christian leadership Conference (SCLC), as well as other activist organizations; and local Black colleges—already existed. These organizations had already tried out many legal and political strategies, often with great success. Boycotts and sit-ins seemed to be the most rational way of challenging the existing segregation laws. These tactics did not represent a radical break away from existing social organization but, rather, were built upon it.

The first boycott, for instance, of the Montgomery, Alabama, bus system, widely regarded as "the watershed of the civil rights movement" (p. 51), was a consequence of "deliberate organizing efforts initiated by community leaders through mass-based organizations" (p. 56). The emergence of a mass, nation-wide civil rights movement, which took place in the 1960s, resulted from a marriage of local networks, structures, and organizations that were already in place, and nationally recognized leaders who attracted national, even international, media attention. In short, the emergence and success of a social movement is dependent on organization and the mobilization of available resources, not on a sudden and inexplicable outburst that represents a break with tradition.

The resource mobilization perspective expands the "cast of characters" (Zurcher and Snow, 1981, pp. 472–477) relevant to the study of social movements to include not only leaders and their lieutenants, rank-and-file supporters, and ordinary members, but also bystanders; opponents and competitors; constituents; potential beneficiaries; the mass media; the state, including agents and agencies of social control; and any and all outside agencies that consciously or unwittingly attempt to damage or facilitate social movements. Each of these set of actors can influence social movement outcomes no less than leaders and members and become aspects of a social movement organization's resources.

The media, for instance, can serve as a morale booster, give publicity to stimulate membership, and serve as a beachhead for support (or opposition) by the government; media coverage may facilitate goal attainment and validate the view that what the movement does matters. While the members of social movements and SMOs often complain of biased reporting of their activities, most are acutely aware of the potential for benefit—and harm— that the media can yield to their cause. The media *filter* social movement activity; they form a *linkage system* between social movements and a variety of mainstream institutions and groups. With their reporting, they may grant *legitimacy* to a movement and influence the formation of a certain *agenda* for authorities (Zald, 1991). In short, "News coverage is critical to sustaining social movements" (Molotch, 1979, p. 91). There is, of course, a symbiotic relationship between the media and social movements; the two share a "bed-fellow dialectic." Just as social movements thrive on certain kinds of media attention, the media benefit from interesting stories about social movements; the two "often need one another," although the relationship is often fraught with tension (Molotch, 1979, p. 71).

As we saw, the resource mobilization perspective is acutely interested in the efforts of nonmembers who represent nonmovement agencies and organizations—such as official agents of social control—who intend to damage (or facilitate) their organization's aims. For instance, clandestine government operations (by the CIA and the FBI) have released damaging information, true or false, to the press about movement figures; private agencies have withdrawn or increased funding for certain social movement organizations in response to government pressure or threats; local governments have withdrawn permission to movements for parade permits; spies and undercover agents have been planted in organizations to create dissent in their ranks; specific actions taken by movement organizers have been sabotaged (Marx, 1979; Marx 1988, pp. 32, 64). One of the most notorious examples of the efforts of external organizations to subvert the leader of a social movement involved the Rev. Martin Luther King, Jr. Fearing that Dr. King and some of his associates were "communists," "subversives," "radicals," and "revolutionaries," J. Edgar Hoover, head of the FBI, at the instigation or with the cooperation of President Lyndon Johnson and Attorney General Robert Kennedy, for six years directed a systematic surveillance of the private activities of Dr. King. Bugs were even placed in bedrooms where he slept to obtain tapes of his sexual activities (Garrow, 1981). These efforts undermined, but did not destroy, the civil rights movement in the 1960s.

Although resource mobilization is now the dominant perspective in the study of social movements, it has been criticized by a number of observers. It has been accused of focusing too much on elites and not enough on rank-and-file members, underplaying grievances altogether too much, and not understanding the relationship between grievances and movement mobilization (McAdam, 1982, pp. 23–35). In my view, the advocates of resource mobilization exaggerate the rationality and institutional basis of social movements and the stability of their goals, as well as underplay the spontaneous, impulsive, expressive, emotional quality of their participant's actions. And, while I agree that collective behavior and most social movement participation represent two more or less distinct species of behavior, I would also argue that they shade off into one another and that some social movement participation is extrainstitutional, spontaneous, and very much like a great deal of collective behavior. Like most perspectives, resource mobilization is a valuable but limited, often overly ambitious, perspective, which works better for some movement processes than others and for some social movements and organizations than others. As such, it deserves the close attention of the student of social movements and collective behavior, but not to the exclusion of other perspectives.

___ SOCIAL MOVEMENTS AS COLLECTIVE BEHAVIOR ___

We've already seen that the classic Chicago school collective behavior theorists (for instance, Turner and Killian, 1957, 1972, 1987; Lang and Lang, 1961), along with Smelser's value-added perspective (1962), saw social movements as a form of collective behavior. In contrast, the more contemporary politico-rational, mainly resource mobilization, theorists regard social movements as distinct from collective behavior and, in fact, seem to want to define what was previously regarded as collective behavior out of existence or, at least, sociological relevance. My position, as I've said, is markedly different from both these approaches. I would argue that, while most social movements and social movement organizations are *not* instances of collective behavior and therefore lie outside the scope of the field of collective behavior, *some* features of social movements and movement organizations *do* display collective behavior-like features. In short, just as some social movements and social movement aspects are *irrelevant* to the field of collective behavior, others are *relevant.*

There are at least two aspects of social movements that lie largely within the scope of the field of collective behavior, that is, those aspects in which relatively spontaneous, relatively noninstitutional behavior dominates: first, *in a social movement's formative stages*, before it becomes a normatively governed organization or institution, and second, *during certain confrontational social movement activities*, such as riots and some protests and demonstrations. In both, hesitancy, tentativeness, spontaneity, impulsiveness, and an impromptu quality dominate over predictability; certainty; decisiveness; explicitness; and a planned, norm-governed quality. What makes spontaneity so crucial a quality in some social movement activity is that *members and leaders can never be certain just what nonmembers are going to do in response to their actions* and hence, can never be sure just how they themselves are going react.

Resource mobilization theorists have three ways of dealing with the collective behavior-like features such as spontaneity that spring up in some social movements and in certain stages of most social movements. First, they can simply minimize them or deny their existence, insisting that what seems like spontaneity and extrainstitutionality to outsiders is really a product of planning and institutional involvements on the part of movement activists (Morris, 1981, 1984). Second, they can shoehorn them into a special kind of planning, claiming that "impromptu" (as distinct from "impulsive") actions have always been a part of social movement behavior (Rosenthal and Schwartz, 1989, pp. 38–43). Third, they can acknowledge their existence and importance, admit that their influence cannot be explained by the resource mobilization perspective, agree that resource mobilization and the collective behavior approaches complement one another, and urge that more research be done on spontaneity's role in social movements (Zald, 1991). Zald, adopting the third of these approaches, argues that the collective behavior school "emphasized some phenomena not well treated in the more contemporary" resource mobilization approach, such as "enthusiasm, spontaneity, and conversion experiences." An analysis of spontaneity "adds much to the hyperrationality that can develop in RM [resource mobilization] theory" (Zald, 1991). It is the third of these positions that guides this discussion.

LATENCY

The most important way that social movements and collective behavior share features in common is *latency*. This idea was discussed in Chapter 9, in the section on fads (see page 358), and will be discussed in more detail in Chapter 11, in which four recent social movements are presented. At a given time, a specific social movement—like a specific novelty item—may or may not possess the capacity to "catch on"; it may or may not be capable of finding a niche or space in that society, or the society may or may not have a niche or space which the behavior or the item can occupy. Some budding social movements fulfill a need and, if their leaders are skillful enough, can translate that need into a stable organization.

ACT UP, a movement organization centered around fighting AIDS, erupted practically overnight; a potentiality or latency or space existed in that society to accommodate its struggle. Other organizations die almost as soon as they are launched. The difference is not, as resource mobilization would have it, solely a matter of the mobilization of relevant resources. It is unlikely that a major mass social movement can emerge over the next few years based on protesting the inclusion of perfume fragrance strips in magazine advertising (although a tiny one does exist). ACT UP served an aching need in American society; it tapped a longing in the lives of a substantial number of Americans. The desire to eliminate fragrance strips does not have that same quality of latency. Latency is the *central* way that social movements and collective behavior overlap. However, once a movement becomes firmly established in a society, its latency—present or absent—is revealed and its collective behavior-like features diminish.

SPONTANEITY

Whether one refers to more or less unplanned, unpremeditated actions and decisions that are made on-the-spot as "impromptu" or "spontaneous" (but *not* "impulsive," *not* "disorganized," and not "thoughtless"), clearly, they are a major element of social movement activity, especially in their initial phases. Spontaneity—that impromptu quality—is also a major (and defining) element of collective behavior *and* it is far less likely to be found in more conventional, more fully institutionalized realms. When we say that behavior is spontaneous or impromptu, that it has an "emergent" quality, this is not to say that it is totally discontinuous with the actor's past, that it has no institutional roots whatsoever (Killian, 1984, p. 780). The roots are there; it is just that the transition from roots to action is more tenuous, less certain, more unpredictable in certain contexts than in others. In some situations, what one should do is far less clear and far more ambiguous than in others. The potential for action at some times is broader, more open, less clearly defined, less clearly spelled out.

Many actions pursued by movement participants are in response to immediate situations; *improvisation* in such a case is the rule, not following a clearly spelled-out path. Engaging in collective behavior—and in some social movement activity—is more similar to playing jazz than classical music; clearly, the former is more spontaneous than the latter, in that some improvisation is permitted, but this does not mean the musician can play absolutely anything that pops into his or her head. Some resource mobilization theorists have misconstrued spontaneity to mean "anything is possible"; clearly, here, we are discussing a matter of degree, not an absolute difference. Social movement activists often pursue actions on a darkened, unclear, obscure path; they know where they want to go, but they aren't sure how to get there or whether what they are doing will get them there. In this sense, we agree with Rosenthal and Schwartz, who say there is an "*intermingling* of spontaneous and planned action," that, in spite of its spontaneous, impromptu quality, "there is an organizational backbone to collective action" (Rosenthal and Schwartz, 1989, p. 37), just as we agree with Killian when he says, in the emergence of social movements, there is always "a mix. There is structure, emphasized by resource mobilization theorists, and process, stressed by collective behaviorists" (1986, p. 10).

UNPREDICTABILITY

Social movement actors frequently act in the face of unpredictability; that is, they can never be certain as to what the results of their actions will be. Especially in the beginning of any movement, activitists cannot know whether, and to what extent, they can mobilize a constituency, nor can they reliably predict the reaction their actions will generate among agents of social control. Most human behavior contains an *element* of unpredictability, it is true; we cannot know *for certain* that when we hand a sales clerk a sum of money for an item we wish to purchase that we will be successful in acquiring that item. At the same time, the initial phases of social movements contain *more than their share* of unpredictability. For instance, in the early phases of the civil rights movement, in the 1950s and early 1960s, Black student, community, and church leaders had no more than "a vague idea of what resources they could rally. Neither the Black churches nor the Black secular organizations had any record of participation in the kind of social action being proposed, action which would require both personal and financial sacrifice. The movement was launched more on faith than on the basis of an inventory of resources" (Killian, 1984, pp. 780–781). A major element of collective behavior is *surprise*—the emergence or eruption of the unexpected. To argue that movement behavior and outcomes are predictable is to argue that there are no surprises for participants or their opponents; in contrast, the social movement literature is replete with unexpected movement participants' behavior, the behavior of their opponents, and the ensuing interaction between them.

In a study of the success of the Yugoslavian communist party, Denitch (1981) concludes that, from the point of view of the resources they commanded, there was nothing about their pre-World War II situation "which could have led an informed observer to suppose that a successful communist-led revolution would have occurred in that country. On the contrary, there were numerous particular specificities . . . which argued against such a prospect" (p. 77). It was something of an indeterminate mix of spontaneity and organization that made it possible for a tiny, 3,000-member pre-war party to emerge from the struggle against the Germans and Italians, over 150,000 members strong, capable of crushing all opposition (p. 79). It is only because we already know that a movement or an organization is successful that we are able to say that the achievement of its goals was inevitable and predictable. In the heat of battle, with the forces of opposition struggling over an issue, outcomes are never certain; when the movement is small, the odds against its success seem extremely slim, the unpredictability of the outcomes it seeks looms even larger. And unpredictability, both of actions and outcomes, is a major ingredient of collective behavior.

EXTRAINSTITUTIONALITY

When engaged in movement activities, participants do not act on a whim or on impulse. For the most part, their actions are an expression of their prior ideological commitments. Morris (1981, 1984) shows us that, prior to the national emergence of the civil rights movement in the late 1950s, early activists had both ideological commitments to equality and institutional involvements in civil rights organizations, such as leaderships in the NAACP. These civil rights workers knew what they were going to do in advance; their actions were planned out, deliberate, normative, and cannot be regarded either as extrainstitutional or as a form of collective behavior. But, in reality, neither beliefs nor institutional involvements entirely predict future behavior. In any realm of life, we can never know for certain what someone is going to do simply from his or her normative or institutional commitments. And the newer, the more uncertain, and the less normatively established a behavioral pattern is, the more extrainstitutional it can be said to be—regardless of the degree to which it corresponds to a budding activist's ideology and commitments.

The fact is, equal access to public facilities and voting rights had not yet been implemented in the South in 1958; they had to be fought for. The interaction between recalcitrant whites and activist Blacks that gave birth to these rights—much of it conflictual, hostile, some of it even lethal—had yet to take place. Simply because one party in a conflict has ideological commitments and institutional involvements does not tell us what the *outcome* of that confrontation will be. Outcomes have to be struggled over, hammered out, negotiated, finessed, and compromised upon. Some resource mobilization theorists give the impression that the events that make up the actions of movement activists and the outcomes of those actions are inevitable, the mechanical unfolding of a certain set of norms and commitments on the part of activists and a set of resources on the part of the organizations of which they are a part. This sort of historical determinism is fine for Greek drama, but it has no place in the volatile "blood and guts" drama of real-life movement activity, in which contingency, ambivalence, hesitance, indecision, backtracking, miscalculation, faith, courage, and a day-to-day or even minute-to-minute give-and-take play a major role.

Moreover, ideological commitments, and even institutional involvements, and the reality of acting are two entirely different phenomena. Doing something that has never been done before and achieving results that were only previously imagined cannot be regarded as part of the established, normative, institutional realm; they represent the *process,* not the *fact,* of institutionalization. McAdam's study (1988) of the "freedom summer" project workers—many of them college and graduate students, mostly white, who went to Mississippi to register Black voters during the summer of 1964—shows this clearly. All of the hundreds of young men and women who worked on the project described the experience as liberating—a liberation from the rigid norms and institutions they grew up with. While, for all, their participation in freedom summer was an expression of their ideological commitment to equality and, for most, an extension of prior institutional involvements with similar organizations, actually working in the real world to achieve a desired goal was an altogether different experience. It was, for them, a form of ecstasy, a sense of liberation that comes from "stepping outside . . . the taken-for-granted routines of society" (McAdam, 1988, p. 67; Berger, 1963, p. 136). Said one worker, "It was just so different from the way I had been raised; you know, to be proper and demure and all that. . . . This whole stiff, uptight way I had been raised felt like it was melting away" (p. 92).

EMOTIONALITY

As we saw in Chapter 1, emotionality is *not* a defining characteristic of collective behavior. Much conventional behavior—love within a family, for instance—is highly charged emotionally, while some unconventional, extrainstitutional behavior is relatively affectless (witness the taken-for-granted, "of course" quality of some legends and paranormal beliefs). At the same time, it cannot be denied that collective behavior is *more likely to be* characterized by strong emotion than conventional, institutional behavior. Fads, fashion, and especially crazes, gossip and rumor (which are generated by strong feeling, or at least interest), miracles, ecstatic crowds, disasters, riots and other collective violence, legend and collective delusion—all are arenas within which strong emotion, even passion, typically dominate. The early stages of social movements are likely to be cut out of the same cloth, just as conventional, mainstream political and organizational activity is less likely to partake of this quality. Yet, some resource mobilization theorists describe social movement activity as something of a bloodless affair; they "neglect the importance of strong passions" (Zurcher and Snow, 1981, p. 477).

McAdam's (1988) workers who participated in the freedom summer project, once again, illustrate the importance of passion in social movement activity. These were idealistic young men and women, mostly white, who were acting out of an intense feeling that things were wrong with this society that had to be set right. They were filled with a sense of righteousness of their cause and fear for the risks their actions entailed. Beginning with their orientation sessions, these activists felt ecstasy, a "giddy, disorienting sense of liberation" (p. 67). It was "intoxicating," said one; "intense," said another. "It was an incredibly moving experience," said a third. "I was frightened by it and awed by it"; "it was a real romantic trip" (pp. 68, 71, 93). After a confrontation with white authorities who eventually backed down, one freedom summer worker said, "It was moments like that you felt . . . practically an erotic feeling" (p. 95). While these young men and women were acting out of their convictions, they also found coming face-to-face with the realities of racism and experiencing what they had to do to struggle against it awesome, moving, frightening, exhilirating, and an ecstatic experience. It is extremely difficult to fit these emotions into the organizational "business as usual" resource mobilization framework. For many, perhaps most, activists attempting to change a major aspect of society they consider wrong, emotionality tends to be a major experiential component.

———— CLAIMS-MAKING IN SOCIAL MOVEMENTS ————

Social movement representatives engage in *claims-making* activities (Spector and Kitsuse, 1977). That is, all social movements begin with a *premise;* more specifically, they begin with the claim that *something is wrong that can and should be remedied.* Thus, the "claims" that social movements make fall into two parts: "What's wrong?" and "What is to be done?" As we saw, the condition that social movements address—"What's wrong?"—may exist and be as serious as they say, may exist but not be as serious as they say, or may not even exist at all. It doesn't matter: In order to attract recruits and donations, motivate activists, gain media attention, and move lawmakers to enact favorable legislation, social movement leaders and publicists must formulate an argument and marshall evidence supporting their position. Claims-making is one of a variety of methods or tools social movements have to help them achieve their goals. It is part of the struggle for the hearts and minds—and consequently, the time and the pocketbooks—of the public, legislators, and the media.

In other words, social movements are engaged in "the politics of reality" (Goode, 1969), that is, using evidence as a means of defining for others how things are and how they ought to be. To convince others that one's definition of reality is correct, that the condition really is serious and in need of solution, represents a kind of victory for a movement, one milestone along the way to achieving its ultimate goals. Definitions of reality are fought over and debated. Much of the struggle and the give-and-take between social movements and their constituents, their opponents, the public, the media, and legislators entails the attempt to legitimate a certain version of the reality of the condition being addressed. Indeed, even getting others to *pay attention* to certain previously ignored conditions represents a major victory for a social movement. Another way of saying this is that movements attempt to define their cause as "politically correct" and opposition to their program—or even simple inaction—as politically *incorrect*, almost unthinkably monstrous behavior. Anti-abortion groups refer to abortion as "killing babies"—what could be worse than murdering infants? Who could possibly be in favor of such monstrous behavior? The animal rights people refer to favoring humans over animals as "speciesism," a sin no less wrong than sexism or racism. Clearly, much social movement activity represents a struggle over *what certain actions should be called, how they are to be defined or referred to.*

Arguments put forth by social movements very rarely weigh the pros and cons of both sides in a reasoned, scholarly fashion and come out with the conclusion, "On the one hand . . ., but then, on the other. . . ." They nearly always "make a case," much as a trial laywer does in arguing for or against a defendant in court. Typically, the evidence is presented in a one-sided fashion. Evidence suggesting that the other side might have a point is presented—if it is—as a foil, a device to demolish their point of view. Movements are more likely to formulate an argument in black-or-white terms than in shades of gray. It must be stressed that social movements defend their positions much as the other participants in this drama do; their opponents, too, engage in one-sided arguments. When Exxon tells us that the 1989 oil spill in Alaska did not do any permanent damage to the environment, it would be wise to be extremely skeptical about that claim. As we saw in Chapter 7 on gossip and rumor, large corporations retain public relations experts who make a living claiming that the damage their clients do is less serious than it really is. Much of the process of claims-making is taken up with not only validating the view of one's own group but also discrediting those of one's opponents.

It is extremely rarely the case—although it sometimes happens—that the conditions a movement focuses on are worse than its activist's claim. With most conditions, nearly all the time, movement participants must make them out to be worse than they are; they tend to focus on the worst aspects of the condition *as if they were typical.* In this sense, the justifications that social movements construct to support their position are similar to gossip, rumor, legends, and paranormal beliefs—that is, they "tell one hell of a good story." In order to grab the observer by the throat, get his or her attention, and insist, "*This condition is important, it is bad, and it must be changed!*," it is almost always necessary to lie or at least exaggerate a little. It would be difficult to contest the point that, while some participants in some social movements describe the conditions they wish to change accurately, *taken as a whole*, social movements tend to exaggerate their extent and seriousness. To be plain about it, exaggeration is a great deal more *effective* as a movement strategy than the complex task of literal, point-for-point truth telling. Movement claims-making makes demands on people's limited time and attention; there are many issues to deal with, and movements must convince potentially interested parties that *this* particular issue needs dealing with.

For instance, in their attack against pornography, anti-pornography groups focus more or less exclusively on violent pornography and pretend not to know, or explicitly deny, that the overwhelming majority of pornography is nonviolent—or they arbitrarily define all nonviolent pornography as violent—and ignore or dismiss evidence that suggests that pornography does not cause or influence men to become violent towards women. To say that a tiny percentage of all pornography depicts violence against women is to elicit a "ho-hum" response from an audience; to say that pornography depicts women being "bound, gagged, sliced up, tortured" (Dworkin, 1982, p. 255) is to stir up a sense of outrage. To say that the evidence suggests that, over the short run, witnessing violent films with sexual content is correlated with men inflicting simulated pain upon women in a laboratory setting, but watching nonviolent films probably is not, does not cause very many women to run out and enlist in the anti-pornography crusade. In contrast, chanting "Rape is the practice, pornography is the theory"—the slogan of Women Against Pornography—does generate that movement-joining fervor. (For some representative anti-pornography claims, see Dworkin, 1981, and the essays in Lederer, 1982; for a summary of the literature, see Malamuth and Donnerstein, 1984; Donnerstein, Linz, and Penrod, 1987; and Goode, 1990, pp. 151–169.)

Anti-abortionist groups claim that abortion is not simply harmful to the fetus, it is also extremely dangerous to the woman who aborts a fetus; after an abortion, women supposedly suffer a serious "syndrome" of "physical or emotional trauma" (Garb, 1989). In contrast to this claim, the evidence is clear-cut: Childbirth is many times more dangerous to a woman's health than is abortion. According to figures released by the National Center for Health Statistics, there were 6.6 maternal deaths per 100,000 births in the United States each year in the late 1980s. In contrast, the risk of death for a woman undergoing an abortion is 0.4 per 100,000 (down from 3.4 per 100,000 in 1973, when abortion first became legal). Anti-abortion forces never mention the increased risk of childbirth when discussing the issue of the impact of abortion on a woman's health. (Of course, in a parallel fashion, the pro-choice forces underplay the fact that abortion always results in death to the fetus—which is, after all, a *potential* human being.) Bringing in all the facts, in all their complexity, makes strong advocacy of a given cause more difficult.

Organizations attempting to induce the government to "do something" about child kidnappings by strangers claim that some 50,000 take place each year in the United States, and perhaps 4,000 of these are victims of murder. In reality, fewer than 1,000 children under the age of 15 are murdered each year, the overwhelming majority of whom are killed by parents, other relatives, and friends. Some 95 percent of missing children are runaways, most of whom return home within three days; most kidnappings of children are by estranged and separated parents; and the actual number of stranger-abducted children is less than 600 per year nationwide, the vast majority of whom are not killed or even physically harmed (Griego and Kilzer, 1985; Best, 1988; Gentry, 1988).

Exaggerated claims such as these stimulate more outrage, attract more attention, and generate more resources for the cause than assertions that are nearer to the truth. To an activist, carefully weighing the evidence is tantamount to saying that the condition really isn't terribly serious and isn't much in need of remedy. It is seen as a *betrayal* of the cause. "Are you for us or against us?" activists will challenge those who insist on factual correctness. "Do you want these horrible conditions to continue?" they will ask, as if facts are little more than a distraction from their goal. Indeed, in terms of generating movement activity, this is often the case.

It should be emphasized, once again, that exaggeration in claims-making is *by no means unique* to social movement participants. Indeed, it is a universal human activity. Individually, every one of us engages in the process; collectively, mainstream organizations also routinely engage in exaggerated claims-making. Public relations, a major part of the activities of conventional, mainstream institutions and organizations, is geared to sanitize their image in the public eye. And what is public relations but claims-making that avoids a rigorous, systematic assessment of the facts? In this respect, social movements are *similar to* rather than different from their more conventional organizational cousins. All efforts to gain attention, to generate action, and to change public opinion—in short, to get one's way—are and must inevitably be based on focusing on what supports one's claims and ignoring what does not—that is, lying a little. While, in general, social movements do not differ from conventional organizations in this respect, social movements do differ among themselves: Some do it more than others. What I've said about exaggeration in claims-making is not to say that social movement activists' claims can drift wildly and unrealistically away from reality, or what much of the public takes to be reality, without negative consequences. Statements that are felt by constituents or potential participants to be completely wrong can discredit a given movement and possibly its aims as well. Thus, there are limits to this process; some reality testing inevitably protrudes into the claims-making process (Bouchier, 1987, 1990).

Aside from exaggerating its claims of the seriousness of a given condition, another type of "claims-making" activity that movement participants engage in is *minimizing the benefits* of the condition, if any are seen by others. Non-movement individuals might grant that a given condition is bad, but argue that, on balance, it is "worth it" to do nothing about it because of certain benefits that accrue as a result of it. For instance, most observers might admit that it is terrible to cut down acres and acres of thousand-year-old redwoods, but, they are likely to say, the alternative—not having the wood for the products we need—is even worse. So activists have to counter the claims made by observers and opponents that, even though the condition might be bad, eliminating it isn't "worth it" because it creates even more undesirable conditions.

For instance, the more militant animal rights activists claim that animal experimentation is ineffective, that human lives are not really saved by medical research using animals as subjects, that animal research has contributed little or nothing to human health and longevity. All animal research could be eliminated and clinical research on humans substituted—or none conducted at all—and humans would lead lives just as long and just as healthy as a consequence (Tiger, 1985; Sharpe, 1988). Most scientists dispute this claim, and argue that, over the course of this century, we live at least 20 years longer and we lead much healthier lives thanks in part to research that was conducted on animals (Goodwin, 1989); notice that scientists, too, engage in claims-making activities. Some of the "miminimizing the benefits" aspect of claims-making represents a *challenge to existing values*. Nearly everyone values a long, healthy life, and so anything that contributes to it is likely to be looked upon favorably. Quite different is the claim that certain values are invalid, and should not be allowed to perpetuate an undesirable condition. A good example of this type of claims-making activity is the charge made, again, by the animal rights activists, that desiring fur coats is an empty, false value; cloth and artificial materials warm the wearer every bit as effectively as fur (Kasindorf, 1990).

Another claims-making tactic that social movement representatives engage in is *discrediting their opponents*, individuals or agencies they *see* or *define* as their opponents. To many movement activists, it seems obvious and self-evident that their cause is just; they simply cannot understand why anyone would disagree with their position. There must be an explanation for *why* others put obstacles in their path. Two readily come to mind: those who do so must be either *stupid* or *evil*. In an argument with them, therefore, this basic fact must be pointed out; bystanders must be made to realize that this is the case. Thus, as we'll see in the next chapter, anti-AIDS activists publicly charge that AIDS workers or observers are liars and guilty of "murdering" AIDS patients. In a similar vein, the animal rights lobby accuses fur trappers, ranchers, manufacturers, the employees of stores that sell fur garments, and purchasers of furs of being "murderers." Likewise, anti-abortionist or pro-life advocates claim that abortionists, women who undergo abortions, and pro-choice advocates are, once again, guilty of "murder." Of course, murder is simply the most extreme charge that movement activists can hurl at their opponents; practically all movements charge them with a wide range of crimes and outrages in an effort to discredit them, their arguments, their behavior, and their position. One of the most important claims-making activities of social movements is *vilification* (Vanderford, 1989).

Another type of claims-making that social movements put forth—and *must* put forth in order to be effective—is *minimizing the difficulty of rectifying the problem*. Although some movement spokespersons will say, "This isn't going to be easy," it is far commoner to hear them say, "All we have to do is this. . . ." All we have to do is to stop animal research, stop eating meat, stop buying and wearing furs, and free all the animals from zoos—and animals won't have to suffer. All we have to do is to stop industry from polluting our air and water and get them to stop cutting down our nation's trees and strip-mining our hills and mountains, and we'll have a purer, cleaner, more natural environment. All we have to do is to give AIDS patients unlimited access to untested experimental drugs, and more of them will live longer lives, a cure for this dread disease will be found much more quickly, and many lives will be saved (DeParle, 1990; Taylor, 1990). The observer is very rarely told of the extreme difficulty and even improbability of making such changes, and their possible negative, and often unanticipated, consequences. This is not to say that changes such as these have not been made; in fact, the impact of activist social movements on the course of twentieth century America is truly impressive. While some changes may have been accomplished with a great deal less difficulty than was anticipated, in fact, most were bought at a very high price and with some negative consequences that even the most realistic movement activists had not conceived of.

The claims-making tactic of minimizing the difficulty of improving conditions is not quite the same thing as Smelser's "if only" process of collective behavior and social movement "short-circuiting" (1962, p. 72). There are at least three differences between them.

One is that such thinking is not unique or distinctive to collective behavior or social movements; it has been abundantly described and documented for people generally, in all areas and walks of life—scientists included (Nisbett and Ross, 1980; Kahneman, Slovic, and Tversky, 1982). Smelser is simply wrong in assuming that it applies to collective behavior or social movement activity more than for other, more conventional, routine spheres of life.

Second, Smelser takes participants' statements about the ease of accomplishing movement goals at face value. In fact, while some may believe in these statements, what is more important is that they are *rhetorical devices*— they are statements that *work better* in achieving movement goals than more accurate and pessimistic assessments would. It is even likely that "insiders" are quite accurate and sophisticated concerning their chances of success and the difficulty of achieving desired movement goals. They espouse more optimistic and simplistic solutions for *tactical* reasons—to attract support and resources. On the other hand, rank-and-file members, in all likelihood, are less likely to be as knowlegeable and are more likely to hold to the more "official" view, that is, one that is fairly optimistic and simplistic. This is not because they hold a "magical" view of the way things work; it is because, like everyone else, they view the world through their own conceptual framework, and because they don't have access to all the facts. In fact, *different* SMOs in the *same* movement will adopt very different approaches with respect to the feasibility of their goals. More radical and more "extreme"— and, presumably, less realistic—SMOs may permit more mainstream groups to look less radical and therefore achieve more of their goals. This is called the *niche theory* of social movements (Scarce, 1990, pp. 6–7).

And third, it is entirely possible that *believing in* such an optimistic view of the ease of change may, in some instances at least, *facilitate the achievement of movement goals.* Few civil rights leaders, looking back at the 1960s from the vantage point of today, would say that they imagined that racial change was going to be as difficult and as partial as it has been. But it is also likely that many would not have endured as much as they put up with had they known this a generation or so ago. Optimism is not magical thinking. It represents the art of the possible; it is an engine for social change.

SUMMARY

Social movements are organized, noninstitutionalized efforts by a large number of people to change or preserve major aspects of a society. In nearly all societies of the world, some people band together to bring about, or prevent, change. By their very nature, social movements express dissatisfaction either with the way things are or the way, some fear, certain people want to make things. Social movements require three basic conditions to come into being: one, a real, potential, or imaginary condition to which some do or may object; two, a subjective feeling that this condition is undesirable and must be changed; and three, an organized means for expressing this dissatisfaction collectively, that is, a social movement organization.

In comparison with collective behavior, social movements are more organized and longer lasting, and their participants are more intentional, goal-directed, and more likely to seek substantial social change. Social movements are not fully institutionalized; they do not work strictly within the mainstream political system—in fact, they tend to be denied direct access to governmental power. Consequently, they attempt to affect change through more unconventional means, such as boycotts, strikes, demonstrations, and, for some, occasionally violence. Still, it must be recognized that they are a central aspect of the political process.

It is necessary to distinguish between social movements and *social movement organizations* (SMOs). A social movement is a broad umbrella for everyone who works for or in relation to a given cause. In contrast, a social movement organization is one of a number of specific groups that fall under the broad umbrella of a given movement.

Social movements and SMOs have been classified in a number of ways. One is according to the direction and degree of change. Reactionary movements seek regressive change; they want to return society or an aspect of it to the way things were in the past. Conservative movements want to resist change, to retain things the way they are now. Reformist movements seek moderate progressive change. Revolutionary movements seek a basic, drastic, thoroughgoing, and sudden transformation of society generally. Escapist movements—not even thought of as movements by most experts—seek to withdraw from society, regarding it too corrupt, and the social order they desire as too pure for them to be able to work within the existing system to affect meaningful change. Expressive movements, also often not seen by many observers as a real social movement type, engage in behavior that is not designed to affect any meaningful change, but to express members' personal or ideological feelings about the way things are.

The grassroots view of why social movements are launched is commonsensical: People form movements to the extent that they are dissatisfied, and they are dissatisfied to the extent that they are objectively deprived. It is now widely recognized that this view is largely incorrect. The relationship between objective deprivation and subjective discontent, and that between subjective discontent and social movement participation, is not automatic; it requires an explanation. How conditions are regarded and what should be done about them are subjective matters, not a simple outgrowth of their objective existence.

At least eight theories have been crucial in explaining social movement participation. The *irrational group mind* perspective holds that, when people organize for a collective goal, they become an unreasoning, frenzied mob; this view has been completely discredited and is of historical interest only. *Marxism* sees social movement participation as an effort by class-conscious members of the working class to throw off bourgeois oppression. While it is widely recognized as an excessively narrow view of social movements, Marxism did stress the importance of movement organization and social control and the central place of rationality and goal-directedness of movement members. The *psychopathology* viewpoint argued that certain movement leaders and participants suffer from an abnormal personality. Hardly anyone accepts this view today. Max Weber introduced the importance of *charisma*, a unique, extraordinary, almost supernatural quality that some leaders have, in the dynamics of social movements. The *mass society* view holds that social movements tend to arise in societies in which there is weak social integration, and likewise tend to attract rootless, alienated individuals; research has more or less thoroughly discredited this view. If anything, such societies seem to generate less movement activity, not more, and such individuals are less likely to join movements than are those more integrated into social networks.

The *Chicago school* or collective behavior approach looks at social movement participation as a type of collective behavior; while still a focus of debate, most contemporary researchers do not hold this view, and regard the two realms of behavior as distinctly different. Smelser's *value-added theory*, like the Chicago school, sees a continuity between collective behavior and social movement participation; they emerge when the conditions of structural conduciveness, structural strain, generalized beliefs, precipitating factors, mobilization for action, and social control are present, and do not arise when they are absent. While most researchers question several of Smelser's points, his theory did focus on two factors of crucial importance in work done today: mobilization and social control. Last, *resource mobilization* downplays the importance of strain and deprivation in social movement participation and success, and stresses factors such as leadership, money, communication networks, links with business and government—in short, the mobilization of resources. Some observers argue that grievance cannot be so easily dismissed, movement participation may not be nearly so rational, and spontaneity and volatility may not be nearly so rare or unimportant as resource mobilization argues.

While many, perhaps most, aspects of social movement participation are not forms of collective behavior, some clearly are. Latency, spontaneity, unpredictability, extrainstitutionality, and emotionality play a role at crucial times in some social movement activities.

In order to mobilize popular support, social movements must engage in claims-making; they must present a case or view of the way things are to the public to win their hearts and minds. This usually entails exaggerating the seriousness of a condition, minimizing its benefits, and minimizing the difficulty of changing it. Such claims-making activities usually facilitate the achievement of movement goals. It does not represent the magical thinking that Smelser claims; instead, it represents practicing the art of the possible.

References

Adorno, Theodor W., et al. 1950. *The Authoritarian Personality.* New York: Harper & Brothers.

Berger, Peter L. 1963. *Invitation to Sociology.* Garden City, N.Y.: Doubleday-Anchor.

Best, Joel. 1988. "Missing Children, Misleading Statistics." *The Public Interest*, no. 92: 84–92.

Bettleheim, Bruno. 1971. "The Roots of Radicalism." *Playboy* (March): 106, 124, 206–208.

Bouchier, David. 1987. *Radical Citizenship: The New American Activism.* New York: Schocken Books.

Bouchier, David. 1990. "Hard Questions for Citizen Radicals." *Social Anarchism*, no.15: 5–19.

Cameron, William Bruce. 1966. *Modern Social Movements: A Sociological Outline.* New York: Random House.

Cantril, Hadley. 1941. *The Psychology of Social Movements.* New York: John Wiley & Sons.

Denitch, Bogdan. 1981. "Spontaneity and Organization: Revolution-ary Party and Modernization." In Ulf Himmelstrand (ed.), *Spontaneity and Planning in Social Development*, pp. 75–85. Newbury Park, Calif.: Sage.

DeParle, Jason. 1990. "Rash, Rude, Effective, Act-Up Gains AIDS Shifts." *The New York Times* (January 3): B1, B4.

Donnerstein, Edward, Daniel Linz, and Stephen Penrod. 1987. *The Question of Pornography: Research Findings and Policy Implications.* New York: Free Press.

Dworkin, Andrea. 1981. *Pornography: Men Possessing Women.* Perigee Books.

Dworkin, Andrea. 1982. "For Men, Freedom of Speech; For Women, Silence Please." In Laura Lederer (ed.), *Take Back the Night: Women on Pornography*, pp. 255–258. New York: Bantam Books.

Feuer, Lewis. 1969. *The Conflict of Generations.* New York: Basic Books.

Fischer, Claude S. 1984. *The Urban Experience* (2nd ed.). San Diego: Harcourt, Brace, Jovanovich.

Gamson, William. 1990. *The Strategy of Social Protest* (2nd ed.). Belmont, Calif.: Wadsworth.

Garb, Maggie. 1989. Abortion Foes Give Birth to a 'Syndrome,'" *In These Times* (February 22–March 1): 3, 22.

Garrow, David J. 1981. *The FBI and Martin Luther King: From "Solo" to Memphis.* New York: W.W. Norton.

Gentry, Cynthia. 1988. "The Social Construction of Abducted Children as a Social Problem." *Sociological Inquiry*, 58 (4): 413–426.

Goode, Erich. 1969. "Marijuana and the Politics of Reality." *Journal of Health and Social Behavior*, 10 (June): 83–94.

Goode, Erich. 1990. *Deviant Behavior* (3rd ed.). Englewood Cliffs, N.J.: Prentice-Hall.

Goodwin, Frederick K. 1989. "We Can't Sacrifice People for the Sake of Animals." *Newsday* (May 21): 5.

Griego, Diana, and Louis Kilzer. 1985. "The Truth About Missing Kids: Exaggerated Statistics Stir National Paranoia." *The Sunday Denver Post* (May 12): 1-A, 12-A.

Hills, Stuart L. 1980. *Demystifying Social Deviance.* New York: McGraw-Hill.

Hoffer, Eric. 1951. *The True Believer: Thoughts on the Nature of Mass Movements.* New York: Harper & Brothers.

Jenkins. J. Craig. 1983. "Resource Mobilization Theory and the Study of Social Movements." *Annual Review of Sociology*, 9: 527–553.

Jenkins, J. Craig. 1986. "Stirring the Masses: Indigenous Roots of the Civil Rights Movement." *Contemporary Sociology*, 15 (May): 354–357.

Kahneman, Daniel, Paul Slovic, and Amos Tversky (eds.). 1982. *Judgement Under Uncertainty: Heuristics and Biases.* Cambridge, England: Cambridge University Press.

Kasindorf, Jeanie. 1990. "The Fur Flies: The Cold War Over Animal Rights." *New York* (January 15): 27–33.

Killian, Lewis M. 1984. "Organization, Rationality and Spontaneity in the Civil Rights Movement." *American Sociological Review,* 49 (December): 770–783.

Killian, Lewis M. 1986. "Courage or Calculation? Theories of Social Movements." Paper Presented at the Southern Sociological Society Meetings, New Orleans.

Kornhauser, William. 1959. *The Politics of Mass Society.* New York: Free Press.

Lang, Kurt, and Gladys Engel Lang. 1961. *Collective Dynamics.* New York: Thomas Y. Crowell.

Lawson, Ronald. 1983. "A Decentralized but Moving Pyramid: The Evolution and Consequences of the Structure of the Tenant Movement." In Jo Freedman (ed.), *Social Movements of the Sixties and Seventies,* pp. 119–132. New York: Longman.

Lederer, Laura (ed.). 1982. *Take Back the Night: Women on Pornography.* New York: Bantam Books.

Lipset, Seymour Martin. 1963. *Political Man.* Garden City, N.Y.: Doubleday/Anchor.

Logan, John. 1978. "Rural-Urban Migration and Working-Class Consciousness: The Spanish Case." *Social Forces,* 56 (6): 1159–1178.

Malamuth, Neil M., and Edward Donnerstein (eds.). 1984. *Pornography and Sexual Aggression.* Orlando, Fla.: Academic Press.

Marx, Gary T. 1979. "External Efforts to Damage or Facilitate Social Movements: Some Patterns, Explanations, Outcomes, and Complications." In Mayer N. Zald and John D. McCarthy (eds.), *The Dynamics of Social Movements: Resource Mobilization, Social Control, and Tactics,* pp. 94–125. Cambridge, Mass.: Winthrop.

Marx, Gary T. 1988. *Under Cover: Police Surveillance in America.* Berkeley: University of California Press.

McAdam, Doug. 1982. *Political Process and the Development of Black Insurgency, 1930–1970.* Chicago: University of Chicago Press.

McAdam, Doug. 1988. *Freedom Summer.* New York: Oxford University Press.

McAdam, Doug, John D. McCarthy, and Mayer D. Zald. 1988. "Social Movements." In Neil J. Smelser (ed.), *Handbook of Sociology,* pp. 695–737. Newbury Park, Calif.: Sage.

Molotch, Harvey. 1979. "Media and Movements." In Mayer N. Zald and John D. McCarthy (eds.), *The Dynamics of Social Movements: Resource Mobilization, Social Control, and Tactics,* pp. 71–93. Cambridge, Mass.: Winthrop.

Morris, Aldon D. 1981. "Black Southern Sit-in Movement: An Analysis of Internal Organization." *American Sociological Review,* 46 (December): 768–767.

Morris, Aldon D. 1984. *The Origins of the Civil Rights Movement: Black Communities Organizing for Change.* New York: Free Press.

Morris, Aldon, and Cedric Herring. 1987. "Theory and Research in Social Movements: A Critical Review." In Samuel Long (ed), *Annual Review of Political Science,* vol. 2, pp. 137–198. Norwood, N.J.: Ablex.

Nisbett, Richard, and Lee Ross. 1980. *Human Inference: Strategies and Shortcomings of Social Judgment.* Englewood Cliffs, N.J.: Prentice-Hall.

Oberschall, Anthony. 1973. *Social Conflict and Social Movements.* Englewood Cliffs, N.J.: Prentice-Hall.

Rosenthal, Naomi, and Michael Schwartz. 1989. "Spontaneity and Democracy in Social Movements." *International Social Movement Research,* 2: 33–59.

Scarce, Rik. 1990. *Eco-Warriors: Understanding the Radical Environmental Movement.* Chicago: Noble Press.

Schwartz, Michael. 1991. Private communication, February 20.

Sharpe, Robert. 1988. *The Cruel Deception.* Wellingborough, England: Northants, Thorsons.

Smelser, Neil J. 1962. *Theory of Collective Behavior.* New York: Free Press.

Spector, Malcom, and John I. Kitsuse. 1977. *Constructing Social Problems.* Menlo Park, Calif.: Benjamin-Cummings.

Taylor, Paul. 1990. "AIDS Guerillas." *New York* (November 12): 66–73.

Tiger, Steven. 1985. "Medical Research Isn't Making Us Healthier." *The New York Times* (August 24): 22.

Toch, Hans. 1965. *The Psychology of Social Movements.* Indianapolis, Ind.: Bobbs-Merrill.

Turner, Ralph H., and Lewis M. Killian. 1957. *Collective Behavior.* Englewood Cliffs, N.J.: Prentice-Hall.

Turner, Ralph H., and Lewis M. Killian. 1972. *Collective Behavior* (2nd ed.). Englewood Cliffs, N.J.: Prentice-Hall.

Turner, Ralph H., and Lewis M. Killian. 1987. *Collective Behavior* (3rd ed.). Englewood Cliffs, N.J.: Prentice-Hall.

Useem, Bert. 1985. "Disorganization and the New Mexico Prison Riot of 1980," *American Sociological Review,* 50 (October): 677–688.

Vanderford, Marsha L. 1989. "Vilification and Social Movements: A Case Study of Pro-Life and Pro-Choice Rhetoric." *Quarterly Journal of Speech,* 75 (May): 166–182.

Weber, Max. 1968. *Economy and Society: An Outline of Interpretive Sociology* (Guenther Roth and Claus Wittich, eds.; Ephraim Fischoff et al., trans.). New York: Bedminster Press.

Wilson, John. 1973. *Introduction to Social Movements.* New York: Basic Books.

Zald, Mayer N. 1991. "Looking Backward to Look Forward: Reflections on the Past and Future of the Resource Mobilization Research Program." In Aldon Morris and Carol Mueller (eds.), *Frontiers of Social Movement Theory.* New Haven, Conn.: Yale University Press.

Zald, Mayer N., and John D. McCarthy (eds.). 1979. *The Dynamics of Social Movements: Resource Mobilization, Social Control, and Tactics.* Cambridge, Mass.: Winthrop.

Zald, Mayer N., and John D. McCarthy (eds.). 1987. *Social Movements in an Organizational Society: Collected Essays.* New Brunswick, N.J.: Transaction Books.

Zurcher, Louis, and David A. Snow. 1981. "Collective Behavior: Social Movements." In Morris Rosenberg and Ralph H. Turner (eds.), *Social Psychology: Sociological Perspectives,* pp. 447–482. New York: Basic Books.

CHAPTER

11

SOCIAL MOVEMENTS AND SMOS: FOUR CASE STUDIES

I t is in the examination of the particular that general principles may best be known. Case studies illuminate how social movements and social movement organizations (SMOs) emerge, attract followers, attempt to overcome the conditions they wish to eliminate, struggle with the entrenched powers that resist their efforts, and sustain themselves over time—or, even more often, meet their demise.

The number and variety of organizations and groups affiliated with social movements in the United States is truly staggering. There are 7,000 groups concerned more or less exclusively with animal rights and welfare, and some 3,000 organizations focusing on gay and lesbian issues. One social movement organization is engaged in a fight against a government requirement that children must have Social Security numbers for parents to be able to claim them as tax exemptions, while another is devoted to barring fragrance strips in magazines. While many social movements and social movement organizations are remarkably long-lived—certainly more so than is true for most forms of collective behavior—many are extremely fleeting, popping up and disappearing with an almost astounding rapidity. Jerome Price, a sociologist, studied the anti-nuclear movement for a book published in 1982; when he updated the book eight years later, he found most of the regional groups active in the earlier period had disappeared by 1990 (1990, p. 28). However, in spite of their diversity and instability, we should be able to locate common themes and principles applicable to movements and SMOs in general.

How do we select a small number to represent social movements and movement organizations in general? The task is not easy. One widely-held stereotype about social movements is that, by their very nature, they seek progressive change. This is most emphatically not the case. It must be emphasized that, as we saw in the last chapter, movements are ideologically all over the map. Some are liberal or reformist, and aim for progressive change, such as the civil rights movement. Some are revolutionary—they wish to overthrow an existing order and replace it with a newer and, in their view, a better one, such as the Communists in the 1930s, or some of the more radical feminists today. Some aim at *resisting* change, like the National Rifle Association, which attempts to block all gun control legislation. Some attempt to turn back the hands of the clock and restore features of an older way of life, like the Moral Majority or the "scientific creationists." Some even attempt to block *another* movement's attempts to thwart progressive reform; an example would be the pro-choice movement that seeks to keep abortion legal. A recent summary of a number of twentieth century movements (Goldberg, 1991) includes the Anti-Saloon League, the Ku Klux Klan, and the John Birch Society—three reactionary movements—along with the Industrial Workers of the World, the Communist Party, the Student Nonviolent Coordinating Committee, the Free Speech Movement, and the National Organization for Women, which range from reformist to revolutionary. Today, just about everyone in the field recognizes the *diversity* of social movements, but until fairly recently, this was not the case.

For instance, two sociologists, Ron Roberts and Robert Kloss (1979), adopting a Marxist-oriented and now clearly out-of-date perspective, claim that there are "three major trends of our time"—industrialization, bureaucratization, and cultural imperialism. Correspondingly, there are, they say, three types of social movements that arise in response to, and attempt to overcome, these trends—egalitarian, antibureaucratic, and nativistic/nationalistic movements. Movements, they say, "may or may not be in harmony" with the three master trends mentioned above (p. 15), but if they are not, "they are doomed to failure" (p. 16). Following their teacher and mentor, Rudolf Heberle (1951), Roberts and Kloss restrict their definition of social movements to "attempts at changing power and income" (p. 14).

This restriction excludes many—in fact, *most*—of the movements active in the United States today. While some movements are directed at certain actions of large corporations or the government, and in this sense, they oppose their uncontrolled power, *very few* movements focus on effecting a major redistribution of power and income in this society. The view of Roberts and Kloss "is dominated by the idea that [movements] develop in class, racial, national, or sexual struggles" (p. 10). Again, only a small minority of social movements are devoted specifically to these struggles, and those that are not cannot in any conceivable way be subsumed by or seen as "subordinate"

(p. 11) to those that are. It is entirely possible that most movements in other, especially less industrialized, countries, are more narrowly focused on changing power and income inequities than on other matters; however, in contrast, in industrialized Western democracies, this is most emphatically not the case. In reality, most social movements and social movement organizations are, at least in the more affluent countries of the world, *pressure groups* or *interest groups* rather than the collectivities that seek the more fundamental and thoroughgoing change that Heberle and Roberts and Kloss stipulate. Because it is almost certain that types of social movements vary enormously from one society and country to another, comparative research is necessary for any broad view of social movements.

In adopting their narrow, restrictive view of the subject matter at hand, Roberts and Kloss dismiss a remarkable range of social movements. For instance, making the assumption that religious fundamentalism does not and cannot spawn a social movement, they claim, "We could not accept the idea . . . that religious fundamentalism is a social movement" (Roberts and Kloss, 1979, p. 10). Only months after this statement was made, a religious fundamentalist movement, led by the Ayatollah Khomenei, toppled the United States-supported regime of the Shah of Iran. Was this movement "in harmony" with the major developing historical trends—or not? Whether it was or it wasn't, it was successful, and its impact is being felt to this day all around the world; dismissing it in this fashion is fatal to any analysis that strives to be meaningful and relevant. Four of the social movements in the United States today that attract the most attention are: the animal rights movement; ACT UP, an anti-AIDS group; Earth First!, a radical ecology organization; and Operation Rescue, a radical anti-abortion group. Not one of these movements or movement organizations even remotely fits the definition offered by Roberts and Kloss; each is geared to changing a condition that is much more specific than the existing distribution of power and income in a society. Where these authors fail is in not recognizing the importance of conditions *that potential social movement members and participants consider vitally important.* They fail in assuming that objectively oppressive conditions will generate specific social movements that attempt to overcome them. In fact, the formation of social movements is a largely *subjective* affair. What is subjectively important to the people who form them covers an immense and almost bewildering ideological and political variety.

Granted, a diversity of social movements exists; again, how are we to select a few to represent or illustrate the many? In this chapter, we'll look at two social movements—the animal rights movement and the right-to-life movement—and two SMOs—ACT UP, or the AIDS Coalition to Unleash Power, a predominantly gay anti-AIDS group, and MADD, or Mothers Against Drunk Driving. Our selection must be to some extent arbitrary; there is no scientifically valid process by which we could make this choice. Still, it is crucial to look at a *range* of movements and SMOs. Two of our movements can be regarded as reformist (ACT UP and the animal rights movement); one is reactionary in the sense that it seeks to return to the historical past (the right-to-life movement); and one, MADD, cannot easily be placed on this continuum at all.

All of these movements are relatively successful in achieving some of their goals, but none, in my view, can be completely successful; they attack problems that are likely to remain a fixture of Western society, possibly forever. (ACT UP may be an exception; it is possible that a cure for AIDS will be found in the not-too-distant future.) But what characterizes them—and what characterizes the overwhelming majority of American social movements—is that they are fairly *specific* in their focus; they attack, and aim to overcome, a relatively *delimited* set of conditions. None attempts to change anything so fundamental as the distribution of power and income in the society. Ours is an age of specialization, and American social movements reflect this fact. In many ways, our two social movements and two SMOs illustrate some of the general principles that are most crucial in an understanding of the emergence, dynamics, and success of social movements.

Our two social movements and two SMOs were selected for another reason as well: They all emerged recently, thereby maximizing the importance of the notion of "latency," that is, the filling of a potential niche by an innovation that "caught on." No one now alive was present at the inception of the older, more established movements, such as the labor movement; hence, it is not possible to come by an adequate description of what happened when they emerged from an idea to an organizational reality. Most likely, many of the older, broader-based movements (again, such as the labor movement) emerged independently in many different places at a number of times. In contrast, we know a great deal about the distinct beginning point, including the specific actors who created them, of the movements and the SMOs I've selected. Since collective behavior focuses on latency, spontaneity, and extrainstitutionality, clearly, it is far more interested in the point at which movements are formed than long-term movement maintenance.

ACT UP

In March 1987, a popular and very successful writer, Nora Ephron, was scheduled to speak at the Lesbian and Gay Community Services Center in New York City's Greenwich Village. She canceled at the last minute, and Larry Kramer, a playwright, advocate for AIDS sufferers, and homosexual activist, filled in for her. This was one of life's truly fortuitous moments, for Kramer gave a spontaneous, impromptu, and impassioned speech that launched a movement. The event illustrates the central theme in all collective behavior and the formation of social movements: *latency*, that is, the potential for certain themes to touch a responsive chord among an audience. That night, Kramer told the audience that two-thirds of them could be dead within five years—casualties, he said, not only of a virus but also an unresponsive medical-industrial complex. If what you're hearing doesn't rouse you to anger, fury, rage—and action—he said, then gay men will have no future here on earth.

ACT UP (the AIDS Coalition to Unleash Power) is a recently emerged, still-in-transition social movement organization. Its membership has been described as "brash, rude, and effective." Unlike most social movements, it has no real leadership, few resources, and it relies mainly on the disruption of some normal, everyday activities and relies on institutions that are felt to sustain the AIDS crisis.

Two days later, 500 people who heard, or heard about, Kramer's speech convened, established a movement, and adopted a name for it—ACT UP, or the AIDS Coalition to Unleash Power. And they devised a symbol, a logo—a pink triangle, pointing up, set on a black background, with Silence = Death inscribed beneath the base of the triangle. Two weeks later, the group held its first demonstration, on Wall Street, to protest the business community's lack of response to the AIDS crisis. (At the time, a year's dosage of AZT, still the most hopeful of the available AIDS drugs, cost $10,000.) The demonstration gave ACT UP immediate notoriety, informed a potential constituency about its existence and its cause, and put the powers that be on notice that more protests were to follow.

The goal of ACT UP is saving lives through the eradication of AIDS. Its members believe that the major parties in the struggle against this dread disease are not sufficiently dedicated and, in fact, actually contribute to the death of its victims through inaction, underfunding, cautiousness, ignorance, and prejudice—or, in the case of the media, biased reporting. ACT UP's adversaries are seen by its membership as "liars, hypocrites—even murderers" (DeParle, 1990, p. B4). On the group's "hit list" are homophobia (hostility toward homosexuals); insensitivity and indifference to gay issues; foot-dragging in the testing and approving of AIDS drugs; a chronic shortage of hospital beds; health-care inequities; discrimination against people with AIDS by employers, insurance companies, landlords, immigration agencies, and religious groups; and profiteering by pharmaceutical companies (Taylor, 1990, p. 67). ACT UP is a militant activist group dedicated to immediate change. Its members see their mission as saving lives that are quite literally at death's door; this gives their actions a sense of urgency, mission, and righteousness.

ACT UP's primary focus has been on speeding up the distribution of new and experimental AIDS drugs. Federal regulations require that, to be marketed, a drug must be tested in both animal and human populations in a large number of experimental and clinical studies; the results of these tests must show that the drug is both safe and effective. AIDS patients say these stringent requirements should not be applied to them; they simply don't have the time to wait for proper testing. ACT UP says that, if the disease had struck a middle-class, heterosexual, nondrug-using population, we would be well on the way to a cure by now. But because AIDS mainly infects a homosexual (and drug-using)—that is, a stigmatized—population, they believe, the media underreports and distorts its reality, the government is maddeningly slow on funding research and approving drug availability, and drug companies exploit its sufferers. Some estimates hold that roughly half of ACT UP's membership is infected with either AIDS itself or the HIV virus, the precursor to AIDS, which both decimates their numbers by the month and imparts a sense of urgency to its actions. And ACT UP's actions have been activist, confrontational, and controversial.

Within a few months of its first demonstration, ACT UP hung an effigy of then-Food and Drug Administration (FDA) commissioner Frank Young outside Trinity Church (which is located near Wall Street); the action was filmed by a news crew and reported on Dan Rather's *CBS Evening News*. Within two days, an FDA spokesperson announced that the agency intended to accelerate the drug testing process.

In 1988, Stephen Joseph, then New York City's commissioner of health, after surveying the available evidence, reduced his estimate of the number of the city's residents who were infected with the virus by half—while, at the same time, cautioning that no one should think that the new estimate "in any way reduces the services needed." In response, ACT UP members accused him of fomenting a plot to do just that. They splashed paint on, and attached anti-AIDS posters to, his house, held a sit-in in his office, and accused him of being a Nazi. (A later independent panel found Dr. Joseph's figures to be "in the ballpark.") Said Dr. Joseph about the incident, "While people in ACT UP want to express their opinions, they don't think that anyone else should" (Taylor, 1990, p. 68; DeParle, 1990, p. B4).

In September 1989, activists forged identification badges, slipped onto the floor of the New York Stock Exchange, chained themselves to a banister, unfurled a banner that said "Sell Wellcome" (referring to Burroughs Wellcome, the manufacturer of AZT), honked foghorns, and stopped trading on the Stock Exchange for the first time in its history. A photograph of the protest appeared the next morning in *The Washington Post*; five days later, Burroughs Wellcome announced a 20 percent reduction in the price of AZT (Taylor, 1990, p. 71). Today, AZT sells for one-fifth of its original price.

In December 1989, some 5,000 ACT UP protesters assembled at St. Patrick's cathedral, some outside, some inside, to assail and mock Cardinal John O'Connor for his (and the Catholic Church's) opposition to the use of condoms and "safe sex" education. Some demonstrators were dressed as clowns, some as nuns, and some as bishops. Several carried a mock condom the size of a huge torpedo, which was labeled "Cardinal O'Condom." Just as the Cardinal was about to give his sermon, protesters staged a "die-in," lying on the floor of the cathedral or chaining themselves to the pews, blowing whistles and chanting slogans. Police were called in and they hauled off demonstrators on stretchers; a total of over 100 arrests were made. During the communion, one ACT UP member, a lapsed Catholic, broke up a communion wafer and said, "Opposing safe-sex education is murder." (Devout Catholics believe that, during communion, the wafer becomes the actual, literal body of Jesus Christ, and so the action, unauthorized by ACT UP, was widely seen as a sacrilege.) The St. Patrick's demonstration attracted a great deal of negative publicity and was regarded by most of the group's membership as a serious mistake. One ACT UP member denounced the protest as an "utter failure," a "selfish, macho thing" (DeParle, 1990, p. B4).

In June, 1990, President Bush's Health and Human Services secretary, Louis Sullivan, addressing the Sixth International AIDS Conference in San Francisco, was drowned out by a loud, vocal ACT UP delegation. Dr. Sullivan vowed never to deal with the group again, and President Bush said that ACT UP's excesses "do not help the cause."

ACT UP also conducts countless "zaps"—"small, instantaneous protests done in response to an emergency or tipoff" (Taylor, 1990, p. 70). When Northwest Airlines announced that it refused to allow people with AIDS to fly its planes, ACT UP jammed its phone and fax lines with "phone zaps" and "fax zaps," mainly complaints and nuisance calls.

ACT UP is "angry, loud, expert, and effective" (DeParle, 1990, p. B4). In 1988, Larry Kramer wrote an article denouncing Anthony Fauci of the National Institutes of Health as "an incompetent idiot" and a "monster." "At first," Dr. Fauci says, "when ACT UP was just getting people's attention, they were very confrontational. I know—I was their target. But now I realize they have a perspective that's extremely valuable. They have some very important people who are informed and decisive and who have pointed out shortcomings in our approach that have led to the implementation of new ideas" (Taylor, 1990, p. 72). One idea developed by ACT UP mentioned by Dr. Fauci was devising and promoting the "parallel track"—administering experimental drugs to AIDS patients unable to get into regular clinical trials, a system with relevance for a number of other diseases, such as Alzheimer's and leukemia.

At this time, ACT UP's weekly meetings attract an audience of roughly 700; 3,000 names are on its list of those willing to participate in demonstrations. New York's ACT UP has some two dozen committees, and there are some 40 affiliated but independent ACT UP groups across the country and in a half-dozen countries. ACT UP does not follow the classic movement pattern described in the resource mobilization literature, with its heavy emphasis on organizational structure. It has "no leaders and every member is a spokesman or spokeswoman" (Taylor, 1990, p. 68). The group's weekly meetings "are an exercise in creative anarchy. There is no board and no paid staff. Anyone who shows up can vote. Some say the group's anti-organizational ethic is a source of its strength since it generates new ideas, people, and energy" (DeParle, 1990, p. B4). Meetings are a mixture of carnaval, Robert's Rules of Order, and psychodrama. Members describe their meetings as "cathartic" and "empowering." Said one member, "I've been waiting for an opportunity to kick ass for years" (Taylor, 1990, p. 68).

No one can predict ACT UP's future with confidence. The group is split between two tendencies or emphases. The first aims to keep the focus on what can be done specifically and concretely with the AIDS problem and the plight of the disease's sufferers, while the second is to attack the larger and more general problem of hostility and discrimination against homosexuals. Whichever way ACT UP goes, at least two things are clear: At a specific time, the group addressed a vital, unmet need, and it has had a profound and lasting impact on the AIDS crisis.

THE ANIMAL RIGHTS MOVEMENT

The treatment of animals in ancient and medieval societies would be thought barbaric nowadays, and their philosophy and theology fostered barbaric treatment. For example, Aristotle argued that animals existed solely to serve the needs of humans, and consequently, possessed no rights whatsoever. Christian theologians, Augustine and Aquinas included, believed that, since animals are "irrational" and have no soul, what happens to them is not God's concern. One of the earliest glimmers of dissent came from the English philosopher and utilitarian Jeremy Bentham (1748–1832), who wrote of animals, in his *Introduction to the Principles of Morals and Legislation* (1789), "The question is not, Can they reason? nor Can they *talk?* but *Can they suffer?*" In 1822, the British Parliament passed a bill "protecting draft and farm animals from unnecessary cruelty," and the Society for the Prevention of Cruelty to Animals was formed to help enforce it. Its principal target was drivers who whipped their horses. (A related effort, the attempt to outlaw vivisection—the dissection of living organisms—proved to be controversial and was eventually dropped.) The animal protection movement began in the United States in the 1860s. During a diplomatic stint in Russia, Henry Berghe witnessed the cruel treatment of carriage horses; on his way home, he stopped off in London, where he attended a meeting of the Society for the Prevention of Cruelty to Animals. Back in New York, he formed an SPCA devoted to preventing cruelty to animals; here, as there, the vivisection emphasis met with no enthusiasm (Jasper and Nelkin, 1989). What brought about this nineteenth century interest in animal protection? It is possible that what sociologist Norbert Elias called "the civilizing process"—learning to respect the feelings of others—gradually extended to animals. As people increasingly moved away from wilderness and farming regions, in which animals were hunted, slaughtered, or otherwise used primarily as resources, existing solely to serve human needs, to towns, where most of the animals humans came into contact with were pets, gradually "compassion replaced cruelty as the accepted mode of behavior" (Jasper and Nelkin, 1989, p. 5).

The nineteenth and early twentieth century movements that focused on animals aimed specifically at animal *welfare* and animal *protection*, that is, the humane treatment of animals. They did not question the premise that animals existed to serve humans. What they *did* question was the view that, since humans owned animals, they had the right to treat them in any way they saw fit, including cruelly and brutally. While these early groups certainly influenced the thinking of the contemporary animal rights movement, the thinking and goals of the latter really represents a quantum leap beyond those of the former. In contrast, animal *rights* supporters argue that, since animals are capable of suffering, they have rights no less than humans; these activists are dedicated to *eliminating all forms of animal exploitation.* While the animal protection movement of the nineteenth century has no precise beginning, the animal rights movement began with two specific, concrete events: first, the appearance of a single, remarkably influential book, Peter Singer's *Animal Liberation* in 1975, and second, a protest against inhumane animal research that was being conducted at the American Museum of Natural History in New York in 1976. These two events launched the animal rights movement on a nationwide, and even international, scale.

The Premise. In *Animal Liberation* (1975, 1990), Singer argued that animals have rights in the same way that humans have them. Singer calls "prejudice or attitude of bias in favor of the interests of members of one's own species and against those of members of other species" (1990, p. 6) *speciesism*, and it is, he says, equivalent to racism and sexism. Beginning with Bentham's observation that animals suffer no less than humans, Singer attacks "the tyranny of human over nonhuman animals"; because of this tyranny, animals are an *oppressed group.* The way that humans routinely treat animals causes immense suffering; it is cruel, inhumane, immoral, and should and must be stopped. Animal liberation is not simply about being nice to your pets. There are roughly five *billion* animals being raised on "factory farms" in the United States right now; most live under exceedingly brutal and painful conditions, and most will be slaughtered for food (meat production), which is, Singer argues, ethically indefensible and shamefully wasteful of the Earth's protein resources. Eating meat is immoral, Singer argues, and anyone who does so collaborates with and supports a cruel and brutal system. Some

60 to 100 million animals are killed in scientific research, most, needlessly, Singer argues. Animals do not deserve such a fate, he says, and we cannot call ourselves moral beings by actively (eating meat, for example) or passively (not fighting it) supporting it. We have a moral obligation to liberate animals from such tyranny in the same way that whites living in a slaveholding society a century and a half ago had a moral obligation to end slavery. Nearly all early animal rights activists mention reading and being influenced by the arguments in *Animal Liberation.*

In the early 1970s, Henry Spira, ex-seaman and former high school teacher, found himself taking care of his girlfriend's cat; "I began to wonder about the appropriateness of cuddling one animal while sticking a knife and fork into another," he said (Feder, 1989b, p. 32). In 1976, he read an especially derogatory review of Singer's book in a Marxist magazine; his curiosity piqued, he decided to read the book himself, and found himself persuaded by its arguments. A handful of pro-animal activists, a number of whom had taken a course on animal rights taught by Peter Singer, had heard about a set of experiments taking place at New York's American Museum of Natural History that involved mutilating, deafening, and blinding cats to find out what effect this had on their sexual performance. Spira joined them and emerged as the leader of their fight against the research. He wrote an exposé of the study in a neighborhood newspaper; then, with a small group of supporters, he began a picket of the museum that was to last every weekend for a year and a half. The research—and the museum—received a great deal of very bad publicity, including derision from then-congressman (later mayor) Ed Koch. The museum received 400 negative letters in June 1976, the month the demonstration began, 650 in July, and 15,000 in August. Finally, funding for the project was withdrawn. This represented a major breakthrough: At the time, there was not a single case of an animal experiment being halted as a result of an animal group who opposed it (Feder, 1989b; Jasper, Nelkin, and Poulsen, 1989). Much as Larry Kramer's impromptu speech did for ACT UP, Singer's book and Spira's protest launched the animal rights movement. With both movements, a few activists and a proto-organization existed at the time of the catalytic events, but, again, with both, a specific event was needed to bring large numbers of people together to create an organization that could set things in motion.

All animal liberationists want to end or drastically reduce the suffering humans inflict upon animals. This would include at least some of the following particulars. First, there should be an end to unnecessary animal experimentation; some say 50 percent of all current animal research is unnecessary, some say 90 percent is, some say 100 percent. Second, we should outlaw using animal pelts in coats and other clothing. Third, while some say that meat-eating can be eliminated altogether and others argue that it can only be drastically reduced, all animal rights activists agree that there should be a radical reform in the way that farm and ranch animals are treated and a sharp reduction in the consumption of animal flesh. Fourth, all hunting of animals for sport—in fact, hunting for any reason at all—must be stopped. Fifth, all animals in zoos must be freed and placed in a humane, supportive environment. Sixth, the use of animals for entertainment—for instance, in rodeos, circuses, and carnivals—must stop. And seventh, the environment must be protected so that no more species in the wild will become extinct.

Animal Rights SMOs.   Animal rights is not a specific SMO like ACT UP, but is an entire movement that consists of literally thousands of social movement organizations. A few of their names include People for the Ethical Treatment of Animals (PETA), Trans-Species Unlimited, the Animal Liberation Front, In Defense of Animals, and the International Society for the Ethical Treatment of Animals. Consequently, it is far more difficult to refer to the policies and actions characteristic of "the movement," as if it were a monolithic entity. A given SMO may approve of a given action, while a second may denounce it; moreover, there is a great deal of variability in this respect from one movement individual to another. In other words, there are a number of wings, factions, tendencies, and emphases within the animal rights movement.

Two dimensions that separate these factions are *how radical the change* they advocate and *how illegal the actions* they endorse or participate in. Among animal liberationists, groups range "from the armed and radical to the simply noisy" (Feder, 1989b, p. 32). "Moderate" animal rights groups aim for moderate change and disapprove of illegal means to achieve it. "Radical" groups aim for radical change and approve of illegal, even violent, means. For instance, the FBI has labeled the Animal Liberation Front a terrorist group. Its members have planted bombs and burned down research labs; Peter Singer (1990, p. xii) has denounced violent actions such as these. Still, while the overwhelming majority of animal rights activists disapprove of violence likely to cause human death or injury, the vast majority of animal liberationists do endorse some of the fairly aggressive tactics used by activists, such as "liberating" animals from labs and shouting derogatory remarks to women on the street who are wearing furs.

For the most part, members of both radical and moderate groups desire the same goal—an end to all animal suffering—but the moderates are more realistic and willing to compromise; they know that the goal of seriously reducing the suffering and killing of all or even a majority of animals simply isn't possible in the real world. In contrast, radicals want it all and they want it now. For instance, radicals say, there should be an end to all animal experimentation as soon as possible. Moderates, knowing that this isn't possible, argue for "the three Rs": *reducing* the number of animals tested; *refining* the tests so that they are less painful; and *replacing* animal testing with alternative tests, for instance, computer simulation or clinical trials on humans. While it is not wise to exaggerate tactical differences within the movement, likewise, it is not wise to ignore them.

The more radical wing of animal rights attracts the most attention from the media and the public; it is, like ACT UP, confrontational, activist, and most decidedly "rude." Some of its actions are illegal, and therefore, technically criminal. Like the members of ACT UP, animal liberationalists believe they are trying to save lives, others are obstructing their efforts, and time is running out. They are the ones who splash red paint and even blood on the windows of stores selling furs, shout obscenities at women wearing furs on the street, set potentially lethal traps for hunters ("better a dead hunter than a dead animal"), and "liberate" animals from research labs (or even bomb or burn such labs to the ground). When thinking about the tactics of this or any social movement, keep in mind the diversity of tactics that different factions within a movement approve of and adopt. Two participants in the same social movement don't necessarily engage in the same actions when they seek to achieve the same goal.

Tactics: The Dimension of Vulnerability. What are some of the tactics that have been employed by the animal rights movement? What results have they achieved?

Movements and SMOs select specific *vulnerable* targets against which to wage their campaigns; in fact, targets are selected as much for their vulnerability as their objectionable behavior. The likelihood of achieving a given specific, short-term objective depends in part on *which target* a movement or SMO selects. Activists are rarely so idealistic or unrealistic that they butt their heads against a condition that outrages them but cannot be changed. Before they mount a campaign, activists are likely to ask one another, "Can we win this one?" For instance, animal research is a better target for the animal rights people than farming because scientists are more vulnerable than agribusiness, their resources are slimmer, their funding is usually dependent on government sources, their work receives less public support, and their "product" is seen as less essential. Research involving animals that are household pets are more vulnerable than that involving animals people don't care as much about. The 1976 campaign against the research being done at the American Museum of Natural History was selected because it could be ridiculed and parodied extremely easily. Each of the specific campaigns described below, likewise, was mounted for strategic rather than exclusively theoretical reasons. Some target organizations are known to be well organized and are therefore formidable opponents; for instance, they may have a skilled public relations staff, or administrators who are experienced in the art of dealing with movement activity. Others are disorganized, incompetent, and inexperienced at dealing with social movements opposed to what they do (Jasper, Nelkin, and Poulsen, 1989).

In 1980, after a year of gathering information about animal testing by the cosmetics industry, Henry Spira approached the Milleneum Guild, a philanthropic organization concerned with animal welfare, and received financial support to run full-page newspaper ads. They depicted rabbits being blinded by tests, and they read: "How many rabbits does Revlon blind for beauty's sake?" The ads were followed up by demonstrations, letter-writing campaigns, and eventually an international boycott (Feder, 1989b, p. 60). Today, nearly all cosmetics manufacturers are using an array of tests that represent alternatives to animal research. Some of the cruellest of the animal tests, such as the Draize test, conducted on the eyes of rabbits, have been scaled down drastically, and a few companies, such as Bennetton, no longer do animal tests at all (Feder, 1989a). Clearly, experiments that blind rabbits in order to produce cosmetics that do little more than pander to women's vanity and fatten the profits of an industry that is seen as nonessential are extremely vulnerable to movement activity.

In 1981, Alex Pacheco, founder of People for the Ethical Treatment of Animals (PETA), got a volunteer "undercover" job at the Institute for Behavioral Research in Silver Spring, Maryland. There, he observed monkeys living a wretched, horrifying existence—with their limbs amputated, bones protruding, cages caked with feces. Secretly, Pacheco took photographs of what he saw, snuck independent veterinarians into the lab at night, and finally, took his evidence to the police, who arrested the lab's director, Edward Taub, and charged him with 17 counts of cruelty to animals. Taub's funding was withdrawn by the National Institutes of Health; in the original trial, he was convicted of the charges against him, a conviction that was overturned on appeal. Like Spira's protest, Pacheco's action was groundbreaking: It resulted in the first instance of a police intervention in a case involving a research facility on a charge relating to animal abuse. This case represented a major coup for the animal rights movement, and it emboldened them to enter more labs for documentation that embarrassed research scientists.

In 1984, the Animal Liberation Front broke into a lab and stole 60 hours of videotapes made by researchers working on a baboon brain-injury research project at the University of Pennsylvania; an edited half-hour version that has been shown around the country depicts researchers making unfeeling, insensitive remarks and causing pain to "inadequately anesthetized baboons living in unsterile conditions." On the tape, one researcher is heard to say, "You better hope the anti-vivisectionists don't get ahold of this film." They did, and only a few days after the tapes were made public, the Department of Health and Human Services withdrew financial support for the project (Boffey, 1985; Ridgeway, 1985, p. 28). The sight of the heads of baboons being crushed by laboratory instruments was extremely effective in furthering movement aims.

In 1984, a group calling itself the Hunt Retribution Squad began digging up the grave of the recently deceased Duke of Beaufort, a prominent organizer of fox and hare hunts. Their intention had been to mail the Duke's severed head to the royal family to protest "blood sports." They were caught in the act and preventing from carrying out their plan. Extreme as this action was, the fact is, few targets are more vulnerable than the pursuit and killing of small, furry animals by a rich, indolent aristocracy; few British—or Americans—would mourn the passing of "riding to hounds."

In 1985, animal rights activists chained and padlocked the front door of the Fur Vault's Fifth Avenue store, locking customers and employees in for 15 minutes. In 1989, at an International Fur Mart sale in Detroit, activists defaced some 75 fur coats with razor blades and chewing gum; they were never caught. The day after Thanksgiving, 1989, demonstrators protested outside department stores that sold furs. They wrote "Murderers" on the sidewalk in front of the Fur Vault. Some shouted insults, even obscenities at women wearing fur coats. Several carried a huge banner that read, "50 Dead Animals = 1 Fur Coat," with several dozen small imitation animal pelts attached to it (Kasindorf, 1990, pp. 28, 29). Fur is an excellent target for the animal rights people. Again, many people regard as vain the killing of animals and the stripping of their hides so that upper-middle class women can parade their affluence before an audience of their peers; after all, every one of us is familiar with the hollowness of "conspicuous consumption." We all do it, of course, but for all of us, there is a point beyond which such displays are considered excessive. For many people, wearing furs crosses that line.

In 1987, Trans-Species Unlimited began picketing the lab of Michiko Okamoto, a Cornell medical scientist experimenting with barbiturate addiction on cats. It also passed out literature at Grand Central Terminal and spoke to a number of members of Congress about the project. Cornell received some 10,000 letters denouncing Dr. Okamoto's research. Several months later, Cornell officials lied and claimed that the research had been completed; two months after that announcement, Dr. Okamoto applied to the National Institute on Drug Abuse (NIDA) for a renewal of the grant, which was funded. When Trans-Species got wind of this, it mounted a massive letter-writing campaign; a year later, feeling personally harassed, the researcher gave up the $600,000 grant and left her 14-year research project unfinished. Except in the case of the death of a researcher, it was the first time a NIDA grant had been returned after it had already been funded (Lyall, 1988). Dr. Okamoto now does research on rats—to an animal liberationist, theoretically no different from cats, but practically speaking, with respect to the ability of nearly all of us to empathize, worlds apart (Lyall, 1989). Most scientists feel the Cornell administration handled the case extremely poorly; it has, in any case, prepared its existing research facilities for similar future actions by the animal rights movement. As a result, this case may be one of the very last instances of an animal research project being shut down by the movement (Jasper, Nelkin, and Poulsen, 1989, p. 13).

Fanaticism or Rationality?   There have been efforts to portray animal liberationists as fanatical, mentally unbalanced, and out of touch with reality (see, for example, Sperling, 1988). Said one scientist, Federick King, director of the Yerkes Primate Center, which works with apes, "I don't believe for one instant that the purpose of these extremist [animal rights] organizations is to further animal welfare. Their purpose is to mock, hinder, and destroy research. They're just a bunch of liars if they say otherwise" (Hopkins, 1988). However, according to Peter Singer, while there are "a few fanatics with bizarre ideas who attach themselves to any movement for change," the vast majority of animal rights activists resemble not the mentally unbalanced fanatics depicted in the media, but the activists, "sometimes idealistic, sometimes entirely realistic, who try to prevent needless and unjustifiable human suffering, for example, by working against nuclear weapons, racism, and apartheid, or for women, the environment, or aid for poor third-world countries." The difference is that animal liberationists "have pushed the boundaries of their concern back one stage further. They see nonhuman animals as another oppressed group, suffering from blatant exploitation by a species that has unlimited power over other species and uses this power for its own selfish interests" (1989, p. 37).

Very few animal liberationists are mentally unbalanced; very few resort to magical thinking; and, while some are extremely idealistic, most are practical and seek more or less attainable goals. As we can see, the movement has already had a substantial impact; dozens of research projects employing cruel and unnecessary tests on animals have been shut down or defunded. Tests on products have cut down drastically on the number of animals used. And, although the fur industry denies it, its revenues have suffered in recent years—in part because of the general economic recession, and, in all probability, at least in part because of the impact of animal liberation (Hochswender, 1989). In some countries, such as the Netherlands, fur sales are down over 80 percent, and the majority of its manufacturers are out of business. And the membership of animal rights organizations has grown explosively in the past few years. For instance, between 1985 and 1990, PETA's membership grew from 23,000 to more than 300,000; it now has a budget of more than $6 million and employs a staff of 60 full-time employees. Judged by the standards of social movements generally, these are remarkable and impressive accomplishments.

The Issue of Moral Resources.   There is another side to the animal rights movement, one that relates directly to the success and dynamics of social movements. It faces several insurmountable obstacles to its effectiveness, obstacles to attaining nearly all of its long-term goals. Some relate to the intrinsic nature of those goals, and some to the society or societies in which the movement operates. Some of these problems have been pointed out by animal activists themselves, such as Peter Singer (1990, pp. xi–xii). Recall that, while some 60 to 100 million animals are killed each year in the United States in animal research, five *billion* live a mostly painful existence in "factory farms." Therefore, at most, the *total elimination* of *all* animal research would result in improving the lives *of one or two percent* of all animals in pain—a fact that puts many of the accomplishments of the movement in the area of reducing animal experimentation in perspective. Even when animals are liberated in a given experiment, "the researchers will simply order another batch of animals"—and if they are removed from farms, "who can find homes for a thousand factory farm pigs or 100,000 hens"? (Singer, 1990, p. xii).

The problems of the animal rights movement are more than practical, however; they are also moral. I don't mean "moral" in the sense that movement philosophical theoreticians do, that is, morality taken in the abstract or absolute sense (Regan, 1983; Singer, 1975, 1990). I mean moral in the sociological sense: Th*e moral boundaries drawn by the movement are not the same as those drawn by the public at large.* One factor that ought not to be largely ignored by resource mobilization researchers, but which is, is the concept of "moral capital" or "moral resources." Moral resources are *the appeals that a given argument has* for the public, for legislators, and for representatives of the media that can be drawn on and used by the movement. Some arguments resonate with what many people feel and believe; they appeal to their sense of justice and moral correctness. For instance, in the 1960s, when African-American civil rights protesters were beaten and hosed by the police and set upon by their dogs, media representatives thought that this was not only newsworthy but *outrageous, unjust,* and *improper*—and so did their audience. Almost nothing, except for the protests themselves, had as much impact on the passage of civil rights legislation in the 1960s as the image of those civil rights workers being victimized and abused. Their cause suddenly had an immense reserve of moral capital to draw upon, and this helped the movement achieve some of its goals.

What sort of moral resources can the animal rights movement draw on? A major problem with the animal rights movement (one that is similar to that of most movements) is that *they must appeal to the public by invoking the most extreme, outrageous cases while, at the same time, ultimately aiming for the elimination of practices where they have no moral capital whatsoever.* Nearly everyone is moved by the sight of a baby seal being clubbed to death, a rabbit being blinded in a lab, a baboon's skull being crushed, a beagle's lungs being poisoned by toxic fumes. However, humans have a limited capacity for empathy; they empathize with animals that look like humans (chimps, monkeys, baboons) or that are cuddly and widely kept as pets (mainly cats and dogs). Few of us care very much about rats and mice—and the vast majority of lab animals are rats and mice. Dr. Okamoto's switch from cats to rats—and the lack of movement activity that was then stirred up by her new work—shows that movement activists, however they might feel personally, are aware that the public's capacity to be outraged is limited by its ability to empathize with the subjects of animal research. In animal rights tactics, unlike its theory, some animals are "more equal than others" (Lyall, 1989).

Most people believe that animals should not suffer needlessly in laboratory tests, but very few believe, as many animal liberationists do, that animals should not be sacrificed for medical research or that such research has not brought about a diminution in human suffering. The animal rights movement may be able to eliminate some of the most painful and unnecessary scientific experiments, especially on animals that induce empathy in humans, but it is totally incapable of doing away with animal research altogether, which is a major goal of the more radical of its activists; it simply doesn't have the moral capital to draw upon to do it.

Moreover, the goal of eliminating the farming and ranching of animals by many of its more radical members is wildly unrealistic. Americans—and citizens of most other countries as well—are simply too attached to eating meat to make a major dent in "factory farming." Again, because of the movement's efforts, some of the crueller farming practices are likely to be eliminated: hens and veal calves will get larger pens; less painful ways of killing animals will be instituted; and the more outrageous farming practices, such as branding the faces of cattle or debeaking baby chicks with a hot knife, will be eliminated. My guess is, roughly the same number of animals will be living on farms and ranches a generation from now as today—roughly five billion—although their lives are very likely to become far less painful. Again, the moral resources the movement has to draw on with respect to the farming question are extremely meager, given how ingrained meat is in our lives.

In addition, the opponents of animal rights score a number of points against the movement. They argue that the restrictions it seeks will lead to even more serious restrictions, in fact, depriving us of many things that most of us value. For instance, many—perhaps most—Americans would not mourn very much to see fur eliminated. But if fur, then why not leather? After all, do cows and horses suffer any less as a result of being killed and stripped of their hides than mink, beaver, and fox when they lose their lives and their pelts? There is no theoretical or moral difference between fur and leather to an animal liberationist; the difference, again, is in moral capital—that is, the difference in the public's perception of the vanity of fur and the practicality of leather. While it is possible that some substitutes might be found for leather, the same aguments that are used for fur do not resonate with the public when it comes to leather. Much of the public finds a number of movement arguments silly; some activists refuse to wear wool because sheep can be nicked in shearing, and some disapprove of the use of goosedown pillows because geese may suffer some discomfort when their feathers are plucked. And, while Peter Singer does make distinctions among different animals according to their capacity for suffering—an earthworm, with its more primitive and less sensitive nervous system cannot feel the same level of pain in response to the same stimulus as humans do—many animal rights activists do not; they believe that *all* animals, mosquitos, cockroaches, and flies included, should be protected from pain and death to the same extent. Again, in this belief, they draw on an empty bank account in the eyes of the American public. (For a social movement that failed in large part because of its inability to draw on much moral capital with the American public, see Weitzer, 1991.)

Counterarguments. Moreover, few Americans are insensitive to the fur industry's counterargument to the movement's charge of its cruelty to animals; namely, that nature itself is cruel. Animals tear one another to shreds, kill and eat one another; kindness to animals is distinctly "unnatural." True, much animal suffering is at the hands of humans and much of this can be eliminated. At the same time, animals in the wild tend to live an extremely painful existence: Many starve to death, get sick and die, or become prey for natural predators; even members of the same species kill and eat one another. Animal extinction is not exclusively a human creation but is mainly a natural process; the overwhelming majority—possibly 96 percent—of the animal species that became extinct did so before humans appeared on Earth (Gould, 1984, 1989). Again, humans should probably not speed up that process, if it can be avoided, but the extinction of one species of spotted owl or a tiny creature called the snail darter as a consequence of cutting down a few trees or diverting a river is not going to cause great consternation in the public, or among legislators, because this sort of thing has been going on for almost as long as distinct species have existed.

Furthermore, some of the ground is being cut out from under the extinction issue by zoos. The animal rights people claim that zoos are little more than animal prisons. In response, representatives of zoos argue that one of their principal functions is to ensure the survival of endangered species by breeding them in captivity and releasing them into the wild. (Some zoos also have programs of rescuing animals after ecological disasters, like oil spills.) Thus, through effective public relations, zoos, one of the targets of the animal liberationists, can make themselves appear to be on the positive, progressive side of an issue, and the movement can be made to seem unreasonable and dogmatic. Whether true or false, claims-making is extremely important in determining the achievement of movement goals, and counterclaims can often block them. This is clearly the case with the animal rights issue.

Counterresponses. Another factor the animal rights movement has to face that will inevitably limit its effectiveness is *the development by its targets of more effective responses to its actions.* In fact, the effectiveness of *countermovement activity* is a major reason for movement success or failure. This is probably true in all movement struggles, but perhaps more so for animal liberation than for most. Until recently, because of its novelty, organizations and groups that have been the target of animal rights activities have not had the experience in developing an institutional response to their actions. "Once burned, twice shy" is the appropriate motto here; target institutions vow not to be burned twice.

A good parallel may be found in the anti-nuclear movement. In the 1960s, anti-nuclear groups—a genuine national anti-nuclear movement had not emerged at that time—had a great deal of success with blocking the construction of nuclear reactors because utilities could simply move their sites to a location that was not contested. But by the early 1970s, all sites became contested, and utilities came to resist such pressure; consequently, the anti-nuclear movement became unable to stop the construction of their plants (Jasper, 1990). When targeted institutions stop thinking that a controversy will simply blow over, they form countermovements. Ironically, at times, the success and increasing size of a movement may make its job more, rather than less, difficult because that stimulates a more effective response to its activities (Jasper, Nelkin, and Poulsen, 1989). Institutionalized responses by movement opponents represent another side of latency: In their earliest stages, movement tactics are often unanticipated, a surprise to opponents; with more experience, they know what to expect, surprises are few, and counterresponses are often effective in blocking movement goals.

This very fate has befallen the animal rights movement. In response to infiltration, animal research labs have instituted more effective background checks. In response to break-ins, they have installed stronger and more sophisticated security devices. In response to protests, they have hired public relation firms and more ruthless administrators. After caving in to animal liberationists' demands, administrators and officials learn to deal with them in a more unyielding fashion. After compromises are made in a particular case, scientists counsel all research labs not to do so in the future—and offer support for those who do not do so. Instead of waiting until they are in trouble with the public and the press, labs now take the initiative and stress their contributions to humanity (Jasper, Nelkin, and Poulsen, 1989). Every movement action results in a target counteraction, making the attainment of movement goals more difficult, and increasing the need for more sophisticated movement strategy. Some observers feel that the animal rights movement may not be up to the task.

Limitations of the Animal Rights' Constituency. One of the most important limitations on the animal rights movement is *the inherent limitation of its constituency.* In almost all cases (the environment is a partial exception), much of the strength and "political momentum" of a movement comes from the individuals and groups who would themselves directly gain if their demand for change were met. In the 1960s, overwhelmingly, African-Americans were in the vanguard in the civil rights movement. In the women's movement, it has almost always been women who have been most effective in demanding change on the sexual and gender front.

In contrast, a movement in which "the oppressed can never by themselves exert leverage" is severely limited. Animals simply cannot *do* anything to further their cause; in fact, they cannot even become aware that there *is* such a thing as an animal rights issue or a cause. Individually, animals will attempt to avoid suffering; collectively, they are incapable of all but the most primitive political action. Everything must be done for them. "To judge from history, this is not a recipe for success. It may forever remain the case that, when it comes time to sit down and do the moral bargaining, nonhuman animals, unlike all past downtrodden [human] organisms, don't have much to bring to the table" (Wright, 1990, p. 27).

Thus, while the animal rights movement has achieved a great deal, there is a vast distance between their members' ideals—that is, what they would like to achieve—and what they can reasonably hope to achieve. Their ceiling is of necessity fairly low; how this and other limitations impact on future movement activities should be interesting to witness (see Jasper and Nelkin, 1992).

THE ANTI-ABORTION RIGHT-TO-LIFE MOVEMENT

Until 1973, abortion was illegal in the United States under all but an extremely restricted number of circumstances in 46 states. Before that time, only in cases where bearing a child would endanger a woman's life, and in a few states, in cases of rape or incest, could a physician legally perform an abortion. In a landmark case, *Roe vs. Wade* (1973), the Supreme Court decided that states may not restrict a woman's access to an abortion; abortion became legal for any reason until the fetus is viable, that is, capable of living outside the woman's womb. During the first trimester, it may be done in a clinic; during the second trimester, an abortion must be performed in an accredited hospital, not in a clinic or physician's office, and such a request must be reviewed by a medical board. In the United States, abortions are not performed at all in the third trimester; if a full-term natural birth would endanger the life of the mother, doctors would induce a premature birth, and then try to save the lives of both the mother and the infant.

Roe vs. Wade touched off one of the most controverial issues now debated the United States today, and generated one of the most committed of all contemporary American social movements. Tiny, scattered, largely local anti-abortion movement organizations existed before 1973 (in California, for instance, because, by 1973, for all practical purposes, abortion was available to almost any woman "on demand"). But *Roe vs. Wade* exploded the abortion issue into the national consciousness, launched the movement careers of thousands, possibly millions of previously politically inactive individuals, and generated a *nationally based* social movement focused around making abortion once again a criminal act.

The Positions.   The two sides of the abortion controversy are the *pro-choice* position, that is, the view that women should have the right to determine what happens to their bodies, and the anti-abortion, *pro-life*, or *right-to-life* position, that is, the view that a fetus is a full-fledged human being, and that abortion therefore is murder and should be illegal. Pro-choicers are not "in favor of" abortion. They simply believe that a nonviable fetus, that is, one that cannot survive out of its mother's womb on its own, is part of its mother's body and is not a full human being, that abortion is a woman's right, and the state does not have the right to restrict a woman's access to abortion. Pro-lifers do not, as they argue, support the absolute sanctity of life, since most support the death penalty, and they are more likely to be in favor of military intervention than pro-choicers. Perhaps it would be better to call their position "anti-abortion" than "pro-life," but the latter is how they refer to their own position. (It should be emphasized that when I refer to abortion here, I mean an *induced* abortion. What people call a miscarriage is technically known as a *spontaneous* abortion; it is not what most of us mean when we use the term "abortion.")

Looking at Biological Processes.   Pro-lifers believe that "life begins at conception." Is this true? During conception, a single male spermatozoon enters the woman's fallopian tube, penetrates and unites with the woman's egg or ovum, and begins the process of cell division. The fertilized egg travels down the fallopian tube and enters the womb, a voyage that takes about five days. There, in slightly less than half the time, within about four days, the fertilized egg implants itself onto the uterine wall. During the first two weeks after conception, the fertilized egg is known as a *zygote;* from two weeks until the fourth to the eighth week—that is, when the heart begins beating—

it is known as an *embryo;* after the eighth week, it is a *fetus.* Before 24 weeks, that is, during the first two trimesters, experts agree that the fetus is not viable outside the womb. Its lungs are too undeveloped to breathe on its own and its veins are too tiny to insert life-support tubes into. Increasingly, because of advances of medical technology, early third trimester fetuses are surviving outside the mother's womb, which is why physicians do not perform abortions that late. In the United States, 99 percent of all abortions are performed by the 20th week of pregnancy.

Clearly, a zygote, an embryo, and a fetus represent "human life"—but so does sperm, the unfertilized egg, or, for that matter, pieces of living tissue taken from someone's body; that is, they are "human life," but not, by their very nature, *a* human life. (However, unlike pieces of living tissue, they also represent *a potential* human life.) In the view of pro-choicers, they cannot be called a baby, a person, *a human being.* Exactly when a fetus may be called a baby is a moral and ideological, and not strictly a medical, matter. Pro-life advocates believe that, *at the moment of conception,* the zygote is a person, a full human being in the most important sense of that term, and hence, may be called a baby. Pro-choice advocates, in contrast, generally grant personhood (and babyhood) to the fetus at the point of *viability,* that is, some time during the last trimester. They do not believe the fertilized human egg a human being; just as a tomato seed is "tomato life," it is not a *tomato plant.* To them, a fetus is a *potential* not an actual human being. To the right-to-lifer, a zygote, an embryo, and a fetus all represent *an unborn baby,* with the same rights as a newborn. The difference between the two positions is theological, not biological: Most right-to-lifers believe that, at the point of conception, the zygote has a soul, and is therefore a human being, while the pro-choicers rarely make use of the concept of the soul, in the abortion controversy at least.

Abortion in the United States. Abortion is extremely common in the United States—far commoner than in all other Western industrialized countries. During the first year following *Roe vs. Wade,* roughly three quarters of a million abortions were performed in the United States; during the 1980s and into the 1990s, the number leveled off at roughly 1.6 million per year. One fifth of all American women have had, or will have, an abortion at least once in their lives. During the entire span of their reproductive years, among every 100 women in the U.S., there will be 76 abortions. This is twice as high as the rate that prevails in Canada, and several times higher than Western European countries. Abortion is high here not only because nonmarital sex is so common, but because contraception is relatively rare. In the United States, over half (51 percent) of all pregnancies are unplanned, as compared with 32 percent in Great Britain and 17 percent in the Netherlands (Kolata, 1988). The AIDS scare has increased the rate of contraception use, but it still remains low relative to that of other affluent nations. Nearly one fourth of all births in the U.S. (23 percent) are out of wedlock. About three out of ten pregnancies in the United States, excluding miscarriages and stillbirths, end in abortion, compared with 14 percent for Canada and 13 percent for West Germany.

About eight out of ten women undergoing an abortion are unmarried, and six out of ten are under the age of 25 (Lacayo, 1989, p. 21).

Ambivalence. American attitudes toward abortion can be characterized by a single word: *ambivalence*. Most Americans see it as a "necessary evil"; that is, they are not pro-abortion, they do not regard abortion lightly, but they feel it is an ugly way of dealing with an even uglier situation. A clear-cut majority of Americans believe that some forms of abortion should remain legal. Only 33 percent of the respondents in a survey conducted in October 1989 by the Gallup Poll organization of a cross-section of Americans age 18 and older said they would like to see *Roe vs. Wade* overturned, 61 percent said they would not like to see it overturned, and the rest said they didn't know or weren't sure (Gallup, 1990, p. 211). This poll tapped the ambivalence most Americans feel concerning the abortion issue: A majority of the respondents (55 percent) said they believe that abortion "is the same thing as murdering a child," and yet, a majority (66 percent) *also* said abortion "is sometimes the best thing in a bad situation" (Clymer, 1986). While most Americans oppose abortion *in principle*, they accept it *in practice*. It is a painful dilemma that cannot be resolved without some violation of principles.

The percentages obtained in a given survey on either side of this controversy depends in part on how the question is asked. At the same time, regardless of the survey and regardless of the wording of its question, there are commonalities in all such surveys. A small minority of all Americans—between 10 and 20 percent—agree with the right-to-lifers in that they are *absolute* anti-abortionists: They believe abortion should be illegal *under any and all circumstances*. A much larger minority—roughly 30 to 40 percent—believe that abortion should remain legal (within the limitation of the first two trimesters) "on demand," that is, *for any reason whatsoever*. And the rest, roughly half the American public, occupies "the uneasy middle ground" (Lacayo, 1989, p. 20), believing abortion should be legal *under certain circumstances but not others*—that is, they swing back and forth, depending on the conditions being asked about. Some draw the line at risk to the woman's life; others do so at rape and incest; still others (about 40 percent) say it is acceptable if the woman is unmarried and does not want to marry the man. In addition, whether the abortion takes place during the first or the second trimester also influences respondents' answers (Lewin, 1989). *Neither* the pro-life *nor* the more extreme pro-choice position (abortion for any reason, on demand) attracts the approval of a majority of the American public; at the same time, the basic pro-choice position, that *Roe vs. Wade* not be overturned, *is* supported by a clear-cut majority.

Intensity of Attitudes. There is a wrinkle in these figures, one that is intimately connected with the study of social movements: For the most part, those who are *opposed* to abortion feel much more strongly about the issue than those who *support* a woman's right to an abortion. Most issues are not decided by referendum; in fact, in many instances, social movements arise *in opposition to* what a majority of the public believes. Ultimately, movements very rarely achieve their goals simply by getting a majority of the public to agree with their position. Social movements do attempt to change public opinion to their views, but swaying public opinion does not guarantee movement success. At least as important as the *size* of the public agreeing with a given position is *how strongly held* those views are. In the same poll as the one cited above, over twice as many respondents who were *opposed* to abortion said that they felt "extremely strongly" about the issue as was true of those who said that they were *in favor*—41 versus 17 percent. Abortion opponents were three times as likey as supporters to say a politician's stance on abortion was "one of the most important considerations when deciding how to vote"—27 versus 8 percent (Gallup, 1990, p. 211). It is important to note that, while there are exceptions, on the whole, abortion opponents feel significantly more strongly about their position than pro-choice supporters do about theirs. This is important, because movement activism is strongly related to how intensely someone feels about a given issue.

Social Factors. In addition, attitudes toward abortion are strongly correlated with education, income, and occupational position. People with more education and higher incomes are least hostile toward abortion; the lower down the individual is on the socioeconomic ladder, the greater the hostility he or she feels toward the abortion and its legality. In one poll, one half the respondents (50 percent) with an income or less than $12,500, but only one fourth (27 percent) of those who earned more than $50,000, believed that there should be a pro-life, anti-abortion constitutional amendment. Almost two thirds without a high school education (64 percent), but only one third of those with a college degree (36 percent), believe that abortion is murder. Attitudes toward abortion are also strongly correlated with age, with younger individuals more tolerant and older ones less so, and regional residence, with Southerners and Midwesterners most hostile and Northeasterners least (Clymer, 1986). As we'll see, the patterning of attitudes toward abortion by social characteristics strongly influences the nature of the debate, as well as pro-life and pro-choice movement activity.

Stage of Pregnancy. The attitude most observers hold toward abortion is strongly influenced by the *stage* of a woman's pregnancy: The earlier it is, the more accepting most Americans are toward her having an abortion; the later it is, the more opposed they are. Both the pro-life and the pro-choice movements engage in claims-making that capitalizes on this dimension. Even though, in principle, pro-lifers believe that "life begins at conception," they depict aborted fetuses as more fully developed at a relatively early stage—that is, as more "baby-like"—than is actually the case. (We saw the same process being used by the animal rights movement when they target the killing of animals the public can identify with, such as dogs, cats, and monkeys, but not those they cannot identify with, such as rats and mice.) On the other side, pro-choicers attempt to do the reverse: They argue that the fetus is merely unwanted, undeveloped "tissue," little if anything like a human baby.

A 1985 pro-life film, *The Silent Scream*, depicts a 12-week-old being aspirated out of a woman's womb, purportedly emitting a scream of pain. In reality, embryologists say, a 12-week-old fetus cannot feel pain, since its nervous system is not fully developed. Though it has reflexes and reacts to stimuli, much the same way an earthworm or a brain-dead individual reacts, its nerve cell pathways have not been established, and hence, electrical messages cannot be sent to the brain to register pain. In addition, a 12-week-old fetus cannot scream, silently or otherwise, since its lungs are not fully developed. Even knowing this, many viewers find the film shocking because the fetus looks so much like a baby—especially when it begins sucking its thumb. On the other side, the pro-choice movement has produced a video, *Abortion: For Survival* (1989), which depicts an abortion as lasting a minute and a half; two aborted embryos are shown out of the womb, constituting only two tablespoons of blood and tissue.

This variation in public attitude will become increasingly crucial in the future as a result of two recent technological developments; first, the marketing of RU-486, and second, the increasing availability of self-administered uterine suction devices. RU-486 is a drug developed in France that, when administered during the first seven weeks of a pregnancy, causes the uterus to eject the fetus. Strictly speaking, according to the prolife position, even at this point, the fetus is a "baby," but it is so un-babylike that, to most Americans, this procedure is far less objectionable than most current abortions. When the use of RU-486 becomes widespread in the United States, the job of pro-life advocates to generate widespread public outrage will become much more difficult.

In the early 1970s, when abortion was still illegal in the U.S., an abortion device was invented; it has a flexible tube that is inserted into the womb, which aspirates fetal tissue out of the womb. Now, with abortion legal and fairly readily available, it is relatively rarely used; if abortion becomes illegal once again, its use will become very widespread (Kolata, 1989). Again, public attitudes toward using the device are likely to vary according to how far along a woman is in her pregnancy; it is less likely to be strongly opposed if it is done in a pregnancy's early weeks. This is likely to influence movement strategy on both sides of the abortion issue.

The Impact of Roe Vs. Wade on Prolifers.   As we saw, one explosive event catapulted most current right-to-life activists into the movement: the Supreme Court's *Roe vs. Wade* decision, which was handed down on January 22, 1973. It stirred potential partisans to political life as almost no single event has for any other social movement. Right-to-life activists prior to that time were tiny in number, local, fairly unorganized, and publicly unrecognized. *Roe vs. Wade* changed all that. The decision came, as many contemporary activists put it, like a "bolt from the blue" (Luker, 1984, p. 137). More activists joined the movement in 1973 than in any other year, before or since; many can recall exactly what they were doing when they heard about the Court's decision. And, unlike many, perhaps most, social movements—and certainly unlike Aldon Morris's characterization of the origin of the civil rights movement (1984, pp. 51–56)—the overwhelming majority of most right-to-life activists who joined the movement in 1973 *had never been involved in political issues or activities.* "They were not members of the League of Women Voters, they had no ties with professional associations or labor unions, they were not active in local party politics, and many of them had not even voted in previous elections. Perhaps more unexpectedly, they were not active in PTA, church groups, scouting, or other political and social activities traditionally thought of as being compatible with the role of wife and homemaker" (Luker, 1984, pp. 138–139). This is largely because they typically had a large number of children (half had four or more) and were totally involved in their wife, homemaker, and motherhood roles. Political activities were seen as distracting from, not adding to, those roles. Clearly, then, right-to-life women did not join the movement because of their prior institutional and organizational involvements. It might seem that the "bolt from the blue" quality of *Roe vs. Wade* puts the role of latency and spontaneity in the forefront as a force in bringing the right-to-life movement into existence.

What Abortion Symbolizes.   At the same time, anti-abortion activism should not have been entirely unpredictable. Convergence theory, discussed in Chapter 2—the view that people come together to engage in collective behavior and social movement activity because of their prior characteristics— has a great deal to say about why right-to-lifers joined the movement. In a nutshell, and perhaps too simply, immediate post-*Roe vs. Wade* pro-choice activists joined the movement in large part because of their social backgrounds and current life circumstances. While few had political or organizational involvements, their lives pointed directly to anti-abortion activism. The social worlds of pro-life and pro-choice advocates are sharply different. In fact, the argument between them is not so much an argument about the status and fate of fetuses but about *ways of life, world views,* what *other* things abortion *represents* or *symbolizes.* On the surface, the debate is about the fate of the fetus, but what the debate is *actually* about is the meaning of women's lives. Abortion is simply the "tip of the iceberg" (Luker, 1984, p. 158). In many ways, for right-to-lifers, abortion represents *an assault on their way of life* and *their entire world view* (p. 158). Knowing this tells us much about the nature and dynamics of the abortion controversy and perhaps even more about some of the causes behind the activities of the representatives of the pro-life and the pro-choice movements.

Although the overwhelming majority of both the pro-life and pro-choice factions are women (over 80 percent), they share very few other social characteristics in common. Typically, the pro-choice activist married at the age of 22, she is most likely to have one or two children, she has some graduate or professional training beyond the B.A. degree, she is employed at a regular paying job (94 percent), her husband is a professional man, and her family income is nearly twice as high as the pro-lifer. She is not religiously active, feels that religion is not important to her, and attends church rarely if at all (Luker, 1984, pp. 196–197). In sharp contrast, the average, "typical," or modal pro-lifer got married at 17, has three or more children, may have some college education or a B.A. but no graduate training, her husband is a small businessman or a lower white collar worker, she is not in the paid labor force (63 percent), and her family income is moderate. Typically, she reports that religion is one of the most important aspects of her life, and she attends church at least once a week (p. 196). While, prior to the late 1980s, most pro-life activists were Catholics, today, about 60 percent are Protestants—born-again, fundamentalist, evangelical Christians. In sum, "the pro-choice women emerge as educated, affluent, liberal professionals, whose lack of religious affiliation suggests a secular, 'modern,' or . . . 'utilitarian' outlook on life. Similarly, the income, education, marital patterns, and religious devotion of pro-life women suggests that they are traditional, hardworking people . . . who hold conservative views of life" (p. 198).

While social backgrounds play a crucial role in molding attitudes and behavior, "the relationship between social worlds and social values is a very complex one" (p. 198). Complex or not, it is clear to see why and how the backgrounds of right-to-lifers and those of pro-choice women influence and fit in with their respective positions on the abortion issue. Pro-life activists believe that men and women are basically and fundamentally different. For them, it is taken-for-granted that women should be wives and mothers first and foremost; mothering is a full-time, not a part-time, job. If women have to work because of economic circumstances, they may, but ideally, a woman belongs in the home. What makes women special is their ability to nourish and nurture human life. Abortion is wrong, they say, because it downgrades woman's primary and traditional role in life; makes motherhood, at one specific time or even throughout her entire life, optional rather than obligatory; and gives women control over their fertility. It plays havoc with natural arrangements in the world (pp. 161–162). The primary purpose of sex, pro-lifers believe, is procreation; abortion (like birth control) makes sex primarily recreational. In fact, they believe, abortion *exploits* women, because it legitimates and excuses male lust by erasing the product of that lust—getting a man "off the hook" for engaging in recreational sex. The generation of life from sex is part of a "Divine Plan" (p. 174); God intended life to spring from sex. Abortion is therefore an unnatural tampering with that plan.

Moreover, the social and economic position of certain American women clearly points them in the direction of a right-to-life position. The fact that they have *already* invested their lives primarily in mothering; or have relatively little education; and, in a majority of cases, have no career or work experience means that they have *foreclosed* their possibilities laid out by the pro-choice position. That is, "*they have made life commitments that now limit their ability to change their minds*" (Luker, 1984, p. 199). Their value and resources are largely or totally invested in the very spheres that pro-choicers challenge or undermine. They have arranged their lives to fit the pro-life world view. "Having made a commitment to the traditional female roles of wife, mother, and homemaker, pro-life women are limited in those kinds of resources—education, class status, recent occupational experience—they would need to compete in what has traditionally been the male sphere, namely, the paid labor force" (p. 200). Attitudes toward abortion, though rooted in childhood, are clearly intimately tied in with present-day interests (p. 200).

The same applies to pro-choice women, of course. Most pro-choice women are secular; do not couch their arguments in theological terms; strongly believe in careers for women; do not believe that a woman "belongs in the home"; believe that motherhood is a matter of individual choice; and advocate recreational sex, if that is a woman's desire. Many pro-choice women are mothers, but very few regard motherhood as their primary role. Most have invested a great deal of time, energy, and emotion in education and their careers, believe that women have the same occupational rights as men, and feel that they should be evaluated at least as much by their achievements in the occupational sphere as by their more traditional female roles. A denial of the right to abortion would undercut a sphere of achievement and value that these women emphasize; it would in effect declare that women's reproductive role should be given primary emphasis, whereas most pro-choices have spent most of their lives demonstrating precisely the opposite (Luker, p. 200). *The pro-choicer is accomplished in those areas which out-lawing abortion would seem to undermine.* Contrarily, *the pro-lifer is accomplished in those areas which abortion itself seems to undermine.* It should not be surprising that each has chosen the abortion issue as a platform on which to express her political sentiments. To each side, abortion *means* very different things because it intersects with their lives in totally contrary ways.

Strategies and Tactics.   Right-to-life activists have engaged in a number of different strategies to achieve their goal, in their words, of "saving babies." They range from those that are fairly traditional among movements, such as protesting and supporting political candidates who agree with their position, to more unconventional, radical, and drastic ones, such as bombing abortion clinics. Given the fact that pro-lifers regard abortion as murder, very few strategies to prevent their occurrence seem immoral to most of them; what counts is saving lives.

1. In 1989, the American Rights Coalition, a pro-life organization based in the South, put up a billboard high above the streets of Atlanta, Georgia. It advertises free legal advice to women who have suffered "emotional or physical trauma" after an abortion. A woman who calls the toll-free number listed on the advertisement is directed to a lawyer who will prepare a malpractice suit against the clinic or physician who performed the abortion on the woman. Only six weeks after the billboard went up, the number received hundreds of calls, and three malpractice suits were filed. Similar billboards have gone up in cities throughout the South. The goal is to drive abortion clinics out of business and, ultimately, to lower the availability and therefore the incidence of abortion (Garb, 1989).

2. Every January 22 since 1973, abortion foes hold a rally in Washington to protest *Roe vs. Wade* and to demand a constitutional

amendment outlawing abortion and affirming the fetus's right to life.

3. In 1985, Joseph Scheidler, a former Benedictine monk and anti-abortion activist, published a book titled *Closed: 99 Ways to Shut Down the Abortion Industry.* Methods include picketing the homes of doctors who perform abortions and using private detectives to dig up embarrassing information about them.

4. On Christmas day, 1984, in Pensacola, Florida, three abortion clinics were demolished by bomb blasts. Two weeks later, federal agents arrested Kaye Wiggins, 18, for setting the bombs. Said Wiggins, the blasts were "a gift to Jesus on his birthday."

5. In 1984, the administrator of North Dakota's only abortion clinic was picketed at her home by protesters carrying signs that read: "Hitler would be proud of you."

6. In 1989, 85 pro-life activists, members of Operation Rescue, crowded into the lobby of a building that held a doctor's office where abortions are performed. They confronted couples and women entering the lobby. One protester thrust the picture of a dismembered fetus at an entering woman. "Don't have an abortion," she said. "The baby inside you is a living thing." Another waved a plastic doll in the woman's face. "Rescuers" locked arms in front of the office door. The woman with the doll screamed, "Don't kill your baby!" Finally, the young woman, now sobbing hysterically, left the building (Tyre, 1989).

7. According to the National Abortion Federation, between the late 1970s and the late 1980s, over 600 abortion clinics have been picketed by demonstrators, 134 have received harassing mail or telephone calls, over 200 have received bomb threats, 32 were actually bombed, 38 were set on fire, hostages were taken in two, and there were 60 clinics whose personnel have received death threats (Chancer, 1989, p. 37). Over time, anti-abortion activities have become more creative and varied. "Demonstrators have passed themselves off as patients, then splashed paint in waiting rooms, dropped stink bombs or chained themselves to examining tables." In one community, "opponents set up their headquarters next door to a . . . clinic, pounded furiously on the windows and even conducted mock funerals over a septic tank" (Beck et al., 1985, p. 23). Garbage men who make pick-ups at abortion clinics have been confronted and asked how they feel hauling away corpses (Adler, 1985).

Summary. Although many right-to-lifers do not condone such extreme actions, few feel they are *unjustified.* After all, they are aimed at saving lives, they would say, and are therefore ugly acts for a just cause. During the first two years of its militant actions (1987–1989), Operation Rescue, a radical anti-abortion organization, mobilized 30,000 protesters who blocked and harassed the activities of abortion clinics around the country, resulting in over 20,000 arrests. Operation Rescue claims that these efforts have saved the

Social movements rely on less-than-fully institutionalized means—protest among them—to achieve their ends. Protests attract attention and recognition and may generate support, new members, and resources. On the other hand, a resort to illegal tactics may be counter-productive and lead to a decline in public support.

lives of more than 125 "unborn babies." The number may be small, says a supporter, a Catholic priest. But "the only survivor of Pharaoh's slaughter of the male Hebrew babies was Moses, and the only survivor of Herod's slaughter of the innocents was Jesus. What price . . . do you put on a baby?" (Connors, 1989, p. 406).

Given the deep and dense entanglement of the abortion question in religious and moral sentiment, and the many entangled things that abortion symbolizes or stands for in a distinct world view for right-to-life and prochoice supporters, it is difficult to see how the issue can possibly be resolved in the foreseeable future. The very *basis* of the argument is irreconcilable. Consequently, the controversy is likely to be with us, my guess is, for generations to come. Currently, legislatures and courts are deciding the legal fate of abortion on a state-by-state basis; each decision, whether pro or con abortion, generates a storm of controversy. It is inconceivable that this situation will change very much unless the entire culture of American society changes; the positions on each side are based on basic and irresolveable assumptions. It is unlikely that the abortion issue will cease to generate social movement activity and collective behavior any time soon.

___ MADD (Mothers Against Drunk Driving) ___

On May 3, 1980, Cari Lightner, 13, was walking along a bicycle lane to a church carnival when a car swerved out of control and hit her. She was struck with such force that she was knocked out of her sandals, landing more than 40 yards down the road. Cari died an hour later; the driver, 46-year-old Clarence Busch, never stopped. Busch's conscience-stricken wife reported him to the police. As it turns out, the man had received three drunk driving convictions in the previous four years, and only two days before, he had been arrested for yet another hit-and-run offense while under the influence; at the time of killing Cari Lightner, Busch was free on bail. The evening before her daughter's funeral, a veteran police officer told Candy, the child's mother, "Lady, you'll be lucky if this guy gets any jail time, much less prison." Totally apolitical when her daughter was killed ("I wasn't even registered to vote"), Lightner decided "to start an organization" to ensure that her daughter's death had some meaning (Wilhelm, 1981; Friedrich, 1985). Eventually, Busch served 21 months in jail and in a community halfway house.

Starting with some personal savings, some insurance money from her daughter's death, some financial assistance from her father and ex-husband, and some donated help from volunteers, Lightner founded MADD—Mothers Against Drunk Drivers. (In 1984, the organization's name was changed to Mothers Against Drunk Driving.) Its goal is to reduce the number of deaths and injuries on the highway caused by alcohol intoxication; its methods include educating the public, passing more stringent legislation as well as stricter enforcement of existing legislation, creating court monitoring programs, and offering assistance to victims of drunk drivers. Within a year, working out of Lightner's small office in Sacramento, 22 local chapters of MADD were formed, a petition urging federal action was signed by 50,000 people, and a formal membership drive got under way; MADD's first-year budget was $41,000, and it targeted a $100,000 goal for its second year from corporate and foundation grants alone.

Today, according to the 1991 edition of the *Encyclopedia of Associations*, MADD boasts a membership of one million, a full-time staff of 40 workers, and a budget of $13,000,000. In reaching many of its goals, MADD has been remarkably successful. It has been instrumental in raising the drinking age to 21 in every state in the country; in June 1984, Congress passed legislation, identical to a proposal written by Lightner, barring federal highway appropriations to states that did not enact a minimum drinking age of 21. Community tolerance for drunk driving has clearly declined; during the 1980s, all 50 states enacted stricter penalties against drunk driving, and the number of alcohol-impaired driving fatalities declined significantly during the decade. Computerized criminal and driving record retrieval systems have been installed in police cars in many states. Plea-bargaining has been eliminated in many jurisdictions for DWI (driving while intoxicated) and DUI (driving under the influence) offenders. Blood-alcohol levels have been reduced in many cases from .10 to .08 and even .05 percent. Liability laws for establishments serving liquor to intoxicated patrons have been enacted. Roadblocks ("sobriety checkpoints") have been set up to stop vehicles randomly (Reinarman, 1988, pp. 107–108). By nearly any conceivable standard, MADD has enjoyed a decade of remarkable success. Clearly, the movement answered an unmet latent need in American society to do something about a widely-felt problem.

MADD's founding and success both verify and challenge some of resource mobilization's most central theses. On the negative side is the modesty of its resources—at least with respect to its *local* chapters—in contrast to its remarkable influence. Most of MADD's efforts are local, grass roots, and focused on citizen activism. In 1985, a typical local chapter of MADD (and a related organization, RID, or Remove Intoxicated Drivers) consisted of 36 members, a mailing list of 120, and an annual budget of $1,200. Most groups "depend exclusively on volunteer labor and operated from the group president's home." Most founders have "little or no previous experience in mounting citizens' action campaigns"; three quarters of the local leaders are women. Given their modest local power base, then, it is surprising that the local chapters of drunk-driving groups have had such a substantial impact. "In alliance with others, including state agencies, law enforcement officials, and insurance companies, they have worked to bring about changes in citizen attitudes toward drinking and driving, shifts in law enforcement patterns directed toward drunk drivers, legislative and administrative changes focused on the control and punishment of drunk drivers, and attention to their own leaders and activities" (McCarthy et al., 1988, pp. 71–72).

In a somewhat different respect, however, resource mobilization's approach is verified by MADD: Counties with a high and growing population and more affluent and highly educated residents are more likely to have an active MADD chapter than those with fewer, less affluent, and less well-educated people. Clearly, some sort of a "critical mass" principle is operating here: If enough activist-oriented people who are concerned about drunk driving live in the same region and can be mobilized by an effective leader, a MADD or MADD-type of chapter can be founded and sustained, but if that number is too small, it cannot (Weed, 1987, 1991). A large number of middle class residents also present another resource for drunk-driving organizations, one closely tied in with the moral resources argument: They are more likely to believe in individual responsibility and tend to be outraged that a failure to adhere to it results in the death of another (Weed, 1991, p. 865).

As we know, resource mobilization underplays grievance; it assumes that there will always be a sufficiently large, constant, and steady supply of individuals who are aggrieved about a variety of issues for a skillful leader to mobilize and thereby found and sustain almost any type of social movement. In contrast, grievance plays a fairly substantial role in MADD and RID; half of local chapter presidents, and 35 percent of their members, are relatives of persons killed in alcohol-related crashes (McCarthy et al., 1988, p. 73; Weed, 1987, p. 266). In addition, there is a statistical relationship, from one county to another, between the rate of alcohol-related crashes and the alcohol-related auto fatality rate and the founding of a local citizen group opposed to drunk driving (McCarthy et al., 1988, pp. 80, 81). The testimony of drunk driving victims lends gravity to the problem and draws on enormous moral capital with the public. Victim activists play a crucial role in the leadership and direction of the anti-drunk driving movement (Weed, 1990). Although the significance of the relationship is reduced when size of community is held constant, it remains as an important variable nontheless. Although this relationship is commonsensical, it does run counter to the prevailing wisdom in the field, and should force us to rethink the role of grievance in social movements.

The number of local anti-drunk driving organizations founded revealed an interesting pattern over time. Between the late 1978s (when RID was founded) and 1983, the number of new chapters increased dramatically. In 1978, two were formed; in 1979, three; in 1980, three; in 1981, 23; in 1982, 95; in 1983, 113. But in 1984 and 1985, the number of new chapters founded declined—99 in 1984, 86 in 1985. Interestingly enough, the trend of publicity received by MADD and RID paralleled the trend of new chapters almost precisely. The number of articles published in newspapers and magazines increased dramatically between the late 1970s and early 1980s to 1983, and declined after that (McCarthy et al., 1988, pp. 78, 83). What we see here is a pattern of "saturation." A new way of looking at, thinking about, and relating to a phenomenon is introduced; in communities with a certain "critical mass" or "threshold" of victims and outraged citizens, it catches on and becomes widely diffused; at some point, a "natural limit" to the number of groups founded is reached, with as many citizens participating in the issue as may ever do so. With this "saturation" point reached, the number of new chapters begins to decline (McCarthy et al., 1988, p. 82). This analysis suggests that, when a movement's goals are too limited and specific, there are also limits on its growth potential.

SUMMARY

There are a bewildering number and variety of social movements and social movement organizations (SMOs) in the United States. Still, to best understand their nature and dynamics, it is necessary to select a few to represent the many. But which ones do we choose to look at closely? One common stereotype of social movements is that they all seek progressive or even revolutionary change. Actually, movements are as likely to be reactionary as reformist or revolutionary. Some conflict-oriented theorists see social movements as organized attempts to change the power structure and income distribution in an unjust society. Although this broad goal does characterize a few movements and SMOs, in Western societies, most are far more specialized and focused.

I have selected two social movements—the animal rights movement and the anti-abortion "right-to-life" movement—and two social movement organizations—ACT UP, or the AIDS Coalition to Unleash Power and MADD, Mothers Against Drunk Driving—to illustrate some of the more central principles or aspects of the workings of social movements; each illuminates a somewhat different principle or aspect. They were selected in part because they illustrate at least one crucial element of collective behavior: latency. Since they are recent, their genesis—easier to examine than older, established movements—is likely to display some spontaneity and extrainstitutionality.

ACT UP was born out of a fortuitous, spontaneous event; it illustrates the principle of latency—the potential for certain themes or appeals to touch a responsive chord in a segment of the public. ACT UP lacks a formal organization, and leaders influence fellow members according to their force of personality, not their position. Its tactics are fairly free flowing, impromptu, and flexible. ACT UP also demonstrates that movements are, like crowds, not necessarily monolithic and completely unified; their membership may be divided according to both goals and tactics. Its successes also show that movements can achieve many of its goals if they are realistic, concrete, and limited, and the tactics chosen to achieve them are confrontational and unorthodox.

The animal rights movement illustrates the principle of the importance of selecting vulnerable targets. Social movement activists are not mentally imbalanced; they are typically rational about tactics, and one aspect of their tactics includes focusing on delimited problems that have a practical solution. On the other hand, animal rights also shows that tactics are a dynamic affair: Targets often change their countertactics according to their experience with movement activities in the past, making the achievement of future goals for movements more difficult. Most movements face certain insurmountable obstacles to their effectiveness. One such obstacle for the animal rights movement is that there is a huge gap between their ultimate goals and what is actually attainable; most members of Western society do not believe in the absolute sanctity of all animal life. The movement, in short, has limited "moral resources" or "moral capital" to draw on from the public's point of view; members will always be frustrated. In addition, the movement's constituency—animals—cannot speak up for themselves, another of its weakness.

Although local anti-abortion or "right-to-life" organizations existed before *Roe vs. Wade* (1973), that momentous Supreme Court decision, for all practical purposes, generated the movement practically overnight. The anti-abortion movement, like the animal rights movement, has a great deal of moral capital to draw on for some of its aims, but it is lacking for many of them. This is because the American public is deeply divided on abortion, not merely from one group to another, but also internally. Most individuals are ambivalent about the issue. The participation of movement members does not follow the classic resource mobilization pattern; most early members, in fact, were apolitical and lacking in organizational experience. On the other hand, participation in either the pro-life or pro-choice organization deeply reflects members' world view. Given the deep and dense entanglements of the abortion question in religious and moral sentiment, it is likely that neither side will see the legitimacy of the other, and the abortion issue will be with us for some time to come.

Like several of the other movements and SMOs, MADD (Mothers Against Drunk Driving) emerged as a result of a single event. One woman, because of the death of her child in a drunk-driving accident, created and built MADD into a well-funded, influential, national-based organization. Although the local chapters of MADD tend to be small, the movement's impact has been enormous, and it has achieved a number of its most important goals. MADD, and its sister organization, RID (Remove Intoxicated Drivers), tend to attract relatives of drunk driving victims—supporting the grievance hypothesis. It is also strongest in populous, growing counties with educated, affluent residents, supporting the resource mobilization hypothesis. The publicity and the number of new chapters for MADD and RID declined after 1983, suggesting a "saturation" of the issue.

Many, in fact, undoubtedly most, features of social movement dynamics lie outside the scope of the field of collective behavior, while some have one foot planted in both realms. The older, more established, more fully institutionalized, more mainstream, more conventional a social movement or SMO, and the more cautious its tactics, the greater the likelihood that its maintenance and dynamics will fall more or less exclusively within the study of social movements. The more recent and the less fully institutionalized it is, the younger its membership and activists, the more unconventional and "radical" its tactics, the greater the seriousness and number of points of confrontation there are between the movement and conventional society—especially agents of social control—and the more frequently they meet, the greater the likelihood that that movement generates instances of collective behavior, and its activities will be of interest to the field.

References

Adler, Jerry, with John McCormick. 1985. "Chicago's Unsilent Scream." *Newsweek* (January 14): 25.

Beck, Melinda, et al. 1985. "America's Abortion Dilemma." *Newsweek* (January 14): 20–25.

Boffey, Philip M. 1985. "The Rights of Animals and Requirements of Science." *The New York Times* (August 11): 8E.

Chancer, Lynn. 1989. "Abortion Without Apology." *The Village Voice* (April 11): 38, 40.

Clymer, Adam. 1986. "One Issue That Seems to Defy a Yes or a No." *The New York Times* (February 23): 22E.

Connors, Joseph M. 1989. "Operation Rescue." *America,* 160 (April 29): 400–402, 406.

DeParle, Jason. 1990. "Rash, Rude, Effective, Act-Up Gains AIDS Shift." *The New York Times* (January 3): B1, B4.

Feder, Barnaby J. 1989a. "Research Looks Away From Laboratory Animals." *The New York Times* (January 29): 24E.

Feder, Barnaby J. 1989b. "Pressuring Purdue." *The New York Times Magazine* (November 26): 32, 34, 60, 72.

Friedrich, Otto. 1985. "Candy Lightner: 'You Can Make a Difference.'" *Time* (January 7): 41.

Gallup, George, Jr. 1990. *The Gallup Poll: Public Opinion, 1989.* Wilmington, Del.: Scholarly Resources.

Garb, Maggie. 1989. "Abortion Foes Give Birth to a Syndrome." *In These Times* (February 22–March 1): 3, 22.

Goldberg, Robert A. 1991. *Grassroots Resistance: Social Movements in Twentieth Century America.* Belmont, Calif.: Wadsworth.

Gould, Stephen Jay. 1984. *Hen's Teeth and Horse's Toes.* New York: W.W. Norton.

Gould, Stephen Jay. 1989. *Wonderful Life: The Burgess Shale and the Nature of History.* New York: W.W. Norton.

Heberle, Rudolf. 1951. *Social Movements: An Introduction to Political Sociology.* New York: Appleton-Century-Crofts.

Hochswender, Woody. 1989. "As Image of Furs Suffer, So Do Revenues." *The New York Times* (March 14): A1, B8.

Hopkins, Ellen. 1988. "Animal Rights." *Newsday Magazine* (February 21): 8–13, 24–29, 34.

Jasper, James M. 1990. *Nuclear Politics: Energy and the State in the United States, Sweden, and France.* Princeton, N.J.: Princeton University Press.

Jasper, James M., and Dorothy Nelkin. 1989. "New Rights, New Fights: Social Forces Behind Animal Rights Claims." Paper Presented at the Annual Meeting of the Society for the Study of Social Problems, Berkeley, California, August.

Jasper, James M., and Dorothy Nelkin. 1992. *The Animal Rights Crusade: The Growth of a Moral Protest.* New York: Free Press.

Jasper, James M., Dorothy Nelkin, and Jane Poulsen. 1989. "When Do Social Movements Win? Three Campaigns Against Animal Experiments." Unpublished Paper, November. New York.

Kasindorf, Jeanie. 1990. "The Fur Flies: The Cold War Over Animal Rights." *New York* (January 15): 27–33.

Kolata, Gina. 1988. "Study Finds Rate of Abortion Is High Among U.S. Women." *The New York Times* (June 2): A22.

Kolata, Gina. 1989. "Self-Help Abortion Movement Gains Momentum." *The New York Times* (October 23): B12.

Lacayo, Richard. 1989. "Whose Life Is It?" *Time* (May 1): 20–24.

Luker, Kristin. 1984. *Abortion and the Politics of Motherhood*. Berkeley: University of California Press.

Lyall, Sarah. 1988. "Pressed on Animal Rights, Researcher Gives Up Grant." *The New York Times* (November 22): B1, B5.

Lyall, Sarah. 1989a. "But Are Some More Equal Than Others?" *The New York Times* (January 29): 24E.

McCarthy, John D. et al. 1988. "The Founding of Social Movement Organizations: Local Citizens' Groups Opposing Drunken Driving." In Glenn R. Carroll (ed.), *Ecological Models of Organizations*, pp. 71–84. Cambridge, Mass.: Ballinger.

Morris, Aldon. 1984. *The Origins of the Civil Rights Movement: Black Communities Organizing for Change*. New York: Free Press.

Price, Jerome. 1990. *The Antinuclear Movement* (rev. ed.). Boston: Twayne.

Regan, Tom. 1983. *The Case for Animal Rights*. Berkeley: University of California Press.

Reinarman, Craig. 1988. "The Social Construction of an Alcohol Problem: The Case of Mothers Against Drunk Drivers and Social Control in the 1980s." *Theory and Society*, 17 (1): 91–120.

Ridgeway, James. 1985. "Animal Talk." *The Village Voice* (August 27):28, 29.

Roberts, Ron E., and Robert Marsh Kloss. 1979. *Social Movements: Between the Balcony and the Barricades* (2nd ed.). St. Louis: C.V. Mosby.

Singer, Peter. 1975. *Animal Liberation*. New York: New York Review of Books.

Singer, Peter. 1989. "Unkind to Animals." *The New York Review of Books* (February 2): 36–38.

Singer, Peter. 1990. Animal Liberation (2nd ed.). New York: New York Review of Books.

Sperling, Susan. 1988. *Animal Liberators: Research and Morality.* Berkeley: University of California Press.

Taylor, Paul. 1990. "AIDS Guerillas." *New York* (November 12): 66–73.

Tyre, Peg. 1989. "Holy War: On the Front Lines with Operation Rescue." *New York* (April 24): 49–51.

Vanderford, Marsha L. 1989. "Vilification and Social Movements: A Case Study of Pro-Life and Pro-Choice Rhetoric." *Quarterly Journal of Speech*, 75 (May): 166–182.

Weed, Frank J. 1987. "Grass-Roots Activism and the Drunk Driving Issue: A Survey of MADD Chapters." *Law and Policy*, 9 (July): 259–278.

Weed, Frank J. 1990. "The Victim-Activist Role in the Anti-Drunk Driving Movement." *The Sociological Quarterly*, 31 (3): 459–473.

Weed, Frank J. 1991. "Organizational Mortality in the Anti-Drunk Driving Movement: Failure Among Local MADD Chapters." *Social Forces*, 69 (March): 851–868.

Weitzer, Ronald. 1991. "Prostitutes' Rights in the United States: The Failure of a Movement." *The Sociological Quarterly*, 31 (1): 23–41.

Wilhelm, Maria. 1981. "A Grieving, Angry Mother Charges That Drunken Drivers Are Getting Away With Murder." *People* (June 29): 24–26.

Wright, Robert. 1990. "Are Animals People Too?" *The New Republic* (March 12): 20–27.

NAME INDEX

Subject Index